5.95

With best wishes

TRANSPORT ORGANISATION IN A GREAT CITY

The Case of London

Figure 1 THE GLC AND THE LONDON BOROUGHS

TRANSPORT ORGANISATION IN A GREAT CITY

The Case of London

MICHAEL F COLLINS and TIMOTHY M PHAROAH
Greater London Group
London School of Economics and Political Science

FOREWORD BY PROFESSOR W A ROBSON

The London School of Economics

LONDON · GEORGE ALLEN & UNWIN LTD
Ruskin House Museum Street

First published in 1974

ISBN 0 04 380018 1

Printed in Great Britain
in 10 point Times Roman type
by Alden & Mowbray Ltd
at the Alden Press, Oxford

CONTENTS

TABLES

FIGURES

FOREWORD

The planning, provision and control of transport are now recognised as of supreme importance in all great cities; and the larger the city the more important is transport. Until recently public transport was regarded as a self-contained function which could be planned and administered separately from highways and other functions. Thus in 1933 the London Passenger Transport Board was set up as an independent body on the initiative of the late Herbert Morrison, for many years leader of the London County Council. In 1937 roads were also dealt with in isolation by the Highway Development Survey for Greater London, undertaken by Sir Charles Bressey and Sir Edwin Lutyens on the invitation of the Minister of Transport. Their report[1] criticised the waste, inadequacy and stunted growth of the highway system caused by the mismanagement of a multitude of district authorities devoid of any common purpose, and put forward a bold and ambitious scheme of improvement. But it made no attempt to relate the highway proposals to the piecemeal planning which then existed or the regional planning which was clearly needed. The Bressey Report merely assumed that ribbon development and other costly mistakes which they observed would not recur in the future. This assumption was no more than a pious hope which could only be achieved by comprehensive planning. I pointed out at the time the obvious need for highway development to be closely co-ordinated with the location of industry and commerce, housing, recreational facilities, etc.[2]

The chief emphasis in the 1930s was on the need for new and improved roads and for extension of the tubes. The threat posed by the private motor-car to public urban transport and the environment of cities was not yet evident, although the main-line railways had been seriously damaged by the successful competition of the motor haulage industry in attracting freight which had previously been consigned by rail. The response of the railways to this challenge was to press Parliament to pass legislation severely restricting the haulage of goods by road if railway facilities were available and following the publication of the Salter Report, the road haulage industry was brought under state regulation in 1933. Motor-bus and motor-coach services were also subjected to a drastic system of regulation by the Road Traffic Act 1930. The object of the legislation in each case was to restrict road competition in the interests of the railways. This aim was achieved to a substantial degree but the railways never recovered the pros-

[1] *Highway Development Survey* (*Greater London*) (1937), HMSO.

[2] W A Robson (1939), *The Government and Misgovernment of London*, pp421–6.

perity they had enjoyed in the days before the mass production of motor vehicles.[1]

No one foresaw that within and around cities the chief threat would come from the private car, and that the chief victim would be the bus. I mention these facts to show what rapid changes the transport problem has undergone in the last thirty years. It is not surprising that neither public opinion nor public policy has caught up with these changes.

Today we are aware that transport has played and still plays a major part in determining the size and shape of cities; in the evolution of the city region as an outstanding phenomenon of the twentieth century; in the ever-lengthening distance between workplace and home; in the blurring of the age-long distinction between town and country life; and in fundamental changes in the pattern of urban life. To comprehend fully the influence of transport on economic, social and political life requires a considerable effort of the imagination as well as a knowledge of recent history.

This is the background against which this book should be set. The research on which it is based was initiated by the Greater London Group from a conviction of the immense importance attached to the proper ordering, planning and development of the transport system for the health, convenience, prosperity and quality of life of the millions who live and work in Greater London. With this in view the Group undertook to study in depth the transport system as a whole. The members of the Group are social scientists, so we were not directly concerned with the technology of transport. What we had in mind in formulating the project was to examine the history of the various authorities in charge of different parts of the system; to consider their institutional roles; to discover what degree of co-ordination existed between them; to find out whether there was any overall system of comprehensive planning; how priorities were determined and the allocation of resources for investment decided; and the relation between the transport and traffic authorities and those responsible for such services as housing, the location of industry, new towns, etc.

This book does, I think, fulfil to a substantial degree the aims set out above. It demanded a very large amount of research, which was carried out by Mr Michael Collins, senior research officer in charge of the project, and Mr Tim Pharoah, research officer. They were responsible for writing the entire text, and for revising the chapters after they had been subjected to detailed scrutiny and often severe criticism by members of the Group at our regular meetings. The Greater London Group is greatly indebted to Mr Collins and Mr Pharoah for their single-minded devotion to the task, for the intellectual ability they displayed in undertaking the research, for their readiness to accept criticism of draft papers with good temper and a willingness to rethink complex problems, and for their skill in presenting the work in a readable form. All the members of the Group participated actively in discussing the work as it proceeded. Mr J Michael Thomson,

[1] D N Chester (1936), *Public Control of Road Passenger Transport*, pp132–48, 171–2; W A Robson (1960), *Nationalised Industry and Public Ownership*, pp32–3.

formerly Rees Jeffreys Research Fellow in Transport at the London School of Economics and Political Science (LSE), was especially helpful.

The present volume is the first academic study in depth of London's transport organisation; and it is probably more comprehensive and complete than any similar studies relating to other great cities which have been carried out at home or abroad. A few individual case studies have been published about transport, but the fifteen case studies included in this book are unique in their range and depth of analysis.

A major conclusion of this study is that the institutional arrangements at present existing in the metropolis are not conducive to the production of a fully integrated approach to the many-sided problems of transport development and traffic management. Moreover, the system of Exchequer grants causes different items of expenditure to be considered in isolation on financial grounds only, rather than from the standpoint of their contribution to a unified programme. Thus, capital grants are at 100% for trunk roads, 75% for principal roads and for most railway investment, and 50% for new buses and various other items. As a result, it is unrealistic to expect that a capital programme will be drawn up which ignores these financial differentials in the interests of a comprehensive scheme of improvement. The authors propose that piecemeal grants should be replaced by a total block grant to the Greater London Council (GLC) for transport to cover a comprehensive programme including every item of public expenditure on principal roads, commuter services by British Rail (BR) and London Transport (LT) buses, interchanges, traffic management schemes and parking. Any future programme would be based on a strategic plan for the metropolis submitted by the GLC to the Department of the Environment (DOE). This would contain alternative investment programmes from which the Secretary of State would be able to make a choice. One result of the general transport grant would be to remove the present bias in favour of highway investment as opposed to capital expenditure on other forms of transport.

Changes of thought on this and other aspects of transport have recently been expressed in the Layfield Report of the Panel of Inquiry into the Greater London Development Plan (GLDP) and the report on Urban Transport Planning from the Select Committee on Expenditure of the House of Commons. The Secretary of State for the Environment, in his statement on the Layfield Report, announced that the Government are already considering altering the system of grants to local authorities to cover the costs of all forms of transport, including roads.

The GLC have at present the power to make financial contributions to BR but are unwilling to do so while lacking any effective voice in deciding policy. Under the Transport (London) Act 1969 the Executive of LT, the Railways Board and the Bus Company have a duty to co-operate in the exercise and performance of their respective functions for the purpose of co-ordinating the passenger transport services. In preparing transport plans for Greater London the GLC must consult with the Minister, the

Railways Board and the LT Executive and any London borough council any part of whose area is likely to be significantly affected by the plan.[1]

The Panel of Inquiry into the Greater London Development Plan considered that the existing arrangements for co-ordination have proved to be inadequate. The interests of BR, LT and the National Bus Company (NBC) are diverse and conflicting, and the bus network is the poor relation of the transport system. The Layfield Report proposed to remedy these defects by creating a single transport authority for London, which might take one of three suggested forms. In their view only by a drastic reorganisation of the structure could the fundamental aims of a co-ordinated development and integrated investment plan be achieved.[2]

The Layfield proposals envisaged as one possible form of reorganisation, that the GLC should become the Passenger Transport Authority for London, instead of having only policy control over LT. This would involve strengthening the Council's functions in relation to both BR and the NBC and give them a more positive role in planning and developing transport services over a wider area. The alternative Layfield proposals were either (a) to make the LT Executive the Passenger Transport Executive for London under the Transport Act 1968, or (b) to set up a new Passenger Transport Authority for London to which LT Executive, BR and NBC would be carrier contractors and of which they would be members.

The Secretary of State for the Environment (Mr Geoffrey Rippon) did not accept the Panel's view that a new transport authority should be set up in the metropolis, for the Government consider the real issues at present are those of policy rather than of organisation. Shortly afterwards, the Minister for Transport Industries announced that Sir David Barron, a former chairman of Shell International Petroleum, would be chairman of a joint study on the future of London's rail services to be carried out by the DOE, the GLC, BR and LT.

The Government's refusal to accept any reorganisation at this stage is understandable in view of the short time which has elapsed since responsibility for LT was transferred to the GLC by the Act of 1969, but it has for long been recognised that some stronger link between BR and the GLC should be considered. The changes recommended in this book might achieve an integrated investment and operating system and a co-ordinated strategy without further disturbing the internal organisations of BR, LT or the GLC.

An important recommendation put forward herein is that the GLC should be given responsibility for planning and policy control of BR's London commuter services, while the management and operation would continue as they are at present. This proposal would mean that the GLC would determine the quantity and quality of BR services in Greater London, and of course assume some financial responsibility. Both current and

[1] Sections 2 and 5.

[2] DOE (1973), *Report of the Panel of Inquiry into the Greater London Development Plan*, vol2, pp359, 363–6.

capital expenditure would be met by the GLC, who would receive the revenues from fares and charges. The authors do not slur over the difficulties inherent in this dichotomy; but the advantages could be very great.

The Layfield Report strongly criticised the GLC for their apathetic and complacent attitude towards public transport, especially the improvement of bus services. Perhaps anticipating these remarks and aware of the possible influence which transport and environmental questions might have in the GLC elections in April 1973, the Council took several steps intended to improve their somewhat tarnished image in these fields. They expressed a desire to be able to decide where buses and underground trains should run, including the siting of new tube stations. They announced their intention of appointing a Pedestrian Commissioner to look after the interests of pedestrians, who for decades have been disgracefully neglected. They issued in July 1972 a Green Paper, *Traffic and the Environment*, which put forward numerous suggestions for improving the traffic situation during the critical years before the major programmes to improve public transport and build new roads such as the Motorway Box could take effect.

After hearing a number of discussions and points of view stated by official bodies and individual citizens, the Council issued a White Paper, *Living with Traffic*, setting out their recommendations concerning future policy. This White Paper dealt mainly with the restriction of both on-street and off-street parking facilities in central London, and the provision of additional parking spaces at railway stations in outer London. The bus lane programme would be extended. More shopping streets would be reserved for pedestrians. In addition to these proposals the White Paper contained a large number of minor suggestions. Like the Green Paper it shrank from drastic measures to curtail motor traffic and lacked any strong conviction that traffic congestion can be dealt with effectively by any measure of traffic control or indeed by any kind of Government action which can be regarded as feasible. The Green Paper was especially lavish in explaining what little difference most of the remedies would make to the total situation. The White Paper ended by saying that one of the criticisms of *Traffic and the Environment* was that it concentrated on traffic problems and said little about the environment and possibly the same comments could be made about the White Paper. Their answer to these criticisms was that any improvements to the environment are indissolubly linked with the task of 'taming traffic.' These promises of a not very brave new world turned out to be too little and too late so far as any impact on the public was concerned. The threat of the Motorway Box overshadowed the belated repentance by the GLC for their slow pace in providing alternative policies to motorways.

A stronger indication of the widespread change in public and political opinion was the Report on Urban Transport Planning from the Select Committee of the House of Commons on Expenditure.[1] The scope of this

[1] *Hansard HC Papers 57–1, 1972–73*, para29 (HMSO 1972).

Report was not confined to London but its recommendations apply with special force to the metropolis. The Committee declared their first objective to be that: 'National policy should be directed towards promoting public transport and discouraging the use of cars for the journey to work in city areas.' They then recommended ways of promoting public transport, several of which follow closely the proposals independently arrived at more than a year earlier by the authors of this book. The Select Committee made numerous proposals designed to restrain traffic, many of them wider in scope and more drastic than those contained in the GLC Green Paper. They urged that local authorities should be encouraged to make more widespread use of pedestrian precincts; that all Trunk and Principal schemes of urban road building which have not reached the exchange-of-contract stage should be re-examined *ab initio*; that the level of fines for serious parking offences should be stepped up, and so forth.

A welcome feature of the Report is the critical scrutiny given to transportation studies, on which very great reliance is placed in adopting highway schemes. The Select Committee criticised (a) the built-in bias in favour of highways inherent in many such studies; (b) the limited value of the techniques employed; (c) the lack of a sufficiently wide choice of alternative schemes resulting from transportation studies; and (d), above all, the failure to ensure that studies are carried out within a clearly defined framework of general policy. The authors' proposals for grants and planning procedures would provide a means of overcoming some of these objections.

The authors of this book make constructive recommendations on a wide variety of topics. They contend that the traffic functions of the Metropolitan Police could be carried out more effectively and economically if they were transferred to a Traffic Corps controlled by the GLC with powers of delegation to the London boroughs. There would be considerable advantages accruing to the Metropolitan Police, although they will almost certainly oppose a change of this kind involving loss of functions. The main arguments for the transfer are that the body responsible for making traffic policy should also be responsible for its enforcement; and that it is unnecessary and extravagant in manpower to use trained police constables on routine traffic duties at a time when the police are hard pressed to cope with the mounting incidence of serious crime.

The concluding chapter also proposes organisational changes both in the GLC and the London boroughs with a view to achieving a comprehensive planning approach which would bring together transport and all the other elements of physical development. The aim is to ensure that highway and traffic planning is carried out by a department responsible for all aspects of transport, the environment and land use planning. A move in this direction is already taking place at County Hall. Another suggested organisational change is that a standing liaison panel should be set up in each borough containing officers of the planning department and officials of the transport operators serving the area.

Traffic management schemes have hitherto been focused almost exclusively on increasing traffic flows. The authors advocate that this narrow objective should be widened to include improvements in the local environment, better facilities for pedestrians, priority lanes for buses, better parking and loading facilities. Can anyone doubt the desirability of these recommendations?

I have indicated the main conclusions which emerge from this research. There are several others which the reader will find in the closely argued concluding chapter.

Although the book concentrates on the transport problems of London, most of these problems exist in greater or lesser degree in other great cities of the world. The relevance of the work is therefore not confined to the metropolis, but extends to other cities in Britain and overseas which are struggling to overcome these problems. Those parts of the book which deal with the relations between the GLC and the London borough councils will be of special interest to the new metropolitan counties and districts created by the Local Government Act 1972, and to other metropolitan cities which have a two-tier structure of government.

I have referred to the Report of the Select Committee on Urban Transport Planning, the Layfield Report, Mr Rippon's statement on that Report, and the GLC's Green and White Papers, to show that the recommendations which were reached independently by Messrs Collins and Pharoah and the Greater London Group a good deal earlier are already receiving a substantial measure of support in official quarters. There is still a very long way to go but I feel sure that the world is moving in our direction.

The research project was financed throughout by the Social Science Research Council, to whom the Greater London Group is deeply indebted for their support. The result is, I believe, a major contribution to a major problem.

William A Robson
Chairman of the Greater London Group

PREFACE

This study was instigated as a result of the Greater London Group's examination of the evolution and early workings of the new system of local government in London, as described in the books written and edited by Gerald Rhodes.[1] These researches revealed that the organisation of transport in London posed particular problems which had not been fully dealt with in the 1965 reforms, a finding reinforced by the White Paper *Transport in London* in 1968 which led to further legislation, and by subsequent Government policies concerning central and metropolitan organisation. This suggested to the Group that the subject warranted deeper study.

It was decided that the study should concentrate on the nature and operation of the complex structure of institutions which was responsible for planning and operating the networks of transport facilities and services in London. The study would involve questions of policy only in so far as they demonstrated the roles played by the institutions, and would not attempt to evaluate the rights and wrongs of particular choices of action.

It was also decided to concentrate on passenger transport, partly because it was considered to present the most pressing and difficult organisational problems, but mainly because the complexity of the passenger system was sufficient in itself for the study to encompass.[2]

A major part of the research undertaken for this book was in the form of fifteen case studies designed to trace important or significant policies and issues from first inception to final (or latest) decision. The purpose of these studies was to show, against a background of more general investigations, how major institutions became involved, the sort of difficulties and delays that arose, the type of arguments used, and the balance of influence which ultimately led to a decision. These studies attempted to cover a wide range of aspects of London's transport system, with the deliberate exception of the furore over urban motorways, which has attracted a great deal of attention elsewhere. An attempt has been made, however, in the general body of the research, to place the motorway controversy in context with other issues.

From the outset, the project was conducted on the assumption that the

[1] *The Government of London: the Struggle for Reform* (1970) and *The New Government of London: the First Five Years* (1972), both published by Weidenfeld & Nicolson and the LSE.

[2] Case Study *P* on Operation Moondrop, although dealing with freight transport by road, was included because one of the key objectives behind the experiment was the easing of daytime traffic congestion in central London, an objective closely bound up with problems of road passenger transport.

basic structure of local government in Greater London created in 1965 would continue for many years. A further major upheaval was considered to be undesirable in the short term and in any case was unlikely to be justified from the standpoint of transport alone. Throughout the period of research the authors have found little difficulty, again from the transport point of view, in accepting in principle the two-tier local government system.

ACKNOWLEDGMENTS

We are indebted to the Greater London Group who met on many occasions throughout the project to discuss and advise upon drafts of the studies and chapters. Special thanks are due to the chairman of the Group, Professor W A Robson, for his help and encouragement throughout the project and for contributing the foreword, and to J Michael Thomson for his expert guidance and criticism.

Many people (more than 200) in or connected with central and local government in Greater London, transport undertakings, academic institutions, voluntary organisations, and other groups and individuals willingly gave their time to meet us and provide information. Some generously agreed to address group meetings on subjects relevant to the project and of which they had particular expert knowledge. To all these people we are deeply indebted and wish to express our gratitude. The only problem encountered was during 1971–72 when pressure of work connected with the GLDP Inquiry unfortunately prevented the GLC from being as generous with help and information as beforehand, and thus we had to rely more heavily on published statements of GLC views and policy, notably with regard to some of the case studies on public transport.

In addition we thank those who contributed to the preparation of the research and manuscript. Mrs W Lamberth and Mr G Peters undertook preliminary work on some of the chapters and case studies. Mr D New-Myer of Drew University, NJ, also helped with Case Studies *E* and *F*. The maps and diagrams were skilfully prepared by Mrs J Baker and Mrs S Wilson of the Geography Department drawing office of the LSE. The typing of drafts and other secretarial assistance was provided, at different stages of the project, by Mrs E Bedford, Miss P Margison, Mrs C Cooper, Mrs J Dethof-Kahn and Miss S Popat. Help in reading and correcting the manuscript was given freely by Mrs C A Pharoah, Mr D Southron and also Mr K MacDonald.

We hope the book is worthy of all these contributions.

M F Collins
T M Pharoah

THE GREATER LONDON GROUP

The Group was formed in 1958, under the chairmanship of Professor W A Robson, from among members of the teaching staff of the LSE. It offered substantial written and oral evidence to the Royal Commission on Local Government in Greater London and has since continued its researches into the problems of government within Greater London as well as in the surrounding areas of South-East England that constitute the Metropolitan Region. In 1966 two reports were commissioned from the Group by the Royal Commission on Local Government in England, and these were published in 1968. Between 1969 and 1971 the Group undertook a major research project which aimed to evaluate the reorganised system of local government in Greater London and this was published in 1972. Its current research projects include studies of politics and democracy in the London boroughs and an analysis of labour supply and employment in Greater London. The Group consists at present of the following members:

Professor W A Robson, Professor Emeritus of Public Administration (chairman).
Professor P J O Self, Professor of Public Administration (vice-chairman).
Mr A J L Barnes, Lecturer in Political Science.
Dr B P Davies, Lecturer in Social Administration.
Mr D R Diamond, Reader in Geography.
Mr C Foster, Director of the Centre for Urban Economics.
Mr J B Goddard, Lecturer in Geography.
Professor J A G Griffith, Professor of English Law.
Professor Emrys Jones, Professor of Geography.
Dr G W Jones, Senior Lecturer in Political Science.
Dr J L Jowell, Research Fellow in Urban Legal Studies.
Dr P H Levin, Lecturer in Social Science and Administration.
Dr D H Metcalf, Lecturer in Economics.
Miss A A Nevitt, Reader in Social Administration.
Professor R A Parker, Professor of Social Administration, University of Bristol.
Mr G J Ponsonby, formerly Sir Ernest Cassel, Reader in Commerce.
Dr D E Regan, Lecturer in Public Administration.
Dr G R J Richardson, Lecturer in Economics.
Mrs E P Tate, Lecturer in Social Administration.
Professor M J Wise, Professor of Geography.
Mr Gerald Rhodes, Royal Institute of Public Administration.

Research Staff
Mr D W D Southron, Research Officer.
Miss P M Chamberlayne, Research Officer.
Mrs C C O'Cleireacain, Research Officer.
Mr J Smith, Research Officer.

ADDENDA

The writing of this book was completed in April 1973 (apart from the case studies, most of which were finished at various earlier dates). Since then a number of developments have taken place, many of which are referred to in my Foreword. But there are still a few further changes to which I wish to draw attention. They are as follows:

(1) In October 1973 the Government decided to reduce public expenditure in 1974–75. One of the main items to suffer cuts is the allocation for Trunk roads and Principal local roads. The cuts will apply both to capital construction and to road maintenance.[1]

(2) Following this announcement the Minister for Transport Industries informed the House of Commons that a switch of resources would take place within the transport sector, mainly from urban roads to railways. Capital investment for the railways would increase over the ensuing five years from £140 million in 1973–74 to £225 million in 1977–78. The total increase during the period would be about £700 million.[2] The Minister explicitly stated that the Government would continue to provide substantial revenue support to the railways.

(3) As forecast by Mr Peter Walker in 1972 (see page 616 *post*) the Department of the Environment set out its proposals for a new system of comprehensive grants for transport.[3] The object of the new system is to facilitate a co-ordinated and comprehensive approach to transport problems and to reduce governmental control over individual projects. The GLC would prepare a comprehensive annual statement of their transport policies and the programme for the area, and the estimated cost. The Government grant would, so far as possible, be paid to the local authority and not direct to the transport operators. Most of the existing specific grants would be replaced by an amount payable through the rate support grant system plus a supplementary grant for local authorities whose

[1] DOE *Circular 77/73*.
[2] *Hansard HC Deb.*, 28 November 1973, cols397–99. See also *Hansard HL Deb.*, for the same date, cols142–50.
[3] DOE *Circular 104/73*.

annual expenditure on transport exceeded a prescribed threshold. The new system would not affect a few grants made direct to LT, such as that for research and development.

The Transport Plan and Programme (TPP) will consist of a statement of the GLC's intentions for transport for the next 10–15 years, together with a five-year rolling programme of phased expenditure. The TPP will take the form of a short statement of general transport strategy, a statement of the GLC's medium-term objectives, a list of the immediate action programme for public transport, restraint and traffic management, highways, environmental improvement, etc., and finally, a forecast of expenditure for each of the next five years.[1] It was not prescribed that the mainline railways are within the scheme although the GLC may include BR projects, so divided responsibility for commuter services between GLC and BR may still continue

(4) After the Labour victory in the GLC elections in April 1973, the new Council decided to abandon the proposals included in the Greater London Development Plan for the two inner Ringways, and the radial roads connected with them. The Council declared itself in favour of an outer orbital route known as Ringway 3, to which they urged the government to give immediate attention.

(5) The GLC also came out strongly as advocates of 'a new and realistic transport policy, whose principal features must be whole-hearted support for public transport, better managment of the existing road system, effective restraint of vehicle use and planning policies compatible with this new approach.'[2] Many factors will make the realisation of these goals extremely difficult, including the problem of recruiting and retaining sufficient staff to man London Transport's trains and buses, and the reluctance of some London boroughs to adopt the standards of off-street parking facilities for new buildings recommended by the GLDP.

(6) Important changes have taken place in the financing of London Transport. Shortly after the GLC became responsible for the undertaking early in 1970, the Executive were directed to meet all their costs on current account from revenue and to make sufficient to transfer £2 million to the general reserve. The following year the GLC decided to make a capital grant of precisely this sum to LT. In November of 1971 the GLC, in dealing with an application by LT for fare increases, withdrew the direction to put £2 million to reserve account that year. The Council repeated their intention of not subsidising London Transport's revenue. They gave the Executive greater latitude in transferring money from capital to current account, thereby making it possible to limit the fare increases requested by LT. At about the same time the Council agreed to contribute 25% towards the cost of a number of London Transport's capital projects, the remaining expenditure being defrayed by the central government.

(7) The first signs of a radical change of policy came in July 1972 when

[1] GLC *Minutes*, 6 November 1973, pp550–1.
[2] GLC *Minutes*, 24 July 1973, pp382–5.

LT again applied for permission to raise the level of fares. On this occasion the GLC decided to limit the increases, particularly on the buses. It then became clear that this would compel the GLC to provide assistance to LT on current account, but no precise commitment was made. In 1973, however, the GLC have undertaken to pay London Transport the substantial sum of £15 million.[1]

All the decisions set out above are moves favouring public transport in comparison with highways and the private motor car; some were in embryo in the policies of the previous GLC; they accord increasingly with public opinion, with increasing prices of fuel, and with many of the policy implications of the studies in this book. They support the conclusions of the authors that the institutional system has been moving towards a greater capability of providing a comprehensive approach to the city's transport system. Suggestions put forward in the book for further changes in the same direction to strengthen this capability have not yet been discussed or accepted publicly.

William A Robson

23 January 1974

[1] GLC *Minutes*, 18 December 1973.

Chapter 1

THE DEVELOPMENT OF TRANSPORT ORGANISATION IN LONDON SINCE THE MID-NINETEENTH CENTURY

The means by which London today meets the challenge, common to all great cities, of providing for the extensive and complex movement of people and goods have developed over many years. The current institutional arrangements reflect how transport problems have been interpreted, how solutions have been sought and how Government influence and control over transport has grown. As the institutional system itself has a profound effect on the quality of transport it is important to understand how it has evolved. Consequently, in this chapter a brief history of institutional developments is set out.

Other studies have described the growth and development of London and its transport facilities.[1] This chapter focuses on the formation and evolution of institutions and other events which from the mid-nineteenth century onwards contributed to the system of transport organisation that existed at the time of the reorganisation of London's government in the mid-1960s. Several main phases of transport development and urban growth during these dozen decades, which help to explain the context within which the institutional changes occurred, are also briefly described.

THE 1850s AND THE FORMATION OF THE LONDON GENERAL OMNIBUS COMPANY

During the nineteenth century Londoners made most of their journeys on foot although, as Barker and Robbins have described, the outward spread of the city and the rapid growth of its population was accompanied by a growing volume of Hackney carriage, short-stage coach and hansom-cab traffic. The horse-drawn omnibus appeared on London's streets in the 1830s, after its success had been demonstrated in Paris, and it provided at first an alternative to making journeys on foot within the city for those able to afford the relatively high fares, and then increasingly a means of distributing passengers to or from the main line railway termini. It has

[1] For examples of the former see R Clayton (ed) (1964), *The Geography of Greater London*, esp chs by J T Coppock. Also H C Prince (1964), *Greater London*, esp ch11 by P Hall. Railway histories include H P White (1963), *A Regional History of the Railways of Great Britain*, vol3, *Greater London*; and E Course (1961), *London's Railways*. Perhaps the most reliable general transport history is H J Dyos and D H Aldcroft (1969), *British Transport*.

been estimated that in 1854 245 000 people entered the City of London each day, of whom 80% travelled on foot, about 9% by bus, 6% by Thames steamboat and 5% by train.[1] Excess omnibus capacity, created to serve the 1851 international exhibition, together with increased operating costs led to fierce competition between the rival proprietors; many went out of business or were taken over.

Between 1853 and 1856 financial interests in a large horse bus company in Paris began operations in London and many of London's bus companies were bought up and operated by their London General Omnibus Company (LGOC). The venture did not match up to the financial aspirations of the French owners, however, and in 1859 the LGOC became an independent British company. After initial difficulties the company's fortunes improved, boosted partly as a result of another international exhibition in 1862, and it was to dominate public road transport in London for the next forty years.

During this period the number and frequency of horse buses on London's streets grew considerably and Barker has reflected that the service provided was the nearest to a continuous system of passenger conveyor belts yet devised.[2] But he has also emphasised that traffic congestion was a common phenomenon at the time:

> The traffic jam is not a product of the motor car age. When the main thoroughfares were narrower and fewer, and when vehicles were more ponderous and speeds slower, it did not take much traffic to cause serious congestion. And, in the 1830s, and 1840s, the volume of traffic was rising quickly.[3]

After the reports on London's traffic problems of a Royal Commission in 1844–51 and a Select Committee in 1854–55, a Metropolitan Board of Works was established in 1855, *inter alia*, in the hope of relieving congestion by improving the city's street pattern. It proceeded to do this vigorously[4] until it was supplanted by the new London County Council in 1888, which implemented some of the later schemes initiated by the Board. Attention also turned to the regulation of traffic, including the requirement of drivers to observe 'the rule of the road' (keeping on the left) and of buses to pick up passengers at the nearside kerb rather than in the middle of the carriageway (bus stops had not yet been designated).[5] It was in such matters that the police became involved in traffic supervision.

[1] Much of this chapter draws on T C Barker and R M Robbins (1963), *A History of London Transport*, vol1, *The Nineteenth Century*. The references to horse buses fall on pp4–39, 56–98.

[2] T C Barker, Lecture at Bedford College, London, 29 October 1970.

[3] Barker and Robbins (1963), p64.

[4] Creating such streets as Victoria Street, Queen Victoria Street, Shaftesbury Avenue, Clerkenwell Road, Charing Cross Road and the Victoria Embankment on the north side of the Thames.

[5] *Metropolitan Streets Act 1867*, ch134, s8.

THE BEGINNINGS OF THE UNDERGROUND AND SUBURBAN RAILWAYS

By 1845 only five radial main-line railways served the capital, with short 'suburban' routes to Blackwall and Greenwich. Fifteen years later four major radial routes had been added, with several branches and the North London Line to serve the docks.[1]

A Royal Commission on Metropolitan termini had prevented the intrusion of railways into the main built-up area, or what now forms the central area of the city. The Great Western Railway (GWR) was anxious to gain a link with the City and subscribed one-fifth of the capital (as did the City Corporation) for the construction of the Metropolitan Railway between 1859 and 1863, using the cut-and-cover method. Its success was immediate, with traffic almost trebling in the first five years.[2] There was a great upsurge in interest in London railways as part of a 'railway mania' and Parliament was overwhelmed with proposals; for example, in 1864 there were 259 projects for over 300 miles of new railway in London alone.

Then, as now, developers' plans were challenged by local interests; residents objected to the prospect of London being 'cut up in such style,' but only some of the proposals actually went ahead. For example, a Joint Select Committee of both Houses of Parliament recommended the establishment of an Inner Circle route including a line along the north bank of the Thames where the Board of Works was embarking on the construction of a new highway.

The Inner Circle route was at first considered too expensive but part of it, the District Line, was opened from Kensington to Westminster in 1868 and extended to Blackfriars in 1870. The line was originally worked by both Metropolitan and District trains but a breakdown in the agreement in 1871 was one factor which prompted the first statutory move towards transport co-ordination in London.[3] The following year Sir Edward Watkin, chairman of the South-Eastern Railway, was appointed general manager of the Metropolitan. Watkin was already a rival to the Managing Director of the District, James Forbes, in the operation of services south of the Thames, for Forbes was also General Manager of the London, Chatham and Dover Railway. The Metropolitan and District companies competed directly for suburban traffic from west London (the Metropolitan to the north, the District to the south)[4] and for traffic to and from the Kensington exhibitions. This rivalry made completion of the Inner Circle seem unlikely, but the Metropolitan and District (City Lines and Extensions) Act of 1879 required that 'each company shall, for the purpose of securing to the public the advantage of continuous working of the said Inner Circle with the other portions of the two organisations' lines, work over the railways

[1] Barker and Robbins (1963), pp44–52, 99–165.
[2] C E Lee (1972), *The Metropolitan Line* (published by London Transport), esp pp8–13.
[3] C E Lee (1968), *100 Years of the District*, pp7–13.
[4] H F Howson (1967), *London's Underground.*

of the other company forming part of such Inner Circle.' This was almost certainly the first statutory obligation for metropolitan transport co-ordination and remained in force until the London Passenger Transport Board (LPTB) was formed in 1933.[1] The complete Inner Circle was eventually opened in 1882.

Meantime a spate of suburban railway development was occurring south of the Thames, following the opening of termini at Charing Cross and Victoria. The horse-buses, while providing feeder services to the railways, found it increasingly difficult to compete with the speed of the railways or with their third-class fares and season tickets in serving the spreading suburbs from Hammersmith to West Ham, and Clapham to Clapton.[2]

HORSE TRAMWAYS

The first horse-drawn tram began operation in 1870. These vehicles were more costly to operate than horse-buses but could carry more passengers more quickly. By 1875 they carried virtually as many passengers as the buses. Under the 1870 Tramway Act either a local authority or a company through a twenty-one-year franchise from the authority could construct a tramway, but schemes could be vetoed by one-third of the frontagers in any street. Not surprisingly this led to a fragmentary development of tramways. Nevertheless, the tram had a considerable influence on the distribution of the working population, partly because the companies were compelled by statute to provide cheap workmen's fares.

After its establishment in 1888, the London County Council (LCC) began to take over these franchises as they expired. This was the first major municipal incursion into public transport but it by no means covered the whole of the built-up area. The Council also obtained powers to build its own tramways in a radical attempt to help the poorer people. In 1900 it obtained powers for electrification, but still had three virtually separate systems only tenuously linked by the Kingsway subway and with few links with tramways independently operated outside the County.[3] The 1905 Royal Commission on London Traffic criticised this lack of integration but suggested no remedy.

THE RAILWAY BOOM OF THE 1890S, ELECTRIFICATION AND THE UNDERGROUND GROUP

During the late nineteenth century as both the size and the wealth of the city grew, particular areas became more specialised in their function, as did the journeys between them. The City of London increasingly became a workplace while shopping and entertainment functions developed in the

[1] Lee (1968), pp12–14; (1972), pp20–2.

[2] J R Kellett (1969), *The Impact of Railways on Victorian Cities*, pp91–2.

[3] Barker and Robbins (1963), pp178–97, 269–70, map pp258–9; W A Robson (1948, 2nd edn), *The Government and Misgovernment of London*, pp143–4; J H Price (1958), 'London's First Electric Tramway,' *J of Tr Hist*, 3, pp205–11.

West End. In the thirty years from 1870 the number of passenger journeys by vehicle quadrupled while London's population grew by 60%.

Part of this growth was in journeys-to-work from the ever-spreading residential suburbs, which were made possible by faster rail transport and made attractive by cheaper land and housing or more pleasant surroundings. Cheap workmen's fares played a key role in this change: they were introduced in 1864 on the Metropolitan Railway, in 1865 on the London, Chatham and Dover, and later were adopted on a widespread scale by the South-Eastern, North London, and Great Eastern. All railways were obliged to offer cheap fares after 1883. Dyos and Kellett describe how these contributed to the suburbs of Camberwell and Edmonton. Likewise suburban estates designed for the growing numbers of clerical and non-manual workers were developing in Wood Green, Enfield, Bedford Park and other places, and land speculation became increasingly associated with railway development.[1] The established underground railway companies also developed suburban services running over the lines of other companies: the District to Richmond in 1877, Hounslow in 1883 and Wimbledon in 1889, the Metropolitan to Harrow in 1880 and as far as Aylesbury by 1892.

Meantime the growth of passenger and goods traffic on the roads made evident the need for a better distribution system for the centre and innermost suburbs and in the 1890s a second wave of underground railway development occurred. This mostly took the form of deep-bored tube railways made possible by new tunnelling technology. In 1886 work started on a 1¼-mile tube railway from King William Street to the Elephant and Castle. It was originally to be cable-hauled but electric traction was installed from the beginning and the line was extended to Stockwell and Clapham. It was opened in 1890 and extended to Moorgate in 1900, in which year it carried 13 million passengers. After extensions to Euston in 1907 traffic rose to 26 million passengers annually.[2] As a result of this early success, in 1892 schemes were approved that formed the core of the present-day Central, Northern and Bakerloo Lines, and in 1899 of the Piccadilly. The first sections of these lines, which were confined mainly to what is now regarded as central London, although extending also to Hampstead and Brompton, were opened between 1900 and 1906.[3]

[1] Further detail on inner suburban development may be found in H J Dyos (1955), 'Railways and Housing in Victorian London,' *J of Tr Hist*, II; and (1961), *Victorian Camberwell: a Study in Urban Growth*. While recognising the role of railways, J R Kellett (1969), ch11, nevertheless stresses the importance of trams and horse-buses in encouraging urban growth. J N Tarn (1968), 'Some Pioneer Suburban Housing Estates,' *Arch Review*, cxviii, pp367–70, deals with artisans' and clerks' suburbs. D A Reeder (1968), 'A Theatre of Suburbs: Some Patterns of Development in West London 1801–1911,' in H J Dyos (ed), *A Study of Local History*, pp253–70, describes the impact of the Central Line. For a note on the 'yearnings' of the Metropolitan to become a main-line company under Watkin, and subsequent land development in North-West London see D White 'Metroland', *New Society*, 1 July 1971, pp5–7.

[2] White (1963), pp97–8.

[3] J Simmons (1966), 'The Pattern of Tube Railways in London,' *J of Tr Hist*, VII; 4, pp234–40.

Finance for some of these schemes was difficult to obtain (because other domestic industrial investment was more profitable) until Charles Yerkes, who had managed street railways in Chicago, arrived with financial backing from Speyer Bros of New York. This venture was a reflection of surplus American finance seeking overseas outlets.[1] Called by some a dreamer, Yerkes foresaw that many people would travel twenty or more miles to work by electric train by 1920 and that the days of the horse-bus were numbered.[2] In 1900 he obtained financial control of the Hampstead tube for £100 000 and in 1901 of the District, Brompton and Strand (later Piccadilly) Lines. In 1902 he bought the assets of the Baker Street and Waterloo (later Bakerloo) for £360 000 after the insurance company which had invested £700 000 in the scheme had gone into liquidation. This illustrates that the poor financial return which hindered the expansion of the railways in London after the Second World War was no new phenomenon.[3]

In 1902 the Piccadilly, financially the strongest of the three lines, was reconstituted as the London Electric Railway Company, and took policy control of the others. In 1905 Yerkes died and his partner Speyer took over as chairman with Sir George Gibb, previously General Manager of the North-Eastern, as his deputy and General Manager of the District. Gibb soon succeeded him and in 1907 established the London Passenger Traffic Conference which sought to co-ordinate fares and services, not only of the Yerkes group but also of other companies.

In 1907 Gibb's successor as chairman of the District board was Albert Stanley, who had successfully run street tramways in Detroit and New Jersey. In 1910 Stanley became chairman of the London Electric Railway and of the Conference; he sought to widen the co-ordination of the Conference to include the private railway companies, the Central London and City and South London railways, and the LGOC. Only the LCC tramways, the Metropolitan Railway and the Tilling bus group remained as major elements of the passenger traffic distribution system outside the Group.[4]

In 1910 the Conference adopted the common UNDERGROUND symbol to give unity to the public image of the network. Under the aegis of the Group common fares and through bookings were developed. Major interchange stations were built at Charing Cross, Leicester Square and Piccadilly Circus; such interchanges made the system attractive to travellers particularly in the 1950s and 1960s when road congestion became severe. Under an Act of 1915 a Common Fund was established 'into which were paid all net receipts of the District railway, the associated tube railways, and the

[1] C E Lee (1973), *The Piccadilly Line*, p9.

[2] White (1963), p99.

[3] When adequate private finance was no longer forthcoming, the Government first guaranteed loans and, as described more fully in Chapter 3, later made grants for capital works (see Case Study *C*).

[4] White (1963), pp104–5; Lee (1968), pp24–6; and C F Klapper (1963), 'Co-ordination,' *Inst of Tr Journal*, pp77–80.

LGOC. The fund was then divided into agreed proportions,[1] although the companies retained their legal identities. A headquarters office was established at 55 The Broadway SW1. Under Stanley's leadership the Group showed that co-ordination worked, and this was to prove the nucleus on which the London Passenger Transport Board was established in 1933, again with Stanley (by then Lord Ashfield) in the chair.

THE LONDON TRAFFIC BRANCH, THE FIRST WORLD WAR AND THE FORMATION OF THE MINISTRY OF TRANSPORT

The last two decades of the nineteenth century saw some major street improvements in London (e.g. Shaftesbury Avenue, 1886, and Charing Cross Road, 1887) and the completion of new Thames bridges (Putney and Hammersmith Bridges, 1887, Tower Bridge, 1894). But road traffic also grew apace, especially passenger traffic by horse-bus and tram. Rival bus companies to the LGOC had become established and towards the end of the century were carrying almost as many passengers—154 million in 1896 compared with 159 million carried by the LGOC. In the same year the trams carried 280 million passengers.

It was not long after the turn of the century that concern again began to mount over London's traffic congestion. Despite the maintenance of very low speed limits, motor-cars, which had been introduced in the 1890s, grew rapidly in popularity (nationally there were 8500 cars in use in 1904 and over 32 000 by 1907[2]). The Royal Commission on London Traffic in 1905 deplored the congestion in London's streets and, like the Metropolitan Board of Works, saw part of the solution in road building, street widening and the construction of new arterial roads. These were to be partly financed from sales of land surplus to the schemes. (Similar arrangements had recently recouped over 80% of the £4.9 million cost of building Kingsway.) But the Commission also urged the development of new residential suburbs by means of new railways built if necessary by local authorities. They did not, however, foresee the imminent growth of the use of the petrol engine to power cabs, commercial vehicles and buses as well as private cars:

> tramways will continue to be the most efficient and the cheapest means of street conveyance, and we cannot recommend the postponement of tramway extension in London on the ground of any visible prospect of the supersession of tramways by motor omnibuses.[3]

To deal with both rail and road transport problems in London, and the planning and management of the proposed new works, the Royal Commission recommended the establishment of a new Traffic Board to advise central government. This was seen as preferable to giving greater powers to

[1] Lee (1973), p19.
[2] W Plowden (1971), *Politics and the Motor Car 1896–1970*, pp31–60.
[3] Royal (Barbour) Commission on London Traffic (1905), *Report*, p42.

the LCC because of conflicts that would arise with other local authorities in Greater London. This administrative proposal was ignored but London's growing transport problems, which the Commission had thoroughly investigated, could hardly be denied.

In 1907 a London Traffic Branch was created within the Board of Trade, which was already responsible for rail and maritime transport, but while recognising the problems to be tackled, had virtually no executive powers for dealing with them. 'Thus,' Robson has written 'matters were allowed to drift on into the motor-car era without any effective steps taken to deal either with the communications of the metropolis or the organisation of its public transport on bold or imaginative lines.'[1] The Traffic Branch did, however, produce a plan for major arterial road schemes which contained the origins of the Great Western Avenue, the North Circular Road and the Brentford by-pass;[2] and it undertook surveys which documented the growth of motor vehicles and the decline of horse-drawn vehicles. This change of motive power contributed, in 1909, to the establishment of the Roads Board, a new national body to administer the income from fuel and vehicle taxation for the purposes of road construction—a unique case of hypothecated taxation. The Roads Board desired to tackle London's traffic problems by means of new road construction, but the LCC wished to concentrate on improving junctions that were notable points of traffic congestion. This dispute was not settled by the time war broke out in 1914.

By means of a Railway Executive, consisting of the chairmen of the major companies, the Government took control of railway operation during the war, guaranteeing each company its receipts as in 1913, or its arrears on maintenance and replacement for the duration of hostilities and two years thereafter. Loss and obsolescence of equipment and a fall in traffic receipts resulted in a cost to the Government of £60 million in 1919 alone. Indeed most railway and canal companies were at that time making losses while the roads involved a net Government expenditure of £20 million per annum. Only municipal tramways showed a net return.[3]

In 1918 the Haldane Committee had advised that the functions of Government departments should be allocated on the basis of services performed so as to ensure a coherence of responsibility, the development of expertise and the fulfilment of primary duties.[4] The Committee was of the opinion that if the railways and canals were nationalised, a Ministry of Transport would have to be established. It was obvious to the Government that the railways could not revert to their pre-war conditions and in 1918 a Select Committee on Transport reported that unification of the railway

[1] W A Robson (1948), p148.

[2] C M Buchanan (1970), *London Road Plans 1900–1970* (GLC Research Report No.11), documents almost a score of plans variously produced up to 1970; a more concise account is to be found in J M Thomson *et al* (1969), *Motorways in London*, pp94–107.

[3] *Hansard HC Papers 119*, cols1767–84, 17 March 1919; and 1950–2048, 18 March 1919; see also Sir G Jenkins (1959), *The Ministry of Transport and Civil Aviation.*

[4] *Report of the Machinery of Government Committee* (1918), Cmnd 9230, HMSO, esp paras12–27.

system was desirable for reasons of rail planning and operation, even disregarding current financial problems. This course was favoured by the acting chairman of the Railway Executive.

After discussion in Parliament, nationalisation of the railways was rejected by the Prime Minister, but a new Ministry called 'Ways and Communications' was proposed (later renamed the Ministry of Transport (MOT)). In the lengthy Parliamentary debates in 1918 and 1919 the dominant questions were the treatment of the railways and whether more Government control was necessary. The more conservative Members disliked the idea of the new Ministry, seeing it as a virtual nationalisation of the railway network. But it was becoming clearer that the cause of many transport problems, both rail and road, was the lack of any overall control. As Sir Eric Geddes said when introducing the Bill for the new Ministry: 'There is no policy (for inland transport) and no one is responsible.'[1] When he became the first Minister of the new department he had the task of preparing a new administrative framework for the railways; as an interim measure the emergency arrangements were extended for a further two years.[2]

The new Ministry was also made responsible for electric power generation and distribution because Geddes was convinced that the main railway routes would be electrified within a few years.[3] Responsibility for this, and for shipping, roads, and rail safety were acquired from the Board of Trade which had accumulated over many years a vast conglomeration of disparate functions. The initial staff of 450 were organised into groups corresponding to the main means of travel,[4] and the additional amount of co-ordination the department achieved initially was not great. In 1921 a Railway Act was passed, merging the pre-war companies, which still numbered over a hundred, into four large units—the GWR, the London Midland and Scottish (LMS), the London and North-Eastern (LNER), and the Southern.

Meanwhile the Ministry's new Roads Department had rapidly begun a classification of the roads according to importance as traffic routes and in 1919 main roads were grouped into class I, eligible for 50% grant for major works, and class II for which 25% was given. Under the 1929 Local Government Act the grants were increased to 75% and 60% respectively and in 1946 a third class, eligible for 50% grant, was introduced. Thus the principles of the present fixed-grant system were established.[5]

[1] *Hansard HC Papers 119*, col1759, 17 March 1919.

[2] Dyos and Aldcroft (1969), pp291–4.

[3] F Willson (1968, 2nd edn), *The Organisation of British Central Government 1914–1964*, pp72–6. In 1918 the Power and Transport Department was established within the greater Department of Commerce and Industry within the Board of Trade. A E Kirkus (1937), 'The Organisation of the MOT,' *Modern Transport*, 940, p6; 941, p5; 942, p11; 943, pp2, 9, 10.

[4] *Hansard HC Papers 122*, col1656 of 11 December 1919.

[5] Buchanan (1970), p15; Jenkins (1959), pp125, 127–8.

THE TRAFFIC ADVISORY COMMITTEE

In 1920 an advisory committee reported to the Minister on action needed to deal with London's traffic problems. In his covering letter the chairman, Kennedy Jones, said that only a complete remodelling of co-ordination machinery and an increase of existing powers, preferably vested in a new three-man Greater London Traffic Authority (GLTA), would suffice. The report stated: 'Above all a just and true preconception of the proper functions of each form of transport is needed in order that wasteful competition may be avoided.' The GLTA would have power to examine individual transport schemes, to arbitrate on their finance, to undertake surveys and research, to prepare a transport plan, to establish building lines, traffic routes and traffic management systems, to comment on traffic aspects of housing and planning schemes, to co-ordinate passenger transport, and to approve the design of vehicles.[1] The Committee believed that the local authorities within the Metropolitan Police area were:

> so numerous, their personnel so changing, and their interests so divergent that . . . there is no possibility of a selection from these sources of a small body such as is required for effective action, which could in any way be considered as representative of the whole. Indeed any authority constituted on these lines would be unwieldy and the difficulties of obtaining a wide range of vision and carrying out a continuous policy would be insuperable.

In 1919–20 the LCC had requested a Government investigation of the whole system of London government. In 1921 the Government appointed the Ullswater Commission to do so, which reported two years later. The LCC, the Labour Party and Mr Herbert Morrison made strong representations that a Greater London Council (GLC) should be established as a multi-purpose authority with boundaries extending over a wide area, nearly three times as large as that of the present GLC.[2] The majority of the Commission, however, felt that no case had been made for abolishing the outer London authorities and establishing such a body.

The Commission, which Robson has described as 'an unmitigated fiasco,'[3] failed to make any significant impact on the problems of London government. It recommended that to deal with transport, town planning, housing and main drainage matters an advisory group with up to 20 members should be formed. Despite the earlier rejection of a large advisory group by the Kennedy Jones Committee, the Ullswater recommendation clearly resulted in the setting up, in 1925, of just such a body for traffic matters:

[1] MOT (1920), *Report of Advisory Committee on London Traffic*, Cmnd 636.
[2] Nearly 2000 square miles, the area covered by the London Electricity Board, and on which the LPTB area was later based.
[3] Robson (1948), pp294–314.

London and Home Counties Traffic Advisory Committee (LHCTAC). It had a membership which eventually reached 45 (2 from central government, 22 from local authorities, 3 from the police forces, 4 from the main line and underground railway companies and 14 selected by the Minister to represent specific interests). It covered the London Traffic Area, roughly 25 miles in radius from the centre of the city. With the exception of occasional reports, the Committee proved as ineffective as the Kennedy Jones committee had feared such a body would be, and dealt mainly with detailed matters of local traffic schemes such as bus stopping places and pedestrian crossings. Nevertheless, the Committee endured until 1962 by which time the MOT had decided to play a direct role in London traffic matters by setting up the London Traffic Management Unit. No doubt the Ministry was influenced in this by the Herbert Commission's verdict on the LHCTAC:

> It is a means, and a very cumbrous means, of trying in the interests of traffic to reconcile the differences or conflicts of interest between the various authorities and classes of road users concerned. In consequence, their work has been slow and tortuous in spite of the devotion of its members and the energy and ingenuity of its Chairman.[1]

As the successor of the Roads Board the MOT, through a series of local conferences, had managed to negotiate with local authorities in London for 65 miles of new roads and 35 miles of widening schemes, but in 1926 the principle of applying road tax solely to road expenditure was abandoned and the Treasury were empowered to retain one-third of the licence duty receipts. In 1927 £7 million were abstracted from the Road Fund and in 1928 £12 million, the whole net balance, to the great wrath of motoring interests.[2] This and the generally poor national financial and employment situation curtailed new road construction severely. Dyos and Aldcroft have suggested that low calibre of the Ministers of this period, their relationship with Chancellors of the Exchequer, and the greater priority given to railway problems were also contributory factors.[3]

THE FORMATION OF THE LONDON PASSENGER TRANSPORT BOARD IN 1933

Throughout the First World War and the period 1919–30 the Underground Group arranged a fares pooling system with the other major operators. A great advantage of this voluntary move towards a co-ordinated system was that some measure of security was given to operators who, like the LGOC, had a large number of services which were unprofitable for part of

[1] The Royal Commission on Local Government in Greater London, 1957–60 (1960), *Report*, Cmnd 1164, para406.
[2] Buchanan (1970), p15; and Plowden (1970), pp183–213.
[3] Dyos and Aldcroft (1969), p371.

their length or at certain times of day. The early 1920s saw the appearance of a number of independent bus operators ('pirates'), who took up what traffic they could get by plying along existing and new routes. This upset the cross-subsidisation patterns of the LGOC rather than its overall financing,[1] but it was stopped by the 1924 Road Traffic Act which gave the LGOC a virtual monopoly by restricting the entry of new operators. From 1926 to 1932 the LGOC bought up forty-eight of these independent companies.

Meantime the Government had sought to help the capital financing of rail development: Government guarantees of loans were assured under the Trade Facilities Act 1922 and by means of this the Hampstead tube was extended to Kennington, and the City and South London Railway to Morden in 1923–26.[2] Likewise in 1929 the Developments (Loans, Guarantees, and Grants) Act was passed with the purpose of encouraging building schemes to alleviate unemployment. The Piccadilly Line was extended northwards and westwards at a cost of £9.9 million.[3] By this means also the Wembley to Stanmore branch of the then Metropolitan Railway was built, the Upminster Line electrified and some District Line track quadrupled as part of an £11 million programme of new works in 1930–33.[4]

Meanwhile in 1926 the LHCTAC initiated a series of investigations into the travelling facilities in north, north-east, east and south-east London which were the areas where problems were thought to be worst. In 1927 the LHCTAC 'blue' report suggested, in addition to the pooling of revenues, the appointment of a public body to oversee questions of fares, services, and the use of existing resources, from the point of view of the consumer and taxpayer.[5] This entailed a common fund and management for the Underground Group and the railways but there was considerable opposition to the creation of what was seen as a private monopoly.

In 1929 the LCC and the London Electric Railway Company both promoted private bills seeking to co-ordinate London's public transport systems, but in the same year the Labour Party was brought to power with Herbert Morrison as Minister of Transport.[6] He introduced a bill to bring all London's transport undertakings within state ownership over an area of 1840 square miles (the same area as that given to the London Electricity Board in 1926). His concept was that of a board running an undertaking on efficient business and technical lines (i.e. without a subsidy), without favour to any sectional interest, whether governmental, municipal, capitalist or

[1] J Hibbs (1972), 'The London Independent Bus Operators 1922–34', *Jnl of Tr Hist*, 5, pp274–83.

[2] Lee (1967), p24.

[3] Lee (1973), p21.

[4] Lee (1968), p28–30; and (1973), p20.

[5] LHCTAC (1927), *London Traffic*, p3.

[6] *Hansard HC Papers 250*, cols47–178, 23 March 1931. His thinking was later expounded in *Socialisation and Transport* (1933). C D Foster has some interesting comments on Morrison's ideas about public trust, the public good, the role of Ministers, in *Politics, Finance, and the Role of Economics* (1971), pp28, 33, 77, 85–6, 223. See also W A Robson (1960), *Nationalised Industries and Public Ownership*.

Labour. He believed such a body was necessary to eliminate 'wasteful' competition and to prevent the separate development of the various networks by individual operators, which would have entailed duplicated investment.

The Bill encountered much opposition: some opposed it on the doctrinaire grounds that nationalisation was not necessary to remove wasteful competition; others because Morrison proposed to give the Minister the unprecedented power to appoint the whole of the management Board; and the shareholders of the Metropolitan Railway, the one transport company who strongly objected to the Bill, because they claimed the proposed compensation was insufficient. By the time the Bill had been through a Joint Committee of both Houses of Parliament in the 1931–32 sessions and Mr Pybus had become Minister of Transport in a new Government, many of the objections had been overcome and terms had been agreed with the Metropolitan. Control over the Board was to be undertaken by a group of five trustees, and a joint committee was to be established with the main-line railways. The revised legislation received Royal Assent in April 1933.[1] The new London Passenger Transport Board (LPTB), which encompassed 5 railway companies, 14 municipal and 3 private tram companies, and 61 bus companies, thus provided the machinery for an altogether greater degree of transport co-ordination in London. But it also placed control with central government and from 1933 until 1970 local authorities in London had no direct means of influencing public transport in their areas; by comparison most of the larger provincial authorities operated their own bus or tram undertakings throughout this period.

Problems rapidly mounted for the London Board: the values of stock transferred to former company shareholders had been 'generous beyond the dreams of avarice' and were costing £4.5 million in interest payments, new vehicles had to be bought, staff compensated, a £7 million outstanding capital debt paid, and savings were less than anticipated. In 1938 the Board defaulted on its *C* stock interest payments (equivalent to ordinary shares). Its duties to the public, its staff and its shareholders were proving difficult to manage.[2]

The LPTB arranged a pooling system with the main-line railways for their stopping services under which the LPTB received 63% of fares revenue. Of the remaining 37%, no less than 25% went to the Southern Region. The LPTB, GWR and LNER formulated the 1935–40 New Works Programme, or '£40 million plan,' under which major new rail schemes were contemplated and overdue works of electrification were to be undertaken (see Case Study *C*). Because of its financial problems the LPTB could not support its borrowing, and the London Electric Revenue Corporation was formed with Treasury backing to guarantee the required capital. Schemes undertaken by the Board with this finance included a new

[1] *Hansard HC Papers 269*, cols1255–1314; *272*, cols657–739; and *274*, col843.

[2] E Davies (1937), 'The LPTB', in W A Robson (ed), *Public Enterprise*; and S F Edwards (1944), 'The LPTB' (unpub MA thesis, Univ of London).

link between Baker Street and Finchley Road to enable the Stanmore branch to be operated by Bakerloo trains, rebuilt stations (e.g. Sloane Square, Aldgate East, Notting Hill Gate) and extensions of the Central Line to Newbury Park in the east and Greenford in the west (completed after the Second World War), and of the Northern Line to East Finchley and Mill Hill.[1]

Tetlow and Goss were of the opinion that 'the LPTB did more to direct (or misdirect) the urban growth of London than any other agency was able to do;'[2] Jackson and Croombe were more critical: 'London was to be shaped to meet the economic needs of the Underground and (later) the (London Passenger Transport) Board . . . the planning was for (rail) transport and not for London.'[3] Robson criticised Frank Pick, vice-chairman of the LPTB, for the views he held about the role of the Board and the development of the City:

> As a transport executive he is naturally satisfied with the unified administration, the satisfactory monopoly, the £40 million of new capital guaranteed by the Government for expansion and improvement works. As the representative of the Transport Board . . . he desires the further growth of London to a population of 12 million persons or such larger size within the 15-mile radius as the straphanger's patience will tolerate.[4]

Certainly explosive population growth followed in parts of 'Metroland': for example Harrow grew from 49 000 to 97 000 people in 1921–31, Hendon from 56 000 to 72 000 in the first five years of the decade; Ruislip and Northwood Urban District grew by 100% in 1931–38, and by 326% in 1931–51. White has described how, after the extension of the Piccadilly Line, 'Arnos Grove, "Old" Southgate, Oakwood, and Cockfosters, some not even villages, all became large suburbs in less than five years.'[5]

Meantime the railways south of the Thames had also undertaken an extensive programme of electrification which had been begun in the inner suburbs in 1913–15 by the LSW and LBSC railways as a defence against competition from the motor-buses, electric trams and new tubes, and later to exploit the cheaper land and pleasant countryside and coasts of Surrey, Kent and Sussex as large areas were opened up by travel speeds considerably faster than those offered by steam traction. By 1933 the Southern Railway had spent £11.8 million on electrifying 800 miles of track, and very large increases of traffic were experienced on some stretches of line. As Moody said:

> From 1925 to 1939 there was intensive housing development in the

[1] Lee (1967), pp25–7; (1968), pp30–1; (1970), pp29–31; (1973), p21.
[2] J Tetlow and A Goss (1965,1st edn), *Homes, Towns and Traffic*, p25.
[3] A A Jackson and D F Croombe (1962), *Rails through the Clay*, p354.
[4] Robson (1948), p336, referring to F Pick (1932), 'The Organisation of Transport,' *Royal Soc Arts*, XXXIV, p211.
[5] White (1963), pp137, 100, 141, 167–9.

> electrified area and while some of it would no doubt have taken place if the lines had continued to be steam-worked, there is no doubt that it was greatly increased by the advantages of the electric services.[1]

Some of the increases were spectacular: the population of Chislehurst and Sidcup Urban District had grown by 9% in the years 1921–25 to 18 500 when the railway was electrified; the growth was 17% during 1926–31 but an incredible 155% in 1931–36 and by 1939 had reached 61 800; Orpington almost doubled in size during 1934–39 and Coulsdon and Purley did so in 1926–36.[2] White has described the similar effects of the extended Southern Railway electric services allowing the separation of homes and workplaces and so permitting the development of 'dormitory' estates—either municipal, like those of the LCC at St Helier, or private, such as Beckenham where nearly 40% travelled to central London jobs.[3] Foster has been as critical of the limited view taken by the Southern Railway and LT of their role in shaping the city as Robson was of the LPTB:

> London Transport, and of course, the Southern Railway, left an indelible mark on the land-use pattern of London. But one does not feel this was done with any conscious understanding of how public transport might mould a city. Whilst this may be easily understood in the 1930s, London Transport did not develop any stronger sense of the relation between transport and land use planning in the 1950s.[4]

Despite the apparent shaping of city growth by the railways, the operating companies themselves showed poor returns to their shareholders: the Southern was the most profitable, yet in 1938 paid only ½% dividend. The LNER paid no ordinary dividend at all between 1925 and 1938.

THE 1939–45 WAR: CONTROL OF PUBLIC TRANSPORT AND NEW ROAD PLANS

With the outbreak of war the Government took control of the railways as it had done 25 years earlier, in order to have total and immediate command of the system. Once again an Executive Committee composed of railway managers was established and each company received a fixed annual net revenue related to a 'normal' pre-war year; that of the LPTB, for example, was £4.7 to 4.8 million. The canals were in decline, and petrol rationing severely curtailed road traffic, so that the burden on the railways was all the greater: freight traffic increased by one-third and passenger traffic nearly doubled; but the quantity of rolling stock remained the same,

[1] G T Moody (1958), *Southern Electric 1909–68*, esp pp85–7.
[2] White (1963), pp68–70.
[3] White (1963), pp65, 202, 211.
[4] C D Foster (1972), *Public Enterprise* ('Fabian' Research Series 300), p10.

and considerable obsolescence and damage was incurred without much repair and replacement.[1]

During the War the Government began to consider desirable post-war policies of planning and reconstruction (for instance through the Scott and Uthwatt Committees on physical planning). In 1943 Abercrombie and Forshaw produced their County of London Plan, partly based on a pre-war road plan for London produced for the MOT by Bressey. It included an arterial *B* ring road with other major inner and outer *A* and *C* rings, and eight major radials, four of which intersected in the centre. In 1944 Abercrombie added an arterial *D* ring and a sub-arterial *E* ring in his Greater London Plan produced for the Minister of Town and Country Planning. This was the pattern subsequently recommended in 1947 to the Minister by the Clement Davies Advisory Committee on London Regional Planning. When preparing their first Development Plan,[2] the LCC hoped to persuade the Government to upgrade the *A* ring to arterial status but this was unacceptable at a cost of £88 million,[3] and a much more modest range of schemes went into the plan. In fact there was little new major road construction in inner London during the 1950s and 1960s, although more in outer London and beyond, mostly undertaken by the MOT. With the exception of the *A* ring, however, the ring and radial proposals of Bressey and Abercrombie formed the antecedents of the urban motorway system proposed by the GLC in the 1960s. Abercrombie also proposed some major improvements to the tubes and the linking up of the BR termini in central London.

NATIONALISATION AND THE BRITISH TRANSPORT COMMISSION

In 1945 the railway system was, if anything, more battered and war-weary and in worse financial straits than in 1919. On the basis of successful war-time control and co-ordination and the working of the LPTB the Labour Government decided (unlike its Conservative counterpart in 1919) that the major transport undertakings should be nationalised and brought under a single body which would control planning and financial policies including fares and charges; separate Executives for the railways, LT, the docks and waterways, road transport, and hotels would undertake operations. The controlling body thus established in 1947 was the British Transport Commission (BTC). Given the size of the undertaking and the scale of its problems it is not surprising that the main-line railways dominated the Commission's activities. After meeting the costs of repairing the wartime damage, a vast modernisation plan was formulated, costing £1200 million at 1955 prices (revised to £1660 million in 1957).[4] This

[1] K M Gwilliam (1964), *Transport and Public Policy*, p92; and C I Savage (1957), *Inland Transport* (History of the Second World War UK Civil Series).
[2] Under the Town and Country Planning Act 1947.
[3] Buchanan (1970), pp21–36.
[4] C N Reid and K Allen (1970), *Nationalised Industries*, ch5, esp pp115–16.

plan included the replacement of steam with diesel or electric locomotives, modernised signalling, track and rolling stock, the electrification of the London and Manchester main line, as well as extended electrification on the Eastern and Southern regions.

The BTC initiated a unified charging system for passenger and freight traffic; Reid and Allen have described succinctly how the charges levied meant that the railways were left with increasingly unprofitable traffic in both sectors. Despite a revised scheme of charges this situation was not improved. In fact, it gave even less room for manoeuvre regarding passenger services, for which the BTC and British Railways (BR) held an ill-defined obligation to maintain services to certain communities or at certain levels for social reasons.[1] Thus by 1963 the railways' operating deficit had reached £75 million.

After severe criticism by the Select Committee for Nationalised Industries in 1960 of the way the Government and the Commission had handled railways and of the methods of capital financing and of fares and charges, a new plan was produced by an advisory group set up by the Government. This group saw the railways and their financial problems as the heart of the Commission's plight and concluded that its activities were 'so large and so diverse that it is virtually impossible to run them as a single undertaking.'[2] This led to the Transport Act of 1962 which broke up the BTC and established separate Boards for railways, ports, waterways and LT, while other activities such as hotels were controlled by a holding company. The LT Board was 'as hitherto' to work closely with the BR Board 'on all matters of common concern' (see below). Much of the railways' capital debt of £705 million was held in suspense, and the new Railway Board's book assets were reassessed at some £312 million less than those of the Commission, partly as a result of having to pay no interest.

In 1963 the Board published a report examining the state of the railways by Lord Beeching, who claimed that only some of the main trunk freight and passenger services were making profits and that many rural lines, stopping and suburban services, were making slight to heavy losses. In 1961 all suburban services lost £25 million, although the loss in the London commuter area, which produced 86% of the suburban revenue, was relatively small.[3]

After Beeching, however, continuing transfers of freight traffic to road haulage and of passengers to cars contributed to a growing annual deficit which by 1969 had reached £92 million on freight operations and £85 million on passenger services, including £24 million on suburban routes. This occurred despite cuts of 4300 miles of loss-making railway routes and 157,000 staff since 1962.[4] The Board was criticised for inaccuracy in its

[1] Reid and Allen (1970), p115; and Gwilliam (1964), ch6.
[2] *Hansard HC Papers 254*, 1960, esp para333 onwards; and MOT (1960), *Proposals for the Reorganisation of the Nationalised Transport Undertakings*, Cmnd 1248, esp paras5–9, 13.
[3] BR Board (1963), *The Reshaping of British Railways.*
[4] BR Board (1969), *Annual Report*, 1967, app1.

costing, pricing and marketing strategy,[1] but there was also a growing belief that it should be relieved of the burden of those loss-making services services provided for social reasons. This led to the provisions of Barbara Castle's mammoth 1968 Transport Act which wiped out the £705 million suspended debt and an additional £557 million that bore interest, gave phasing-out grants for surplus track, removed 'sundries' freight traffic to National Carriers Ltd, and enabled the Minister to pay grants for unremunerative passenger services.

During the period under the aegis of the BTC, the LT Executive had been criticised for failing to obtain approval and finance for essential programmes of modernisation and rationalisation, and for inadequately improving the productivity and pay scales of their workers.[2] In 1948 the Commission had reviewed major rail extensions put forward by a committee chaired by Professor Sir Charles Inglis in 1944–46, including proposals for increasing the mileage of underground railway in London from 67 to 116. The Commission said:

> If the planning needs of the metropolis make new facilities essential, the labour and materials which will be required must be found from sources additional to those which are at present available to the Commission, and the cost should not be met from their financial resources.[3]

War damage was repaired and some of the New Works schemes were completed or carried out; for example, the Central Line was extended to Stratford in 1946 and Leytonstone in 1947 and Loughton (via LNER lines) and West Ruislip in 1948. The Metropolitan Line was electrified to Chesham in 1960.[4] The establishment of the Green Belt round London checked the outward spread of the suburbs and hence the growth in traffic envisaged by Ashfield and Pick before the War (see Case Study *N*). From the late 1940s no new works were undertaken until the Victoria Line was begun in December 1961. Thereafter the amount spent on new works grew to about £20 million in 1968. Of the expenditure on replacement and renewal, £5 to 6 million p.a. was spent between 1948 and 1954 on new buses (many to replace the trams and trolley buses) and £2 million p.a. in the four years after 1959. Between 1960 and 1963 there was a burst of capital expenditure on new tubes of £6 to 7 million annually, which was renewed after 1970.[5]

During the period in which they remained part of the BTC, the LT Executive had pressed for a more independent voice and initiative; from 1958 they published their own *Annual Review*, as a result of which coverage

[1] National Board for Prices and Incomes (1968), *Proposed Increases by BRB in certain countrywide fares and charges* (Report No.72).

[2] Select Committee on LT (1965), *Report* (vol1); *Proceedings and Evidence* (vol2). See Case Study *C*.

[3] BTC (1948), *1st Annual Report*, 1947, p5.

[4] Lee (1970), pp29–31; and (1972), pp30–1.

[5] GLC (1970), *The Future of London Transport*, app3.

in the BTC's reports shrank to a few pages. In the *Review* for 1958 the Executive hoped that they might 'play some part in closing the gap between what is happening and what ought to be happening in London today.'

DEVELOPMENTS IN THE 1960s

Under the 1962 Act the Executive was recast as a Board responsible directly to the Minister of Transport, although a Passenger Transport Committee for London was formed as a link with BR, with two subcommittees to co-ordinate long-term planning and day-to-day operation respectively. The Board's initial capital debt was £162 million, equivalent to LT's share of the BTC's indebtedness to stockholders and the Minister (other than loans of £14.4 million in respect of revenue deficit which were written off). Beside the long and costly job of replacing worn out and obsolete equipment and vehicles both the Executive and the Board had to cope with major losses of passenger traffic. Growing car ownership and use cut both peak and especially off-peak usage of the buses. Off-peak travel was also reduced by the growing popularity of television and the associated decline of the cinema and other spectator activities. At the same time the roads became more congested making the speedy and reliable operation of bus services increasingly difficult. With relatively full employment and a rising standard of living the labour-intensive bus industry suffered badly from increased wages which comprised 75% of its costs. Thus passengers transferred to other modes and services became more costly and less viable; fares were successively raised and services 'trimmed.' Between 1950 and 1970 the number of bus passengers dropped by 40% and the services provided were run at only 55% of their 1951 levels (see table). At the same time some passengers transferred from the buses to the more reliable Underground services. Thus while it was said in the 1930s that 'the buses kept the tubes alive . . . to the tune of £500 000' annually, from 1965 to 1971 the buses made an average net loss on traffic receipts of £5.2 million annually while tubes showed an average surplus of £2.5 million.[1]

(1962 = 100)	CENTRAL BUS MILES	FARES	RETAIL PRICES (NATIONAL)
1951	130	—	—
1962	100	100	100
1969	80	140	132
1970	78	167	140
1971	77	191	153
1972	74	218	165

As a result of this combination of factors the Board's finances continued to decline after 1963, and the Government made provision in the Trans-

[1] *Hansard HC Papers 269*, col1296, 27 October 1932; LT Board *Annual Reports*, 1965–69; and LT Executive, *Annual Reports*, 1970–1.

port Finance Act 1966 to cover revenue deficits of up to £16 million for the three-year period to 1968. In the event greater losses were incurred and further provision was made in the 1968 Transport Act; the revenue deficit grant was £10 million in 1968 alone. By 1968 the Board's capital liabilities had grown by an average of over £15 million annually to £255 million.

As far as travel by private car was concerned, the twelve years following 1939 saw what Plowden has called 'austerity motoring' with petrol rationing lasting until 1951,[1] and the number of cars produced for the home market being very limited. There was little Government discussion of major problems connected with motoring such as the demand for road space or action on road safety. Thus despite the fact that bad road congestion in London continued, and was the precursor of similar problems in the provincial towns and cities, the LHCTAC in a special study questioned 'whether it would be desirable at the present time, after so many years of severely restrictive private motoring, to impose new restrictions on the freedom of movement of private cars in Inner London.'[2] The Committee suggested increasing off-street parking accommodation, but also experiments with meter schemes as a means of providing revenue for such works. Their arguments were mostly accepted by the Minister, who in 1953 rejected proposals for further waiting restrictions.[3] 'Government policy towards the car as a method of transport appeared to allow it to develop as fast as its users wanted, provided this did not lead to embarrassing frictions with other users.'[4] The traditional assumption was that whatever problems of urban transport developed, the remedies would eventually catch up. Such a Micawber-like view indicated that the Government's priorities lay elsewhere: the Minister of Transport was outside the Cabinet from 1940 to 1957 and between 1947 and 1959 his senior official was a Permanent Secretary whose career lay in shipping; also, it was only in the latter year that the 'loose coalition' of Transport and Civil Aviation was broken up.[5]

Plowden has summarised the attitude of successive Governments to the motor-car in the twenty years up to 1970 thus:

> Only in the late 1950s did it start to become clear that it might not be possible . . . to satisfy all the demands on resources made by the car. This realisation was not followed by action. Comprehensive planning—in the sense of trying to maximise the advantages derived from the car by deliberately reconciling demands and resources—was still impracticable. This was partly due to the structure of British government: the policy outputs from the Cabinet continued to be little more than the sum of the several departmental inputs. Equally important, after sixty-odd years of broadly laissez-faire policy towards the car, any move to work out a

[1] Plowden (1971), chs15–16, esp pp318, 325, 328–9.
[2] LHCTAC (1951), *London Traffic Congestion*, para54.
[3] *Hansard HC Papers*, cols 2214–15, 15 July 1953.
[4] Plowden (1971), p342.
[5] Plowden (1971), p342; and Willson (1968), p360.

> positive policy, whatever its objects, could be attacked as 'against' the car. . . . The result of the government having no case to present was that the motorists prevailed by default; there was no adequate challenge to the view that in normal economic times as many cars should be provided for as the industry could turn out.[1]

The inability of the local authorities in London either individually or in concert (through the LHCTAC) to tackle the growing problems of traffic congestion led to the formation of the London Traffic Management Unit at the MOT which pioneered techniques for easing more traffic along existing urban roads, such as raising speed limits from 30 to 40 m.p.h. on certain main roads, one-way systems, limiting pedestrian crossings, linking traffic signals, and prohibiting parking at certain places and times. The LCC and the MOT co-operated to institute the London Traffic Survey in 1961–62.[2] Also, in 1959, the Minister of Transport had established the London Travel Committee to 'take action on the widest possible fronts in a new attack on London's peak-hour problems of overcrowded public transport and congested roads.' The chairman was also the chairman of the LHCTAC.[3]

By this time the Herbert Commission had been appointed to review London's complex local government, and they paid a great deal of attention to the undesirability of fragmented responsibility for roads and planning:

> A consequence of this divorce between transport and planning has been the grave increase in congestion on roads, railways and underground railways. The siting of offices in central London and the siting of the office workers' houses have fallen within the sphere of planning. The provision of necessary communications between the two have not been co-ordinated with the growth either of houses at the one end or offices at the other.[4]

Public transport provision depended on the financial position of the BTC, and for highway construction the ability of the Minister of Transport to make funds available was crucial. At the same time the divorce of the various elements in planning led to a lack of information, or of a comprehensive view or analysis of schemes for road or rail. The financial criteria for rail and road construction were, as Herbert pointed out, very different:[5]

[1] Plowden (1971), pp419–20.

[2] For the background to the establishment of the Survey and the operation of phases 1 and 2 see M D Goldrick (1967), 'The Administration of Transport in Greater London' (unpub PhD thesis, Univ of London).

[3] Royal Commission on Local Government in Greater London (1960), *Report*, Cmnd 1164, p116. There were four subcommittees—on railway developments (see Case Study *C*), new building developments, road traffic, and staggering of working hours (see Case Study *B*).

[4] Cmnd 1164, para347.

[5] Cmnd 1164, para439.

on the railways (including tubes), capital construction was justified only if the expenditure and expected return conformed to the necessity to balance the accounts in any one year; but the road schemes depended on a local authority's ability to convince central government of the need for a grant and to raise its share of the cost; unlike the railways there was no direct return, or any requirement to compute a notional one.

Robson has made the point that opportunities for co-ordinating transport planning have been missed on several occasions such as between 1831 and 1851 when a rational pattern of terminals could have been established enabling suburban lines to develop in a less tangled way, when the tramways were built after 1870 and as they were taken over by the local authorities in the 1890s, during the underground railway extensions of the 1890s and 1900s, and after the Royal Commissions of 1905 and 1923 and when the LHCTAC was formed in 1924.[1] The exclusion of public transport from the purview of the Herbert Commission was considered to be an unfortunate limitation not only by their critics but also by the Commission themselves.

Nevertheless the last 130 years have seen an increasing amount of co-ordination first by private takeover and agreement, and increasingly since the First World War, by a growing influence and control by central and (since 1965) local government. Control over the operation of and provision for passenger travel in London may be seen to have reached a peak in the early 1950s when all means of travel apart from the relatively small numbers of private vehicles were wholly within public control. Since then the growing number of car owners (and thus of individual transport decision makers) has led administrators to seek new forms of control.

The work of the Herbert Commission and its report, subsequent changes in the London Government Bill, and the provisions of the Act and its early operation, have been closely studied by Rhodes and others.[2] Against the general background of these studies and the brief historical account in this chapter, the remainder of this book examines the arrangements since 1965 for transport administration as one function, but a highly important one, of London's government.

[1] Robson (1948), p140.

[2] See G Rhodes (1970), *The Government of London: the Struggle for Reform*, esp pp65, 77, 95, 174–7, 180–2; and G Rhodes (ed) (1972), *The New Government of London: The First Five Years*, ch8, pp263–98.

Chapter 2

THE ROLES OF THE INSTITUTIONS

A study of transport organisation must be concerned with the statutory framework within which plans are made and decisions are taken. This chapter describes the various institutions which administer the planning and operation of London's transport system and their powers and responsibilities in this field as set out in legislation or policy statements. The way authorities are organised to carry out their functions and their methods of communication, consultation and co-ordination with related institutions, and how these in turn modify the statutory conception are considered in the following chapter.

STATUTORY BODIES

Throughout the 1960s it was a consistent aim of the Government to divest itself of functions that could be dealt with by local authorities, not least in the field of transport. A transfer of functions, however, from central to local government depended on strengthening the local government structure. This was certainly a major factor leading to the London Government Act 1963 and the consequent reforms of 1965.[1] The reorganisation of local government in the rest of the country which was to come later was also founded on the principle of a new relationship between central and local government, as well as on a need for restructuring the local authority system. A similar principle lay behind the creation, in 1968, of the four conurbation transport authorities.[2] Accompanying these changes, and inseparable from them, was the concept of a much firmer role for the Government in co-ordinating policy at the national level and setting the framework within which local government would operate. It was considered that the role of central government departments in this respect had become obscured by an increasing accumulation of executive and often very detailed or local functions. Again, this had become particularly true of the work of the Ministry of Transport (MOT).

The Government also believed that better central co-ordination of policy and decision making at the national level depended on the integration of related functions within Government departments. This led, in October 1970, to the publication of a White Paper announcing a general reshuffle of

[1] For a detailed analysis of the history and purpose behind the reform of London government see G Rhodes (1970), *The Government of London: The Struggle for Reform*, Weidenfeld & Nicolson/LSE.
[2] *Transport Act 1968*, ch73, ptII.

the Government's departmental structure. The Department of the Environment (DOE) became (on 12 November) the major of several new departments, and aimed to bring together related fields. Planning, development and transport were accepted as being inextricably related:

> These are among the main functions of local authorities . . . and because they give rise to acute and conflicting requirements, a new form of organisation is needed at the centre of the administrative system.[1]

The DOE took over the responsibilities of the former Ministries—Housing and Local Government, Public Building and Works, and Transport—under one cabinet minister, the Secretary of State for the Environment. Within the Department, functions were divided and placed under the charge of three ministers. (These were not cabinet ministers, nor were they responsible for separate ministries as such, but took responsibility for related groups of functions within the Department.) These were:

Minister for Housing and Construction. Responsible for, amongst other things, housing programmes, finance and improvement, new towns and building research and development.

Minister for Transport Industries. Responsible for the various nationalised transport undertakings with which the Government was directly involved together with road and vehicle safety.

Minister for Local Government and Development. Responsible for local government, regional land use and transport planning, roads and road passenger transport.

Regional economic policy and the control of air transport became the responsibility of a new Department of Trade and Industry, successor to the Board of Trade and the Department of Economic Affairs, but ultimate responsibility for all the principal matters affecting transport was, for the first time, in the hands of one cabinet minister, the Secretary of State for the Environment.

The integration of related functions within the DOE, rather than the mere stitching together of those of its three constituent ministries, could not be achieved overnight and was the aim behind continuing evolution of the internal organisation. Indeed the three former ministries themselves had moved some way towards internal functional co-ordination prior to the merger. Statements issued by the Ministries of both Housing and Transport had increasingly stressed the need for an integrated approach to land use and transport. In 1963, for example, a White Paper entitled *London: Employment, Housing, Land*[2] emphasised the adverse effects on London's

[1] *The Reorganisation of Central Government* (1970), Cmnd 4506.
[2] MOHLG and Minister for Welsh Affairs, Cmnd 1952.

transport system arising from an increasing separation of homes and work-places. In 1967 the Minister of Transport said:

> The provision of transport . . . can no longer be considered in isolation from other developments. It must be built into the whole planning of our community life so that no factory is sited, no housing estate or 'over-spill' developed, no town replanned without the implications for the movement of people and goods having been studied and incorporated from the outset.[1]

The move towards functional integration has characterised structural and legislative changes in both local and central government, and the creation of the Greater London Council (GLC) in 1965 and the DOE in 1970 may be regarded as milestones in this process.

The Department of the Environment

Statutory functions. The examination and approval of local development plans is a major function of the DOE (and formerly the Ministry of Housing and Local Government (MOHLG)) and is intended to be a means by which the work of local planning authorities can be co-ordinated and influenced by considerations of national and regional policy. In the particular case of London, the London Government Act 1963 created for the first time a system whereby local planning functions were formally divided between two types of authority within the same area.[2] 'The GLC,' it said, 'shall be the local planning authority for Greater London as a whole' and 'the local planning authority as respects any London borough shall be the council of the borough and as respects the City shall be the Common Council.'[3] The GLC would first prepare a development plan for Greater London as a whole (the Greater London Development Plan (GLDP)) for submission to the Minister for his approval (with or without modifications) after the formal objection and inquiry procedure. It would then be the task of the London boroughs and the City to prepare local development plans for their areas (see page 62). In the meantime development was to be controlled by an 'initial development plan' which was a patchwork of the plans drawn up by the former county and county borough authorities in Greater London.[4]

The character of development plans was revised by the Town and Country Planning Act 1968 which replaced the provisions of the Act of 1947. The new plans were to be much less concerned with detailed land-use allocations and much more with the broad pattern of development and policies related to it. They were to be backed up by more detailed local plans for

[1] MOT (1967) *Public Transport and Traffic*, Cmnd 3481, p1.
[2] As opposed to delegation arrangements operated by counties and districts.
[3] *London Government Act 1963*, ch33, s24 (2) and (3).
[4] Ch33 (1963), s25 (superseded by Town and Country Planning Act 1968).

particular areas which would also be subject to ministerial approval.[1] The first GLDP which appeared in mid-1969 is regarded (after approval) as one of these 'structure' plans although its preparation preceded the statutory regulations on the form and content of such plans and it was too late to incorporate the advice of a departmental manual.[2] Its form was determined by the 1963 Act and by a series of ministerial regulations before the 1968 Act came into force, although these were influenced by the recommendations of the Planning Advisory Group (PAG) (1965), and by the expectation that the borough plans would also be statutory documents.

Responsibility for the control of development was also split between the two levels of local government in London. The 1963 Act established that planning applications should be made to the boroughs or the City, but that not all would be determined by them. The Act itself did not specify how these powers were to be divided but provided for the Minister to make regulations setting out certain classes of application which would be decided either by the GLC or (in some cases) by himself.[3] This division of responsibility became the subject of continuing debate and modification, particularly between the boroughs and the GLC.[4]

The principal role of the DOE in the determination of planning applications is that of an 'independent' arbitrator where appeals are lodged against a refusal of planning permission by the borough or the GLC or, as in the case of the Hammersmith Air Terminal (see Case Study *E*), where the borough cannot agree with the GLC's determination. As with the approval of development plans, this quasi-judicial role is based upon the system of planning inquiries.[5] Non-statutory inquiries into matters of special importance such as that for the third London airport (the Roskill Commission) may also be conducted by the DOE.

In the field of transport in London, the DOE now has few functions of a purely executive character. Most of the traffic functions formerly carried out by the MOT became the responsibility of the GLC in 1965 while the nationalised transport undertakings have been increasingly organised to reduce the involvement of central government in their management. The prime function of the DOE in transport is the formulation of Government policy and, in conjunction with this, the responsibility for securing an appropriate transport share of the 'national cake' and then for allocating this between the various transport interests. In securing this money through the parliamentary vote system the DOE is in competition with the interests represented by other departments of State. There is also competi-

[1] *Town and Country Planning Act 1968*, ch72, ss1–14. Superseded by *Town and Country Planning Act 1971*, ch78, ss6–21. The provisions of the Act in this respect stemmed largely from the report of the Planning Advisory Group (PAG) (1965), *The Future of Development Plans*, HMSO.

[2] MOHLG (1970), *Development Plans: A Manual on Form and Content.*

[3] Ch33 (1963), s24 (6).

[4] For a discussion of this see G Rhodes (ed) (1972), *The New Government of London: The First Five Years*, ch9, pp299–346, by P Self.

[5] *Town and Country Planning Act 1971*, ch78, ss9, 13, 36, 47–50.

tion in this respect between transport and other interests such as housing and new towns within the DOE itself.

Second, as the head of the institutional hierarchy, the Secretary of State for the Environment is chief arbiter of any conflicts that arise between bodies involved in the organisation of transport. In London these are primarily the GLC and London Transport (LT), the London boroughs, the City and British Rail (BR), but other authorities such as the Port of London Authority and the British Waterways Board are also involved.[1]

The direct executive functions of the DOE in relation to roads and traffic in London are largely confined to Trunk roads for which it remained the traffic and highway authority after the 1963 Act.[2] The DOE has a duty to 'keep under review the national system of routes for through traffic in England and Wales.'[3] Responsibilities of the DOE for other roads in London are largely confined to appellate jurisdiction for certain highway improvement schemes (but not traffic management schemes)[4] and to arbitrate in schemes to build or improve Principal roads eligible for a Government grant.[5] The DOE also determines after negotiation the element of rate support grant to be paid to local authorities for the maintenance and administration of highways.

The transfer of responsibility for LT in 1970 to the GLC considerably reduced the Government's stake in the organisation of public transport in London but the DOE carries important responsibilities with regard to other bodies including the BR Board and the other nationalised undertakings, the National Freight Corporation, the Port of London Authority, and the British Waterways Board. The powers of the DOE concerning these undertakings can be summarised as follows:

1 Powers to appoint top management and consultative committees (e.g. BR Board, the Transport Users' Consultative Committees).
2 Powers to obtain information (e.g. through annual reports).
3 Powers to direct development (through authorising capital investment programmes, e.g. of the BR Board).
4 Powers, occasionally represented as a duty, to make specific regulations regarding the conduct of business.
5 Powers to direct in cases of conflict between the Boards and the Government or other authorities (e.g. to the BR Board over subsidies to the London commuter rail services).

As far as public transport investment is concerned, the DOE determines

[1] The British Airports Authority is under the control of the Secretary of State for the Department of Trade and Industry.
[2] That is, for the purposes of the Road Traffic and Highways Acts. For the background to this see Gerald Rhodes (1970), *The Government of London: The Struggle for Reform*, esp pp181–2.
[3] *Highways Act 1959*, ch25, s7 (2).
[4] This situation was under review at the time of writing.
[5] Under s235 of Highways Act 1959.

ceilings of capital expenditure and levels of loans by the bodies mentioned, and also LT, and may make grants in aid of capital expenditure on major fixed assets (e.g. railway track, signals, interchanges), and other items such as new railway rolling stock and buses. In addition it can pay operating grants for unremunerative but socially desirable rail services (but not bus services) in London. The provisions with regard to BR and LT are dealt with more fully below.

The 'assumed' role of the DOE. The 1960s saw a growth of interest in physical and economic planning problems at the regional scale and especially in the South-East of England. The MOHLG produced the South-East Study in 1964. In 1965 the Department of Economic Affairs (DEA) appointed the South-East Economic Planning Council (SEEPC) to advise on regional issues and to assist a planning board of departmental officials created at the same time. The SEEPC also produced a plan for the South-East in 1967. This central government interest was shared by the constituent planning authorities of South-East England who had in 1962 formed a joint advisory committee later known as the Standing Conference on London and South-East Regional Planning (SCLSERP). After some difference of opinion on long-term strategies between the Council and the Conference it was a team of planners drawn jointly from the DEA, MOHLG and the Standing Conference that produced, in 1970, the third plan for the region[1] which was approved by the Secretary of State in 1971.

Matters of South-East regional planning became, in the same year, the responsibility of the Minister for Local Government and Development within the DOE. But although the DOE clearly plays a role in regional planning and policy, this role is nowhere statutorily defined and may be described as advisory and exhortative. The 'Strategic Plan for the South-East' for example, although endorsed by the DOE in 1971, depends for its implementation on the will and co-operation of several bodies (e.g. BR, GLC, County Councils) with differing interests and commitments.

Particular attention was paid by the former MOT to the role it played in London after the reforms of 1965 and the description of its 'assumed' rather than statutory responsibilities serves as a guide to those adopted, at least initially, by the DOE. In July 1968 the MOT produced a White Paper setting out the thinking behind the Transport (London) Act 1969. (An earlier White Paper had indicated the Ministry's recognition of 'special difficulties' in London.)[2] In this the Government clarified its views on the division of responsibility between the GLC and the Minister:

[1] The three plans were: MOHLG (1964), *The South-East Study 1961–1981*; SEEPC (1967), *A Strategy for the South-East*; South-East Joint Planning Team (1970), *Strategic Plan for the South-East.*

[2] MOT (1966), *Transport Policy*, Cmnd 3057, para64 reads: 'London's transport problems are unique in their size and complexity. And the ways in which they are being tackled represent the new approach which will be needed in other conurbations.'

> Urban transport is essentially a local rather than a national matter. Local people should be the best judges of the standard and quality of services they want and are prepared to pay for. In London the Greater London Council can appropriately take on this major task.[1]

After setting out proposals for major additions to the GLC's powers and responsibilities (in particular the take-over of LT) the White Paper set out 'a new role for the Ministry of Transport'. Five areas of responsibility were defined:

1 '*To ensure that the GLC receive the right guidance on national considerations* that affect the framework within which they must work,' notably the share of national resources for transport investment that can be made available for London (para 96).
2 *To collaborate* in devising with various interests represented in the Planning Group,[2] 'the best allocation of resources between the various alternatives (for capital investment) which may present themselves' (para 97).
3 *To mediate* ('whatever new relationship is ultimately established between British Rail and the GLC') between the GLC and BR on railway matters, not least because of the effect of the London network on the national system for which the minister has responsibility (para 98).
4 *To inform* and seek assistance from the GLC over individual problems in London which are of national significance (para 99).
5 *To alert* the GLC to technical and scientific developments relevant to transport and traffic in London (para 100).

The Greater London Council

A major reason for the creation of the GLC was the need for a single local authority 'to administer functions which require to be dealt with over the whole of Greater London'[3] and this reasoning was applied particularly in the fields of planning, highways, traffic management and housing. In discussing the functions of the GLC, Rhodes and Ruck have said:

[1] MOT (1968), *Transport in London*, Cmnd 3686, para38.
[2] The second item expressed the Government's desire to continue to participate in the co-ordination of transport in London which was initiated on a permanent formal basis by Barbara Castle in 1966 when she set up the Transport Co-ordinating Council for London (TCCL). Paragraph 43 of the White Paper said that 'the Government understands that proposals will be coming before the GLC to set up a Greater London Transport Planning Group under the Director of Highways and Transportation. The Group will consist of representatives of the GLC, the Ministry of Transport, London Transport and British Rail.' Although non-statutory in itself, the Group was eventually established (the Greater London Transport Group, see p142) to deal with consultation between those institutions statutorily required by the Transport (London) Act 1969 (s2), and was largely a replacement for the TCCL.
[3] *London Government: Government Proposals for Reorganisation*, Cmnd 1562 (1961), para8.

> . . . it is useful to consider planning, highways and traffic together, not only because of the links between them but also because, apart from housing, most other functions of the GLC, although important in themselves, do not add up to an argument for a large authority of this type. The GLC is a strategic planning authority . . . or it is nothing.[1]

A matter omitted not only from the provisions of the 1963 Act but also from the brief of the Royal Commission (the Herbert Commission) upon whose report the London government reorganisation was largely based, was public transport.[2] The need to plan public transport, land use, highways and traffic together was recognised by the Transport Act 1968 which created Passenger Transport Authorities for four provincial conurbations (Tyneside, the West Midlands, Merseyside and South-East Lancashire–North-East Cheshire) to carry out this task. London was the subject of separate legislation the following year giving the GLC a new status as transport planning authority for London. This was enacted by giving the GLC overall control of LT together with further plan-making and highway and traffic responsibilities.[3] Thus the character of the GLC as a strategic authority in the sense described by Rhodes and Ruck has been considerably reinforced, and the role of central government in the planning of London's transport system correspondingly reduced.

The GLC has become the most powerful body concerned with transport in London. But it has by no means comprehensive and exclusive powers in this field; other authorities (the London boroughs and BR for example) have powers and responsibilities which influence transport in London which are independent of or shared with the GLC.

The distribution of powers and responsibilities between central and local government, despite the reforms of 1965 and subsequent changes, is complex, as are the problems of the city and its transport system. One question which this book attempts to answer is how well, despite these complexities, the system carries out the tasks for which it has been established. Inevitably, the role of the GLC lies at the centre of such an inquiry, and of fundamental importance is the way in which the GLC is distinguished as a 'strategic' local government unit from the 'primary units' of local government—the London boroughs and the City of London. But first it is necessary to describe the statutory duty of the GLC.

The Planning of Greater London. The provision of the London Government Act 1963 relating to development plans reflected the intention that the GLC should be concerned with general policy for matters such as highways which it was considered should be treated for London as a whole. The Act required the GLC to produce a development plan to 'lay

[1] G Rhodes and S K Ruck (1970), *The Government of Greater London*, p96.
[2] *Report of the Royal Commission on Local Government in Greater London 1957–60*, Cmnd 1164.
[3] *Transport (London) Act 1969*, ch35.

down considerations of general policy with respect to the use of land in the various parts of London including, in particular, guidance as to the future road system.'[1] The Town and Country Planning Act of 1968 superseded this original provision but not before the form of the first GLDP (1969) had been determined.[2] The GLDP, when approved, will replace the initial development plan but the implementation of its land-use provisions will depend not only on the GLC but also on the London boroughs. All planning applications have to be made in the first instance to the London boroughs (or the City of London) but, as already noted, the Minister[3] can determine which class of applications are decided by the GLC. Regulations have included planning applications which fall within specified areas of comprehensive redevelopment and within 220 feet of the centre of a Metropolitan road[4] (see page 56). The Minister may also 'call in' certain applications for his own determination.

The GLC's role in transport. The Government's intention that the responsibility for transport planning and control in London should rest primarily with the GLC was made clear in the 1968 White Paper entitled *Transport in London*.[5] The subsequent Act of 1969 charged the GLC with the general duty to:

> Develop policies, and to encourage, organise and, where appropriate, carry out measures, which will promote the provision of integrated, efficient and economic transport facilities and services for Greater London.[6]

One of the basic purposes of the 'structure' type development plans required by the Town and Country Planning Act 1968 was that they should link 'land-use planning and transportation in a more basic and systematic way.'[7] But because of the time scale involved in their preparation and approval, and because they must relate to longer-term solutions, the Minister of Transport in 1968 asked urban authorities outside London to produce 'traffic and transport plans' for their areas.[8] These were to show traffic and transport policies and their relationships to longer-term objectives. The measures contained in these plans were to be designed specifically for the following main objectives:

1 *London Government Act 1963*, ch33, s25 (3).
2 *Town and Country Planning Act 1968*, ch72, ss1–5, 14 and sch1. See also consolidating *Act 1971*, ch78, ss5, 6–10, 19.
3 Previously the Minister of Housing and Local Government, but now the Secretary of State for the Environment.
4 *The Town and Country Planning (Local Planning Authorities in Greater London) Regulations 1965* (SI 1965, No.679), regs3, 4.
5 MOT (1968), Cmnd 3686.
6 *Transport (London) Act 1969*, ch35, s1.
7 MOT (1968), *Roads Circular No.1/68*, para2.
8 MOT (1968), *Traffic and Transport Plans*, HMSO, incorporating *Roads Circular No.1/68*.

a To relieve congestion.
b To help public transport.
c To build road safety measures into highway and traffic plans.
d To protect the environment by traffic management.[1]

This was an indication of what the Government expected of local authorities in terms of their transport functions, and how they would like to see policies developing. Although Greater London was excluded from the scope of *Traffic and Transport Plans* the Transport (London) Act 1969 went further and imposed on the GLC a statutory requirement to produce transport plans in addition to the GLDP. Unlike those to be prepared by other local authorities, the GLC transport plans had to pay 'due regard' to 'transport facilities and services outside (as well as within) Greater London.'[2] Their form and content has to be agreed by the Minister and prepared in consultation with BR and the LT Executive as well as with the London boroughs and other local authorities affected.

These plans, together with the GLDP, will eventually become the visible expression of the GLC's interpretation of its general duty to promote a system of integrated and efficient transport in London referred to earlier. But the GLC's various powers over public transport, roads and road traffic will be a major determinant in this process.

The transfer of overall responsibility for LT from the Minister of Transport through the 1969 Act gave the GLC a large measure of control over public passenger services in London. Apart from appointing (and paying) members of the newly created LT Executive, the GLC was given the task of laying down the broad principles under which the Executive should operate. 'The GLC, representing the users of (London Transport) services, (must) decide on the broad levels of service which the Executive should provide, and on their financial objectives.'[3]

The GLC also has the power to make either capital or revenue grants:

a to the Executive for any purpose; or
b to the (British) Railways Board in respect of passenger transport services or other passenger transport amenities . . . which appear to the Council to be required to meet the needs of Greater London.[4]

Thus the GLC is able to influence directly the services operated by the LT Executive, and less directly (through consultation and payment of grants) those operated by the BR Board.

[1] MOT (1968), para4.
[2] *Transport (London) Act 1969*, ch35, s2.
[3] MOT (1968), *Transport in London*, Cmnd 3686, para53, enacted by *Transport (London) Act 1969*, ch35, ss5 (1), 7.
[4] Ch35 (1969), s3 (1). Such expenditure, however, is not eligible for rate support grant in terms of the *Local Government Act 1966*, ch42, s1.

Road Traffic, Highways and Motor Vehicles. Under this heading in the London Government Act 1963 a general duty was placed on the GLC:

> To secure the expeditious, convenient and safe movement of vehicular and other traffic (including foot passengers) and the provision of suitable and adequate parking facilities on and off the highway [whilst paying] due regard to [the need to maintain reasonable access to premises, the effect on amenity and] any other matters appearing to the Council to be relevant.[1]

This general duty was repeated in the Road Traffic Regulation Act 1967 and in the Transport Act 1968 which, significantly, added 'the importance of facilitating the passage of public service vehicles' as a matter to be taken into account.[2]

It is important to distinguish the Council's role as a 'highway authority' and as a 'traffic authority.' Although in practice they are closely related, as far as legislation is concerned these terms have quite specific meanings.

A highway authority has powers to create, alter and improve roads (i.e. carriageways and footways) and is responsible for maintaining them.[3] New roads may be created by local highway authorities although Ministerial approval is required for roads connecting with a Trunk road and for Special roads (i.e. those whose use is limited to prescribed classes of motor traffic). The Minister himself may, of course, create new roads in consultation with the local authorities affected.[4]

Powers of improvement are complex but the most important are summarised in the 1959 Act as follows:

a The division of carriageways, provision of roundabouts, variation of the relative widths of carriageways and footways.
b Construction of cycle tracks.
c The provision of subways, refuges, pillars, walls, rails, fences or posts for the use or protection of persons using a highway.
d The construction and reconstruction of bridges and alteration of level of highways.
e The planting of trees, shrubs and other vegetation and laying out of grass verges. . . .[5]

Highways authorities have the power to prescribe 'improvement lines' for the widening of streets when redevelopment takes place; 'building lines' in front of which new buildings must not protrude; and 'frontage lines' determining the position of the front of new buildings.[6]

[1] Ch33 (1963), s9 (2).
[2] Ch76 (1967), s84 (1); and ch73 (1968), s130 (3).
[3] These powers and responsibilities are given largely by the *Highways Act 1959*, ch25. Also *London Government Act 1963*, ch33, s16.
[4] Ch25 (1959), ss11 and 26.
[5] Ch25 (1959), s64.
[6] Ch25 (1959), ss72–4 and sch9.

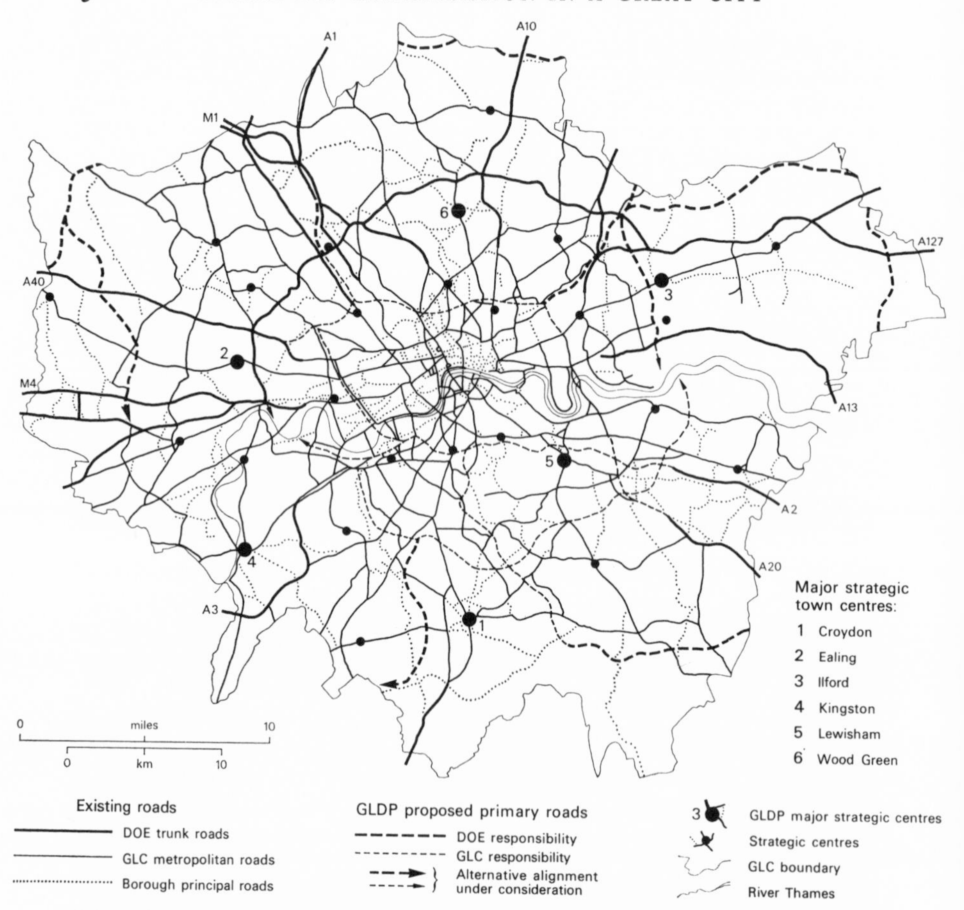

Figure 2 LONDON'S EXISTING AND PROPOSED MAIN ROADS AND THEIR HIGHWAY AUTHORITIES, 1970

The GLC is highway authority for about 560 miles of Metropolitan roads in London. The term 'Metropolitan road' has never been defined but relates to certain roads listed in the London Government Act 1963[1] which have a major traffic-carrying function. They are not, however, the only major traffic routes in London; there are in addition about 150 miles of Trunk roads for which the DOE is the highway authority, and about 320 miles of 'borough Principal roads' for which the London boroughs and the City of London are the highway authority[2] (see Figure 2). The London

[1] Ch33 (1963), s17, and sch7 (plus subsequent amending regulations).

[2] 'Principal roads' are those which are eligible for Government grants (normally 75%) under section 235 of the Highways Act 1959. In 1970 there were 877 miles of Principal road in London of which 64% were Metropolitan (GLC) roads and 36% were borough Principal roads. (See GLC (1972), *Annual Abstract of Greater London Statistics 1970*, vol5, p86.) The Transport (London) Act 1969, s29, provided for the transfer of the

boroughs are also the highway authority for local roads; that is, the remainder of the network other than Trunk or Principal roads—some 6800 miles. There are, consequently, thirty-five highway authorities in London.

Arrangements can be made whereby the GLC may plan, build, improve and maintain Trunk roads, while the boroughs can similarly act as agents for either the DOE or the GLC on Trunk and Metropolitan roads respectively.

The quantity of legislation relating specifically to footways is small compared to that relating to carriageways or highways generally. The Highways Act 1959 devoted12 of its 313 sections to footways. It gave highway authorities the power to create footpaths by agreement with land owners, or by compulsory purchase powers.[1] It also provided for compensation to owners of property demolished as a result of the creation of footpaths and for the maintenance of footpaths by local highway authority.[2] Other sections related to footpaths in urban streets, and these are grouped under the heading 'Safety Provisions'. The duty of highway authorities is to provide a 'proper and sufficient footway as part of the highway in any case where they consider the provision thereof necessary or desirable for the safety or accommodation of pedestrians.' In addition to this duty—which is permissive rather than mandatory—powers are given for lighting footpaths and providing 'raised paving, pillars, walls, rails or fences . . . for the purpose of safeguarding persons using the highway.'[3] Refuges can be provided in a carriageway 'for the protection of pedestrians crossing the carriageway,' while the provision of pedestrian subways is said to be 'for the purpose of protecting traffic along a highway . . . from danger, or of making the crossing of it less dangerous to pedestrians . . . .'[4]

The Act also empowers highway authorities to widen both carriageways and footpaths, using compulsory purchase if necessary, and to vary the width of either the carriageway or the footway at the expense of the other.[5] However, an indication of the relative importance to be attached to each is given by section 20 of the Road Traffic and Roads Improvement Act 1960[6] (which has not been repealed by subsequent legislation). It states that the widening of a carriageway shall not cease to be regarded as an 'improvement' (e.g. for grant purposes) simply because it involves reducing the width of or removing a footway.

A 'highway authority', then, is concerned with the extent, character and state of repair of roads. A 'traffic authority' is responsible for the regulation and control of traffic using them. The major powers and responsibilities of traffic authorities are contained in the Road Traffic Regulation Act

boroughs' 320 miles of Principal roads to the GLC, although at the time of writing this had not been implemented (see also page 109).

[1] Ch25 (1959), ss27, 28, 30, 31.

[2] Ch25 (1959), ss31 and 30 respectively.

[3] Ch25 (1959), s67.

[4] Ch25 (1959), ss68, 69.

[5] Ch25 (1959), ss71, 76.

[6] Ch16 (1960). This Act was produced during the Ministry of Ernest Marples and gave teeth to the management of traffic by the London Traffic Management Unit (see page 98).

1967 and subsequent modifications referring to London in the Transport (London) Act 1969.

The GLC is traffic authority for all roads in Greater London including (with the consent of the Minister) trunk roads, and its powers in this respect are therefore much more comprehensive than those relating to its role as a highway authority. The GLC's power to make traffic regulation orders, either for permanent or experimental schemes, embraces virtually all aspects of road traffic. The 1967 Act lists twenty-two different aspects[1] of which the most important are:

1 For prescribing the routes to be followed by any class or classes of traffic or vehicles, from one specified point to another, either generally or between any specified times.
2 For prescribing streets which are not to be used . . . by vehicles . . . either generally or at specified times.
3 For regulating the relative position in the roadway of traffic of differing speeds or types.
7 For prescribing the conditions subject to which, and the times at which, articles may be loaded . . . or unloaded . . . on streets.
15 Places in streets where vehicles . . . may or may not wait either generally or at particular times.
21 Priority of entry to public vehicles.

Other matters include *U* turns, movement of heavy vehicles and loads, traffic signs, taxi ranks, obstructions, and so on.

The 1969 Act gave the GLC further powers in the traffic field including the transfer of responsibility for providing pedestrian crossings from the Minister.[2] The Act also enables the GLC to transfer the operation and maintenance of metered parking spaces to a borough, whether or not the borough has agreed to accept them.[3]

The most important extension of the GLC's traffic powers was the control of off-street parking. Off-street parking places which are made available for public use can now be controlled by a system of licences in areas designated by the GLC. The licence may specify various conditions under which the parking spaces can be used, namely:

a The maximum number of spaces that may be used and the allocation of space as between long term, short term and so on;
b the scale of charges;
c the times of opening and closing; and
d the keeping of records on the use of the spaces.[4]

[1] Ch76 (1967), sch1.
[2] Ch35 (1969), s32.
[3] Ch35 (1969), s35. Formerly a borough's consent was required.
[4] Ch35 (1969), s36.

The Secretary of State for the Environment can also make an order specifying the control of parking places within a designated control area, but only 'if it appears to him expedient to do so by reason of any emergency. . . .'[1] The GLC now has wider powers over parking than any other local authority, being able to control the operation of all parking except off-street spaces for private use. The standard of provision of off-street parking spaces in new development is a separate issue and is subject to planning control.

Apart from the limited powers retained by the DOE over their traffic regulation activities, the only statutory obligation of the GLC towards other institutions is to consult with them before approving any traffic scheme. In the case of other local authorities the GLC must consult with any 'within whose area any road affected by the proposed (traffic) order lies or whose area appears to the Council likely to be affected by that order.'[2] The London boroughs are themselves able to initiate schemes but, because it is the GLC who make the necessary orders, in these cases consultation is inevitable. The GLC must also consult the police over any scheme whether it originated from them or a borough so that the statutory procedure is at the minimum a three-cornered affair. In practice there is a need also for consultation with bodies affected such as the LT Executive (with regard to bus routes, station accesses, etc.) and the statutory undertakers whose sub-soil services are frequently affected by road works.

Finally, for the function of registering and licensing motor-vehicles, the GLC acts for Greater London as if it were a County Council.[3]

To summarise, the GLC as traffic authority for London has wide powers and responsibilities to control traffic on all roads in London except Trunk roads where schemes require Ministerial consent. They also have an obligation to take account of other interests affected, in drawing up and examining schemes particularly those presented by the boroughs and the police.

The London Transport Executive

On 1 January 1970 the responsibility for LT's services was transferred from the Minister of Transport to the GLC and a new LT Executive took over from the former LT Board. It was constituted by the Transport (London) Act 1969 as a 'body corporate with perpetual succession and a common seal' for the express purpose of implementing the transport policies which the GLC under the same Act had to develop. Consequently the role of the LT Executive, whose members are appointed by the GLC, is subsumed into that of the GLC to 'promote the provision of integrated, efficient and economic transport facilities and services for Greater London.'[4]

[1] Ch35 (1969), s36 (15).
[2] Ch76 (1967), s8 (i).
[3] *London Government Act 1963*, ch33, s20. The Metropolitan Police's Public Carriage Office deals with licences for public service vehicles, including taxicabs.
[4] Ch35 (1969), ss4 and 1 respectively.

The general duty of the Executive, which is subject both to principles laid down by the GLC and to a statutory requirement to break even financially, is to 'provide or secure the provision of such public passenger transport services as best meet the needs for the time being of Greater London.' They must do this 'in conjunction with the (British) Railways Board and the (National) Bus Company, and with due regard to efficiency, economy and safety of operation. . . .'[1]

The principal financial duties of the Executive under the 1969 Act are to allow for the depreciation of their capital assets in their revenue (or operating) account, to establish a general reserve (the amount of which may be determined by the GLC) and to ensure 'so far as practicable' that their accounts balance for each accounting period or if there is a deficit in one period to make it good in the next. The length of the accounting period has to be agreed with the GLC.[2] These requirements were tempered initially by the writing-off of LT's capital debt by the Government at the end of 1969, and on a permanent basis by the powers given to the GLC and other authorities to make grants to the Executive. The GLC may make grants for any purpose; the Government can pay infrastructure grants (for fixed capital or rolling stock) under the Transport Act 1968[3] and (under the 1969 Act) operating grants for socially desirable but unremunerative Underground services which the Secretary of State for the Environment refuses to sanction the Executive to close.

Other local authorities may assist the Executive (or BR), using powers under the Local Government Act 1948, section 136 of which says:

> A local authority in England or Wales may, with the consent of the Minister given either generally or specially, contribute towards the expenses of any body carrying on activities within the area of that authority, being activities for the purpose of furthering the development of trade, industry or commerce therein, or of giving advice, information or other assistance to persons resident therein, or otherwise for the benefit of that area or those persons.[4]

The principles upon which the Executive must operate are, as already mentioned, largely for the GLC to decide, and the powers of the GLC in this respect are sufficiently comprehensive to be comparable with those of the Government in relation to the Railways and other Boards. It was the Government's intention in drawing up the Transport (London) Act 1969 that the GLC would set for the Executive 'interlocking "level of service" and financial objectives.'[5] The Act itself, however, although setting out the general duties of both the GLC and LT Executive contained provisions

[1] Ch35 (1969), s5 (1).
[2] Ch35 (1969), s7 (1), (2), (3).
[3] Ch35 (1969), s3 (1); and ch73 (1968), s56.
[4] *Local Government Act 1948*, ch26, s136.
[5] MOT (1968), *Transport in London*, Cmnd 3686 para52.

which were more specifically related to the financial performance of the Executive. The main provisions were for:

a The GLC to determine the amount and management of the Executive's general reserve (section 7 (2));
b the GLC to approve the Executive's capital expenditure programme (section 7 (5));
c the GLC to give general directions to the Executive 'in relation to matters appearing to the Council to affect the policies and measures which it is the duty of the Council . . . to develop, organise or carry out' (sections 11 (1) and 5 (5)); and
d the Executive to 'submit to the Council and obtain the Council's approval of':
  i 'Annual or other estimates of income or expenditure. . . .'
  ii 'Any major change proposed to be made in any of those estimates after their approval by the Council.'
  iii Proposals for major capital expenditure.
  iv The 'general level and structure' of fares.
  v Proposals to set up or co-operate with other companies (section 11 (2)).

Provision was also made for the GLC to review the organisation of the Executive and to direct changes thought to be necessary for efficient operation (section 11 (6)). Further, the Secretary of State for the Environment retained certain default powers with regard to the Executive and is able, if he wishes, to control the upper limit of their capital expenditure from year to year (section 7 (5)).

Within their 'operating brief' from the GLC, the Executive have certain specific powers directly related to their general duty of providing public passenger services (section 6 (1)). They can, for example, commission or carry out research (with the approval of the GLC), extend to such activities as hiring-out public service vehicles, providing car parks with or without garages attached, and designing and manufacturing their own buses and rolling stock and spare parts. The Executive can, moreover, operate services using any mode of transport on land or water, which may extend beyond the Greater London boundary—a provision which relates partly to the need for continuity of the services formerly provided by the LT Board and partly to the need for co-ordinating LT's services with those of other operators.

A major objective of the 1969 Act was to co-ordinate public passenger services. It laid on the Executive the duty to work where necessary with both BR and the National Bus Company (NBC) (which operates bus services outside Greater London) including its subsidiary London Country Bus Services Limited which operates the former LT Board's Green Line services.

The London boroughs

The thirty-two London borough councils and the Common Council of the City of London (referred to generally as the London boroughs hereafter) are the local planning authorities for their areas, while the GLC is the local planning authority for matters concerning London as a whole (see Figure 1). The division of planning powers and responsibilities between the two tiers is complex in detail and subject to change but is basically intended to reflect differing breadth rather than level of interest.

Under the Town and Country Planning Act 1971 the London boroughs have a duty to prepare structure plans for their areas but none had been completed during the period of research and preparation of this book.[1] These plans will guide long-term development and have to be consistent with relevant provisions in the GLDP (which will be the structure plan for Greater London). The information on which they are based must include the physical and economic characteristics of the area, population structure, communications, the transport system and traffic.[2] In addition the Secretary of State for the Environment or the GLC can direct the boroughs to incorporate other matters.[3] As already mentioned the borough structure plans will not require the approval of the Secretary of State. In addition local plans may be prepared for particular areas to show in greater detail relatively short-term proposals for development including measures 'for the improvement of the physical environment and the management of traffic.'[4] Meanwhile control over development is exercised in accordance with the Initial Development Plan.

The highways and traffic functions of the boroughs, at least in relation to London's transport system generally, are very limited. The Herbert Commission reported in 1960 that 'the only possible solution to the present administrative muddle, is for the organisation (of highways and traffic) to be in the hands of the Council for Greater London.'[5] As already described this recommendation was adopted with regard to traffic but highway functions were shared between the boroughs, the DOE (formerly the MOT) and the GLC. In terms of mileage alone the boroughs taken together are the predominant highway authorities in London, but the roads for which they are responsible are of lesser traffic importance than those administered by the GLC and the DOE. This difference will become even more marked when the GLC takes responsibility for all Principal roads in London.[6]

The boroughs can, at their own expense, close local roads (i.e. not Principal roads) to vehicular traffic for amenity purposes and carry out

[1] *Town and Country Planning Act 1971*, ch78.
[2] Ch78 (1971), s6 (3).
[3] Ch78 (1971), s7 (4), sch4 (7).
[4] Ch78 (1971), s11 (3).
[5] *Report of the Royal Commission on Local Government in Greater London 1957–60*, Cmnd 1164 (1960), para779.
[6] As provided for by the *Transport (London) Act 1969*, ch35, s29.

improvements such as paving and planting trees.[1] Although the GLC is traffic authority for Greater London the boroughs can devise traffic management schemes and submit them for the GLC's approval and they must be consulted on the GLC's own schemes affecting their areas.

With regard to car parking, the boroughs have considerable freedom as to the provision of car spaces in new development (through the exercise of planning control). On-street parking control schemes whether initiated by a borough or the GLC require the approval of the latter. The GLC may require a borough to operate parking meter schemes in its area. Boroughs may also be called upon to operate the licensing of off-street car parks open to the public in controlled areas designated by the GLC under section 36 of the Transport (London) Act 1969.[2] The use of private off-street parking space cannot be controlled either by the boroughs or the GLC with their present powers.

The role of the boroughs in traffic matters has been summarised by Camden Council in the following way:

> In the final event a London Borough . . . has no power. Its influence is thus by persuasion and is largely dependent on demonstrating by expertise in the transportation field the benefits to be derived from its own proposals or where appropriate . . . the undesirable consequences at the local level of the GLC's strategic policies.[3]

The boroughs may also act as agents for the DOE and the GLC in maintaining and improving their roads (in some cases designing new highways and works) and in devising traffic management schemes. For this they receive an agency fee, usually of about 2½% of the contract price.[4]

With regard to public transport the boroughs' powers are limited to providing, either singly or in conjunction, financial assistance to LT and BR. Section 56 of the Transport Act 1968 enables them to make grants towards capital expenditure for the 'improvement or development of any facilities for public passenger transport . . .' while the more general provisions of the Local Government Act 1948 enable them (with the Minister's consent) to pay operating grants (see page 60).[5]

British Railways Board

The BR Board was set up together with three other Boards for LT, Docks and Waterways by the Transport Act 1962 in succession to the British Transport Commission. It has the duty to provide railway and ancillary

[1] *Town and Country Planning Act 1971*, ch78, ss212, 213. (Provision first made in Act of 1968, ch72, ss92–3.)
[2] By the end of 1972, the GLC had not taken up these powers.
[3] London borough of Camden (1971), *Camden Scene: A Planning Survey*, para3.7.
[4] *London Government Act 1963*, ch33, s5.
[5] *Transport Act 1968*, ch73, s56 (2); and *Local Government Act 1948*, ch26, s136.

services in Great Britain having due regard to 'efficiency, economy and safety of operation.'[1] Like the other Boards, BR was required to pay its way taking one year with another,[2] but after six years of deficit on the revenue account the concept of this requirement to 'break even' financially was substantially altered by the Transport Act 1968. In 1966 the Government had said that:

> The touchstone of a sound railway policy is the extent to which it meets the country's overall transport needs. Commercial viability is important, but secondary . . . it is now widely recognised that the railway system cannot play its proper role in the economy of the country and also comply with the 1962 Act.[3]

The Transport Act 1968 maintained the requirement of viability but removed the responsibility of operating unremunerative services. It was for the Government to decide which unremunerative services were socially desirable and to pay the Board specific grants for their continued operation.[4] Furthermore, provision was made for infrastructure (capital) grants for the provision, improvement or development of facilities for public passenger transport in Great Britain.[5]

These statutory provisions relate to the BR Board as a national undertaking. It is also broadly true that BR is not organised with special reference to services for the London area (see page 116). The Transport Act 1968 removed the earlier requirement that six regional boards should share responsibility for the railway system with the central board, but executive matters continue to be handled by four regional offices.[6] None of these regional organisations was designed to handle the London railway services as an entity.

Following the review of transport policy by the Ministry of Transport under Barbara Castle, however, more attention was paid to the regional significance of railway services in the conurbations. As already mentioned the Transport Act 1968 set up the four Passenger Transport Authorities (and Executives) in the provinces while London was the subject of special consideration. The White Paper, *Transport in London*, declared that:

> BR services provided essentially for the needs of London cover places as far afield as Southend, Ashford, Brighton, Reading and Bletchley. Greater London, much smaller than the 'commuter area', has no special significance in terms of BR operations. The network of services in and around London is much denser than in other conurbations, and the

[1] Ch46 (1962), ss1, 3.
[2] Ch46 (1962), s18.
[3] MOT (1966), *Transport Policy*, Cmnd 3057, paras14 and 16.
[4] Ch73 (1968), s39. See also MOT (1967), *Railway Policy*, Cmnd 3439, paras2, 8 and 11.
[5] Ch73 (1968), s56 (1).
[6] Ch73 (1968), s38 (4), superseding s1 (3) of the *Transport Act 1962*, ch46.

> interrelation and operational interworking between services (and with long-distance services) is more complex. . . . In these respects the London situation is quite different from that in the provincial conurbations, so different arrangements for the organisation and financing of BR commuter services are required.[1]

But the Transport (London) Act 1969 which arose from the White Paper left these arrangements to a rather complex relationship between the Government, BR and the GLC which was shaped only in part by the statute, and for the rest relied on Government policy. The broad intention was that 'the London commuter area services will be treated as a network' and that 'the GLC must necessarily have a role in transport needs.'[2] The major element of Government policy was the decision to achieve financial viability for the London network as a whole, the means to be worked out between BR, the Minister and the GLC.[3] The statutory provisions of the 1969 Act relating to BR were mainly concerned with the planning of the commuter network, the financing of improvements and unremunerative services and fares. The general duties of the GLC in relation to transport planning and their obligation to consult the BR Board have already been described. In addition the Act required the Minister and the Board to 'have regard to any plan prepared' in drawing up or deciding on major railway investment proposals affecting Greater London.[4] Both the Minister and the GLC (and other local authorities) were enabled to make grants to BR for improvements or for the continued operation of loss-making services on the London network. The removal of control by the Transport Tribunal over passenger fares in London[5] was a corollary of giving greater responsibility for passenger services to the GLC. But the fixing of both fares and levels of service for the London network became the subject of tripartite consultation and agreement between the BR Board, the Minister and the GLC.

The 1969 Act provided for the GLC to lay down principles upon which fares are determined for services required to meet the needs of Greater London. The BR Board must fix fares in accordance with these principles. The Board must also take account of 'such financial objectives for those services as the Minister (after consultation with the Council) and the Board may from time to time agree.' Furthermore, the Board must consult the GLC each year about the general level and structure of fares for journeys wholly within Greater London and the general level of service. They must also inform the GLC of any proposed 'changes of substance in any such fares or in the level of provision. . . .'[6]

[1] MOT (1968), *Transport in London*, Cmnd 3686, para55.
[2] Cmnd 3686 (1968), paras55, 58.
[3] Cmnd 3686 (1968), para55.
[4] Ch35 (1969), s2 (3).
[5] Ch35 (1969), s27 (1).
[6] Ch35 (1969), s28.

Railway services in the London area have been treated as a whole for the purposes of co-ordination at an executive level. There have in fact been statutory provisions for the co-ordination of 'main-line' services with those of the LT system since the formation of the London Passenger Transport Board in 1933. Under the Transport (London) Act 1969 it is the duty of the BR Board, the LT Executive and the NBC 'to co-operate with one another' for the purpose of co-ordinating their passenger services and meeting the LT Executive's general duty of providing services which 'best meet the needs for the time being of Greater London.'[1]

British Airports Authority

The British Airports Authority was established in 1965 to 'provide at its aerodromes such services or facilities as are in its opinion necessary or desirable for their operation,' although it could only provide navigation services with the consent of the (then) Minister for Aviation.[2] It initially controlled the three major London airports (Heathrow, Gatwick, Stanstead) and one in Scotland (Prestwick). This functionally specialised body whose origins have been said to 'lie more in the chance of history than in the application of any general policy for airports' is obviously overwhelmingly concerned with the air traffic generated by the Metropolis, and as will be seen in Case Study *E*, is thereby involved in the impact of air travel on the road and rail transport systems.

Other statutory bodies, such as the British Waterways Board and the Port of London Authority, serve the metropolis but are concerned with freight transport which falls largely outside the scope of this book.

Statutory consumer bodies

There are two statutory bodies representing public transport users in Greater London, the Transport Users Consultative Committee (TUCC) for London and the London Transport Passengers' Committee (LTPC). The TUCC for London is one of several area committees which together cover the whole of Great Britain and which report to a Central Transport Consultative Committee. The Central Committee is directly responsible to the Secretary of State for the Environment. The chairman and the members of both the Central and area committees are appointed by the Secretary of State after consultation 'with such bodies as appear to him to be representative of the interests of persons likely to be concerned with matters within the competence of the committee.' It is the duty of the TUCCs to consider representations about the services provided by any of the nationalised transport undertakings except those relating to fares and charges and those 'appearing to (the) committee to be frivolous.' They must also consider

[1] Ch35 (1969), s5 (2) and (1) respectively.
[2] *Airports Authority Act 1965*, ch16, s2 (1).

matters referred to them by the Secretary of State or by one of the transport Boards, and can also consider other matters on their own initiative.[1]

The situation in London is complicated by the fact that LT is no longer a nationalised undertaking. The Transport (London) Act 1969 required the GLC to establish a new body to take over most of the functions of the TUCC for London with regard to LT services; this was set up in 1970 and called the LTPC. Its terms of reference, like those of the TUCCs, excludes consideration of fares and charges, but includes permanent closures of LT railways and stations. The Government's intention as expressed in the White Paper *Transport in London* had been to abolish the TUCC for London and to transfer the functions not to be taken over by the LTPC (i.e. matters relating to BR services in London and LT rail closures) to the TUCC for South-East England.[2] The latter body, however, was reluctant to accept the additional responsibility. Moreover, another objective in the White Paper—that of bringing the London commuter services under a single TUCC—would not have been met because commuter services already penetrated into the areas covered by two further TUCCs.

On the recommendation of the Central Committee the Minister of Transport finally decided to retain the TUCC for London.[3] Consequently the BR London commuter services are covered by four TUCCs, for London, the South-East, East Anglia and the West Midlands.

As explained above, fares and charges fall outside the scope of both the TUCC and the LTPC, but again the position in London is different from the rest of the country. Until 1970, the Transport Tribunal[4] could hear objections to proposals to raise public transport fares and charges anywhere in Great Britain, but the Transport (London) Act 1969 removed the function of the Tribunal with respect to Greater London.[5] The GLC is now ultimately responsible for LT fares and charges and is not compelled to investigate complaints or representations made by other bodies.

Permanent rail closures, whether BR or LT, are dealt with by the TUCCs who must report on any hardship that would arise from a closure but the Minister's decision is required. Before permitting a closure within Greater London, the Minister must consult the GLC, but if he refuses permission to close a line or station and if he is satisfied that the line is running at a loss, then he may pay a grant for its continued operation.[6]

The Metropolitan Police

While the major functions and responsibilities of the police in London are

[1] *Transport Act 1962*, ch46, s56. (The TUCCs and the Central Committee were first established by the *Transport Act 1947*, ch49, s6.)

[2] MOT (1968), *Transport in London*, Cmnd 3686, p12.

[3] Central Transport Consultative Committee for Great Britain, *Annual Report 1969*, p45.

[4] Established in succession to the Railway Rates Tribunal by the *Transport Act 1947*, ch49, s72.

[5] *Transport (London) Act 1969*, ch35, s27 (1).

[6] Ch35 (1969), ss25 (3), 26.

similar to those throughout the country, police organisation in the capital is unique in Britain, and this gives rise to certain differences in the operation of police matters. Not only has the major force, the Metropolitan Police, grown up largely independently of local government in its area of jurisdiction but also this area omits the one square mile of the City of London which has its own police force. Thus Greater London has two statutory police forces which are both geographically and administratively independent. In addition, the British Airports Authority, the Port of London Authority and the BR Board each have their own police forces which operate within and beyond Greater London; their officers have the same powers, privileges, duties and responsibilities as ordinary constables but they are under the direct control of the bodies concerned.[1]

The Metropolitan Police operate within an area of approximately 700 square miles known as the Metropolitan Police District of which approximately 100 square miles lies beyond the administrative area of the GLC in the north and in the south-west.[2] Consequently they are responsible not only for the thirty-two London boroughs but also for thirteen other local authorities in Essex, Hertfordshire and Surrey. This lack of coincidence with local authority boundaries is associated with a further unique feature of the Metropolitan Police: it comes directly under the control of central government through the Home Office and, unlike provincial forces, is in no way responsible to or controlled by any local authority. Like other police forces throughout the country, however, the Metropolitan Police are in part financed from rate precepts on the local authorities whose areas they serve.

The ultimate responsibility for the Force rests with the Home Secretary who also deals with general policy matters, including discipline, pay and conditions. Day to day operation is entrusted to the Commissioner of the Metropolitan Police who is appointed by the Crown. Responsible to him is a Deputy Commissioner and four Assistant Commissioners, one of whom is responsible for the Traffic Department. They are also appointed by the Crown on the recommendation of the Home Secretary.

The City of London Police were established in 1839, ten years after the Metropolitan Police, and operate under the direction of a Commissioner of Police appointed by the Common Council of the City but with the approval of the Home Secretary. The Force is financed by Government grants (since 1919) to the extent of one-third of its cost. Despite the tiny area for which they are responsible and their consequently small establishment, the City of London Police have similar functions to the Metropolitan Police with respect to transport and traffic, without of course having such specific

[1] *Airport Authority Act 1965*, s10; *The Port of London Act 1967*, s10; *The British Transport Commission Act 1949*, s53, as amended by the *Transport Act 1962*, ss69–71.

[2] When the London Government Act was implemented on 1 April 1965, the eastern boundary of the Metropolitan Police District was adjusted to coincide with the Greater London boundary which involved including an area previously under the Essex County Constabulary. (See section 76 of that Act.)

responsibilities as those towards the taxi trade or such wide interest in general police matters. The City Police, however, because of their independence, do enjoy a similar status to the Metropolitan Police in such matters as representation on consultative committees and working groups.

Whilst the overriding purpose and priority of the police is to maintain public order and safety by the prevention and detection of crime, the supervision of road traffic, enforcement of traffic regulations and inspection and regulation of vehicles form significant parts of the policing function.

The Metropolitan Police have certain specific responsibilities for road vehicles in use for transporting the general public. They license drivers and conductors of all public service vehicles (i.e. taxis, buses and coaches) through the public carriage office with the exception of private hire cars. They also have powers for checking the roadworthiness of vehicles, and the positioning of cab ranks. They have a general duty to enforce orders made by highway and traffic authorities and to help in this work they have been made responsible for the traffic warden force. Traffic wardens deal with routine traffic supervision and enforcement matters prescribed by order of the Home Secretary. But the police role regarding traffic is very largely the outcome of history: the police took over the control of traffic simply because they were the only ubiquitous representatives of authority on the streets who could perform this function. Since the police have a statutory duty to attend to accidents, it is hardly surprising that their role has been seen to include aspects of traffic supervision which contribute to their prevention.

The powers for initiating and developing traffic management and highway schemes lie largely with the various highway and traffic authorities, but the police have a right to consultation where traffic is involved since the extent and nature of traffic schemes introduced must pay some regard to the possibility of their being enforced. The main purposes for which the police must be included in the consultation process are traffic regulation orders in London,[1] bus routes and stopping places in the Metropolitan Police District[2] and the installation of pedestrian crossings.[3] Despite the statutory inclusion of the police in the consultation procedures of traffic authorities, there is no compulsion for account to be taken of police views. The police also have power to introduce traffic experiments or temporary schemes (covering all the aspects listed on page 58), but this is subject to the consent of the GLC.[4]

To summarise, the police in London have no statutory role in the formation of traffic policy or schemes. Their participation in this field is limited to consultation with the 'parent' traffic and highway authorities. Consequently the influence of the police in traffic matters is dependent more on

[1] *Road Traffic Regulation Act 1967*, ch76, s11.
[2] *Road Traffic Act 1960*, ch16, s141.
[3] *Road Traffic Regulation Act 1967*, ch76, s21.
[4] *Transport (London) Act 1969*, ch35, s11, sch2.

the view of the police role held by the traffic authorities than on the statutory institutional arrangements. Where the police do exercise an executive role is in enforcing legislation concerning driver behaviour and regulating traffic on the one hand, and coping with accidents and other emergency situations on the other. Both historical and practical factors may extend the role of police into the traffic management and surveillance fields and into wider aspects of road safety, but precisely where statutory duty begins or ends is largely a question of interpretation both by the police themselves and in their relations with the other authorities concerned.

NON-STATUTORY BODIES

Advisory, pressure and professional groups

This chapter has so far been concerned with the role of the statutory bodies involved in transport in London, but it is important also briefly to describe the constitution and functions of some of the major non-statutory bodies. The various regional planning agencies for South-East England, which are closely related to the statutory bodies, are dealt with first.

The South-East Economic Planning Council and Board. The Government decided in October 1964 to set up a Department of Economic Affairs which would produce a National Economic Plan and coordinate regional plans. To formulate the latter, eight regional councils were established including one for the South-East; these were advisory bodies of part-time members drawn from local government, industry, the universities and other fields.[1] The official role of the SEEPC (as it was entitled) was 'to advise the Secretary of State (for Economic Affairs) on regional issues and to assist a regional planning board' of departmental officials which was simultaneously created. In 1969, when the DEA was abolished, the SEEPC and Board became the responsibility of the Secretary of State for Local Government and Regional Planning (who was overlord to the MOHLG) and with the creation of the DOE in 1970, the Secretary of State for the Environment.[2]

The Standing Conference on London and South-East Regional Planning (SCLSERP). The Standing Conference (as it is generally known) is a joint advisory committee of local planning authorities in South-East England.[3] It was formed in 1962 because 'by the late 1950s the authorities of the London region were facing the most serious problems arising from the size and location of the population and employment increases in the

[1] DEA (1966), *Economic Planning in the Regions*, pp4, 7.
[2] Peter Self (1971), *Metropolitan Planning: The Planning System of Greater London*, Greater London Paper No.14 (LSE), pp38–9.
[3] There are eight similar groups elsewhere in England and South Wales.

region.'[1] Professor Peter Self has described the constitution of the Standing Conference as follows:

> It enlarged and standardised its area to coincide with the economic planning region established by 13 counties, and 10 county boroughs. It covered a similar area to the South-East Study south and west of London, but a much smaller area to the north and east where a separate region was created for East Anglia. The Conference comprised a body of local councillors nominated by the constituent authorities plus a technical committee of planning officers, and had the aid of a small planning staff. It had of course no executive powers, and action depended upon the constituent authorities.[2]

The South-East Joint Planning Team. The differing origins, composition and approaches of the SEEPC and the Standing Conference led the Government to invite them in 1969 to participate in a joint study on the region's long-term planning problems. The resulting study team comprised staff drawn from the DEA, the MOHLG and the Standing Conference and produced its *Strategic Plan for the South-East* in 1970. Like the earlier South-East Study (MOHLG, 1964), Strategy for the South-East (SEEPC, 1967) and Standing Conference papers, this was an advisory document but it received general approval from the DOE in 1971.

Voluntary pressure and interest groups. The interests of vehicle users and manufacturers were formally represented from an early date. The Society of Motor Manufacturers and Traders was formed in 1902, the Automobile Centre (later the Royal Automobile Club) in 1897, and the Automobile Association in 1905. Later additions included the British Road Federation (which was basically composed of firms and trade associations from the road construction and vehicle manufacture and operating interests), the Roads Campaign Council, the Road Haulage Association, the Freight Transport Association and others. All these bodies, which are often loosely referred to as the 'roads' or 'motor lobby,' are national rather than Metropolitan bodies.

The era of the motor-vehicle was preceded (and overlapped) by a time when the bicycle provided personal mobility for great numbers of people. The Cyclists' Touring Club was formed in 1896 to represent the interests of cyclists and continues to exist despite the fact that the use of cycles has declined sharply since the Second World War. The motor-vehicle brought with it a rising number of road accidents and in 1916 the Royal Society for the Prevention of Accidents was established. This was followed in 1933 by the Pedestrians' Association for Road Safety. These bodies, too, are organised on a national basis.

[1] SCLSERP (1965), *The Conference—A Stock-taking*, Joint Report of Administrative and Technical Panels to the Conference.

[2] P Self (1971), p39. The enlargement of the Conference area involved the inclusion of Oxfordshire, the Isle of Wight and seven county boroughs.

There are many other voluntary groups some national, some London-wide and many local, with varying interests, resources and sponsorship. To catalogue them all would be a considerable task and one of little value to this study, but their importance in the overall picture of transport organisation in London may be judged in part from the case studies which follow Chapter 3.

Professional bodies. The representative bodies of the professions in transport and planning are concerned with setting standards of professional practice and education and the varying interests of their members working in government, private practice, universities and elsewhere. They all operate either on a national or international basis. They include the Royal Town Planning Institute, the Institute of Transport, the Institutions of Civil Engineers, Municipal Engineers and Highway Engineers, the Royal Institute of Chartered Surveyors, and the Royal Institute of British Architects. They can, and often do, act as pressure groups through memoranda, reports and conferences on particular topics.

Political parties and elected members

As in Parliament, politics in London (at Metropolitan and borough level) are basically organised on the two-party system although there is scope for independent members and other parties both permanent (such as the Liberals) and *ad hoc* (such as the Homes Before Roads group which fielded candidates in the 1970 GLC elections). Members have been elected to each council every three years, the GLC cycle being 1964, 1967, 1970, 1973 and that of the boroughs 1964, 1968, 1971 and 1974. After 1973 both will operate on a four-year cycle to be consistent with other local authorities.

Constituency areas up to 1973 were differently drawn for the boroughs, the GLC and Parliament. Borough representation is usually on the basis of three members from each ward and the majority party is that holding the greatest number of seats rather than wards. The GLC system was re-organised for the 1973 elections. It was always the intention with the reform of local government in London in 1965 that GLC members would be drawn from parliamentary constituencies, but this was not possible until the boundaries had been redrawn to coincide with borough boundaries. Consequently GLC representation through the elections of 1964, 1967 and 1970 were on a multi-member constituency basis—each constituency being a London borough returning three or four members. For the 1973 elections and after the GLC draws single members for each parliamentary constituency which will fall within borough boundaries.

As the following figures show, the same party held control of the GLC and the majority of the boroughs in the first two terms but at the time of writing there was a Conservative-held GLC and a majority of Labour-held boroughs.

The organisation of the political parties themselves has been well described by Young[1] and need not be repeated here, but a mention is required of the London Boroughs Association. This is a joint committee of London boroughs' elected representatives[2] representing common borough interests but it has no statutory obligation or functions.

		CONSERVATIVE	LABOUR
GLC majority	1964–67	—	√
	1967–70	√	—
	1970–73	√	—
No. of boroughs in each party's control	1964–68	11	21
	1968–71	28	4
	1971–74	10	22

[1] In G Rhodes (ed) (1972), *The New Government of London: The First Five Years*, Weidenfeld and Nicolson/LSE.
[2] Within the terms of the Local Government Act 1933.

Chapter 3

THE OPERATION OF THE SYSTEM

The previous chapter sought to show the powers and responsibilities of the major institutions and the roles they are required to play. By contrast this chapter attempts to describe how the system is organised and operated in practice and to consider what additional roles, responsibilities, and constraints are imposed on the institutions in this process, and to see how formally and informally they co-operate with one another and co-ordinate their related functions.

The chapter is divided into two sections. The first shows how the major bodies are structured to undertake their tasks, how their role in transport relates to their other tasks, and summarises their major policies and decisions. The short second section describes the formal co-ordination machinery. This chapter is followed by fifteen case studies which examine in detail particular policies or decisions.

THE DEPARTMENT OF THE ENVIRONMENT

The period covered by this book includes not only the first years of the Department of the Environment (DOE) but also the latter years of its constituent ministries (particularly from 1965 to 1970) and it is therefore necessary to understand the structure of each and their major policies affecting transport in London.

As Harrop has pointed out,[1] the DOE was formed from three very different ministries. The Ministry of Public Building and Works (MOPBW) was a very large department (24 200 staff) with mainly executive functions, an integrated hierarchy of professional and administrative classes, and a large regional organisation. The Ministry of Housing and Local Government (MOHLG) by contrast was a small department (4800 staff) mainly with regulatory functions, organised as two parallel administrative and professional staffs, with relatively little delegation to regional offices. The Ministry of Transport (MOT), with 10 200 staff, had both executive and regulatory tasks (e.g. concerned with Trunk roads and nationalised transport undertakings respectively) which it carried out with considerable staff integration and considerable delegation of executive work to its regional Road Construction Units.

The work undertaken by any Government department is always influenced by its political masters who may require advice on new policies or

[1] P J Harrop (1971), 'Setting up the Department of the Environment,' *O & M Bulletin*, 26; 3, pp129–41.

a modification or cessation of current ones. The degree of uncertainty which frequently surrounds final decisions on matters of major importance inevitably gives rise within a department to considerable speculation as to the minister's attitudes. Preventing abortive work or seeking to influence major decisions is, for departmental officials, a matter of knowing what the minister is likely to accept and advising accordingly.[1] This political constraint tends to become predictable (except perhaps in the first year of a new political regime) and helps a department or ministry to wear one 'face' in dealing with other bodies; to the officials, a decision by the minister is a decision by the Ministry. In looking at the operation of a central Government department, therefore, it is important not to underestimate the role of the minister himself. Even if a particular minister plays a relatively small part in the initiation of policies and ideas, he will still be the figurehead by which the public can judge the work of the machine he controls. This was particularly important in the case of Peter Walker in 1970–72 as he attempted to demonstrate that his large new department with its ministerial team could meet the brave claims which attended its establishment.

The MOT was headed by six ministers during the last decade of its existence:

October 1959 to October 1964, Mr Ernest Marples.
October 1964 to December 1965, Mr Tom Fraser.
December 1965 to April 1968, Mrs Barbara Castle.
April 1968 to October 1969, Mr Richard Marsh.
October 1969 to June 1970, Mr Fred Mulley.
June 1970 to November 1970, Mr John Peyton.

Those that held the office for the longest periods, Mr Marples and Mrs Castle, were particularly active and 'interventionist.' Marples was responsible for the examination of British Railways (BR) headed by Dr Beeching and for expanding the inter-city road building programme, for setting up the London Traffic Management Unit (LTMU) and for the development of on-street parking controls, particularly in the central area of London. It was his Ministry too that began research into environmental and traffic restraint matters (in the Buchanan and Smeed reports respectively). Mrs Castle was keen to see the integration of different modes of transport, particularly freight transport, to increase the rate of improvement to urban road and rail systems, to provide capital and revenue subsidies for public transport in recognition of the consequent social benefits, and to improve transport planning in the conurbations by placing it in the hands of new authorities created for the task. These were the main aims embodied in the 1968 Transport Act which was one of the largest

[1] See, for example, Case Study *K* where the Secretary of State, Peter Walker, turned down the recommendation of his inspector following the public inquiry into his own department's scheme to widen the A1 Trunk road through Hampstead Garden Suburb.

pieces of non-financial legislation for many years. Paul Johnson (then editor of the *New Statesman*) expressed the opinion that:

> Barbara Castle had a very powerful effect because for the first time she was able to reconstruct the MOT and to reconstruct the policy into an integrated system . . . not only did she bring economists into the system . . . but she herself was able to see transport as a whole and act accordingly.[1]

Succeeding her, Richard Marsh had the task of seeing through the Transport (London) Act 1969 and the establishment of the Passenger Transport Authorities in the provincial conurbations. By comparison, Marsh's successor, Fred Mulley, considered himself to be 'very much a slave to [his] inheritance' (i.e. to the 1968 and 1969 Transport Acts).[2]

During the 1960s there were several changes in the internal organisation of the MOT of significance to its role in London. The LTMU set up in 1960 as a relatively autonomous group within the MOT, was included in a new London Highways division in 1964 under the Director General of Highways (then Sir William Harris). Apart from traffic management including parking control, London matters were also included in the work of groups and divisions concerned with railways, Trunk roads, urban passenger transport, freight and the Channel tunnel which were co-ordinated at deputy secretary level or (in some cases) by the Permanent Secretary.

The London Highways Division was the first (in 1964) to merge the professional and administrative hierarchies, and proceeded to combine with its traffic functions certain highway matters formerly dealt with by other divisions. These changes were found to reduce consultation procedures, to speed decision making within the ministry and to simplify communication with local authorities and outside bodies.[3] In October 1965 a new London Policy division was established within the Urban Policy Group to deal with long-term highway and transport planning in London, while a third division was responsible for traffic surveys and road traffic regulation.[4] By this time, of course, the Greater London Council (GLC) had taken over most of the MOT's traffic regulation functions in London, but the new arrangements helped to overcome the functional division between highways and public transport, for which the Ministry retained considerable responsibility.

When Barbara Castle took charge the co-ordination of urban transport policy was handled at deputy secretary level. Below this the London Group comprised three divisions headed by assistant secretaries: London Transportation Planning, London General and London Highways. This

[1] W de'Ath (1970), *Barbara Castle: A Portrait from Life*, p47. See also the *Guardian*, 22 July 1968.

[2] The *Guardian*, 2 March 1970.

[3] MOT Annual Report, *Roads in England and Wales 1964*, p35.

[4] MOT Establishment Minute 262/65 and Chart No. 22; the *Guardian* 10 January 1966.

structure remained broadly the same until the creation of the DOE in 1970.

The Ministry of Housing and Local Government, like the MOT, was led by a number of ministers during the 1960s:

January 1957 to October 1961, H Brook.
October 1961 to July 1962, C Hill.
July 1962 to October 1964, Sir K Joseph.
October 1964 to August 1966, R Crossman.
August 1966 to June 1970, A Greenwood.
Nineteen days in June 1970, R Mellish.
June 1970 to November 1970, P Walker.

During the period 1960–63 the MOHLG was involved in the drafting and passage of the London Government Bill[1] and subsequently in the preparation of regulations for the Greater London Development Plan (GLDP) and for the division of development control responsibilities between the GLC and the London boroughs. The preparation for structure planning (from the report of the Planning Advisory Group[2] to the Town and Country Planning Act 1968), the undertaking of regional studies including the South-East Study (1964), the introduction of new measures to improve housing and the environment, and initiating the reorganisation of local government outside London were other major tasks.[3]

The Ministry was also involved in the examination of the county and county borough development plans (as these were produced) some of which became part of the Initial Development Plan for Greater London. The first review of those for the counties of London and Middlesex were approved in 1962 and 1965 respectively. This work was mainly undertaken by a London Planning division led by an under-secretary whose scope was subsequently widened to include the South-East region.

When the Department of Economic Affairs was abolished in October 1969 the MOHLG took over its regional planning functions (including those of the South-East Economic Planning Council). On these matters the Ministry reported not (as with its other planning work) to the Minister of Housing and Local Government but to a newly created Secretary of State for Local Government and Regional Planning. This latter post was one of 'overlord' minister to the MOHLG and MOT and foreshadowed the creation of the DOE by the Conservative administration a year later.[4]

The objectives underlying the reorganisation of central government and the formation of the DOE in particular have already been described in Chapter 2. For the first time 'the whole range of functions which affect people's living environment' became the responsibility of a single depart-

[1] See G Rhodes (1970), *The Government of London: The Struggle for Reform*, ch12.
[2] MOHLG (1965), *The Future of Development Plans.*
[3] *Report of the Ministry of Housing and Local Government 1969* and *1970* (*passim*).
[4] *Report of the Ministry of Housing and Local Government 1969* and *1970* (biennial), p1.

ment under a Secretary of State. Supporting the Secretary of State (Peter Walker for most of the period covered by this book) are the three ministers for Local Government and Development, Housing and Construction, and Transport Industries, each 'by delegation from the Secretary of State, [in] full charge of his functional wing of the Department. . . . They will have subordinate ministers working to them within the field of policy which falls to each.'[1]

The Secretary of State for the Environment and his ministers are responsible for one of the largest central government departments with a very wide range of functions, a total establishment of about 80 000 civil servants and an annual budget in the region of £3000 million, about an eighth of all public expenditure in Great Britain. The internal organisation of a department of this size is inevitably complex.

Initially, three groups of directorates were appointed within the DOE, reporting respectively to the three ministers, and a fourth group was created to service the whole Department. During the first months there were major organisational tasks involving the structure of the central services (establishing directorates for establishment, resource allocation, finance, strategic planning, legal and research functions), and preparing for the move from buildings scattered throughout central London to a huge new building in Marsham Street, where 3500 of the 18 500 headquarters staff of the DOE were to be accommodated.[2] After this had been achieved, the shape of the Department was reviewed for its ability to carry out the Secretary of State's policies (e.g. with regard to the links between land use and transportation planning and increased decentralisation to regional offices) and to move from amalgamation to integration.

Considerable changes took place with regard to the planning of land use and transport in London and the South-East. The Government's decision to site the third London airport at Foulness led to the setting up of a coordinating group headed by the under-secretary responsible for the London and South-East Planning directorate.[3] In August 1971 a separate directorate for the third airport was created.[4] At the same time the former MOT London directorate and the MOHLG South-East Planning Directorate exchanged responsibilities so that the London directorate 'took aboard' land-use planning in the conurbation while the South-East directorate received the onus of regional transport planning matters in the South-East (except for BR commuter services).[5] Later in 1971 a new regional organisation was established for the rest of the country, providing six offices headed by under-secretaries who also chaired the Economic Planning Boards, aided by two regional controllers for roads and transportation,

[1] *The Reorganisation of Central Government*, Cmnd 4506 (1970), paras31–2.
[2] Departmental Notice 1/70.
[3] Departmental Notices 18/70, 25/70.
[4] Departmental Notices 12/70, 37/71, 48/71.
[5] Departmental Notice 45/71. The London Group still relies on the central organisation for specialist services such as economic evaluation of projects for grant or loan sanction, but specialist manpower may be seconded or placed within it.

and housing and planning (the former divisional road engineers and principal regional officers).[1]

Thus by 1972 the headquarters organisation consisted of three major groups, comprising the third London airport, South-East and London directorates. The London Directorate was organised as follows:[2]

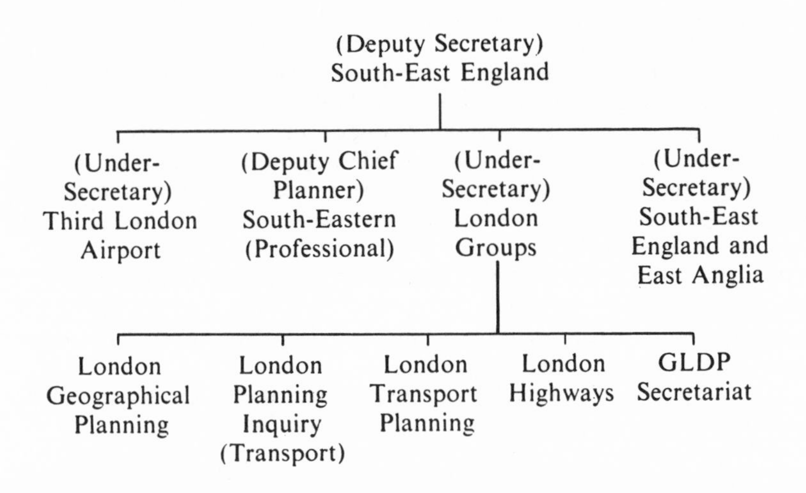

The other two groups contained specialist services enabling the headquarters to concentrate on national policy and co-ordination, while allowing greater autonomy of decision making within the regions.[3] The first group covered regional development and economic policy, countryside matters and minerals, the second development plans, urban policy, land-use policy and urban and passenger transport. The first deputy secretary appointed to lead the second group, Dr Wilfred Burns, was the first specialist professional to fill one of the top posts.

In November 1971 Peter Walker announced a further change in departmental responsibilities. The Minister for Local Government and Development became responsible for planning policy generally and for 'casework' outside London, and planning and transport casework in London fell to the Minister for Transport Industries (e.g. such matters as the Docklands study (see below), the West Cross Route of the GLC's proposed Ringway 1, and the redevelopment of Piccadilly Circus). The aim was to ease the workload on the former Minister who had the burden of the reorganisation of local government outside the metropolis.[4]

Thus the new department underwent considerable reorganisation in its

[1] Departmental Notice 26/72.
[2] Departmental Notice 49/72, 2 October 1972.
[3] *The Times* and the *Guardian*, 22 October 1971; and *Surveyor* 29 October 1971.
[4] DOE *Press Release 336M*, 5 November 1971.

first two years; in fact Sir David Serpell who retired from his post as its Permanent Secretary in August 1972 was reported to have:

> made no secret of his regret that as much as two-thirds of his time during the first eighteen months had been absorbed by managerial cares rather than policy, adding that he would expect to see a different mix once the reorganisation was over.[1]

A year later Geoffrey Rippon replaced Peter Walker as Secretary of State, and changed his ministers' responsibilities. Mr Rippon himself took over general London policy, the third London airport and land availability; the Minister for Transport Industries, Mr Peyton, receiving road matters from Mr Page, the Minister for Local Government and Development; and London planning casework becoming the responsibility of Mr Channon, another of the ministerial team.[2]

Initially, therefore, the DOE's central role of co-ordinating the work of all levels of government, the methods it employed and its underlying policies, were of necessity largely inherited or evolved from those established by the three former ministries.

The means by which the DOE's role is exercised, and the actual policies pursued, may be described under six broad headings:

a Control over public expenditure.
b Legislation and regulation.
c Involvement in schemes of national significance.
d Plans and projects by other authorities.
e Arbitration between conflicting interests.
f Research and advice to other authorities.

There is considerable overlap, as for example with the GLDP which embraces all six aspects.

Control over public expenditure

The DOE's most powerful influence in urban transport is through the control of public expenditure. Besides discussing and negotiating with local authorities over the amounts they receive through rate support grants, the DOE decides on the allocation of specific Government grants and ceilings of expenditure by transport operators. The Department's philosophy, as expressed in a memorandum to the Parliamentary Committee on public expenditure in the 1971–72 session, was that there was no universal formula by which transport expenditure could be judged because circumstances vary from area to area:

> The responsibility for the initiation and execution of urban transport

[1] *The Times*, 8 May 1972.
[2] Departmental Notices 59/72 and 60/72, 24 November 1972.

projects in conurbations lies with the local authorities . . . except in the case of a limited number of trunk roads mainly in London.[1]

Nevertheless, the DOE must form some view (which may be interpreted as national policy) as to the appropriate total level of expenditure in each area and the allocation of this between different types of transport expenditure. In these respects policy has relied to a large extent on major transportation studies carried out in the conurbations (a study of inter-urban traffic has also been commissioned). The DOE's confidence in these studies has been helped by the fact that it 'normally bears half the cost . . . and participates in their technical direction.'[2] In London, a major input to the first GLDP was the London Traffic Survey (LTS), a study begun in 1962 'with the limited objectives of producing traffic forecasts for 1971 and 1981 and relating those forecasts to highway networks envisaged for those years.'[3] The GLC's motorway and other transport proposals were modified to some extent by the later stages of the LTS (renamed by the GLC 'London Transportation Study') for inclusion in the GLDP (see page 96).

At the time of writing the Secretary of State had taken no decision on the GLDP and the DOE therefore had no approved strategy for London as a whole which could be used as a basis for deciding transport expenditure. But the implementation of many individual projects, even major ones, was not interrupted. By the end of 1972, for example, the East Cross Route motorway (part of the GLC's proposed Ringway 1) had been approved and largely constructed; the West Cross Route had been assured Government grant, subject to the various local planning procedures; the DOE were continuing with schemes to increase the traffic capacity of the North Circular Trunk road (the northern half of Ringway 2 in the GLDP strategy); grant aid had been approved and construction had begun on the first stage of the new Fleet Line (see Case Study *C*); and a £35 million scheme to electrify certain suburban services into King's Cross had been approved for grant aid.

Thus, as far as the DOE is concerned, it is possible to draw a distinction between the approval of individual transport projects and the ratification of an overall transport strategy into which these schemes might fit. In the absence of an approved strategy, the process of evaluating individual projects for grant aid is of crucial importance to the final result. There are broadly three elements in the DOE's evaluation process. First, the rates of grant aid towards various categories of transport expenditure 'are fixed by administrative decision and can be varied.'[4] In 1972 the position for public transport was that major projects were eligible for 75% grant; new buses,

[1] Expenditure Committee (Environment and Home Office Subcommittee) Session 1971–72, *Minutes of Evidence*, 25 January *1972*, *Hansard HC Papers 107* (*i*), p2

[2] *Hansard HC Papers 107* (*i*), 1971–72, p3.

[3] *Ibid.*

[4] *Hansard HC Papers 107* (*i*), 1971–72, p5. Neither the basis of these grants nor the rules by which they are applied have been published.

improvements at stations, interchanges and bus lanes 50%; and bus stations 25%. For new roads or improvements to existing ones central government bore 75% of the cost on Principal roads and the entire cost on Trunk roads.

Second, methods are devised and applied to ensure that 'schemes submitted for grant represent value for money.' As far as public transport projects are concerned they 'must be based on detailed traffic, operational and engineering studies which evaluate the main features of the project as compared with the alternative options, and include an assessment both of commercial prospects and wider social costs and benefits. All major schemes are subjected to a detailed cost-benefit analysis.'[1] For urban road schemes, however, the DOE has considered it difficult to carry out such detailed appraisals because, as one senior official explained:

> When one improves a road or builds a new road in an urban area the effect of this spreads itself so far afield that it is very difficult to say . . . what will be the effect of that particular exercise.[2]

Third, in evaluating projects the DOE inevitably applies its own attitudes and policies whether or not these have been explicitly stated; indeed the influence of such policies is implicit in the other two elements. The DOE itself, for example, has said that:

> The differing grant rates are intended to concentrate the funds available on those types of project which overall are likely to be the most beneficial to the travelling public, but which operators and authorities might find too costly and unattractive as commercial investments.[3]

The 1968 Transport Act itself was based on the policy view that public transport should receive financial aid as well as roads and that the best way to achieve improvements was to provide capital grants rather than to increase revenue subsidies (except for unremunerative rail services thought to be socially necessary).

It has been the DOE's policy to eliminate revenue subsidies for BR (see below) and central government has no power to pay them for London Transport (LT) services, but the rates of capital grant affecting both undertakings were increased in 1971—namely, grants for new buses were increased from 25% to 50%, and additional categories of investment (mainly new and replacement rolling stock and signalling) became eligible for grant aid. A senior BR official commented at the time that this would not necessarily increase the total amount of money available, but the DOE later gave these changes in grant rates as one major reason for expected increases in infrastructure investment 'from £8.1 million in 1970–71 to £23

[1] *Hansard HC Papers 107* (*i*), 1971–72, p2.
[2] *Hansard HC Papers 107* (*i*), 1971–72, p13.
[3] *Hansard HC Papers 107* (*i*), 1971–72, p5.

million in 1971–72 and £44.1 million in 1972–73.'[1] The other reason given was the approval of major railway schemes, particularly in London. Table 1 shows the major urban public transport schemes approved for grant up to February 1972. (Actual expenditure, of course, is spread over a number of years.)

		COST OF PROJECT (£ MILLION)	GRANT AUTHORISED (£ MILLION)
London	Great Northern Suburban electrification and resignalling	35	26
	Fleet Line (Stage I)	26	19.5
	Improvement of south-east approaches to BR termini	13.8	9
	LT rolling stock	11.8	8.8
	Feltham area resignalling	6.2	4
Total		92.8	67.3
Outside London	Liverpool Terminal Loop	12	9
	Bradford Interchange	6.6	1.9
	Redditch Busway	3.5	1*
Total		22.1	11.9
GRAND TOTAL		114.9	79.2

Table 1 MAJOR PROJECTS APPROVED FOR GRANT AID TO FEBRUARY 1972

* With prospect of further grant later

Source: Hansard HC Papers 107 (*iv*), (1971–72), p56

Individual decisions on capital grants, however, have not suggested any hard and fast policy. For example the Government decided at first not to pay a grant to LT for its Heathrow extension (see Case Study *C*) but shortly afterwards granted 75% towards the cost of the first section of the Fleet Line and the Great Northern Suburban and South-Eastern Approaches improvements (see Case Study *H*).[2] In the intervening period the GLC had been 'disappointed' by the Heathrow decision and sent a deputation to discuss grants policy with Mr Graham Page, then Minister for Local Government and Development. The GLC contended that the grant arrangements operated 'to the disadvantage of public transport as

[1] *Hansard HC Papers 107* (*i*), 1971–72, p4.

[2] DOE *Press Notices 25M*, 18 August 1971; and *347M*, 8 November 1971.

compared to road schemes'[1] and that public transport should receive the the same treatment as roads. It was reported that Mr Page opposed this view because public transport could be financed in part from fares whereas roads could not. Nevertheless he promised that the grant system would be reviewed and that GLC officers would be involved. Subsequently the Government decided to pay a grant for the Heathrow extension amounting to £5.67 million.[2]

Policy is also implicit in the way different transport projects are drawn up and implemented. The DOE has increasingly adopted a policy of promoting the improvement of public transport in urban areas. The DOE explained this aspect of its role to the Parliamentary Committee already referred to as:

a To make sure that public transport operation is organised in the most efficient and effective way possible.
b To help to improve the infrastructure and stock by capital grants.
c To provide revenue support for unremunerative rail services needed for their community value and to provide fuel tax relief for buses.
d To encourage local authorities and public transport operators to co-operate with each other in producing the best overall local transport network.
e To promote research and experiments.[3]

Regarding road schemes the DOE has continued the 'preparation list' procedure introduced by the MOT in 1965 which has been described as follows:

> Trunk and principal road schemes are prepared in two stages. Those considered to have sufficient priority to get into the Road Programme later are first included in the Preparation Pool (or List). When the design is advanced enough, the cost and probable benefits are assessed. The schemes are then considered for allocation to the Road Programme for a particular target year in the light of funds likely to be available.[4]

Policy is inevitably involved in according priority to one scheme as opposed to another. For example,

> In selecting which urban schemes to place in the Preparation List the Secretary of State will, apart from *traffic relief*, look in particular for those which produce *environmental benefits* . . . and those which are *consistent with an agreed transport strategy* for the sub-region as well as for the urban area itself [our italics].[5]

[1] *The Times*, 19 January 1971.
[2] DOE *Press Notice 835M*, 21 July 1972.
[3] *Hansard HC Papers 107* (*i*), 1971–72, p56.
[4] Footnote to DOE press notices on Trunk and Principal road schemes.
[5] *Hansard HC Papers 107* (*i*), 1971–72, p5.

Control over expenditure, then, is not only a major responsibility of the DOE but is also (in the way that it is exercised) an indicator, even if only in the broadest terms, of national policy. In turning now to the other aspects of the DOE's role in transport it is important to recognise how these influence and are influenced by policy attitudes at the national level.

Legislation and regulation

The DOE concerns itself with the legislative framework within which local authorities make basic decisions concerning, for example, the relative priorities of public and private transport in their areas. In March 1972 Peter Walker announced studies in three towns and three inner city areas to develop a 'total approach' to the problems of the urban environment. One of the aspects to be considered in these studies was the possibility of a 'thorough-going reform of the present system of transport grants.'[1]

The DOE gives positive guidance on policy through legislation and regulations, many of which were introduced by the former ministries. For example the MOHLG produced guidance for local planning authorities through Development Control Policy Notes dealing with such matters as parking provision in residential areas and town centres.[2] But it would be inaccurate to suggest that the relationship between national policy and local or executive decision taking was uni-directional: the DOE, like other central departments, takes account of movements in both public and professional opinion and the introduction of 'consultative' or 'Green Papers' indicates the Government's recognition of this need. Increasingly the DOE has been concerned with environmental matters and has introduced or prepared for legislation dealing with, for example, better compensation for those adversely affected by new road schemes,[3] and the limitation of noise and fumes created by motor-vehicles.

The DOE's housing policies (as embodied in legislation) are concerned primarily with questions of rents, subsidies, conditions of tenure, building programmes, cost yardsticks, grants for house improvements and conservation. These policies, although they may have a significant impact on transport matters, have not been formulated with this in mind. The DOE has so far developed few national policies or guidelines that consciously influence the spatial relationship between houses and other uses and hence the transport facilities which serve them. The outstanding exception as far as London is concerned was the DOE's approval in October 1971 of the *Strategic Plan for the South-East* (in which the MOHLG had been one of the chief participants). One of the Plan's objectives was an 'efficient distribution of employment within the region' and the matching 'as far as possible (of) population and employment growth.' The plan proposed

[1] DOE *Press Release 683M*, 9 June 1972. Announcement by Keith Speed, Parliamentary Under-Secretary of State.
[2] See MOHLG, *Development Control Policy Notes*, 2 and 5 respectively.
[3] See DOE (1972), *Development and Compensation—Putting People First*, Cmnd 5124.

growth centres outside London intended, in terms of population and employment, to be largely self-contained. This was expected to accommodate growth 'without posing journey-to-work and congestion problems.'[1]

Despite being undertaken on an advisory rather than a statutory basis, regional planning is an important part of the DOE's role in matters beyond (or considered to be beyond) the scope of the statutory 'structure' planning of local authorities. Blake has suggested that there is a distinction to be made between 'strategic' social and economic planning at the national and regional level, and essentially physical local 'structure' planning, and criticises the GLC for attempting to do both in the GLDP, blurring the distinction between them and not succeeding in doing either.[2]

Involvement in schemes of national significance

The DOE may also become involved in specific planning issues such as the siting of the third London airport and the Heathrow Link (see Case Study *E*) and may 'call in' planning applications of major importance such as those relating to the redevelopment of Piccadilly Circus. The DOE has also pursued a major Trunk road building programme in London, its proposals mostly forming part of the GLDP proposed network of 'primary roads' (see Figure 2). The justification for involvement has usually been either that the project is of national significance or that it poses particularly difficult problems of co-ordination. On the other hand the DOE decided to carry out a study of London's Dockland for which no such justification was publicly put forward.[3]

Plans and projects of other authorities

The DOE's role in deciding on individual transport projects as recipients of grant aid and the importance of overall plans has already been described. In London the preparation and approval of the first GLDP was a lengthy process in which central government was involved at several levels. The GLDP was prepared by the GLC on lines agreed with the MOHLG which were significantly influenced by the 1965 report of the Planning Advisory Group. The former MOT was closely involved in the formulation of the motorway proposals incorporated into the plan through an officers group called the Highways Development Review Group, and in the financing and direction of the LTS which aimed to validate one of the alternative networks. Indeed the motorway proposals in the GLDP may be regarded as a joint effort between the MOT and the GLC (and formerly the London

[1] South-East Joint Planning Team (1970), *Strategic Plan for the South-East*, pp19, 79.
[2] J L Blake (1971), 'The Philosophy of the Structure Planning Process,' (a Paper to the CES/TPI conference, University of Birmingham 23–4 April).
[3] Indeed the DOE was criticised for pre-empting a joint study by the GLC, London boroughs and Essex County Council of the whole South Essex corridor. See *The Times*, 6 May 1971.

County Council (LCC)). There were more than 20 000 objections to the published plan, over 18 000 of which were against the motorway proposals. Whilst most of these were objections to particular roads in particular parts of London, some were concerned with the whole motorway plan as part of the GLC's transport strategy. The Minister of Housing and Local Government was strongly urged by two major pressure groups[1] and others to set up a Planning Inquiry Commission under the provisions of the Town and Country Planning Act 1968.[2] Although this request was not met the eventual form of the inquiry was similar to that of a planning commission in that it could hear representations from people not directly affected by the Plan's proposals and could initiate research. The Minister appointed a Panel of Inquiry consisting of seven members chaired by Mr Frank Layfield QC and assisted by specialist assessors 'to enable the variety of issues posed by the Plan and the objections to it to be considered in greater depth than might normally be possible in a development plan inquiry.'[3] On approval (with or without modifications) by the Secretary of State, the GLDP will become the first statutory development plan drawn up for Greater London as a whole.

Prior to this decision a major change—which also forms an example of how the DOE can influence the structure of the planning system as well as its operation in practice—was that the London borough development plans would not need ministerial approval. This was announced by Mr Graham Page (then Minister for Local Government and Development) in November 1970, shortly after the commencement of the GLDP Inquiry.[4] The aim was to cut down the length of time involved in the development plan process. It was seen that under the system laid down by the London Government Act, the GLDP would be coming up for review before the borough plans had been formally adopted. Information on the scope and content of borough plans had not, at the time of writing, been published, but they will have to be broadly consistent with the GLDP and to incorporate local 'action area' plans.[5]

The Secretary of State as arbiter

In his role as 'arbiter' between conflicting interests, the Secretary of State for the Environment is concerned primarily with objections to planning and transport projects or with appeals against a refusal of planning permission. Whilst conflict does arise between the two tiers of local government in London, disputes have rarely been considered serious enough to

[1] The London Motorway Action Group led by the Rt Hon Douglas Jay MP and the London Amenity and Transport Association. See J M Thomson *et al* (1969), *Motorways in London*.
[2] Ch72 (1968), ss61–3.
[3] *GLDP Inquiry*, Opening statement by the Chairman of the Panel, 7 July 1970.
[4] DOE, *Press Release 139*, 12 November 1971. Enacted by *Town and Country Planning (Amendment) Act 1972*, ch 42, s3 and sch1.
[5] *Town and Country Planning Act 1971*, ch78, ss7, 11, 14, 19 and sch4–6.

warrant the Secretary of State's intervention. One example was when he held a public inquiry into the proposal to build an air terminal at Hammersmith (Case Study *E*). He has also called in major planning applications or project proposals when local objections have become very strong, as in the case of the proposal to build an exhibition centre at Northolt.

Research and advice

The last aspect of the DOE's role dealt with here, but one which is closely associated with the other aspects already described, is that of undertaking research and experiments into various planning and transport matters. The subjects covered may form part of a continuing programme of research and development, or may be decided on an *ad hoc* basis as issues arise. Work may also be carried out within DOE research groups or in collaboration with other authorities, universities or consultants. The two principal aims are to inform policy and decision making at the national level (i.e. by the DOE itself) and to assist or advise local authorities, particularly on matters which are beyond their resources to study.

The Road Research Laboratory set up by the MOT has maintained a continuing programme of research into various aspects of road design and safety.[1] In 1964 it provided expertise for the first official report on road pricing[2] followed by a review of traffic restraint measures.[3] The scope of the Laboratory's work, particularly since the creation of the DOE, and its renaming as the Transport and Road Research Laboratory, has steadily broadened to include, for example, bus operation[4] and the assessment of the environmental effects of road traffic.

Examples of transport problems of national (or rather widespread) significance with which the DOE has been involved are the possibilities of giving buses priority over other traffic and the environmental nuisance caused by lorry parking in urban areas. A number of bus demonstration projects were sponsored by the Department, some of which were in London (see Case Study *M*). The lorry parking study was a theoretical rather than a demonstration one. (The GLC, however, were undertaking their own studies at the time and Greater London was excluded from the working group's terms of reference.) Some work was also undertaken by the MOHLG on the implications of the Buchanan Report, *Traffic in Towns*, published by the MOT in 1963. Examples were 'environmental area' studies in Deeplish (Rochdale) and Barnsbury (see Case Study *G*).

The Department has its own research and development programmes some of which are carried out by commissioned agencies. The Secretary of

[1] For example, continuing research into the relationships between traffic speeds, flow and the physical characteristics of roads, and the development of standards of road design. See MOT (1966), *Roads in Urban Areas.*

[2] MOT (1964), *Road Pricing: The Economic and Technical Possibilities.*

[3] MOT (1967), *Better Use of Town Roads.*

[4] See, for example, F V Webster and R H Oldfield (1972), *A Theoretical Study of Bus and Car Travel in Central London*, TRRL report No. LR451.

State established two new advisory councils chaired by two of his ministers, Messrs Amery and Peyton, to co-ordinate research in their respective fields.[1] The former was to head the Construction and Housing Research Advisory Council (including construction problems of roads and ports). The latter was to chair a Planning and Transport Research Advisory Council. The two tasks of the Council were to advise the Secretary of State, first on his Department's requirements for applied research and internal priorities, and second on his statutory duties regarding the research and development programmes of the nationalised transport undertakings and the National Ports Council. These Councils were broadly based and set the Department's need in the context of the specialist research fields. For its internal research needs the Department established a Directorate of Research Requirements which handled programmes of work totalling £17 million in 1972–73. Each programme was formulated by a Research Requirements Committee, which reported to three Review Committees for planning and transportation, building and construction, and environmental pollution and resources.[2]

GREATER LONDON COUNCIL

Organisation

The evolution of the GLC's initial internal structure has been described by Rhodes and others,[3] so that it is necessary here only to bring the reader up to the 1972 position and to enlarge upon the Council's organisation relating to transport matters.

As the GLC began with a predominance of former LCC chief officers heading departments (14 out of 18) and LCC members as committee chairmen (11 out of 14), it is perhaps not surprising that its departmental and committee structures reflected this inheritance; in this sense the GLC was the LCC 'writ large.' Initially in the planning and transport fields it had separate Planning and Communications and Highways and Traffic Committees, a separate Housing Committee and a General Purposes Committee which (as in most local authorities) handled any public transport matters. There were separate departments for Housing, Planning, and Highways and Transportation. As some of the problems of operating at a regional scale became apparent (the Council was often referred to in its minutes as a 'regional authority') and after the recommendations of the Maud Report on local government management, the Council established a special committee to investigate any necessary changes in structure.

Immediately after their successful campaign in the 1967 elections on the

[1] As reported in *Surveyor*, 3 December 1971.
[2] White Paper, *Framework for Government Research and Development*, Cmnd 5046 (1972), paras18–19.
[3] GLC *Minutes*; and G Rhodes (ed) (1972), *The New Government of London: The First Five Years*, chs9, 10 and esp 11 and 13.

twin platform of a 'war on waste' at County Hall and a programme of highway and traffic policies to 'get London moving,' the new Conservative administration decided to appoint a Traffic Commissioner to head a new Traffic Branch within the Department of Highways and Transportation. He was expected to 'cut through the red tape' and 'get traffic moving, speed its flow and get the greatest possible operational efficiency out of our roads with the fullest possible regard for pedestrian and road safety.' He was also expected ultimately to have wider powers over traffic, some of which were then vested in the borough councils, the police and the MOT.[1] The other work of the Department under the Director of Highways and Transportation was to be organised into three branches (administration, research, and liaison and construction) co-ordinated by a Chief Executive.

While the transfer of wider traffic powers was being negotiated (and it was clear that legislation could not come forward until the 1968–69 session of Parliament because of pressure of business) 103 and 74 candidates respectively applied for the posts of Traffic Commissioner and Chief Executive but the staff subcommittee was unable to recommend suitable candidates to the General Purposes Committee. Reviewing the situation the committee felt that they had to relieve the Director of day to day work so that he could 'concentrate on external relationships and on the formation of basic policies.' They therefore designated him to be Traffic Commissioner and appointed a Chief Executive to run the department. This took place in 1968[2] and suggested an acceptance of the Maud Committee's conclusion that some distinction was necessary between the role of the Council as a forum for discussing and devising long-term policies and as a machine for taking decisions.

At member level, the special committee recommended the establishment of three forward planning committees (Leaders' Co-ordinating, Policy Steering, and Strategic Planning) and nine executive committees. The Policy Steering committee was to be responsible for the long-term formulation of objectives for the Council's services and the allocation of resources, as suggested earlier.[3] It was also responsible for the negotiations for taking over control of LT, carried out under the direction of the Chief Executive of the Highways and Transportation (H & T) Department. The Strategic Planning Committee was to be concerned with the longer-term functions of the former Highways and Traffic and Planning and Communications committees including the GLDP and relations with the boroughs and other planning bodies. The Leaders' Co-ordinating Committee was to consist of the committee chairmen (i.e. majority party members only) in order to co-ordinate policy 'in a regular way'. An unofficial policy group had advised the previous Labour administration but formalisation of this function meant that the members could now have the benefit of officers'

[1] GLC *Press Release 150*, 15 May 1967. Statement by Sir Desmond Plummer, Leader of the Council.
[2] GLC *Minutes*, 23 July 1968, pp428–41.
[3] GLC *Minutes*, 21 November 1967, p682.

advice. Amongst the executive committees was a Planning and Transportation Committee (to deal with immediate schemes) and a Housing Committee. The former was serviced by four area boards to deal with matters concerning primary roads, historic buildings and planning applications and local traffic schemes, in the central, north-east, south and west parts of the conurbation.[1]

Further minor but significant changes in the officers' management structure occurred. In the previous year (1967) the special committee had emphasized the co-ordinating role for the Clerk to the Council and recommended his designation as Director General.[2] He now headed a chief officers' board to prepare advice on long-term policies and the allocation of resources.

Once the arrangements for the Council to become the statutory local transport planning authority for Greater London (including taking over LT) were negotiated,[3] the Director General and a Special Committee on Procedure reviewed the situation, as a result of which it was discovered that five departments had overlapping responsibilities for matters of strategic planning and transportation:

	ESTABLISHMENT
Architect's Department (civic design and general divisions)	70
Highways and Transportation Department	900
Planning Department	470
Research and Intelligence Unit	50
Director General's Department (co-ordination)	small

It was decided to combine the first four of these into a Planning and Transportation Department headed by two joint directors (the former directors of the Highways and Transportation and Planning departments). Their responsibilities were to be split roughly between departmental operation, and the GLDP and regional relationships. The Executive Director (H & T Department) became Traffic Commissioner and Director of Development (i.e. with responsibility for executive architectural, engineering and development control work). The new department had a strategic planning wing with three branches, namely strategy, plans (those for Greater London and the boroughs) and the Intelligence Unit,[4] and an executive wing with a chief engineer (construction), a chief planning architect, and a chief engineer (traffic) jointly controlling interdisciplinary area teams. The aim of this reorganisation, which took effect from 1 October 1969, was said to be four-fold:

[1] GLC *Minutes*, 29 July 1968, p521.
[2] GLC *Minutes*, 21 November 1967, p684.
[3] GLC *Minutes*, 9 July 1968, pp380–7.
[4] GLC *Minutes*, 22 July 1969, pp449–52. Rhodes (1972) described the furore over the absorption of the Research and Intelligence Unit more fully.

1 To facilitate the formation of multidisciplinary teams.
2 To simplify communications with the public.
3 To achieve economies of scale in staffing.
4 To widen career prospects.

The joint directors of Planning and Transportation and the Traffic Commissioner (initially Messrs Stott, Collins and Morrison respectively) became members of a new strategic planning board to co-ordinate also with the Council's Chief Valuer and Chief Architect under the Director General to advise the Strategic Planning Committee.

The Council thought that control of the new LT Executive could be 'most effectively and economically exercised through the Council's existing departmental organisation and that it is neither necessary nor desirable to set up a special unit within the Council's organisation to deal comprehensively with London Transport matters. We propose that co-ordination of the Council's functions in relation to the Executive shall be effected through the medium of the chief officers' board'.[1]

The responsibilities for links with the LT Executive on policy matters, particularly long-term planning aims, thus had to be co-ordinated through several officers in the Planning and Transportation, Director General's and Treasurer's departments and, in February 1970, Mr Morrison was asked to take a chief officer's post in the Director General's Department as controller of services with special responsibility for a standing liaison group with the LT Executive.[2]

Later in 1970 the organisation was again reviewed with particular attention to the strategic planning wing after Dr Benjamin had resigned as the head of the Research and Intelligence Unit. It was thought that research should become more closely allied with the formulation of planning and transport policy. Accordingly socio-economic studies became the responsibility of a (renamed) Intelligence Unit. Transportation policy, 'a major management task in its own right' became the work of a new branch created for the purpose,[3] led by a chief planner.

The chief officer's board had also been considering the implementation of a planning, programming and budgeting system (PPBS) to aid the Council's policy making, decision taking and co-ordination, and the Council decided in principle to adopt such a scheme in February 1970. A programme office was established to devise a programme structure. Initially at least this covered five major fields each with subprogrammes and related five-year and one-year budgets. It was hoped to have the system in operation by 1973–74.[4] One of the programmes related to transportation, whose goal was 'to ensure the availability of a transportation system

[1] GLC *Minutes*, 4 November 1969, pp13–18.
[2] GLC *Minutes*, 10 February 1970, p113.
[3] GLC *Minutes*, 9 June 1970, p356.
[4] GLC *Minutes*, 10 February 1970, p130–1; and 20 July 1971, p398–9. A sixth programme group related to internal management matters, or external activities.

Committees	Leaders Co-ordinating Committee	Policy and resources Committee	Strategic Planning Committee	Environmental Planning Committee	Housing Committee	Public Services Committee	Arts and Recreation Committee
Corresponding Officers Board (working through Director General)	CHIEF OFFICERS BOARD	GLC-LTE LIAISON GROUP	STRATEGIC PLANNING BOARD	TRANS-PORTATION BOARD	HOUSING BOARD	HEALTH AND SAFETY BOARD	ARTS AND RECREATION BOARD
Principal Subcommittees		Finance and Scrutiny Committee Establishments Committee General Purposes Committee	Covent Garden Joint Development Committee	Four area boards (central, north-east, south, west) Primary Roads Board Historic Buildings Board	Town Development Committee Thamesmead Committee	Ambulance Committee Fire Brigade Committee	Thames Action Subcommittee Arts Subcommittee

Table 2 MANAGEMENT STRUCTURE OF THE GLC, JULY 1972

appropriate to the social, economic and environmental needs of Greater London.' Like the others, the transportation programme was to be co-ordinated by a Chief Officers Board[1] and had six main areas (Highway Construction and Improvement, Traffic Management and Maintenance, Railways, Public Road Transport and Interchanges). After the 1970 elections the Policy Steering Committee was renamed the Policy and Resources Committee, partly to reflect this innovation, and the Planning and Transportation Committee became the Environmental Planning Committee. The former was increased from 13 to 15 members, the latter from 30 to 33. Nine of these could be co-opted rather than elected members and there was reciprocal *ex officio* representation on the Strategic and Environmental Planning Committees. These changes brought the management structure of the GLC to the situation shown in Table 2.

As far as the officers' structure is concerned two further changes affecting transport have occurred. First, pressure from LT and the encouragement of the MOT and DOE led to the setting up of a new unit to examine traffic measures to aid buses (see Case Study *M*); second, manpower shortages within the police (leading to a withdrawal of their road safety training functions) and exhortation by the Minister of Transport Industries influenced the establishment of a Greater London Road Safety Unit. Both of these are in the Traffic and Development Branch.[2] This produced a departmental structure as shown in Figure 3. The notable thing about this form of 'branch' organisation is that responsibility for policy co-ordination within the large department mainly lies with the joint directors (as opposed to the executive co-ordination falling to the assistant director), who are additionally involved in many external liaison matters (see page 145).

Further changes were made in 1972. In response to 'strains on the top structure' the joint directors were appointed joint controllers of the department with an executive Director of Planning to undertake the running of the department together with the Director of Development and Traffic Commissioner, so as to 'give proper attention . . . to their wider role of co-ordinating.'[3]

The LTS, the motorways and traffic management

During the first four years of its existence, the Council was not only preparing the first GLDP but was also carrying out a large programme of work developing or continuing policies and proposals inherited from the LCC and other authorities. A major inheritance, which greatly influenced the work of the GLC and the policies and proposals in the GLDP, was the

[1] GLC *Minutes*, 10 February 1970, p129–31.

[2] GLC *Minutes*, 22 June 1971, p303; and *Press Release 254*, 17 June 1971.

[3] GLC *Minutes*, 20 June 1972, pp273–7; and 3 October 1972, pp412–13. Controllers were also appointed for personnel and administrative services, financial services, and the architect was given similar status; the controller of services post continued with the added description 'operational.'

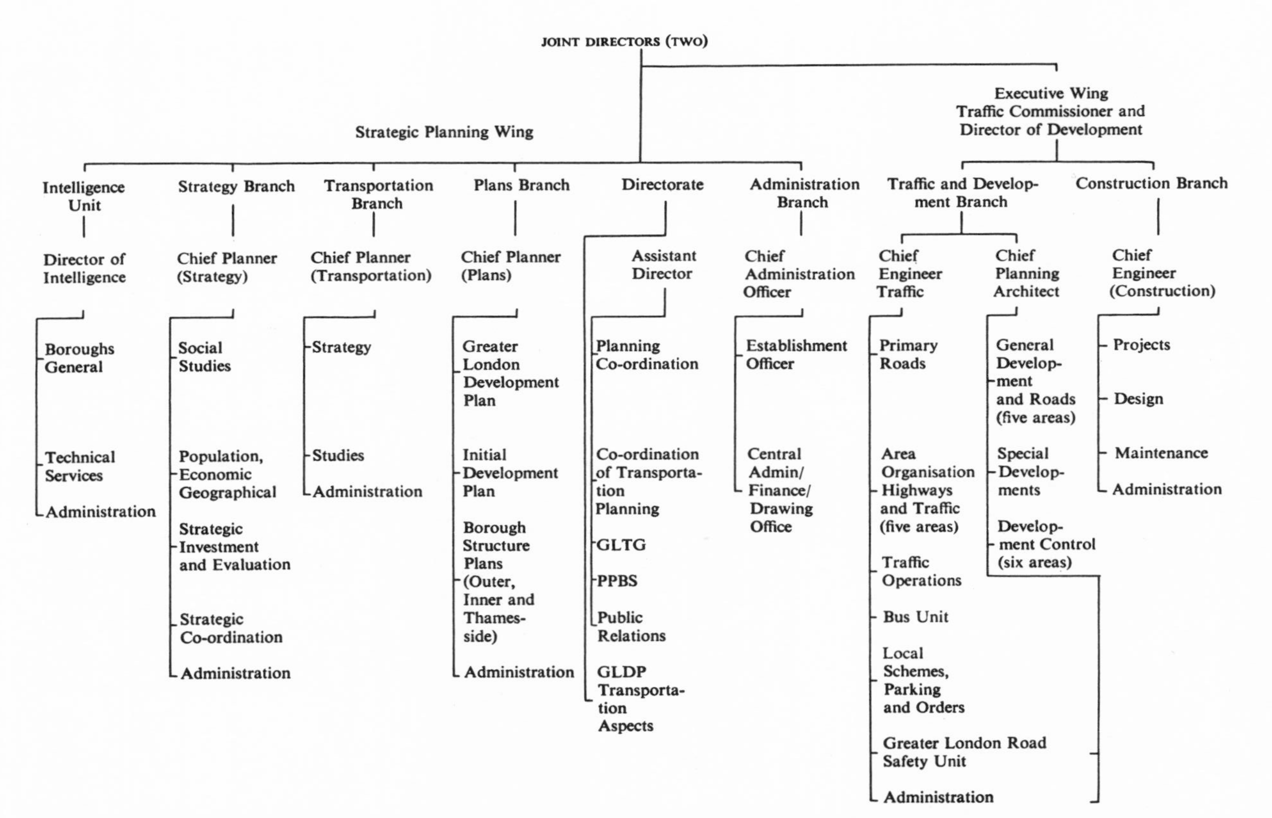

Figure 3 STRUCTURE OF THE GLC'S PLANNING AND TRANSPORTATION DEPARTMENT, OCTOBER 1971.

massive London Traffic Survey (LTS) begun in 1962 by the LCC in conjunction with the MOT. Although the survey was large in scale, its purpose, especially at first, was narrowly conceived as providing information with which to justify major highway proposals in London that had evolved over a number of years.[1]

When the GLC took over the direction of the work in 1965 (the study itself was carried out by consultants) Phase I, which reported on the survey of personal and travel characteristics carried out in 1962, had been completed and Phase II was well under way. Phase II, published in 1966, made initial forecasts of future potential travel demand by road but not by public transport. Later, in Phase III, the study was extended to include an evaluation of three alternative road plans and two public transport plans and to take account of restraint on the use of the car, and the whole exercise was renamed the London Transportation Study. The cost of the study, more than £1 million, was shared 60:40% by the Government and the GLC.

The methods employed by the study, particularly the forecasts of travel demand and the assumptions upon which they were based, and also the way in which the results were interpreted by the GLC, have been heavily criticised.[2] Some of those involved in the study have themselves readily admitted that it has major limitations and that care is required if its results are not to be misinterpreted.[3] Nevertheless the GLC said that the LTS data 'became the foundation of the Council's road planning and transportation proposals incorporated in the GLDP; it has also been used by Government Departments for planning trunk roads in the London area.'[4]

The Council had, however, taken the need for a system of major new roads in London as its starting point and had wasted no time after its creation in 1965 in deciding on a massive programme of investment for the coming decades. As Table 3 shows, the motorway proposals were decided before both the publication of the GLDP and the completion of Phase III of the LTS. The 'Motorway Box' (Ringway 1) was approved in April 1965 as 'the minimum need' and the basic pattern of three orbital motorways and the connecting radial motorways was approved in July 1966. Some of the roads were already either under construction or at an advanced stage of design.

[1] The historical background to the GLC's motorway proposals has been described in J M Thomson, *et al* (1969), *Motorways in London*; London Motorway Action Group/ London Amenity and Transport Association (1971), *Transport Strategy in London: Proof of Evidence E12/20*, GLDP Inquiry Stage 1; C M Buchanan (1971), *London Road Plans 1900–1970*, GLC Research Report No.11.

[2] See, for example, J M Thomson, *et al* (1969) *Motorways in London*; John Blake (1970), 'London's Proposed Motorways: Their Cost and Benefits,' *Surveyor*, 13 March 1970.

[3] See papers by T M Ridley, J O Tressidder, and D Bayliss, in *Regional Studies*, 4, 1, May 1970; and D Bayliss as witness for the GLC: GLDP Inquiry, Stage 1 (transcripts).

[4] Expenditure Committee (Environment and Home Office subcommittee) *Minutes of Evidence, 8 March 1972, Hansard HC Papers 107* (*vii*), 1971–72, p125 (Memorandum submitted by GLC).

DATE	REFERENCE	SUBJECT
July 1964	LTS, volI	LTS Phase I published describing existing situation
6 April 1965	*Minutes*, p347	Motorway Box (Ringway 1) approved as 'the minimum need'
July 1966	LTS, volII	LTS Phase II published projecting future changes
19 July 1966	*Minutes*, p424	Acceptance of basic concept of three ringways and connecting radials
21 November 1967	*Minutes*, p694	Acceptance of possible construction programme from 1971–83. Completion of the network contained in this report expected by 1990s
November 1968	LTS Phase III, volI	Completion of LTS Phase III (analysis completed late 1968, not made public until GLDP Inquiry, September 1970)
25 March 1969	*Minutes*, p207	Draft GLDP approved for statutory consultation containing primary network, basically as contained in the report of 21 November 1967
8 July 1969	*Minutes*, p222	GLDP final approval for submission to MOHLG. Network basically unaltered after statutory consultations
27 January 1970	*Minutes*, p42	Review of road investment (1) Previous proposals to build motorways in two stages (half-width first, full width later) abandoned (except West Cross Route) (2) Construction of network planned in two phases. North and South Cross Routes of Ringway 1 put in Phase II (1990s)
21 January 1970	*Minutes*, p491	Phase I more clearly defined (1970–81). Further consideration of primary roads but no decisions taken
14 November 1972	*Minutes*, pp528–31	Rephasing agreed to link South, East and West Cross Routes of Ringway 1 to North Circular by 1987

Table 3 GLC PRIMARY ROADS: MAIN POLICY DECISIONS, 1964–72

In November 1967 Sir Desmond Plummer, leader of the GLC, announced that his Council had decided 'to adopt as its immediate objective an £860 million investment programme to give London an integrated primary-cum-secondary road network by the early 1980s.' The approved roads plan and its subsequent detailed design would, he believed, provide an end to a long period of 'doubts about what should be done and uncertainties about where and when the new highways should be built.' Concern about the adverse effects of the major road proposals on people's lives and property led the Council in 1966 to urge upon the Government the need for wider powers of compensation.[1] Initially the failure of the Government to make the necessary changes was to be no reason for delaying schemes, but by March 1972 the GLC, presumably in anticipation of forthcoming legislation, announced that the West Cross Route would not be built until the 'additional powers and adequate financial arrangements to deal with the environmental problems of property alongside the road' had been 'assured.'[2] At the same time he also referred to the need for improvements to public transport, although no firm commitment or investment programme existed. He explained that the Council was developing 'a comprehensive transportation policy which besides the road programme *allows* [our italics] also for investment in improved public transport facilities and for the control of movement on the roads.'[3]

More positive policies for public transport did not appear until the GLDP and, more particularly, after the GLC's takeover of responsibility for LT in January 1970, whereas policies had been developed to control road traffic, namely parking control and traffic management.

The first real impetus to traffic management had been given by the MOT's London Traffic Management Unit (LTMU) in the early 1960s which had carried out a considerable number of schemes with the objective of easing traffic flow or allowing for growth in traffic. Examples were the complementary one-way systems in Tottenham Court Road/Gower Street, Baker Street/Gloucester Place and Piccadilly/Pall Mall. It concentrated most of its efforts on the traffic problems of central London. The GLC subsequently implemented other schemes which the LTMU had drawn up, and began to develop its own programme including, for example, the introduction between 1967 and 1969 of peak-hour 'clearways' on 240 miles of main radial roads.

The Council had also from the start attached great importance to the continuation and development of parking control as a method of improving traffic flow, road safety and, later, traffic restraint (see Case Study *Q*).

[1] GLC *Minutes*, 21 June 1966. Various indirect effects of new roads were identified where hardship might arise. (For example, property affected by the noise, fumes and vibration of traffic on new roads and overshadowing by their structures and for which compensation should properly be paid.) The LCC had previously made a similar approach to the Government over properties it wished to acquire in connection with the West Cross Route.

[2] GLC *Press Release 128*, 14 March 1972. The Council had also pressed its case in oral evidence to the GLDP Inquiry and in its suggested revision of the Written Statement. The Government's proposals for a new compensation code were put forward in a White Paper, *Development and Compensation—Putting People First*, Cmnd 5124, October 1972.

[3] Sir Desmond Plummer, leader of the GLC, addressing a British Road Federation symposium 28 November 1967 (GLC *Press Release 450*).

Standards for the provision of parking in new development, operated through planning control procedures, were inherited from the LCC, but were later substantially changed. Also inherited from the former County authorities and exercised through planning control were plans to safeguard the ultimate widening of many existing main roads in London (to what are known as widening lines) as and when frontage redevelopment occurred: the Council itself was responsible, of course, only for widening lines on Metropolitan roads. A continuing programme of 'improvement' schemes on Metropolitan roads has formed a major part of the work of the GLC's highway engineers. Again, many of the schemes constructed during the first four or five years of the GLC's existence were inherited. Subsequently, submissions by the GLC to the preparation list or preparation pool system operated by the MOT ensured a reasonably steady programme (but see Case Study *K*).

The first Greater London Development Plan

Thus the GLC's role in transport before the publication of the GLDP was largely confined to a concern with roads and road traffic, although some decisions had been of a major and far-reaching nature. The GLDP itself incorporated and brought together for the first time most of the policies and proposals which the Council had developed during the first four years. It was prepared 'with the close collaboration of the borough councils both in carrying out surveys and in the formulation of views'[1] as well as with the advice and direction of the MOHLG as regards form and content and the MOT with regard to Trunk road proposals in the London area. The Plan was published in mid-1969 and consisted principally of a Written Statement and a map showing the major existing and proposed roads. It was supported by a bulky *Report of Studies* describing the statistical data and analysis on which the Plan was based. It is necessary here only to outline the broad strategy and to describe the major transport policies and proposals, namely those relating to roads, parking, traffic management and public transport.

The GLDP, although paying some regard to expected changes in the structure of the South-East region and accepting the Metropolitan Green Belt as a constraint, was primarily concerned with the GLC area itself. The main problems identified in the Plan were: the possibility of imbalance between population and employment (paragraph 2.6), poor housing conditions in some areas, poor environmental conditions particularly due to road traffic (paragraph 2.7, 2.8) and the 'inconvenience of movement in Greater London' (paragraph 2.9). The Plan's primary concern, however, was not so much with programmes to solve problems as with a strategy 'to foster the commercial and industrial prosperity of London and its cultural status . . . the social conditions which the people of London are to enjoy will depend upon this prosperity and the flourishing economy and

[1] GLC *Minutes*, 25 March 1969, p209.

culture which it should produce' (paragraph 2.1). This aim was central to the Council's policies for the three critical elements of long-term planning—population and housing, employment, and transport.

The movement of population out of London and beyond the Green Belt that had taken place over the years was thought to have brought benefits particularly to the inner parts of London through reduced overcrowding. But concern was expressed that 'continued decline [in population] would begin to be harmful to the economy of Greater London' (paragraph 2.4) through a reduction in the labour force. The Council's population policy was consequently based on a distinction between 'the many industrial and commercial concerns which have *good cause* to be in London' including the '*vitally important* central functions' and those 'which have *no need* to be in or near the centre of London' (paragraphs 2.2, 2.4—our italics). This distinction was fundamental to the concept of growth and helped to rationalise the Council's target population of 7.3 million by 1981 which was thought to be 'not so great that it militates against the creation of good living conditions nor so small that it gives rise to difficulties in the maintenance of the labour force' (paragraph 2.5).

A similar distinction lay behind the intention to develop the road system 'to cater efficiently for the enormous amount of road traffic which is *essential* to the proper functioning of London' (paragraph 2.9—our italics). At the same time the Plan had the objective of 'improving public transport in all possible ways' (paragraph 2.9) although this objective appeared to relate mainly to the needs of commuters.[1] But most important, the Council saw (with apparent reluctance) 'no way of avoiding, over a period of years, a massive programme for the improvement of the road system' (paragraph 2.10). These proposals were considered to be 'what is necessary so that each element [of the transport system] shall play its proper part' (paragraph 5.2). They were intended to produce a balance not only between the various forms of transport but also between transport and 'the needs of housing, employment and services and facilities of all kinds' (paragraph 5.1).

The most important proposal in the Plan (indeed the largest and most expensive ever put forward by a local authority in Britain) was for the construction of the network of motorway or near-motorway standard roads. These new 'primary roads' were to form 'the uppermost tier in a hierarchy of roads consisting of primary roads, secondary roads and local roads' (paragraph 5.13) and responsibility for them was divided between the GLC and MOT. Figure 2 shows the new primary roads as proposed at October 1970. The secondary road network broadly corresponded with the Metropolitan and borough Principal roads (also shown on Figure 2) with some additional links of local roads. Secondary road policy was not developed in the plan itself although it was recognised that major investment would be required to increase their traffic-carrying capacity if the primary roads were going to fulfil their function. It was expected that the existing main

[1] See report on draft GLDP, GLC *Minutes*, 25 March 1969, p211.

roads would play an interim traffic role until they could be 'improved' or 'relieved' by the primary roads, and those which would not be relieved in the short term assumed a higher priority for improvement. No significant increase was contemplated in the mileage of these roads, and 'thus no further disruption of the environment through which they pass. The level of use [would] be such as to avoid the creation of new barriers to local movement on foot and in vehicles.' However, these roads would have to become as efficient as possible to take long-distance traffic (for which no primary roads existed) and local traffic diverted from environmental areas. In achieving this the boroughs were expected to play a major role by preparing detailed plans delineating 'environmental areas' and enabling the design of both the primary and secondary road proposals to be completed. The GLC for its part would 'use its traffic management powers both to assist the creation of environmental areas . . . and to ensure the best use of the road system. . . .'[1] Examples of how these policies have been handled in practice are given in the Case Studies on environmental areas (*G*), secondary road schemes (*K*) and pedestrian improvements (*L*).

The most important aspect of traffic control policy from the point of view of the GLDP roads strategy was parking control. In central London and at other areas of intense activity (i.e. parts of inner London and many of the suburban centres) the GLC recognised at an early stage that 'full motorisation' could not be provided for, even with a vastly bigger road building programme than it was proposing. Some form of traffic restraint was therefore required and by 1969 the GLC saw parking control as the 'best means' within 'the foreseeable future' (paragraph 5.33). The use of parking meters and yellow lines had evolved (as shown in Case Study *Q*) from a measure of expediency to tidy up on-street parking and to ease traffic flow to one of restraining all-day parkers, and of giving priorities to certain groups of motorists. As the purpose of parking control broadened so did the Council's powers for dealing with it. The Transport (London) Act 1969 gave powers to control all off-street parking spaces available for public use. Although at the time of writing the Council had not taken up these powers it had stated the intention of doing so by 1975 and had indicated a device to gain some control of private off-street spaces.[2]

Standards for parking provision in new office and shop development were also radically altered to reflect the objective of restricting the availability of parking spaces to match the capacity of the road system. The original standards, which required a minimum number of spaces according to the total floorspace and the use to which it was to be put, were changed to a maximum permissible number, related to the operational needs (i.e. service traffic) of the development. These new standards (GLDP, paragraph 13.14) were not mandatory but the GLC expected them to be applied by the borough councils according to local circumstances. The

[1] GLDP Written Statement, paras 5.24–5.26.

[2] GLC (1971), *Paper B483. Future Assessment and Development of Parking Policies as a Means of Restraint*, GLDP Inquiry Stage 1.

GLC for its part, however, envisaged large increases in parking space in the Central Area including, for example, a large parking provision in Covent Garden, a redevelopment area for which it was directly responsible.[1]

The GLDP put forward the concept of balance between different forms of transport and the twin objectives of improving both public transport and roads, but it contained few positive proposals for public transport and certainly nothing to match the scale or level of specification of the proposed primary roads. The public transport proposals consisted merely of some long-standing schemes devised by LT and BR. The Council was heavily criticised for this at the Inquiry and elsewhere, but believed that in order to create a balance major investment in new roads was necessary to make up for the lack of it in the past, whereas the railway system was 'well suited to London's needs and will continue to provide for the majority of personal journeys to central London, particularly the peak journey to work movements' (paragraph 5.50). Bus services were expected to undergo a reshaping programme (see Case Study *N*; and paragraph 5.64 of GLDP) and the GLC believed that they would benefit from reduced congestion on the secondary roads.

In the period between the publication of the GLDP, and the examination of its transport strategy at the public inquiry, certain aspects of the GLC's policy were further developed partly, it seemed, in response to initial criticisms that some of the Plan's proposals were too vague. In January 1970 a revised programme for implementing the primary road network was approved based on a reassessment of the amount of grant aid likely to be available from the MOT, a revised capital expenditure programme for the Council as a whole and increased cost estimates of the road programme itself.[2] This involved delaying the construction until the 1990s of the North and South Cross Routes of the 'motorway box' which besides being the most expensive links, seemed the least likely to produce a reasonable economic return on their investment.[3] The report also emphasised the priority to be attached to completing Ringway 2 which had to be built *de novo* south of the Thames, involving much rehousing.

Later the same year the Council published a document on secondary roads policy, for consultation with the boroughs, other authorities and the public. In contrast to the primary roads policy this contained no detailed plans for investment, nor even a list of schemes for early consideration, but reiterated as a general principle the decision taken in 1967 that expenditure should continue at about half the rate on primary roads. It also gave some general criteria for determining the priority of secondary road schemes and general design standards. For example, high priorities were considered to be the widening of sections near interchanges with the primary roads and

[1] GLC (1971), *Proof of Evidence E12/1*, GLDP Inquiry Stage 1, Table 8; (1971) *Summary* of proposed Covent Garden CDA plan.

[2] GLC *Minutes*, 27 January 1970, pp42–6.

[3] The GLC later stated at the Inquiry that the return on Ringway 1 as a whole was unlikely to exceed 5% p.a.

the widening of intersections rather than whole lengths of road. The document was revised after consultation in 1970 to take account of the latest programme for the primary roads and Professor Colin Buchanan's recommendations, in a study commissioned by the Council in North-East London, that two types of secondary road should be defined to reflect differences in the function of existing main roads.[1]

By the end of 1970 the Council had received programmes for capital expenditure on public transport from LT and BR. These were incorporated into the GLC's proposed capital programme for transport in their proof of evidence on transport submitted to the GLDP Inquiry in November 1970.[2] As Table 4 shows, this brought the total investment envisaged for the period 1971–90 up to £2900 million and the amount to be spent on public transport to something approaching that on roads. The figure for BR, however, included investment over a much wider area than Greater London, and those for BR and LT included replacement of capital assets. The GLC considered the total investment for London, at one-third of the total amount likely to be available for the country as a whole, 'a not unreasonable proportion.'[3]

	£ MILLION
Primary roads	1100
Secondary roads	500
LT Rail	525
LT Buses	125
BR services (London and South-East)	650
Total	2900

TABLE 4 PROPOSED TRANSPORT INVESTMENT IN LONDON, 1971–90

The roads plan, as already mentioned, had evolved over a considerable period of time in negotiation with the MOT and (latterly) the DOE through the joint highways planning machinery (see page 142) and the DOE itself suggested to the Inquiry that it seemed reasonable to commit expenditure on Trunk and Principal roads in London to a total of £1200 million in the period 1971–81, approximately that required to meet the GLC's programme. The proposed public transport investment, however, which had been arrived at by largely separate considerations of BR and LT was simply added to that for roads and apparently did not affect the DOE's or the

[1] GLC (1970), *A Secondary Roads Policy* (revised after consultation), and *Minutes*, 21 July 1970, pp494–5. Colin Buchanan and partners (1970), *North-East London—Some Implications of the GLDP* (A report to the GLC), pp85–7.

[2] GLC (1970), *Proof of Evidence E12/1*, GLDP Inquiry Stage 1.

[3] GLC (1970), p156.

GLC's conception of a reasonable total for transport as a whole. The DOE indicated that public transport investment could amount to £675 million in the period 1971–81 mainly for the replacement and renewal of capital assets while

> the long-term requirements for improvements and additions will *depend ultimately on what view is taken of the role of public transport within the overall transport system of London as a whole* [our italic], and this in turn depends on the view ultimately taken of the future development of London generally, in the light of the present GLDP Inquiry. Until a long-term strategy for public transport has been defined, investment decisions will have to continue to be made in the light of the needs for public transport *as they can be seen at the time*.[1]

In view of this apparent separateness of the roads and public transport elements of the GLDP it was hardly surprising that an important part of the Inquiry proceedings was taken up with an examination of the GLC's overall concept of a balanced strategy for transport. The GLDP Inquiry itself was the most lengthy, complex and broad-ranging ever held into a statutory development plan. The public hearings spanned eighteen months from autumn 1970 to spring 1972 (with a total of about 250 days of sittings) and were split into three stages. The first stage dealt purely with strategic issues and the second was concerned with local objections to the plan, some of which were heard in the locality affected. The purpose of Stage 3 was to allow the panel to collate the vast amount of evidence and call for any further evidence or information required. After the conclusion of the hearings the Panel prepared their report to the Secretary of State; in a remarkably brief time, by November 1972. A decision on the Plan was not expected until well into 1973.

Not surprisingly the most contentious issue was the GLC's transport strategy and in particular the motorway proposals. To attempt to summarise the Inquiry proceedings would be a major task not directly relevant to the purpose of this book but there can be little doubt that the exercise had a profound influence on the development of GLC policies. Not only did it coincide with a period when the GLC was attempting to come to grips with its new responsibilities under the 1969 Act but the panel also sought clarification and elaboration *inter alia* of a number of aspects of the GLDP's transport strategy, notably public transport, evaluation of the motorway and secondary road proposals, and the importance and feasibility of traffic restraint. They also examined the co-ordination and consultation procedures used by the GLC in evolving their policies. Consequently, in describing developments since late 1969, it is difficult and probably unrealistic to distinguish between work arising from the rigorous proceedings at the Inquiry and that which would have been carried out in

[1] DOE (1971), *Paper B612*, GLDP Inquiry Stage 1.

any case, although the latter was clarified and speeded up by the exposure to criticism and explanation that the Inquiry process afforded.

New responsibilities for public transport

By the time the Stage 1 transport hearings were under way early in 1971, the effects of the GLC's control of LT were already becoming apparent. Financial targets for the undertaking had been set early in 1970 including the requirement that LT was not only to cover its costs year by year (as required by the 1969 Act) but was also to put aside £2 million each year as a general reserve. The Council had also determined from the outset that this was to be achieved without the payment of operating subsidies, a decision which led to major fare increases in August 1970 designed to combat rising costs and falling passenger demand on the bus services in particular. In October 1970 the GLC sought to formulate a more comprehensive policy for LT and issued a consultative 'Green Paper' which set out the problems and put forward a number of possible courses of action including, for example, a 'flat fare' or 'fares free' system, staggered working hours (see Case Study *B*) and measures to give buses priority over other traffic (see Case Study *M*).[1] The public consultation process was extended by holding a number of public meetings to discuss the contents of the Green Paper. By July 1971 the Council had formulated and agreed a range of policies for LT, and made a number of further directives. The main elements of the 'policy package' were:

a To improve the 'context' within which LT operates, through the GLC's planning, highway and traffic powers (e.g. by concentrating development at stations, and many traffic management measures to assist bus operation).
b To help finance LT's capital investment (it was decided, for example, to pay a capital grant of £2 million to LT for 1970–71) and to press the government to 'shoulder its full responsibilities' (i.e. by increasing bus and infrastructure grants).
c To reappraise LT's fare structure; to examine proposals to coarsen the bus fare structure; to examine the marginal costs of running off-peak services on both buses and tubes; to examine flat fare or fare zone systems; to investigate new means of issuing tickets and the possibility of experimental minibus services.

The following directions were given to the Executive:[2]

1 *On levels of service*
a To improve the reliability and regularity of peak-hour services.

[1] GLC (1970), *The Future of London Transport.*
GLC *Minutes*, 6 July 1971, pp348–9.

b To give local authorities (including the GLC) three months within which to make representations about proposed changes in services (see Case Study *N*).

2 *On fares*

a To maximise passenger mileage and to minimise the loss of passengers caused by any fare increases.

b To cover peak-hour costs from fares, including full fares for children.

c To simplify fare structures.

3 *To report on the matters outlined in* (c) *above*

Later in 1971 LT made an application for further fare increases averaging from 13 to 15%, again mainly to meet steadily rising costs and falling passenger demand on the bus services. Although the GLC remained determined not to pay any operating subsidy they decided to waive the necessity for LT to put £2 million into its general reserve, influenced no doubt by the Government's desire to keep price increases below 5%. This, together with increased capital grants for public transport announced at the same time which allowed LT to divert some resources, enabling them to cut fare increases to an average of about 10%. This action was approved by the Council in November 1971 and implemented in January 1972.[1]

Having decided to make contributions to LT's capital investment programme, the Council approved 25% towards the cost of the Piccadilly Line extension and the first stage of the Fleet Line. Contributions were also approved towards new rolling stock on the Northern and Piccadilly Lines and also towards the reconstruction of Bond Street and Strand stations (see Case Study *C*). The Council was much less concerned with BR policies and, although expressing general approval of BR's maximum investment plan before the GLDP Inquiry, decided to make no financial contribution to the London commuter services on capital or revenue account. Speaking about this decision Mr Horace Cutler (Chairman of the Policy and Resources Committee) said: 'Every penny we have available is being invested in London Transport... this is our first responsibility.'[2] It appeared, however, that co-ordination between the GLC and BR on the broad levels of service that should be provided, fare levels and so on, was limited by the GLC's decision not to exercise their powers to give grants to BR; as Mr Peter Stott (Joint Director of Planning and Transportation) later said: 'In the absence of any *direct policy control* (the Council) has not exercised them'[3] [our italics].

As explained in Chapter 2, under the provisions of the 1969 Act the GLC must take account of the broad levels of service to be provided both in its consultations with BR on fare structure and in setting financial policies for LT. It was clearly difficult for them to set down standards of provision for BR while refusing to consider any financial contribution. The

[1] GLC *Minutes*, 15 November 1971, pp576–80.

[2] GLC *Press Release 556*, 25 November 1970.

[3] *Hansard HC Papers 107* (*vii*), 1971–72, p124.

same difficulty did not apply to LT, at least not to the same degree. Yet it was not until February 1972 that the GLC set out even in quite general terms the level of services expected from the Underground and LT's buses, in the suggested modifications to the GLDP. These guidelines, however, were not regarded by LT as being very helpful since they could easily be met if there were no problems such as traffic congestion and staff shortages, problems which the guidelines themselves could not help to overcome.

Revision of the GLDP

During 1972 there began to emerge some shift of emphasis in the GLC's policies and approach. Probably the most significant move was the publication in February 1972 of a revised version of the GLDP Written Statement. The revisions did not 'rank as a statutory part of the submitted plan but the Secretary of State will be able to take account of them when considering what modification he may wish to propose to the plan.'[1]

Apart from including much of the previous GLDP material already described (e.g. the LT and BR capital programmes and the primary and secondary roads policies) the revised Statement gave a much fuller account of what the GLC considered London's transport problems to be and the specific measures that would be taken to deal with them. In particular the role of public transport in the overall strategy was much more clearly defined and standards (albeit very general ones) were suggested for the levels of service to be achieved on LT's bus and Underground services. There was also much greater emphasis on restraining the use of private cars 'to achieve the most effective use of the road system.[2] The need to relate transport and land-use patterns was also clearly established in principle.

In sharp contrast to the GLDP itself, the revised Statement put much less emphasis on the roadbuilding proposals, and in particular the motorways which had provoked so much criticism. Indeed, shortly after the new document had been approved the leader of the Council, Sir Desmond Plummer, when asked why other cities had found it easier to construct ring roads, replied: '. . . I do not want to over-emphasise the roads because the roads are only a small part of this and in fact probably public transport is our main concern.'[3] Of course, nearly five years had passed since he had presented the Council's primary road programme to the British Road Federation (see pp97–8) but when asked if there was considerable opposition to the GLDP he replied: 'Oh, yes. There is opposition to every plan irrespective of its merits or demerits. . . .'[4]

There were other significant events in 1972. In July a further Green Paper was published entitled *Traffic and the Environment* in which the

[1] GLC *Minutes*, 8 February 1972, p74.
[2] GLC (1972), *GLDP Revised Statement*, para5.8.5.
[3] Expenditure Committee (Environment and Home Office Subcommittee) Session 1971–72, *Minutes of Evidence*, *Hansard HC Papers 107* (*vii*), p138
[4] *Hansard HC Papers 107* (*vii*), p143.

Council invited comments on measures designed to place much stricter control over the use of cars to central London (including the possibility of a daily supplementary licence system and the introduction of control over public off-street car parks). Other measures were also put forward for discussion including the use of bus lanes to restrain other traffic and the banning of heavy lorries in residential streets. Also indicative of an increasingly flexible approach to the problems of road traffic was the introduction before Christmas 1972 of an experimental scheme closing Oxford Street to all traffic except buses and taxis during the busiest part of the day, including widening the pavements to improve conditions for pedestrians. The significance of this scheme lay in the fact that the GLC accepted it despite the statement by their consultants that it would only be successful if total traffic in the area was reduced. It was, in other words, the first time that the GLC had promoted the restraint of traffic by deliberately reducing the amount of available roadspace.

A further major change in policy came in July 1972 when the Council, faced with yet another application by LT to increase fares by an average of about 7%, decided to give some revenue assistance to LT to reduce the increases to about 4%.[1] In the same month that these fare increases were implemented (September) the Council announced that alternative phasings of the primary road programme were being investigated with a view to completing a ringway in inner London by the end of the 1980s. In November it was decided to 'shelve' the south side of Ringway 2 and the north side of Ringway 1 and to press ahead with a 'hybrid' ringway composed of Ringway 2 in the north and Ringway 1 in the south, linked by the East and West Cross routes, even though this had not been presented to the GLDP Inquiry.[2]

Control of new development

One of the GLC's continuing functions is that of development control; it has to deal with a considerable number of planning applications referred to it for observation or direction under section 24 of the London Government Act 1963. As the figures in the table show, about half of the total may have transport implications concerning development near railway stations or Metropolitan roads or involve a large car park.

PLANNING APPLICATIONS 1969[3]	FOR OBSERVATION	FOR DIRECTION
Near railway station	107	23
Affecting Metropolitan road	1701	546
Including major car park	50	22
Others	1491	743
Total	3349	1324

[1] GLC *Minutes*, 18 July 1972, pp357–9.
[2] GLC *Minutes*, 14 November 1972, pp528–31.
[3] GLC *Minutes*, 24 February 1970, pp184–6.

The transfer of Principal roads from the boroughs to the GLC will reduce this proportion, but some will still be referred on other planning grounds. In the meantime the GLC, the DOE and the London Boroughs Association (LBA) formed a joint working party to improve the processing of those that have to be referred to the GLC, and to decrease their numbers; category *A* roads continue to be subject to GLC screening, category *B* to be referred only in a limited number of cases. At the time of writing the schedule had not been published and the matter was still under consultation.[1]

Constraints on the GLC's activities

Having outlined what are probably the main policies and decisions of the GLC with regard to transport, it is important to balance the activities of the Council with an account of some of the constraints under which they operate. The availability of Government funds for the implementation of road and public transport investment has already been mentioned. In addition the Council were concerned about the length of time taken to complete the various planning and consultation procedures before a new project could be started. Delays were regarded as harmful on two scores: they increased the extent to which people were uncertain about the future of their areas or properties (i.e. 'planning blight') and each year of delay saw increases in the cost of the programme.[2] The GLDP Inquiry in particular was considered to be a constraint on the machinery of planning in London.

> Until there is a decision the Council is unable to make progress on schemes which are an integral part of the Plan. The Council's resources are strained to meet the requirements of the Plan's investigation. And the Department of the Environment is constrained by the fact that the Secretary of State will have to decide upon issues in the Plan when he comes to determine the question of approval.[3]

Progress in introducing traffic management schemes (including parking controls) was considered by the Council to be limited by the ability of the police to enforce them. Shortage of police officer and traffic warden manpower and difficulties in enforcing fines for parking and traffic offences stemming from the need to trace the driver of the vehicle were considered to be major constraints on, for example, the extension of the Inner London Parking Area (Case Study *Q*), the introduction of more station car parks (Case Study *F*), bans on lorry parking in residential streets, prescribed lorry routes and bus priority schemes (Case Study *M*).[4]

A further and more general constraint upon the GLC's activities was considered to be the fact that 'the Council is not its own master in the

[1] London Borough (LB) of Enfield *Minutes*, 14 December 1972, item1068, pp329–30.
[2] See, for example, GLC *Minutes*, 19 October 1971, p531, Report on West Cross Route.
[3] *Hansard HC Papers 107* (*vii*), p122.
[4] *Hansard HC Papers 107* (*vii*), pp131–5.

implementation of its policies,'[1] and co-ordination and consultation was therefore required with the borough councils, BR, and the DOE as well as the police and other agencies involved in transport in London. The co-ordination machinery set up to deal with this is described later in this chapter.

LONDON TRANSPORT EXECUTIVE

After existing from 1933 to 1947 as an independent public corporation under the title London Passenger Transport Board, and as a nationalised undertaking responsible to the British Transport Commission from 1947 to 1962 when its members felt it had languished for lack of priority in investment and replacement of equipment,[2] the LT Executive became a separate Board directly responsible to the Minister of Transport. Under the Transport Act 1968 it received extra powers with regard to research, manufacturing and the development of land.[3] It was section 9 of the same Act, however, that established the Passenger Transport Authorities and Executives for four provincial conurbations responsible for integrating public transport and local authority town planning, traffic and parking policies. The GLC and the Minister of Transport engaged in prolonged negotiations over moves towards similar integration in London and the terms on which LT was to become the GLC's responsibility. The principal issue was the financial position of the undertaking. The GLC was determined that in assuming responsibility it should not take over the Board's large debt and that the new Executive should be required by statute to pay its way subject only to grants from central or local government. The Government eventually agreed to write off the LT Board's accumulated debt of about £270 million and thus relieve the Executive of a burden of about £13 million annually in interest charges. 'Having had this debt written off the Executive (was) determined to avoid the accumulation of a further large load of unrepayable debt.'[4]

The new Executive was made responsible for the day-to-day management of LT services and was to consist of a chairman appointed by the Council and from 4 to 10 members appointed by them after consulting with the chairman. This compared with a chairman and from 5 to 9 members of the former LT Board under the 1962 Act.[5] The GLC appointed Sir Richard Way as the first chairman of the Executive. Mr Anthony Bull, the vice-chairman of the former Board, remained as vice-chairman of the Executive until he retired in 1971, to be succeeded by Mr Ralph Bennett. By 1971 only two members of the 1969 Board remained: Messrs Robbins and Shave.

[1] *Hansard HC Papers 107 (vii)*, p126.
[2] Select Committee on Nationalised Industries, *London Transport voll Report*, p118; *Hansard HC Papers 313*, 1965, vol2; *Minutes*, Q1506; *Hansard HC Papers 313-1*.
[3] *Transport Act 1968*, ch73, s546–8.
[4] LT Executive *Annual Report*, 1970, p7.
[5] *Transport (London) Act 1969*, ch33, s4; and *Transport Act 1962*, ch46, s1 (4).

RESPONSIBILITIES OF FULL-TIME EXECUTIVE MEMBERS (TOTAL OF SIX)	CHIEF OFFICERS REPORTING DIRECTLY TO EXECUTIVE MEMBERS
Chairman	Secretary to the Executive
	Solicitor
	Claims and Insurance Officer
Managing Director (Buses) (Deputy-Chairman)	Chief Operating Manager (Buses)
	Director of Transportation Planning
	Director of Transportation Policy
	Director of Commercial Policy
	Director of Operations Research
Managing Director (Railways)	Chief Operating Manager (Railways)
	Public Relations Officer
	Supplies Officer
	Commercial Advertising Officer
	Railway Development Officer
Engineering	Chief Civil Engineer
	Chief Mechanical Engineer
	Chief Signal Engineer
	Chief Electrical Engineer
	Mechanical Engineer, Design and Development
	Director General Research and Development
	Architect
Finance	Chief Finance Officer
	Chief Estate Manager
	Data Processing Manager
	Director of Marketing
	Director of Capital Planning
Personnel and Industrial Relations	Chief Establishment Officer
	Chief Industrial Relations Officer
	Chief Medical Officer
	Catering Officer
Part Time Executive Members (two)	

Table 5 LT EXECUTIVE ORGANISATION, OCTOBER 1971

The management structure of the new Executive (Table 5) showed a clear functional division and direct line of responsibility to individual members of the Executive, in charge of managing buses, managing railways, engineering functions (formerly split between railways and buses) personnel and finance (augmented by a Marketing department for all the Executive's services including consultancy). This division left the chairman much freer than his predecessor on the Board to consider the overall policies of the Executive but at the same time put an onus for co-ordination directly on his shoulders. The structure of the Executive reflected the views of the Directing Group of the LT Joint Review established by the MOT and the LT Board in 1966 which reported in 1968. They believed that the Chairman should have more time for corporate planning and external co-ordination matters,[1] whereas the Select Committee of 1965 had decided to spread the executive responsibilities over all full-time members of the (smaller) Board including the chairman.[2] The appointment of a member responsible for finance was recommended by both of these bodies and the Select Committee had also recommended that one member should hold specific responsibility for personnel.

Initially at least the GLC's policy control of LT corresponded very closely to the Joint Review's conclusion that LT 'must have clearly defined objectives relating to financial viability and to the services they are expected to provide . . . an appropriate practical one for them would be to carry as many passengers as possible while continuing to provide a network of services and operating within viability.'[3] The Executive realised that 'its overriding duty is to conduct its affairs on a commercial basis and in such a way as to meet the financial objectives set for it by the Council.' It expected to have to meet expenditure from revenue (for maintenance, depreciation, and improvement) except to the extent that GLC or Government grants were available.[4]

The actual financial policies and directives which the GLC set out for the Executive have been described earlier in this chapter while the terms of the 1969 Act on which they were based were outlined in Chapter 2. The Executive's reaction to the first year of control by the GLC was indicated in their annual report:[5]

> It must surely be right that a local public transport system, however large, should be the political responsibility of the elected representatives of the area which it serves.
>
> The new relationship between the London Transport Executive and the Greater London Council has created a fresh atmosphere in which it has become possible to discuss the whole concept of the place of public transport in the life of the community, and its function in the process of urban planning, in a new setting.

As the Executive is responsible for the day-to-day management of the LT system its relationship with the GLC is primarily concerned with matters of overall policy and forward planning. Its programme of capital expenditure is submitted each year for inclusion in the GLC's overall corporate programme. In the first years the programme consisted largely of plans drawn up over a period of years by the former Board, the main items

[1] MOT (1968), *Transport in London*, Cmnd 3686, Annex, especially pp60–3.
[2] *Hansard HC Papers 313*, 1965, pp13–14, 148.
[3] Annex to Cmnd 3686 (1968), paras151–2.
[4] LT *Annual Report*, 1970, pp4, 7.
[5] LT *Annual Report*, 1970, pp9, 23

being extensions to the Underground system (see Case Study *C*), the modernisation of stations (for example, South Kensington) and the replacement and improvement of signalling and rolling stock. These were expected to require expenditure of £290 million by 1980 and a further £235 million by 1990 (at 1970 prices, see page 103). For the bus services the emphasis was on a reshaping programme first proposed in 1966 including the conversion to one-man operation of all services by the late 1970s (to overcome staff shortages and reduce operating costs by a reduction in manpower of 12 000), and the shortening of bus routes to combat the adverse effects of traffic congestion. The investment required was much smaller than for the Underground amounting to about £125 million in the period 1971–90. This figure included expenditure on new buses, garages, control equipment and other items such as bus stations.[1]

The implementation of the bus reshaping plan had begun in 1968 with the introduction of the first six Red Arrow flat-fare, limited-stop services in central London and the 'recasting' of services in the Wood Green and Walthamstow areas. Conversion to one-man operation continued and by January 1972 about 25% of the Executive's bus fleet was one-man operated. The original concept of the reshaping plan was, however, gradually modified over the years in the light of experience of the early schemes. Less emphasis was placed, for example, on the shortening of routes since it was found difficult to achieve without disturbing (and consequently reducing) established patterns of passenger demand.[2] Moreover, in 1972 LT announced something of a *volte-face* with regard to the extension of one-man operation in central London. Experience of delays with the new buses due to increased passenger boarding times led the Executive to conclude that in the congested conditions of central London complete conversion would give rise to unacceptable delays to bus and other traffic.[3]

The Executive appeared increasingly to believe that their bus operating problems could not be solved by the reshaping plan and accompanying investment alone, and began to take a more positive attitude towards the contribution which the GLC could make as traffic authority by considering a widespread introduction of bus priority schemes (see Case Study *M*).[4]

The financial duties of the former Board and particularly of the Executive have always been quite clearly defined, but the relationship of this duty to that of providing 'such public passenger transport services as best meets the needs for the time being of Greater London' has been couched in more general terms. The LT Board had set itself operational criteria for the network coverage of buses and the frequency of bus and tube services (see Case Study *N*) but it was not known (or at least never made public) to

[1] LT *Annual Report*, 1970; LT (1970), *Proof of Evidence, E12/2*, GLDP Inquiry Stage 1.
[2] LT (1971), *Paper S27/366*, GLDP Inquiry Stage 2.
[3] LT *Press Release, GPN 367* of 9 November 1972.
[4] LT *Annual Report*, 1971, p7.

what extent these standards were achieved. The GLC directed the Executive to improve the regularity and reliability of peak hour services,[1] and included its own standards relating to level of service in the revised version of the GLDP (see page 107) but again there was no indication of how realistic these were either as a measure of present services or as an objective to be sought in the future.

LT's involvement in transport planning is further discussed in the case studies on Thamesmead (*A*), Staggering of hours (*B*), New tube railways (*C*), Development at Stations (*D*), and Station Car Parks (*F*). Its role more specifically as a transport operator is also discussed in the case studies on Alterations to Services (*N*) and Inner London Parking Area (*Q*).

BRITISH RAILWAYS

The Labour Government elected in 1964 sought to change some of the railway policies of its predecessor including those relating to management, the manufacturing powers of the Board and social considerations in determining rail closures, and to introduce new policies particularly with regard to the co-ordination of road and rail freight traffic and the integration of public transport in the conurbations. Subsequently BR was reconstituted under the 1968 Transport Act which abolished the Regional Boards established under the 1962 Act, and slightly reduced the size of the Board, as suggested by its management consultants (Cooper Brothers).[2] Furthermore the Board was to review its organisation within a year, and consequently management consultants were appointed who produced a series of reports culminating in a document called 'Organising for the 1970s' which was approved by the Minister of Transport in December 1969.[3] The report proposed that the Board should have a non-executive, corporate planning, and policy-making role over the railways and associated businesses, with the exception of one full-time member, who was to be the Chief Executive (Railways). The Board members would each have a specific field of responsibility 'in which they possess or will develop special interests or expertise' while the part-time members were 'to bring a wider range of experience and judgement, and perhaps a greater degree of objectivity to bear on the deliberations of the Board.'

The new organisation (Table 6) clearly distinguished the corporate and railway functions with their separate structures.[4] The Railway Management Group consisted of six executive directors with specific functions and five Regional General Managers. The hotel, hovercraft, property, engineering, shipping and consultancy subsidiaries each had an executive director.

[1] GLC *Minutes*, 6 July 1971, pp336–53.

[2] *Transport Act 1968*, ch73, s38 replacing *Transport Act 1962*, ch73, s1 (3).

[3] Published as House of Commons Paper, *BRB Report on Organisation* (HCP 50, 1969/70, HMSO). Further detail on the Board's history and organisation can be found in M R Bonavia (1971), *The Organisation of British Railways.*

[4] Although the personnel, planning and finance positions were shared between the corporate and railway departments.

BOARD MEMBERS	RESPONSIBILITIES AND OFFICERS REPORTING
FULL-TIME MEMBERS (8)	
1 Chairman	Property Board; Public Relations; Management Development
2 Deputy Chairman	Railway Management Group and shared responsibilities with Chief Executive (Railways)
3 Chief Executive (Railways) (Joint Deputy Chairman)	*Regional General Managers* Eastern London Midland Scottish Southern Western *Executive Directors* Managing Director, BR Engineering Ltd Planning Finance Systems and Operation Freight Passenger
4 Vice-Chairman	Corporate Finance Corporate Planning Transportation Systems and Mechanical Research Ltd BR Engineering Ltd
5	BR Hotels Ltd BR Hovercraft Ltd
6	Personnel
7	Research; Engineering Technology
8	London and South-East Passenger Services; Shipping and International Services; BR Advertising Ltd; Publicity; Films; Channel Tunnel
PART-TIME MEMBERS (6)	

Table 6 BR BOARD ORGANISATION, FEBRUARY 1971

One Board member was to have special responsibility for the London commuter services.[1]

In addition to these reorganisations the Board received a new chairman in September 1971 when Mr Richard Marsh, Minister of Transport in 1967–68, succeeded Sir Henry Johnson, who had been chairman from 1967. Marsh saw it as his job to 'operate wholly and solely commercially' while it was the responsibility of the Government to define those services

[1] At the time of writing this was Mr D McKenna, a former general manager of Southern Region.

which needed subsidies for social reasons. He believed that the future quality of the London commuter services depended on how much capital the Government was willing to invest.[1]

By early 1971 the consultants had looked at the local area management of the railways (i.e. below headquarters level) and suggested that it should be simplified. A principal aim was to reduce its size to match the smaller responsibilities left after the formation of the National Freight Corporation in 1968[2] and the formation of subsidiary companies for workshops, ports, shipping and properties. The consultants also considered that the abolition of the Regional Boards of 1962–68 required some concentration of business and functional planning at the centre and a devolution of day-to-day functions to 8 or 10 territorial organisations under a general manager with his own functional managers.

The second report on BR organisation appeared in April 1972 and consolidated these suggestions, confirming the main proposal to eliminate a whole level of management by replacing the 5 regions and 20 divisions with 8 'territories.' The territorial boundaries were drawn so that the major provincial conurbations were not split. The Greater London services were split between four territories but this was not considered to be an anomaly because the 'local service groups are generally radial and would be confined to one of four territories.'[3]

A corporate planning department was established during 1968 and 1969 with the aim of producing plans at two time-scales—one year and five (or more) years. The corporate plan for 1971–75 suggested a total investment of £557 million for the whole country with approximately £75 million recoverable through infrastructure grants. This compared with a ten-year programme for the improvement of the whole Southern Region (mainly London commuter services) costing £217 million, submitted to the Minister of Transport in 1969.[4] Within the national framework of the whole of BR's operations the GLC area has little significance; much more important is the area covered by the London and South-East (L & SE) 'pool' services,[5] which includes all London commuter lines south-east of a line drawn through Clacton, Cambridge, Bedford, Reading and Bournemouth. This is considered as an entity for financial and planning purposes even though four separate regions (or territories) run the trains, and by 1971 BR had put forward alternative levels of investment.

The Board has developed three main objectives for the L & SE pool services. The first is the provision and maintenance of an efficient commuter service to central London. This largely entails the provision of radial peak-

[1] The *Guardian*, 15 September 1971.
[2] *Transport Act 1968*, ch73, s1.
[3] BR Board (1972), *Second Report of the Board on Organisation*, HMSO, p11.
[4] *Evening News*, 2 December 1969; BR Board (1970), *Proof of Evidence, E12/7*, p23, GLDP Inquiry Stage 1.
[5] So called because revenue grants under section 56 of the 1968 Act were pooled for all passenger services within the area other than Inter-City and freight services. See paragraph 55 of Cmnd 3686 (1968).

hour services and may conflict with the Board's other functions of providing Inter-City and non-radial passenger services and freight services in the London area. Off-peak traffic on the commuter lines is considered to be 'subsidiary to commuting in terms of volume of movement and social significance.'[1] BR has no criteria for defining adequate or desirable frequency of service (or, apart from desirable loading standards, for quality of service). This is partly because BR prefers to consider separately the particular circumstances of each service, which has both influenced and been influenced by people's locational decisions and travel habits.

The second objective is to improve the quality of the services to keep pace with the public's rising standards and expectations: in particular to keep passenger loadings down to a comfortable level, especially on the longer-distance journeys, and to provide an attractive alternative to the car for all journeys to and from central London. BR regards improvements to the quality of service as vital to their role of helping to reduce or avoid road traffic congestion and of lessening the need for road construction with its attendant environmental difficulties.[2]

The third objective which may appear to conflict with the first two, is to make the services financially viable, which is interpreted as securing a sufficient surplus to replace assets and build up reserves. The reasoning behind this objective is primarily that viability would allow a greater degree of freedom from government control (i.e. by removing dependence on revenue grants from either central government or the GLC) while contributing to the statutory duty of BR as a whole not to make a loss.

Within the context of these three objectives BR also has more specific financial objectives. One is to reduce the extent to which cross-subsidy occurs between services, or at least to prevent it from becoming any more pronounced. For example, BR considers that the inner suburban services are too heavily subsidised by the longer distance services. Another objective is to maintain a given level of services in the face of fluctuating demand or costs, even if this means higher fares.

In seeking to achieve financial viability on the L & SE services BR has increasingly applied 'commercial' criteria, or at least a 'commercial' approach, in determining its operational and investment priorities. In order to obtain the maximum return on existing assets, priority has been given to investment schemes that would promote traffic growth (for example the electrification of the ex-Great Northern suburban lines) or improve the quality of services to overcome the counter-productive effects of fare increases (for example the new signalling schemes at London Bridge and Feltham). Services have also been adapted to cater for an increasing number of longer-distance commuters and a declining number of commuters from inner London; the longer-distance services are usually more profitable than the inner London stopping services (see Case Study *H*). Further examples of

[1] *Hansard HC Papers 107* (*xvi*), 1971–72, p357.

[2] See BRB *Annual Report*, 1969, pp12–13; 1970, p7; and BR Board (1970), *Proof of Evidence*, *E12/7*, p5, GLDP Inquiry Stage 1.

the 'commercial approach' are BR's increased concern to realise the full value of its property assets (see Case Study *D*) and to introduce fare structures that reflect more closely the demand for services and the costs of providing them.

Despite the clear objectives of BR with regard to the L & SE rail services, the Board is by no means the sole agency for achieving them. As with the undertaking as a whole, Government decisions on the general level of fares to be charged and on capital and operating grants have been a continuing and often tight constraint on BR activities. In more recent years the move towards central government responsibility for unremunerative services and local responsibility for transport planning has introduced a further dimension to this constraint. The Board has commented on this in the following terms:

> . . . the machinery of specific grant aid from Central Government, which has emerged from the Transport Act 1968, has led to the joint involvement of the Board and the Department (of the Environment) in developing action plans for local rail passenger services, and as the providers of both revenue grants and, where appropriate and necessary, investment grants, the Department will remain an integral part of the whole transportation planning process.
>
> The emergence of new transportation planning authorities concerned with local transport in the shape of the Passenger Transport Authorities and Executives is, however, particularly welcomed, as is the new relationship with the GLC provided by the Transport (London) Act 1969.[1]

Within this framework the role which BR has played with regard to the L & SE services may be conveniently described under the separate general headings of operations and planning and investment.

Operation of the L & SE services

BR has pointed out that in all the conurbations they have to:

> maintain four different types of service and generally to run them over the same complex and usually intensely used network:
>
> Local passenger services
> Longer-distance (commuter) services
> Freight services
> Inter-City passenger services

The latter two types are mostly profitable but the local and longer-distance commuter services to central London incurred a deficit every year from 1968 to 1972. The Government, while continuing to pay grants to meet this deficit (e.g. about £15 million for each of the years 1968–71) has been

[1] *Hansard HC Papers 107* (*xvi*), 1971–72, p356.

anxious to rid itself of this particular burden. The Labour Government stated in 1968 that the London pool services would have to pay their way by 1973[1] and the Conservatives, four months after coming to power in 1970, decided to eliminate the grants by 1973.[2] The BR Board also wanted their London Service to be financially self-supporting, and believed that there was:

> a reasonable prospect of attaining balance within a few years provided that fares increases of a moderate size, after discounting inflation, are permitted. The Board, however, recognises that there is bound to be intense political interest in the services provided and fare levels in this area.[3]

Government intervention in the fixing of BR fares has always been of major importance to the question of viability.[4] In 1971, for example, a period of rapid inflation throughout the British economy led the Confederation of British Industries to take the initiative of calling for a voluntary 5% ceiling on price increases. The Government (which fully supported this move) asked BR to limit fare increases to that amount and subsequently agreed to pay the Board special assistance to meet rising costs on BR as a whole (totalling £27 million for 1972) so that this could be achieved. *The Times* commented that this arrangement was:

> particularly ironic in the case of the railways, where the strict financial discipline imposed for the first time by a Labour Government is being relaxed by a Conservative Government—and one dedicated to the proposition of financial control—after only three years.[5]

Faced with a situation of continuing deficit on the pool services and the withdrawal of Government aid, BR would have the choice (if meeting its statutory obligation to break even) of raising fares or cutting costs. The Board has indicated that it would prefer the former course rather than drastically reducing the level of service. But inevitably the Board was considering possible closure (if grants were not forthcoming) of some of the services making the heavier losses, particularly those not intensely used, such as the Broad Street–Richmond (see Case Study *N*) and North Woolwich services. Other ways of cutting costs to bridge the revenue gap could involve withdrawing some inner suburban services or removing the 'top of the peak' on some services,[6] measures which would be more likely to affect commuters from within the GLC area than those from further afield. BR has recognised that all this has important implications for their relationship with the GLC as well as the Government:

[1] MOT (1968) *Transport in London*, Cmnd 3686, p14.
[2] Announced by the Chancellor of the Exchequer, 27 October 1970.
[3] *Hansard HC Papers 107* (*xvi*), 1971–72, p357.
[4] BR Board *Annual Report*, 1971, p2.
[5] *The Times*, 23 December 1971.
[6] BR (1972), *Paper S30/75*, GLDP Inquiry Stage 3.

> The prospect of overall viability conceals . . . the fact that the short-distance services—those of primary interest to the GLC—are very much more uneconomic than the longer-distance services. The planning interest of the GLC, related primarily to the inner suburban services, therefore presents a number of problems. These relate to the determination of appropriate priorities where there are competing demands of different services or limited track capacity. They relate also to priorities for investment, and to the successful financial management of the whole area of London and the South-East.[1]

Planning and investment

The grants paid for unremunerative passenger services, including those for the L & SE pool, have only covered the maintenance of the services and not their overall improvement. The infrastructure grants under the Transport Act 1968 have therefore been regarded by BR as crucial to the achievement of their objectives for improving the quality of the London services. The extension by the Government in 1971 of the infrastructure grant system to cover most investment projects in the conurbations was therefore particularly welcome. But the Government wishes to ensure that each scheme will bring value for money and, as with most public investment projects, the Treasury demands certain minimum rates of return from railway improvements receiving grant aid; this is known as the 'test discount rate' and is currently 10%.

Influenced by this requirement, BR has increasingly used cost-benefit analysis as a means of justifying its investment schemes. Although cost-benefit analysis is not regarded as an infallible decision-making tool, it has helped to clarify the relative merits of investment in road and rail, or different rail schemes (see Case Studies *C* and *H*). The need to determine the relationship between road and rail traffic has also been important to BR since the MOT's decision that preference should be given to infrastructure grants for schemes which would either transfer traffic from road to rail, or would prevent a possible transfer from rail to road.

In putting forward its plans, BR has made it increasingly clear, not only to the Government and the GLC but also to the public at large, that the railways will be unable to play what is considered to be their proper role (as set out in the statutes and the GLDP, and as interpreted by BR) without substantial investment over the period 1971–81. Richard Marsh, on taking over as chairman of BR, said that if road investment was given priority over investment in public transport 'then as a prescription for total chaos it would be difficult to beat.'[2]

Three alternative 'prescriptions' for the L & SE services were produced by BR in the form of three levels of investment over a ten-year period. The first would be a minimum investment aimed simply at maintaining

[1] *Hansard HC Papers 107* (*xvi*), 1971–72, p357.
[2] The *Guardian*, 20 May 1971.

the most essential services while reducing first the quality and then the volume of other services. This 'option' was discarded with the agreement of the DOE.[1] The intermediate level would maintain a better quality of services and include certain improvements such as the scheme to improve reliability at London Bridge (see Case Study *H*) and to electrify the former Great Northern suburban lines into the City. This intermediate level would total £250 million over a ten-year period with an expenditure in the first five years (1972–76) of about £110 million (with about £35 million expected to be recoverable through infrastructure grants).[2]

The third level would include all this together with more comprehensive improvements to the whole system. BR advocated this 'progressive' level of investment and considered that it would produce a network of services which would keep pace with rising public standards and could also produce the greatest social benefit by avoiding road traffic costly to accommodate either in investment or environmental terms.[3] The sum proposed to the GLDP Inquiry was £350 million (at 1969 prices) over a ten-year period, of which £155 million would be spent in the first five years (1972–76) mainly on track and signalling, electrification and rolling stock.[4]

The 'intermediate' and 'progressive' levels of investment comprised a package of individual investment schemes, each costed and justified individually. It was thus possible for the Government to consider and decide each scheme on its own merits whilst being aware of its general 'level' of priority. It was reported in October 1971 that initially only the first five years of the intermediate programme had been approved.[5] As with the major investment proposals of the GLC, Government approval beyond the short term (i.e. five years) seemed unlikely until the Secretary of State had taken a decision on the GLDP.

The role of BR as a transport operator is further discussed in the case studies on Thamesmead, Station Car Parks, the Heathrow Link, South-East Approaches (*A*, *F*, *E* and *H*) and as property developer also in the case study on Development at Stations (*D*).

THE LONDON BOROUGHS

The characteristics of the thirty-two boroughs (and the City of London) vary very widely[6] and this is reflected in their differing organisation, policies and the problems which they face. To survey each one in detail would require considerable research, certainly beyond the resources of this study, but to provide a reasonable coverage, Chief and Deputy Engineers, and in

[1] *Hansard HC Papers 107* (*xvi*), 1971–72, p358.
[2] Interviews with senior BR officers.
[3] BR Board (1970), *Proof of Evidence*, *E12/7*, para4.27, GLDP Inquiry Stage 1.
[4] BR Board (1970), para4.29 and table 9, GLDP Inquiry Stage 1.
[5] *Evening Standard*, 27 October 1971.
[6] See G Rhodes (ed) (1972), *The New Government of London: The First Five Years*, Weidenfeld & Nicolson/LSE, ch12.

some cases Planning Officers, were interviewed in twelve selected boroughs,[1] and the information collected was supplemented by published material.

The arrangement of committees for dealing with planning, highway and transport matters varied considerably and was subject to change. Nine of the twelve boroughs had separate Highways (sometimes Highways and Works) and Planning Committees; Hammersmith had a Borough Development Group Committee with Highways Planning, Development Control and Development Plan subcommittees and a similar arrangement was found in Barnet whose Development and Resources Committee had three 'service' committees reporting to it (Building, Development and Public Works); only Havering combined the two functions. In four boroughs (Westminster, Hammersmith, Bromley and Greenwich) the 'service' committees were co-ordinated by a policy committee or panel consisting of majority-party members;[2] three of the other eight boroughs also had a policy committee of equal status to the functional committees. Road safety and development control matters were usually delegated to subcommittees whilst the Highways and Works committees often handled other aspects of public services (e.g. parks as in Harrow). Car parking policy and management was one rapidly growing area of transport policy receiving particular attention: in Westminster this was a function of the main Highways Committee, but of subcommittees in Croydon and Lambeth.

Officers commented in particular on two aspects of the adequacy of these structures for decision making. First, the problem of demarcation of responsibility between the Highways and Planning committees increasingly arose as the councils sought a more comprehensive approach to the planning and management of highways and land use. In Camden this problem had been tackled by including highways planning and car parking policy in the responsibilities of the Planning and Communications Committee. Second, there were difficulties in distinguishing between matters of strategy and of detail. Attempts to 'streamline' procedures by reducing the number of committees had sometimes been stultified by the need to cope with an immense workload; examples were quoted of a resulting need for more frequent meetings or a large number of panels or subcommittees. In one borough the Highways and Services Committee had an average agenda of from 40 to 50 items (a record at one meeting of 114) despite the existence of a separate committee for technical matters, and had to impose a guillotine on committee business.

[1] Comprising five inner boroughs (Westminster, Hammersmith, Camden, Kensington and Chelsea and Lambeth) and seven outer boroughs (Barnet, Bromley, Croydon, Greenwich, Harrow, Havering and Waltham Forest). The interviews were carried out during 1970.

[2] This may be regarded as an adapted form of the Board of Management suggested in the Maud Committee Report (1967, vol1) sometimes incorporating financial programming as well; seventeen out of twenty London boroughs considering reform had adopted such machinery by 1969. See *Recent Reforms in Management Structure of Local Authorities*, Inlogov Occasional Paper No.2, Univ of Birmingham, 1969.

DEPARTMENTAL STRUCTURE	INNER		OUTER	
	SAMPLE (6)	TOTAL (12)	SAMPLE (6)	TOTAL (20)
COL 1	COL 2	COL 3	COL 4	COL 5
Separate Engineering	5	11	4	12
Joint Eng/Planning	0	0	1	7
Joint Pl/Architecture	3	4	1	5
Separate Planning	2	7	3	7
Tech Directorate (incorporating engineering, planning and architectural functions)	1	1	1	1

Table 7 ORGANISATION OF LONDON BOROUGH'S TECHNICAL DEPARTMENTS, JUNE 1970

Cols (3) and (5) from *Departmental Organisation in Local Government*, Booz, Allen & Hamilton, January 1970. Cols (2) and (4) from research in 1970 for this study.

The organisation of departments likewise demonstrated considerable variety (see Table 7) and did not always match up exactly with the committee structure. Croydon's Chief Planning Officer and Engineer, for example, reported to two separate committees. The division of functions between departments was if anything more complex than between committees and this was particularly evident in two fields: the forward planning of the road network and its relationship to land use; and the environmental aspects of highways and traffic. The most common pattern was for traffic and highways planning to be carried out within the engineering department and for land use and environmental matters to be carried out within the planning department. Where these matters overlapped joint reports would often be produced for consideration by the highways and planning committees. There did not appear to be any specific arrangements for combining both functions in the preparation of borough development plans, invariably the responsibility of the planning department, and working relationships between planning and engineering departments varied considerably. Interchange of ideas and information at every level from major policies to design details was not always helped by geographical separation of the planning and engineering departments, as in Camden and Islington. In Camden the computer on which the land-use and transportation data were processed was in a third location. The Chief Planning Officer and Engineer of Croydon was convinced that his joint department greatly facilitated co-ordination and that duplication of functions had been eliminated and staff numbers held down by this form of organisation. The Chief Engineer of Bromley thought that problems of two separate departments did not arise because both he and the Chief Planning Officer had training in both disciplines.

The borough engineers' departments sampled ranged in size from twenty to fifty professional and supporting technical staff. The most usual divisions were between highways and traffic sections, and civil engineering sections which had the support of specialists on such matters as structural engineering, drainage, and lighting. Road safety was usually dealt with by a separate group. Where traffic or transportation studies were being undertaken, a separate group was usually established for this purpose. Particular local circumstances were also sometimes expressed in terms of staff requirements; for example Westminster, Croydon and Lambeth had separate sections to administer parking control and Havering, with a major concern for Romford town centre's ring road, devoted nineteen of its thirty-four technical staff to this project. Harrow and Havering both had groups concerned with vetting, supervising, and approving work on private streets, which were numerous in some of the outer boroughs.

Some boroughs have adopted new management techniques in an attempt to improve efficiency. The Borough Engineer of Bromley considered that a management-by-objectives approach had maintained a high level of staff morale and more accurate results in costing and timing schemes, whilst the introduction of a Planning, Programme and Budgeting system was being planned in Westminster and Islington.

A review of borough policies in relation to transport presents difficulties not only because of wide variations but also because many policies are subject to considerable and sometimes rapid change. Moreover, at the time of this study no borough development plans had been published, or even reached an advanced stage of preparation. The remainder of this section should therefore be regarded as an illustration rather than a review of the way in which the London boroughs performed.

Primary roads

By 1969, most boroughs had decided to accept the concept of ring and radial motorways as put forward by the GLC, though they differed in their views on how this concept should be carried through. Lambeth, for example, in its views on the draft GLDP thought that the Ringway 1 proposal was premature because it did not form part of an integrated land-use and transportation policy,[1] while Southwark considered that it should take low priority compared with the improvement of the secondary road network. Harrow, Westminster, Haringey and the City of London (who had no motorways proposed within their areas) expressed general approval. Tower Hamlets had major reservations about the lack of GLC traffic restraint and public transport proposals, but accepted the need for a new primary road network.[2]

The majority of boroughs were concerned overwhelmingly with the impact of the proposed motorways on their own areas. Those boroughs

[1] LBA (then Committee), *Minutes*, 23 June 1966, p30.

[2] LB Tower Hamlets (1970), *Proof of Evidence*, *S12/30*, GLDP Inquiry Stage 1.

directly affected also expressed general approval but often had reservations either about the loss of housing (e.g. Hackney) or about the environmental effects; Kensington and Chelsea for example supported the West Cross Route but were anxious about the possibility of extra traffic in the vicinity of Cheyne Walk and the Embankment. A few boroughs suggested alternative alignments for sections of the motorways, for example Wandsworth proposed a different routing of Ringway 1 in their area which they claimed would be cheaper and would involve the demolition of 700 homes instead of 1750.[1] Richmond suggested that the motorways should be routed so as to avoid the borough altogether because of its exceptional environmental quality.[2]

Other major causes of concern were uncertainty about the phasing of construction, and about the routing of the proposed motorways. Lambeth, for example, believed that it was inequitable to safeguard the route of Parkway East until the 1990s and that it should be excluded from the GLDP. The Borough Engineer of Bromley on the other hand thought that because the route had been safeguarded for so long (since before the Second World War) it had become accepted by the community. Bromley Council was concerned about the blighting effects on property in the vicinity of Ringway 2 for which no definite alignment was published until 1969.[3] Hackney was concerned about the effects of increased traffic in the borough during the time between the building of the East Cross Route of Ringway 1 (which was well advanced) and the North Cross Route which had been put back to the 1990s. They suggested that an existing east–west road should be widened in time for the opening of the East Cross Route.[4]

Although discussion of the GLDP draft produced many and varied comments on the primary road proposals, only four boroughs—Camden, Croydon, Greenwich and Hounslow—eventually submitted strategic objections to them (e.g. on the grounds that the LTS projections of demand and allocation of traffic between public and private transport were wrong). Even these boroughs, in their evidence to the GLDP Inquiry, tended to restrict their objections to the motorways directly affecting their own areas. (Camden, for example, objected only to the North Cross Route.)[5]

It was perhaps not surprising that the boroughs' attitudes were determined primarily by local considerations since they (and their pre-1965 constituent authorities) had little experience of or responsibility for the planning of major new roads. In general they accepted that major road planning was properly the responsibility of the GLC. Kensington and Chelsea's Borough Engineer, for example, said that the motorway box proposal showed the 'essential rightness' of the existence of a strategic

[1] *Evening Standard*, 12 October 1970.
[2] LB Richmond consultants' report, *Study of Ringway 2*, September 1971.
[3] GLC *Minutes*, 11 February 1969, p73.
[4] LB Hackney, *Minutes*, 15 April 1970, item 630.
[5] *Proofs of Evidence, E12/29* (Camden); *E12/15* (Croydon and Greenwich); and *E12/32* (Hounslow). GLDP Inquiry Stage 1.

authority. Even Camden, who submitted evidence to the GLDP Inquiry against the Ringway 1 proposal, accepted that the boroughs should play no part in the forward planning of such roads. The objections of Lambeth and Wandsworth both stressed the need for more information about the primary road network in order to assess its efficiency in solving their traffic problems[1] (for example regarding the number of lanes, the siting, type and size of intersections).

Towards mid-1971, while strategic objections to the primary roads were being heard at the Inquiry, borough attitudes began to change radically. Up to that time both the London Labour and Conservative parties had acknowledged the need for motorways; a programme had been adopted by the Labour GLC as early as 1965 and was developed by the Conservatives after 1967. But in May 1971 the London Labour Party expressed 'clear and unequivocal opposition to Ringways 1 and 2.'[2] In the same month the Labour party won twenty-two of the boroughs, and the significance of this change soon became apparent. In particular Wandsworth Council passed a resolution stating:[3]

> that the Council, recognising that Wandsworth's opposition to the GLC's destructive motorway programme can only be effective if linked to general opposition to that programme, expresses its unequivocal opposition to Ringways 1 and 2 as they affect London in general as well as Wandsworth in particular; and that the Council calls on the GLC in consultation with the Government, London Transport and the London Boroughs to initiate discussions on a public transport alternative.

By mid-1972 at least six other boroughs had announced their opposition to Ringways 1 and 2.[4] The LBA (which was now also Labour dominated) also voted in support of Wandsworth's resolution in October 1971.[5]

Secondary roads

The boroughs had a more intense interest in the management and planning of the existing main roads. They had highway planning powers for some of these (i.e. *pro tem* for the borough Principal roads) and in the case of the remainder often acted as agents for the GLC. The GLDP roads map showed the existing roads which were to form London's 'secondary roads' and as already noted the policy for these had not been included in the GLDP itself but was the subject of a GLC document produced in November 1969 for consultation with the boroughs and other bodies. The bulk of the secondary roads were Principal roads (shown on Figure 2). Borough

[1] *Proofs of Evidence*, *E12/21*; and *E12/19*. GLDP Inquiry Stage 1.
[2] R Mellish at Press Conference after the Conference of the Greater London Regional Council of the Labour Party, 6 May 1971.
[3] LB Wandsworth *Minutes*, 22 June 1971.
[4] Bexley, Hammersmith, Hackney, Lambeth, Lewisham and Merton.
[5] LBA *Minutes*, 13 October 1971, p74.

views varied widely from those of the GLC as to the function of and responsibilities for the existing main roads. In discussions prior to the Transport (London) Act 1969, for example, the LBA aimed to reduce the mileage of Metropolitan roads (i.e. those for which the GLC held responsibility under the 1963 Act).[1]

But whatever views the boroughs had on responsibility for the roads, concern for the traffic movement on them was intense. Islington,[2] for example, wanted the GLDP to weigh more carefully the proposed balance of expenditure between the primary and secondary networks while Camden and Westminster wanted a larger share of the available investment.[3] Camden were of the opinion that without a much higher allocation of funds to secondary roads:

> we can look forward sadly to many fields of friction in negotiations as efforts are made to squeeze traffic through shopping centres, making a minor environmental improvement here and there but balancing this against loss of environmental quality elsewhere.[4]

The GLC expected the secondary network to be modified as the boroughs produced structure plans and the primary network was built, but Hounslow, for one, believed that this added another element of uncertainty and delay to an already difficult situation:

> the detailing of local plans will in many instances rely upon the alterations to the secondary network and we can foresee that many boroughs will be seriously inhibited in their efforts to evolve plans by the need to wait on GLC decisions on modifications to the Roads Map. There is here a potential for serious conflict between the boroughs and the GLC.[5]

When secondary road schemes were proposed by the GLC or other authorities the boroughs were often strong in their defence of local interests. Haringey and Westminster, for example, were concerned about complaints from traders in Tottenham High Road and Piccadilly respectively over GLC bus-lane proposals (see Case Study *M*); Kensington and Chelsea flatly rejected in 1966 a proposal by the MOT to divert traffic through residential streets when the Cromwell and Brompton Roads became congested (see Case Study *G*). The boroughs' concern for local environmental and other interests did not, however, prevent them from supporting schemes which conflicted with these interests. Haringey and Barnet, for example, were both anxious about the environmental effects of

[1] LBA *Minutes*, 27 July 1971, p81. Also LB Hackney *Minutes*, 23 November 1966 refer to LBA report calling for reduction of Metropolitan road mileage from 546 to 243 miles.

[2] *Paper S12/46*, GLDP Inquiry Stage 1.

[3] Westminster CC (1972), *Paper E27/68*, GLDP Inquiry Stage 2.

[4] LB Camden (1971), *Proof of Evidence*, *E27/104*, p49, GLDP Inquiry Stage 2.

[5] LB Hounslow (1971), *Proof of Evidence*, *E27/34*, p3, GLDP Inquiry Stage 2.

the A1 widening put forward by the MOT but did not oppose the widening in principle (see Case Study *K*).

The boroughs also often initiated schemes (such as new roads) which provoked an adverse response from local interests. A major example was Bromley's proposal for a system of new distribution roads, to take traffic (except buses) out of the main shopping streets of its town centre.

Most boroughs have proceeded with the forward planning of their road networks and some have carried out transportation studies either individually (as in the case of Ealing and Camden) or in liaison (as with the member boroughs of the West and South-East groups).[1] These studies generally accepted the London Transportation Study 1981 traffic predictions as an input (assuming that the primary roads would be constructed) and the results were expected to show where and when changes in the capacity of the secondary and local roads would be necessary. On the other hand, regardless of these studies, most boroughs continued to implement road widening schemes (drawn up many years previously in some cases) as and when frontage redevelopment allowed. A few boroughs, for example Camden and Westminster (see page 578), had abandoned or modified individual safeguarding lines but none had undertaken a comprehensive review of their implications. Indeed, many road widening schemes had never been ratified by the new boroughs and were mainly regarded as the officers' responsibility.

Most boroughs regarded forward road planning as an input to their structure plans. Some (Greenwich, for example) did not expect to complete their transportation studies before the drafting of their physical plans, but a common aim was at least to define the road network on the Buchanan principles of a hierarchy of distributor roads. Islington had in fact decided on a preliminary road hierarchy by the end of 1968.[2] As a complementary policy to a definition of the relative traffic roles of roads, some of the boroughs defined proposals for the creation of 'environmental areas', i.e. areas from which through traffic would be excluded or discouraged by traffic management schemes. Camden and Islington, for example, had by the end of 1971 virtually completed the planning of these areas on paper. The fact that there were only a few implemented was often considered to be due to the traffic difficulties which the GLC envisaged would result from them (see Case Study *G*). A further difficulty which was also strongly emphasised in relation to other traffic management schemes was the length of time from the approval of a scheme to the completion of the necessary traffic orders by the GLC, rarely less than six months and sometimes two years or more.

Probably the most important projects of the boroughs were those associated with the improvement or redevelopment of their major centres. Most of them were plans for areas of comprehensive development con-

[1] Thirteen boroughs in the West group and seven in the South-East group, Croydon being common to both.

[2] LB Islington Policy Paper No.5 (1968), *Hierarchy of Roads* (see Case Study *G*).

tained in the Initial Development Plan or, more recently, were the subject of action area plans being prepared within the framework of the GLDP.[1] The following centres were amongst those for which major schemes were proposed: Woolwich (LB Greenwich), Kingston, Sutton, Lewisham, Ealing, Putney (LB Wandsworth), Enfield, Wood Green (LB Haringey), and Harrow. All of these schemes incorporated major new road and parking facilities but problems of obtaining grants had been considerable, and the GLC consultation document on secondary roads envisaged an allocation of only 10% of the secondary roads capital expenditure in the 1970s and 1980s to road schemes in town centres (i.e. just over 3% of the total roads expenditure) with provisos that schemes should be staged, and should consist mainly of improving existing roads. Following criticism[2] that the GLDP's designation of strategic and major strategic centres should involve a commitment to priorities for both private and public investment, the revised secondary roads document increased the allocation from 10% to 15%.

A further constraint on the boroughs with regard to town centres can be the strategic land-use planning considerations of the GLC. A major conflict arose, for example, between Hammersmith who wanted their existing centre to be designated a 'major strategic centre,'[3] and the GLC who gave it only strategic status (see Figure 2).

Parking

The 'inner' boroughs have inevitably been the most closely involved with the control of parking as it was mainly in central and inner London that pressure from increased car use was first experienced. The effects of this pressure—in terms of hindrance of traffic flow, environmental intrusion and local access and servicing problems—have persuaded all of the boroughs concerned of the necessity of controlling at least on-street parking (see Case Study *Q*). The pressure of on-street parking has also been growing in outer London particularly at suburban centres and some railway stations. The boroughs concerned have usually introduced on-street control schemes although some have not been keen to accept the principle of charging. Havering introduced a new type of scheme aimed at preventing commuters from leaving their cars in the residential streets adjoining Gidea Park station (see page 282).

Many of the outer borough councils have considered the provision of station car parks but decided in most cases either that they should not pay for such facilities (because the main beneficiaries would be ratepayers from other areas) or that their powers were inadequate to deal with the problems of co-ordination involved (see Case Study *F*). The provision of off-

[1] *Paper B382*, GLDP Inquiry Stage 1.
[2] For example, J Blake, 'Town Centres or Motorways?' *Surveyor*, 19 September 1968.
[3] LB Hammersmith *Minutes*, 14 May 1969, p492; and *GLDP Written Statement*, para8.16.

street parking was considered a desirable aim by the twelve boroughs studied, even if only as a long-term policy, but the problems of financing were universal. Off-street parking was provided free by some boroughs (Enfield) or subsidised (Havering) and was charged for by others (Redbridge). All were being encouraged by the GLC and DOE to seek contributions from private developers. Bromley, on the other hand, had a firm policy of owning and operating all car parks in the borough and of making the total parking account balance. Camden and Westminster also sought to make their own car parks self-financing.

Lorry parking in residential streets was considered by many boroughs to be a major nuisance and was a major issue taken up by the LBA who expressed considerable dissatisfaction with the way the GLC was handling the problem. The GLC devised an experimental scheme together with the Metropolitan Police and Tower Hamlets council (in whose area the scheme was implemented), but the time taken to implement the scheme, and the expected delay while its success was measured, led one borough, Haringey, to promote its own Act of Parliament which gave it powers to ban the parking of lorries in residential streets. Haringey also obtained powers to employ its own attendants to enforce the law.[1] By the time Haringey's ban came into force, however (autumn 1972), the GLC had announced its intention to extend night-time lorry parking controls to cover sixty square miles of inner London (i.e. an area half as large again as that proposed for ILPA—see Figure 19).[2]

Public transport

Relations between the boroughs and BR and LT appeared to be generally good at an operational level (e.g. the co-ordination of physical works at stations and traffic management for buses) but many boroughs felt they should be more closely involved in alterations to services. Hackney and Lambeth, for example, both made representations to this end on the Transport (London) Bill 1969[3] (see also Case Study *N*).

No borough put forward the view that it should have a hand in policy-making for public transport, even amongst those which were keen to gain more control over major roads, and only Tower Hamlets submitted to the GLDP Inquiry a plea for a major policy impetus to improve public transport.[4] Individual matters, however, were often taken up by certain boroughs. Westminster wanted the introduction of tickets which were interchangeable between buses and the Underground (particularly since the introduction of the 5p minimum fare on the latter) and referred this sug-

[1] *Haringey Corporation Act 1971*, ch li.
[2] GLC (July 1972), *Traffic and the Environment: A Paper for Discussion*, p26.
[3] LB Hackney *Minutes*, 25 September 1968; 27 January 1971.
[4] LB Tower Hamlets (1971), *Proof of Evidence*, *E12/30*, GLDP Inquiry Stage 1. Although Wandsworth and other boroughs attempted to do so after the borough elections in May 1971.

gestion to the LTPC.[1] Greenwich and Lewisham both supported the Fleet Line proposal, Southwark took up the considerations given by the former Metropolitan Borough of Camberwell to the possible extension of the Bakerloo Line to Camberwell,[2] and Hackney had for many years been pressing for a new tube line to serve its area (see Case Study *C*). Southwark also took an active interest in bus services, for example by providing a subsidy to maintain a Sunday service through Surrey Docks,[3] and discussing the proposed bus reshaping plan with LT.[4] Camden took the initiative in preparing a bus-lane network feasibility study for its part of the central area (see Case Study *M*) and persuaded LT to introduce new bus services in their area. Westminster initiated a study (with representatives of the MOT, Ministry of Technology, GLC and other central London boroughs) of possible new transport systems for central London.[5]

While these boroughs (mainly in south and east London) pressed for better or more public transport services, most, whether they were in inner or outer London, were quick to defend the services which they had but were in danger of losing. Camden, for example, defended both bus and rail services in its area (see Parliament Hill and Broad Street–Richmond sections of Case Study *N*), and in outer London and beyond the GLC boundary boroughs also fought to retain services threatened with closure and sometimes co-operated in their efforts (see Epping–Ongar and bus route 151 sections of Case Study *N*). While claiming that unremunerative public transport services in their areas were socially necessary, rarely were boroughs prepared to pay a subsidy to LT or BR to keep these services going. Through the LBA, however, the boroughs agreed to pay for the provision of concessionary fares for old people. Discussions had been initiated by the LCC with the LTB and were continued by the LBA which approved the principle of such payments in February 1966. The GLC claimed that concessionary fares were a borough rather than a Greater London matter.[6] Camden Council (then under Conservative control) was the first to introduce concessionary fares in 1970. Although the system of fare concessions was generally introduced in 1970–71, its basis was strongly criticised and was soon reviewed by the LBA when Labour took control in 1971.[7]

Housing

Almost without exception housing was the overriding policy issue in the inner boroughs. Some were mainly concerned about poor housing and

[1] Westminster CC *Minutes*, 2 February 1970; LB Hackney *Minutes*, 4 March 1970.
[2] LB Southwark *Minutes*, 29 June 1966, p55.
[3] LB Southwark *Minutes*, Summary of Year's Work 1967–68 (Document C25).
[4] LB Southwark *Minutes*, 28 June 1967, p53.
[5] Westminster CC, *et al* (1971), *An Aid to Pedestrian Movement*.
[6] GLC *Minutes*, 12 May 1970, pp310–11.
[7] LBA *Minutes*, 1 February 1966, p7; 17 March 1971, p22; 13 September 1971, p80.

social conditions (e.g. Islington) and others with a particular shortage of land for building (e.g. Lambeth), although usually the two problems went hand in hand. But despite their concern for housing, few inner boroughs expressed immediate opposition to the Ringways on grounds of housing loss, even though Ringway 1 alone was expected (by the GLC) to involve the direct loss of 7585 dwellings.[1] Even Camden who objected to Ringway 1 from the start were concerned more with its traffic and environmental effects than resulting housing loss.[2] This is particularly interesting in view of the inner boroughs' recognition that in order to achieve their aim of redeveloping housing to lower densities, sites would have to be made available outside inner London to rehouse surplus population. Moreover, the outer boroughs were generally unreceptive to the idea of raising densities to house people from inner London. The GLC believed that inter-borough co-operation was essential if London's housing problem was to be effectively tackled. Some reconciliation of these differences was achieved in 1971 when the LBA decided to set up a housing office to deal with the problem.[3] It was suggested that the reconciliation was due to the boroughs' fear that the GLC would itself take over the policy role. For example, Judy Hillman, planning correspondent of the *Guardian*, said that the boroughs 'may dislike each other, but they dislike the regional authority even more.'[4]

The only boroughs to contest the GLC's projections of population (with their housing implications) were Brent and Enfield whose officers, at the request of the Inquiry Panel, argued at length that the capital would benefit from a lower population than that provided for in the Written Statement.[5]

The boroughs' relationship with other bodies

As the foregoing paragraphs suggest, borough relationships with the GLC are certainly varied and often complex. The boroughs had to deal with the GLC on so many matters that head-on conflict over individual issues tended to be avoided if possible. At the day-to-day working level contacts were often both friendly and, especially in the case of the boroughs nearest to County Hall, frequent. The boroughs often expressed the general view that the GLC had yet to define its strategic role, and to learn when to delegate matters of detail and local consideration on planning schemes. For example, Camden believed that local needs should predominate in the determination of proposals for the King's Cross area, whereas the GLC considered the site to be of metropolitan if not national

[1] GLC (1970), *Proof of Evidence, E12/1*, Table 6.5, p108, GLDP Inquiry Stage 1.
[2] LB Camden (1971), *Proof of Evidence, E12/29*, GLDP Inquiry Stage 1.
[3] The *Guardian*, 29 September 1971; and LBA *Minutes*, 13 October 1971, pp34–5.
[4] The concept of a new housing agency to deal with London's housing problems at the Metropolitan level was put forward by Professor B Cullingworth in 1970, *Report to the MOHLG*, volI, September 1970, pp728.
[5] LB Brent and LB Enfield (1972), *Paper S11/161*, GLDP Inquiry Stage 1.

importance and therefore an appropriate one for the metropolitan authority to handle.[1] Conflict also arose with Hammersmith over a proposed air terminal.[2] Conflict appeared to be common over certain highway and traffic matters such as the designation of secondary roads and the implementation of environmental area schemes.

After 1965 the boroughs dealt with the MOT only on agency work for the maintenance or improvement of Trunk roads, on major road schemes in the Ministry's rolling programme that attracted Government grants and (until 1972) on pedestrian crossings. Those borough engineers who had experience of contact with the Ministry generally viewed its ability to delegate with favour, but reservations were expressed on two counts: one was that the checking and approval of statutory orders, estimates and tenders was a very slow process and the other was that a high turnover of Ministry staff often made continuity of contact on the planning and implementation of schemes difficult to maintain.

Relationships with the police seemed generally to be good, but comments contained some criticisms. Some officers, while appreciating that the traffic branch of Scotland Yard had long experience of traffic control, disliked their tendency to criticise the design of traffic management schemes without proper qualifications for doing so. Also the low priority that the police gave to enforcing schemes designed to improve amenity was often directly opposed to the interests of the boroughs (see Case Study *F*). Some boroughs felt that they could more effectively carry out parking control with their own paid attendants, and claimed that this represented better value than the contribution paid to the police for schemes controlled by wardens. Borough officers who had formerly been employed by counties and county boroughs with control of their own police forces were the most trenchant in their comments, claiming that sympathy of interests and cooperation in action were much greater than with the Metropolitan Police over whom local authorities in London had no control. It was sometimes suggested that the GLC should at least have been given control of the Metropolitan Police traffic branch, especially in the light of the growing importance of environmental considerations.

As far as the operators of public transport were concerned, most boroughs found liaison with the engineering and operations staff of LT and BR easy and effective on day-to-day matters but contact on longer-term projects was much slower and more difficult where matters of regional policy or estate development were concerned. This was especially true of BR when decisions were needed which involved reference from the Region to the Board. BR were also criticised for failing to have a clear policy for suburban lines and by at least one borough for not taking a more cooperative attitude to the provision of station car parks. LT's central bus

[1] E Wistrich (1972), *Local Government Reorganisation: The First Years of Camden*, pp169, 174–7; and LB Camden, *Proof of Evidence*, *XE21/19*, GLDP Inquiry Stage 2.
[2] LB Hammersmith Local Planning Inquiry, 2 February 1968. See also Case Study *E*.

division was criticised for sometimes taking a narrow operational view of traffic management schemes involving buses, particularly in relation to the provision of bus interchange facilities.

Contacts between adjacent boroughs were entirely *ad hoc* as far as executive matters concerning individual schemes were concerned. On long-term planning and study methods the West and South-East London Working Parties mentioned above were the mechanisms for liaison. A similar joint group was later set up by east London boroughs to handle transportation studies.

The LBA was seen very differently by the various authorities: some officers thought that it performed an active and useful watchdog role over the balance of powers and responsibilities between the boroughs and the GLC; some were convinced that it should take a stronger line against 'such a powerful umbrella authority'; others thought that it was a very slow means of co-ordination and that it depended greatly for its impetus on its advisory committees of professional officers (e.g. the Associations of London Borough Engineers and Planning Officers). But to several officers it appeared that most matters (other than national legislation) arose through the initiative of individual boroughs with particular problems to air. Examples included Hounslow on aircraft noise, Haringey and Islington on lorry parking.

Publicity and public relations

The boroughs' attitudes to the use of press and general publicity procedures, and to consultation and participation with local societies and the public in general varied greatly, although all but one of the sample boroughs had a press or public relations officer. The exception, Croydon, was also the only one to indicate that it was not customary for officers or members to enter into discussion of problems or policies in the local press, partly because it was thought to be a poor means of communication particularly on strategic issues, and partly because it had not proved fruitful in the past. At the other extreme there were several boroughs where the attitude at both officer and member level was that the council's activities could not be over-publicised. In general, relationships with the local press were good, although officers usually had reservations about the accuracy of reporting and felt that the editors for their part could more actively seek the local authority's views on problems raised by readers and local groups. In Bromley, however, the local press contacted the Borough Engineer as often as three or four times a week for comments on topical issues.

Amongst all the boroughs there appeared to be an increasing move towards local publicity and discussion of schemes or policies before ultimate decision, as opposed to the traditional method of publicity in the time gap between decision and implementation. Westminster, for example, had published 'green paper' type reports for discussion which although dealing with technical matters were written for the layman,[1] and Hammersmith had found that many problems and objections to the implementation of an ILPA scheme could be overcome by local public meetings.[2] Most boroughs intended that discussion documents, public meetings and exhibitions would be increasingly used as Local Development Plan, action area, and improvement area activities proceeded.[3]

The growth of concern about environmental matters, spurred on in London by the controversy over the motorway proposals, had led to a substantial increase in the number of local pressure groups; for example the London Motorway Action Group had a corporate membership of about thirty local groups of which at least ten were set up to oppose the GLDP motorway proposals. Many boroughs had a large number of local amenity groups; some had developed from ratepayers associations, some were specifically concerned with planning and amenity matters. Some had been in existence for many years and were well organised with strong professional backing (e.g. the Societies for Hampstead, Highgate, Barnsbury, Islington, Greenwich, Norwood and Richmond) while others were very much *ad hoc* groups of more recent birth concerned with individual local problems. In Camden for instance the South End Green Society was formed largely to influence proposals for the rebuilding and widening of a railway bridge, and ATTAC (the Archway–Tufnell Park Transport Action Committee) to press for improved east–west bus routes and Northern Line tube services. The borough officers in general thought that such local groups performed a useful function and many were keen to consult them as early as possible over proposals, although in no case was there any formal machinery for doing so.

THE METROPOLITAN POLICE

To enforce law and order, including traffic and parking offences, the Metropolitan Police in 1970 employed 20 700 men in the uniform and CID branches, 820 women and 10 000 civilian staff. The City of London Police employed about 1000 uniformed officers plus a small number of civilian staff and traffic wardens.[4]

The police have accumulated responsibilities for ensuring the safe, orderly and expeditious movement of traffic since their institution in 1839,

[1] For example, *Future Parking Policy* (December 1966); and *Charter Coaches in Westminster* (1971).

[2] In a survey of public attitudes to the proposed pedestrianisation of shopping streets in Chichester, Sussex, a strong correlation was found between those who disapproved of the scheme and those who knew least about it. See P Hart and B Thomson (1970) 'Attitudes to Pedestrianisation in the City Centre,' *High-Speed Ground Transportation Journal*, I, 1970, p47.

[3] For example, Haringey's exhibition *This is Haringey* and Camden's exhibition *Camden Scene*, which set out broad planning issues in their respective boroughs.

[4] *Annual Report of Commissioner of Police for Metropolis*, 1970, Cmnd 4680; and City of London Corporation *Minutes*, 12 November 1970.

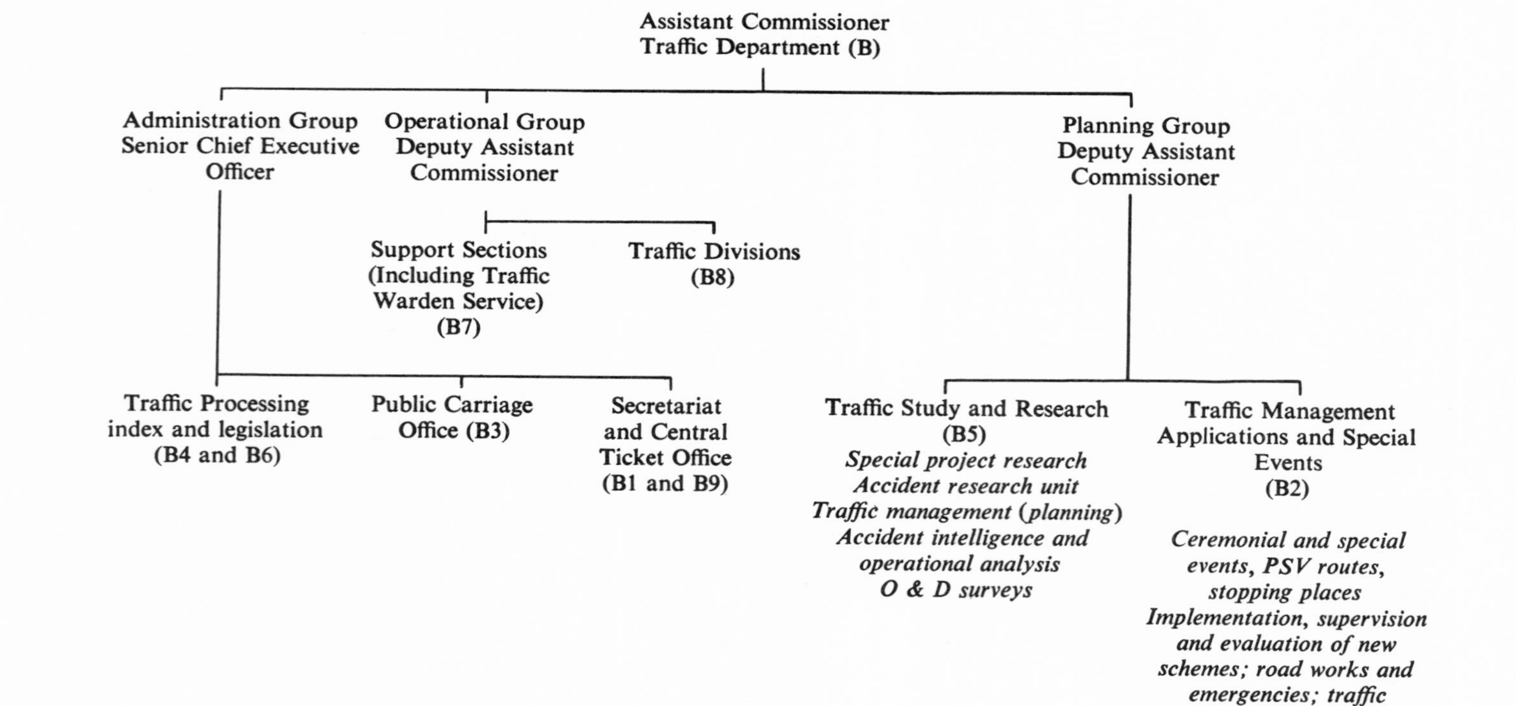

Figure 4 METROPOLITAN POLICE TRAFFIC DEPARTMENT, JULY 1971

and since 1919, the year in which the MOT was established, have had a separate traffic department (although there had been some separation of traffic responsibilities from 1884). Apart from traffic, there were eight other major and two subsidiary departments.[1] In 1971 the staff employed wholly or mainly on traffic matters numbered about 3500 people comprising 300–350 in the headquarters branches B1–B9, some 1300 officers in the traffic division and over 1800 traffic wardens. This traffic staff was roughly the same size as that of the CID.

As traffic engineering and traffic planning techniques developed in the early 1950s, the police decided that they should add some knowledge of these matters to their expertise in supervision and enforcement if they were to be fully involved in traffic management as advisers and consultants as well as being the enforcement agency. The importance attached by the police to their role in traffic is evidenced by the Commissioner's Annual Reports which consistently refer to traffic problems. In 1966, for example, they were described as 'pressing, varied, and intractable.'[2] After the establishment of the GLC with its overall traffic powers, the police formed a new Study and Research branch (B5, see Figure 4) responsible for undertaking surveys on traffic speed and flow, for devising and operating traffic control systems (e.g. on the M4 and in West London), for investigating the pattern and cause of accidents, and for investigating proposed traffic management and parking schemes. In 1968 during a general review of the organisation and functions of the force, PA Management Consultants Ltd said that the control of traffic:

> 'could be defined as a continuous mission embracing supervision of pedestrian and vehicular road traffic, prevention of accidents and assistance if they occur, and enforcement of traffic legislation.' In those few phrases were outlined activities which touch every person in the Metropolitan Police District more nearly and more frequently than any others in which police are engaged. The moral issues posed by the problems of crime and traffic ordinarily differ, but it would be unrealistic not to recognise that the effect of motor traffic on the community in terms of death and injury, of aggravation of the human lot and of economic loss, far exceeds in severity that resulting from crime. There are not, therefore, any good reasons for regarding the traffic mission as of less importance than any other but it differs from our control of crime in that the strategy is dictated by other authorities.[3]

Two major organisational changes followed the consultants' recommendations. First, the functions of the Receiver were merged with those of the

[1] The others were uniform (A), CID (C), Personnel and Training (D), Civil Staff (E) Finance (F), Administration (G); and those of the Architect and Engineer.

[2] *Annual Report*, 1966, Cmnd 3315, p11.

[3] *Annual Report*, 1969, Cmnd 4355, p14.

Commissioner, and the Receiver became responsible for all civilian staff. Historically the Commissioner was head of the force with responsibility for its conduct, discipline and organisation, while the Receiver was independently responsible to the Secretary of State for the Home Office for all police expenditure and property. This change eliminated the complete independence of the financial and operational hierarchies, the latter with its strong military traditions, and began to make the police organisation more like other modern bureaucratic structures with an emphasis on functional links. Second, the headquarters departments were reorganised. A new Management Services Department was created and the Traffic Department was reorganised to bring together all police officers and auxiliaries involved in the traffic mission. The traffic branch had three groups: one for planning, consisting of the Study and Research branch (B5) mentioned above and a group for processing traffic management schemes (B2); an operations group (B7 and B8) consisting of 1200 mobile patrols and 1800 traffic wardens; and an administrative group processing fines, public service vehicle licences and legislation (B1, 3, 4, 6, and 9).[1]

Despite the importance given to traffic matters, the prevention and detection of crime and maintenance of public order have received first priority in a situation of rising crime and chronic shortage of police manpower—in 1970, for example, staff was 4700 (18.5%) below establishment. One senior officer of the Traffic Department expressed the view in 1971 that given the shortage of both finance and staff, the proportions devoted to crime and traffic were 'about right,' but this did not mean that the Traffic Department was able to do all that it should or would like to do.

These shortages also have compelled the police to examine their priorities within the traffic division and these may be summarised as safety, traffic circulation and amenity, in that order.[2] The police have tried to alleviate this problem of shortage of skilled manpower in three ways, first by handing over an increasing share of the more routine matters to auxilliary staff; increasingly, traffic and parking control (using the fixed penalty system), point duty and the patrolling of school crossings has been undertaken by traffic wardens.[3] Second, some functions have been relinquished altogether including traffic census work, road safety training (some London boroughs have appointed road safety officers and the GLC set up a road safety unit) and follow-up procedures on motorists who fail to pay parking meter excess charges (now the responsibility of the boroughs); details of the latter change are given in Case Study *Q*.[4] Third,

[1] A third proposal for reorganising the local subdivisions was rejected because it would have involved changing boundaries and responsibilities only recently reorganised (in 1965) under section 76 of the London Government Act 1963. See LBA *Minutes*, 31 March 1965, p29.

[2] Interviews with senior officers, *Annual Reports*, 1966, p11; 1969, p57; and 1970, p17. See also Case Study *F*.

[3] *Annual Reports* 1966, pp13, 66, 86; 1967, pp12, 92; 1970, p78.

[4] *Annual Reports* 1967, p17; 1968, p18; 1970, pp16, 17, 57.

to ease the enforcement task the police have pressed for a simplification of the law, for example by reducing the types of waiting restrictions and other regulations and by introducing owner rather than driver liability for minor traffic offences (see Case Study *Q*).

The traffic policeman undergoes specialist training as well as the basic training and two years 'on the beat,' and having the cachet of technological aids (such as high-speed patrol vehicles, automatic traffic control and monitoring equipment) he is considered within the force to be a 'policeman plus.'[1]

The period since 1965 has, therefore, been one in which the Metropolitan Police have sought to make their involvement in traffic more efficient in terms of organisation, more specialised in terms of the functions undertaken and more sophisticated in terms of the techniques employed. But a steady increase in traffic and the consequent need for more regulations and controls has ensured that the strain on police resources has not diminished. The police have admitted that while surveillance is widespread, enforcement is selective,[2] and have consistently made clear to the GLC that the number and range of schemes that can be adequately enforced is limited by the manpower available (see Case Studies *F* and *Q*). They have also tried to resist schemes which are not to a degree self-enforcing because of a fear that inadequate enforcement induces a lack of respect for the law. Equally, the police are sensitive about the 'public acceptability' of measures, and resist schemes which they think unreasonable.[3]

Although the GLC have no duty to take account of police views, in practice they have done so and have tended not to recommend schemes to which the police are firmly opposed. The need for continual co-operation between the GLC and the police on traffic matters means in practice that each attempts to understand the other's point of view. Thus a constraint on police activities such as lack of manpower has become accepted by the GLC as a constraint on their own activities.

The police have a very close working arrangement with the GLC through the Joint Traffic Executive (see below), and with the boroughs through a liaison group with the Association of London Borough Engineers and Surveyors, and also through a steering group chaired by the GLC's Traffic Commissioner concerned specifically with the extension of automatic traffic control.

The police role as an advisory and enforcement agency is further discussed in the case studies on parking control (*Q*) station car parks (*F*), environmental management (*G*), pedestrians (*L*), Operation Moondrop (*P*) and bus priorities (*M*).

[1] Interviews and conversations with staff of the Survey Research Centre undertaking a study for the Home Office of the police and the public.

[2] *Annual Reports* 1966, p77; 1969, p15.

[3] Paper by Deputy Assistant Commissioner Candy to the British Parking Association Conference, May 1971, and *Evidence to Expenditure Committee* (Environment and Home Office subcommittee) 6 June 1972, *Hansard HC Papers 107* (*xviii*), 1971–72.

BRITISH AIRPORTS AUTHORITY

After four years of operation of its airports (Stansted, Gatwick and Heathrow in London, and Prestwick in Scotland) the British Airports Authority (BAA) described themselves as a 'public enterprise run on business lines'[1] and indeed in 1970–71 they made a net profit of £5.7 million on their operations. Their structure consisted of a four-man board to whom the Chief Executive, Secretary and Financial Controller were responsible. Six directors were responsible to the Chief Executive, for Planning, Engineering, Personnel, Operations, Commerce, and Co-ordinating the four airports' General Managers, of whom the Heathrow manager had a seat on the management team. In 1971 the Director of Planning was also given a direct responsibility to the Board. His remit was overwhelmingly the planning of the Authority's property, although he was to co-operate in wider problems such as ground access and aircraft noise. The BAA were closely involved in the proposals to link Heathrow airport with central London (see Case Study *E*).

CO-ORDINATION MACHINERY

The bodies referred to in this section and their relationship with the major institutions are shown in Figure 5. Prior to 1965, co-ordination other than that of the MOT and MOHLG lay with the London and Home Counties Traffic Advisory Committee (LHCTAC) (see Chapter 1) and the Standing Conference (see Chapter 2). The latter continues but in general considers matters connected with the conurbation only in so far as they impinge on the other parts of the region (e.g. the growth of office employment, the relocation of population and industry). The GLC has a regional policy group consisting of members of the Planning and Transportation, Architect's, Housing and Valuation departments[2] which co-ordinates the Council's input to this body.

The LHCTAC was an unusually large body of forty-five people whose major work was done through a number of working parties concerned with traffic regulation and circulation. After 1960 an increasing number of traffic schemes in the central area were handled by the LTMU[3] and the Committee was wound up when the traffic and transport functions of the GLC were clearly emerging, presumably because it was hoped that the proposed distribution of functions and day-to-day contacts would suffice. The 1963 Act provided for no similar machinery to succeed the LHCTAC.

When Barbara Castle succeeded Tom Fraser as Minister of Transport in November 1965 she was 'horrified that there was no forum where everyone involved in transport in London could meet.'[4] In February 1966 she there-

[1] BAA *Annual Report*, 1970–71; *Hansard HC Papers 527*, 23 July 1971, pp1–11.
[2] GLC, *P & T Departmental Handbook*, item 6A, April 1971.
[3] LHTAC Report, *London Traffic*, 1962, p5.
[4] GLC *Press Release*, 31 July 1967. At a press conference to launch Operation Moondrop (see Case Study *P*).

fore established the Transport Co-ordinating Council for London (TCCL—the mnemonic 'Tickle' soon stuck). The Council consisted of the following members: the leader of the GLC, the chairman and one other member of the BR and LT Boards, the chairmen of the LBA and of the South-East Regional Economic Planning Council, and the general secretaries of the National Union of Railwaymen and the Transport and General Workers Union. The Commissioner of the Metropolitan Police later became a

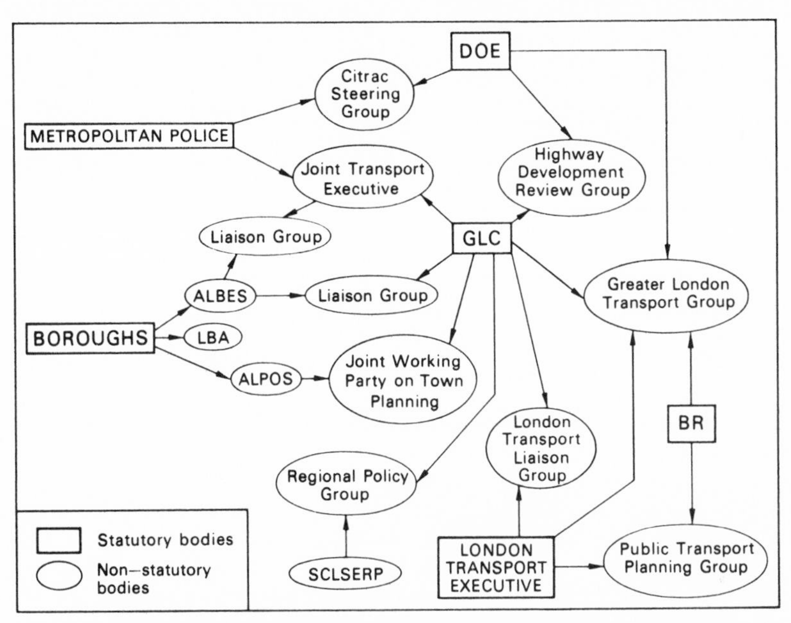

Figure 5 TRANSPORT CO-ORDINATING BODIES FOR LONDON, 1972

member. The Minister herself chaired the Council and saw it as 'the spearhead of a concerted attack upon the growing problems of the movement of people and goods in London.'[1]

TCCL appointed a committee of deputies to supervise work that it initiated. All TCCL's work had to be done by officers of its constituent organisations because it had no staff of its own. Both the Council and the Committee of deputies met infrequently and most work was done in five working groups whose terms of reference were as follows:

1 *Operations Group*—to keep under review the effectiveness of public transport and traffic operations and the arrangements for co-ordination in these fields, and to consider suggestions for improvement and as appropriate pursue them with authorities concerned.

[1] The *Guardian*, 25 February 1966.

2 *Interchanges Group*—to examine and keep under review facilities for interchange between different elements of the transport system and to recommend a programme of improvements in relation to present and future transport demands.
3 *Public Transport Investment Group*—to formulate programmes of investment in public transport in London in the light of developing transport and traffic policies, and to make recommendations for action on specific proposals.
4 *Highways Planning Group*—to plan and exercise surveillance over the development of a strategic primary road network for London and to this end to formulate and keep under review, in the light of other traffic measures, a continuing programme of work on motorways, trunk and metropolitan roads. [This grew out of a Joint Steering Group (supported by a committee and delegated staff) of the GLC and MOT to oversee and review the highways programmes of the former authorities.]
5 *Freight Group*—to consider the problems of freight movement in the London area.

The working groups often included representatives of other bodies such as the Board of Trade, Port of London Authority, BAA, and the Traders Road Transport Association. Their activities and influence varied greatly: the Operations Group for instance faded away after less than two years' existence; the Highways Planning Group was very busy devising and designing the Primary and Trunk roads programmes; the Public Transport Investment Group discussed many schemes but was permanently hampered by the divided responsibilities for investment; the Freight Group was involved for example in Operation Moondrop (see Case Study *P*) and the move of Covent Garden Market to Nine Elms; the Interchanges Group was concerned with questions of improving the central BR termini (particularly Waterloo and Victoria for which separate working parties were established) and parking at stations (see Case Studies *D*, *E* and *F*). All groups contributed critiques of the GLDP drafts from their specialist viewpoints. The members achieved better understanding of one another's problems but TCCL remained 'a talking shop.'

When two years later the Government sought to improve transport planning in London it assessed TCCL as part of the 'holding arrangements . . . a useful means of initiating joint planning' but 'far from ideal as a body for planning continuously and regularly; and still less suitable for overseeing the execution of plans once made.' Certainly TCCL was not directly responsible for any new policy initiatives and became bogged down where the co-ordination of several bodies, each with its own vested interests, was vital, as for interchange schemes. There were no proposals to legislate for a successor to TCCL because the GLC were instigating a new Greater London Transport Group (GLTG) consisting of representatives of the GLC, MOT, LT, and BR (see Figure 5).[1] Based on the precedent of the

[1] MOT (1968), *Transport in London*, Cmnd 3686, paras5, 36, 43.

Joint Highways Planning machinery it was thought that GLTG 'in the longer run' might have its own staff, but this has not yet happened. GLTG was seen to have three functions: to act as a forum for considering transport needs and facilities, as a means of guiding the preparation of transport plans as required by the 1969 Act, and for co-ordinating such plans and their implementation through programmes of schemes.

The GLTG, like its predecessor, has operated at a high level, the GLC being represented by its Joint Directors of Planning and Transportation, assistant director and chief planners of the strategy and transportation branches; LT and BR each represented by a board member, and the DOE by the under-secretary for its London Group. It does not have the support of such a full range of formal subgroups as TCCL, though there is a Public Transport and General Standing Committee where senior officers meet. Although fewer bodies are formally represented the GLTG has been regarded by those involved as an advance on the TCCL machinery. Little information was available by the end of its first two years of operation to judge its full range of activities and the functional transport plans (whose preparation was to be guided by the GLTG) had not appeared, but the GLTG was involved in individual projects such as the Fleet Line and BR's south-eastern approaches scheme (see Case Studies *C* and *H*). The GLC considered that the GLTG would not be able fully to perform its advisory function until the GLDP had been finalised.[1]

Another important agency for co-ordination is the Joint Traffic Executive (JTE) established between the Traffic Department of Scotland Yard and the Traffic Commissioner at County Hall in 1968. This sought to agree priorities in traffic matters and to ensure the speedy implementation and economical enforcement of traffic schemes.[2] The JTE is served by three working groups, one on road safety, one on traffic control systems and one on traffic management. The traffic management group has three subgroups dealing respectively with major and local traffic schemes and parking control schemes. Some of the work of the Control Systems group has been taken over by the Central Integrated Traffic Control (CITRAC) Steering Group established to implement the extension of computerised traffic control from west London to the whole of central London. The Road Safety Group has been superseded by a Greater London Road Safety Unit comprising representatives of the City and Metropolitan Police, GLC, DOE, LBA and the Royal Society for the Prevention of Accidents (RoSPA) (see page 94).

A third main agency for co-ordination is the LBA[3] which seeks to represent the interests of the thirty-two London boroughs. Each inner

[1] *Hansard HC Papers 107* (*vii*), 1971–72, p122.
[2] Commissioner of Police *Annual Report*, 1968, p7.
[3] The London Boroughs' Committee from 1964 to 1966. For the background to this organisation see ch11 of G Rhodes (ed) (1972), *The New Government of London: The First Five Years.*

London borough appoints three members, and each outer borough four.[1] The LBA has sought to retain or extend the boroughs' powers when considering legislation such as the 1968 Transport Bill or the 1969 Transport (London) Bill. It deals with transport and planning matters mainly through its Works Committee, although public transport matters are handled by a General Purposes Committee and concessionary fares, for instance, by a Social Services Committee. The Works Committee is serviced by two advisory committees composed of the Chief Planning Officers and Engineers of the boroughs (the Association of London Planning Officers and the Association of London Borough Engineers and Surveyors—ALPOS and ALBES).

The major recurrent matters before the Works Committee in the period 1964–71 were the problems of lorry parking in residential areas, the provision of station car parks, the cost and supply of traffic wardens, and the cost and implementation of various types of traffic schemes. Many of these issues arose out of locally acute problems brought to the Association's attention by one or more of the member boroughs. It could not be said that the LBA had decisively altered a major policy, although it collectively protected borough interests. For example, its response to the question in the GLC's 1970 Green Paper on the future of LT, 'what additional specific financial contributions to public transport facilities should the GLC press other local authorities and public bodies to make?' was 'no comment' but the Association wanted LT to be aided by both revenue and capital grants. The elections of 1971 which brought the majority of the boroughs (and consequently the LBA) under Labour control were significant in terms of the LBA's activities. By 1972 it had become clear that the LBA was playing a more active role and was being used by the Labour boroughs as a further channel of opposition to certain GLC policies, particularly on the inner ringway proposals and LT financial policies.

The Association of Engineers (ALBES) is represented on two liaison groups (Figure 5), one with the GLC and one with the JTE. The function of the former is 'to discuss and ventilate matters of joint interest' and of the latter 'to exchange views.'

Apart from *ad hoc* co-ordination between adjacent boroughs formal joint machinery has existed since 1965 to advise on planning in central London. This machinery, generally known as the Central London Planning Conference, had both officer and member representation from all the boroughs with part of the Central Area together with the City of London. During its first seven years, however, despite the creation of several working groups and many meetings, no advisory plan had been produced.

Co-ordination of LT policy matters between LT and the GLC has been handled (since 1970) by a joint liaison group which reports to the Policy and Resources Committee and is chaired by the Controller of Services. It

[1] That is, one to sit on each of the General Purposes, Works and Social Services committees, and on Education committees for the outer boroughs that are education authorities.

was intended to be 'the accepted agency for the development of relations with London Transport and the predigestion of all matters of policy intended in due course to come before the Council and Executive for final decision,'[1] although matters concerning LT policy are also discussed by the GLC's Chief Officer's Board. Additional GLC involvement in a policy co-ordination group concerned with regional planning and, from 1971, the Central London Planning Conference, adds up to a complex pattern of co-ordination. While it cannot be denied that the policies and problems are complex, this system does throw a great deal of responsibility for co-ordination on to relatively few people who also have major policy formulation and/or management responsibilities within their respective authorities. This is especially true as far as the GLC is concerned where those officers who serve on GLTG are also members of two, three or four other standing groups.

One particular aid to co-ordination is the involvement of the public in the policy or decision-making processes, not through their elected representatives or as consumers (for example, through the TUCC or LTPC) but directly as envisaged by the Skeffington Report on public participation in planning initiated by the MOHLG.[2] The GLC considered that in applying its ideas to London there were problems in relation to the size of the conurbation, the capacity of the public to understand strategic problems, the danger of widespread and long-term blight of property and business values, and of encroaching on the role of elected members, and pressures of cost and price.[3]

Other than the opportunity to make objections to the Plan, the GLDP process of public participation consisted of an exhibition in thirty-two town halls and County Hall accompanied by a series of public meetings in different localities which dealt predominantly with local matters, particularly the effects of the road proposals.[4] As a result, the GLC saw a much more structured process with a clearly defined time scale as desirable for consultation on transport plans, consisting of three stages:

1. A draft stage where proposals are devised and discussed within the Council via the GLTG after discussion with such bodies as the LBA, the SEEPC and Standing Conference, the CBI, and TUC.
2. A publication stage after the Council has approved the draft, when a Green Paper (similar to those on LT and Hotels policy issued in 1970 and 1971) would be sent to other organisations and made available to the public for comment.
3. A finalisation stage.[5]

[1] It includes the Treasurer, the Joint Director of P & T and two LTE members; see GLC *Minutes*, 7 July 1970, p426.
[2] MOHLG (1969), *People and Planning*.
[3] GLC *Minutes*, 10 February 1970, pp122–3.
[4] M Harris and M Myers (1969), 'The Public Meeting as a Means of Participation in Development Planning,' *GLC Qtly Bull*, 9, pp3–7.
[5] GLC *Minutes*, 7 July 1970, p437/8.

The description in the foregoing chapters of how the various transport agencies in London have developed and pursued their roles since the reform of London government in 1965 provides a background to the fifteen case studies which comprise the next part of this book. These studies, to which the major share of the research was devoted, explore in greater depth how transport is organised in London, using specific policies or decisions as examples of the many, varied and complicated issues with which the system has to deal.

In order to illuminate the relevant factors in the decision-making process the approach to the studies was as flexible as possible. Some continuity has been attempted by summarising, at the beginning of each case study, the specific areas of concern and responsibilities of the bodies involved and by making comparisons with the roles they actually played, in a concluding section.

Case Study A

THAMESMEAD

INTERNAL AND EXTERNAL TRANSPORT LINKS FOR A NEW COMMUNITY

'One of those imaginative ideas that will prove to be a complete failure in practice.' Witness at Thamesmead Public Inquiry, October 1967.

1 INTRODUCTION

Thamesmead is a major urban development, originally for 60 000 people, being built on the south bank of the Thames between the already developed areas of Woolwich and Erith to the east and west, and the London County Council's (LCC) Abbey Wood housing estate to the south. The 1300-acre site, the last large 'virgin' area in London, consists partly of unreclaimed marshland and partly of slightly more solid ground once used for the production, testing and storage of armaments by the former Woolwich Arsenal. It is by far the largest single project ever undertaken by the LCC or the Greater London Council (GLC).[1] and of similar size to the first two 'generations' of new towns: indeed it has social, economic, and design objectives in common with or derived from them. Unlike the new towns, which were physically free-standing and intended to be so socially, Thamesmead is situated within the conurbation and needs to be fully integrated. When one allies these two facts with the local problems associated with the site (drainage problems concomitant with a high water table, liability to flooding, difficulties of building foundations), the decline of local job opportunities, relatively poor communications (congested local roads and an overloaded railway service to central London) and environment (the site is overlooked by two power stations, a sewage works and a swathe of riverside industry in Barking), one might say that Thamesmead is being developed despite its circumstances.

Besides its overall powers as metropolitan planning and highway authority and Inner London Education Authority (ILEA), the GLC is implementing the scheme under its continuing housing powers to provide replacement housing for people displaced as a result of inner area re-

[1] *The Architect's Journal* (23 March 1966, p733) commented: 'Only a few years ago the LCC would have considered a scheme one-quarter of this size as a major development,' and other current major projects are much smaller—Kidbrooke and Hendon Aerodrome 2500 dwellings each, Lea Valley 4000, compared with Thamesmead's 17 000.

developments,[1] but many other authorities are also concerned. The London boroughs of Greenwich and Bexley will take over responsibility for the schools, open spaces, welfare and cultural facilities and local roads, footpaths and cycleways, while facilities in the town centre, the marina, industrial estates and one-third of the housing areas are intended to be provided by private developers. London Transport (LT) and British Rail (BR) are involved as transport operators, the Ministries of Housing and Transport (and now the Department of the Environment (DOE)) as grant-aid authorities.[2]

In view of this complex of responsibilities and the nature of the scheme it is instructive to look at its planning process, in particular its internal transport network and external links. Was the network determined by the form of existing facilities, in order to conform with plans for the metropolitan area as a whole, or by the form and needs of the development itself? Was it ever considered that such a new development could support or was worthy of a new form of transport? What practical and institutional problems arose during the formulation and implementation of the plan?

These questions are discussed below, but first it is necessary to understand the sequence of events that led to the site being chosen for development, and the contribution that Thamesmead was intended to make to London housing problems.

London's housing problems since 1945

After the immediate post-war problems of reconstruction the LCC became increasingly concerned with the problems of slums and severe overcrowding of housing and sought a series of solutions outside its own boundaries: first, the out-county estates which were basically dormitory settlements for commuters; second, the eight new towns, much more complete communities; and third, negotiated arrangements with local authorities to expand existing towns with overspill population. Nevertheless the county's housing deficit continued to rise and it was clear that some larger, quicker and more directly controlled remedy was needed.[3]

The LCC began a search for its own new town in 1952, intensified its efforts in 1955 and, after considering seventy sites, chose Hook in north-east Hampshire in October 1958.[4] A plan was prepared but Hampshire County Council strongly opposed it[5] and the Minister, stepping in to

[1] *London Government Act 1963*, ch33, s21.
[2] *Transport Act 1968*, ch73, s56; *Transport (London) Act 1969*, ch35, ss2, 5; *Road Traffic Regulation Act 1967*, ch76, s6.
[3] See W E Jackson (1965), *Achievement—a Short History of the LCC*, pp97, 109–10; LCC (1965), *London Statistics 1952–61*, NS, VI, pp94–5; and LCC (1960), *Development Plan First Review: County Report*, p100.
[4] LCC (1961), *The Planning of a New Town*; the criteria used were evolved from the experience of the earlier new towns—see Major-General A C Duff (1961), *Britain's New Towns*, ch3 'The Selection of Sites.'
[5] LCC (1961), *The Planning of a New Town*. Hampshire's opposition can be attributed to

reconcile the two main parties, secured a substitute programme of town expansion at Andover, Basingstoke and Tadley.

Thus the LCC was thrown back on its own resources. The strategy then evolved was for further 'infill' schemes within the LCC area and the development of 'windfall' sites, such as land surplus to the requirements of Government departments and public utility companies.

An opportunity for a major scheme

In the 1950s the LCC had built the Abbey Wood housing estate for 10 000 people, between the North Kent railway line and the dyke carrying a major sewer to the Crossness treatment works (see Figure 6). In addition the LCC owned 700 acres of the Plumstead Marshes acquired between 1905 and 1911. In 1962 the LCC devised a plan for a very large housing estate (25 000 people) on this land[1] and arranged for industrial development on part of the Woolwich Arsenal site. The remainder of the Arsenal site was to be given over to industrial uses including electricity generation, a heliport and Government supplies and storage depots.

In December 1963 the Government's considerations of London's housing land problems led it to offer 500 acres of the Woolwich site to the LCC, who responded by requesting to be allowed to develop the whole site.[2] Other prospective users were persuaded not to press their claims to the land, and in February 1965 the land was released to the LCC for a housing scheme for an estimated 50 000 people, and later in the year a price was agreed.[3] Five other factors combined to enable this land to be developed. New methods of sewage treatment meant that some of the land zoned for extensions to the Crossness sewage works could be released; reduced air and water pollution made the site less noxious; by 1965–66 the GLC was evolving a ring-and-radial system of urban motorways, of which the second (known as Ringway 2) was planned to cross the river at Woolwich and intersect with the Dover Radial, greatly improving road accessibility to the site; deep piling techniques enabled tower block housing to be built on such marshy sites; and finally, it was thought that industrialised building techniques would produce economies of scale which would offset some of the extra costs of developing such a difficult site.

In July 1966 the GLC formally announced that it would be responsible for the development but after prolonged negotiation it was decided that many of the services (local roads, open space, schools, etc.) would be

its desire not to lose too much income and power by having another large independent authority carved out of its fabric in addition to the rapidly growing Southampton area.

[1] The 'town on stilts' to be built 8 ft (2.4 metres) above sea level to prevent flooding.

[2] In the White Paper, *London: Employment, Housing Land*, Cmnd 1952 (February 1963), especially paras52–7.

[3] £6.8 million for 1016 acres or £6700 per acre. GLC *Minutes*, 19 December 1965, p582.

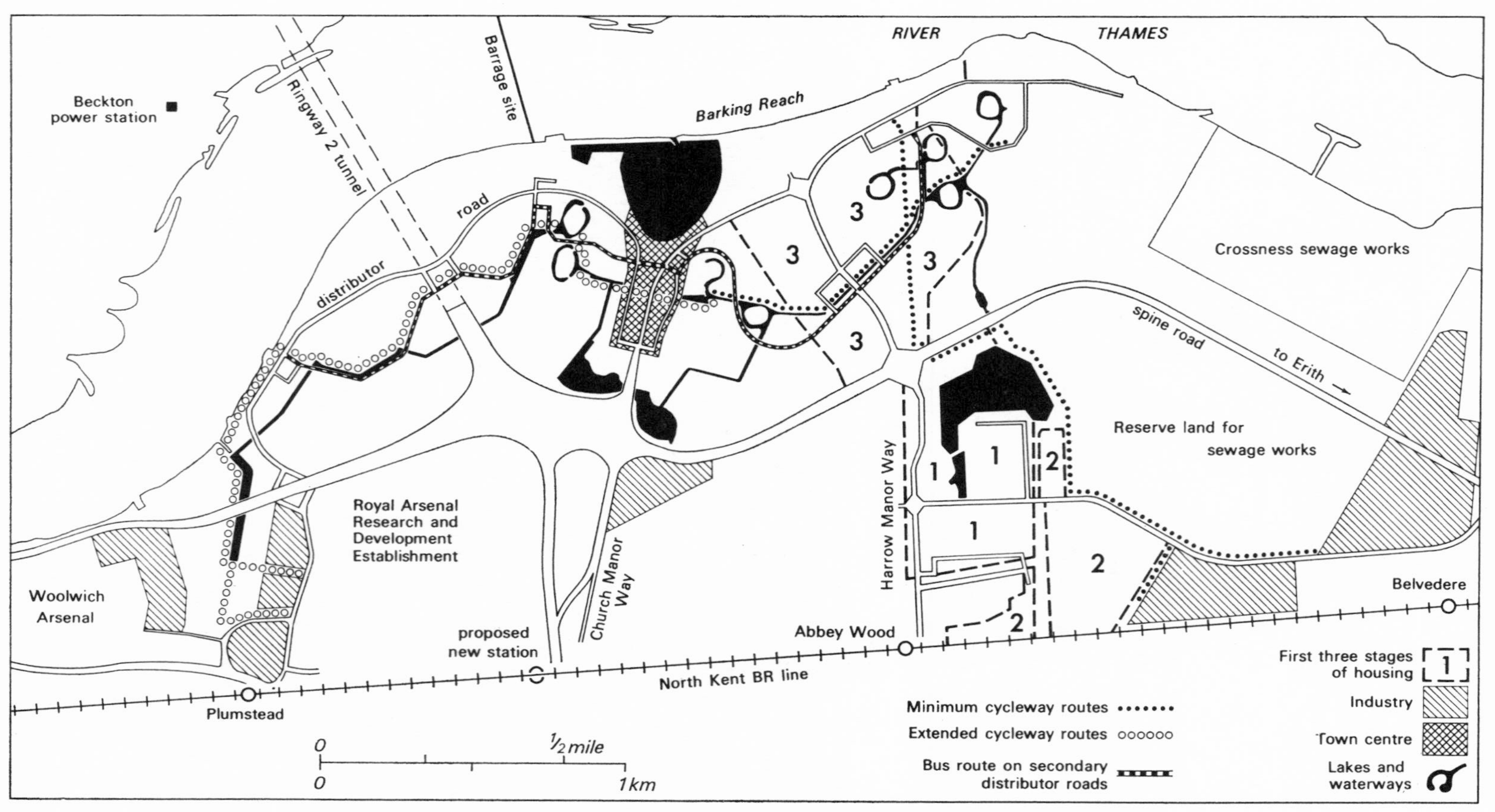

Figure 6 THAMESMEAD AND ITS TRANSPORT FACILITIES

provided by the two boroughs.[1] It was undisputed that such a large scheme (1340 acres or 2 square miles) required a master plan to guide and relate the different phases of construction. In this work the GLC were greatly influenced by contemporary planning concepts about new towns.

The nature of Thamesmead

Two closely related major aims of the British new towns were the attainment of 'self-containment' and 'social balance.' Self-containment in terms of a low proportion of workers travelling into or out of the new town has been basic to the decision to establish a new free-standing settlement, and the existing new towns clearly demonstrate this.[2] Social balance was also believed to be a rather nebulous but laudatory aim, implying an average cross-section of population by age, sex, and socio-economic status not only in the town as a whole, but also within its constituent neighbourhoods. Some critics have claimed that this has meant in practice that the lower-paid semi-skilled and unskilled groups, whose severe housing problems the new towns were supposed to solve, were under-represented, as were the highly paid professional groups. Thomas and others have demonstrated that this was due mainly to housing policies,[3] particularly:

1 the allocation of housing to those already holding jobs (the new towns have a predilection for light industries with a high proportion of skilled manual and administrative jobs);
2 the limitation of housing for purchase to new dwellings only (giving high average mortgage repayments not attainable by the lower paid); and
3 lack of suitable housing for the professionals (who often live in surrounding villages).

In the sense that it was the 'heir apparent' to the abortive Hook plan, Thamesmead was cherished by the GLC at both professional and political levels; policy and publicity statements were invested with the pioneering spirit, the sense of enterprise, and the architectural and social aspirations associated with the new towns. Indeed it has often been loosely referred to as a new town, but it is embedded in south-east London suburbia and it will rely on surrounding areas for many services and for much of its employment, certainly in its early years.

The aim of avoiding social imbalance and isolation has been explicit

[1] In the case of schools, the London Borough of Bexley is an education authority in its own right, Greenwich is part of ILEA.
[2] See A A Ogilvy (1968), 'The Self-contained New Town,' *Town Pl Rev*, 39, 1, pp38–54; and R Thomas (1969), *London's New Towns*, PEP Broadsheet 510, chI–IV.
[3] B J Herauld (1966), 'The New Towns and London's Housing Problem,' *Urban Studies* 3, 1, pp8–21, and (1968), 'Social Class and the New Towns,' *Urban Studies*, 5, 1, pp33–58; V Karn (1970), *Occasional Papers 8–11*, Birmingham University Centre for Urban and Regional Studies; and W P Roderick (1970), *Town Planning Review*, 42, 4, p323.

from the beginning: on the day he released the site to the GLC in 1965 the Minister of Housing, Mr Robert Mellish said: 'I do not want this to be a sea of council flats, but the greatest thing London has ever done.' The policy implications of the new town concept of Thamesmead for housing, jobs, transport and social services, were not clear in the early and critical days of the planning process, and were only clarified in a slow and a piecemeal fashion. Many statements about the 'new town,' 'limiting commuting' and 'social balance' continued to be made.[1]

2 THE PLANNING PROCESS

The draft Master Plan

In March 1966 a draft Master Plan for the site was published by the GLC which described two main influences on the town's structure as:

1 'The need to seize the visual opportunity the Thames waterfront offers.' The solution chosen was to provide a spine of high density housing along the river bank with a branch at right-angles to incorporate the town centre 'giving the new town [*sic*] a firm riverside identity and creating a scale of development to balance the [industrial] structures on the north bank.' It was also claimed that this high density 'spine' would achieve the same sense of community as the neighbourhood unit in the lower density new towns.
2 'The need to create strong but separate links for both pedestrians and vehicles' by creating a functional hierarchy of roads enclosing nine environmental areas, and a separate network of footpaths.[2]

This was considered 'an imaginative and exciting architectural solution';[3] it was certainly an architecturally determined one. There was little discussion of wider planning matters such as what would be the sources and characteristics of the population coming to live in Thamesmead, where they would work, and whether Thamesmead was meant to provide extra industry or office jobs for an area where job opportunities had been contracting. Moreover, there were no firm estimates of the total cost of the development or how it would be divided between the public and private sectors, or between central government, the GLC, and the London boroughs of Bexley and Greenwich.[4]

[1] See, for example, GLC (1969), *Initial Development Plan Amendment*, No.107, Written Statement p1; *Guidance Notes for Conservative Candidates*, No.1, GLC, 1967–70, pp35–6; *First Annual Report of Thamesmead Committee*, p23; and Seton Forbes-Cockell, the chairman of the Committee on 17 June 1971 (GLC *Press Release 251*).
[2] GLC (1966), *Woolwich–Erith, a Riverside Project*, pp9–11.
[3] Comment in the *Architect's Journal*, 23 March 1966, 145, pp733–5.
[4] A GLC standing order had to be suspended to allow the General Purposes Committee to approve the plan without such figures (GLC *Minutes*, 22 March 1966, pp171–4.)

The Plan and its accompanying report to the Council merely stated possible land-use requirements:

1 *Housing*. The development could accommodate 60 000 people at an average density of 100 per acre; one-third of the housing would be provided by Housing Associations or speculative builders for private purchase or renting.
2 *Industry*. Three major sites were allocated (see Figure 6).
3 *Offices*. 'We hope there will be a good deal of office employment in order to make the development self-contained and to ease the commuter problem.'
4 *Open space*. Provision of 190 acres (3 per 1000 people) was proposed, which was lower than either the LCC or Kent Development Plan standards, but 'took into account' the adjacent Bostall and Lesnes Abbey Woods.
5 *Education*. Sites for primary and secondary schools were shown but the ILEA and Bexley had yet to agree standards of provision.
6 *The central area*. A multi-level centre was proposed, including an unspecified amount of shopping floorspace great enough to ensure self-sufficiency but not so large as to compete with Woolwich, Erith and Bexleyheath.
7 *External communications—public transport*. Existing train capacity on the North Kent Line was used to the maximum; expansion could only be achieved at great expense; the report concluded that the most effective long-term measure 'may well be the transfer of commuters from either the Bexleyheath or mid-Kent lines to London Transport's proposed Fleet line tube with a percentage of the released capacity being assigned to the North Kent line.'[1] A 'possible new station' was shown at Church Manor Way on the Master Plan, linked by a new road to the town centre, but this was not mentioned in the text.

   As far as buses were concerned a need for 'very considerable increases' in services was forseen, particularly for people working a few miles from their home (i.e. in Crayford, Dartford, Greenwich, Eltham, Lewisham and north of the river); discussions were proceeding with the LT Board.
8 *External communications—road*. A cross-Thames motorway linking the northern and southern parts of Ringway 2 was to cross the site and a route had been safeguarded for a dual three-lane road; they showed a preference for tunnel construction rather than a bridge; east-west communications were to be provided by means of a four- or six-lane spine road, as it was called, running from Woolwich via two inter-

[1] When the report was received by the Council on 22 March 1966, Mr Vigars, a member of the minority party, unsuccessfully tried to amend the Council's resolution of approval to specifically include further study of the commuter problem.

changes with the motorway and the town centre road system to Erith; the GLC believed that it was essential to construct this at an early stage 'to facilitate development' of the site.

9 *Local roads*. These were to consist of one-way loops linked to the spine road and passing through the high density housing along the river frontage; the one-way system was meant to prevent traffic conflicts by eliminating right turns and to minimise through traffic in the residential areas; these distributor 'loop' roads were intended as bus routes (see Figure 6). Garaging would be generous (1 to 1.5 spaces per dwelling) and convenient for the householder.

During the following months a great deal of work was undertaken on the general plan for the scheme and on detailed designs for 1500 houses in Stage 1 fronting Harrow Manor Way (see Figure 6).[1] In March 1967 a revised Master Plan was produced. The basic principles were unchanged but an increased area of industry was allocated, the central area was re-designed in a *Y* shape and given a specified area of shopping floorspace,[2] the standards of school provision had been agreed, Bexley Borough Council had decided to provide a health centre. The road and pedestrian networks had been designed as well as a system of waterways for drainage and recreational use. A preliminary costing of £160 million public invest-ment (£216 million total) was also made (see Table 8). The one-way loop roads now had been replaced by a main road along the river front beside the higher density housing and a meandering route through the low density housing 'which should be unattractive to through traffic but which will bring buses within easy reach of all the housing and thus will enable a frequent service to be provided on an economic basis' (see Figure 6).

Some conflict of objectives began to show, for although the roads and car-parking facilities 'will cater for expected increases in ownership the aim is also to produce a *first class* public transport service that will *mini-mise* the need to use the private car.'[3] (our italics).

Two months later the new Conservative administration at County Hall decided that Thamesmead should be handled by a separate committee (instead of being under the aegis of the General Purposes and Housing committees). It was hoped that this would speed the pace of building and encourage private investments.[4] A complex system of liaison groups was set up to co-ordinate with the London boroughs, statutory undertakers, and central government (see section 6). In June 1967 a one-day conference

[1] GLC *Minutes*, 14 March 1967, pp207–12; and GLC (August 1970) *Thamesmead—a Riverside Development*.

[2] Totalling 220 000 square feet gross, of which 180 000 were in the central area, 15 000 in Stage I, and the remainder in nine other shopping groups.

[3] *Thamesmead—a Riverside Development*, p7.

[4] Thereafter annual reports were produced (GLC *Minutes*, 25 June 1968, 24 June 1969, 23 June 1970, 22 June 1971).

was held at Woolwich Town Hall to inform people in south-east London about the proposals and to promote interest in living and working in Thamesmead.

(a) *By Function* (*March 1967*)	£M
Land	13.4
Roads	25.9
Public housing (65% of total)	76.6
Central area	4.0
Education	8.7
Other functions	1.4
Parks and open spaces	6.8
River walls	7.9
Fees, etc.	15.0
	159.9
Private housing (35% of total)	41.0
Industry and Polytechnic	15.1
	216.0
(b) *By Sector* (*June 1968*)	
GLC	100.0
ILEA	14.3
London Borough of Bexley	5.0
London Borough of Greenwich	2.5
Central government	9.0
Other developers	80.2
	211.0

Table 8 COSTS OF THAMESMEAD

The Minister of Housing's public inquiry into the GLC's application for approval of the plan as a departure from the Initial Development Plan was held at County Hall during October 1967. Much of the time of the inquiry was taken up with the question of whether the GLC's proposed town centre at Thamesmead would compete with the town centres of Woolwich and particularly Erith, where a major private town centre redevelopment, approved by the Minister in 1966, had begun. The property company suggested an overall reduction in Thamesmead's floorspace and a ceiling of 50 000 square feet on the central area for a few years to give Erith a head start and an improvement in road connections and bus services. In 1970 the Minister indicated that he would limit the town centre to 100 000 square feet until 1978.

Work on Stage I proceeded, and the first show flat opened in May 1968; a delaying factor on Stages I and II was that the degree of housing subsidy could not be finalised with the Ministry. The planning of Stage III and the central area of Thamesmead was also held up for at least six months in 1969–70 by studies on the problem of whether to carry Ringway 2 across the river by a bridge or a tunnel (see section 4). The Thamesmead Committee decided to radically reappraise its employment policies when the AEI factory at Woolwich closed, leaving 5000 redundant. In 1969, the firm of C A Parsons (which employed 2000 people) closed and another 4500 losses were expected.[1] The building of the eastern industrial estate was hastened in the hope of attracting replacement jobs.

By late 1971 a reduction in the rate of building the public housing, slow development in the private sector and rising costs, led the GLC to undertake a reappraisal of the whole project which was published in 1972. The 65:35 public–private housing split remained as before, with 8800 GLC dwellings to be completed by 1986. But the density of the private housing was to be lowered and the timescale of its provision lengthened to 1988. This meant a reduction in target population from 60 000 to 48 000 or 45 000, or by 20 to 25%. The acreage of land required for roads, community services and the central area increased, while of the reserve industrial sites, 60 acres was reallocated for housing. The central area provision for shopping was unchanged at 200 000 square feet; but 160 000 square feet of extra commercial space was allocated and provision was made for the office area to be increased from 200 000 to over 400 000 square feet.[2]

The GLC then consulted the DOE and the two boroughs on these revisions, who had reason to have severe doubts about them, because the reduced population meant increased unit costs for all infrastructure and social services, and all the changes taken together threw doubts upon the validity of the original social concept. Nevertheless, the Thamesmead Committee chairman declared 'apart from a realistic updating of earlier forecasts of the population and price of development, the broad picture which emerges from this reappraisal in depth is that the pattern remaining is much the same. It fully bears out the Council's intention to press ahead vigorously with the development on the lines laid down in the 1967 Master Plan.'[3] Greenwich Borough Council, however, was seeking a new public inquiry in mid-1972 and hoping to enlist Bexley's support.[4] Their fears must have been accentuated by the growth envisaged for the town centre, and its possible impact on Woolwich and Erith developments in the

[1] GLC *Press Release 251*, 17 June 1971.
[2] GLC *Minutes*, 25 January 1972, p5.
[3] GLC *Press Release 20*, 19 January 1972.
[4] *Building Design*, 20 June 1972, pp287–93.

1980s. No strategic implications were possible, however, for the revised version of the Greater London Development Plan (GLDP) only gave development target figures for 1972–76. The slower pace of actual and planned development, the Conservatives' desire to ensure at least 35% private development and the subsequent lowering of average density to some fifty-two persons per acre all have considerable bearings on the scheme's transport problems and particularly that of rail commuting, to which we now turn.

3 COMMUTER CAPACITY OF THE RAILWAYS AND THE QUESTION OF A NEW STATION

At the time of the draft Master Plan very little was said about the type of work that the residents would do and where they would find it except that there would be some local movement into south-east London and some commuting to the central area.[1] One year later the first figures were given in the revised Master Plan: 30 000 of the 60 000 residents were expected to work (indicating a high activity rate amongst the women); of these some 8000 would be office workers going to Erith and Woolwich town centres and central London (page 13) although elsewhere all 8000 were said to commute to the centre (page 23). Jobs for 6000 people were proposed in the town centre (transport, sales and service groups); some sales, service and professional staff would be scattered through the development, and 8000–14 000 industrial jobs provided on the three estates (page 13).

It was estimated that only 2500 of the 8000 could be carried by adding extra coaches to existing trains,[2] or two new trains brought in by retimetabling, but new capacity would be needed including better access to the central London terminals through costly improvement of the notorious Borough Market and Nunhead junctions[3] (see Case Study *H*). It was also proposed to build a new station at Church Manor Way to replace that at Plumstead, in order to improve passenger interchange from car and bus and to allow better train operations (trains would turn here and at Abbey Wood). A new link road from Thamesmead town centre and a flyover over the railway[4] would have to be provided before the station, which would cost £500 000.

At the public inquiry held later in 1967 the problem arose on eight of the twelve days.[5] Considerable doubts were expressed about the rail capacity particularly by Mr J Wellbeloved, MP for Erith and Crayford. He questioned whether the system could cope with 2000 extra commuters by 1971

[1] Except that Alderman R Stucke, leader of Greenwich Council and a member of the GLC subcommittee, called for at least half of all employment to be on-site: anything less would make the commuting situation 'impossible.' See the *Guardian* 17 September 1965.
[2] This point appeared in the GLC Minutes but not in the draft plan.
[3] *Guardian*, 9 March 1967.
[4] See also *Transportation and Thamesmead*, paper T17, item 5, of Thamesmead Committee, 11 July 1967, pp2, 3.
[5] See *Transcripts* of inquiry, especially days 8 and 11.

(out of an expected population of 14 000) when it had taken three years to get one extra train into the timetables; whether it was wise to provide a large car park at the new station which would provide space for other park-and-ride commuters from outside Thamesmead who should entrain further 'down the line'; whether the timing of Thamesmead and Kidbrooke developments could bring the existing services to breaking point;[1] and whether an extra 1000 commuters from Thamesmead, brought about by an increase of private housing from 35 to 50%,[2] could be accommodated. A GLC engineer, Mr Copas, had to admit that 'things would be difficult, particularly in the period until British Railways could do things' and later a planner, Mr Craig, said 'nobody is happy with the present arrangements.' Mr Heath, MP for Bexley and leader of the Opposition, had questioned the Minister of Transport, Mrs Castle, on this matter who replied: 'British Railways' plans are not finalised but I can say that they are likely to involve a major investment of perhaps some £10 million in new works to provide the necessary extra capacity in time for the inflow of population. It will be for me to consider the detailed investment proposals when they are ready. I shall do so sympathetically.'[3]

One other matter was brought up at the inquiry. Giving evidence Mr Hurlstone, the Bexley Borough Engineer, said that 'some reliance appears to be placed on encouraging travellers to use new services to Victoria whereas the greater demand is probably to London Bridge and the City.'[4] This indeed was BR's intention both in the short term and after the re-signalling and junction improvements proposed in 1971 and the mid-1970s.[5] In fact, subsequent evidence proved BR's case to some extent[6] (see Case Study *H* and Table 23).

In 1968[7] further information was given of the station improvements, including programming. As well as the new Church Manor station, Abbey Wood and Belvedere were to have flyovers built to replace existing level crossings. Abbey Wood was to be rebuilt by 1971, the new station as soon

[1] Based on a statement to that effect by Mr D McKenna, General Manager of Southern Region, in the *Kentish Reporter*, 22 September 1967, and in a letter to Sir William Hart, Clerk to the GLC, on 26 August 1967 making the following points: 'The line . . . already carries some 12 000 commuters to Charing Cross and Cannon Street through the most difficult railway operating conditions in the world. Thus it must be accepted that the development [Thamesmead] poses very difficult problems for the railways. . . . However, we are now at an advanced stage of preparing a scheme of major physical works . . . [which] will adequately service the requirements of the Thamesmead development in due course [by 1975] subject to their ultimate approval by the Minister of Transport. I make this proviso since it is highly unlikely that we can provide the additional capacity required and meet our financial obligations under the 1962 Transport Act. In other words, the works will need to be justified in terms of social benefits to the community.'

[2] Referring to paper 357 of the GLC General Purposes Committee, 17 January 1965.

[3] *Kentish Times* 20 October 1967.

[4] Day 6 of inquiry.

[5] *Thamesmead Rail Services*, paper T121, item 6, of Thamesmead Committee, 2 July 1968.

[6] BR Board (1970), *Proof of Evidence, E12/7*, table 13, GLDP Inquiry Stage 1.

[7] *Thamesmead's Rail Services*, 2 July 1968.

as the central area and Stage IV housing neared completion (then assessed as late 1972). Of the 1971 situation, with an extra train running, the report said 'conditions would be comparable with those before the introduction of the 1967 timetable.'

The Policy and Research Branch of the Department of Highways and Transportation carried out a study into journey-to-work movements in 1968 which attempted to calculate and assign car flows to a road network, incidentally calculating the proportion of people using each mode within Thamesmead travelling to the nearby areas and to central London.[1] The study used a division of trips as follows:

	Employed resident population 30 000
of which	Travelling to central London (20%) 6000
	Travelling to south-east London (50%) 15 000
	Working in Thamesmead (30%) 9000
	Travelling in from south-east London 1800
	Population working in Thamesmead 10 800

The proportion commuting was estimated from a job opportunities model which gave a range of variations from 15 to 25%. Other job opportunity distributions gave figures of commuting to central London of 4400 and 8600. Using data from Kent Development Plan studies, research in Essex by Thomas[2] and at Abbey Wood by the Hornsey College of Art, it is possible to calculate varying ranges of commuting to central London based on assumptions about the proportion of owner occupiers (35 or 50%), the number likely to commute (40%), and the proportion of council tenants likely to commute (15 or 25%). These calculations produce a range from 7100 to 9700 people.

The other vital factor is obviously that of employment: whether Thamesmead can provide jobs for 2300–3000 people in its town centre (depending on which figures one takes for shop and office floorspaces), 6000 people in industrial estates and 15 000 people in the local community where over 10 000 industrial jobs have been lost in industrial closures in recent years.[3] The essential link between homes and jobs in the planned migration process is priorities for allocating housing, and we shall return to this matter. In the formal planning statement about Thamesmead in 1969[4] the GLC reiterated its desire to limit commuting. In the meantime as our rough cross-check calculation has shown, 8000 commuters was a reasonable 'guestimate' in view of the uncertainty about the vital controlling parameters.

[1] GLC Department of Highways and Transportation, *Thamesmead—The Journey to Work*, RM 62, by G M Lamb, October 1968.

[2] R Thomas (1969), *London's New Towns* (PEP Broadsheet 510), p433.

[3] *The Times*, 17 June 1969.

[4] *GLC Initial Development Plan Amendment No.107* (1969), written statement and explanatory statement.

There now entered on the scene two factors of delay which have been very fortuitous in moving towards a solution of the interim problem of lack of capacity, one acting on BR, the other on the GLC.

Although BR continued to plan for improvements to Southern Region lines and in particular the south-eastern approaches[1] (see Case Study *H*), further examination of trends in the pattern of commuting verified suspicions that had begun to develop at Board level that the number of long-distance trips were increasing while the inner suburban commuting was falling (see Table 9). As far as the south-eastern lines were concerned this would mean that peak period arrivals (0700–0959) would drop from 136 000 to 110 000 and peak hour (0815–0914) arrivals from 84 000 to

	1951		1969		CHANGE	
TYPE OF SERVICE	NO. (000)	(%)	NO. (000)	(%)	NO. (000)	(%)
Inner suburban	183.6	68	172.3	57	−11.3	−16
Outer suburban	53.3	20	69.2	23	+15.9	+16
Long distance	31.6	12	58.6	20	+27.0	+65
Total	286.5	100	300.1	100	+31.6	+12

Table 9 PASSENGER ARRIVALS SOUTHERN REGION TERMINI, 1951–69, DURING MORNING PEAK PERIOD (0700–0959)

Source: BRB (1970) *Proof of Evidence E12/7* Table 12 p51, GLDP Inquiry Stage 1

74 000 even allowing for new commuting from Thamesmead and Kidbrooke.

Also in early 1970 Southern Region announced two management changes involving fare structures which could help to overcome interim problems.[2] First, tickets on all south-eastern division lines would be available to any London terminal (instead of specifying which one); this could encourage more people to use Charing Cross and particularly Victoria. Second, on eight North Kent Line stations (Charlton to Slade Green) a special fare reduction of about 20% was offered to passengers travelling before 0810 or after 1910 to overcome the 'peak-of-the-peak overcrowding.'

On the GLC side 'external' delays arose because of problems concerning the river crossing (see section 4) combined with lengthy design processes, slow negotiations over housing subsidies related to the Ministry's cost yardstick[3] and a slow rate of lettings. This meant that early estimates of the build up of Thamesmead's population had to be revised downwards:

[1] White Paper, *Transport in London* (July 1968), Cmnd 3686, para20; BR Board (1970), *Proof of Evidence E12/7*, esp paras4.6, 4.44, A4.1. GLDP Inquiry Stage 1.

[2] *Southern Region Report*, No.1, February 1970.

[3] See *The Times*, 12 February 1971; and *Third Annual Report of the Thamesmead Committee*, pp2, 7–9.

Public inquiry (October 1967), 14 000 people by 1971.
Council minutes (10 March 1970), 15 000 people by 1976.
Third annual report (June 1970), 1400 people resident.
Council minutes (21 July 1970), 12 000 people by 1976.
Fourth annual report (June 1971), 4000 people resident.

In January 1972 the population of the whole scheme was revised downwards by 20–25% and the timescale was lengthened, thus postponing the growth of commuting.

Another outcome of the GLC's investigations was that the link road from the town centre to serve the new station, estimated to cost £1.2 million, would be only very lightly used between Church Manor Way and Woolwich and thus would not rank for a 75% grant from the Ministry of Transport (MOT). Moreover, BR could foresee no major operating benefit from the new station, and implied that the GLC would have to finance it if they considered it important on planning grounds. After deliberation it was decided instead to rehabilitate the existing Plumstead station and provide bus laybys and station car parking.[1] LT and BR were quite happy not to disturb the journey patterns of existing passengers. Thus the commuter problem in one sense 'disappeared' without any conscious action from the bodies involved.

The question of the Fleet Line did not arise after its mention in the draft Master Plan because traffic estimates looked more hopeful for the Lewisham route (see Case Study *C*), although some people have urged that a branch should run to Thamesmead.[2] The BR Board indicated that in this case they would not be worried by railheading (see station car parks Case Study *F*). The major question of the socio-economic status and job location of Thamesmead's workers remained surrounded by severe doubts.

4 BRIDGE OR TUNNEL? THE CONTROVERSY OVER A THAMES CROSSING[3]

As already mentioned, the planning of Thamesmead was hindered by the prolonged decision-making procedure over the river crossing of the primary road system. Surprisingly enough this question had been aired for over forty years.

In 1926 the only facilities for crossing the river Thames below Tower Bridge were the congested Rotherhithe and Blackwall tunnels, and the ferries at Woolwich and Gravesend. A Royal Commission[4] examined three

[1] GLC *Minutes*, 3 November 1970, p597; and interviews with BR Board and GLC officers.
[2] The Greenwich Society suggested that the proposed Greenwich bypass and the Fleet Line could run in a double tunnel from the Surrey Docks via the Isle of Dogs to Woolwich. See P Hall's Report, 'Transport under the Thames,' *New Society*, 14 January 1971.
[3] The authors are grateful for the opportunity to discuss this issue with Mr L Goldman of Princeton University, NJ, who was studying Thamesmead for his PhD thesis in 1971–72.
[4] *Report of the Royal Commission on Cross-River Traffic in London*, 1926.

proposals for new links: a high-level bridge at Woolwich and tunnels at Gravesend/Tilbury and Dartford/Purfleet. They concluded that the Dartford tunnel provided the best location and value for money at £2.95 million; they also recommended improving the approaches to the Dartford site and to the Woolwich Ferry, and to acquire the Gravesend ferry, and operate it free of charge.[1] The high level bridge (150 feet) at Woolwich was dismissed on the grounds that it was 'beyond the range of practical politics', since the MOT did not believe it would show a good return on its high cost (£4 million).

The debate continued because traffic using Woolwich ferry doubled in the period 1926–36. Bressey and Lutyens in their 1938 highways plan gave a high priority to improving the approaches to the ferry (Bressey's Route 38) and ultimately to providing a permanent link at Woolwich. They discarded a high-level bridge on aesthetic grounds, a barrage because of its frequent interruptions of both road and river traffic (remembering that the docks near the Pool of London were still very busy at this period) and also favoured a tunnel as being cheaper to build and having fewer operational difficulties.[2]

A few years later Abercrombie suggested in his *County of London Plan* (1943) that either the Woolwich free ferry be replaced by a high-level bridge or that a tunnel be driven farther east to take his *C* Ring road away from residential and shopping areas. In his *Greater London Plan* a year later he recommended both. The LCC's 1951 County Development Plan did not discuss the matter as it did not include any new major road proposals.

During the processing of Phase II of the London Traffic Survey (1964–66) the newly-formed GLC were evolving a primary road system of urban motorways (since admitted to be derived from Abercrombie's ideas of twenty years earlier). Their traffic consultants, Freeman Fox, Wilbur Smith and Associates, had tested a motorway network in north-east London including the problem of cross-river traffic.[3] Assuming that the other motorway links north and south of the river were completed, their traffic projections for 1981 indicated a demand for 80 000 vehicles per day or nearly three times as great as the 1962 traffic in the Blackwall tunnel. This would require a crossing of dual three-lane carriageways.[4] The GLC consulted Sir Harold Hardy on the costs of three alternative forms of construction: a high-level bridge, a deep-bored tunnel and an immersed tube, i.e. set in a trench on the river bed. He reported in February 1966 that the immersed tube would be cheapest at £11 million compared with £20 million for the bridge and £40–45 million for the bored tunnel.[5] The

[1] The Dartford tunnel was opened in 1963, the Woolwich approaches improved in 1967.

[2] *Highway Development Survey 1937* (Greater London) by Sir Charles Bressey and Sir Edwin Lutyens, 1938.

[3] T Bendixson, the *Guardian*, 29 December 1965.

[4] *Draft Master Plan*, p8, March 1966.

[5] *Construction News*, 25 April 1968.

draft Master Plan proposed an immersed tube tunnel capable of taking such flows and expressed a preference for a westerly location.

In January 1967 the Council recommended a change of route for the *C* Ring (i.e. Ringway 2) in south London and mentioned that the river crossing should be of dual four-lane standard, based upon a new traffic assignment figure of 130 000 vehicles per day (or 60% higher than the previous one)[1] although a year later the revised Master Plan still indicated a dual three-lane crossing.

The implications of these two extra lanes became evident when costings were undertaken later in the year. The additional cost of a tunnel with four lanes was likely to bring the total cost to well above that for a dual four-lane bridge (three sunken tubes would be needed instead of two). In addition, new developments in bridge technology (for example, box girder rather than suspension bridges) seemed to offer savings on the original estimates. In addition, the Port of London Authority were willing to consider lower clearances for the bridge. Freeman Fox's structural specialists informally confirmed this. In view of the advanced state of planning for both the tunnel and the Thamesmead project, the GLC officers decided to approach the chairmen of the relevant committees for a directive regarding further studies. The chairmen felt that it was a major policy matter and so referred it to the Leader's Co-ordinating Committee who approved further work by Freeman Fox and Sir Harold Hardy. The consultants' report, received in March 1968, confirmed the GLC engineers' suspicions that the bridge was cheaper than the tunnel: £12.6 million against £20.7 million, or almost the exact reverse of Hardy's estimates in 1966.

The GLC officers, particularly the architects and planners, reacted to this situation in an interesting way. Despite a price differential that would decide the choice in many circumstances they resisted the idea of a bridge. They argued that if a bridge were built:

1 the amenity value of the whole site and the visual value of Thameside would be impaired by a bridge 150 feet above the river, carried by 350-foot towers;[2]
2 large areas of housing land would be lost directly where land was required for bridge works, and indirectly in adjacent areas where traffic noise and fumes would render living conditions intolerable;[3] and
3 besides these losses, three years of planning work on the majority of Thamesmead's housing areas and open spaces and the town centre would have to be radically revised (if not begun afresh) and that the consequent delays would vitiate one of the objectives of the scheme, a rapid attack on the housing problem.

[1] GLC *Minutes*, 31 January 1967, p70.
[2] See question in Council, GLC *Minutes*, 25 June 1968, p317.
[3] See *The Times*, 24 January 1968.

They did not even attempt contingency planning; they proposed to await a clear decision on the problem. The architects in particular felt that the housing loss and delay factors would put up overall costs considerably, but the Engineer's and Treasurer's officers could not support this. It was agreed that the delay might cost £2.5 million to set against the bridge, and some 80 acres of land for housing (enough for 2500 dwellings or 7500 people) would be lost. The degree of concern about this is evident from the leaked information in the press.[1]

These points were accepted by the Council who expressed the opinion that the extra construction costs of the tunnel were small compared with the overall long-term social losses connected with the bridge,[2] and asked the officers to elaborate on these factors. However, the decision lay with the MOT, from whom the GLC were expecting a 75% grant. As a subsequent report to the Council showed, the GLC feared the grant might be paid only for the equivalent cost of the bridge, or even withheld, for the Ministry's traditional criterion did not allow payments of grants for amenity matters, certainly on this scale: these, it could claim, were within the purview of the Ministry of Housing. The GLC made a proposal to raise any shortfall in the final grant through tolls of from 1 to 2 shillings (5–10p) per vehicle[3] although by July 1968 the Ministry had agreed that there should be no toll.

Despite pleas by GLC members for an urgent decision both in public and behind the scenes, matters continued to hang fire, indicating the severity of the department's problem, first in assessing the total costs and benefits and secondly in deciding on the grant. By this stage planning for Stage III of Thamesmead's housing and central area had reached the point where more detailed work had to begin, which would be completely abortive if the Minister preferred a bridge. After consultations within the Leader's Co-ordinating Committee it was decided to stop further work until the outcome was known. This was interpreted by some as an attempt at 'shot-gun tactics to enforce a speedy decision.'[4] If so, it was not conspicuously successful, despite further supporting statements.[5] The GLC and central government officers continued to meet, each time at a more senior level but by November it was obvious that the gap had not been closed and that the politicians of each body would have to meet. During this period the Minister of Transport's economic advisers undertook a cost-benefit exercise. It is difficult to see why a full cost-benefit study was needed because the traffic benefits of both proposals were equal (with the minor qualification that certain sorts of abnormal and dangerous loads would not be

[1] *Evening News* and *Evening Standard*, 23 January 1968.

[2] David Thornton had already expressed this belief: see *The Times*, 13 and 24 January 1968; see also *Thamesmead Annual Report* 25 June 1968; GLC *Minutes*, pp345–6; and an interview by Seton Forbes-Cockell in *Architect's Journal*, 17 January 1968, 147, p158–61.

[3] GLC *Minutes*, 25 June 1968, pp345–6; 3 December 1968, pp697–8.

[4] *The Times*, 'An Agonising Muddle,' 7 November 1968.

[5] For example, GLC *Press Release 101*, 18 February 1969, urging the Minister to 'consider the welfare of future generations' and choose a tunnel.

allowed in the tunnel) so that it was basically a question of whether the amenity and land-use benefits of a tunnel (mainly intangibles) would be worth the extra construction costs, delays, etc.[1] It demanded an informed value judgement. In one sense the extra cost of the tunnel (about £6.5 million) could be attributed to the Thamesmead development because without it the cheaper bridge solution could have been adopted.

On 18 December Mr (later Sir Desmond) Plummer and his colleagues met Richard Marsh the Minister of Transport and stressed not only the points they had already made, but also the fact that Thamesmead's design standards would be compromised by a bridge and that the scheme might be less attractive to private capital as a result. The Ministry economists produced a paper which showed smaller cost differences between the schemes. Whether influenced by the GLC's arguments, the cost-benefit analysis, the fear of public disapproval at holding up such a prominent public housing scheme, or all three, Mr Marsh approved the tunnel for grant aid in March 1970. Mr Plummer welcomed this decision saying that 'the Minister has shown his concern for future generations of residents at Thamesmead who will not now be threatened with a dominant structure in this new town development.'[2]

Further design work proceeded although it was almost a year later that details of the new tunnel were published. The cost had risen considerably, although it now included 1¾ miles of approach roads, a traffic surveillance system, and PLA costs for radar installations, attendance, pilotage, etc., while construction was proceeding.

	WORKS	PROPERTY	TOTAL £M
Thamesmead gyratory	2.20	0.42	2.62
Tunnel and approaches	22.75	3.07	25.82
Total	22.55	3.49	29.04

Thus the tunnel occasioned a delay of six months in the planning of Thamesmead after creating many months of uncertainty[3] and once again emphasized the importance of financial liability between local and central government.

The GLC through the instigation of its architects and planners were in this case 'on the side of the angels' in preferring the tunnel. They had a vested interest in the sense that they had committed a good deal of work based on it. They also incurred no overt displeasure from the engineers to whom either proposal was an interesting technical challenge, and gave

[1] According to a *Seminar on Treatment of Land Infrastructure and Amenity in Cost-benefit Studies* (HM Treasury Management Accounting Unit, November 1969, p2) it attempted to measure these 'externalities.'

[2] Reply to Question in Council, GLC *Minutes*, 10 March 1970, pp236–8.

[3] Conservative Central Office, *Guidance Note for Candidates*, 1970, No.1, p35; and *Third Annual Report of the Thamesmead Committee*, 1971.

equal traffic benefit, although the bridge would have been a more evident testimony to their skills.

Whilst the GLC planners were in the forefront of the Thamesmead debate there is no evidence that the same situation occurred at central government level. The issue seems to have been treated basically as a traffic problem despite the existence of a liaison committee with central government (see section 6). This may also account for the surprising fact that no regional view was taken of the river crossing situation: the improvements to the Blackwall tunnel and Woolwich ferry approaches, the Ringway 2 crossing, the duplication of the Dartford tunnel and a proposal for a new crossing in the Tilbury area[1] surely demanded some joint consideration of financial priority. In the absence of a regional body, only the Ministries of Housing or Transport could do this; the latter's introduction of the preparation pool system for road schemes could have enabled this to be done. It was not, despite pressure also from the Dartford Tunnel Joint Committees and Kent and Essex County Councils for urgent consideration of a second Dartford tunnel (which was separately approved in April 1971).[2] The Ministry appeared still unduly 'project orientated.'

One other doubt remained: the immersed tube method of building tunnels was an untried technology in this country and, irrespective of inflation, new techniques have a habit of costing far more than their original estimates. On the other hand the new box girder bridge-building technique pioneered by Freeman Fox has had its image tarnished by the collapse of two box-girder bridges under construction at Milford Haven and Melbourne. Far from becoming an established technique, it is now admitted to be 'pioneer work that is pushed towards the limits of the engineer's knowledge.' The Secretary of State for the Environment set up a committee to examine the basis of design and method of erection of such bridges in November 1970.[3] From this point of view the choice of a tunnel may prove fortuitous.

5 MOVEMENT IN THAMESMEAD

This section examines the means of moving within and immediately around Thamesmead—on foot, on cycles, by car, by bus or by some newer system.

Pedestrians

Thamesmead was planned with footpaths separate from the primary and secondary roads, a feature which has been maintained throughout the

[1] Proposed by the South-East Planning team in their *Strategic Plan for the South-East: a Framework* (HMSO 1970) to serve developments along the lower Thames, pp59, 61, 105.

[2] The *Guardian*, 14 March and 7 June 1968, and 23 April 1966; DOE *Press Release 264*, 28 April 1971.

[3] MOT *Press Release 609*, 5 November; and The *Guardian*, 6 November 1970.

evolution of the design.[1] Much of the system is on the deck level of the housing areas (i.e. above possible flood levels), and some roads are crossed by bridges; in both situations travellers tend to be rather exposed to wind, rain, and cold mist in Thamesmead's environment. In other areas roads are crossed via shallow underpasses under slightly ramped roads.

The cycleways

As part of the concept of a traffic-segregated town it was always intended that Thamesmead should have a cycleway system segregated from the main roads as well as a system of pedestrian ways.[2] The flat nature of the site and the heavy traffic flows on the major distributor roads which serve

	BASIC ROUTE (2.25 MILES)	EXTENDED ROUTE (2.1 MILES)	TOTAL (4.35 MILES)
a: Thamesmead			
Land cost (£000)	59.5	55.5	115.0
Construction cost[a] (£000)	211.9	174.3	386.2
Total	271.4	229.8	501.2
Annual maintenance (£000)	0.6	0.4	1.0
Daily trips	5800	5400	11 200
	EXISTING (20 MILES)[b]		
b: Stevenage			
Daily trips—workers	10 000		
Daily trips—school children	5 000		

Table 10 CYCLEWAYS IN THAMESMEAD AND STEVENAGE

[a] Sixty per cent of this cost consisted of structural items (bridges, subways); 40% was for the tracks themselves
[b] The Stevenage system has 80 cycle underpasses at junctions; when extended it will cover 30 miles and have 100 underpasses

the chief employment areas should encourage the use of a separate system. Experience at Harlow and Stevenage[3] had shown great benefits in saving

[1] The draft Master Plan (p16) said rather patronisingly (as if it were a gift rather than a right): 'Only in the projected Hook scheme has planning provided for the pedestrian to be given this scale of freedom.' See also p18 and *Revised Master Plan*, p5; and brochure *Thamesmead: Movement.*
[2] See Report to *Thamesmead Committee*, 10 December 1964; *Revised Master Plan*, p24; and brochure *Thamesmead: Movement.*
[3] Systems exist also at Hemel Hempstead, Telford, Daventry and Cramlington, and are proposed at Peterborough.

road and parking space costs, in almost eliminating accidents to cyclists, and in providing a healthy and cheap means of travel to school, work and shops. In Stevenage (where the total working population is similar to that planned for Thamesmead) this allowed 13% of workers to cycle to work in 1966, and a total of 15 000 trips daily were made by cycle.

In December 1968 when Stages I and II of the housing were beginning to be constructed and Stage III was being planned and costed, the Finance Committee requested the Thamesmead Committee to consider the justification for the system 'in the light of shortage of capital.' Drawing on the experience of the new towns and the engineers' estimate that 11 200 trips would be made daily, the officers reported that the system costing £270 000[1] was justified (see Table 10). Pressed again to see if costs could be reduced they later explained that construction costs at Thamesmead were higher than at Stevenage, first because of site conditions and second in order to minimise maintenance costs (see Table 10*a*). This was a consideration on which pressure had also been put by the boroughs of Bexley and Greenwich because these authorities would become responsible for maintenance.

Costs were also kept at a high level by insistence from the Valuer's Department that cycleways' land should be itemised and costed separately from the roads, at a cost of over £17 000 per acre which is far more than, for example, a 'notional' costing for open space use.[2] Even the police objected to what one might have felt was a road safety aid; they said that the cycleways gave a sense of false security to the cyclist which lasted until after he passed onto ordinary roads, where his behaviour might be an extra accident hazard.

The cycleways have been retained in the scheme only by stout defence by the planners and architects involved in their design.[3] Experience in other new towns, even with a high car ownership, a clearly defined road hierarchy, and high motor traffic capacity shows that cycleways bring considerable benefits; in Thamesmead's environment they may be as attractive as the pedestrian ways, if not more so.

Roads and the use of the car

As noted in section 2, Thamesmead was deliberately designed for a high car ownership (0.30 cars per person or 1 per household by the design date of 1981 and possibly a saturation level of 1.5 cars per household by the year 2000) and usage, encouraged by high-capacity roads, free-flow multi-level intersections and plentiful residential parking spaces.[4] Access to the main roads should be fairly easy and once on the main roads movement to the

[1] Paper T171, item 9 of report to Thamesmead Committee 15 May 1969.
[2] Paper T190, item 6 of report to Thamesmead Committee 15 May 1969.
[3] The chairman of the Thamesmead Committee was also said to be strongly in favour of cycleways.
[4] See draft Master Plan, p11; revised Master Plan, p23; and Paper T17, item 5, *Transportation and Thamesmead*, report to Thamesmead Committee, 11 July 1967.

town centre or industrial areas would be quicker than by any other mode according to present plans.

Thus in calculating both journey to work and off-peak flows of car traffic a GLC engineer could write: '...certainly whatever public transport system is finally adopted it is extremely unlikely that the percentage by car will ever fall below 60%' (for the journey to work), and implied that it might exceed 80%;[1] and 'it can generally be assumed that as car ownership grows, and in a situation like Thamesmead, the inhabitants can be expected to walk less for shopping journeys than others.[2] In this case the car was assumed to be used for 25% of trips lasting from 1 to 3 minutes but for 58% of journeys in excess of 5 minutes. In contrast a recent survey of Hammersmith shoppers showed that 67% of trips to local shopping centres were on foot and 27% were by bus or train.

Buses

Section 2 described how the revised Master Plan provided for a meandering secondary route which served both the high-density riverfront housing and the lower-density inner areas. A service frequency of 5 minutes during the peak period and 10 minutes off-peak was hoped for; experience elsewhere suggested that 'frequent bus services are always asked for by new town inhabitants most of whom have come from urban areas of high density with correspondingly frequent buses.'[3]

This was much more acceptable than the draft Master Plan with its one-way systems produced apparently without any consultation with LT. After LT's rather shocked reaction to this plan, a working party was established under the chairmanship of J D C Churchill (then GLC adviser on transportation policy and a former LT Board senior officer) bringing RB and LT into liaison with the GLC. LT subsequently suggested that in addition to the basic network, supplementary express bus services might limit car usage, but would need subsidy.[4] These services would be one-man operated, and some would be run as satellite 'loop routes' running from Woolwich town centre. More detail than this was not given, although the matter was discussed by the Greater London Transport Group.

A matter continuously stressed by LT was a design detail, but an important one: bus stopping places must be linked with the pedestrian systems, especially in low-density areas. As E R Ellen, Director of Transportation Planning for London Transport wrote: 'Nobody would have thought of segregating pedestrians from buses if it had not become necessary to segregate them from private cars.'[5]

[1] G M Lamb (1968), *Thamesmead: The Journey to Work*, RM 62.
[2] G M Lamb (1968), *Off-Peak Journeys in Thamesmead*, RM 113.
[3] A J Dickens (1963), 'The Busman's Ideal New Town,' *Modern Transport*, 22 June, pp11–12.
[4] *Transportation and Thamesmead*, July 1967; and *Thamesmead Bus Services*, paper T104, item 4, of Thamesmead Committee, 2 May 1968.
[5] E R Ellen (1967), 'Design for Buses: the Operator's View,' *Town and Country Planning*, XXV, 1, pp16–20.

The GLC officers claimed that the 'low (general traffic) loadings on the secondary distributors preserve environmental standards and give the buses a free run.'[1] Eventually, however, the buses must join the main traffic flow on the distributors within Thamesmead, and the secondary routes leading to other local town centres or employment areas. The likely efficiency of the bus services can be gauged by present conditions on the A106 through Woolwich, Plumstead (where it is the High Street) and Erith. In 1967, GLC officers were reporting that the greatest passenger flows anticipated would require no more than thirty buses per hour and that nowhere would this justify a bus lane, let alone a busway (buses-only road). By 1968 they admitted that 'some special facilities for buses may be required in the main shopping centre, to provide free access to the bus station.' Moreover, however frequent and reliable the bus services prove to be, they will find it hard to compete with the car, for which such generous provision is being made in Thamesmead.

New forms of transport

From the early days of Thamesmead's planning, a professional group sought to promote new forms of public transport. Through its studies of provision for cars and conventional forms of public transport, the Advanced Studies Group of Hornsey College of Art (HCA) came to the conclusion in 1967 that what was needed in Thamesmead and new towns of a similar size was a form of 'bus-train' called the 'overground,' running on an elevated track (similar to the American Westinghouse Skybus).[2] GLC Labour member Ellis Hillman was in touch with the HCA Group. Other well-known architects working on new movement systems (e.g. Brian Richards, David Wager) could have had an influence on the architects and planners working on Thamesmead's design. Certainly automatic vehicle systems or monorails could add extra excitement to a futuristic architectural concept.

The designers started to look at the problems of fitting in such a system, or at least of safeguarding a route, and in 1967 the new Conservative Council promoted interest by commissioning the Highways Department to study monorails (see Case Study *J*) but the study was confined to large systems in a central London situation. The decision not to proceed diverted attention from lighter and more adaptable systems, such as the minirail and Cabtrack.

The Highways Department (and LT) disliked such systems; they labelled them 'the funnies,' and thought them costly, inflexible, and

[1] *Thamesmead Bus Services*, 2 May 1968 (by the Architect and Director of Planning and Transportation).

[2] See *Transport in Cities* (1965), First HCA Conference on Transportation and the *Observer*, 19 February 1967.

unnecessary since they claimed the future road system would be uncongested.[1] As the financial squeeze increased, the idea became less and less attractive, even in terms of safeguarding land, and it faded away.

6 CONCLUSIONS

In the foreword to the first draft Master Plan of Thamesmead, Sir William Fiske wrote: 'It is in such projects as this that we learn to use the machinery of Greater London's local government and make it work effectively.' In this context it is instructive to see what sort of administrative structure was devised to handle such a large and complex project, before evaluating the various aspects of the transport planning process.

Thamesmead was initially one of the responsibilities of the Labour GLC's General Purposes Committee, but in July 1965 it became the total responsibility of a Woolwich–Erith development subcommittee chaired by the leader of the Council, and including the leader of Bexley Borough Council and the chairman of Greenwich's General Purposes Committee. This was a novel form of co-operation amongst members, obviating the need for a more cumbersome joint committee procedure. At officer level the architects and planners formed a joint team who liaised with other GLC departments, the boroughs, and the statutory undertakers, and produced the two versions of the Master Plan.

In May 1967, the new Conservative Council appointed a Thamesmead 'project' committee of twenty-eight members, including four from each of the boroughs. The Master Plan team was dispersed and a new officers' structure was formed, co-ordinated to an increasing extent by the Clerk's department. The deputy Clerk, Mr Fitzpatrick chaired two groups: one co-ordinating the specialist activities of nine departments and ILEA, the other linking the GLC to the officers of Bexley and Greenwich to agree standards of provision and conditions for taking over facilities and local rate burdens. A Ministry liaison group chaired by a representative of the Ministry of Housing and Local Government was also established, representing virtually all Government departments, the GLC and the boroughs. This group had a transport subcommittee whose effectiveness was limited by its size: as many as forty people are said to have attended meetings at a time and the railways Board, for example, found it too cumbersome for discussion of vital planning matters. Its usefulness was mainly as a sounding board and clearing house for information. A construction consultative group was established to facilitate site work, as this began.

In July 1968 two extra members were added to the Thamesmead Committee. In April 1970 it came within the purview of the Housing Committee, presumably on the grounds that the development was now proceeding steadily, and that the main job was to house the newcomers. Later the

[1] *Evening Standard*, 31 January 1967.

same year the borough representation was reduced to two members each, with two more members acting as 'observers'.

Section 1 traced the origins of Thamesmead to the LCC's desire to achieve a more rapid and direct impact on London's housing problems and the failure to achieve this at Hook. When the Woolwich–Erith marshes were obtained as a windfall site, the GLC set about the task of designing it with the same much-proclaimed vigour as a new town corporation, and implicitly with the same social aims (e.g. social balance, self-containment) and design parameters (e.g. pedestrian segregation). The new towns, however, were directly financed and controlled in their policies (for industrial relocation and housing allocation, for example) by central government[1] whereas despite its considerable dependence on Whitehall grants and subsidies, Thamesmead was not. It could be argued that Thamesmead should have been given a special area, a special status, and a separate agency to run it, but this probably would have complicated the practical problems of co-ordination and implementation while separating the scheme even more widely from the control of the metropolitan and local planning agencies.

The new-town image was translated into a design, but a design which was not influenced by vital metropolitan and regional considerations of homes, workplaces and transport, or by the design needs of an internal transport system. In fact, the GLC's concepts about these fundamental relationships were vague, not surprisingly perhaps when it is realised that they had few powers to ensure that jobs, housing and transport were in balance; they had to rely on any residual impetus after the central government's priorities had been satisfied. This points to the possibility of similar problems on an even larger scale in the docklands redevelopment.

Section 3 on rail commuting proved the need to take a regional view, particularly in BR's case, and emphasised the parochial view taken by the GLC, which added to its contemporary problems, for example over the new station. A broader and longer-term view might have clarified the situation, while the postponement of the target date and the lowering of densities may have eased this particular problem but have added to uncertainties over traffic generation and modal split generally.

The river-crossing issue also had regional implications, and raised the question of what financial responsibility central and local government should bear for such large projects. It also demonstrated how the GLC could effectively put political pressure on central government when the latter was committed to solving housing problems as a high priority; to have approved the bridge would have reduced the amount of housing and prolonged the time-scale of the project.

The engineers took over the detailed design work for Thamesmead's internal transport system where the architects left off, each working to their own sets of criteria, resulting in difficulties for public transport in particular. The passivity of LT and the institutional separation of the

[1] See Major-General A C Duff (1961), *Britain's New Towns*.

operators, combined to virtually exclude them from all three stages of the design process (civic design, programming and working drawings, and estate management) through which Thamesmead has passed.

Relationships between the boroughs and the GLC have been strained: Bexley and Greenwich were worried about the encroachment that Thamesmead's needs for personal health and education services would make upon their own priorities, and about the extra burden of cost that would fall on them after taking over roads, cycleways and open spaces. Differences about the relationships of the three town centres and their road access and about the Crossness Sewage Works seemed to have been largely settled until the 1971–72 reappraisal, but worries about the practical problems of 'integration' with the rest of the boroughs remain. The delays that so frustrated the GLC as promoters of Thamesmead did not bother borough officials so greatly: as one put it, 'there will be problems enough once the people start to arrive.'

As far as provision for bus services was concerned what seems strange is that after Messrs Churchill and Ellen of LT had established a good contact with Mr Rookwood, the LCC Architect's planner in charge of the 'town on stilts' scheme, this understanding should have waned so badly during the preparation of the basic designs for Thamesmead. In fact none of the traditional new towns had an outstanding record of planning for public transport, and the LCC have some notable failures to co-operate (e.g. in not providing for any bus stands, lay-bys or turn-rounds on the much-praised Roehampton Estate) but these had mainly been overcome by this time.[1]

In fact the personal and institutional contact was broken: Mr Rookwood was seconded to the Covent Garden study when the GLC succeeded the LCC and initially the planning of Thamesmead was put under the Architect to the GLC rather than the Chief Planner, perhaps indicating that it was seen as the implementation of an unusually large civic design project. What is certain is that during that time the bus operators missed an opportunity to influence the basic housing design on the broad scale: when it was revised a bus system was feasible but certainly not optimal. LT officers still hope to influence the detailed design of each phase, but seem resigned to occupying the residual role allocated to them by the architects and engineers.

LT had not thought seriously of any real bus innovations in terms of either of route or junction priorities or of flexible systems like dial-a-bus. Surely this was a situation where, if anywhere, the LT Board could have pressed for a grant from the GLC and MOT for a demonstration project. Experimentation seemed an alien concept to 55 Broadway.[2] The limit of the LT Board's ambitions seems to have been the one-man operated bus with automated fare collection. The prime example of planning for public

[1] The *Guardian*, 9 January 1967.

[2] Although LT later agreed to run some experimental minibuses in other parts of London with a GLC subsidy, GLC *Minutes*, 9 May 1972, pp222–3.

transport based on current rather than 'futuristic' technology in the current series of new towns is that of Runcorn, which has been designed around its bus system which will run on a segregated figure-of-eight bus-only route. The close relationship holds from the general level (relationship of the town centre, industrial and housing areas) to the smallest details (individual housing layouts and footpaths in relation to bus stops, the busway elevated to meet the main shopping level on the first floor in the town centre).[1]

The GLC–central government relationship was mainly centred on financial matters once the Master Plan was approved. Having obtained agreement to the development in the first place, the GLC was successful in persuading the Government to pay for the increasingly expensive housing and for major projects of value to London as a whole (such as the river crossing). They had increasing difficulty over the housing, however, having to reduce design standards and density.[2] In all these negotiations the political channels were the ultimate ones and were often resorted to, and the personalities of Ministers and senior GLC members were significant.

The links between the GLC and BR, LT and the Port of London Authority tended to be at official level and were much less effective; in fact, it could reasonably be said that in the whole nexus of planning relationships, transport suffered the most, being left as a technicality to be solved by the GLC's engineers. The transport operators were not involved during the critical early days of the planning process and were consulted only belatedly. After the 1967 reorganisation they were still not represented on the steering groups and so their influence on the scheme has been small and *post-hoc*. LT and BR were in a better position to negotiate after the 1969 Act through the Greater London Transport Group, but this came rather late in the day.

The GLC, despite its monolithic appearance, has so many departments and functions that even when organised to co-ordinate on a single scheme, differences are bound to arise as they did over the provision for buses, cycleways and the bridge–tunnel issue.

The last point here concerns the GLC as a 'regional body,' since this is how it has frequently described itself in policy statements. In the preparation of the plan for Thamesmead, as in that for Greater London, the basic parameters were of jobs, housing and transport, but instruments for their control were not defined. Priorities for relocating employers and workers were announced in 1967[3] but they were meaningless without an indication of how each was expected to contribute to the scheme, or how they ranked for priority against national policies of regional development. As far as statutory controls like ODP's were concerned it became clear that the Board of Trade considered Thamesmead less important than other new

[1] Runcorn Development Corporation (1971), 'Runcorn Busway, and Runcorn Shopping Centre ' *Architect's Journal*, 21 June 1972, pp1371–92.
[2] The *Guardian*, 22 August 1970; *The Times*, 12 February 1971; and *Evening Standard*, 25 August 1971.
[3] GLC *Minutes*, 4 July 1967, pp434–5.

towns and development areas. Indeed, after approving the *Strategic Plan for the South-East* in 1971, it became clear that Thamesmead and similar GLC priority areas for development came fifth after Development Areas; 'Grey' areas; new towns and the Strategic Plan's 'growth' areas.[1]

What, then, could be done? First, the GLC should settle the overriding question of finance. The GLC's attitude was that 'the Government knew it was expensive when the land was made available . . . they should accept it as part of the housing problem or leave it' (Mr Craig on day 8 of the public inquiry). Mr Forbes-Cockell emphasised that 'Thamesmead is a difficult site which no one in his right mind would use if it were not for housing need; and one should not have to apply yardsticks.'[2] More recently Maurice Ash has said: 'It is its siting that brings Thamesmead into question: its lack of relationship to employment, its inadequate transport links and its social isolation. But to question the siting is to question the concept.'[3] Concern over the financing of Thamesmead led Mr Wellbeloved, MP for Erith and Crayford, to call for an inquiry in the House of Commons and, together with the reappraisal, threatened to make Thamesmead the subject of party politics within the GLC as it had never been before.[4]

The principles on which money will be allocated to this expensive housing scheme must be decided as a prerequisite to settling the GLC's priorities for moving jobs and workers to Thamesmead. Solving this second problem requires some knowledge of the sort of jobs and people that one desires to accept in the scheme or that are being displaced elsewhere, and preferably both. Ensuring that the desired pattern of immigration takes place may mean increasing incentives at Thamesmead through housing subsidies or lower ground rents for private developers (which were rumoured to be under consideration in mid-1972) or a better system of promotion and selection in areas of redevelopment. This would require some change in form or function of the Industrial Selection Scheme or the GLC Valuer's Department's Industrial Centre.

A third step would be for the GLC to come to some reasoned view as to the desirable division of housing and commercial development between the public and private sectors, its form and its needs.

The trials and tribulations of Thamesmead in conception and practice have, not surprisingly, attracted a good deal of adverse criticism including a sardonic comment from *Private Eye*.[5] The scheme has proceeded, despite shortcomings of the institutional framework, due in large part to the commitment of both the politicians and the professionals involved. There is still time for major changes in its final physical and social form and it is to be hoped that the transport implications of any changes, whether internally or in its links with the rest of the city, will be better handled in the future than hitherto.

[1] DOE *Press Release 234*, 12 October 1971. [2] *The Times*, 12 February 1971.
[3] M Ash (1972), *A Guide to the Structure of London*, p73.
[4] *The Times*, 29 July 1971; and GLC *Minutes*, 18 July 1971, p234.
[5] 'Nooks and Corners', *Private Eye*, 5 November 1972, No.258.

Case Study B

STAGGERING OF WORKING HOURS

INTRODUCTION: THE PROBLEM OF THE PEAK

Journeys to work comprise a large proportion of the total trips made in urban areas; in London the figure was 47.5% in 1962.[1] Because of uniformity of working hours, they are concentrated into two periods of the day (roughly 0830–1000 and 1630–1830 hours). This peaking of demand for transport facilities imposes great economic costs on transport operators and great stress and social costs on the community as a whole.

First, and most important, the problem is one of dissatisfaction among those who cannot easily avoid the most congested times and have to suffer overcrowded and uncomfortable travelling conditions on both the roads and railways each morning and evening. Journeys by road in particular are often slow and unpredictable. The frustrations of the journey to work are a serious disadvantage of life in big cities, and London is certainly no exception.

Second, business efficiency is inevitably affected and employers suffer when they cannot rely on the punctual arrival of their staff.

Third, the peaking of travel demand creates serious economic difficulties for transport operators. A large proportion of the manpower, rolling stock and fixed equipment employed by both British Rail (BR) and London Transport (LT) is fully utilised only during the peak hours, and lies idle at

	TRAINS	CARS
1 Peak period (a.m.)	480	3464
2 Mid-day	272	1821
3 Peak period (p.m.)	482	3476
4 Evening	217	1497
5 2 as a percentage of 3	57	52
6 4 as a percentage of 3	45	43

Table 11 ESTIMATED USE OF LT RAIL ROLLING STOCK AT DIFFERENT TIMES

Note: as 5 and 6 show, some trains are operated with fewer cars in the off-peak periods.

Source: Interviews with LT officers, January 1971 (see also Table 43).

[1] GLC (1969), *GLDP Report of Studies*, figure 6.15.

other times. For example, on the LT rail system the number of trains in service is often no more than half the number required to meet peak hour demand (see Table 11).

In London, peak-hour travel problems have been intensified over the years as homes and work places have become more separated. Housing in central London has been displaced by the expansion of commercial activities and the workforce has progressively moved to the outer suburbs and beyond the Green Belt. The 1966 census showed that of 1.3 million people employed in the statistical central area, only 8% lived there. The majority commuted from inner and outer London (40% and 36% respectively), the rest came from outside Greater London.[1] In addition, there has been a continuing movement towards shorter and more uniform working hours, aided by the decline in manufacturing and the growth of office and service trades in central London.

Figure 7 shows the morning and evening concentrations of trips on the

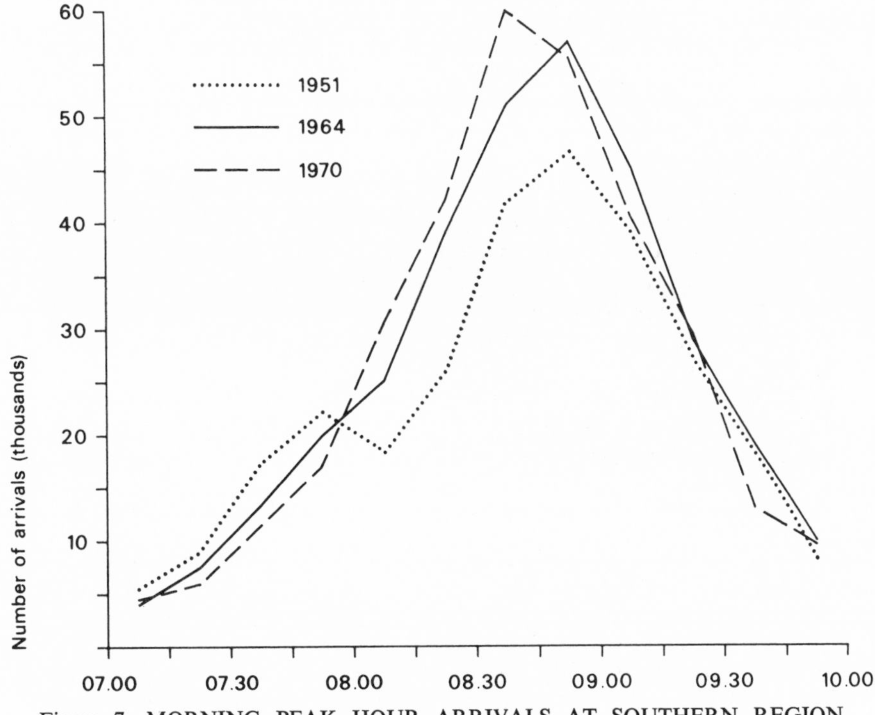

Figure 7 MORNING PEAK HOUR ARRIVALS AT SOUTHERN REGION TERMINI, 1951–70

[1] South-East Joint Planning Team (1970), *Strategic Plan for the South-East*, p12.

Southern Region commuter lines of BR, and also how the peak sharpened between 1951 and 1970.

Peak-hour travel problems may be ameliorated in three ways: by relocating activities, particularly homes and workplaces, to gain a more even spread of demand for transport facilities; by providing extra capacity on the transport system; and by creating a wider diversity in the times people make their journeys, particularly work journeys. The first of these requires the rigorous application of planning controls designed specifically to improve the relationship between land use and transport facilities, and can only produce large-scale improvements in the long term. The second alternative of providing more transport capacity is also, because of the scale of investment required, unlikely to produce widespread benefits in the short term and may need subsidies if it fails to produce a good return to the transport operator.

The third alternative, that of staggering work, shopping, school and other hours, to spread the peak demands for travel, is capable, in theory at least, of giving more immediate benefits. Consequently, the concept of staggered hours has attracted a great deal of attention and it has been advocated with a regularity no less remarkable than the lack of any great success in putting it into practice.

Implementation of staggered hours inevitably involves (or could involve) a wide range of interests and institutions. First, there are the employers whose business may be affected and who are responsible for the organisation of staff hours. Second, there are the public transport operators—BR and LT—who have a powerful financial incentive to act or at least co-operate. Third, both central government and the Greater London Council (GLC) are concerned with the efficient use of road and rail transport facilities and can provide the resources to promote and support any comprehensive scheme for staggered hours. Fourth, staggered working hours involves the travelling public as a whole whose interests may be represented by trade unions and other organisations such as commuter associations and parent–teacher associations.

This case study looks at the way in which various attempts to introduce staggered hours in London, both on a wide scale and in particular localities have been handled.

COMPREHENSIVE SCHEMES

In 1969, Mr Richard Marsh, then Minister of Transport, told the House of Commons that 'the question of staggered working hours to reduce peak hour congestion has been studied on and off for about fifty years.'[1] Certainly as early as 1938, both the London and Home Counties Traffic Advisory Committee (LHCTAC) and the London Passenger Transport Board (LPTB) had specifically urged that action should be taken.[2] The

[1] *House of Commons Debates*, 3 February 1969, cols25–6.

[2] LHCTAC *Annual Report to Ministry of Transport* (January 1938); *The Times* 11 January 1938; LPTB statement in *The Times*, 12 January 1938.

first real impetus, however, was a comprehensive scheme drawn up in the early years of the Second World War by the Board of Trade (London and South-Eastern Regional Board), for maintaining, co-ordinating and protecting armament production. As part of this plan, local transport groups were set up for fifty-five districts within the metropolitan area, each concerned with a number of factories to ensure smooth shift working and a spreading of the traffic burden on the attenuated public transport system. Although the scheme concentrated on industrial jobs in the outer areas of London, by the end of the War 600 000 people were working staggered hours to fit in with the capacity of the public transport system. The scheme was heralded as a success, bringing benefits to both workers and transport undertakings, and in 1945 both the Regional Board and representatives of the local transport groups were anxious to see the arrangements maintained and extended in peacetime, an objective shared also by the LPTB and the four major railway companies.[1] The local transport groups have continued to function and LT recorded in 1962 that a total of sixty-eight were active, covering 1000 establishments and 700 000 workers. The number of active groups had, however, dropped to forty-one by 1971.[2]

Whatever the achievements of the local transport groups, it was soon recognised that the introduction of staggered hours in central London posed a special problem. The Railway (London Plan) Committee reported in 1946, for example, that there had been:

> a progressively greater concentration of traffic movement into the peak hours brought about by the shortening of working hours and their greater standardisation. Staggering of working hours on a really effective basis has not hitherto proved acceptable in the inner zone, and it must be admitted that the prospect of securing material relief by breaking down peak-hour concentrations is not encouraging.[3]

However, as Sargeant has pointed out, in 1946 the public transport operators had 'little option but to try and eke out the existing resources in trying to provide for the return to peacetime activity in central London.' Urged by the LPTB, the Minister of Transport took up the challenge of promoting staggered hours and, having gained considerable support from trade unions and commercial federations, embarked on a campaign to devise and implement proposals.[4]

Fourteen districts were defined, for each of which a committee was appointed to collect data on the numbers of employees and the hours worked. The LPTB then used this information to draw up district plans for

[1] Conference held 27 February 1945 attended by representatives from L & SE Regional Board, LPTB and the major railway companies (LMS, LNER, SR, GWR).

[2] See P W Sargeant (1971), 'Staggering of Hours in Relation to Town Planning,' thesis submitted to University College, London, for Diploma in Town Planning.

[3] Railway (London Plan) Committee (1946), *Report to Ministry of War Transport.*

[4] Sargeant (1971), p48.

staggered hours, and sought the co-operation of employers to put them into effect.

The objective was to remove 120 000 (20%) travellers from the 5 to 6 p.m. peak period and to achieve a more even spread between 4.30 and 6.30 p.m.[1] Initially, at least, progress was made and by the end of 1947 94 000 people (including 22 000 civil servants) were working hours specifically designed to fit in with the LPTB's plans. It is unlikely, however, that any noticeable improvement was made in peak-hour travelling because progress was overtaken by other factors: in 1947 alone, the number of workers in central London was estimated to have increased by well over 100 000; in addition, greater uniformity of hours resulted from the widespread adoption of a five-day week and shorter working day.[2]

The campaign continued in 1948 and achieved a total of about 138 000 participants, including 74 000 diverted out of the 5 to 6 p.m. period. But although the Minister of Transport made further suggestions, such as later closing times for West End shops and alteration of theatre hours, the campaign appeared to have run out of steam by the end of 1948. Moreover, while the results achieved were significant in terms of the original objectives, the two-year campaign secured the participation of a small number of people compared with the wartime schemes in outer London.

Interest was revived by the Committee of Inquiry into LT in 1955, which asserted that the staggering of working hours could 'do more than anything else to get rid of the acute discomfort of travel on the railways in the morning and evening and would do it more economically than any of the other very costly alternatives which have been suggested.'[3]

The Ministry of Transport (MOT) at about the same time asked the Transport Users' Consultative Committee to examine ways of introducing staggered hours. The Committee carried out some pilot projects (involving about 7000 government and privately employed staff in central London), and in 1956 recommended the MOT to conduct a full-scale campaign. The Ministry responded with the appointment in the same year of the Committee for Staggering of Working Hours in Central London.[4]

The Committee embarked on a similar campaign to that of 1947, by setting up six inner zones (covering 8½ square miles), and appealing to firms within these areas to adjust their hours of work. But progress was slower than in 1947. After one year's work the Committee stated that it had secured adjusted working hours for 21 419 people and another report stated that this had grown to only 25 000 after a further year.[5] The Com-

[1] Conference held by the Ministry of Transport (MOT) on 19 November 1946, attended by local authorities, chambers of commerce, business firms, trade unions and the LPTB.
[2] *The Times*, 8 April 1948.
[3] Report of Committee of Inquiry on LT to MOT (February 1955), quoted in *Crush Hour Travel in Central London*, MOT and Local Authorities, HMSO 1958, p41.
[4] This committee included representatives of employers and employees in central London, the local authorities, the Transport Users' Consultative Committee for London and the British Transport Commission.
[5] *Crush Hour Committee Report* (1958), p15; *The Times*, 24 October 1958.

mittee ceased effective operation in 1964, by which time a total of 60 000 staff were said to be involved in hours adjusted by its efforts.[1] Again, in relation to the total volume of commuter movement (over a million people to and from central London in 1956 within the hours 7–10 a.m. and 4.30–7 p.m.) the rewards from the Committee's efforts were not very great.[2]

It is difficult to say how many people are now working hours that were fixed as a result of conscious efforts to relieve peak-hour travel. The effects of the 1947 and 1956 campaigns, for example, were probably not cumulative since the same firms could have co-operated on both occasions. Moreover, since no continued efforts were made to monitor the schemes, there is no indication as to whether employers have maintained the agreed hours. Even more difficult to assess is whether the hours that were agreed as part of the staggering plans are still relevant in terms of present day peak-hour travel conditions. Many factors could have significantly altered the location and the timing of the heaviest peaks, for example the opening of the Victoria Line or the growth of office jobs at the expense of manufacturing jobs.

Whether or not the comprehensive schemes discussed produced any lasting benefits, large concentrations of employment have continued to pose considerable transport problems, and conscious efforts have been made by individual employers to alleviate the situation in particular localities. The next section of this study describes efforts made by one private company, Shell International Petroleum, and by the public sector in London to introduce staggered hours.

LOCAL SCHEMES—THE EXAMPLE OF SHELL

Shell International Petroleum was one of the first large firms to respond to the Committee for Staggered Hours' campaign in 1956. The second-in-command of Shell's Estates and General Services Division, Mr G H Harris, was appointed chairman of the committee for one of the six central zones set up by the Committee, and his direct involvement in the campaign established a continuing interest in staff travel at Shell. The firm was located in thirty-eight separate offices in the City of London, employing 5000 people whose hours were subject to a scheme of staggered hours in their particular zones. Prior to the scheme, the majority of the staff worked uniform hours.

A need (and an opportunity) for a further rearrangement of working-hours presented itself in 1961 with the concentration of operations at Shell Centre, a single new building on the south bank of the Thames, almost adjacent and linked to Waterloo station. The Estates and General Services Division, which was briefed in 1959–60 to make all the necessary arrangements to ensure a smooth transfer, was anxious to discover two facts: whether, on balance, the Centre would represent a more or a less con-

[1] MOT (1969), unpublished internal document.
[2] *Crush Hour Committee Report* (1958), p6.

venient location than the previous offices from the point of view of staff travel, and whether times of starting and finishing work might be adjusted to minimise the impact on travel facilities of such a large concentration of workers.

In order to establish facts from which the most convenient working hours could be derived, a survey was conducted amongst employees in November 1960 before the move began. Mr Harris was largely responsible for the survey which established place of residence, mode of travel to work and journey times of the majority of the staff, and was the basis for deciding the hours of work in the new building. After the transfer to Shell Centre was completed and the new arrangements had had a chance to settle down, it was thought that some employees might have changed their place of residence and journey to work arrangements. A follow-up survey was conducted in 1964, again under the supervision of Mr Harris.

The move from their City offices to the South Bank was bound to inconvenience some employees, such as those commuting from the north-east, whilst benefiting those from the south and south-west, but the 1964 survey showed that on balance there had been a general improvement in terms of employee's travel convenience. For example, in 1960 (before the move to Shell Centre) only 14% of staff could leave home after 8 a.m. and arrive on time whereas 45% were able to do so by 1965. Nevertheless, the survey indicated the possibility of further improvement and to this end working hours were further adjusted.

The Shell Centre continues to operate with a measure of staggered hours, 57% of the staff working from 9.05 a.m. to 5.20 p.m. (introduced 1960) and 35% from 8.40 a.m. to 4.55 p.m. (introduced 1964). Although these hours do not give wide variation from the most congested times for travel on public transport (around 9 a.m. and 5.30 p.m.) they are generally regarded as having some ameliorative effects on peak-hour travel while being satisfactory from the point of view of the staff themselves. A further benefit is that now that the management have data on travel patterns, they are able to warn their staff of rail delays. Similarly, it has been possible to improve emergency transport arrangements for use in the event of strikes or other interruptions to public transport services.

The interest shown by Mr Harris in the relationship between working hours and peak travel problems was undoubtedly a most important factor in Shell's adoption of staggered hours. While it was the objective of the 1947 and 1956 campaigns to encourage similar interest and action by other large firms, most had shown only lukewarm interest. This may have been explained by a lack of any real incentive to act, together with a feeling that the peak-hour travel problems of both the employees and the transport operators were outside the employer's responsibility.

LOCAL SCHEMES—THE EXAMPLE OF GOVERNMENT DEPARTMENTS

Gaining the voluntary co-operation of a large number of private companies had presented difficulties to the 1947 and 1956 campaigns in central London, but it was recognised from the start that progress could be easier in dealing with public sector employment. Indeed, nearly one-third of participants in the 1947 scheme were civil servants. Not only did the public sector employ a large number of people under some form of unified management, but it could be expected also to be sympathetic towards the social and economic aims of the staggering idea.

The MOT has arranged its working hours to suit local transport conditions since 1947, when a scheme for its 2000 staff in Berkeley Square was drawn up in consultation with staff representatives and the local transport group for that area.[1] The hours selected at that time were maintained after the Ministry's move in the late 1950s to St Christopher House in Southwark Street SE1. It had first been established, however, after consultation with the Committee for Staggering of Hours in Central London, that the hours would in general be different from those of other workers in the locality, thus creating a degree of staggering. There was no internal staggering of hours, however, and virtually everyone except the top ranking officials worked from 8.30 a.m. to 4.45 p.m. (4.30 Friday). In planning a further move in 1971 to Horseferry Road SW1 the Ministry contacted LT and large firms in the area to ensure that the hours to be worked in the new building would not impose a major burden on the local transport facilities at peak times.

Since 1956 each department of the Civil Service has been requested to stagger working hours as far as business permits to relieve pressure on transport facilities. Working hours in general are subject to discussions with the Whitley Council, but in practice there appears to be a good deal of freedom within individual departments.[2] A degree of staggering exists mostly within the range 8.30 a.m. to 6 p.m. which allows contact with outside offices to be made over this time.

The GLC also staggered working hours for 13 000 of its 36 000 employees of whom between 8000 and 9000 were based at central offices (including County Hall). The hours range from 8.30 to 9.45 in the morning and 4.35 to 5.35 in the evening and are spaced at quarter-hour intervals. As with the Civil Service, there is considerable departmental freedom. Some departments have a single starting and finishing time, while others offer more individual choice.

CONCLUSIONS

The public transport operators, who have a direct financial interest in achieving a more even distribution of travel demand, played an important role in the few attempts that have been made to secure staggered working hours on a wide scale. The LPTB, for example, both urged the MOT to

[1] One of the fourteen groups established by the MOT itself to cover selected areas of central London as the 'grassroots' basis for the 1947 staggering of hours campaign.
[2] *Estacode*, section DA20 (Estacode is the Civil Service code of management practice).

act and played a key part in devising and co-ordinating the 1947 campaign. Although past efforts have not produced noticeably improved peak-hour travel conditions on a large scale, both LT and BR have continued to press for staggered hours (see Case Study *H*).

The MOT responded positively to representations, particularly those of the transport operators, by initiating the 1947 and 1956 campaigns. The Board of Trade also recognised the value of staggered hours as evidenced by their agreement to allow the wartime local transport groups to continue in operation during peacetime. Although many of these groups still exist, they operate mainly outside central London and thus deal with more localised travel problems.

The question arises of whether the success of staggered working hours in central London has been limited by some inadequacy in the way in which the two major campaigns were conducted, or by the inherent difficulties of the problem itself. Both the 1947 and 1956 campaigns, of course, relied on the voluntary co-operation of employers in central London and it may well be that the achievement of staggered hours on a greater scale would require the introduction of financial incentives or legislative measures. But it seems fairly clear that the MOT and the public transport operators were keen to do all that could be done using exhortative methods. Given that constraint, the experience of the two central London compaigns indicated that the difficulties of introducing staggered hours on a large scale were disproportionately great in relation to the benefits which could be achieved.

Other towns and cities have made various attempts to stagger working hours including (as cities of comparable size to London) Tokyo and New York. The Japan National Railways reported that in 1969 more than a million people were working staggered hours in the Tokyo area involving 192 government and public offices, 1650 industrial organisations and 566 schools.[1] It seems unlikely, however, that this situation was achieved through the application of a positive staggered hours policy and it has certainly made no noticeable impact on Tokyo's appalling peak-hour travel conditions.

An experiment by the Port of New York Authority in 1969 to stagger the hours of 2500 headquarters staff succeeded in making their journey to work less arduous and in reducing overcrowding on the Authority's building's lifts. This success lead the Authority to adopt the new hours on a permanent basis and to co-operate with the Downtown–Lower Manhattan Association in an experiment aimed at staggering the working hours of 100 000 people in the lower Manhattan district. By 1971 it had altered the working times of 60 000 people working in about seventy private firms and public agencies from the normal 9 a.m.–5 p.m. to 8.30 a.m.–4.30 p.m. This experiment apparently succeeded in reducing the rush at peak times on some of the commuter lines. Compared with central London, however, there was a greater degree of uniformity of working

[1] Japan National Railways (1971), *Urban Rail Transport*, table 11.

hours in Manhattan; it was estimated that 65% worked from 9 a.m.–5 p.m.[1]

The speed with which the New York experiment achieved 60 000 participants (one year as opposed to eight years to achieve the same number in central London) suggests that more could be achieved in London. The problem may well depend on the effectiveness of a simple staggering operation such as that applied in New York, but the diversity of employment, location and the pattern of railways and surface transport in central London may require more complex arrangements.

There is inevitably a large amount of work involved in collecting detailed data from a large number of employers on hours of work and the capacity and use of transport facilities, and collating this information to prepare a scheme of adjusted hours which would ease congestion. Moreover, having achieved the implementation of the scheme, continued co-operation with employers is necessary to ensure that hours are only altered by agreement to take account of changes in land use, employment or transport facilities.

It appears, then, that the wider implementation of staggered hours has been limited more by practical difficulties involved than by any obvious inadequacy in the institutional machinery. In 1969 Mr Richard Marsh said in reply to a request for further action to secure staggered hours in London, that experience had shown that peak-hour congestion was best tackled on a local rather than a city-wide basis.[2] The GLC felt that little more could be achieved in terms of persuasion but that fares incentives might bring pressure from employees for staggered hours.[3]

Without the application of financial incentives or legislative action, however, efforts made by individual employers may produce better travelling conditions in particular localities. The Shell Centre example has shown what can be done in the private sector, although the presence of someone with sufficient interest, such as Mr Harris, would seem to be a prerequisite. Public sector employment in London has also, by operating fairly flexible working hours, enabled staff to make a choice of several starting and finishing times. Perhaps the answer in both the public and private sectors is to try to strike the right balance between operational needs and freedom of choice for individual members of staff.

Finally, the recurrent appeals for staggered working hours, despite the difficulties which have been experienced in implementing them on a wide scale, perhaps indicate that London's peak-hour travel problems can only really be ameliorated by much more far reaching or expensive solutions which the various governmental bodies have been reluctant to undertake. As Leipmann said in 1944 'the excessive costs and hardships of daily travel can be taken as a symptom that something is wrong with the form of the town or conurbation.'[4]

1 Downtown–Lower Manhattan Association and The Port of New York Authority (1971), *Staggered Work Hours in Lower Manhattan—First Anniversary Report.*

2 *House of Commons Debates*, 3 February 1969, cols25–6.

3 Letter received from GLC dated 3 May 1971.

4 K Leipmann (1944), *The Journey to Work.*

Case Study C

NEW TUBE RAILWAYS IN LONDON

1 INTRODUCTION AND BACKGROUND

When the Victoria Line was opened in 1969 it was widely acclaimed as the first new tube railway in central London for sixty-two years and a great technological breakthrough with its automatic train operation and its new methods of tube construction. Professor Theo Barker, writing in 1966, suggested that two great phases of railway building had solved previous crises in London's transport system:[1] that of the 1860s which extended the main lines to their major termini, established the framework for the southern suburban lines, provided the North London Line, and began the Inner Circle at a time when London threatened to jam solid with horse-drawn vehicles; and that of the 1890s when not only the central streets were again congested, but also the surface railways, and this time the solution was a network of deep-level tubes. He said that in the 1950s there was a similar crisis when road congestion (this time through motor vehicles) and increasing long-distance commuting combined to produce major distribution problems in the central and inner city.

Yet, he argued, only the Victoria Line had been approved and was being built. 'Why is it,' he asked, 'that a population half as large again as that of 1900 and well over twice as wealthy has not contrived to afford anything like what was then achieved.' He attributed this partly to 'a mistaken belief that the motor-car might come to the rescue' and partly to London Transport's (LT) subordinate position within the British Transport Commission (BTC). He still questioned, however, why LT had not found other means of lobbying for support (e.g. via MPs and councillors) and, even more strongly, why more had not been achieved since 1963 with direct access to the Ministry of Transport (MOT) and a new Board of management.

In the years since Professor Barker made these remarks, the Brixton extension of the Victoria Line was built and opened, while by 1972 the extension of the Piccadilly Line to Heathrow and the first stage of the Fleet Line had been approved and construction was proceeding. Means of grant-aiding the capital costs of these lines were found even though the expected financial return was only marginally or no better than those on lines built in the 1860s, 1890s and 1900s. Other projects were being discussed. How had this change come about, compared with the painful gestation of the Victoria Line which was substantively proposed in 1946,

[1] T C Barker, 'London's Third Traffic Crisis,' *New Society*, 3 December 1966, pp15–16.

received parliamentary powers in 1955, was not authorised to proceed until 1962, and then took seven years to complete? What was the role of the main bodies involved, particularly the Greater London Council (GLC) with its new powers as controller of LT plans and finances instead of the MOT,[1] and transportation authority for London since 1970? How did LT respond to such direct democratic control? Did this make any difference to the preparation and assessment of new tube schemes? As it sought to expand its network what were LT's relationships with British Rail (BR), the other railway operator, and with the London boroughs as local planning and highway authorities? How did the Department of the Environment (DOE) exercise its power as author of national transport policies and authoriser of grants towards capital works?[2] What co-ordinating machinery linked these institutions together, and how did the Greater London Transport Group (GLTG), the major of these bodies, function?

This study investigates some of these questions with reference to the new and proposed lines (except for the Heathrow link which is covered separately in Case Study *E*). Section 2 examines the main section of the Victoria Line, section 3 its extension to Brixton, section 4 the Fleet Line, and section 5 other proposals and the question of orbital lines. A brief resumé of the major plans and reports will help to give an historical perspective to these schemes.

The London Passenger Transport Board, after its formation in 1933 to take over all the underground railways (except the Southern Railway's Waterloo and City Line), combined with the Great Western and London and North Eastern Railways to propose the 1935–40 New Works Programme, or '£40 million plan,' to extend the underground system and to electrify suburban lines (see Chapter 1, pages 35–37). Of the extensive works proposed, some were only partly completed by the beginning of the Second World War, some were completed after the War, some modified, and some abandoned. Forshaw and Abercrombie's plan for the London County Council (LCC) in 1943 and Abercrombie's Greater London Plan in 1944 stressed the vital role of railways in London but also pointed out that many railway works and installations in the central area were obstacles to good land-use planning. They proposed that many lines and some termini should be put underground and that central BR terminals should be linked up.

In 1944 the Minister of Transport set up a special committee chaired by Professor Sir Charles Inglis to investigate the technical and operational aspects of the Forshaw and Abercrombie proposals but in their report in 1946[3] they could not agree with most of the individual schemes and put forward their own proposals for tube and main-line railways. When the BTC was formed in 1948 the Minister of Transport, Alfred Barnes, agreed that it should have the opportunity to review these proposals and a com-

[1] *Transport (London) Act 1969*, ch35.
[2] *Transport Act 1968*, ch73, s56.
[3] MOT (1946), *The Railway (London Plan) Committee*, Final Report.

mittee headed by the chairman of the Commission set up a working party chaired by V M (later Sir Michael) Barrington-Ward, a member of the BR Executive. This recommended in 1949 a series of improvements to both the BR and LT networks.[1]

The LCC's development plan and review incorporated these proposals, showing what had been achieved (mainly by BR).[2] Meanwhile in 1955 a special committee of inquiry into LT (the Chambers Committee) had specifically recommended the construction of one of them—Route *C*—similar to the present Victoria Line.[3]

Ten years later in 1965 the Select Committee on Nationalised Industries[4] surveyed LT (by this time directly responsible via a Board to the MOT) and critically examined the progress of the Victoria Line and other schemes (see section 2). Also in 1965 the GLC became metropolitan planning authority. Phases I and II of the London Traffic Survey were complete and it was decided to widen Phase III to include an examination of public transport. About the same time LT and BR had combined through their co-ordinating body, the Passenger Transport Committee for London, to produce a Railway Plan for London which the Permanent Secretary to the MOT described as 'a preliminary first sketch . . . no more than half baked and not ready for publication.' The Select Committee found this attitude 'regrettable' and thought that LT's views were 'defined clearly enough to warrant publication.'[5]

The Select Committee believed that LT could meet both of its statutory obligations (to provide an adequate service and pay its way) provided it was accepted that (amongst other things):

> So far as the construction of underground lines, such as the Victoria Line, and other capital schemes are justified by calculations of social benefit, wider than the benefits they will produce for London Transport, these costs should not have to be borne by the Board.

Also they argued:

> London Transport need more automated equipment, especially on the railways . . . and, above all, more underground railways to match the increasing pressure of peak-hour commuter traffic.[6]

When the report was debated in the House of Commons in December 1965

[1] BTC (1949), London Plan Working Party: *Report to MOT*, HMSO
[2] LCC (1951), *Development Plan Analysis*, pp165–73, and (1960), *First Review*, pp77–80.
[3] *Special Committee of Inquiry into London Transport* (1955).
[4] Select Committee on Nationalised Industries, *London Transport HC Papers 313*, and *313-I* of 1965.
[5] BR Board/LT Board (1965), *A Railway Plan for London*. Although never published, it was circulated to local authorities and other interested bodies for discussion. The references to the Select Committee are *Report* (1965), paras462, 480, 481; and QQ1591–5.
[6] *Sel Comm LT* (1965), pp147–8.

the Minister announced that the Government would take measures to ensure that public transport in London was improved and that a 'more equitable' means of financing all forms of transport was needed.

In 1966 LT made a loss of £11 million and the Joint Review[1] forecast a continuing loss of £12 million annually, which could only be overcome by either allowing fares increases or undertaking a capital reconstruction. In fact fare increases were postponed or reduced by revenue deficit subsidies from the central government which amounted to £5.9 million in 1966; £10.9 million in 1967; £9.9 million in 1968 and £10.7 million in 1969. The introduction of infrastructure grants in 1968 (sections 3 and 4), was followed by a capital reconstruction when LT was transferred to the GLC.[2]

The 1965 'Railway Plan' schemes and ideas for tube lines to link up the central BR termini were included in the tests of alternative transport networks in Phase III of the London Transportation Study but the consultants' view was basically that 'London's railway system fulfils its traffic requirements very well.'[3] The Study has been criticised on the grounds that the public transport survey data were inadequate, that the projections of demand were biased to car usage, and that the computer model which simulated the distribution of public transport traffic was inadequately developed compared with the road traffic model.

In the Greater London Development Plan (GLDP) Written Statement, however, the GLC broadly accepted their consultants' view (paragraph 5.3):

> The present rail system is well suited to its essential function of carrying workers to the vital central area. The underground railways also provide a key distribution service in that crowded hub of activity. The general scale of demand which the trains can serve will not be significantly increased in future and there is little need for new railways on a large scale outside central London. But the railways must remain competitive in a changing world and the Council's objective is that the rail system must develop and improve to provide higher levels of service.

The tube proposals were mentioned in a single paragraph.[4] The GLC's early evidence to the GLDP Inquiry embodied LT and BR schemes which had been 'suggested' as a 'first appraisal' (with regard to LT) and a 'broad indication' of how money would be spent between 1971 and 1991.[5]

LT's evidence to the GLDP Inquiry mentioned the Fleet Line (see section 4), the Hainault–Wimbledon Line, and possible extensions of the Bakerloo and Victoria lines (see section 5). LT wrote (paragraph 13):

[1] 'Joint Review of LT' printed in *Transport in London*, Cmnd 3686, 1969, pp33, 69–70.
[2] *LT Annual Reports and Accounts*, 1967–69, table BS6.
[3] Freeman Fox, Wilbur Smith and Associates for GLC (1968), *London Transportation Study Phase III*. The quotation is from paragraph 21/130.
[4] GLC (1969), *GLDP Statement*, para5.51.
[5] GLC (1970) *Proof of Evidence, E12/1*, ch4, paras4.4.3, 4.4.7, 4.4.10. GLDP Inquiry Stage 1.

> The proposals for extension of the underground are designed to improve personal mobility in London *by filling gaps in the present system*, give relief to overcrowded sections of existing lines, and bring the benefits of underground railway facilities to areas not yet enjoying them. The proposals will thus further the aims of the GLDP in *maintaining the dynamism of central London* and in *revitalising inner suburban areas*. [our italics].

LT suggested a rail investment programme of £525 million of which £250 million would be spent on new tubes (see Table 12).[1] The GLC had already endorsed the Fleet Line (after discussions in GLTG, see section 3) and the Heathrow and BR south-eastern approaches schemes (see case studies *E* and *H*), but commented 'each is important and would improve public transport in London, but none has the major implications for strategy of, say, a new orbital road.'[2]

	1971–80	1981–91	TOTAL 1971–91
Total investment programme for LT railways	290	235	525
Brixton extension (completion)	4	—	4
Fleet Line	88	—	88
Heathrow link	15	—	15
Bakerloo extension	20	3	23
Hainault–Wimbledon Line	—	90	90
Southern extension of Victoria Line	—	30	30
Total for new underground railways	127	123	250

Table 12 INVESTMENT PROGRAMME FOR NEW UNDERGROUND RAILWAYS, 1971–91

Experience of involvement in managing LT in 1970 and 1971, criticisms of the GLDP strategy by objectors (both municipal and voluntary organisations and individuals), and requests by the Inquiry Panel to elucidate the future demand situation for public transport, all contributed to change the GLC's attitudes. They produced a major policy statement on LT's future, increased their capital grants and ratified again the ten-year investment programme,[3] undeterred by the fact that after only one year the

[1] LT (1970), *Proof of Evidence E12/2, Paper S12/56*, GLDP Inquiry Stage 1; and GLC *Minutes*, 9 March 1971, p141–2.
[2] GLC (1970) *E12/1*, para4.4.5. GLDP Inquiry Stage 1.
[3] See *Strategy for London Transport*, GLC *Minutes*, 7 July 1970 and 5 October 1971, p451.

cost of the tube projects had risen to £140 million and of all rail projects to £322 million in the period 1972–80. They also became aware of the need to relate transport and land use more closely (see Case Studies *A* on Thamesmead, *D* on Development at Stations) and conscious of the potential of railways, in particular in reviving areas of the city that were economically depressed and in need of physical redevelopment (see sections 3, 4 and 5 below). These changes were all reflected in a modified version of the Written Statement.[1]

2 THE VICTORIA LINE[2]

The Inglis Committee in 1946 proposed a new tube (Route 8) of main-line size from East Croydon to Finsbury Park via Brixton, Stockwell, Vauxhall, Victoria, Hyde Park Corner, Bond Street, Euston and King's Cross. Except for the more westerly alignment via Bond Street this followed a very similar line to that of the present Victoria Line and the main objectives of this scheme were relevant to the later proposal. These were: improved railway links between Victoria and Oxford Street, a more direct link between Victoria and King's Cross, and relief of the Piccadilly Line between Finsbury Park and King's Cross.

The Barrington–Ward working party reviewed the Inglis schemes in 1948 and produced some new ones of its own, headed by a Route *C* tube from East Croydon to Tottenham; this was to follow a more easterly alignment via Oxford Circus to improve traffic generation. An additional reason given for building the tube was to facilitate interchange with the Eastern and Southern Regions of BR (which was implicit in Inglis's Route 8). The working party also gave high priority to a tube line from BR's Chingford lines via Fleet Street to Victoria (Route *D*). The BTC commented that the schemes suggested were not included in any investment programme and involved 'vast capital expenditure by no means all of which can be represented as directly remunerative or economically justifiable from the angle of transport.' Additional sources of finance would be required.[3]

LT Executive staff began appraisals of Route *C* but were still considering possible variations. For example, in 1951 it was suggested that the line might run from Victoria to Fulham Broadway and incorporate the Wimbledon branch of the District Line.[4] Repeating this suggestion in 1954 Mr L C Hawkins, an Executive member, pointed out that this line also would probably not be financially self-supporting.

The Chambers Committee of Inquiry into London Transport set up in 1953 and reporting in 1955 commented (paragraph 452):

[1] GLC (1972) *GLDP Written Statement* (possible revisions), paras5.4.3, 5.5.4, 5.5.14, 5.9.4, 5.9.6, and Appendix *M*.

[2] This section draws on J R Day (1969), *The Story of the Victoria Line*, London Transport, *passim*.

[3] BTC *First Annual Report*, 1948, pp30–1.

[4] BTC *Fourth Annual Report*, 1951, p3.

> Although the proposed railway may not in the near future pay its way directly we are of the opinion that the indirect advantages to London Transport and to London's economy as a whole are so important that this project should not be abandoned or postponed because on the basis of direct revenue or direct expenditure it appears to be unprofitable. We are particularly concerned with the very heavy expenditure on roads which will be necessary if London's tube railways are unable to cope with passenger traffic effectively. Expenditure on new tube railways may prove to be less costly than expenditure on roads and more effective in moving large numbers of passengers. Adequate tube railways may prove to be a more effective means of relieving traffic congestion than many more controversial and more expensive schemes which have been put forward.

In December 1953 the Minister of Transport had authorised detailed work to begin.[1] He also gave the BTC permission to seek parliamentary powers for the line so that no hold-up should occur if its construction was authorised, and a BTC Act was ratified by the end of 1955. It included some changes to Route *C* in order to include elements of Route *D*, since it had become clear that capital would not be available to do both. These changes were an extension to Walthamstow on the Eastern Region and an interchange at Highbury with the Northern Line. Sir John Elliot, chairman of the LT Executive, christened Route *C* the Victoria Line in December 1955.[2] In the same year the route was commended by the London and Home Counties' Traffic Advisory Committee (LHCTAC):

> We believe that there is an overwhelming case for this scheme which should do much to relieve pressure on the roads in the inner area and those entering London from the north-east and east, and that it will in fact be virtually necessary in the next few years if only to help to maintain the present speed of traffic.[3]

It also recommended that a definite starting date should be set.

In 1956, £500 000 was allocated for experimental tunnelling (later increased to £1 million). It was half a century since the last new tube railway was built and new techniques had to be learned from abroad or developed *in situ*.[4] Boreholes were sunk along the route to test subsoil conditions and interchange designs at BR stations were discussed with BR, but despite questions in Parliament and discussions between the MOT and BTC on problems of financing the line, no progress was forthcoming.

[1] After representations by the BTC, LT Executive and some north London local authorities, see *Sel Comm LT* (1965), app12.

[2] In a paper to the Institute of Transport, 5 December 1965.

[3] LHCTAC (1955), *London's Traffic*.

[4] This exploratory tunnelling was said later to have saved £3 million on the cost of the whole line; see Day (1969).

By the late 1950s strong pressures were building up for improvements to London's transport system: road congestion was rapidly worsening in the central area; central sections of several other tube lines were severely overloaded at peak hours; and several major tube interchanges were in need of modernisation whether the Victoria Line was built or not. LT reported that the project was essential if they were to discharge their statutory duty of providing an adequate service.[1] By the end of the decade LT's chairman, Sir John Elliot, was really 'banging the table' in an attempt to get finance. However, both LT and the 1965 Select Committee said 'as he had to work through the British Transport Commission the sound must have been rather muffled by the time it reached the Ministry.'[2] LT, as a small part of the BTC, felt that its capital programme had been starved because of the overriding concern of the BTC with BR's modernisation and financing.

In answer to a parliamentary question in March 1959 Harold Watkinson, then Minister of Transport, said that the BTC now estimated the cost of the Victoria Line at £55 million and its likely annual loss at £3 million including £2¼ to 2½ million for interest charges.

In February 1959 the London Travel Committee had set up a working party to examine the 'desirability, practicability and economics' of further railway construction, which concentrated on the Victoria Line proposal and reported in May. The report listed the benefits of the line as follows:

a it would provide a new direct link between BR's main-line terminus at Victoria and the West End;
b it would provide a new direct service between Victoria and the northern main-line termini at Euston, King's Cross and St Pancras, and between these northern stations and Oxford Circus;
c it would provide a new direct connection between the north-eastern suburbs of Walthamstow and Tottenham and the West End, and through convenient interchange stations between Enfield, Edmonton, Chingford and the West End;
d it would provide faster travel between various points in central London; halving many existing journey times;
e it would relieve the intense pressure on other lines at peak times; particularly the Central, Piccadilly and District Lines; and
f it would provide easy interchange facilities with other lines (interchange with other tube and BR lines was planned at eleven of the thirteen stations.)[3]

It set out estimates of passenger use including new (generated) traffic and diversions from other tube lines, BR and bus services (see Table 13). The expected cost of the line was £55 million, averaging £9 million annually

[1] BTC *Tenth Annual Report*, 1957, p42.
[2] *Sel Comm LT* (1965), p118, and QQ1504, 1506.
[3] London Travel Committee (1959), *The Victoria Line*, MOT, p10.

			ESTIMATED					ACTUAL		
	1955	1958	(%)	1967	1969	(%)	1969	(%)	1970	(%)
DIVERTED										
from tube and BR			51			55		82		70
from bus and car			19			15		9		8.5
'NEW' TRAFFIC			30			30		9		21.5
Total (million passenger miles p.a.)	242	255		203	169		165		229	

Table 13 ACTUAL AND ESTIMATED VICTORIA LINE TRAFFIC

CAPITAL COST (1959)	(£M)	CURRENT ACCOUNT (1959)	(£M)
Land	2.6	Receipts	+1.94
Tunnels	19.4	Working expenses	−1.34
Stations	17.1		
Equipment and depot	7.4	Net operating profit	+0.60
Plant	4.0	Loss to other tubes	−0.69
		Loss to other buses	−0.54
Total	50.5		
		Total loss on other services	−1.23
Rolling stock	4.5	Savings on other tubes	+0.05
		Savings on other buses	+0.36
GRAND TOTAL	55.0		
		Net gain on other services	+0.41
		Net loss to LT	−0.22
		Net loss to BR	Not known

Table 14 VICTORIA LINE: ESTIMATED CAPITAL COST AND CURRENT ACCOUNT, 1959

over a seven-year planning and construction period, but reaching a peak of £16 million in the fifth year. There was an expected annual operating loss to LT Executive of £219 000 because greater traffic losses than cost savings on other services offset an operating profit on the line itself (Table 14).[1] The working party also examined alternative measures including other tube improvements, building only some sections of the line, doing the most urgent road improvements in London, road improvements along the Victoria Line route, and providing off-street parking. Although no direct economic comparison had been made in terms of value for solving traffic problems, the London Travel Committee was of the opinion that none of these could do the job that the Victoria Line could do, or in the case of the roadworks be built as quickly. The report concluded that the Victoria Line was an essential improvement to the tube network, and a necessary improvement to the whole of London's transport system that 'should be authorised forthwith and construction put in hand as soon as possible.'[2] The scheme was also endorsed by the LCC in the first review of its Development Plan.[3]

Nevertheless there ensued another quiet period. LT continued to work on the scheme and in December 1961 proposed to terminate the line at Hoe Street (now Walthamstow Central) rather than Wood Street (see Figure 8). This change reduced the estimated capital cost by £1.4 million.

[1] There was also, of course, a revenue loss to BR from an estimated reduction of 22 million passenger-miles a year, London Travel Committee ission, 1959, p18.
[2] London Travel Committee (1959), pp23–9.
[3] LCC (1961), *London Plan, First Review Report*, p78.

Revised traffic and financial estimates were submitted in December 1960 and again in April 1962. The Minister finally indicated the Government's approval of the construction of the line in August 1962, and work began immediately on the station works at Oxford Circus.

In 1961 and 1962 two economists, C D Foster and M E Beesley, undertook a study to estimate the social benefit of building the Victoria Line, using LT data. Their preliminary report was sent to the MOT in May 1962 and the full report was presented in a paper later in the year to the Royal Statistical Society.[1] This study is often regarded as the decisive factor in securing the Government's approval, but it came very late in a protracted process and was more in the nature of a clear confirmation of views on the wider needs and benefits of the line. Discussing the study Mr R M Robbins of LT said 'we thought it might come in very handy indeed in hastening the decision,' and Mr P Sheaf of the MOT: 'I would suggest that the calculation will nearly always be a valuable help to decision making even if there are all sorts of difficulties and reservations about it.'[2] As the permanent secretary to the MOT, Sir Thomas Padmore, later told the Select Committee:

> I would judge that that is why at the end of the day the Victoria Line project was approved, not because it was a particularly attractive thing to do financially, not because the demand for it was such that there was a good prospect of its paying its way, but because it was highly desirable in relation to congestion, in relation to the problems of rush hour travel in London and the absence of an underground line in the area which it will serve—all these things no doubt were the reasons fundamentally why in 1962 it was approved.[3]

The study was a pioneer in Britain in its methods and application, however, and very important in the light of later events concerning capital investment in transport and is worthy of further consideration here before considering the construction and early operation of the Victoria Line. Foster and Beesley argued that a social cost-benefit analysis was required because: (a) LT had to undertake its costings on an average rather than marginal cost basis, i.e. that their whole undertaking should cover its costs taking one year with another; and (b) vehicle-users in London did not pay the true costs of the trips they made; if they did the Victoria Line would be in a relatively much better position 'when there could be hardly any doubt that it would pay to build [it].' Even if charging for both on the same basis was considered impolitic or impractical there was no reason 'why this distortion need be reflected in its investment policy.'[4]

[1] C D Foster and M E Beesley (1963), 'Estimating the Social Benefit of Constructing an Underground Railway in London,' *J R Stat Soc* (A), pp46–92. The principles of the problem were outlined in two articles by Foster in *The Times*, 11, 12 December 1962.
[2] Foster and Beesley (1963), pp82, 85.
[3] *Sel Comm LT* (1965), Q1577.
[4] Foster and Beesley (1963), p47; and *The Times*, 4 December 1962.

The analysis depended on estimating the social benefits from time saved by travellers, savings in the cost of operating public or private transport vehicles, and the value of extra comfort and convenience as a result of the new facility. These were estimated for travellers whose habits remained unchanged, those who diverted to the new facility and those who made new trips; the numbers in each category were estimated by LT. Of the benefits calculated in the study, 52% went to the first group, particularly motorists whose journey was quicker and cheaper (35% of all benefits); 34% accrued to those who diverted to the line; and 14% resulted from generated traffic.

The outcome of the calculation then depended to a considerable degree on the assumptions about the *value* of the gains and losses particularly of the value of time, and upon what rate of interest was used to convert (discount) future costs and benefits to present values. The values of time Foster and Beesley used were 7s 3d (36½p) per hour for trips in working time and 5s (25p) per hour for other trips. At the chosen values of time at a 6% annual discount rate, the net current benefit was £70 million compared with the estimated capital cost of £55 million; at lower and higher discount rates (4% and 8%) the net current benefit was £106 million and £49 million respectively. The sensitivity of the calculation to the value of time is shown by changing working time to 3s or 10s (15p or 50p) per hour which produced the benefits of £52 million or £115 million respectively.

Foster and Beesley's calculations on generated traffic showed a gain for BR compared with a loss in the LT Executive's 1959 estimates. The whole project showed a social gain of £32 million but if LT had to finance the investment, they 'lost' £28 million. Discussing the paper, C B Winsten pointed out that the study assumed that the scheme would not be financed from fares increases: if these were necessary either on the Victoria Line or over the whole system, the benefits claimed would not accrue. Foster and Beesley did not at first think that a large increase would be needed: a further study showed that traditional financing methods (capitalised interest repaid from year 1 of operation) could lead to large social losses. They considered various ways of increasing fares to help raise the revenue, but all led to losses of passengers, and they preferred to see a system of road pricing introduced which would, amongst other things, transfer motorists to LT and BR services.[1]

The MOT indicated to LT that they should finance the Victoria Line by means of loans, with the interest capitalised until March 1969. A spate of tenders was let in 1962 and 1963 and work began on forty different sites. Day described the very complex structures needed for some of the stations, the extensive accommodation works needed, especially at Oxford Circus, and the technical experimentation with signalling and automatic train control, new rolling stock and automatic fare collection.[2]

It was at first hoped that the line would be completed by the end of 1967

[1] M E Beesley and C D Foster (1965), 'The Victoria Line: Social Benefit and Finances,' *J R Stat Soc* (A), pp67–88.

[2] Day (1969), *passim.*

but some time was lost on tendering and working drawings by consultants and contractors, and also through shortages of construction staff (particularly for tunnelling) during the building boom of the early 1960s. As a result tunnelling was not completed until September 1966. The first stretch of the line was opened from Walthamstow to Highbury in September 1968, the second from Highbury to Warren Street in December and the remainder to Victoria in March 1969. (Section 3 deals with the subsequent extension to Brixton.)

During 1969 the GLC began negotiating the terms of their takeover of LT and by February were able to announce that 90% of LT's capital debt and accrued interest would be 'written off' by the Government including the expenditure on the Victoria Line and the Brixton extension on which work was then well advanced; in October it was agreed that the whole of LT's debt of £250 million plus £12 million interest would be erased.[1] As far as tube railways were concerned this left only the outstanding expenditure on the Brixton extension which was eligible for an infrastructure grant.

How did the line fulfil its purposes in the early years of its operation? LT undertook counts and surveys of passengers at stations in May and

	1969		1970		1970 INDEX
	(000)	(%)	(000)	(%)	(1969 = 100)
Victoria	42.0	22.5	61.0	23.5	147
Green Park		9.5		9.5	136
Oxford Circus	38.0	20.5	56.0	21.5	140
Warren Street		5.0		5.0	130
Euston		8.5		8.5	144
King's Cross		8.5		8.5	134
In-town sub-total	138.5	74.0	198.0	76.0	143
Highbury and Islington		4.5		4.5	136
Finsbury Park	20.3	11.0	26.1	10.0	131
Seven Sisters		3.5		4.0	165
Tottenham Hale		1.5		1.0	116
Blackhorse Road		2.0		1.5	112
Walthamstow Central		3.5		3.0	120
Out-of-town sub-total	47.5	26.0	63.0	24.0	132
GRAND TOTAL	186.0	100.0	261.0	100.0	140

Table 15 DAILY NUMBERS OF PASSENGERS ENTERING THE VICTORIA LINE PLATFORMS, 1969 AND 1970

Source: LT planning office (1971) drafts of report on Victoria Line traffic.

[1] GLC *Minutes*, 21 February 1969, pp21–2; and 21 October 1969, pp571–3.

June 1969 and 1970 and the GLC undertook a sample before-and-after home interview survey in areas along the line north of Finsbury Park. LT had found automatic train operation more efficient and fault-free than manual control, and automatic fare and ticket collection was gradually being accepted by the public, with increasingly reliable equipment. The least satisfactory aspects were considered to be the noise levels and parsimonious space standards at station booking halls, subways and platforms.[1]

As far as passenger traffic was concerned the line soon reached its estimated levels: the level of use estimated early in 1969 (a rate of 169 million passenger miles annually) was achieved only three months after the line had opened (Table 13). A year later this figure had increased by 41% and by 1971 was expected to reach the higher levels estimated in the early 1950s schemes, when bus usage was much greater, the line proposed was longer (to Wood Street) and the Great Northern Line was assumed to be electrified, bringing more passengers to Highbury station.

The survey results showed that three-quarters of the total traffic arose on the in-town section and only one-quarter north of Finsbury Park. Moreover, Oxford Circus and Victoria each had more than a fifth of the total traffic and were increasing their share: by 1970, 19% of all trips were on the section of line between these two stations. By far the most heavily used section was that between Green Park and Oxford Circus (94 000 daily or 29.5 million annually in 1969 and 133 000 and 41.7 million in 1970). Of all passengers, 31% came from other tube lines of which the Piccadilly Line with three interchanges was the most important (35 000 trip ends) and 42% of all tube–tube interchange occurred at the four stations with cross-platform connections. Victoria took over half the BR trip ends (62 800), while Finsbury Park was the main bus feeder centre particularly from the Muswell Hill area which has no tube line of its own. The majority of access on foot occurred in the central area where Oxford Circus (59 700) claimed 28% of all foot trips. Feeder bus and 'park-and-ride' or 'kiss-and-ride' trips increased faster between 1969 and 1970 than access trips by tube or BR services. Only in this period, apparently, did Northern Line passengers become aware that Euston provided an easier interchange with the Victoria Line than Warren Street.

According to interviews in the West End the Victoria Line served people travelling to or from various parts of the city and as Foster had pointed out from early estimates, the benefit to BR commuters was considerable: of the 29% from south of the river, 6% were in the LCC area, 5.5% in Kent and 17.5% in Surrey and Sussex. Sixty per cent of all trips were from areas not directly served. Origins of Victoria Line trips are shown below:

[1] Based on R M Robbins (1970), 'Passenger Reactions to London's new Victoria Line,' *High-Speed Ground Transportation Journal*, IV, 2, pp193–6; F G Maxwell (1970), 'The Victoria Line After a Year's Operation,' *Railway Students Association Bulletin*, 12, pp18–41; LT Executive planning office (1971–72) drafts of report on the traffic results (unpublished).

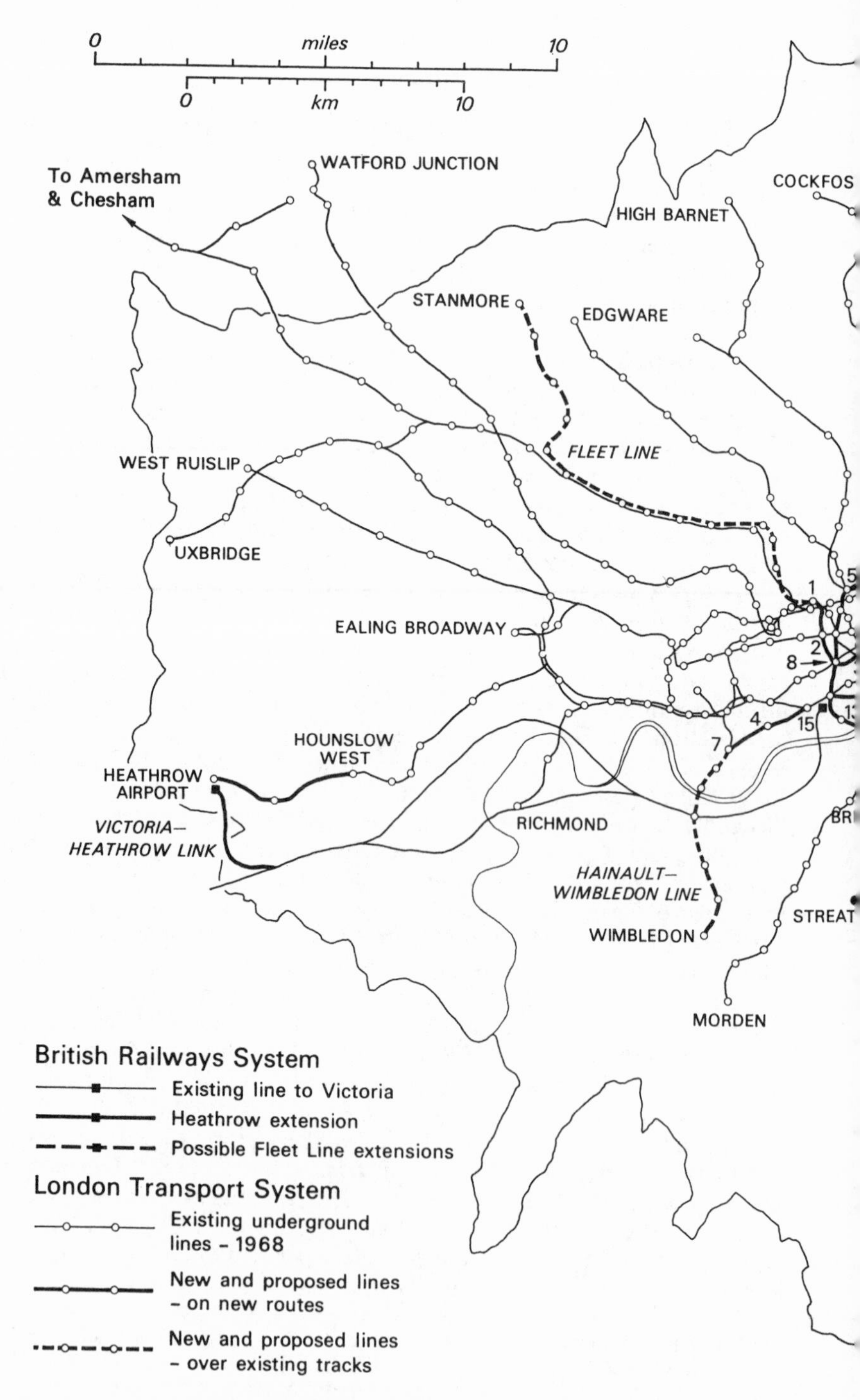

Figure 8 LONDON'S EXISTING UNDERGROUND SYSTEM AND PROPOSED ADDITIONS

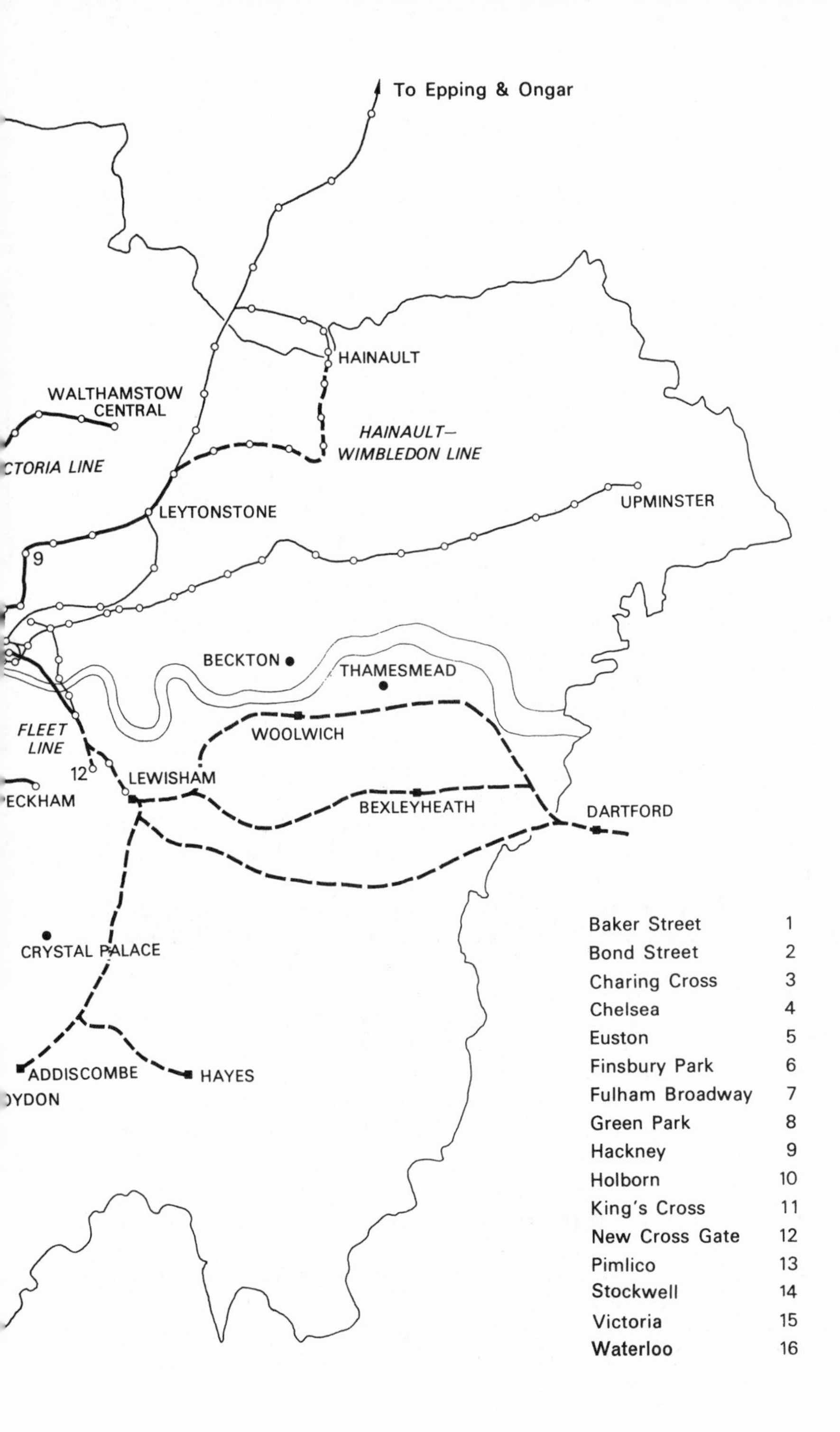
To Epping & Ongar
HAINAULT
WALTHAMSTOW CENTRAL
HAINAULT–WIMBLEDON LINE
LEYTONSTONE
UPMINSTER
9
BECKTON
THAMESMEAD
FLEET LINE
WOOLWICH
12
LEWISHAM
BEXLEYHEATH
DARTFORD
CRYSTAL PALACE
ADDISCOMBE
HAYES
Baker Street 1
Bond Street 2
Charing Cross 3
Chelsea 4
Euston 5
Finsbury Park 6
Fulham Broadway 7
Green Park 8
Hackney 9
Holborn 10
King's Cross 11
New Cross Gate 12
Pimlico 13
Stockwell 14
Victoria 15
Waterloo 16

	(%)
West End and inner areas	23.0
North-east suburbs on the line	17.5
Other north-east suburbs	12.0
North and west suburbs	14.0
South of river	29.0
Other	4.5
	100.0

There was a considerable change in the amount of 'generated' traffic between 1969 and 1970 (7.5% to 20% of total traffic) even allowing for the difficulties of identifying generated trips (Would you have made this trip without the Victoria Line? Have your circumstances, i.e. job or home changed within the last year?). Regarding diverted traffic, by 1970 it was estimated that 4000 road vehicle trips daily were no longer being made as a result of the line being available, although 5000 (shorter) park- or kiss-and-ride journeys had been generated. There was a net decline of 34 000 bus trips daily. Comparing the 1970 results with the various forecasts (Table 13) the following generalisations can be made:

1 Total traffic and journey to work flows were reasonably accurately predicted (1970 was 107% of the 1955 predicted figure).
2 Day-time off-peak traffic and evening short trips especially between Victoria and Oxford Circus were underestimated (1970 was 128% of 1955).
3 The relief of the most heavily laden parts of the District, Circle, Northern and Piccadilly Lines was underestimated (by an average of 19%) and so were the increases on parts of the Central and Bakerloo.
4 The transfer of BR Southern Region passengers from Waterloo and London Bridge to Victoria was underestimated (the inter-availability of BR tickets between termini encouraged this).
5 The transfer from BR and other tube services was greater than estimated; that from buses was growing but was not up to the forecast level; that from cars and generated traffic was still below the early 1969 estimate.

LT's Estates Department also attempted to assess the change in property values within the vicinity of the line. The increase (above that which might have occurred without the line) was assessed at £35 million mostly in residential property. This nearly equalled the cost of the northern part of the line and the depot at Northumberland Park. In the long term it was expected that, as in Toronto (see Case Study *D*, Development at Stations), a great proportion of new office development was expected to occur near the line. By the time this evaluation was proceeding, the extension of the Victoria Line to Brixton had been opened; we now turn to this.

3 THE BRIXTON EXTENSION OF THE VICTORIA LINE[1]

The original concept of Barrington–Ward's 'Route *C*' was that it should be extended beyond Victoria and the scheme was one of three contained in the unpublished London Railway plan of 1965. After he had worked on the original Victoria cost-benefit study Professor Beesley was asked by LT to help with the assessment of the proposed extension for which there were the options of joining up with the District Line branch at Fulham Broadway, or of going to Brixton and possibly beyond. Studies of traffic diverted from cars and newly generated traffic showed that the Brixton option would attract more traffic.[2]

The Select Committee in 1965 heard from LT that the Brixton extension would be the most convenient scheme to undertake after the Victoria Line and would enable about half the specialist teams of tunnellers and their plant and subcontractors to be retained, saving about £1 million in construction costs. The main planning item outstanding was negotiation with Lambeth Borough Council over the exact location of the Brixton terminus.

LT sought powers in the following parliamentary session (1965–66) and hoped to start work early in 1967 but in view of the fact that no commitment had been made by the MOT, and the lengthy process of gaining rights-of-way, purchasing land and designing and tendering for works, the Select Committee was 'obliged to record that the Board have prejudiced the retention for other lines of the teams assembled for the Victoria Line by leaving too little time for the preparatory process.'[3] The Ministry's witness was doubtful if the consideration of keeping the construction teams together would influence the decision to embark on the line at all. In any case, other uses could be found for this labour.[4]

However, LT were supported by the GLC in their concern about this aspect of the problem.[5] In reply to the criticism by the Select Committee, LT pointed out that they had already sought authorisation from the Ministry, and that a start early in 1967 would enable a 'limited proportion' of the construction teams to be employed (already in 1966 they were reduced to 50% of their peak level).[6]

Parliamentary powers were granted in 1966 and in March of that year the Minister allowed LT to order segments to line the tunnels. Despite this commitment, the Minister of Transport did not announce approval for the

1 See LT (1971), *The Brixton Extension of the Victoria Line* (44pp), *passim.*

2 7.7 million passenger miles per route-mile annually compared with 2.4 million per mile; see *Sel Comm LT* (1965), Q1498 and interviews.

3 *Sel Comm LT* (1965), p122–3.

4 *Sel Comm LT*, volII, QQ1597 and 1619.

5 The *Guardian*, 4 March 1967, by Mrs Jane Phillips, chairman of the Highways and Traffic Committee; see also GLC *Minutes*, 16 November 1965, p737.

6 *Second Special Report to Sel Comm HC Papers 14*, 1965, p4; and *LT Annual Report* (1966), p12.

project until August 1967. Work started almost immediately; some thirty miners were completing work on the main line, but could only form the nucleus of the 200-strong team needed.

The scheme for the 3½-mile extension with intermediate stations at Vauxhall and Stockwell was expected to carry 18 million passengers in the first full year. The Minister, Mrs Barbara Castle said:

> I have approved this scheme simply and solely because I think it will improve the lot of the travelling public in London. The new line will bring LT relatively little new revenue, because most of the 18 million passengers a year who will be attracted to it already use the Northern or Bakerloo lines or London Transport buses. It will actually cost the Board money. But, after carefully examining the case for the project against rival calls on our resources I have decided that *the benefit of the line to the public*, not least in relieving the congested conditions in which many of them have to travel, *will outweigh any accounting loss* [our italics].[1]

Mr A Bull, a member of the LT Board, commented that the revenue on the line itself would equal 2½% of the capital cost on the extension and 2% over the whole line, as much as was expected from any of the other lines. The Minister was currently steering her mammoth Transport Bill through Parliament, and hoped that the extension would be the first scheme to benefit from its infrastructure grant provisions.

The use of the tunnelling techniques and the management methods developed for the Walthamstow–Victoria section enabled the target date for the line to be advanced from 1972 and the line was opened on 23 July 1971.[2]

When the Minister gave approval for the scheme she also may have been influenced by two events connected with the possible transfer of road traffic to the line. First, the extension of the Inner London Parking Area (ILPA) to cover the whole of Lambeth north of Brixton was programmed for completion by 1969. Second, Ringway 1 (the Motorway Box) was proposed to pass through Brixton with interchanges to the east and west of the town centre, which could provide a convenient 'park and ride' point on a large scale.[3] In fact the ILPA programme rapidly fell behind schedule and it later became clear that this area would not be controlled until 1972–73 (see Case Study *Q*); Ringway 1 South was reprogrammed for the 1990s rather than the 1980s, and although a new bus station and car park was being planned for the town centre, a heavy car–rail interchange movement was not expected.[4]

The Brixton extension was originally estimated to cost £15.9 million

[1] *Financial Times*, 5 August 1967.
[2] LT (1971), p28.
[3] Day (1969), p118.
[4] Interviews with officers of GLC, LT, and the London Borough of Lambeth.

including extra rolling stock. By the time LT was transferred to the GLC, £14 million had been spent and written off; after January 1970 the GLC contributed 25% and the remainder of the capital was met from central government infrastructure grants.[1]

The line ran under Pimlico and although no station was proposed, the idea for one was suggested in 1964–65. It was considered by the Westminster City Council (CC) Planning Committee in January 1966[2] when it was reported that LT was not willing to provide the money (originally estimated at £1.4 to £1.6 million but later almost £2.0 million), but they were willing to make provision for station tunnels in their Parliamentary powers. Westminster CC decided to press the matter with the Transport Co-ordinating Council for London in May 1966. At that time the Victoria Transportation Centre project was active (see Case Study *E*) and it was thought that a station at Pimlico would partly relieve its traffic problems.[3] Later Barbara Castle, Minister of Transport, was reported to have suggested that Westminster should contribute part of the cost; LT believed that they or the GLC should do so.[4]

The Crown Estate Commissioners were keen for improved transport facilities for their tenants in the area, who might increase from 1200 to 2500 in number, and they offered to make available the surface land necessary for access to a new station at no charge. The Dolphin Square Trust with 3000 tenants, and other residents' groups expressed their support in the press and in letters to the Minister, as did some large firms on Millbank (Vickers, the Electricity Council and the Ministry of Defence) and ILEA who were completing a large comprehensive school nearby.[5]

The possible exchange of riverfront commercial zoning with the (residential) block in which the station was sited was considered and discussions continue.[6] After undertaking a brief cost-benefit evaluation (in which the chief benefit of the station was to relieve surface traffic) the Ministry approved the construction of the tunnels in June 1968, and in 1969 the Minister, now Richard Marsh, awarded an infrastructure grant for the station itself on similar grounds.[7] The station was opened on 14 September 1972.

The evaluation of the station had included an element of benefit from reduced road congestion in the area using a method evolved by a Ministry economist, H Neuberger.[8] This measured the congestion costs of adding

[1] GLC *Minutes*, 10 February 1970, p133–4.

[2] Westminster CC *Minutes*, 6 November 1966 and 25 April 1968.

[3] Question in Council, Westminster CC *Minutes*, 27 July 1967, p209.

[4] *Westminster and Pimlico News*, 11 August 1967.

[5] After the station was approved, the needs of these groups also helped to justify a pedestrian subway from the station across Bessborough street.

[6] See *Crown Estate Millbank: Proposals for Redevelopment* (1972), by Chapman Taylor and Partners, especially pages 39–43. Proposals for offices, including a headquarters for the CBI for which an ODP for 125 000 square feet had been granted, and an hotel were mooted, relying heavily on access to Pimlico and Victoria stations.

[7] The *Guardian*, 5 August 1969.

[8] Appendix *J*, Cmnd 3686, 1969.

extra vehicles to given traffic flows by measuring and valuing the time lost by added delays at junctions (whose capacity largely determines that of the whole road system). This formula was used 'in reverse' to measure the reduced delays resulting from *removing* vehicles from the flow, and this was the means of evaluating the benefits of transferring traffic to railways. This element had been identified in Foster and Beesley's studies of the main Victoria Line, and proved to be more important in the studies of the Brixton extension and Pimlico station, and in the studies of the Fleet Line.

By the time the Victoria Line was opened the property management of LT had become interested in its potential land-use benefits (see Case Study *D*), and were undertaking a survey of the effects of the Walthamstow–Victoria section.[1] Residential property prices (which had risen in Tottenham and Walthamstow) showed considerable rises in Stockwell as middle-class owner-occupiers moved in in anticipation of the line opening.[2] Developers became interested in office developments around Vauxhall station and employment in the area was likely to increase with the transfer of Covent Garden Market to Nine Elms and the building of a new Government office building near Vauxhall bridge.

There were suggestions by local groups at the GLDP Inquiry that the Victoria Line should also be extended at its northern end to Leytonstone (to relieve the Central Line and to provide a park-and-ride facility for the growing traffic on the Eastern Avenue) and later to Barking or Ilford (to relieve BR lines into Liverpool Street).[3] In their evidence to the GLDP Inquiry and their Brixton booklet (page 39) LT suggested that an extension beyond Brixton might be considered, but this had not actually been investigated. The early traffic results from the northern section of the Victoria Line suggest that in suburbs with a long-established BR rail service which is *not* being taken over, the potential traffic for new tubes is limited.[4]

4 THE FLEET LINE

The BTC's London Plan Working Party report of 1949 did not contain any proposals that definitely previewed the Fleet Line although parts of a proposed main-line tube to link Gillingham and Sevenoaks services with those to Tring and Aylesbury (Route *F*) were on a similar alignment. The LCC were particularly keen to see Route *F* built to relieve congestion on the south-eastern BR routes.[5]

By the time the 1965 Railway Plan for London was formulated the Fleet Line was the largest of LT's proposals, having been 'seriously considered'

[1] DOE economists dispute the value of their findings (interviews with officers of LT, GLC, DOE).

[2] *Evening Standard*, 27 July 1971.

[3] Wanstead Residents' Society (1970), Papers *S27/63 Rail in the East* and *S27/62*, GLDP Inquiry Stage 2.

[4] Interviews with GLC and LT officers.

[5] LCC (1951), *Development Plan—Analysis*, p168.

by the LT–BR co-ordinating committee[1] and discussed by a Parliamentary committee. The scheme was envisaged to link one of the branches of the Bakerloo Line via a new section interchanging with the Central Line (at Bond Street), Piccadilly and Victoria Lines (at Green Park), Northern and Bakerloo Lines (at Trafalgar Square), thence along Fleet Street, 'north or south of St Pauls, and via Fenchurch Street to the New Cross–Lewisham area and possibly absorbing an existing Southern Region branch beyond.' It was claimed to relieve the existing Central, District and Bakerloo lines, to enable more trains to be run on the current Bakerloo network (which was now the most congested with peak overloading of 41% above LT's 'acceptable capacity') and, if extended over Southern Region lines, to relieve the approaches to the South-eastern BR termini (see Case Study *H*). It also improved in-town distribution by interchanging with all eight existing lines.

At this stage LT estimated that the scheme would cost £57 million. Survey work for the alignments and discussions on local planning effects had still to be undertaken, and construction was not envisaged until after the Brixton extension of the Victoria Line and the Aldwych–Waterloo extension of the Piccadilly Line had at least been started.[2] LT pointed out that there were three constraints on the rate of tube construction: the problems of safeguarding the route with existing Parliamentary and local authority planning powers; the maintenance of a regular programme of work to employ specialist design and construction teams; and the limit of the overall flow of finance for tube railways permitted by central government (set at £19–20 million p.a. by the MOT during the construction of the Victoria Line).[3]

LT continued planning work for the line and traffic estimates were made during 1967, when alternative extensions of the line beyond Lewisham were discussed with BR. LT and MOT agreed Parliamentary powers should be sought in 1968, but general cut-backs in public spending made sure that no start of works could be considered until 1970.[4] In 1968 authorisation was granted to seek the necessary powers as far as the Strand, and a firm line was established to Fenchurch Street. Cost-benefit studies of the whole project and further examination of the south-eastern section continued.[5]

During 1969, while the GLC were negotiating the take-over of LT, the comment was made that 'the GLC is not at all likely to embark on projects that will place extra loads on London ratepayers' and that the Government's view on the write-down of LT's capital debt and on capital grants would be a crucial factor.[6] The Transport Act 1968 was then in force and the GLC

[1] The Passenger Transport Planning Committee for London, set up by Ernest Marples after 20 March 1963, which formulated the 1965 Plan.

[2] *Sel Comm LT* (1965), *Report*, paras466, 472; and *Proceedings*, QQ149–58. Also app7, Memo by LT, 19 March 1965, pp336–8.

[3] The *Guardian*, 14 December 1965 (LT's comments on Select Committee Report).

[4] *LT Annual Report*, 1967, p21.

[5] *LT Annual Report*, 1968, p43. The Act was chxviii of 1968.

[6] *The Sunday Times*, 1 September 1968.

and LT both hoped that the Fleet Line would receive an infrastructure grant. However, in the GLDP the scheme was still baldly described as 'a proposal by LT.'[1] By September 1969 LT submitted their traffic, financial and social benefit studies to the Ministry. They elaborated their previous arguments, and produced a new cost estimate of £74 million including rolling stock.[2]

In November one of the GLC's senior engineers expressed the view that the GLC should provide the remaining 25% of capital costs for schemes ranking for infrastructure grant, one of which was suggested to be the Fleet Line. The leader of the Council and chairman of the Policy Steering Committee replied 'at this stage it is quite impossible to generalise or dogmatise on the extent to which the Council should or could make a direct contribution to the cost of a new project.'[3]

On 1 December 1969 the Policy Steering Committee decided to refer the matter to the newly formed Greater London Transport Group.[4] The Public Transport and General Standing Committee of the GLTG (which included the senior planners of BR, LT and the GLC and senior administrators and economists from the DOE) examined the scheme. The LT Executive formally asked the GLC in May 1970[5] for authority to proceed. In July a definitive joint report was put to the GLC by the Policy and Resources, Strategic and Environmental Planning committees. The scheme was then estimated to cost £86 million. The traffic estimates of the line were:

	(MILLION PASSENGER MILES P.A.)	(%)	(%)
Diverted from other tubes	57	25	
Diverted from buses	43	19	45
Diverted from BR	57	25	
New traffic (latent demand, ex-motorists and new passengers, e.g. from Surrey Docks)	67	31	19
Total	224	100	
Existing passengers on Stanmore and east London sections	127		36
GRAND TOTAL	351		100

[1] GLC (1969), *GLDP Written Statement*, para5.60.
[2] *LT Annual Report*, 1969, pp37–8.
[3] *Evening Standard*, 7 November 1969; and GLC *Minutes*, 18 November 1969, p622.
[4] GLC *Minutes*, 2 December 1969, p680.
[5] *LT Annual Report*, 1970, p19.

The financial estimates were:

	(£M P.A.)
Net revenue (including rents, advertising, etc.)	2.5
Net working expenses (including bus savings)	1.7
Net surplus	0.8
Loss of revenue to BR	0.7

The capital cost of the scheme was spread over nine years but excluded £3.5 million for replacing obsolete Bakerloo Line rolling stock and £2 million for new signalling on the Stanmore branch, and £4.5 million for improvements to Strand and Bond Street stations, which would be necessary in any case. The report continued:

> Benefits arising from a major new transport facility in a large town are of two kinds: benefit to users of transport and the less tangible but equally important benefits to the community as a whole, relating to changes in urban life which might result from the new facility. Transport user benefits are capable of reasonably precise quantification in money terms. They include savings in travel time, increased reliability of travel, reduced road congestion from diversion of car travellers to the new line, improved comfort and the value of the extra traffic which the line itself generates. An assessment of the value of all these things set against the cost shows the value of the benefits to be about one-half the cost. But a complete comparison of costs and benefits must include the less tangible benefits to which we refer. There is no generally accepted method by which these can be expressed in money terms. Whether expressed in money terms or not they are a vital part of the consideration and we have therefore examined what the community of London might expect to get from the Fleet Line.[1]

These were discussed under three headings:

1 *Benefits to the central area.* Chiefly in providing the quick safe interchanging and rapid travel that cannot be had by bus or car, particularly necessary in the main 'spine' of commercial development running from the City to Oxford Street.

2 *Benefits to inner London.* In opening up new employment and cultural prospects for the residents of south-east London including those in the future Deptford and Surrey Docks schemes; in providing access to a wider housing market for central London workers; and in generally encouraging development in the sector.

3 *Relation to the general investment situation.* Large-scale investment in

[1] GLC *Minutes*, 7 July 1970, p429.

housing and supporting facilities will be needed in the 1980s and 1990s in this sector. LT estimated that south of the Thames the Fleet Line would promote £70 million worth of development on sites with access to its stations. Members of the Estates Department of LT were very interested in this potential (see Case Study *D*, Development at Stations). 'General investment on this scale would not be regarded as sound if it were based on an inadequate transport infrastructure. The Fleet Line investment must therefore be seen as one aspect of the means of matching transport investment to general investment.'[1]

On 'the basis of the total benefits' the Council concluded that the scheme was in accordance with its strategy and 'gave good value for money' and approved the scheme with a 25% grant (£22 million) subject to a 75% grant from the DOE, and subject to further examination regarding the possibility of giving priority to the south-eastern section and of providing a station to serve the GLC redevelopment at St Katherine's dock. The *Economist*, which viewed the building of new tubes as an expensive and old-fashioned means of solving transport problems (compared with solutions such as hover trains), criticised any approach which did not expect users to pay for the costs of the facility, pointing out that only a small proportion of the Victoria and Fleet Line traffic would transfer from cars.[2]

The scheme was then referred for consideration to central government, together with the Heathrow Link which was approved at the same Council meeting. LT continued to stress the importance of new projects in maintaining their construction and management teams.[3] Extension of the Piccadilly Line to Heathrow was the first to be authorised by the Government in November 1970 but initially without any grant (see Heathrow link Case Study *E*). The GLC confirmed that it would still give a 25% grant but sent a deputation to the DOE in January 1971, complaining about the unequal consideration given to grants for road and rail schemes, and threatening not to proceed with the Fleet Line unless grant was forthcoming. The leader of the GLC said that it would cripple LT if they had to provide £64 million (75% of the total capital).[4]

The Secretary of State for the Environment, Mr Peter Walker, announced that he would give a 75% grant to the £35 million first stage of the Fleet Line (to the Strand) on 18 August 1971, after he had made a tour of the Brixton extension.[5] The first stage was expected to carry 192 million passenger miles annually, 60% inherited from the Bakerloo Line, 15% from other tube lines, 13% from buses and 7% from car travellers and generated traffic. The Secretary of State commented of this grant and of

[1] T R Wacher (1970), 'The Effects of Rapid Transit Systems on Urban Property Development,' *Chartered Surveyor*, pp420–8.

[2] *Economist*, 12 July 1969 and 21 August 1971.

[3] LT (1971), *Brixton Extension of the Victoria Line*, p43.

[4] *Evening Standard*, 24 November 1970.

[5] *DOE Press Release 25M*, 18 August 1971. The £35 million included an allowance of £3 million (subject to revision) for works at Bond Street and Strand stations.

that for the electrification of BR's Great Northern Line announced at the same time (a total of £52 million): 'This is three times as much as has ever previously been given out by central government to London's transport system . . . every family of four in the country will be paying £4 towards it.'[1] He intended to consider a grant for the rest of the line when the conclusions of the commissioned study of the redevelopment of London's dockland were clear: these were expected late in 1972.

It was hoped that Stage I of the Fleet Line would be completed by 1977. Tenders were invited immediately for preliminary work near Bond Street station whose reconstruction was a critical factor in the programming of the line. LT also began negotiating with BR for land at Stonebridge Park for a depot for the line.[2]

The GLC Policy and Resources Committee commented that Mr Walker's reservation about the outcome of the docklands study really only applied beyond Fenchurch Street and, subject to marginal changes at Fenchurch Street station itself, Stage II need not be delayed.[3] The question of the third stage was therefore still open, although LT had hoped to obtain powers for it by late 1972. The GLC and Southwark Borough Council were very keen to see the extension built, particularly to serve the 400-acre redevelopment area of the Surrey Docks.[4] The London Borough of Southwark–Port of London Authority consultants were in no doubt about the role of the Fleet Line in relation to the Docklands generally and the Surrey Docks in particular: 'This route could be the link which finally breaks down the area's sense of isolation and draws it into an integral working relationship with the rest of central London . . . it is of the utmost importance for the Surrey Docks that the Fleet Line, as presently planned, should be constructed.'[5] Before the Docklands Study was published planning consultants were commissioned to produce, before the end of August 1972, a study of the development prospects along the line of Stage III of the Fleet Line.[6]

It has also been suggested that the Fleet Line could be built on a line running east from New Cross to Thamesmead with a station on the Isle of Dogs.[7] Professor Buchanan's report on Greenwich expressed the hope that the Fleet Line and improvements to BR's rail approaches to Charing Cross and Cannon Street (see Case Study *H*) would relieve roads in the area of some traffic.[8]

[1] *The Times* and the *Guardian*, 19 August 1971.
[2] *LT Magazine*, 25, 7, October 1971, p4.
[3] GLC *Minutes*, 5 October 1971, p450.
[4] *The Times*, 5 February 1971; L. B. Southwark (1971), *Proof of Evidence, E27/105*, GLDP Inquiry Stage 2.
[5] Shankland Cox and Partners (1972), *A Report on the Future of the Surrey Commercial Docks*, paras2.9, 1.2 respectively of vol2.
[6] *Architect's Journal*, 9 August 1972, p299.
[7] E.g. *Building Design* 3 March 1972.
[8] C Buchanan and Partners (1971), *Greenwich and Blackheath Study*, pp35, 37, 66; and GLC *Minutes*, 20 July 1971, pp408–10.

BR were still not very enthusiastic about the Lewisham extension, being concerned that they would lose passenger revenue without concomitant savings in costs. They later feared that it might be necessary to raise fares or even close some stations within Lewisham's hinterland, although they 'would not wish to be thought trying to force on our own initiative a decision on the alignment of that line one way or another.' According to Mr Cutler, Chairman of the GLC's Policy and Resources Committee, the GLC was not consulted before this statement was made. The Labour opposition on the GLC tabled a motion at the same meeting asking the Committee to report by July on the steps to be taken to secure the necessary legislation and Government authority to commence construction at the earliest possible date.[1]

Within a month of Mr Walker's decision the GLC approved an LT Executive proposal to rebuild Bond Street station, whose passenger flow was expected to increase from 12 to over 20 million annually when Stage I of the Fleet Line was open. The proposal involved improved subway and escalator access to the surface and interchange with the Central Line. The GLC proposed to give a 25% grant to the Fleet Line element and a 50% grant to the Central Line element thus:

(£M)	TOTAL COST	GOVERNMENT	GLC
Fleet Line	1.94	1.46	0.48 (25%)
Central Line	1.85	0.93	0.92 (50%)
	3.79	2.39	1.40

The Central Line element was expected to bring benefits of £35 000 annually in revenue from newly generated traffic and social benefits in improved pedestrian convenience and time savings, as well as enabling the station to function while existing escalators were replaced. These benefits were considered 'more than enough to justify the project.'[2] The Minister approved the whole scheme with a £2.4 million grant in January 1972.[3]

The rebuilding of Strand station was approved by the GLC in March 1972. The existing Northern Line station, serving 10 million passengers annually and relying solely on lifts, was to be rebuilt with escalators to serve about 20 million passengers expected after the opening of the Fleet Line. A working party of GLC and Westminster planners was examining the pedestrian subway links with Charing Cross BR station, Covent Garden and Trafalgar Square. The costs were given[4] on the same basis as for Bond Street, namely:

[1] GLC *Minutes*, 7 March 1972, p135.
[2] GLC *Minutes* 2 November 1971, pp552–3; and *Press Release 468*, 27 October 1971.
[3] DOE *Press Release 34M*, 11 January 1972.
[4] GLC *Minutes*, 21 March 1972, pp159–60; and *Press Release 125*, 15 March 1972.

(£M)	TOTAL COST	GOVERNMENT	GLC
Fleet Line	1.90	1.43	0.47 (25%)
Northern Line	1.10	0.55	0.55 (50%)
	3.00	1.98	1.02

Strand Northern Line station would have to be closed for 2½ years. Consideration was given to the alternative of providing new lifts but this would have involved extending the subsurface concourse and might delay the opening of the Fleet Line station by a year. Although £250 000 cheaper it would also lengthen pavement to platform journeys for Fleet Line passengers (although slightly shorten them for Northern Line travellers) and on balance the escalator scheme was preferred.

Having proceeded thus far, and with high hopes of further grants, in July 1972 the GLC received a rude shock. The estimated costs of Stage I including work at the two stations and rolling stock had risen to £52.9 million compared with £35 million two years earlier, an increase of 51%. Of the increase of £17.9 million, over £10 million was attributable to inflation and £3.5 million to revised plans for the new Bakerloo Line depot. The balance of the increase was due mainly to necessary extra works and equipment at the Strand and Bond Street.

Mr Cutler, the chairman of the Policy and Resources Committee, said: 'The possibility in my view is that the estimates for the Fleet Line were not properly processed; perhaps because London Transport had not got very much hope of its succeeding. This is no excuse and we are expecting much more accurate estimates even in these days of speculation and high inflation.'[1] Certainly LT had had a sudden boost to its hopes and a great deal of new work to do on the project from December 1969 to mid-1970. (It was a sharp contrast with the apparent accuracy of its estimating on the Heathrow link, see Case Study *E*.) This increase meant that a Government grant of £13.5 million was needed and some of this, for the Strand works, had to be forthcoming by the end of July 1972 if the project was not to be held up. In fact the Government approved a 65% (£2 million) grant towards the Strand station works in October 1972 but by the end of the year had still not indicated any intention to grant aid Stages II and III.[2]

The question of a station to serve St Katherine's and London Docks was also still not settled. LT, dubious of its overall traffic prospects and financial benefits, suggested that it could be provided if Tower Hamlets Borough Council paid the capital cost. In evidence to the GLDP Inquiry the Borough's principal planning officer Mr William Briggs said 'It must be wrong that a London borough, whose limited financial resources are already strained between so many competing social needs should be asked to expend a large capital sum without return when, on the other hand, the

[1] Question in Council, GLC *Minutes*, 18 July 1972.
[2] DOE *Press Release 1174M*; and GLC *Press Release 512*, 24 October 1972.

costs of another transport element, that is roads, falls largely on national and Greater London funds.'[1]

5 OTHER PROPOSALS

Besides the lines being built there have been various other proposals including an extension of the Bakerloo Line from Elephant and Castle to Peckham, an extension of the Aldwych branch of the Piccadilly Line to Waterloo, a line from Hainault to Wimbledon, and an orbital line.

The Bakerloo extension

An extension of the Bakerloo Line from the Elephant and Castle to Camberwell was proposed as early as the mid-1920s and Parliamentary powers were obtained in 1931, but closer investigation demonstrated that the scheme would not be remunerative, and the powers lapsed. It was, however, included in the BTC's working party report of 1949 as Route *H* with possible further extensions to Crystal Palace via Bricklayers Arms and Peckham (Route *K*).[2] This extension, by allowing trains to reverse more easily at the southern terminus, would permit a greater peak-hour capacity on the whole line. Parliamentary powers were again obtained in 1950 and work was to have started quickly.[3] When reviewing its investment priorities, however, the BTC thought that this scheme at its latest costing of £6 million (including rolling stock and new depot at Stanmore) was expensive and 'not directly revenue earning.' It was therefore postponed indefinitely.

The scheme was not one of those included in the 1965 Railway Plan although the metropolitan boroughs of Camberwell, Southwark and Bermondsey had often pressed for a new tube. When the Aldwych and Fleet Line schemes received higher priority, members of LB Southwark met the vice-chairman of the LT Board in June 1966 to press their case for the extension.[4] After another meeting in May 1967 the Chairman of Southwark's General Purposes Committee said, referring to deputations he could remember in 1924 and 1956: 'One has heard of the continuing story of Peyton Place. This is as nothing compared with the time this Council and the metropolitan boroughs have spent on this matter.'[5]

In March 1969 LT told Southwark that the scheme had a lower priority than the Fleet Line but greater than any work on the Northern Line. In 1971 LT described it as a scheme for the 1980s,[6] but suggested that it would be helpful if Southwark could safeguard sites for stations and a depot for rolling stock.[7]

[1] LB Tower Hamlets (1971), *Proof of Evidence, E12/30*, para4, GLDP Inquiry Stage 1.
[2] BTC *First Annual Report HC Papers 235*, 1948–49, p145.
[3] BTC *Third Annual Report HC Papers 210*, 1950–51, p20.
[4] LB Southwark *Minutes*, 29 June 1966, p55.
[5] LB Southwark *Minutes*, 27 November 1968, p234.
[6] LT (1971), *Brixton Extension of the Victoria Line*, p39.
[7] LB Southwark *Minutes*, 19 March 1969, pp379–80.

An LT–LB Southwark working party was established which examined the line of the route and sites for stations at Camberwell and Peckham Rye (Figure 8). The latter was particularly difficult because it lay in a hollow where two BR lines ran on viaducts. The only feasible depot site lay to the east of Peckham on higher land. Two alternatives were examined: an underground line and station with trains coming to the surface into the depot, and a scheme whereby the railway came to the surface to the west of Peckham and crossed the hollow, also on a viaduct, and then returned to ground level to run into the depot. The latter had the advantage of providing easier interchange with BR and of not interfering with the local road network or redevelopment of the town centre. Although no detailed costing was done LT officers thought that the two-track viaduct was considerably cheaper than the tunnel.[1] In August 1972 Southwark Council were asked to ratify the working party's choice of the elevated solution, and LT sought data from Southwark on which to work up reasonably detailed traffic estimates.

In his evidence to Stage 2 of the GLDP Inquiry the Borough Planner, Mr I Lacey, said:

> Extension of the Bakerloo Line from the Elephant and Castle to Peckham would improve accessibility to the network in a way that would bring considerable benefit not only to residents, an increasing proportion of whom find employment in the central area, but to centres such as Peckham which urgently need to realise their development potential and maintain their prosperity. The realisation of this extension will remedy a long-standing deficiency in this sector of London.[2]

Although LT had always assumed that the extension would run via Camberwell Green, some of the Southwark officers would have liked to see a more detailed evaluation of an alternative route via Bricklayers Arms. This option was mentioned in the 1949 report and would have brought a tube line to an area less well served by bus than Camberwell Green, and one which was soon to undergo widespread redevelopment.

The Hainault–Wimbledon Line

The third of the three new schemes in the 1965 plan was the extension of the Aldwych branch of the Piccadilly Line across the river to Waterloo to improve distribution from Waterloo and relieve the Northern Line. Powers were obtained for this in 1965 and it was hoped to begin work in 1967 but in the latter year the scheme was postponed *inter alia* because of general cuts in public expenditure.[3] By 1968 several factors led to the formulation of a new proposal for a line linking sections of the existing Central

[1] Interviews with LT and LB Southwark officers.
[2] LB Southwark (1972), *Proof of Evidence*, *E27/105*, p2, GLDP Inquiry Stage 2.
[3] *Sel Comm LT*, 1965. LT *Annual Reports*, 1966, p16; 1967, p20.

Line (Hainault to Leyton) and the District Line (Fulham to Wimbledon) and incorporating the Aldwych branch of the Piccadilly Line. These factors were:

1 Long-standing complaints from councils and residents in areas without a tube, that they were underprivileged, notably Fulham and Chelsea, Wandsworth and especially Hackney.
2 A desire by LT to simplify operation and improve peak-hour capacity by eliminating branches on existing lines.
3 A need to further relieve the in-town distribution system particularly on parts of the District and Central Lines and on the lines crossing the river.
4 The need for some new links, e.g. between Victoria and Waterloo.

The proposal (Figure 8) was described as the 'skilful stitching together of existing tubes and disused sections of BR track.'[1] Despite this it was estimated to cost £100 million and to be a scheme for consideration as part of LT's future investment programme (see pages 112–13 and Table 4).[2]

Local councillors and GLC members for Hackney had been particularly vociferous in their demands for a tube line, pointing out that there was no line truly serving the borough, the Piccadilly Line only peripherally touching Hackney at Manor House station and the Northern at Old Street.[3] Between October 1969 and March 1970 LT and Hackney Borough Council organised a working party to consider the line and invited representatives of the GLC to join them so that problems of alignment could be considered in conjunction with the Ringway 1 and radial link motorway proposals (the East Cross section of Ringway 1 had been approved).[4]

It was agreed that as dates for the construction of both road and rail schemes had yet to be fixed, they had best be planned so as to be built independently, although near Dalston Junction the motorway might have to be elevated to accommodate the railway on the surface. The whole line might take ten years to build. LT emphasised that the railway could only be built if land for a depot could be found, possibly by extending the existing Hainault depot and by providing extra sidings at Wimbledon and Newbury Park. They pointed out that the line would not make any contribution to capital costs out of revenue, that it would therefore be important to establish a social benefit case drawing on the studies for the Victoria and Fleet Lines and the Bakerloo proposals, and that Hackney could help by making land available for the line and by re-zoning land for commercial development near the sites of stations.[5]

[1] Wanstead Residents Society (1970), *Rail in the East* (*Paper S27/63*), GLDP Inquiry Stage 2.
[2] LB Hackney *Minutes*, item 534, 4 March 1960; and *The Times* 2 January 1970.
[3] E.g. GLC *Minutes*, 31 January 1967, p10; and 10 March 1970, pp219–21. LB Hackney *Minutes*, item 567, 27 January 1971.
[4] LT *Annual Report*, 1969, p37.
[5] LB Hackney–LT Executive (1971), *Possible Underground Railway Facilities for Hackney.*

Thus the proposal is still in embryo, with major questions unresolved such as the route between Old Street and Holborn, the design of the junction and a sharp curve needed at Holborn, and whether the line between Victoria and Fulham should run north of the river through Chelsea or south of the Thames via Battersea and Wandsworth. No pressures as strong as those in Hackney or Southwark had been brought to bear on this point.

An orbital tube line

The furore in the GLDP Inquiry over the GLC's Ringway proposals engendered some discussions about the possibility of a second 'Circle Line' tube for the middle or outer suburbs. Some of the objectors pointed out that the orbital motorways, particularly the inner ones, were very expensive and could not carry as many passengers as a tube line. The case was clearly put by consultant witnesses for the boroughs of Croydon, Greenwich and Hounslow.[1] Using a route roughly on the line of Ringway 2 (the North and South Circular Roads) with a station interval of 1 mile they suggested each station might generate 6000 trips (50 000 passenger-miles) daily. Changing the alignment to serve the major strategic centres might increase the traffic. This was an attempt to counter the traditional argument that railways were not flexible enough to cope with outer suburban trips with widely dispersed origins and destinations. The GLC disputed the assumption behind this calculation reckoning the figures to be much nearer 3000 trips and 20 000 passenger miles,[2] while altering the alignment would lower the population density in the catchment areas of the stations.

Railway enthusiasts' groups and others have suggested that the makings of a loop line already exist both north and south of the river, and need only new links between Poplar and St Johns to the east and Fulham[3] or Gunnersbury[4] in the west. Later analysis of both the inner and outer suburban routes convinced the GLC and LT that the lines would show a very poor return for a very large investment.[5]

OVERSEAS EXPERIENCE AND CONCLUSIONS

As LT pointed out in 1971, over 40 of the 50 cities in the world with under-

[1] W S Atkins and Partners for LBs Croydon, Greenwich (1971), *Paper S12/51*, GLDP Inquiry Stage 1.
[2] GLC (1971), *Paper S12/69*; although in *Paper B486* the GLC estimated that a line serving Croydon might generate 40 000 passenger miles daily (pp29–30), GLDP Inquiry Stage 1.
[3] National Council for Inland Transport (1971), *Proof of Evidence*, *E12/9* and *Paper S12/125*, GLDP Inquiry Stage 1.
[4] London Liberal Party (1971), *Paper S12/37*, GLDP Inquiry Stage 1.
[5] GLC (1971), *Alternative Public Transport Plans* (*Paper B487*), pp25–7, GLDP Inquiry Stage 1.

ground railways were planning to extend them, 20 were planning or building entirely new lines and 20 were considering doing so.[1] Few of these systems undergo such rigorous planning, financial, economic and social investigation as the schemes looked at in this study;[2] San Francisco[3] with BARTD is an exception. Indeed, LT engineering and planning staff were increasingly requested to apply their expertise as consultants to such cities.

If the London schemes under discussion were implemented by 1990 the LT tube network would be extended by over 10% in size. What has led to the possibility of a third wave of tube construction after a period of sixty years? There are three main aspects of the current situation: a changed national policy towards public transport; the way in which schemes are evaluated; and the role and influence of the GLC.

First, there has been a major change of policy attitude towards underground railway construction. During the 1950s and early 1960s new tubes were considered an expensive luxury and, as such, secondary to the needs of national rail improvements, national and metropolitan road improvements, and replacement of tube rolling stock and power generators and other equipment. During Barbara Castle's Ministry, however, national priorities turned increasingly to urban transport and particularly public transport problems. At the same time these were reinforced by institutional changes. The GLC as highway and planning authority for the conurbation found itself with new responsibilities for LT at a time when its first long-term plan was undergoing rigorous examination. They were severely criticised at the GLDP Inquiry for failing to include a coherent public transport strategy to balance the highways and traffic proposals. In the eyes of the critics and the wider public the GLC felt, therefore, that they had to be seen to be improving the quality and quantity of public transport services, particularly if, as soon proved necessary, the fares were to be increased to avoid paying operating subsidies.

From LT's viewpoint, after the long and difficult negotiations over the Victoria Line and the slightly easier ones over its extension, they were still not too sanguine about the maintenance of a 'rolling programme' of schemes akin to the roads programme until the approval of the Heathrow link and Stage I of the Fleet Line. Indeed the cost revision of the latter added to these doubts, which continued despite continuous pressure on the Government on the grounds that the special construction team 'is not easy to get together but only too easy to disperse.'[4] But the dovetailing of the

[1] LT (1971), *The Brixton Extension of the Victoria Line*, p9.

[2] Information from LT officers, and Mr J M Thomson who visited over twenty cities throughout the world in 1971 to obtain information on their traffic and transport policies.

[3] Because the finances for BARTD were raised by local bonds and sales taxes there was a great deal of direct opposition from the motoring lobby, which is unknown in the London situation. See F C Colcord Jnr (1971), *Urban Transportation Decision-making in San Francisco: a Case Study* (Tufts U/MIT) esp ch6.

[4] Day (1969), p124.

Victoria Line and Brixton extension was not tight enough to prevent this dispersal from substantially happening, and the small transfer of manpower that took place could not have saved much money, nor could the subsequent transfer from Brixton to Heathrow.

Second, there have been some changes in the way the planning process has been handled. The responsibility for devising, designing, costing and (until 1970) evaluating the schemes remained primarily the responsibility of London Transport who submitted them successively to the BTC, the MOT, the GLC and DOE for approval. The GLC, despite having powers over the planning of all transport facilities except Trunk roads under the 1969 Act, did not intervene substantially in this process, partly because of the number of other matters involved in LT policy making, partly because it did not want to become too engrossed in detail, and partly because LT's long-established planning and design sections were technically competent as the demand for their advice has demonstrated.

This situation has had two results: LT have undertaken the evaluation of alternatives (such as the decision as to where railheads or stations should be, which alternative route to take for a particular stretch of line) on engineering cost and traffic criteria. Projects have been refined within the organisation and then presented to the GLC and DOE as desirable objectives ranked in order of importance.[1] Thus the proposals current in 1970, with the exception of parts of the Hainault–Wimbledon Line, dated back beyond the 1965 working party report to the schemes of the BTC and Ministry working parties. LT officers had great faith in the value of their schemes which were based on long operating experience and skill and evolved in careful and detailed discussion, but they could not transcend LT's own area of responsibility.

Moreover, having a fairly dense city centre network and widespread coverage of the suburbs north of the Thames, LT engineers could not foresee that any further major schemes were necessary to 'fill the gaps in the system.'[2] As the gaps have been successively filled, it is not surprising that the projects have shown increasingly poor returns, even with the extension of methods of evaluation to attempt to quantify values of comfort, convenience, reliability and the benefits of decongesting roads and other lines. The exception (see Case Study *E*) was the Heathrow link which has a specific function to serve a market with great capacity for growth and diversion from other means of travel, as is demonstrated by its estimated profitability.

The use of social cost-benefit analysis for large capital schemes eligible for grant aid has virtually become obligatory but as yet accepted techniques have not become available which adequately represent improvements in

[1] Although LT attempt to rank capital projects in terms of their 'real' return rather than the net cost to LT. Information from Mr D Quarmby Director of Operational Research, February 1972.

[2] Interviews with officers and LT Executive (1970), *Proof of Evidence, E12/2*, para13, GLDP Inquiry Stage 1.

the quality of travel which accrue mainly to existing users (i.e. most of the benefits of line extensions, relief routes or route options and improved interchanges) or of the side benefits that major new facilities like tube lines may have in stimulating development or providing mobility. Economists, particularly in the Treasury, have claimed that some of these effects are 'double-counting' or are cancelled out by losses elsewhere. This must remain a moot point, but it is possible that there are benefits which can only be generated by a new railway with its high capacity.[1]

Thus the time-saving element (especially that for former road travellers) has come to play a very important part in evaluation, to the point where one might assume that it is either being used as a proxy for benefits which cannot be readily given a monetary value, or for other factors which are omitted or undervalued elsewhere in the decision-making process. Indeed as far as the Fleet Line is concerned this seems to have been the case for the quantifiable benefits only gave ratios to costs of 0.7–0.9, and as a senior LT officer put it: 'If you cannot justify the Fleet Line, you certainly cannot justify any of the later schemes.' Also, although the use of cost-benefit analysis has become an accepted part of the evaluation process, no means have yet been found of comparing railways with other forms of transport investment, a fact deplored by economists working in the system, who are too few to do more than prepare and check evaluations of some major individual projects that arise. The wider planning considerations were a very strong factor in GLTG's examination of the Fleet Line and its subsequent consideration by the GLC.

Third, the new responsibilities of the GLC have led to a much more direct pressure to improve the tube system in several ways besides the building of new tube lines. The GLC showed great willingness to put considerable capital sums into tube investment provided the Government contributed capital on the same basis (75%) as for Principal road schemes. Moreover, in negotiations about grants, the GLC were instrumental in getting the criteria widened.

The GLC were keen to help LT in any way that did not mean a revenue subsidy which they feared could escalate as it had done in the mid-1960s. The uncertain state of their road proposals until the Minister's decision on the GLDP, and the relatively labour-intensive nature of the bus services were thought to preclude any rapid and major improvement to LT's bus activities other than new vehicles. Tube investment, on the other hand, gave the GLC the opportunity to make a major financial contribution, to take advantage of the available grants, and thus to promote part of their public transport strategy as it evolved in the period 1970–72, culminating in the suggested revision of the GLDP.

In the longer term, however, there are some major questions to which the GLC should address themselves. Are they going to take a more active role in the forward planning process by suggesting alternative

[1] R Thomas discusses social desirability and profitability with reference to the Victoria Line in his (1968), *Journeys to Work* (PEP Broadsheet No. 504, pp331–8).

schemes to be evaluated, or to demand a list of schemes from which to choose rather than evaluating individual projects in turn?

If the schemes discussed fill the last 'gaps in the system' what is to follow—schemes on existing lines to improve the capacity and quality of service such as improving interchanges, rebuilding junctions and separating branches (e.g. the Northern Line between Euston and Camden Town); new schemes to serve areas that need general revitalisation (e.g. the possible idea of a 'dockland' or 'river' line from Fenchurch Street via the London and Surrey Docks and Beckton to Thamesmead,[1] or a line along the south bank); the development of an express service in full-size tunnels linking BR's suburban services with more widely spaced stops (like the Reseau Express Regional in Paris), or an extension of the tube routes with their frequent services over some BR lines in the GLC area?

There is also the problem of relating the rate of development of the tube system with the reorganisation and freeing from congestion of the bus services (because every new tube causes a considerable diversion of traffic leading to the withdrawal of some services and the reduction of others) and with the spread of parking control and other traffic restraint measures. This means a continuous process of internal co-ordination in the GLC on a comprehensive basis, unknown prior to the 1969 Act.

All of these possibilities demand a close policy and organisational involvement of the GLC with LT and an increasing amount of strategic planning at County Hall. They place a large onus on GLTG as a co-ordinating body particularly if BR planning remains a separate responsibility; indeed they raise the whole problem of the GLC's relationship with BR. The astonishing increases in the cost estimates of Stage I of the Fleet Line may, however, be a spur to a closer involvement of the GLC in the preparation of future schemes.

The criteria and methods for evaluating the social benefits was still very imperfect. Policies were evolving in favour of public transport, but perhaps the methods had not been sufficiently developed and tested to withstand the momentum of the post-war programmes with their strong emphasis on highway investment. They were certainly not sufficiently developed to enable comparisons to be made with other investments, but were accepted as tools of the trade for looking at individual proposals. The GLC now has two major responsibilities: to assess the future long-term role of the tubes within the context of land-use development and the whole transport system, and to consider whether its own role is merely as a co-ordinator through GLTG or as an initiator of future plans, in which case further powers may be needed if this means changing the relationships with BR in London.

[1] Discussed in GLC (1971), *Paper B487*, *Public Transport Alternatives*, s2.4 and Figure 4, GLDP Inquiry Stage 2. This has been mentioned as more feasible if Stage III of the Fleet Line does not proceed.

Case Study D

DEVELOPMENT AT STATIONS

1 INTRODUCTION

The siting of development at railway stations is no new thing: in the nineteenth century the main termini in London and provincial cities were chosen as the natural and symbolic location for large hotels and offices belonging to their operating companies, and smaller stations for parades of shops and showrooms with flats or small office suites above. The idea of concentrating a very large amount of development at stations, particularly office development, gained prominence during the great central London office boom of the late 1950s, although the British Rail (BR) Board had hoped to have commercial development at Euston and Kings Cross as early as 1952.[1]

The main benefits of commercial development at stations are:

1 Income to the rail operator as landlord of whole or part of the site.
2 Income to the operators from any increased travel along the line on which the development is situated, or its interconnecting bus and rail services.
3 Possible transfer of traffic from the roads.
4 Saving of in-town distribution capacity from terminals because people tend to 'live along the line' on which they work and therefore do not need to change in the centre to buses, tubes, or to the pavement.
5 Having a direct service to their offices, workers would tend to travel, if not outside the peak, on the 'shoulders' of the peak in morning and evening thus producing a marginal 'staggering' of demand.[2]

The most tangible benefits accrue directly to the operators. Indeed, the last three benefits would only accrue if the development was relocated rather than being additional to what would otherwise take place. BR claim that without commercial development, desirable operating and interchange improvements could not be carried out; this is invariably true of the central London termini where schemes are especially costly.[3] Improved stations may generate extra rail travel and minimise opposition to fares

[1] The British Transport Commission *Annual Report for 1952*, para24.

[2] For a detailed survey of this effect see P W Sargeant (1971), *Staggering of Hours* (Dip TP thesis, Univ Coll London). Also GLC (1970), *Proof of Evidence*, *E12/1*, para8.44, GLDP Inquiry Stage 1.

[3] See London Transport (LT) and BR Annual Reports; and BR (1971), *Proof of Evidence*, *E12/32*, pp1–5, GLDP Inquiry Stage 1.

increases. Some would go further than this and claim that the public transport system can only play its proper role if the whole structure of the city is related to it, including the pattern of residential densities (see section 4 below). On the other hand some economists would claim that the benefits of development at stations are merely transferred from other places where the development might have occurred, but if it avoids road traffic which could cause congestion (and concomitant lost time) and bad environmental effects, these could be claimed as benefits to the community even if difficult to measure.

In London BR and London Transport (LT) are involved as transport operators. Both have groups specifically charged with looking after property interests; BR have an independent property Board and LT an estates department. The Greater London Council (GLC) is concerned as the strategic planning and transport authority responsible for specifying the broad pattern of land use, employment and transport facilities. The London boroughs are also involved, partly because of their interest as recipients of rate income, sometimes as landlords, and partly because of the local planning and transport effects of such development. The Department of the Environment (DOE) is also involved as arbiter of GLC plans and of capital grants for the transport element of interchange improvement schemes (now 75% of the cost of approved projects). Since 1969 the Ministry of Housing and Local Government (MOHLG) (and subsequently the DOE) has been responsible for scrutinising applications for permits to build new offices in London and the South-East under the Control of Office and Industrial Development Act 1965. This function was formerly carried out by the Board of Trade.

The background of office development in London and attempts to control it are relevant to the whole of this case study. At the end of the war there were 77 million square feet of offices in central London. After some initial rebuilding, the real boom came when building controls were relaxed and over 5 million square feet of offices were approved in each year from 1948 to 1961. By 1961 there was 168 million square feet of office floorspace in central London (Table 16) and it was believed that 15 000 new jobs were being created annually.

The London County Council's (LCC) worries about runaway employment and commuting growth were shared by the Town and Country Planning Association, the regional Standing Conference[1] and the Government. The Location of Offices Bureau was set up to encourage decentralisation in 1963 and in November 1964 the newly elected Labour Government introduced the 'Brown ban' requiring any development producing more than 3000 square feet of net new space to be scrutinised for its necessity and suitability to London and the region, before being given an Office Development Permit (ODP) and being eligible for planning permission (see section 3 below).

[1] Standing Conference *Report LRP 279*, 8 July 1964; see also M Ash (1962), *The Paper Metropolis* (TCPA).

DATE	NET GROWTH	CENTRAL LONDON	INNER LONDON	OUTER LONDON	GREATER LONDON
1939	—	87	—	—	—
1945	—	77	—	—	—
1961	—	168	44	59	271
	1961–66	11	4	10	25
1966	—	179	48	69	296
	Actual 1966–71	8	2	11	21
	Target 1966–71	7	2	7	16
1971	(probable)	187	50	80	317
	Target 1972–76	12	5	12	29
Target 1976	—	199	55	92	346

Table 16 OFFICE FLOORSPACE IN LONDON, 1939–76 (MILLIONS OF SQUARE FEET)

Sources: Marriott (1969), app3; *Standing Conference*, paper 1852, 1 December 1971; *GLDP Paper* B452; and DOE *Returns under COID Act 1965*, 1965–70

	CENTRAL LONDON	INNER LONDON	OUTER LONDON	GREATER LONDON
1 Target 1972–76	12.0	5.0	12.0	29.0
2 Permissions 1968–70 for completion 1972–76	3.7	1.9	1.9	7.5
3 'Remainder'	8.3	3.1	10.1	21.5
4 Permissions needed 1971–74 to achieve 'remainder'	16.6	6.2	16.9	39.7
5 Annual average 1971–74	3.7	1.25	3.5	8.45
6 ODPs. granted: 1966	0.5	0.8 (Inner and Outer)		1.3
1967	1.4	1.2		2.6
1968	2.6	1.6		4.2
1969	4.1	2.8		6.9
1970	6.1	4.2		10.3

Table 17 PLANNING PERMISSIONS AND ODPs (MILLIONS OF SQUARE FEET)

Source: Tables III.8 – III.10 of *B452*, GLDP Inquiry Stage 1

After the control system had been in operation for a few years doubts about its efficiency were raised. The Standing Conference used 1961 census figures to show that total employment increases in central London had only been 55 000 in the previous decade compared with 160 000 as feared, due to losses in industry and other sectors.[1] There were also complaints that the pressure of demand was forcing up rents for both new and existing offices to levels where international companies might be deterred from settling in London, and that this would be particularly disadvantageous if Britain joined the European Economic Community.[2] As a result, markedly more ODP's were granted in 1970 and 1971, and the GLC's sector 'targets' for 1972–76 (see section 2) were almost 80% higher than for 1966–71 (Table 16).

The following sections examine the GLC's policies for offices particularly at stations (section 2), and the plans of BR and LT (sections 3 and 4).

2 THE GLC'S POLICIES

In 1965 the GLC became responsible for producing a Greater London Development Plan (GLDP) and for granting or refusing planning permission for office developments greater than 3000 square feet, but they inherited from the LCC a policy of very strict zoning and granting of permissions under the County of London Plan. (The LCC's policies are given in greater detail in section 3.) The GLC also had to operate within the Government's policy of controlling new office development in London and South-East England through the ODP system.

In the GLC's Preliminary Outline of Policy for the GLDP and the first draft of the *Written Statement* in 1967[3] no specific policy for offices was set out although it was suggested that activity in central London might be stabilised, and certain essential white-collar activities encouraged. Neither document suggested that any form of development could be concentrated around public transport interchanges. The third (consultation) draft text circulated in March 1969 showed the net amount of new office space allocated to various sectors in the period 1966–71 (Table 16) and said:

> In the development of central London termini it should be possible to recoup part of the capital cost of reconstruction by including housing, office, entertainment or retail centres in the plans. The development of offices over selected main-line termini rather than elsewhere would avoid adding to the 'peak of the peak', to the commuters' journey times, and to the burden on the central area distributor system.[4]

[1] Standing Conference *Report LRP 721*, 23 November 1966.

[2] For example, the *Guardian*, 5 October 1971; *The Times*, 17 November 1971; and *Building Design*, 17 December 1971.

[3] GLC (1967), *GLDP Inquiry Paper B13*, pp7, 17; and *B14*, pp5, 6, 9.

[4] GLC (1969), *GLDP Inquiry Paper B16*, pp15, 24, 25, 44. The passage quoted became para5.56 of the *Written Statement* as published in 1969.

The draft GLDP mentioned interchange improvements at King's Cross and Victoria but said little about suburban stations. With respect to central London offices, it said (page 44) 'renewal and such added floorspace as may be appropriate in the general policy should be encouraged generally on the most accessible sites.'

Later that year the *Written Statement* was published incorporating these figures which represented a 4% increase in central and inner London and 10–12½% in outer London. The implementation of the policy would depend on criteria being researched by the GLC, and on local siting considerations such as:

> What benefits will a particular project bring to a particular district? How will it fit in with other buildings planned in the area, with roads and with car parking? What contribution can it make to the restructuring of London? What assistance can it give to larger developments of which it could form part? How is it placed for workers to reach it?[1]

These questions were described as 'within the competence of the local planning authorities to solve.' The statement concerning central London offices was elaborated to read (paragraph 7.22):

> The proposal to allow an addition of approximately 4% of central London's total office floorspace should be used to assist a gradual redistribution of offices to the most suitable locations. Accessibility is one of the principal considerations, and the vicinities of the railway termini and other important traffic interchange points have advantages in that respect.

Perhaps the most interesting remarks were reserved for the (non-statutory) *Report of Studies* in discussing land use and redevelopment changes that could affect the chosen policy.[2]

> *Concentration of activities.* Office development *adjacent to select mainline railway termini* would reduce the need for transport investment within the central area whilst facilitating the use of railways for work journeys.
>
> Outside the central area, economies of scale arise from concentrating the growth of office, shopping and entertainment facilities at suburban centres or transport nodes. This growth is best located at centres *where public transport accessibility is already high* and which have the capacity for additional development. If levels of employment were increased in centres in other parts of London, additional transport investment might be required.
>
> Suburban growth centres might also be located at intersections created

[1] GLC (1969), *GLDP Written Statement*, paras4.21, 4.22.
[2] GLC (1969), *Report of Studies*, paras6.215–6.218.

by additional primary roads, since these will also be centres of high accessibility. However, priority might be given to the development of public transport nodes in order to reap the full advantage of the public transport infrastructure.

Residential density. Residential population densities should *be designed to obtain the benefits of public transport accessibility*. A major problem of building to high densities is the large amount of land needed for car parking and accessibility, but the construction of high-density residential buildings adjacent to good public transport facilities would *tend to minimise the demand for private cars and parking space* [our italics].[1]

Despite these cautious statements and the work of the TCCL group concerned with interchanges (see Chapter 3 and Case Study *F*), a special interchanges study undertaken to support the brief statement in the GLDP contained no information on the relationship of interchanges to land use, or on the problems of implementing interchange improvements.[2] It merely designated as such the central London termini and nine other major and twenty-eight secondary interchanges and analysed them from the point of view of transport movements. However, during 1969 the Group had studied development at terminals using 1960–64 data including the Shell Centre surveys (see Case Study *B*). On the grounds of accessibility it was thought that the terminals handling the most commuters (see Figure 15) should be chosen for development but generally these had little or no spare train or seat capacity for more workers.[3]

In 1970 the GLC analysed some of the data collected by the South-East Joint Planning Team, which suggested that the north London job market was relatively self-contained, so that offices at the northern terminals might draw workers from south of the Thames, particularly when the Victoria and Fleet Lines were available. Notwithstanding this, the GLC estimated that from 3 to 4 million square feet of the 20 million or so to be allowed in central London up to 1981 could be over terminals; this would represent about 20 000 additional workers, and 6% more peak-hour arrivals on BR trains or 2% more on the total peak arrivals.[4]

Neither of these reports was published, but in response to the GLDP Inquiry Panel, BR gave as an example the Liverpool Street scheme—there they claimed that 2½ million square feet of offices, a hotel and shops could provide 9000 jobs, and if 50% of the workers lived along the line (as at the Shell Centre) a 'normal' pattern of travel could relieve the peak 15 minutes by 1%. But a prescribed starting time of, say, 9.30 a.m. could relieve the

[1] Mr Lees, one of the GLDP Inquiry Panel, commented on this point: 'To my mind as an Inspector, what is contained in other documents is not really part of the Development Plan and I could not pay much attention to these. What I would like to see is a clear indication of policy in the *Written Statement*' (*Transcript*, day 66, p26).

[2] GLC (1969), *GLDP Interchanges Study*.

[3] *Paper ICG/89A*, February 1969.

[4] GLC draft report on central London terminals, 1970.

peak half-hour by from 4 to 6%—'a really significant improvement.'[1]

The relationship between transport and land use was referred to by Mr B J Collins (joint director of Planning and Transportation) in the GLC's opening evidence to the GLDP Inquiry in the following terms:

> The present patterns of activity in London are if anything too dispersed to be consistent with good service by public transport particularly in outer areas. Within the Strategic Plan new development generating high passenger demands should be related to the *focal points of the transport system and in particular to railway stations* [our italics].[2]

Mr Collins went on to say that the Council hoped to stimulate beneficial land-use changes through transport investment, and instanced Thamesmead and the Docklands area. In their transportation evidence, this point was set out as one of the six principles governing the formulation of strategy, but added little to Mr Collins's statement, namely:

> Land use and transport development must be planned together and in particular major new public transport facilities must go hand in hand with commercial, industrial and residential development so as to concentrate the demand for movement *in such a manner that public transport will again come into its own* [our italics].[3]

The same document gave one reference to development at stations:

> The opportunities for improvement to interchanges will often present themselves as part of major schemes for renewal on redevelopment. For instance the rebuilding of London Bridge station, to which the BR Board accord high priority, should provide opportunities for better interchange from bus to rail and from surface to underground rail. To the extent that the rebuilding of stations involves general development in their vicinity, it is to be expected that a contribution to total cost will come from private development.[4]

No elaboration was given in the assessment of the transport strategy, and no other background documentation appeared to give any substance to the above statements of policy. During the Inquiry the Town and Country Planning Association (TCPA) criticised the GLC amongst other things for failing to take advantage of the likely changes in land use and for not developing alternative land-use plans (particularly beyond 1981).[5]

[1] BR (1972), *Paper S30/76*, GLDP Inquiry Stage 3.
[2] GLC (1970), *Proof of Evidence, E11/1*, paras8.54–8.55, GLDP Inquiry Stage 1.
[3] GLC (1970), *Proof of Evidence, E12/1*, paras3.2.8, 4.3.17, GLDP Inquiry Stage 1.
[4] GLC (1970), *Proof of Evidence, E12/1*, para4.4.23, GLDP Inquiry Stage 1.
[5] TCPA (1971), *Paper S12/127*. The GLC replied in *Paper S12/240* relying on the documentation already mentioned above.

After consulting the boroughs, the GLC published new office floorspace allocations during Stage 1 of the Inquiry suggesting increases in 1972–76 of 6% for central London, 10% for inner London and 17% for outer London, a rate of provision which was considerably higher than that for the previous quinquennium.[1] As Table 17 shows this could mean giving planning permission for 40 million square feet of offices after allowing for schemes 'in the pipeline' and permissions not taken up because of lack of ODPs. As Table 17 also shows, the required average annual rate of ODPs is less than that allowed in 1970 by the DOE.[2]

It was not surprising, therefore, that towards the end of Stage 1 of the Inquiry the GLC sought to explain their intentions in the evidence given by Dr Eversley, then Chief Planner Strategy Branch.[3]

> For the forseeable future, by far the easiest journey to work, and the one causing fewest social dis-benefits, is the radial rail journey to central London. . . . It is the Council's policy to advocate the strengthening of this rail network, but the matter is not entirely under its control (paragraph 1.70).
>
> All the Council can say, on the evidence before it, is that the rail network is quite capable, with some relatively modest improvements, of bringing half a million workers into central London in comfort every day. This belief also underlies the location policies of the Council in relation to railway terminals. Large new developments have been encouraged, and will be further encouraged, over, or in relation to, the main commuter termini, especially those which commuters use heavily (paragraph 1.71).
>
> Central area locations and offices at termini, however, are not the whole story. The Council is also encouraging office development at or near intermediate stations and interchanges wherever there is apparent spare capacity on the rail lines. This is also in accord with the expressed intentions of the LT Executive and BR. (See *E12/2*, p7, para26 for LT Executive; and *E12/7*, p30, para449 for BR.) Many London boroughs have included such schemes in their local redevelopment plans. The advantages of such locations are that they minimise the call on road space and take the greatest advantage of rail capacity: the under-used outer sections, the possibility of reverse commuting, employment within easy walking distance of railway stations. LT bus networks are also being concentrated on certain suburban rail stations especially where these are well located in relation to shopping centres (paragraph 1.72).

[1] GLC (1971), *Paper B452, Industrial and Office Floorspace Targets, 1972–76*, GLDP Inquiry Stage 1.

[2] There are also office projects which have been granted ODPs but not planning permission; 20 of 35 million square feet of ODPs granted in 1965–72 fell into this category. Question in Council, GLC *Minutes*, 8 February 1972, p39.

[3] GLC (1971), *Proof E11/1, General Strategy and Implementation*, GLDP Inquiry Stage 1.

As a further development of these policies in January 1972 the GLC's Strategic Planning Committee specified six locational criteria for offices two of which were:

> Provision of residential accommodation in conjunction with the (office) development. . . . Improvement of the public transport system, especially in relation to interchanges and railway termini. . . . Growth may also be allowed, subject as above, in other locations which are either in close proximity to central London termini, or to places which provide significant facilities for interchange of passengers provided that the development will not cause passenger traffic exceeding the transport capacity.[1]

Mr Vigars, chairman of the Committee, said that the criteria would apply immediately and 'will give London the benefits of better distribution of jobs, will ease the transport problems and also help to make jobs available locally for married women and part-time workers.' The Committee then specified forty-two locations for priority in receiving new offices. Of these, twenty-five were strategic town centres, including all six major strategic centres, seven were central London rail termini, some were related to the Victoria and Fleet Lines, and the others were proposed redevelopment areas. The list included twelve of the fourteen areas chosen for development by LT a few weeks earlier (see section 4).

These areas were included in a suggested revision of the *Written Statement* in February 1972 where it was clearly stated that a major feature of the new structure of London would be 'that a larger part of total activity and a high proportion of new activity should be located in close relation to the public transport network (underground and railways) and to the new primary and secondary road system.'[2] The report also said that:

> New offices should be located as close to railway stations in central London as other considerations permit. Outside central London it will be most worthwhile to locate large office buildings at major junctions in the rail system and at important public transport interchanges. *The density of housing development should generally be higher in areas most convenient to railway stations than elsewhere. The better the service from a station the more appropriate higher densities will be* [our italics].[3]

This last statement was a major policy movement towards the viewpoint of many of the GLC's critics, notably the TCPA.

[1] The *Guardian*; and GLC *Press Release 28*, 20 January 1972.
[2] GLC *Minutes*, 8 February 1972, pp73–81 appl, para2.20; see also paras5.2.20–5.2.22.
[3] GLC (1972), *Written Statement Revisions*, para5.9.7.

3 BRITISH RAILWAYS: EUSTON STATION, OTHER CENTRAL LONDON TERMINI AND SUBURBAN STATIONS

BR management has been heavily criticised for being slow to recognise the value of its own sites. As Marriott has pointed out, during the office boom developers did approach the Board but few schemes were negotiated partly because of the tight terms required by BR. In London three schemes were negotiated with Town & City Properties at Cannon Street, Holborn Viaduct and Waterloo. But schemes for the bigger stations did not mature until the LCC and the Government had started to apply restrictive policies for office building, and the British Transport Commission (BTC) did not set up a property subsidiary (Railways Sites Ltd) until October 1961, nearly the peak of the property boom.[1]

Under the Transport Act 1962, the transport Boards were empowered to undertake non-operational development on land that they owned or to combine it with schemes for transport facilities. With regard to London, however, the Boards had to consult the LCC as to its use and satisfy the Minister of Housing and Local Government that their proposals were:

> Consistent with the need for keeping a proper balance in the use of their land as between new office accommodation and other accommodation, for trade, business and industry on the one hand, and new living accommodation (with the amenities required by a resident community on the other hand).[2]

This embodied the concern to make all suitable land available for housing, as expressed in a White Paper soon afterwards.[3]

The Railways Board examined its land holdings and put forward proposals to the LCC in November 1963, suggesting that housing land and open space for 35 000 people could be provided in the LCC area and around stations within 2 miles of its boundary. The Board argued that this housing would hold 15 000 workers and that in return it should be given permission over a period of fifteen years to develop offices and other commercial uses at its stations to employ that number. The LCC Town Planning Committee thought that the Board had over-estimated the area of surplus land suitable for housing within the LCC area, and had taken in too much land outside. It suggested that only 18 000 people could be accommodated, representing 7500 workers, of whom only 2500 would be office workers.[4]

Later the Board, the GLC and the boroughs began negotiating about land for housing, which resulted in schemes such as those for Marylebone (Lisson Green) and West Kensington goods yards, which will produce

[1] O Marriott (1967), *The Property Boom*, Pan Books, 1969, pp117–20.
[2] *Transport Act 1962*, ch46, ss11, 87.
[3] *London Employment: Housing: Land*, Cmnd 1952, HMSO 1963, para57.
[4] LCC *Minutes*, 14 July 1964, pp739–43.

1500 and 600 dwellings for Westminster and Hammersmith respectively.[1]

Euston

The rebuilding of Euston has been described as 'one of the classic stories of confusion in post-war British planning.'[2] Against the general planning background just described, electrification of the Euston–Birmingham–Manchester line had been under consideration during the 1950s and the Railways Board were keen to rebuild the station to improve train operations and interchange with the tube system (at that time the new Victoria Line was expected to be completed to Euston by the end of 1963). BR's intentions to demolish and rebuild the station were first revealed to the LCC late in 1959.[3] The Board was keen to include office provision on a large scale to offset the costs of the terminal and its new parcels, car parking and concourse facilities which ultimately cost £15 million. The offices and an hotel were planned in four tower blocks, the tallest of which was to be 365 feet high.[4]

Expenditure on the electrification was approved in January 1964 but decisions on rebuilding the station were bedevilled by the question of destroying or removing the Euston Arch. The furore over this is well documented elsewhere.[5] Subsequently, aesthetic objections to tower blocks by the Royal Fine Arts Commission and others led to a considerable delay. In March 1963 the LCC suggested that only operational offices (i.e. for BR staff) could be included. They had recently examined the office development stituation and feared that there was likely to be considerable growth in office employment because of outstanding planning permissions, and the potential extra floorspace allowed when rebuilding under the Third Schedule of the 1947 Town and Country Planning Act. They therefore recommended further re-zoning of some office areas,[6] decreasing plot ratios in others, encouraging decentralisation (in collaboration with the newly established Location of Offices Bureau) and investigating licensing of new schemes as a form of control. The LCC concluded:

> Were it a case of choosing locations most suitable for office development the Town Planning Committee might agree that there were advantages in such development taking place at the main-line stations. In the

[1] Under MOHLG Circular 57/66, October 1966, nationalised industries and statutory undertakers had to give local authorities first refusal of surplus land. See the *Guardian*, 9 September 1970; and *Daily Telegraph*, 16 March 1970.

[2] P Hall, *New Society*, 9 April 1971, p587.

[3] A A Jackson (1969), *London's Termini*, pp50, 53.

[4] LCC *Minutes*, 26 January 1960, p22; 10 May 1960, pp294–5; 28 February 1961, p92.

[5] For example, A and P Smithson (1968), *The Euston Arch and the Growth of the London, Midland and Scottish Railway*. A lengthy campaign in the press by the Victorian Society and eminent architects, accompanied by questions in Parliament and a public appeal for funds, all came to naught.

[6] LCC *Minutes*, 19 March 1963, pp212–18. The LCC had already reduced plot ratios in 1957 and re-zoned some land in 1959.

present situation, however, these advantages are negligible in comparison with the disadvantages of allowing so substantial an increase in employment in central London.

They recommended that BR's proposals should be strongly resisted and suggested that the Board could seek other uses such as further education, university, hostel and hotel and car park development, although at the time none of these showed as high a return as shops or offices.

As a result, the Minister of Housing and Local Government was unwilling to approve BR's proposals. In September 1964 the Board suggested development on a new basis: the same quantity of housing land in exchange for office space for 5000 workers over a period of fifteen years, plus permission to rebuild their existing offices with a Third Schedule allowance. The LCC feared that this might still result in 15 000 extra jobs. Then, on 4 November, came the Government's decision to licence office development in South-East England, and numerous BR schemes under negotiation were stopped. Two weeks later the Minister told the Board that he could not approve development under the 1962 Act, and that they should release land suitable for housing. Not surprisingly the Board objected but the Minister insisted, fearing employment growth as great as that of the 1950s.[1] The Board later described 1964 as 'a frustrating and unproductive year for property development'.[2]

Operational requirements at Euston, however, made the need for modernisation urgent and in 1963 the rebuilding proceeded without any speculative offices above the station. Moreover, no provision was made for stronger foundations and columns which could later support an office tower, because the cost would have had to be borne by public funds, without any guarantee of return.[3] The Board was particularly disappointed at the lost opportunity to use the vast airspace above Euston because the LCC had approved the private Euston Tower development containing 500 000 square feet of offices, 150 000 square feet of showrooms and 120 000 square feet of shops only 500 yards away, partly as a 'deal' with the developers to gain land for widening Euston Road without paying compensation for lost development rights.[4] This scheme may well have made a profit of £22 million for its developers.[5]

The new Euston station was completed in October 1968 and has since been strongly criticised both in terms of its architecture and its standard of facilities for passengers.[6] Although interchange with the Victoria Line is reasonably good, that with Euston Square has not been improved, and

[1] GLC *Minutes*, 26 May 1965, pp436–8.
[2] *Annual Report*, 1964, p67.
[3] Interviews with officers of the Railways and Property Boards.
[4] BR Board *Annual Report*, 1968, pp356–7.
[5] Marriott (1969), ch11, pp181–95, and app8.
[6] For example, *The Economist* said: 'It would be unfair to say "c'est magnifique, mais ce n'est pas la gare," it is simply, solely and unmistakeably a station,' vol229, 19 October 1968, p84; and 21 December 1968, p42.

still involves a quarter mile walk at ground level.[1] Taxi access is improved compared with the old station but no opportunity was taken to improve access for pedestrians or bus passengers, despite major traffic management schemes to ease the general traffic flow at nearby junctions and prolonged and expensive works to widen Euston Road.[2]

The Board continued to hope for and seek the grant of an 'open' ODP (i.e. a permit for a given quantity of space which could be let by negotiation) or for agreement with a client already granted an ODP. Their efforts were fortified by the establishment in 1968 of a separate Property Board 'with particular regard to the commercial development of its property, including air-space over stations,' and they drew attention to the GLDP's recommendation in September 1969 (see page 226) that the main-line terminals were suitable locations for offices.[3]

In 1967 it was reported that the BR Board were negotiating for an hotel to be built by an American company, but this was dropped in 1968 partly as a result of cutbacks in public spending, and because various factions preferred not to deal with a foreign developer.[4]

In November 1970 the DOE unexpectedly granted BR an ODP for some 500 000 square feet of offices at Euston and the Board immediately appointed consultant architects, estate agents and valuers to undertake a feasibility study and approach various property companies. The *Guardian* commented that the GLC might be willing to approve such a development, which represented a considerable share of its annual central area office space allocation, in return for an environmental *quid pro quo*. Its editorial said 'the office block that BR may now build at Euston Station may make some lucky commuters' lives more civilised. It ought also to be good for BR's budget. And it ought to point the way for similar projects at the other stations.'[5] An outline planning application for 530 000 square feet of offices including a 34-storey tower block and a 440-bed hotel to be built in front of the station was submitted to Camden Council, who had to refer it to the GLC for a direction under section 24 (6) of the 1963 London Government Act. The chairman of Camden's planning committee, Mr Alan Greengross, was concerned to negotiate a package deal over railway land in Camden, with an eye particularly on surplus goods yards which could be used for housing (see below). He said:

> I made it clear that I would only support its approval if it were made part of an overall and binding agreement covering a much larger area of BR land. BR continually paid lip service to the concept. But still the

[1] *New Society* commented: 'All that tunnelling, sapping, mining and excavating, and no Metropolitan Line connection,' 6 November 1969, p734.

[2] GLC *Minutes*, esp 17 December 1968, p775; 28 January 1969, p3; 20 October 1970, p552; and 17 November 1970, p607.

[3] BR Board *Annual Report 1969*, pp52–3; the work of the Railways Estates Department and the company Railway Sites Ltd had been merged in March 1965.

[4] *The Times*, 10 January 1968.

[5] The *Guardian*, 24 November 1970.

> application for 500 000 square feet of offices comes to us in isolation. I believe, if we really care for the community as a whole, we will, when the time comes, reject any such application in isolation so that we can achieve and maintain a balance in the use of our most valuable asset, land.[1]

In June 1971, however, the Central Area Board of the GLC's Environmental Planning Committee directed Camden to refuse the scheme on the following grounds: high buildings were inappropriate here (they were also described as obliterating the western half of Euston Gardens), arrangements to cope with the increased traffic were not satisfactory, and no sufficient justification was seen for the large amount of offices proposed. The chairman of the Central Area Board, Mr Neil Thorne, said:

> These proposals were totally unacceptable. We are very concerned about Euston Square. Redevelopment of the square requires much detailed thought. The only proper solution is for the GLC to sit round a table with the Board of British Rail and other interested parties and discuss what they propose.[2]

The situation was made worse by the fact that through a fault in communications Camden and BR were not notified before the GLC's public announcement was made.[3]

The Railways Board subsequently added to their consultant team Colonel Richard Seifert, author of many major London office schemes, who was acting for the company that had been selected to pursue the detailed planning negotiations. The proposal was modified to avoid encroaching on Euston Gardens although this meant an increase in the height of the tower block to 390 feet and the hotel block to 200 feet.[4] This scheme was submitted to Camden in December 1971.

In June 1972 the GLC's Environment Planning Committee made a statement about the type of scheme which they would be able to accept: they would set the limit (on grounds of traffic generation) at an office block of 405 000 square feet and a hotel of from 250 to 300 beds; they would also need to be satisfied as to the height and bulk of the building, the preservation of Euston Gardens for the public, and improvements to the road system.[4] This prompted Ivor Walker, Chairman of Camden's Planning and Communications Committee, to write to *The Times* to point out that the GLC was not the local planning authority, and that it would have power of direction over only the floorspace and height of the buildings and access to the hotel from the metropolitan (Euston) road. He continued:

[1] The *Guardian*, 2 April 1971.
[2] GLC *Press Release 233*, 8 June 1971; and the *Guardian*, 10 June 1971.
[3] *Building Design*, 18 June 1971.
[4] *Building Design*, 28 January 1972.
[5] GLC *Press Release 328*, 28 June 1972; and *Minutes*, 18 July 1972, pp382–3.

Environmental questions, like most of the planning considerations, are the responsibility of the boroughs but perhaps the GLC, having lost its planning powers, has not yet come to terms with the real situation.[1]

Other central London termini

While the Euston story is a long and tangled one, it is not the only terminus over which there has been controversy about development proposals. The others are surveyed below.[2]

Kings Cross and St Pancras. After the rationalisation of goods services and the establishment of a freightliner depot at York Way north of King's Cross station the Railways Board considered transferring the St Pancras main-line services to Euston and the suburban services to King's Cross and Moorgate (assuming the King's Cross to Royston and Euston to Leicester lines to be electrified).[3] This view was reached after a working party on land use, set up under the aegis of the Transport Co-ordinating Council for London (TCCL) in 1966, had produced an interim report in 1967 on the future land-use patterns and the planning benefits of retaining one or the other station (see below). BR's proposal would have freed the St Pancras site for sale and redevelopment and helped to offset the cost of electrification (estimated at a total of £30 million). There was a proposal to put an office block on the site of Sir George Gilbert Scott's hotel but both this and W H Barlow's train shed were vociferously defended by the Victorian Society, the GLC's historic buildings section and other preservation interests. In November 1967 St Pancras was declared a listed historic building and the project foundered for lack of finance in 1968.

During 1968 another scheme for an office tower above a rebuilt King's Cross concourse proved abortive. Later a minor scheme to improve what Jackson called 'the sad jumble' of buildings obscuring the façade of King's Cross was approved.[4]

The BR evidence to the Roskill Commission's Inquiry into the site for a third London airport suggested that King's Cross was the best site for an air terminal if the airport was to be north of the Thames, and the early deliberations of the DOE Third London Airport Directorate (formed after the decision in favour of the Foulness site) supported this view in January 1972. King's Cross provides an interchange with five tube lines, twenty bus routes and a coach station, and taxis,[5] and would be an attractive site

[1] Letter to *The Times*, 6 July 1972.

[2] Much of the historical information in this section is based on Jackson (1969).

[3] *The Financial Times* and *The Times* 20 September 1967.

[4] To provide new ticket offices, bus and taxi interchanges, GLC *Press Release 581*, 30 December 1971.

[5] Traffic and parking congestion was reported to be blocking taxi access to the station at peak periods. Road improvements were included in the 1972–73 to 1978–79 programme period, but were contingent upon the effects of a possible air terminal. See Question in Council, GLC *Minutes*, 1 December 1970, p637.

for international hotels and offices. Comprehensive redevelopment to form a transportation centre of the type envisaged for Victoria (see below) became a real possibility, subject to the requirements of the airport being more clearly specified. But problems of local redevelopment were tangled with arguments about planning responsibilities between the GLC and Camden Council.

The working party report on land use mentioned above suggested that 140 acres of land were needed for comprehensive planning around the station. A transportation working party (which included LT but not the Ministry of Housing and Local Government, but otherwise represented the same bodies as the land use working party, namely GLC, BR Board, London boroughs of Camden and Islington) reported in September 1968 that a maximum of 49 acres would be needed for all the transportation elements, even if each was to have its own site; this compared with 36 acres proposed for the Victoria scheme. The GLDP *Written Statement* showed the area immediately around King's Cross and St Pancras as an action area which the GLC believed it should implement, but also a larger area of about 200 acres as an 'area of opportunity' for major development. Camden Council immediately lodged an objection because they were of the opinion that this large area of railway and Gas Board land could be used to solve local housing problems and that they should control the action area.

Camden was further perturbed when in 1971 the GLC gave more details about the action area to the GLDP Inquiry Panel. It was shown as 225 acres and the GLC claimed that if such major traffic generators as the stations, an air terminal, and new hotels and offices were to be included in the scheme, housing would also be needed. Camden responded by arguing that:

1 Since King's Cross was one of the most accessible points in London it was unlikely that all its workers would live nearby.
2 Even if they did, a much smaller amount of land would be needed.
3 Camden's own housing and open space needs were great and the area lay adjacent to a large 'area of housing stress' identified in the GLDP.

Camden then suggested either that they should be allowed to prepare and implement the action area plan 'subject only to the need to receive strategic direction from the GLC on the nature and extent of the essential transportation element' or that the GLC should control only a small action area encompassing the Transportation Centre.[1] The matter then (presumably) awaited recommendations and decisions on the GLDP as a whole although BR continued to examine the possibilities of refurbishing Scott's hotel in conjunction with a small office scheme.

One other worry for Camden concerning this land was raised by BR's schemes for Euston in 1970, namely that commercial pressures might lead

[1] LB Camden (1971), *Proof of Evidence*, *XE 21/19*, GLDP Inquiry Stage 2; and interviews with officers.

them to seek piecemeal development of their surplus land. Camden's Planning and Communications chairman offered to talk to BR about a 'package deal' to purchase and develop several sites and the chairman of the Board, Sir Henry Johnson, said 'if someone came along and sounded us out we should be very willing to listen,'[1] which seemed a curiously negative reply in view of the TCCL working party conclusions. Early in 1971, however, a BR statement showed a more accommodating attitude:

> BR see this scheme as a significant step in their policy of achieving the maximum use of their many properties within a proper framework of planning and social needs.
>
> In this matter they share the view of Camden that this method of working in co-operation can represent a major advance in central urban renewal and set a pattern for responsible redevelopment for the community as a whole.[2]

Waterloo. Waterloo is the newest of BR's major central London termini (apart from Euston), having been rebuilt between 1900 and 1922. After the completion in the early 1960s of the massive Shell Centre on an adjacent site, BR negotiated the development in two phases of offices (180 000 and 82 000 square feet) fronting onto York Road. The GLC and London borough of Lambeth were interested to develop the whole of the south bank area in a comprehensive manner, and BR were keen to obtain operational and interchange improvements (for buses, taxis and pedestrians) at the station, with some profitable elements if possible. The GLC highway engineers wanted to increase the capacity of roads near the station. Appendix *H* of the GLDP stated of Waterloo that 'its site and environment might be thought to lend themselves to large-scale development.'

Under the auspices of TCCL's Interchanges Group a working party was convened representing Lambeth, the GLC, LT, and BR (both the Board and Southern Region). It prepared a scheme in late 1966 which proved too costly and adverse in its traffic effects. But modified schemes were prepared until November 1968 when Lambeth and the transport operators believed that they had a scheme which improved access for pedestrians and taxis, provided convenient covered bus access, improved traffic flow in Waterloo Road, and provided a revenue to help offset the improvement costs by including over 300 000 square feet of offices on land owned by Lambeth and the GLC.

The GLC's officers undertook a cost-benefit analysis to test the viability of the scheme which showed a return of 3% on the interchange improvement. Since this was well below the current rate of return expected by the Treasury of 8%, the GLC officers felt that they could not recommend the scheme. The benefits included rail passengers' time saved, comfort and convenience, car passengers' time saved in Waterloo Road and the release

[1] *The Times*, 1 December 1970.
[2] *The Times*, 1 April 1971.

of an acre of land for housing. But operating benefits, the possible benefits from generating new passenger traffic and the large benefits of providing the office accommodation were not included.[1] Lambeth were very annoyed and at a press conference to explain their views, the chairman of the Planning and Development Committee, Alderman Charles Blackstone, said:

> All the experts agree that it would be a good solution . . . it could benefit thousands of people and yet it is frustrated because quite artificial criteria are used to assess the apparent financial returns, and because it is not accepted that the interchange construction costs can be financed from commercial developments which could easily pay for it.[2]

Despite subsequent questions in Council the GLC decided not to approve the scheme.

Meanwhile the BR Property Board had briefed architectural and estates consultants to appraise the potential of Waterloo and in 1971 a major redevelopment of the station was discussed, reputedly involving 2 million square feet of offices, an hotel, and shopping space. This worried the GLC both from the point of view of its relation to other office schemes and because it might prejudice the rebuilding of some of BR's older stations.[3]

Victoria. Victoria station is also one of BR's newer termini. It underwent major extensions in 1901–09, and the Imperial Airways (later BOAC) and BUA air terminals were built adjacent in 1939 and 1962.[4] BR had investigated its rebuilding in 1956 but Westminster City Council feared that traffic congestion, at that time rapidly worsening throughout central London, would be significantly increased by any major scheme. BR subsequently discussed with the LCC the possibility of rebuilding to include a new hotel.[5]

In 1966 the TCCL Interchanges Group set up a working party to consider the problem of a rail link to Heathrow, together with a central London air terminal and multiple transport interchange at Victoria, and consultants were employed to undertake a feasibility study. Twenty months later the GLC reported that the need for a transportation centre was urgent (including the possibility of a channel tunnel terminal by 1975) but that 'formidable problems in land use, associated redevelopment and urban design would emerge.' The development might include 'a large terminus hotel and offices for the railway and airline authorities.' The consultants reported that the development was feasible, that the air terminal could be

[1] Interviews with officers; LB Lambeth (1970), *Waterloo Interchange*; and *Architects Journal*, 26 May 1970, p1235.
[2] *Evening Standard*, 4 May 1970, the *Guardian*, 5 May 1970.
[3] *Observer*, 25 May 1971.
[4] Jackson (1969), pp281–9.
[5] LCC (1960), *County of London Plan First Review Report*, para299.

satisfactorily located over the railway tracks nearest to Buckingham Palace Road, that the building mass would not damage the local environment, and that road traffic could be accommodated by relatively small (£8 million) road improvements.[1] Work on the feasibility studies continued after the TCCL group recommended that the BR line was the best means of reaching the airport but Westminster City Council became very anxious once again about the traffic effects,[2] having just implemented the Pimlico traffic management scheme to improve the local residential environment nearby (see Case Study *G*).

In September 1969 the President of the Board of Trade and the Minister of Transport ordered a reassessment of the Heathrow link and their new study recommended in 1970 that the LT Piccadilly Line extension was a much cheaper and more beneficial solution (see Case Study *E*). This was confirmed by the Government. It did not require a central London air terminal and so the original reason for developing the Victoria transportation centre virtually disappeared, and with it the need for speculative offices at the station to provide a revenue to fund the improved transport facilities. Westminster City Council welcomed the decision, commenting that:

> The BR proposal would have resulted in traffic in the vicinity of Victoria which the existing road system is quite incapable of carrying, and neither the GLC nor the Government have been willing to provide the money required to carry out the road improvements necessary to safeguard the adjacent residential areas.[3]

There the matter rested until late 1971 when the BR Property Board briefed consultants to prepare and evaluate new schemes in consultation with officers of the Westminster and Greater London Councils.

Blackfriars–Holborn Viaduct. A small (80 000 square feet) office block was developed above Holborn Viaduct in the mid-1960s and at the same period there was a suggestion that a new station at Ludgate Hill could replace both Blackfriars and Holborn Viaduct.[4] In 1971 a new scheme in conjunction with King's College Cambridge for a 152 000 square feet office block above Blackfriars station was approved, to be completed in 1975, which would also finance a greatly improved passenger interchange with the tube station and access to the City of London's proposed elevated walkway system.[5]

Cannon Street. After extensive station works in 1955–57, rebuilding was

[1] GLC *Minutes*, 7 November 1967, pp658–60; and *Press Release 403*, 31 October 1967.
[2] Westminster CC *Minutes*, 5 December 1968; *The Sunday Times*, 30 June 1968.
[3] Westminster CC *Minutes*, 20 July 1970.
[4] Jackson (1969), pp204–6; BR (1970), *Southern Region in the 1970s*.
[5] *Evening Standard*, 1 March 1972; and GLC *Press Release 112*, 1 March 1972.

considered necessary and BR submitted a planning application for a new concourse with offices above, but this was refused after the City of London objected that the 220-feet high tower block would obstruct views of St Pauls (a reason also advanced by the City against a scheme over Blackfriars LT station in 1959). The tower blocks were redesigned to a height of 170 feet and the scheme of 154 000 square feet was completed in 1965 except for the frontage shops and pedestrian walkway to link up with other pedestrian ways, all of which depended upon works to strengthen the LT station structure and to widen Cannon Street.[1]

London Bridge. During the 1960s schemes to rebuild the BR station and provide offices were refused, although after 1967 the Underground station was rebuilt by LT. The original idea had been to ensure a much improved interchange (including subways and escalators) with the Underground by designing the surface and subsurface links jointly, but the development company did not receive an ODP until 1970. The project for 238 000 square feet of offices should be complete in 1975 including a new access to the Underground station.[2]

Charing Cross, Fenchurch Street, Liverpool Street, Broad Street, Marylebone. By 1972 schemes were being considered at these stations and BR applied to the DOE for ODPs for all of them except Charing Cross. The BR Property Board was particularly anxious to see developments at Liverpool Street and Broad Street which could provide a major office development on the fringes of the City and would enable major operational and interchange improvements to be made. Here an application for an ODP was made as early as December 1970 and at the time of writing (1972) discussions were continuing. The scheme proposed 1½ million square feet of offices, 250 000 square feet of shops and an hotel.[3]

Marylebone was considered by BR for closure on more than one occasion during the 1960s, but the costs of transferring its services elsewhere proved considerable. Later, BR objected when the GLC failed to designate it as a central London terminus and major interchange in the GLDP, pointing out that it carried as many 'London pool services commuters as King's Cross, Broad Street, Paddington and Euston.'[4]

Suburban and provincial stations

By the late 1960s BR were eager to stimulate development at stations in the GLC and South-East areas other than the main London termini. In their

[1] Jackson (1969), pp183–5; *The Times*, 26 June 1959; *Evening Standard*, 2 December 1969.
[2] Jackson (1969), pp162–8.
[3] The *Guardian*, 14 June 1972.
[4] BR (1971), *Proof of Evidence*, *E12/34*, p6; and *Transcript*, day 87, pp45–9, 58, GLDP Inquiry Stage 1.

evidence to the GLDP Inquiry they emphasised that improving suburban stations decreased operating costs and improved revenue, besides establishing land-use patterns, travel habits and consumer attitudes that favoured public transport use. Studies at Charlton, Slade Green and Belvedere on the Southern Region had shown a revenue increase of 12% after station improvement.[1] One airspace scheme for shops and offices and car parking 'rafted' over a cutting was completed by a developer at Wembley Central in 1966 giving BR a ground rent of £35 000 per year and a share of future rack rent.[2]

By 1972 other schemes to utilise airspace over railway land were emerging. At Wimbledon a scheme including 100 000 square feet of shops, 300 000 square feet of offices, and an 800-space multi-storey car park was under discussion.[3] A 350-bed hotel was being built on a raft over LT and BR lines near Lords cricket ground, and another large raft was planned to carry 640 dwellings above a BR line in Ealing.[4] BR had conceived schemes for most of the major suburban stations, with emphasis on ones that were BR–LT interchanges (such as Sutton where an ODP had been obtained for 500 000 square feet of offices, and major town centres such as Bromley and Kingston). The main stumbling blocks were that these and other locations often conflicted with a borough's objectives for the area (e.g. that it should remain predominantly residential) or with its priorities for redevelopment elsewhere in the borough. Sometimes BR's desire to develop offices has conflicted with a borough's desire to do so. Then there is the thorny problem of ODPs. While, for example, many large office developments have appeared in Wellesley, Dingwall and Addiscombe Roads around East Croydon station, the station itself has remained undeveloped for lack of an ODP; *The Times* called it 'an obvious gap.'[5] Yet Croydon is the outstanding example of a large-scale subcentre (7 million square feet of offices and 35 000 workers) that has developed its own commuting 'hinterland'. It has been estimated that in 1969–70 some 7300 people or 20% of Croydon's total workforce commuted into Croydon by rail, just over half from the south and the remainder from the north, i.e. 'against the peak.'[6]

BR's evidence to the GLDP Inquiry and subsequent events

BR made it quite clear to the GLDP Inquiry that operating improvements at the many stations which are 'unattractive, inefficient and expensive to maintain and operate' and above all interchange improvements, had to be financed by association with commercial development, and that the BR Property Board kept constantly under review all situations where viable schemes seemed likely.[7]

[1] *Proof of Evidence, E12/34*, pp3–4, GLDP Inquiry Stage 1.
[2] BR *Annual Report*, 1963, p64.
[3] *The Times*, 6 July 1970. [4] The *Guardian*, 15 June 1972.
[5] *The Times*, 11 September 1970.
[6] GLDP *Paper B486 Public Transport Demand*, p29, and Location of Offices Bureau (1971), *Research Paper No.5*.
[7] BR (1970), *Proof of Evidence, E12/7*, pp30–2, GLDP Inquiry Stage 1.

BR also criticised the basic statement of the GLDP about development at stations for failing to mention that some suburban stations were suitable points for development which would also aid decentralisation of office staff (mentioned in paragraph 4.15 of the Statement), although this point had been made in the *Report of Studies* (paragraphs 6.215–6.217).[1] The GLC resisted the application of the same principles to suburban stations as to central termini, because of their great variation in type. In 1970 they told BR that the details of interchange, development and car parking provision at suburban stations would have to await borough plans.[2] BR prayed in aid paragraph 7.22 of the GLDP *Written Statement* which encouraged borough councils to locate office development whenever possible so as to take advantage of rail accessibility, while the GLC's counsel at the Inquiry, Mr Boydell, reiterated that the GLC would resist the application of this principle to the whole of London because it 'would in our submission tend to upset the balance and consideration of all the factors which need to be taken into account.'[3]

Other important events occurred after 1970. Early in 1971 it was hinted that the BR Property Board had a 'property plan' for redeveloping their terminals and major stations with a capital value of £1000 million.[4] Later that year Mr Marsh, the Chairman of the BR Board, indicated that he regarded the redevelopment of stations to improve interchange and provide income as very important. He said, 'they are . . . valuable sites, and could bring in a lot of money and they are worth a great deal; and all that gorgeous air floating around up there at £10 a square foot—you know, it makes me weep every time I go through it.'[5] At the same time the GLC published their target figures for office development for 1972–76 and it became obvious that BR's aspirations would be a major factor in the central London 'market' for offices.

As a result a high level meeting, chaired by the Minister for Transport Industries, Mr Peyton[6] (who at the time also dealt with planning casework for the metropolis), was held in January 1972 at which all aspects of BR's property proposals were discussed including their effects on BR profitability, interchange improvements, LT services and their social benefits to commuters and workers. Six days later the GLC produced six criteria for indicating areas of priority for office development, of which office development at terminals was one.[7]

[1] BR Board (1971), *Proof of Evidence*, *E12/34*, p7, and apps*A–C*.
[2] Letter to BR, 26 June 1970, reproduced as app *B* of *E12/34*, GLDP Inquiry Stage 1.
[3] GLDP Inquiry Stage 1, *Transcript*, day 66, p58.
[4] *Daily Telegraph*, 4 August 1971. This might indicate an office content of the order of 10 million square feet.
[5] The *Guardian*, Supplement, 'By Rail into the Seventies,' 15 September 1971.
[6] Also present were Mr Bosworth (the vice-Chairman of BR and also chairman of BR Property Board and the BR Investment Committee); Sir Desmond Plummer, Mr R Brew and Messrs Peterson, Stott, Collins and Blessley of the GLC; and Sir James Jones of the DOE.
[7] GLC *Press Release 28*, 20 January 1972.

In addition at the end of 1971 BR had announced a scheme of sale and leaseback to a private company which would enable BR to finance capital equipment purchases more cheaply and which would enable the company's backers to claim tax relief. A similar scheme was under discussion for property whereby the private companies would provide cash for BR subsidiaries to carry out developments, and allow the tax benefit to be shared.[1]

In 1972 the railways were given a grant of £27 million nominally to cover the deficit that would have arisen as a result of the Government's decision to hold down fare increases, but the deficit seemed likely still to reach £30 million. Mr Bosworth (see footnote 6 on page 243) gave a press conference to explain that the Board's property potential could relieve its deficits, but was being hindered from being realised. He estimated that BR's sites were potentially worth from £600 to 700 million which could mean an annual revenue by 1980 of £10 million a year; 80% of this was in London. The sources of frustration, he said, were two-fold: a financial one from central government and a planning–economic one from the GLC. Central government would not allow BR to borrow from the national loan fund, which was reasonable, or from the City, which was not as it meant that financing had to be through a developer and the profits split three ways instead of two. The GLC seemed to be of the view that only enough offices should be permitted as would cover interchange improvement cost. This, Mr Bosworth claimed, put BR in a worse position than private developers.[2]

The leader of the GLC, Sir Desmond Plummer, felt it necessary to answer this point. He wrote:

> The GLC's office policies are designed to promote the general good of the community, not to serve sectional interests . . . the Council will be looking for planning advantages (including improved stations) regardless of who is the developer. This does not mean the amount of offices permitted will necessarily be BR's original figure. It does mean that it should be possible to find a meeting point between BR's commercial objectives and the Council's planning objectives, and over the past months we have been working hard with BR to this end. To talk of frustration in this situation is completely out of place.[3]

4 LONDON TRANSPORT EXECUTIVE

LT did not own such large areas of land in the central area as BR, because it had no central termini or depots and most of its stations were underground.[4] In the outer suburbs the former Metropolitan Railway had taken

[1] *The Times*, 20, 21 October 1971.

[2] *The Times*, 9 June 1972; *The Times* and the *Guardian* 14 June 1972.

[3] Letter to *The Times*, 16 June 1972.

[4] Its central area developments have been limited to its own offices over St James's Park Station, some shopping attached to station concourses and the residential blocks of Chiltern and Chalfont Courts in Baker Street.

a major role as promoter of new residential developments in 'metroland' through its Surplus Lands Committee.[1] Nevertheless accessibility to a tube service was a significant factor for many employers and employees and LT's Estates Department headed by Ian McGillivray did what it could with the Board's small-holdings in promoting and sharing in development in the early and mid-1960s.[2]

In September 1968 Mr Ralph Bennett was appointed to the Board; he had been particularly interested in the development of new public transport facilities and their relationship to urban structure through his involvement in the Manchester Rapid Transit Study. The Board commented, of the consultation draft of the GLDP, that there was a 'need to associate new development of offices, shopping centres, regional schools, hospitals, and high-density residential areas much more closely with the existing public transport infrastructure (much of which contains considerable spare capacity).' This was reiterated the following year[3] and in October Mr Bennett suggested that ten stations in particular were suitable for new commercial development, which would provide additional revenue for the Board in rents, and extra fares from new 'reverse-flow commuting;'[4] the GLC were reported to be 'sympathetic' but the ideas took some of the boroughs involved by surprise and in January 1970 Mr Bennett and his estates staff met some of the planning officers to discuss them.

Early in 1970 (after the GLC's assumption of policy control over LT) Messrs Sullivan and Wacher of LT's Estates Department undertook a 'whistle-stop' tour of Canada, the USA, Scandinavia, Germany and the Low Countries to see what railway operators in other countries were doing in the way of policies for linking development to public transport. Their findings strengthened their belief that considerable corporate and community benefits could be gained from such policies even though the design and implementation processes would need to be different to suit the London situation (see below). They then began to apply two principal ideas to LT's network: to encourage commercial development around suburban stations which were in major commercial centres and acted as major interchanges or railheads; and to encourage a higher residential density zoning within walking distance of all tube stations. This work led to the inclusion of the following statement in the Executive's proof of evidence to the GLDP Inquiry:

> In LT's view, therefore, there is a strong case for deliberate planning for concentrated development along underground lines. Housing within, say, 500 metres of underground stations should be at the highest

[1] Later the Metropolitan Railway Country Estates Ltd (established in 1919) which still operates from an office in Gerrards Cross.

[2] Marriott (1967), p120.

[3] LTB *Annual Reports*, 1968, p44; 1969, p36.

[4] *The Times*, 27 October 1969. The stations were Farringdon, Blackfriars, Liverpool Street, Pimlico, Earls Court, Barons Court, White City, Edgware, Turnpike Lane and Golders Green.

> density. Special priority should be given to the allocation of new office space at key suburban stations on the underground system, especially at bus–rail interchange points, and existing commercial and retail sub-centres on the underground system should be encouraged to grow.[1]

During 1969 the Greater London Transport Group (GLTG) also discussed the problem of office development at stations.[2] As already mentioned, the GLC's own evidence to the Inquiry (*Proof of Evidence, E12/1*, Chapter 4) envisaged no reciprocal relationship between public transport and development which could be used as an arm of planning strategy, nor did its Green (consultation) Paper on *The Future of London Transport*, beyond suggesting that there was a case for the Government to relax its ODP controls at points on the rail network where capacity existed for further work journeys.[3]

After receiving and considering comments on this latter document the GLC devised and approved a *Strategy for London Transport* in July 1971 which showed a move towards a specific policy along at least the first of these lines. The report said:

> The general policy of seeking to encourage development around certain focal points on the rail system, with easy accessibility and adequate interchange facilities, is already being pursued. It is now proposed, in particular, that the Council shall encourage the concentration of offices and other developments on or around underground stations outside the central area. In this way some measure of reverse-flow commuting will be possible and employers can be helped to attract employees from a wider area. We have asked the Environmental Planning Committee to seek the co-operation of the DOE in granting office development permits and to make early approaches to the borough councils for assistance as local planning authorities.[4]

During 1970 and 1971 the GLC, LT and the DOE were considering, through GLTG, the application for an infrastructure grant for the Fleet Line and in a report to the GLC in July 1971 the possible value of development promoted by the Line in inner south-east London to the possible value of £70 million was emphasised.[5]

Also in July Mr Wacher published an article elaborating his general ideas. He selected fourteen places in outer London where new commercial development should be concentrated: Ealing, Lewisham, Wood Green, Stratford, Finchley, Edgware, Golders Green, Wembley, Harrow, Houns-

[1] LTE (1971), *Proof of Evidence, E12/2*, GLDP Inquiry Stage 1, para26.
[2] LT *Annual Report*, 1970, pp23–4.
[3] GLC (1970), p40.
[4] GLC *Minutes*, 6 July 1971, p339.
[5] GLC *Minutes*, 7 July 1970, p430.

low, Hammersmith, Wimbledon, Brixton and Peckham.[1] All were designated in the GLDP as strategic shopping centres or interchanges of importance. He considered that virtually all the 17 million square feet of new office space 'targets' allocated to outer London for 1972–76 by the GLC should be concentrated in these centres, with a greater concentration in the longer term (2 million square feet) at Hammersmith because of its soon-to-be improved access to Heathrow airport. He also suggested that if higher density residential redevelopment within 500 metres of the tube stations was permitted and encouraged at, say, 100 persons to the acre in the outer suburbs and up to 200 persons to the acre in the inner suburbs, it might be possible to house 750 000 people in these areas and the dockland redevelopments.

The Estates Department continued to negotiate schemes (see items 1–4 in Table 18) but also prepared a strategy to embody the subcentres idea. This

PLACE	(SQ FT)	DESCRIPTION
Projects		
1 South Kensington	—	Hotel for 515 beds over new tube station. Cost £3.4 million, approved in July 1970 by GLC to take advantage of Government subsidy for hotels
2 Moorgate	170 000	Office development to open in 1973
3 Aldgate	80 000	Office block over station £165 000 p.a. airspace lease
4 Edgware Road	—	Hotel for 400 beds over tube station applied for
Proposals		
5 Hammersmith	500 to 750 000	Offices and hotel, shops, car parking, bus station, library
6 Harrow on the Hill	300 000	Shops, car parking, bus station, warehousing
7 Wembley Park	250 000	No firm scheme
8 Golders Green	200 000	No firm scheme
9 Edgware	200 000	No firm scheme
10 Hounslow West	150 to 200 000	No firm scheme

Table 18 LT STATION DEVELOPMENTS AND PROPOSALS, 1972[2]

[1] T Wacher (1971), 'Public Transport and Land Use: a Strategy for London' (reprinted from *Chartered Surveyor*); see also *Daily Telegraph*, 11 September 1971.
[2] *The Times*, 8 November 1971; *Evening Standard*, 15 March 1970; *Building Design*, 28 May 1971; *Kensington Post and Mercury*, 6 July 1970; GLC *Minutes*, 21 July 1970, p455; and *Economist*, 22 January 1972.

was announced in November 1971.[1] It suggested several schemes which were being discussed with the GLC, the boroughs, private developers and the Government, notably at Hammersmith and Harrow (see items 5–10 in Table 18). The latter was, incidentally, one of the pilot projects for TCCL's study of rafting-over cuttings (see station car parks Case Study *F*). LT hoped that extra revenue from such developments might total £2 million p.a. As fare increases became necessary to cover increasing costs during 1970–72, it was suggested that LT should take advantage of their property potential to produce both rental income and new passengers.[2] LT also obtained the freedom to spend up to £500 000 on a development without specific reference to the GLC.[3]

As already noted in section 2 (pages 229–30) the principle of LT's development strategy was included in the GLC's suggested revisions to the GLDP published three months later, but widened to include all railways. Later in 1972 planning consultants were commissioned to assess the property potential along the site of stage III of the Fleet Line.[4]

5 CONCLUSIONS

Lessons from abroad

Commercial developments at or over central termini and suburban stations and high residential densities around stations are widely accepted overseas. Some are individual large schemes such as the Ville Place Marie over Montreal's Canadian Central Railway tracks, the Penn Center built over Philadelphia's Central station, the offices over the Gare Montparnasse in Paris and Berne's Central station, and the offices and department stores over Shinjuku and other Tokyo termini. Others are part of a major restructuring of central areas, e.g. around the Yonge Street and Bloor Street subways in Toronto and the BARTD line in San Francisco (the latter offers density bonuses for offices within 750 feet (228 metres) of stations). A serious attempt has been made to develop major suburban centres in Paris, with the prototype at La Defence with 11 million square feet of office, exhibition and entertainment facilities around a new Metro station. Hamburg has produced similar proposals on a smaller scale.

Schemes for residential restructuring around the railway system mainly occur in the smaller cities or relate to the establishment of new suburbs or satellite townships (e.g. Stockholm, Oslo, Cologne, Frankfurt) although some major urban areas are thinking in terms of restructuring existing areas (Rotterdam, Amsterdam, Paris, Tokyo).

[1] *LT Magazine*, 25; 8, November 1971; and *The Times Business News*, 8 November 1971.

[2] *Economist*, 22 January 1972.

[3] GLC *Minutes*, 21 March 1972, p160–1. This was the ceiling for other forms of capital expenditure.

[4] *Architect's Journal*, 9 August 1972, p229.

Toronto perhaps presents the most striking case. Density bonuses were allowed for development within 1500 feet (557 metres) of stations or bus feeder routes. In the period 1959–63, 50% of all new high-density housing was near the Yonge Street subway stations and, even more strikingly, 90% of all central office development. In fact, two-thirds of all new building occurred within 5 minutes' walking distance of the stations, to a value of some $1000 million. The subway itself cost $67 million. More recently a massive scheme was proposed for a 'Metro Center' of 5 million square feet of shop, office and hotel accommodation over the Canadian National–Canadian Pacific tracks along the Toronto waterfront.[1]

These schemes demonstrate that considerable benefits in land use, property development and transport operation can be obtained. Allowing for cultural differences affecting density or design parameters, there seems no reason why application of the principle in London should be any less successful. It requires all the bodies involved to recognise the validity of the idea, to accept the need for a firm policy and co-operation in the preparation and implementation of both plans and individual schemes, perhaps also involving financial co-operation.

The London situation

The last decade in London has seen three periods of distinctly different policies towards office developments: the end of the *laisser-faire* boom period, a period of restraint which reached its peak in the 1965 Act and the two years immediately afterwards, and a subsequent relaxation of controls. Development at railway stations exemplified the need to bring physical planning and transport considerations and their parent institutions together, and created a situation which would test the effectiveness of any planning and administrative system. But the performance has been poor: no clear plans have emerged, proposals have been slow to appear and piecemeal in nature, and decisions on them have been even slower. There was no firm view taken by the GLC or the Government on the effects of such schemes on the structure of the central area, nor in all cases could the GLC and the boroughs agree on the effects on the immediate vicinity as the Euston and King's Cross cases show. There were no clear criteria for judging the strategic value of each scheme, and so, rightly or wrongly, the influence of local interest was often decisive.

One result of this situation is that BR, as the freeholder of some of the most attractive sites for offices in London, has in practice been put in a worse position than the private developer, despite the intentions of the 1962 Act. While they could have capitalised on their opportunities in the early 1960s, BR were slow to realise the potential of their assets: by the time they had done so, the concern of the LCC and central government over employment growth had led to controls over office development in

[1] M Baily compares this scheme with the potential of the King's Cross area, *The Times*, 4 August 1969.

London, and the institution of ODPs. Moreover, in the period of relaxation since 1968 the GLC have sought planning gains over and above operational improvements, a requirement which has usually involved limiting the amount of office space allowed.

The lack of any clear concept of the particular transport and planning implications of locating offices at stations was not helped by failure to develop an overall interchange policy (see Case Study *F*), but was also the result of confusion over office policies. It certainly resulted in a lack of criteria by which the GLC could judge individual proposals and give guidance to the boroughs, the transport operators and private developers *before* proposals were formulated or submitted. This in turn led to the tangled discussions already described.

Without any of these three ingredients of a comprehensive policy, the decision-making process became at best a problem of resolving conflicting interests and at worst a running fight between the various parties inevitably involved in any interchange decision. The GLC was participant as well as referee (namely, the 1971–72 Euston offices issue) and the other parties were the boroughs, LT and BR and, on occasions, the DOE.

Some means of reconciling the various interests must be found, but reconciliation becomes more difficult as the scale of schemes grows: the latest BR provincial and suburban proposals are several times as large as their predecessors, and two or three central projects are of a different order of magnitude again. The roles played by these bodies with their different interests are summarised below.

The DOE were concerned with offices policy indirectly through regional planning and directly through ODP controls which it took over from the Board of Trade. Even so its policy has not been wholly consistent. One critic has ascribed five policies to different groups of the Department: one wanted decentralisation but did not specify where the offices should go; the regional planners wanted to steer office employment to certain areas; a third granted ODPs, and had granted them at a faster rate than planning permission could absorb; a fourth concerned with London planning often had different ideas from those of the GLC; and the Department's newly established Property Services Agency was seeking its own major office schemes in central London.[1] Except in its role as arbiter of the GLDP and authority for transport infrastructure grants, however, the transport aspects of development at stations was of little concern to the DOE. LT's problems were (since 1970) the responsibility of the GLC and BR had established their own property board. The local effects of such schemes were to be resolved by the boroughs if necessary with the help of the GLC.

The attitude of the London boroughs to development at stations was not always clear and varied according to local circumstance. Although the local authority was unlikely to refuse a substantial increase in rateable value resulting from an office development at a station, it had to consider

[1] Dr D Eversley, formerly Chief Planner (Strategy) within the GLC's Planning and Transportation Department, as reported in *The Times*, 1 November 1972.

whether the same gain could be achieved with greater benefits to the community elsewhere. Thus Westminster City Council was consistently concerned with the possible adverse effects on road traffic of further development at Victoria station, already intensively developed. Their anxiety included the environmental disturbance that would attend any major works. The City of London objected to BR office developments that would obscure St Pauls on the City skyline, although other office schemes were permitted elsewhere in the City that have been criticised on precisely these grounds.

Lambeth Council were keen to take the opportunity offered by the proposed Waterloo redevelopment to bring new uses into the south bank area, even to the point of suggesting a 4000-seat conference centre to be built above the station. In the meantime, however, they were keen to finance an interchange improvement and were very annoyed that the viability of the scheme was assessed solely on its transport elements. During this period local authorities had been accustomed to hearing MOHLG and DOE officers advising that schemes such as transport infrastructure, libraries, recreation and arts facilities should so far as possible be financed in whole or part by revenue-producing commercial elements. In their comments on the GLDP, Lambeth had previously pointed out that the Plan gave no indication of how the responsibility for implementing and financing interchange improvements was to be shared, and said, ironically as it turned out: 'this is the stumbling block over which, if it is not settled, so many schemes will come to grief.'[1]

Other boroughs were concerned that the potential of suburban stations for development should not be forgotten.[2] Camden Council was concerned to see terminal development in its local context and to press the GLC to specify what was strategic about the King's Cross interchange, in other words to identify the statutory responsibilities just as Lambeth wished to identify the financial ones. Thus although the boroughs wished to protect some local interests, both from the points of view of local land-use planning and transport development, and of judging schemes produced by private companies or the transport operators, they would generally have welcomed some clear metropolitan policy.

BR, with statutory duties (and Government aid) to improve their planning methods, services and financial performance, were very keen to realise the maximum return from their property assets. Many stations were very old-fashioned and needed improvements to train operations and passenger facilities which could not be undertaken quickly enough with public money alone. After the Property Board was established a national appraisal of property holdings was undertaken and for the most urgent and valuable sites, 'soundings' were taken from the property market. The Board then approached the borough for planning permission and the DOE for an

[1] LB Lambeth *Minutes*, 7 May 1969.

[2] LB Merton (1971), *Proof of Evidence, E12/42*; and LB Havering (1971), *Paper S12/52*, GLDP Inquiry Stage 1.

ODP, sometimes with their consultants, and sometimes with a client for the proposed office space. They had hopes of a 'package deal' with the GLC and DOE for all the London termini, but this was not achieved and each scheme had to be processed separately. They still sought to maximise their returns and were inclined to see the GLC's allocation of 'targets,' as in the 1972 exercise, as conflicting with their interests. Property developments sometimes do not permit long delays: office clients, or developers' staff or money can be better deployed elsewhere. BR were usually willing to modify their proposals as several of the London cases show, but this inevitably led to delays. This points, however, to the need to involve BR in the overall planning process as early as possible.

LT, on the other hand, have much smaller and less attractive property holdings and thus must exploit their ability to provide access to sites for large numbers of people, and so generate fare rather than rent revenue. The Estates Department, like BR Property Board, surveyed its potential assets and with the example of overseas operators to help them, pressed the GLC for a much closer relationship between land use and public transport, and were a substantial influence on the GLC in its modification of the GLDP. It is very doubtful if this concept would have been as clearly developed or its influence as strong, if LT had remained responsible to the MOT or DOE.

The GLC inherited the LCC's restrictive office policy and in its early years could find no means of satisfying the transport operators' needs amongst the other claims to the limited supply of ODPs. Moreover, during the evolution of the GLDP policies, the Council became concerned that the growth of office employment in central London was encouraging long-distance commuting and doing nothing to combat the social and economic polarisation which it believed was occurring. The interchange studies undertaken for TCCL paid little attention to the land use–transport relationship and none to how interchange improvement could help the operators' financial problems. Only when the GLC became responsible for transport planning and for LT and there was an easing of office control did a change take place. The urgings of LT and rigorous criticisms by the boroughs and private objectors at the GLDP Inquiry evoked the first firm statements and views, which were incorporated in the suggested revisions of the GLDP and in Council policy.

The agency used by the GLC for co-ordination since 1969 has been the GLTG, but it cannot claim any outstanding improvement on the ineffective efforts of TCCL to improve interchanges. The working parties set up for individual schemes fared no better: that for Victoria faded away, that for Waterloo could not produce an acceptable scheme, and the King's Cross working parties seemed to have been deliberately buried.

The 1972 GLDP statements provided for the first time some basis for developing both policy and machinery for co-ordinating interchange schemes, but there are still four improvements needed. First, the GLC has barely recognised the importance of the totality of the urban structure in relation to the transport network. No alternative patterns of residential densities for the suburbs have been studied, nor has any borough looked at this problem in more detail.

Second, criteria for interchange development need to be stated by the GLC to guide both public and private investment, and this requires more detailed information from LT, BR and the boroughs on both transport and planning factors.

Third, the relative importance of station sites *vis-à-vis* other demands for new offices must be made public, probably by the GLC after discussion with the DOE.

Finally, an agreed methodology is needed for assessing the benefits of interchange developments. The Waterloo case shows that methods such as those used for road schemes are not suitable; some way must be found of taking into account the (financial) property benefits, the financial benefits of better bus or train operation, the social transport benefits, and the social land-use benefits. In the present situation there is a danger that improvements to individual parts of the transport system (new buses, bus priorities, new railway stock, new railway lines, etc.) will not be matched by improved facilities for linking them. Since this extends beyond Greater London it should be partly a DOE affair but the central London termini situation is important enough to warrant a major GLC role. Once the method is adopted the GLC and the transport operators should use it to settle priorities and programming for schemes in their interchange plan.

To summarise, there has been no clear concept of the role that stations with large associated development should play in the land-use and transport strategy for London, and as a result there has been no clear policy or definitions of responsibility for finance or implementation. Government control of offices has been a major determinant of the rate of progress, given that both BR and LT developed their interests in property belatedly. The initiative for individual schemes came principally from the two railway operators, with their strong financial interests, but the planning and implementation process was fragmented between several agencies with differing objectives.

There was no satisfactory meeting point for these agencies to co-operate in developing policies although the GLTG could have played this role if the GLC had translated its 1972 policies into more concrete terms by evolving priorities for interchange development and criteria for judging proposals and by relating interchange priorities to those of other office developments. If the DOE (on the assumption that this is a wider than metropolitan problem) could evolve a method of assessing benefits from interchange improvements, sufficient confidence amongst the parties involved could bring them together. As Parker observed, development at stations is often 'not so much a technical problem as a matter of broad policy and a determined belief that this type of development can be profitable and beneficial.'[1]

[1] J Parker (1967) *Transport Interchanges* (Report on Winston Churchill Travelling Fellowship) p19.

Case Study E

HEATHROW AIRPORT RAILWAY LINK AND TERMINALS

1 INTRODUCTION

Greater demand for air travel and the growth in size and speed of aeroplanes, certainly presage considerable problems of distributing passengers and their baggage on the ground,[1] even if the magnitude and rate of growth cannot be accurately foreseen. As aircraft became faster the proportionate costs in time and distance of the trip between home and airport became increasingly important. Many of these trips may exceed the time spent in the air. To travel to Heathrow and Gatwick, for example, may take from between 35 to 40 minutes compared with from 10 to 20 minutes to Tempelhof from central Berlin, from 20 to 45 minutes from the centre of Paris to le Bourget, and from 28 to 80 minutes to Orly, or from 40 to 60 minutes to Fiumicino from Rome.[2] The ground links distributing the traffic, the terminal buildings where it is handled and interchange with existing transport systems can create difficult planning problems.

The way in which these problems were tackled in London between 1965 and 1972 provides an illuminating case study, particularly because there was a reversal of opinion about how the ground link to Heathrow should be provided, and considerable policy confusion over the matter of air terminals.

The Greater London Council (GLC) as strategic planning authority was concerned with the location and scale of airport terminals, but it was also involved in the approval of individual schemes since these form one of the categories of development reserved to the GLC by statute.[3] Since 1970 it has also been involved as transport planning authority for London. British Rail (BR) and London Transport (LT) were involved as operators of railways and the British Airports Authority (BAA) as the body responsible for airports.[4] The Secretary of State for the Environment (formerly the Minister of Transport) held the authority to allocate central government finance for capital investment in transport, which included major items such as new ground access systems and in-town terminals.

The next section examines two studies of a new rail link to Heathrow

[1] See, for example, *The Sunday Times*, 8 September 1968; *The Times Business News*, 5 May 1969; *Building Design* 26 March 1971; the *Guardian*, editorial, 12 January 1970, 'Jumbo-sized Problems.'

[2] 'Noise, Speed and the Transport Slum,' *Observer*, 2 July 1967.

[3] Under section 24 (4) of the *London Government Act 1963*, ch33.

[4] Under the *Airports Authority Act 1965*, ch16.

carried out in 1967 by the Transport Co-ordinating Council for London (TCCL) and in 1969–70 by the Heathrow Steering Group (HSG), and the reasons why they arrived at very different conclusions. The third section looks at the air-terminal problems at Victoria, Hammersmith and West London.

2 THE TCCL AND HEATHROW STEERING GROUP STUDIES

By 1965 it was thought that the growth of air traffic and of road congestion would necessitate additional means of access to Heathrow airport although £10 million had been spent on building the M4 and improving other roads in the previous ten years. A working party was established under the aegis of the interchanges group of TCCL (see page 142) to study the problem. The bodies represented were the GLC as strategic planning and traffic body, the Ministry of Housing and Local Government (MOHLG) as authority for planning matters of national importance, the Ministry of Transport (MOT) as arbiter on public transport investment, BR and LT as possible operators of the link, the Board of Trade as the body responsible for licensing air traffic and overseeing the development of airports and the BAA as owners and operators of Heathrow.

The TCCL group examined several possibilities (see Table 19).[1] The first two were improved coach services from the West London Air Terminal which were used by 40% of all passengers in 1966. In one case the journey time was maintained (I) and in the other it was improved by ten minutes (I*a*); both demanded considerable investment in roads and major improvements at the terminal. The third possibility was the improvement of existing BR tracks (II) to provide a 22-minute service to Heathrow every 10 minutes by means of eight new trains; check-in facilities would be provided at a new Victoria terminal. The fourth was the extension of LT's existing Piccadilly Line from Hounslow West station, with an intermediate station at Hatton Cross (see Figure 8) (III). Frequency would be every 8 minutes, with a 30-minute trip to Gloucester Road (the nearest station to the West London Air Terminal (WLAT)), and 39 minutes to Piccadilly Circus. There would be no in-town terminal and air travellers and their luggage would, of course, have to share the trains with other passengers. Under both these rail options the coach services would be completely withdrawn.

The next two options consisted of new systems. The working group felt that 'the proponents of non-conventional transport systems should have a fair chance' to make their case. One (IV) was a Safege suspended monorail running through the Crane Valley and then over main roads to Victoria; the other (V) was a straddle-type Alweg monorail following the M4 and Piccadilly Line on a more northerly route. These would require completely new infrastructure, terminals, interchanges and equipment. The last three

[1] Table based on TCCL Interchange Group paper 67 (11), July 1967: *A Report on Links for Heathrow Airport*. The different options are described in Part II.

LINK	TOTAL COST[a]	TOTAL REVENUE[b]	DISCOUNTED BENEFITS COMPARED WITH I[c]	QUANTIFIED FACTORS TOTAL ASSOCIATED CAPITAL COSTS UP TO 1982					UNQUANTIFIED FACTORS			
				LINK	IN-TOWN TERMINAL	AIRPORT	ROADS[d]	TOTAL	COMFORT	BAGGAGE-HANDLING FACILITIES	RELIABILITY	CAPACITY FOR IMPROVEMENT
I. Coach services from west London (35-minute journey)	19.7	16.0	0	1.5	3.5	0.5	28.0	33.5	Fair	Good	Fair	Fair
I*a*. Coach service from west London (25-minute journey)	21.0	18.2	+6.2	1.1	3.8	0.5	37.0	42.4	Fair	Good	Fair	Poor
II. BR service from Victoria (shared track)	25.5	22.8	+7.6	16.2	4.4	4.4	3.2	23.2	Good	Good	Good	Good
III. LT Board extension of Piccadilly Line	19.8	12.5	+3.5	13.5	0	10.8	0	24.3	Fair–Poor	Poor	Good	Fair
IV. Safege monorail to Victoria	39.1	25.6	+15.1	27.6	4.5	4.4	3.2	39.7	Good	Good	Potentially very good	Fair
IV*a*. Alweg monorail to west London	30.1	20.2	+12.4	19.2	5.0	4.4	0	28.6	Good	Good	Potentially very good	Fair
V. LT Board extension III and coach service maximum	30.5	17.1	+3.1	14.6	1.2	2.2	28.0	46.0	Fair	Good	Fair	Fair
V*a*. LT Board extension III and coach service minimum	30.6	14.5	+3.2	14.4	0.6	7.5	28.0	50.5	Fair–Poor	Poor	Good	Fair
VI. BR service II and LT Board extension III	35.9	20.2	+8.7	29.3	3.0	4.6	3.2	40.1	Good	Good	Good	Good

Table 19 COST-BENEFIT SUMMARY: TCCL 1967 HEATHROW LINK STUDY (£MILLION, ASSESSED OVER FIFTEEN YEARS)

Notes

[a] Capital and operating costs

[b] Revenue from fares only—taken as 6*s* (30p) per trip from west London and 7*s* (35p) from Victoria

[c] Benefits are included for passenger time saved, reduction in traffic on roads to airport, and in-town congestion

[d] Road costs are for total works, part of which would be used by other traffic

options consisted of combinations of the LT link with two levels of coach service taking 70% and 30% of the traffic (V, V*a*), and of the BR and LT links (VI).

The schemes were assessed partly by a form of cost-benefit analysis in which the costs of the link and of the associated works at Heathrow, the in-town terminal, or of the roads were included. The benefits consisted of a set of quantified factors (time saved or lost compared with Scheme I valued as for road network assessments in the London Transportation Study).[1] To examine profitability as opposed to social benefits, expected fare revenues were computed. Unquantifiable factors were also taken into account (comfort, baggage handling capability, etc.—see last four columns of Table 19).

In its report of July 1967 the group concluded that the BR scheme (II) was 'clearly the best proposal.' Its capital cost, estimated at £25 million, was bettered only by the coach and LT schemes, and it ranked second in the cost-benefit analysis, while it was clearly first in the profitability test partly because of its higher fares, and it was claimed to provide a fast, comfortable service with guaranteed seating and baggage handling. The LT scheme ranked second; although it helped airport workers, it enabled a much better distribution of passengers in central London, had relatively low fares and reasonable profitability, high frequency and very good reliability. The group was obviously of the opinion that the lack of an in-town terminal and of a guaranteed seat for passengers, outweighed these benefits. They said 'the nature of the service . . . makes it *prima facie* less good than is necessary to meet the needs of the large numbers wishing to travel to central London.'[2] It could be considered as a second link although, as the BAA had already pointed out, this would have to be allowed for in designing the Heathrow terminal.

Monorails were rejected as being too costly, environmentally damaging and operationally unproven (see Case Study *J*). The coach schemes could only operate from west London with massive roadworks expenditure, and proved to have low financial and social returns, as did the 'mixed' schemes. Not surprisingly the LT member of the working party, Mr F J Lloyd, dissented from the majority view. He believed the overall forecasts for Heathrow passengers and the numbers using a single in-town terminal were unreliable, and that trends in the USA were for more people to travel directly to the airport by independent means (although he did not mention that car ownership was much higher there). Moreover:

> The implementation of the full Victoria town terminal scheme requires a large capital investment . . . major road works at Victoria, the abandonment of the BEA town terminal at west London and the very profitable coach service, also the possible abandonment of the BOAC terminal.[3]

[1] Namely, 3*s* 4*d* (16½p) per hour for leisure and 9*s* 11*d* (50p) for working time. TCCL (1967), para40.

[2] TCCL (1967), paras63–70 and p4 of summary.

[3] TCCL (1967), p65.

While the Minister was considering the TCCL report, Parliamentary powers were obtained to build either scheme so that the preferred one should suffer no procedural delays. The GLC set up a study group to examine the Victoria terminal (see next section and Case Study *D*).

The further studies showed that the transportation centre at Victoria was feasible, economically viable if including commercial offices, but needing roadworks for which Westminster City Council could see no reasonable prospect of finance. BR and LT officers meanwhile refined their costings and designs and much more work was undertaken on the feasibility of an efficient and cheap baggage-handling system for the Victoria terminal. The problem proved intractable in terms of cost and reliability to 'process' the large numbers of people involved. In addition the major airlines (particularly the British Overseas Airways Corporation (BOAC) and British European Airways (BEA)) pressed their claims to be heard; they had not been represented on the working party. They wished to retain the coach services as an option and a contingency against a failure in rail services, and with the advent of larger aircraft, they were less keen to operate from a single large central terminal.

It must also be remembered that the Government were at the same time reconsidering the Stanstead site for the third London airport, and appointed the Roskill Commission in mid-summer 1968. When it had not proved possible to come to a decision by the middle of 1969, the Minister of Transport and the President of the Board of Trade asked for a re-examination of the Heathrow link issue. A new Steering Group was established with the same membership as before except that the MOHLG was not represented, and BEA, BOAC and Westminster City Council were added. The Group studied four alternatives. These were an extension of the Piccadilly Line plus airline coaches (like TCCL's alternative V) and three BR options—one without coaches and check-in at Victoria (like the TCCL Scheme II), one with coaches and a check-in at Victoria, and one with coaches but without a check-in at Victoria (see Table 20).

The study was based on another cost-benefit analysis.[1] There were three main cost elements:

1 User costs including the time, vehicle operating costs and fares of the users of the links; £1.90 per hour, based on the average income of air travellers in 1968. The figures applied, of course, to all four schemes.
2 Indirect costs, mainly in road congestion affecting other users by delaying them, using a formula for calculating and valuing delays developed in the White Paper, *Transport in London*.[2]
3 Direct capital costs for the link and terminals.

The benefits were defined as the savings in operating costs, time saving by

[1] MOT (1970), *Report of a Study of Rail Links with Heathrow Airport*, pts I and II, HMSO.

[2] Cmnd 3686 of 1968, app *J*.

(£M)	COACHES ONLY (Capital	Annual)	LT (c)	LT (a)	BR1 (c)	BR1 (a)	BR2 (c)	BR2 (a)	BR3 (c)	BR3 (a)
1 User costs										
a Passengers—existing public transport users		0		−24.3		−17.1		−17.1		−28.8
Passengers—diverted from private vehicles		0		−10.2		−2.3		−2.3		−6.6
b Workers—existing public transport users		0		−0.6		0		0		0
Total 1		0		−35.1		−19.4		−19.4		−35.4
2 Indirect costs (congestion)		0		−1.7		−0.9		−0.6		−0.9
3 Direct costs										
a Link	0.8	18.3	11.4	10.4	15.2	6.8	14.7	14.8	14.1	13.3
b Town terminals	0.4	7.3	0	5.7	5.3	11.8	5.1	13.3	0.04	5.7
c Heathrow terminals	0.03	0	2.3	2.9	3.2	2.0	3.1	1.7	3.1	2.8
(a)+(b)+(c) subtotal	1.2	25.6	13.7	19.0	23.7	20.6	22.9	29.8	17.2	21.8
d Road works and airport parking	0.9	—	0.2	—	0.9	—	0.8	—	0.8	—
Total 3	2.1	25.6	13.9	19.0	24.6	20.6	23.7	29.8	18.0	21.8
TOTAL ALL COSTS (1+2+3)	2.1	25.6	13.9	−17.8	24.6	0.3	23.7	9.8	18.0	−14.5
Less coaches only	0	0	11.9	−43.4	22.0	−25.2	21.7	−15.8	15.9	−40.1
TOTAL COST (net present value)				−31.5		−2.7		−6.0		−24.1

Table 20 COST-BENEFIT SUMMARY: 1970 HEATHROW STEERING GROUP STUDY

users and reduced road congestion costs by comparison with a coach link. As in 1967 unquantifiable factors were included in the evaluation. Three of these factors remained the same, but that of potential for development was dropped and replaced by the value of choice of mode, choice of checking-in at central London or at Heathrow, and by acceptability of the link in planning terms. More sophistication was introduced in so far as the final 'matrix' of factors was tested with different rates of interest for discounting and different assumptions for future values of costs and benefits.

The Group reported in 1970 that the LT scheme was the cheapest (£19 million compared with £38, £35 and £26 million for the three respective BR schemes) and could be built most quickly (four years as opposed to five for the BR schemes). The LT scheme also showed up best in the financial assessment (single-year rate of return by 1985 of 15% compared with 13, 6 and 10%). As the study said:

> The LT scheme shows much the highest total return, and the highest return per pound invested. . . . We see the real choice to be between the BR3 and LT schemes. The BR scheme offers its passengers a shorter journey time in transit, a guaranteed seat and rather better baggage facilities. It provides a direct link between the airport and a single point in central London. Those factors have to be set against LT's cheaper fare, slight advantage in reliability and its much better showing both in the cost-benefit analysis and in the financial assessment. It provides, as distinct from BR, dispersed access over central London, and an added facility for workers within the airport complex.[1]

The sensitivity analysis, even using the assumptions most favourable to the BR schemes and least favourable to LT, still showed the LT scheme to be the best option.

What factors had contributed to this dramatic change of view within less than three years? They may be classified as changes in the study method, changes in input elements such as costs, and external factors. First, there are a number of changes associated with the second study which heavily influenced the outcome of the calculations:[2]

1 The TCCL method of accounting for bad congestion set £28 million of roadworks against the coach and LT plus coach schemes (I+V); the 1970 report said 'the possibility that these would in fact have been made was at best hypothetical.' The direct and indirect road costs (congestion costs) were much smaller and more evenly spread in the 1970 study (Table 20, items 2 and 3*d*).

[1] MOT (1970), ptII, para5.1.2; and ptI, para4.3.

[2] MOT (1970), ptII, paras3.1.1, 4.6.2–4.6.4, 4.3.16, 5.1.4 and 7.4.1.

2 The TCCL report estimated the operating costs of coaches on the basis that they would all operate from the West London Terminal. In 1970 costs were based on individual airlines operating from separate terminals; this gave lower load factors. In addition coach costs were 30% higher in 1970 for comparable traffic conditions. This reduced the differential between the schemes as only the BR1 scheme operated without coach services.

3 BR and LT cost-estimates changed dramatically during the three years between the studies, thus:

	(LT)	(BR)	
capital	marginal	+140%	(inflation, extra costs realised)
operating	+60%	+20%	

The LT scheme proved to be costed and designed more completely; as BR examined their schemes more closely, new operational problems were foreseen.

4 Associated with the last two points, the rail options cut out the cost of a coach terminal which was included in the TCCL study; in 1970 the LT, BR2 and BR3 schemes had to bear this (£5.7 million) but the BR1 and BR2 schemes had much greater net terminal costs at Victoria and Heathrow (items 3*a* and 3*d* in Table 20). Because of the problems of a mass baggage-handling system these two schemes also had an extra delay factor built into the computed journey times.

5 The TCCL report assumed that only existing public transport trips from around Hounslow would transfer to the LT link, but more detailed zonal analysis of the traffic data suggested to the Group that double this number would travel immediately the link opened and that this number would double again by 1981. Many people using the BR links would also have used a tube to reach Victoria, including some who would have to 'back-track' from the west; the LT scheme saved them from having to do this.

The second group of factors related chiefly to changes in policies and attitudes:

6 As already mentioned the airlines did not wish to give up the option of having a coach system. This helped to overcome one problem with the LT scheme, that the line would be closed in the early hours of the morning for maintenance. The 2% of travellers who arrive or leave during this period could have a comfortable and swift coach journey.

7 The multiple accesses of the tube increased its availability to passengers throughout the network, especially along the Piccadilly Line and the hotel areas of Bloomsbury, Mayfair and Cromwell Road served directly by it. Half the central London hotel capacity (26 000 beds, or more) was within half a mile of the line, including 17 hotels of over 500 beds

each of which may be of some importance to those travelling by jumbo jet.[1]

8 King's Cross was suggested as the site for the third London airport terminal as early as January 1968[2] (see also pages 236–7). The LT link would enable Heathrow transfer passengers to change directly onto the third airport rail link.

Two other objections to the LT scheme raised in 1967 remained to be covered:[3] its inability to guarantee a seat, and to offer baggage-handling facilities. In the former problem, however, the worst situation was estimated to be at the evening peak when 2% of the total air passengers would have to stand for part of their journey, and this was generally considered acceptable. The latter problem was not resolved.

The same month as the 1970 study was published the LT Executive, now under the GLC's control, requested authority to proceed with the Piccadilly extension at a cost of £14.9 million including land and rolling stock, with £2.85 million interest. Emphasising the advantages outlined above the Executive pointed to an estimated profit of from £0.4 to 0.9 million p.a. in 1975 and from £1.1 to 2 million p.a. by 1981. If the Heathrow terminal costs (from £2.5 to 3 million) were not borne by the BAA those figures would be reduced by £0.5 million p.a. The Council decided to 'accept a changed situation'[4] and recommended the scheme in the interest of both the nation and the capital, and pressed the Government to give a 75% grant to the scheme.

Five months later, the Secretaries of State for Trade and Industry and Environment approved the scheme but refused any grant-aid, on the grounds that the line would make a profit and would greatly benefit London.[5] Within a fortnight the GLC agreed to pay a 25% grant (£3.7 million) expressing disappointment at the view taken by the Government. LT were to borrow the remainder and repay it within ten years. A GLC deputation in January 1971 did not effect any change, but were influential in persuading the Government to widen the scope of its grant applications (see Chapter 3 and Case Study *C*). LT prepared tenders for the scheme and work began in April 1971; eighty-six new trains with baggage storage space were ordered for the Piccadilly Line in June.[6]

Over a year later the Government had a change of heart and decided to give a 25% grant towards the capital cost, now estimated at £22.7 million. This reduced the incidence of cost on LT to 50%.[7] BR continued to press their case, mainly on the grounds that their link 'will be required because

[1] *LT Magazine*, 12, 5, March 1972; GLC (1971), Green Paper: *Tourism and Hotels in London*, p28; GLC *Press Release 498*, 10 November 1971.
[2] *Official Architecture and Planning*, January 1968, pp83–4.
[3] MOT (1970), ptII, para7.4.1.
[4] GLC *Minutes*, 7 July 1970, pp432–6.
[5] MOT *Press Release*, 6 November 1970; GLC *Minutes*, 1 December 1970, pp654–5.
[6] GLC *Minutes*, 6 August 1971, pp349–50.
[7] DOE *Press Notice 835M*, 21 July 1972.

the Piccadilly Line will be unable to cope with the forecast volume in the long-term future' and that it would be an exclusive link with spare capacity.[1] BAA had supported the BR link in 1967; one of their main criteria was that it was most important that a high proportion of the traffic should be processed outside the airport,'[2] another was that an exclusive link was very important.

BEA on the other hand were strongly in favour of the LT scheme on several grounds: it involved no 'back-haul' to Victoria, it would be ready earlier, it did not require the withdrawal of coach services, it required no capital contribution from the airlines, it would carry some of their staff to work, and it would encourage airport check-in which BEA favoured, and 'which research suggests most passengers prefer.'[3]

The third London airport and airport links overseas

As the Heathrow link was a scheme that had to be implemented in the short term, it was perhaps not surprising that conventional rail systems were the only ones seriously considered. While examining the siting of the third London airport, the Roskill Commission 'encouraged' evidence on unconventional means of transport, but concluded that this would present constructional and operational problems: 'the nation cannot afford a repetition of the delays in providing proper fast road and rail links from which Heathrow has suffered.'[4]

A monorail has been built to link Tokyo with its main airport, but has proved costly in operation. In North America[5] cities do not usually have a rail service to their airports, even when these run nearby as in the case of Boston, Chicago, San Francisco (Oakland) and Toronto; shuttle buses link the airports to the rail system or city centre for those travellers not met by cars or taxis. Even New York's three major airports are served by bus from the East Side terminal. Mexico City's airport is served by one stop on its metro system, and Cleveland likewise. Conventional rail extensions have been suggested for Boston, Chicago, New York (to Newark and J F Kennedy airports), and San Francisco (International and Oakland). A monorail has been suggested to serve Kansas City International airport and a form of tracked hovercraft powered by linear induction motors for Los Angeles' International and Washington's Dulles airports. The new Paris Nord airport will have a bus or rail link, perhaps complemented by an Aerotrain link. None of these proposed systems has undergone the

[1] BR Board (1970), *Proof of Evidence, E12/7*, p36, GLDP Inquiry Stage 1.
[2] BAA Annual Reports: 1968–69, p21, *Hansard HC Papers 377* 1969–70, p54; and *Hansard HC Papers 67*; TCCL (1967), p15; letter from BAA Director of Planning.
[3] *First Report Select Committee on Nationalised Industries, Hansard HC Papers 275*, 1970 pp227–9 and QQ594–5.
[4] Commission on the Third London Airport (1971), *Report*, pp105, 109; and BR Board (1970), *Proof of Evidence, E12/7*, p37, GLDP Inquiry Stage 1.
[5] For information on American systems our thanks are due to Mr D NewMyer of North Western University Transportation Centre, Illinois.

broad appraisal process to which the Heathrow link was subjected, the analysis usually stopping short of estimates of demand, capital and current costs and financial viability.[1]

3 AIR TERMINALS

The Victoria terminal and transportation centre

As explained in Case Study *D* BR, LT, the GLC and Westminster City Council jointly commissioned a study from consultants on the feasibility of rebuilding Victoria station together with an air terminal, offices, an hotel and improved transport interchange to cope with the following complex of movements:[2]

BR international traffic: 2000 passengers hourly, many arriving by taxi.
BR domestic traffic: 90 000 passengers daily, 30 000 in the peak hour.
Buses: 400 in each direction in the peak hour.
Tubes: Interchange with the Circle, District and Victoria Lines.
Airport link: Uni-directional peak-hour flows of 3000–5000 passengers.
Coaches: 250 depart at peak period (Saturday morning).
Taxis: Up to 2000 per hour; hire cars in addition.
Parking: Sufficient to operate transporation centre.[3]

The consultants reported in 1967 that the development scheme was feasible, subject to certain conditions, and the leader of the GLC Mr (now Sir) Desmond Plummer commented: 'If we are to maintain London's position as a premier international airport it is essential that we should proceed with the scheme . . . provided it fits in with the environment.'[4] Subsequently Westminster City Council became very concerned at the local environmental problems which the traffic generated by the terminal would create. It was thought that road works costing from £8 to 10 millions could be required in the Victoria area. Public concern over the effects of such a large scheme and uncertainty over the Hammersmith scheme (see below) led Mr Plummer to deny that anything was being kept hidden, and to promise a public exhibition and discussion when plans were finalised.[5] Within the TCCL working party there were also differences of opinion: the BAA were very worried about the scale of check-in facilities needed at Heathrow,

[1] For example, see Systems Analysis and Research Corporation (1970), *Evaluation of High-speed Ground Access between Los Angeles International Airport and the San Fernando Valley*.
[2] Westminster CC *Minutes*, 26 October 1967.
[3] *TCCL Interchanges Group* paper, December 1966.
[4] GLC *Press Release 403*, 31 October 1967.
[5] *The Sunday Times*, 30 August 1968; GLC *Press Release 439*, 17 August 1968; Westminster CC *Minutes*, 7 November 1968.

while BEA and BOAC could not agree on passenger and baggage facilities at Victoria and the airport.[1]

Nevertheless the GLC wrote in the GLDP that the scheme 'offers great promise: the Council looks forward to an early decision by the authorities concerned which will enable this development to be realised.'[2] Subsequently the publication of any scheme was held up as the viability of the BR link and the Victoria check-in came into doubt.[3] The project finally disappeared when the Piccadilly Line proposal was accepted by the GLC and the Government.

In supporting the LT link in 1970, the GLC said 'while the BR link would have promoted the redevelopment of Victoria, such redevelopment could also be promoted by the Channel Tunnel . . . or by the grant of office development permits.'[4]

In their suggested revisions to the GLDP the Council mentioned the possibility of a terminal for the third London airport, but omitted the Victoria scheme, stating 'additional air terminal facilities must be provided within London at places which are selected in accordance with environmental and transport considerations.'[5] From the beginning the Victoria scheme had been severely criticised:

> It is entirely wasteful to construct a line between airport and city that would result in the creation of traffic holdups and chaos at the city terminal, and the building of the proposed air and sea gateway at Victoria would do just that.[6]

Hammersmith air terminal proposal

Whilst the Victoria scheme was under consideration another issue arose. In December 1969 a development company submitted an application for an hotel and air terminal on a site just east of the Hammersmith tube station. This had to be referred to the GLC for decision,[7] but when the GLC failed to give a decision within the statutory period, the company appealed to the Minister, and a local public inquiry was held in February 1968 at County Hall.

The borough of Hammersmith supported the scheme on the following grounds:

[1] Westminster CC, reports of Town Planning Committee, 4 February 1968; and Highways and Traffic Committee, 13 February 1968.
[2] GLC (1969), *GLDP Written Statement*, para5.74.
[3] GLC *Minutes*, 18 November 1969, pp626, 632.
[4] GLC *Minutes*, 17 July 1970, pp435–6.
[5] *GLDP Statement Revisions*, app1 to report 1 February 1972 of Strategic Planning Committee, para5.5.25.
[6] Editorial: *Official Architecture and Planning*, February 1967, p203.
[7] Under *London Government Act 1963*, ch33, s24 (4).

1 Earlier planning appeals had been decided in favour of the Council on the condition that a comprehensive plan was prepared for the town centre and that compatible schemes were allowed to proceed: this scheme related well to the plans prepared, including road widening and a proposed interchange development over the tube station.
2 The centre could not be redeveloped comprehensively without such private schemes and this scheme would be likely to attract further investment.
3 It would enable road widening to proceed by exchange of land.
4 The air terminal represented one of the few suitable options left for the site since the GLC and the Government were strictly controlling industry, shopping and offices.
5 The air terminal at Hammersmith would be needed to cope with the immediate growth in demand, even if the Victoria scheme proceeded.
6 It was well placed in relation to central London, the hotel districts, London airport, and bus and tube routes including the Piccadilly Line which might be extended at some stage to Heathrow.

The GLC opposed the scheme on grounds of transportation policy and traffic considerations. Regarding transportation policy they suggested that this scheme did not relate well to the proposed Victoria terminal and transportation centre and access to the airport which they had approved. The borough retorted that it was not valid to refuse planning permissions to prevent competition, and that many factors in both the Heathrow link and Victoria terminal issues were still unsettled. Also they believed that much greater traffic problems would be created by the Victoria scheme than by the one proposed at Hammersmith.

Concerning traffic, the GLC claimed that the borough's plans did not make adequate provision for both a general increase in traffic (including some expected to accompany proposed major new roads in the area) and for that generated by the terminal. The borough replied that the GLC had not published any future road patterns for the area and that it was satisfied that its own proposals would accommodate local needs and traffic generated by the scheme.[1]

In June 1968 the Highways and Planning committees of the GLC announced that they had made the following decision about air terminals, and referred to Hammersmith:

> The increase in numbers of aircraft using London's airports has resulted in a growing demand for more in-town terminal facilities.
>
> Because the tendency in recent applications has been for the airlines to use part of an existing building or one being built, usually located on the fringe of central London, the Highways and Planning committees of the GLC have recommended general policies to be followed when

[1] E G Sames, Hammersmith Borough Architect and Planning Officer, *Proof of Evidence*, 19 February 1968.

considering future applications for establishing air terminals in London.

They say that planning permission should normally be given for seven years so that airlines will not be discouraged from capital expenditure and the site or premises should be suitable for the purpose.

Other points to be borne in mind are:

1 The effect the terminal would have on the amenities of adjacent premises.
2 The amount and type of traffic the air terminal will generate and its effect on surrounding streets.
3 The facilities available for coach and car parking and for the picking up and setting down of passengers.
4 The proximity of underground and bus services.
5 The proximity to main areas of passenger origin and destination in the West End and Kensington.

A footnote to the report said:

A major international transportation centre, incorporating an air terminal, is planned by the GLC for Victoria and another is under consideration for Kings Cross.

The Victoria terminal would serve Heathrow and Gatwick airports while the one at Kings Cross could serve the third London airport to be built and also those at Luton and Southend.

Consistent with these policies the Council recently rejected a proposed terminal at Hammersmith. [our italics].[1]

This statement of criteria, however, was not presented to the full Council for ratification. The borough council nevertheless adhered to its view that Hammersmith was a suitable location for an air terminal and that it should be developed as a major strategic shopping centre. This was apparent not only in their comments on early drafts of the GLDP (in 1968 and 1969)[2] but also later in their evidence to the GLDP Inquiry.

After the local public inquiry in February 1968 the Inspector recommended approval of the Hammersmith terminal scheme in outline form, on the grounds that:

1 The terminal would not create any more traffic problems than any other development on the site.
2 The GLC's long-term plans for by-passing the centre were 'too remote and indefinite' to warrant refusal.
3 The terminal would be needed in advance of the Heathrow link and Victoria scheme being completed.

[1] GLC *Press Release 365*, 24 June 1968.
[2] Borough Development Group Report, LB Hammersmith *Minutes*, 13 March 1968, pp498–50; and 14 May 1969, pp492–5.

4 If the terminal were closed in the long term it could usefully be converted to a hotel.

When the Steering Group's report on the Heathrow link was published, the Minister had still not come to a decision and, in the light of this 'new evidence', he gave interested parties twenty-one days to comment.[1] On the Hammersmith inquiry in the same week the GLC affirmed that they were re-examining their own policy on air terminals and would not pursue their objection to the Hammersmith scheme.[2] The Minister adopted his Inspector's recommendation and allowed the appeal in September 1970, and granted an outline planning permission for a terminal building of 370 000 square feet and a 500-bedroom hotel of 340 000 square feet. A detailed scheme was prepared by April 1971.[3]

In 1971 the GLC decided to consult other bodies about their 1968 criteria but, after hearing the views of the boroughs, LT, BR and the BAA, adopted these criteria with minor changes in November 1972. The changes related to consideration of possible future expansion in air traffic, and of ensuring that any 'comprehensive central London air terminal' was not prejudiced and that present coach links were not 'unnecessarily perpetuated.'[4]

The West London Air Terminal

The WLAT was built above the junction of LT's Circle and District tracks chiefly to serve BEA and opened in 1963. It could not be built over Gloucester Road or Earls Court stations because although these were convenient sites, they were not readily available for new building. Soon after it had been opened it was criticised for having no convenient access to Gloucester Road, the nearest tube station. There was a 400-yard walk between them involving crossing a major road (Cromwell Road), which was especially inconvenient for people with luggage. LT and BEA set up a working party in 1960 which concluded that the provision of some form of travelator (moving pavement) was desirable and an undoubted amenity. It was estimated to cost £800 000 (or £50 000 annually) and would only bring in an estimated £1000 p.a. in extra revenue. Even the growth of air passenger traffic to 1973, when 1 million passengers were expected to pass through Gloucester Road station to the WLAT, would only result in £40 000 annually.

In 1963 LT raised the matter again after a developer's scheme to rebuild Gloucester Road station with a sub-surface ticket hall nearer the WLAT

[1] Borough Development Group Report to Council. LB Hammersmith *Minutes*, 8 July 1970, pp26–7.

[2] GLC *Minutes*, 7 July 1970, pp432–6.

[3] The hotel was increased to 670 beds and contained facilities for 2000-strong conferences, *LT Magazine*, 24, 5, 1970, p3; and LT *Press Release 130*, 1 April 1971.

[4] GLC *Press Release 546*, 9 November 1972; and *Minutes*, 28 November 1972, pp574–5.

was refused by the LCC on various town planning grounds. However, in 1964 the chairmen of the two bodies (LT and BEA) agreed that nothing could be done except in conjunction with redevelopment.[1] In 1965 the Select Committee on Nationalised Industries commented that 'the "missing link" at this important interchange is unworthy of a major centre of international communications. The Committee hope it will be proceeded with as soon as possible.'[2]

In 1967 and 1968 Maxwell Joseph's Grand Metropolitan Hotel Group proposed a 400-foot high 2000-bed hotel opposite the terminal and, after discussions with Kensington and Chelsea Council, were willing in principle to incorporate a travelator from Gloucester Road station to a point opposite the terminal. Public money might have had to be found for a bridge over Cromwell Road. The GLC turned down the hotel scheme because of building bulk and traffic generation but a permission for a 640-bed hotel on the same site had already been granted.[3] In 1970 a majority interest in this scheme was sold to the European Hotel Corporation (a company in which BEA and BOAC held interests). The plans still allowed for a link to be included at a later date, but no commitment or financial responsibility was settled. On the north side of Cromwell Road another hotel planning permission was granted but there was dispute over ownership of the site and progress there seemed uncertain.[4]

Thus after a decade this interchange remains inconvenient and unimproved despite Parliamentary concern. The reasons for this are epitomised in the reply to a question in Parliament in 1969 by Richard Marsh (then Minister of Transport): 'I have at present no such proposal (to link the WLAT with the tube) before me. Various possibilities have been considered in the past, but all are either very expensive or of limited benefit.'[5]

The WLAT seems eccentrically sited in relation to the Victoria terminal and certainly received less attention even by the TCCL study which proposed the removal of its coach services (and thus presumably also the closure of WLAT when the Victoria scheme was ready). But the spread of the hotel area and the tendency for individual airlines to seek their own termini[6] make WLAT seem less isolated. Nevertheless the Kensington and Chelsea borough council only received formal notification of the Hammersmith scheme and had not been invited to become involved with the Victoria proposals. The BAA had never taken any interest in the problems of WLAT although the borough's Director of Development wrote to them offering to discuss possibilities.

In 1972 BEA decided to withdraw passenger check-in facilities at the terminal by the summer of 1973 because the Piccadilly extension would

[1] *Hansard HC Papers 313–1*, 3 August 1965, vol2, app70, p480–1.

[2] *Hansard HC Papers 313*, 3 August 1965, vol1; *Report*, para126.

[3] *The Times*, 8 October 1968; *Evening Standard*, 6 March 1970 and 23 March 1970.

[4] *Evening Standard*, 26 May 1971, and interviews.

[5] In a written answer to Mr Biggs Davison MP (*HC Written Answers*, 21 July 1969, Col258).

[6] Interviews with officers and GLC *Press Release 365*, 24 June 1968.

provide speedier movement to the check-in facilities at Heathrow. Since 50% of BEA's 3 million passengers annually used the WLAT facilities, this would put great strain on the BAA's facilities at Heathrow. BOAC on the other hand modernised their check-in facilities at Victoria and aimed to reduce the number of people checking-in at Heathrow.[1]

Terminals for the third London airport and overseas airports

A working party consisting of GLC, LT, BR and MOT officers undertook for the Roskill Commission a study of suitable terminal locations. Having evaluated twenty-five sites in terms of site suitability, access, traffic conditions and interchange factors, the working party preferred King's Cross for all four possible airport sites. The only dissident voice at the Inquiry was that of the Thames Airport Group (TAG) which preferred St Katherine's Dock (the Port of London Authority was one of TAG's sponsors); later it accepted Kings' Cross, as did the Roskill Commission,[2] the GLC and the Government.[3] Immediately after this, officers began detailed feasibility studies.[4]

In-town terminals are the exception rather than the rule overseas and airlines rarely share terminals, although the New York Port Authority rents space to all the major airlines flying from La Guardia, Newark and J F Kennedy airports. In America many more people drive to the airports, but it is interesting that consultants preparing an aviation master plan for South California should suggest that a system of terminals in the centres of the large cities could enable the airports to handle more passengers without having to build new facilities.[5]

CONCLUSIONS

Heathrow link

One conclusion is that delay in implementing a project, at least on some occasions, can be beneficial by providing the opportunity to learn from earlier mistakes or to acquire sufficient knowledge. In the light of present circumstances the BR link might well have been an expensive and under-used facility with considerable operating problems particularly at the in-town terminal.

Both study groups completed their reports within a fairly short period. The TCCL study may be criticised for the assumptions used about trends in passenger behaviour and traffic effects, and lack of representation of the

[1] The *Guardian*, 12 May 1972.
[2] *Papers and Proceedings* of the Commission on the Third London Airport (1969–70), volII, 2, app2; and *Report* (1971), paras10.67–10.70, p109.
[3] GLC *Minutes*, 24 February 1970, p190.
[4] GLC *Minutes*, 4 May 1971, p198.
[5] *Los Angeles Times*, 5 February 1972.

airlines as consumers, but the former can be partly excused on the grounds that cost-benefit analysis methodology was very undeveloped. The processing of the second study was reasonably rapid, spurred on by central government who wanted to be seen to be keeping pace with air traffic demand. (The whole issue was much in the public eye as the Roskill Commission was sitting.) Moreover, the GLC and BAA were concerned about rapidly deteriorating road traffic conditions in and near Heathrow.

LT were always convinced of the merits of their case whereas by 1970 BR had doubts about their scheme on grounds of cost and revenue. As one LT officer described the Piccadilly Line extension: 'It's an operator's dream: Heathrow at one end, central London at the other, evening-up opposing flows, using much existing capacity, and generating extra traffic.' The benefits of multiple access both for airport workers and travellers were fully stressed. The airlines supported it for this reason (particularly BEA with its site on the Cromwell Road) and because it enabled them to continue with their coaches, a point stressed in the HSG study.[1]

The BAA did not represent the airlines' interests in the TCCL group but strongly backed the BR scheme throughout 1966–72,[2] believing that an exclusive system with spare capacity was needed, and would have been glad to see some of the access, parking and check-in problems moved from Heathrow to Victoria. Even after central government's decision the BAA and BR continued to hold the opinion that something more than the Piccadilly extension would be needed to carry the future levels of traffic at Heathrow.

The GLC as strategic planning and transportation authority found it reasonably easy to switch horses when the time came for a decision; perhaps it would not have been quite as easy if Parliamentary powers for both had not been available, or if they had not acquired responsibility for LT. On the other hand without responsibility for LT, the GLC would almost certainly not have given a 25% grant or pressed the Government to reconsider its decision not to grant aid the project. They were instrumental in getting the grant rules changed (see Chapter 3) with the result that, for example, the new Piccadilly rolling stock became eligible for grant in November 1971.

It is interesting that the link was generally discussed (though not by LT officers) as a 'self-contained' scheme with implications of national importance rather than as part of London's transport network.

It is too soon to say what consumers might think of the choice, but a London Chamber of Commerce committee became very interested in the airport link after hearing the cases presented by the BAA (supporting BR) and LT.[3] Thus it sent out a questionnaire to its member companies of whom 1626 made returns. The results were reported as follows:

[1] *Hansard HC Papers 275*, 10 February 1971, *Select Committee on Nationalised Industries: BAA*, Q170; and BEA memo, pp227–9.
[2] *Hansard HC Papers 67*, 17 July 1970; BAA *Annual Report*, p54.
[3] Information from interviews.

On a crude basis, the returns showed an almost equal division by firms of preference between rail and underground—44.8% favoured a BR link from Victoria station and 44.6% the extension of the LT Piccadilly Underground line from Hounslow. The balance either had no preference or found neither link satisfactory.

Of the firms undertaking ten or less journeys a year, half expressed preference for the underground link. On the other hand, rather more than half of the largest users (more than 2500 journeys annually) preferred the BR link. Elsewhere the figures were about equal.

The firms that expressed a preference were responsible for a total of 260 000 flight departures from the airport during 1969—159 000 favouring the BR link and 101 000 the underground.[1]

The London Chamber of Commerce sent the results to the MOT, the GLC, BR Board, LT Executive and BAA, implying that this might mean a need for both links.

Terminals

The situation over air terminals is much less clear. The GLC originally had the 'grand conception' of the Victoria centre and after Roskill's short-listed third airport sites had been confirmed to the north and east of London, they expressed the idea of a similar centre at King's Cross for which the Victoria scheme could act as prototype.[2] Realising, however, the practical problems of handling 6600 passengers in the peak hour by 1981, and facing the doubts of Westminster City Council about the traffic implications they were relieved to drop the Victoria air terminal. This decision made the BR link virtually unfeasible and at the same time cleared the way for approval of the Hammersmith scheme.

Subsequently the GLC were willing to consider applications for each terminal on its merits, as airline operators moved out of the BEA and BOAC buildings and sought their own terminals. LT favoured this approach while BR and the BAA opposed it: BR feared a loss of traffic, the BAA felt that the management of coach traffic at Heathrow would be much easier from Victoria than from many scattered sites.[3] While this approach to new terminals was tortuously evolved, the system failed to deal with the interchange problems at the WLAT which has been described as 'one of the worst examples of how-not-to-do-it'.[4]

[1] London Chamber of Commerce, *Home and Economic Affairs Newsletter*, 1 July 1970 of 2 October 1970.
[2] Letter received from BAA, 20 January 1972.
[3] *Ibid.*
[4] *Official Architecture and Planning*, February 1967, p229.

Case Study F

STATION CAR PARKS[1]

INTRODUCTION

The provision of station car parks in London is not a new idea: there was one at Morden as early as 1924. By 1970 there were 13 600 spaces in Greater London and over 48 000 in the London commuter area (see Figure 9).[2]

The original purpose of providing car parks at railway stations was to get people out of their cars and onto the trains as near to their home as possible, i.e. to maintain rail passenger traffic by providing convenient parking facilities, particularly in the outer suburbs, for the growing numbers of commuters who had bought a car. The transport operators therefore began programmes of constructing car parks and the highway authorities assisted in some cases by designating on-street parking spaces near stations.[3]

As traffic congestion increased the station car park gained a second function, of relieving the radial roads and car parks serving central London.[4] In order to secure a measure of traffic restraint, it was also suggested in 1965 that grants for car parks should be regarded as an alternative way of spending public money which would otherwise be used for road building, and that 'a loss sustained on a railway service might well be less than the cost of the highway improvements required to accommodate the railway travellers by road transport.'[5] Others were advocating the provision of low-priced parking at stations both as a means of road traffic restraint and of using surplus railway capacity.[6]

The provision of station car parks as a form of interchange is by its very nature a matter of co-operation and co-ordination between those in control of rail and road transport and the planning authorities. In London the railway operators have traditionally provided them, currently under

[1] Much of the research for this study was undertaken by Mr D NewMyer and formed part of his thesis, submitted to Drew University, New Jersey, USA for the degree of MA (1971).

[2] Information from LT, BR and the Automobile Association (1969), *Off-street Parking in London*, pp26–36. Not all of the car parks in the latter were open to commuters.

[3] See Reports of London Traffic Advisory Committee, *London Traffic*, 1957–59.

[4] *Report of Select Committee on Nationalised Industries: London Transport*, vol1, *Hansard HC Papers 313*, 1965, para423.

[5] *Memorandum* by Standing Joint Committee of Institutions of Civil and Municipal Engineers, RICS, RIBA and TPI, 28 September 1965.

[6] V H Ramsey (1966), 'Station Car Park Policy,' *Modern Transport*, No.95, pp12–14; W J Anson (1966), 'An Alternative to Road Pricing,' *Modern Transport*, No.95, pp14–15.

powers in the Transport Act 1968 and the Transport (London) Act 1969.[1] The Greater London Council (GLC) became responsible for interchange planning as part of the general planning powers under the London Government Act 1963 but much more specifically as transport planning authority in 1970. The Metropolitan Police are involved as enforcement agency of the law regarding on-street parking.

The GLC decided to handle the liaison aspects of this problem through the Interchanges Group of the Transport Co-ordinating Council for London (TCCL). The enforcement problem was discussed with the police and the Home Office via the Joint Traffic Executive, but it also became a political issue at a high level when the GLC were negotiating the transfer of responsibilities for the whole of London Transport (LT). Since the demise of TCCL discussions on interchange matters have been handled in the Greater London Transport Group (GLTG). This study now examines how the bodies have handled policy and project decisions.

LONDON TRANSPORT

As car ownership grew in London, LT added to the number and size of its station car parks at a rate which varied between 100 and 300 spaces annually by the early 1960s, mostly in the outer suburbs (see Figure 9). Scope for car parks was limited on many of the early lines because they served densely built areas where there was little land available adjacent to the stations, for example on the Morden and Edgware lines.

Just before and after the Second World War tube services were extended over some outer suburban lines owned by British Rail (BR), although BR continued to run freight trains over these lines until the mid-1960s. With the rationalisation of BR's services, especially in freight, LT gained sole use of the lines and many small goods yards became redundant. Some had continuing concessions for storing coal supplies, but this function dwindled with the growth of gas, oil and electricity as fuels, so that more sites became available. As a result over 2100 spaces were added to the total in each of the years 1966–68, and by 1971, 68 of LT's 344 stations had car parks.[2] Two-thirds of these were in the GLC area and the sizes ranged from a handful of spaces to 600 at Epping, averaging 155 in the GLC area and 177 outside (Table 21).

The pattern of this provision was determined by land availability and ownership by LT and by no means reflected demand, for average usage in 1971 was only 56%. This low level of usage was also influenced by another factor outside LT's control but about which the Board constantly complained, namely the lack of control of on-street parking near the stations. This needed full co-operation between the GLC, the Metropolitan Police and the London boroughs[3] (see page 282 below). LT's dwindling supply of

[1] 1968, ch73, s48 (2) (c); 1969 ch35, s6 (1) (j) amending 1962, ch46, s14 (1) (d).
[2] See LT *Annual Reports* and *Evening Standard*, 21 September 1968.
[3] See *Annual Reports*, British Transport Commission, 1957, p42; LT, 1967, para74; 1968, para101; 1969, para80.

AREA	CAPACITY	AVERAGE USAGE	USE (%)
LT			
GLC area	7 890	4 708	60
Other	2 999	1 419	47
LT Total	10 889	6 127	56
BR			
ER	1 005	946	94
LMR	890	467	52
SR	3 661	2 086	57
WR (est)	180	130	72
GLC Area total	5 736	3 629	63
ER	5 281	4 984	94
LMR	5 328	3 546	67
WR (est)	4 125	2 996	73
SR	17 303	10 921	63
Outer area total	32 037	22 447	70
BR Total	37 773	26 076	69
LT and BR			
GLC area total	13 626	8 337	61
Outer area total	35 036	23 866	68
GRAND TOTAL	48 662	32 203	66

Table 21 STATION CAR PARKS IN LONDON AND THE SOUTH-EAST, 1971

Source: BR letter Ref PP2012/E and PP2090 of 4 May 1971, and interviews with LT and BR officers

land together with the lack of on-street parking control to ensure the use of station car parks led the Board to complain of the problems of financing multi-storey parking[1] over existing stations or railway cuttings as an alternative source of supply. In 1965 the Board had suggested that facilities for servicing vehicles could help to pay for this or at least help to reduce losses,[2] and powers for such activities were eventually given to LT and BR in section 48 of the 1968 Transport Act.

This Act also provided for infrastructure grants for capital investments including car parks. The Board hoped that this would encourage the provision of station car parks, but their 1969 report said:

Very few additional spaces were provided in 1969. Until free parking on

[1] *Annual Reports*, 1965, para53; 1967; para74; 1968, para101; 1969, para80.

[2] LT repeated this claim in 1967 (GLC *Minutes*, 6 June 1967, Question in Council, p294).

streets adjacent to stations is restricted or grants are provided by the Ministry of Transport to local authorities for multi-storey or other expensive car parks at stations, a significant increase over the present total of 11 000 spaces is unlikely to be financially justifiable.

In 1970 one new car park was provided at Willesden Green station.[1] Although LT's powers to provide car servicing facilities were continued in the 1969 Transport (London) Act, subject to GLC direction, this did not stimulate any schemes by the Executive.

LT has itself operated its car parks in recent years at a rate of 10p per day. Tickets were available through booking offices but methods of payment and parking control have been increasingly automated, both by the provision of 'rising arm' and 'rising kerb' barriers, and 60 or 70% of parks were automatic by 1971. More recently a pre-payment discount scheme has been introduced where five tokens can be purchased for 30p (i.e. a discount of 40%).[2]

Thus despite the early realisation that station car parks could increase passenger usage and also relieve traffic on the main radial roads and in central London,[3] and despite the intention to promote them expressed in subsequent policy documents,[4] LT have been bedevilled by lack of control over other factors affecting transport, and by lack of money.

BRITISH RAILWAYS

Improvements in signalling and conversion to electric traction enabled BR to encourage longer-distance commuting in the 1930s and 1960s by extolling the virtures of living in the country and by the sea. This policy was successful particularly to the south and east of London. More recently the Board has sought to make use of spare capacity on the lines, promoting population dispersal to related areas.[5]

The dominance of the Southern Region commuter services is partly reflected in the distribution of BR's car parks (Table 21 and Figure 9), 3700 of the 5500 spaces in Greater London are at stations south of the Thames, and of the 32 000 spaces in the outer area, 17 000 are in the south.[6] Since the car parks have been provided on relatively cheap land and in less densely built areas, they tend to be larger (from 200 to 400 spaces) than LT's parks. They tend to be better used, moreover, as there are often no bus services or only limited ones to compete for traffic to and from stations. Nevertheless,

[1] LT Executive (1970), *Annual Report*, p18.

[2] *Annual Reports*, 1963, para65; 1964, para22; 1965, para52; 1968, para100; *LT Magazine*, No.24, 8 November 1970, pp3, 22; GLC *Minutes*, 30 November 1971.

[3] *Annual Report*, 1958, paras53–4.

[4] E.g. Binder, Hamlyn & Co, *LT Board Joint Review: Consultants' Management Report*, April 1967.

[5] South-East Joint Planning Team (1970), *Strategic Plan for the South-East*, HMSO.

[6] See BR Board (1970), *Proof of Evidence*, *E12/7*, GLDP Inquiry Stage 1, paras4.6, 4.14, 4.44; Western Region leaflet, *You Can Get to London in Only 60 Minutes . . .*; and *Evening News*, 4 February 1971.

much the same caveats apply as in LT's case; the location of station car parks has been a compromise between the local demand and the availability of land adjacent to the stations and in BR's ownership. The provision was also swelled in the late 1960s by the conversion of goods yards and coal yards[1] (2800 spaces were provided in 1967 and 3500 in 1968).

BR had further plans for development in 1971–72, for instance some 350 new spaces were planned for Greater London and 6000 for the outer area. The planning of new car parks, however, was entirely a matter to be handled within each region by divisional works sections reporting to the regional planning manager. The Board took little part in car-parking matters.

BR's operating policy is that parking fees should cover the cost of the park and not be subsidised from fares revenue. The capital costs may be as low as £150 per car space, for example when all that is required is a skin of tarmac over a goods yard, which requires a daily average payment by commuters of 6p (1s 3d)[2] to repay its outlay fairly quickly. Prices vary from region to region (e.g. from £5 to 20 for a year) and are generally higher in Greater London. In a few places where BR is trying to encourage traffic, parking is free.[3] Increasingly, passengers are being attracted to a scheme of buying an annual combined train and car park season ticket.

Like LT, BR have complained about local authorities that fail to control on-street parking or provide competing off-street parking of their own in locations of considerable activity such as town centres. Under the Transport Act 1962 BR also have a responsibility to break even on revenue account and to establish a reserve (section 18) but may only develop land for purposes other than transport by consent of the Minister of Transport, although they may rent or sell the land to private developers (section 11). Capital has never been plentiful enough to do the former and in the latter cases some sites have been sold for commercial development, because this showed a better financial return than any form of car park. Linking a multi-storey park with commercial development is possible in town centres (such as Wembley, Bromley, and Orpington) but on several occasions other sites have directly conflicted with the local planning authority's location policies for retail and office development.[4]

BR had hoped that the infrastructure grant scheme would allow them to invest in schemes which would show a reasonable return on their 50% share, whilst the central or local government contribution would represent a 'social' subsidy, showing a nil or low return. This has not proved possible, partly because of the generally short supply of capital, particularly in the public sector. Moreover, the Treasury expect a test discount rate of return of 10% on the whole sum of such transport infrastructure schemes.

[1] See A L Cooper (1969), 'Park and Ride,' *Modern Railways*, 25, pp11–14.

[2] A L Cooper, 'Significance of Parking in Rapid Transit,' *Proceedings of PATRAC Seminar*, 3 July 1968, pp6–15.

[3] For example, the area centred on Newbury. Six village stations have free parking, while the charges at Newbury are 15p per day, 50p per week, £1.50 per month and £12 per year.

[4] Cooper (1968) and (1969), and interviews with BR staff.

Land values and the costs of multi-storey structures have also increased considerably.

A more specific factor which has complicated the use of grants for BR is its national rather than metropolitan role. At some heavily used stations where a new car park or an extension would seem to be justified the traffic consists of a mixture of commuters and inter-city travellers. The commuter's needs would be eligible for a 'social' grant on the grounds that road traffic congestion costs would be reduced; this case could not be made for the second group many of whom travel at off-peak times.

The problem of allocating spaces to different users has proved to be a difficult one, for example, at Watford and Croydon stations. The system of only opening a proportion during the morning rush hour does not seem to have been tried possibly because it would mean higher supervisory costs (see below).

The BR Board's policy proposals for developing station car parks and safeguards against railheading (i.e. people motoring further into the city with a consequent loss of revenue) were set out in their evidence to the Greater London Development Plan (GLDP) Inquiry:

> As a general policy BR will concentrate on locating car-parking facilities at strategic stations in the outer metropolitan area and beyond. The closer the stations to the central area the greater the benefit from 'beaming' the bus services from the surrounding areas on to the stations and this policy is being actively pursued between BR and LT.

BR also thought that the responsibility for producing a programme of interchange development including station parking provision should lie jointly with the GLC, the London boroughs and the transport operators, and that any additional developments to those shown in the GLDP should be shown in the boroughs' local plans.[1]

Thus from the transport operators' standpoint the following conclusions emerge:

1 LT generally and BR in certain areas are running out of suitable sites for car parks at reasonable costs.
2 Both would be prepared to meet demands by building over stations and tracks, but can only do so if they can cover the extra land or structural costs with infrastructure grants or revenue from associated commercial development.
3 Grants have been very limited and commercial development depends on local and strategic planning policy.
4 In the case of existing and especially new car parks provision depends on ensuring good usage. This depends on control and/or pricing of on-street parking nearby which entails co-operation by the local planning

[1] BR Board (1970), *Proof of Evidence*, *E12/7*, paras4.5.5–4.5.8; and *E12/34*, app *C*, GLDP Inquiry Stage 1.

authority, the Metropolitan or County Police and the highways authorities (GLC or county council or county borough).

5 LT's role is mainly a conurbation one, whereas BR serve the South-East region and the nation; the latter's regional organisation results in differences in the pattern and pricing of provision and complicates co-ordination; the GLC's takeover of LT gives it direct control of all its policies but has not brought about any obvious changes of intent.

THE LONDON BOROUGHS AND THE LBA

The London boroughs have been concerned in station car park policy both individually and collectively since they were established. In 1965 the London Boroughs' Committee (LBC) (now Association) commented on the desirability of making station parking cheap and convenient.[1] Their involvement generally arose out of conflicting interests, where commuters were parking on the streets near railway stations and annoying residents, or in local authority car parks at town centres. The London Borough of Haringey, for example, was worried about the lack of provision for parking in the Parliamentary powers granted for building the Victoria Line, and Hillingdon complained that over 50% of the capacity of a shoppers' car park at Northwood was pre-empted by commuters.[2] The TCCL interchanges group had begun work by this time and in July 1966 the LBC's advisory officers produced a report on station car parks suggesting five objectives for 'the appropriate authorities' to consider when providing station car parks,[3] including the need:

1 To prevent traffic congestion (the beneficiaries being the GLC, the inner London boroughs and road users in general).
2 To eliminate the nuisance caused by all-day parking in residential streets (beneficiaries being the outer London boroughs).
3 To encourage use of rail services (beneficiaries being BR and LT).

They also recommended that the LBC should be represented on the TCCL interchanges group; that TCCL should investigate the costs of providing car parks on concrete rafts over railway cuttings;[4] that the powers of traffic wardens should be widened so that they could handle parking offences outside parking control zones (for instance, if a limited no-parking order around stations was applied in the morning peak 0730–0930 commuters could be effectively controlled by traffic wardens without extra burdens on the police); and that the railway authorities should be given powers to open their parks to other than railway users.

[1] LBC (later LBA) *Minutes*, 26 June 1965, p50.
[2] LBC *Minutes*, 20 July 1965, p62; and 4 May 1966, p45.
[3] LBC *Minutes*, 27 June 1966, pp82–4.
[4] LT and BR had quoted prohibitive costs (£2000 per parking space) that would only be reduced by economies of scale.

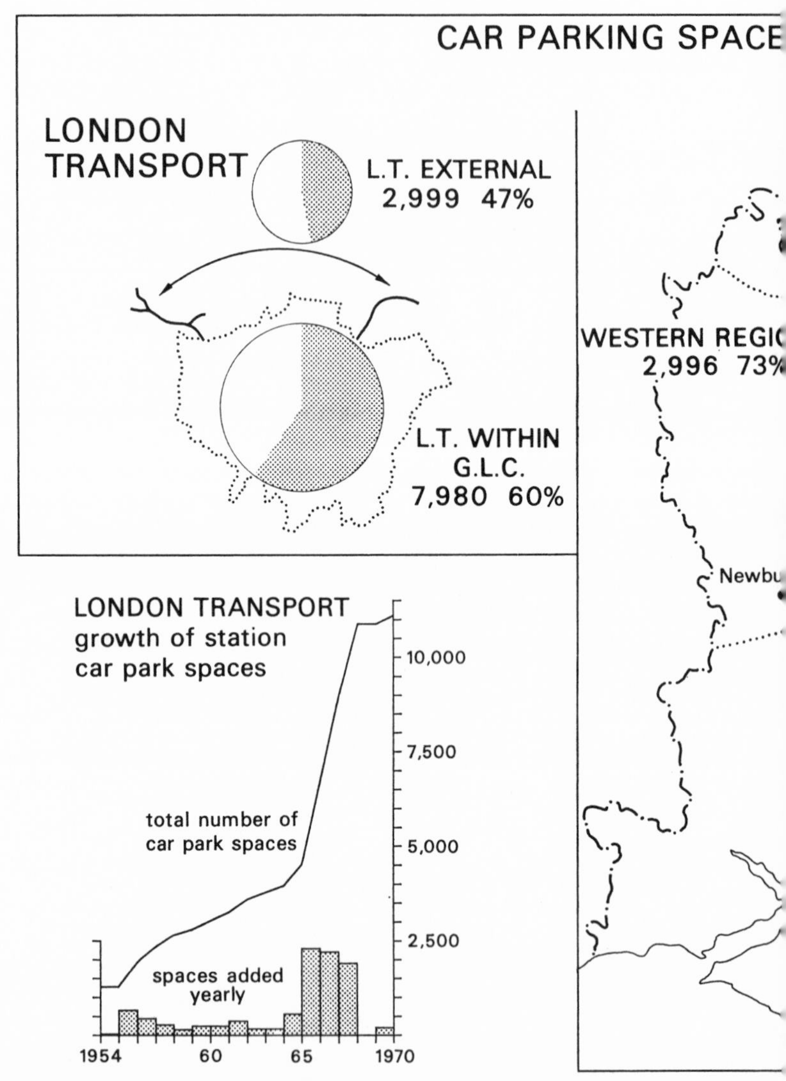

Figure 9 BR AND LT STATION CAR-PARKING SPACES AND USAGE, 1970

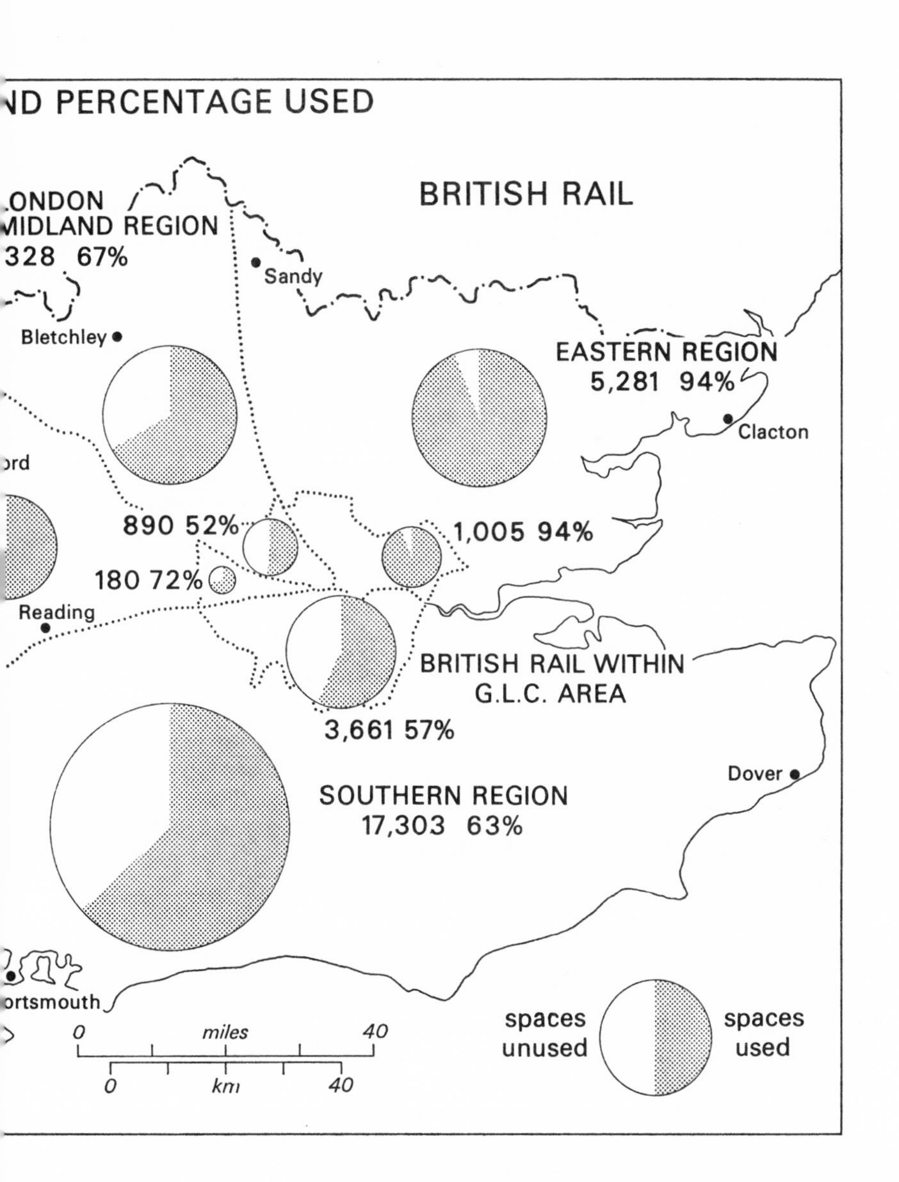

ND PERCENTAGE USED
BRITISH RAIL
.ONDON
MIDLAND REGION
328 67%
Sandy
Bletchley
EASTERN REGION
5,281 94%
Clacton
rd
890 52%
1,005 94%
180 72%
Reading
BRITISH RAIL WITHIN
G.L.C. AREA
3,661 57%
Dover
SOUTHERN REGION
17,303 63%
ortsmouth
0
miles
40
0
km
40
spaces
unused
spaces
used

Although the LBC did not pursue the matter immediately, they were invited to nominate four members to TCCL. TCCL also took up the LBC's idea of a technical study of the problems of rafting and found that costs could be from £600 to 700 per car space (compared with £600 for a multi-storey park at ground level, at 1969 prices) and that this could be covered from revenue.[1] This, it was felt, was a realistic basis for negotiating with commercial companies, although the LBA's officers were of the opinion that financing such schemes should be shared (presumably between the Government, the GLC, the operators and the boroughs themselves). Such a scheme still depends upon loans or infrastructure grants being available and, irrespective of how the car parks are financed, on-street parking being controlled. By mid-1971 no grants had been given for such schemes even at the much-studied site at Harrow or at a major interchange such as Ealing Broadway.

Also, despite the fact that commuter parking near stations constituted a problem in almost every outer borough[2] the idea of controlling this by enforcing a parking ban for a short period each morning lay dormant. In particular the Metropolitan Police were not keen to add yet another type of control to the list of fifty-seven types which they were trying to reduce and simplify.[3] In 1969 the London Borough of Havering pressed the GLC's North-East Area Board of the Environmental Planning Committee and the Metropolitan Police to institute such a control zone around Gidea Park station where prolonged complaints had been made by local residents. Eventually they were successful and the scheme started in April 1971.[4] It was expected to displace 200 commuters who could park at stations farther down the line or drive another three miles to Romford station where parking facilities were available. If this scheme is a success it may set a precedent for other areas with similar problems (e.g. Harold Wood, Eltham, Beckenham, Petts Wood, and Orpington where the residents have petitioned the GLC for action).[5]

THE GLC, TCCL AND GLTG

During their first year of existence the GLC were mainly occupied in preparing to take over responsibility for traffic management, but in December 1965 Mr Fraser the Minister of Transport invited some members of the Council to discuss with him problems of car commuting and methods of controlling the parking in the central area which they involved.

[1] LBA *Minutes*, 30 July 1969, pp58, 62–3. The study used Burnt Oak and Harrow-on-the-Hill as examples.

[2] Information from interviews. The Borough Engineer of Bromley, Mr Collins, considered that in residential areas it was a greater problem than that caused by the use of local streets as 'rat-runs.'

[3] LBA *Minutes*, 26 November 1969, pp95–6; and 17 March 1971, p18.

[4] Information from interviews and GLC *Press Release 37*, 27 January 1971.

[5] In Orpington the Bromley borough council had sought to overcome the problem by building a multi-storey car park but without on-street control it was very little used. GLC *Press Release 402*, 10 August 1970.

In February 1966 he told the Council that 'it would be wrong to take measures which would make the use of private cars for some purposes less attractive, except as part of an integral policy providing also for improving the attractiveness of the alternatives.' Three policies were mentioned: improvements and extensions to the rail and tube networks, improvements of interchanges, particularly at central stations and, most importantly for the purpose of this study, better suburban interchange facilities including new and extended station car parks as a matter of urgency.[1] Unlike the parking policy for central and inner London put forward at the same time (see Case Study *Q*) there were no specific proposals for station car parks.

In June 1967 the GLC admitted that they were not undertaking feasibility studies and that BR and LT were proceeding with their programmes of provision on the commercial basis of increasing passenger usage but also covering the cost of the parks themselves. LT, for example, were reported to have a programme of 10 000 new spaces for 1967.[2] The following month, however, the provision of station car parks was represented as one of the three main 'arms' of parking policy in the preliminary ideas for the GLDP.[3]

The desire of the GLC to ease congestion on the road network, particularly in the central area, by discouraging car commuters, and of the London boroughs to improve amenity by clearing parking out of residential streets near stations, demanded some action.[4] The Transport Co-ordinating Council for London established a new working party to consider the problem, under the auspices of its Interchanges Group. It was chaired by the GLC's then adviser on transport policy Mr J D C Churchill, and contained representatives from the Council's Planning and Highways departments, BR, LT, LBA and later the Metropolitan Police.

In May 1968 the GLC produced a major policy statement on various aspects of car parking which with modifications was still in force at the time of writing. This included the following statements on station car parks:

> The Co-ordinating Council considers that station car parks should pay their way and that charges should, as far as possible, be standard within a particular area and similar to those for nearby local authority car parks. The principle of higher charges nearer to central London should be adopted.
>
> The provision of station and interchange car parking must be a basic part of the Council's comprehensive transport policy and the Council should develop with BR and LT a major interchange plan to take advantage of the payment of grant for schemes envisaged in the

[1] GLC *Minutes*, 22 February 1966, pp115–16.
[2] GLC *Minutes*, 6 June 1967, p294 (Question in Council).
[3] GLC *Minutes*, 4 July 1967, pp428–9.
[4] GLC *Minutes*, 5 December 1967, p719, Q15 on 'Difficulties of Commuter Car Parking in Outer London.'

Transport Bill now before Parliament. We propose to ask the borough councils to look for available land near to railway stations and to make it available for station car parks, to be controlled either by themselves, BR or LT.[1]

It was quickly realised that each authority was constrained in meeting the requirements of the others by their statutory obligation or general policies. BR, for example, were anxious not to see car parks built too close to the centre of London since this was believed to encourage 'railheading.'[2] LT had great problems of shortages of sites and capital. The GLC had no powers to aid the operators and were very concerned about problems of enforcing traffic regulations near stations.[3]

With the need for some comprehensive data to aid GLDP policy formulation, a series of interview surveys were instituted in four phases, covering fifty stations in all.[4] The surveys discovered that:

1 On average 11% of rail passengers used park-and-ride methods and another 5% 'kiss-and-ride' (being delivered in a car driven away) but some outer stations showed much higher proportions (32% park-and-ride at Stanmore, 20% at Osterley, 19% at Hounslow West and Cockfosters, 17% at Wembley Park and 16% at Morden, Surbiton and Redbridge).
2 The great majority used their nearest station and lived fairly close by (98% within five miles).
3 However, some outer stations had wider and growing catchments, particularly if they were termini or had a particularly fast or more frequent service to the centre or provided a direct journey (minimising central area interchange or distribution trips). Examples of this were Cockfosters and Morden in the first group, and Acton, Wembley, Surbiton and White City in the second.[5]
4 South of the river some people from the outer suburbs preferred driving to LT stations in inner London (Elephant and Castle, Clapham South, Oval) rather than to nearer BR stations.
5 Some used major roads to railhead to stations either far in or with good services (e.g. Osterley, Leytonstone, Swiss Cottage and Shepherd's Bush).[6]

[1] *Parking Policy in London*, GLC *Minutes*, 7 May 1968, p262, paras28–9.
[2] GLC *Minutes*, 28 July 1968, p424, Q37; Department of Highways and Transportation, *Research Memo 162*, June 1969 (M Balint; *Railheading Study*).
[3] Interviews with present and former GLC officers.
[4] *SCP Working Party Papers* 35, 37 and 68.
[5] See also D Maltby and C N Cheney 'Factors Affecting the Design of Transport Interchanges,' *Tr Eng and Control*, April 1971, pp625–7.
[6] This led the officers to wonder what effects the proposed primary road network might have, and studies were tentatively begun on the effects of a series of large car parks where Ringway 1 intersected the rail and tube lines, but this was not pursued. See also R F Bennett; 'Road Transport in a Rapid Transit System,' *Inst Tpt Jnl*, March 1968, p14.

While these studies were proceeding, the Working Party also examined individual situations that were referred to them such as the problems of provision on the Victoria Line, cases where residential amenity was threatened (e.g. Petts Wood, Gidea Park), examples of suitable situations for 'rafting' across cuttings (e.g. Bexleyheath, Harrow-on-the-Hill). In the end, however, the problems remained of ensuring the best use of existing car parks where it was considered impracticable to introduce on-street parking control,[1] and of overcoming the shortage of capital and fragmented financial responsibility for new parks.

Thus in October 1969 a statement on parking policy for Greater London incorporating changes to the proposals of May 1968 said:

> Much progress has been made by BR and LT, in consultation with the LBC and with other local authorities outside Greater London, in establishing car parks at railway stations. The aim must be to get car parks provided for the benefit of commuters, and to encourage the longest possible rail journeys by instituting progressively higher parking charges nearer central London, so reducing the attraction of commuting by car. The possibility of meter parking near particularly convenient railway stations, where commuters at present park outside the station without payment, has already been mentioned. Elsewhere, it may be found desirable to introduce waiting restrictions on amenity grounds under the wider traffic management powers conferred by the Transport Act 1968. The provision of station car parks presents problems of finance; and at the same time restrictions on parking in the street outside such car parks can be effective only if they are adequately enforced.[2]

The TCCL Working Party information was supplemented by a wider study on all types of interchange in and outside Greater London prepared in support of the GLDP.[3] This said that 'a significant deficiency of the public transport system in Greater London is the inability to change between services.' Interchange policy should 'extract maximum benefit from the investment in the rail and bus systems' with regard to the effects of interchanges on rail capacity, on workers and shoppers in town centres (when competing for parking space) and on 'encouraging extra road traffic from outside the GLC area.'

The study classified major and secondary interchanges. The former either had large car parks (e.g. Edgware 276 spaces and Morden 452) or were in congested town centres with high land values; the latter consisted of a group of seven stations classified as mainly car commuting centres, with a

[1] E.g. *SCP Working Party Paper 58*, misleadingly entitled 'Economics of Station Car Parks,' which suggested improving access, selectively lowering prices, and publicising the security of station car parks.

[2] *Parking Policy in London*, p13, compare pages 283–4 above.

[3] *GLDP Interchange Study*, July 1969, GLC Planning Department, Ref PL/LV/DG/6344, paras1.1, 3.1, 6.5, 6.6 and 7.2.

total of over 2200 spaces. The report said that there was a need to avoid railheading, and so 'large interchange car parks should not therefore be provided on or near the primary roads in such locations as to encourage railheading but should be located in relation to the secondary road network and to serve residential catchment areas.'

They should also be sited so as not to 'steal' bus passengers.[1]

The report proposed that after consultation with the boroughs and the police the GLC should produce 'a draft policy statement on interchanges indicating the investment level, form of works, and general locations' which could also be used as a context for programming. Two months later the GLDP was published and the *Written Statement* and *Structure Map* indicated the location of major and secondary interchanges. It was suggested that three criteria should be applied to establish priorities for improving interchanges, one of which was the convenience of changing from bus or car to rail (the others were speed of service to the central area and ability to change from train to tube).[2]

The *Statement* said 'there is no basis for assuming that there is at present a large unsatisfied demand for station car parking'[3] and mentioned only three 'immediate' proposals: Harrow-on-the-Hill (a scheme of several years' standing), Ealing Broadway (part of the town centre redevelopment scheme), and Abbey Wood or Plumstead (to serve the growing population of Thamesmead). Four other town centres were suggested to have spare parking capacity which could be used (Wimbledon, Ilford, Lewisham and Croydon) and four other 'less immediate' proposals were listed: Acton Town, Boston Manor, White City and Hatton Cross (to serve the new Piccadilly Line extension to Heathrow airport).[4]

The *GLDP Report of Studies* embodied the Interchanges Study material showing the distribution of car parks and mentioning some of the railheading problems, but neither document gave any indication of what each classification meant in terms of investment or development prospects or priorities. The *Report* finally stated (paragraph 6.302) that

> The deficiency (of interchanging) is primarily the result of the division of responsibility between the various transportation and highway

[1] Data produced by Maltby & Cheney (1971), for instance, suggested that this happened at Kenton station when a new car park was built at Harrow and Wealdstone.

[2] *GLDP Written Statement*, September 1969, paras5.34, 5.61; and *Metropolitan Structure Map*.

[3] Later LT figures for 1970 (document 931/MLG/A3–12), however, suggest that while commuter parking around stations with spare capacity was virtually unchanged from 1968, the number of cars parked around full station car parks increased from 1300 to 2400. This might confirm Maltby & Cheney's idea that outer suburban station catchments were expanding. Choudhury (1969, p56) mentions a GLC estimate that the level of demand could rise from about 40 000 spaces at present to 60 000 by 1981, 'Park-and-Ride for the Journey to Work,' unpub MSc thesis, Imperial Coll, Univ of London.

[4] These had already been before the Council. See GLC *Minutes*, 7 July 1970, pp429, 434; 3 November 1970, p597; 1 December 1970, p659.

> authorities. It is the intention of the Council to ensure that a concentrated effort is made to improve this weak link. The new Government grants . . . will become a spur for action.[1]

It must be remembered, however, that although important, it was a non-statutory document. A general policy document was produced just before the GLDP Inquiry began, but this merely mentioned the Council's past policy and future intentions of 'encouraging' the provision of station car parks.[2]

At the same time the GLC were negotiating the takeover of policy responsibility for LT and one of the conditions they were seeking from the Government was the assurance of adequate police manpower for enforcing parking controls. This was at a time when the Home Office had restricted police recruitment for financial reasons (see Case Study *Q*). Even though this restriction was lifted and funds were made available for recruiting 500 wardens in 1969–70 and 1970–71,[3] this did not help in the provision of station car parks.

There the situation rested until in response to some questioning on park-and-ride during the Inquiry, the GLC produced some slightly more specific comments.[4] It was suggested that:

> In practice a car park is only likely to operate successfully in the following circumstances:
>
> *a* Where there is a proven substantial demand in the station catchment area.
>
> *b* Where the station offers a fast and frequent service to town.
>
> *c* Where the car park is easily accessible, well advertised, supervised and close to the station.
>
> *d* Where free long-term parking in the surrounding streets is either not available or effectively prohibited.
>
> *e* Where the scale of charges is in line with permitted on- or off-street parking in the locality.

The GLC pointed out that parking might be most attractive in terms of use and revenue and also have a weekend use in town centres and suggested that in many such locations park-and-ride facilities should form part of the town centre parking supply. This implied that the GLC themselves or the borough councils or private operators should provide the car parks, but begged the difficult question of who should finance them. Outside the town centres, the GLC foresaw them probably operating 'in the face of un-

[1] *GLDP Report of Studies* (September 1969), fig6.9, para6.18, Table 6.8 and paras6.302–6.308.

[2] GLC (1970), *Transport in London: A Balanced Policy*, pp4, 18.

[3] See GLC *Minutes*, 9 July 1968, p383; 17 February 1968, pp709–10; 21 October 1969, p572.

[4] GLDP Inquiry *Transcript*, day 81, p38A; and *Paper S12/181*, May 1971.

controlled on-street parking.' The leader of the GLC said in November 1971 that the GLC were concerned to fill the gaps in the pattern of provision and that 'in the first instance the London boroughs and the transport undertakings should be involved in the finance. With our limited means we must concentrate on strategic problems.'[1]

In the revised version of the *GLDP Statement* in 1972 greater emphasis was laid on the role of public transport. It said that stations where it was 'convenient to change from car or bus to train should be one of four categories of interchange with priority' and that 'car parking at railway stations in outer London and beyond should be provided to encourage journeys into central London to be made by rail. The amount provided must be consistent with local needs and the policies for traffic restraint.'[2]

THE METROPOLITAN POLICE

The role and the problems of the police have already been mentioned above but are perhaps more clearly set out in their annual report for 1969:

> With regard to the protection of residential amenities, two aspects came up for discussion by the Joint Traffic Executive during the year: overnight parking of heavy lorries and all-day parking of commuters' cars in streets surrounding some suburban railway stations. It was emphasised from the police side that whilst the need for traffic orders for preserving or improving amenities is fully appreciated, the enforcement of such orders must come low in the scale of priorities. This is because only a limited proportion of the total resources of the Force can be allocated to traffic duties . . . and have to be committed primarily to securing the safe and orderly movement of main-road traffic.[3]

EXPERIENCE ELSEWHERE IN BRITAIN AND OVERSEAS

A deliberate policy of providing park-and-ride car parks has been pursued in some other British towns: Glasgow, for example, provided one on its underground and the Greater Glasgow plan proposed nine more sites.[4] As a result of a very successful experiment in 1966 Leicester Corporation decided to provide further car parks around the central area to serve the city's bus services, mainly for shoppers rather than commuters; it was estimated that some 2000 spaces would be needed by 1975.[5]

[1] *Evening News*, 1 November 1971.
[2] GLC (1972), *GLDP Statement Revisions*, paras5.5.20–5.5.22.
[3] *Report of commissioner of Police for Metropolis for 1969*, Cmnd 4355, HMSO 1970, p57. See also the paper by Commander Candy to the British Parking Association Conference, May 1971.
[4] A R Choudhury (1969), pp34–5. Much of the overseas data is from this source.
[5] City of Leicester: *Park 'n' Ride—Reporting an Experiment* (1967); *Traffic and Transport Policy* (1969), p10; *Park 'n' Ride: Five Years' Experience*, 1972.

In North America several cities have provided park-and-ride facilities on a large scale and, as Table 22 shows, several more have ambitious programmes as a result of demonstration projects under the 1964 Federal Mass Transportation Act which provided grants.[1] For example, the Boston rail operators believe they have attracted $165 000 extra annual income from commuter travel, and the White Plains Line's traffic grew by 11% as a result of increasing the parking spaces at seven stations from 2000 to 3000. Perhaps the most successful of all has been the Go Transit Line in Toronto which intercepted a considerable percentage of road traffic along a particular corridor route.[2]

In Europe, Hamburg has a co-ordinated interchange system based mainly on bus–rail interchanges but with some park-and-ride provision, while one professional planning body has urged their more systematic use in Paris to combat central area parking problems and to help in restructuring the suburban centres.[3]

Existing		
Toronto	(Go Transit)	2400 spaces at 12 stations
Boston	(Met Transit Auth)	6300 spaces at 26 stations
New Brunswick	(Jersey Ave Subway)	300 spaces
Chicago	(Ch Tr Auth)	2300 spaces at 6 stations
	(Illinois Central Railroad)	600 spaces
	(Skokie–Swift Railroad)	3300 spaces
Cleveland		5300 spaces at 7 stations
Hamburg	(Hamburg Tpt Commy)	10 000 spaces
Planned		
Philadelphia	(Lindenwold Line)	5000 spaces at 6 stations
Toronto	(Bloor St Subway)	5000 spaces
San Francisco	(Bay Area Rapid Tr)	16 500 spaces at 23 stations
Los Angeles	(S Cal Rapid Tr D)	28 000 spaces at 29 stations
Chicago	(NE Ill Plng Cmsn)	7000 spaces at 8 stations
Hamburg	(Hamburg Tpt Commy)	50 000 spaces

Table 22 PARK-AND-RIDE IN OVERSEAS CITIES

CONCLUSIONS

Station car park provision has so far been almost exclusively by BR and LT, on land that was surplus to the needs of train operations. In this

[1] E.g. Tri-State-Transportation Commission (1967), *Final Report on Demonstration Grant Project* (White Plains Line), pp1, 15, 22. See also J Parker (1967), *Transport Interchanges* (Report on Winston Churchill Travelling Fellowship), pp16–23.
[2] Urban Railway Revival in Toronto, *Modern Railways* 23, 1967, pp417–18, Travelling costs 1½*d* compared with 2*d* per mile by car; parking free compared with 7*s* (35p) per day in the city centre.
[3] Inst d'Amenagement et d'Urbanisme de la Region Parisienne 1970, *Les Transports Urbains*, Fasc3, *Stationnement aux gares*, Cahiers 17–18.

situation there was relatively little need for co-ordination, but despite their planning and traffic powers the GLC showed little concern for the wider aspects of station car parks as an element of a total transport policy. This was demonstrated by their attitude in 1966 that parking controls should not be implemented until improved public transport (the responsibility of BR, LT and the Department of the Environment) was available.

By 1971 land supply had virtually run out in the case of LT and was dwindling for BR. The GLC had formulated a parking policy which included exhortation to the boroughs and rail operators to continue to provide station car parks initially as a means of improving traffic movement (see Case Study *Q*). Their transport-planning functions under the 1969 Act, and the rigours of the GLDP preparation and Inquiry, however, encouraged them to think in wider terms. Thus station car parks began to be dimly seen as one element in a strategy which sought to affect the use of cars and roads and public transport so that the amount of station car parking was now to be 'comparable with the degree of restraint.'

Nevertheless the GLC had not worked out any detailed policy for interchanges as a whole or station car parks as a particular type. There was still only consideration of individual problems, such as Redbridge station and possible car commuting on the M11, or Mitcham and the M23, or possible car parks to serve the proposed Hainault–Wimbledon tube line.[1]

Although some individual cases could be implemented (for instance between a borough and LT or BR, or between a borough and a commercial developer), co-ordination is needed once an interchange problem becomes part of a wider strategy. The machinery for undertaking this function cannot operate without proper terms of reference or major policy guides, yet this was the situation of the LBA and TCCL working groups and remained the situation for GLTG.

Despite the claims of the 1965 Select Committee and the GLC's own officers and members that the interchange problem, including station car parking, was one of the transport network's greatest deficiencies and that the co-ordination machinery was one of the weakest links in the institutional system, there was little progress after 1969. And this was true despite the 1968 Act grants, the 1969 Act provisions for GLC grants and LT car-servicing facilities, the GLC's co-ordinating machinery (e.g. GLTG), an assured supply of traffic wardens, and evidence from overseas that station car parks are an effective means of encouraging rail ridership and reducing car commuting. The GLDP was non-committal about policy priorities, but later statements appeared to accept the *status quo*, with new car parks at best accommodating any growth in demand for the use of cars to reach railheads which resulted from rising car ownership particularly in the outer areas and beyond the Greater London boundary.

The London Transport Executive can only extend its provision by pur-

[1] GLC (1969), *Report of Department of Highways and Transportation*, p12; and *Paper S27/282*, GLDP Inquiry Stage 2.

chasing land or using 'air-rights' over cuttings and stations—both expensive solutions which are within the sanction of the GLC and the DOE. The BR Board continues to finance new and extended parks on its own sites, overwhelmingly in the outer metropolitan area where its traffic is growing fastest, as it did in the mid-1960s.

Perhaps the greatest single lacuna is the lack of definite responsibility for finance, which bedevils individual proposals even when these can be formulated. The GLC indicated to the GLDP Inquiry in 1971 that they still considered that the boroughs and the railway operators should 'initially' take care of this; the Council has, of course, influence over any expenditure LT wishes to make but as far as BR is concerned this leaves any decision to the regional organisations, or in rare cases to the Board and indirectly the DOE. Where car parks and associated control zones around stations are proposed in order to improve residents' amenity there is a good case that the former should be built and the latter staffed with a contribution from the boroughs. Where, however, the purpose is to divert traffic from the roads this is surely a strategic matter in which the GLC is involved.

This case study reveals a failure of policy formulation and implementation for station car parks, and a neglect of their potential role in an overall transport strategy. This failure was due more than anything else to the GLC's rather narrow interpretation of its statutory responsibilities to promote an integrated transport system and its weak efforts to reconcile the varying and often conflicting interests of the other bodies involved—the boroughs, BR, LT and the police. Problems such as finance, land availability and of ensuring that station car parks fulfil a strategic rather than a simply local role emphasise the need for the GLC as transport planning authority to take a strong lead. In this respect at least the intentions of the 1969 Act showed few signs of being realised.

Case Study G

ENVIRONMENTAL MANAGEMENT SOME LONDON EXAMPLES

1 BACKGROUND

Over the last decade there has been such a growing public interest in improving the physical environment in town and country that it has become a major political issue. A major impetus was given by the Buchanan Report[1] in 1963 which focused attention on the conflict between motor traffic and the quality of the urban environment. It provided also a number of concepts such as 'environmental management' and 'environmental areas' which related specifically to methods of ameliorating this conflict. 'Environmental areas' were those from which extraneous traffic was excluded and 'environmental management' was the application of traffic management to achieve this purpose.

As a direct result of the report both the Ministry of Housing and Local Government (MOHLG) and the London County Council (LCC) decided to examine the possibilities and implications of environmental planning for which Buchanan had provided a theoretical groundwork. But while Buchanan had concentrated on improving environmental conditions by segregating various types of road traffic, much of the interest in his proposals for dealing with this manifested itself as a broader concern for upgrading existing environments by improving structurally-sound old houses and by rearranging communal areas to provide off-street parking and traffic-free play spaces. Thus the MOHLG study of Deeplish, a 'twilight area' in Rochdale, Lancashire,[2] contained environmental management as part of an 'improvement package' of which the rehabilitation of old houses was the most important element. Other studies followed that of Deeplish[3] and the rehabilitation of old property was increasingly encouraged by the Government through the provision of more generous improvement grants.[4] Although in practice rehabilitation of old property and environmental management may be carried out separately, both techniques are aimed at the general upgrading of an area and thus extending its useful life.

[1] C D Buchanan (1963), *Traffic in Towns*, HMSO.
[2] MOHLG (1966), *The Deeplish Study: Improvement Possibilities in a District of Rochdale*, HMSO.
[3] For example: the Halliwell Report, summarised in the *Surveyor*, 15 October 1968, pp21–4, and in *The Times*, 13 October 1966, p11.
[4] *Housing Act 1969*, ch33.

This study looks at three schemes in London, one of which, Barnsbury, was characterised at first by the 'improvement package' approach. The other two, Kensington and Pimlico, were environmental management schemes aimed mainly at traffic and parking problems. The various institutions involved in devising and implementing these environmental management schemes are set out below.

The MOHLG had a general interest in environmental planning, its own research influencing central government policy formation and providing methodological guidelines for local authorities, in this case for the Greater London Council (GLC) and the London boroughs.

The Ministry of Transport (*MOT*) were involved as grant aid authority on Principal and Metropolitan road schemes. They had an interest in transport research and were, for example, represented on the MOHLG study of the Barnsbury area. The roles of the MOHLG and the MOT were, of course, subsumed within the Department of the Environment (DOE) in 1970.

The GLC were involved as traffic authority for London and as highway authority for Metropolitan roads. They had the sole power to make orders for the regulation of traffic (including those for amenity purposes) and had a stated objective of improving environmental conditions through their highway and traffic policies.

The London boroughs concerned (Islington, Westminster, and Kensington and Chelsea) were highway authorities for all roads other than Metropolitan roads in their areas, but traffic management schemes on these local roads required GLC approval.

The Metropolitan Police had a statutory right to consultation on proposed environmental management schemes, though no ultimate powers in this respect, and had the responsibility to enforce these schemes once implemented.

Pressure groups were generally local voluntary organisations concerned with a variety of specific problems. Some (e.g. the Barnsbury Association (BA)) had considerable technical and political expertise. They usually assumed the role of watchdogs, only biting when authority encroached on their interests or failed to defend them.

This case study concentrates on the Barnsbury scheme, partly because it involved more widespread co-ordination (and attracted more attention) than either the Kensington or Pimlico schemes, but mainly because it was the first real test of the 'environmental area' concept in the context of London's government system. It was necessary for the bodies involved to face the problems of defining their respective roles in implementing what each claimed to be the common objective of environmental improvement. That such roles should be defined and agreed upon was (and still is) important for London if the creation of 'environmental areas' on a large scale was to be achieved. While the Barnsbury scheme did not in itself lead to the clear definition of the areas of responsibility, it showed where

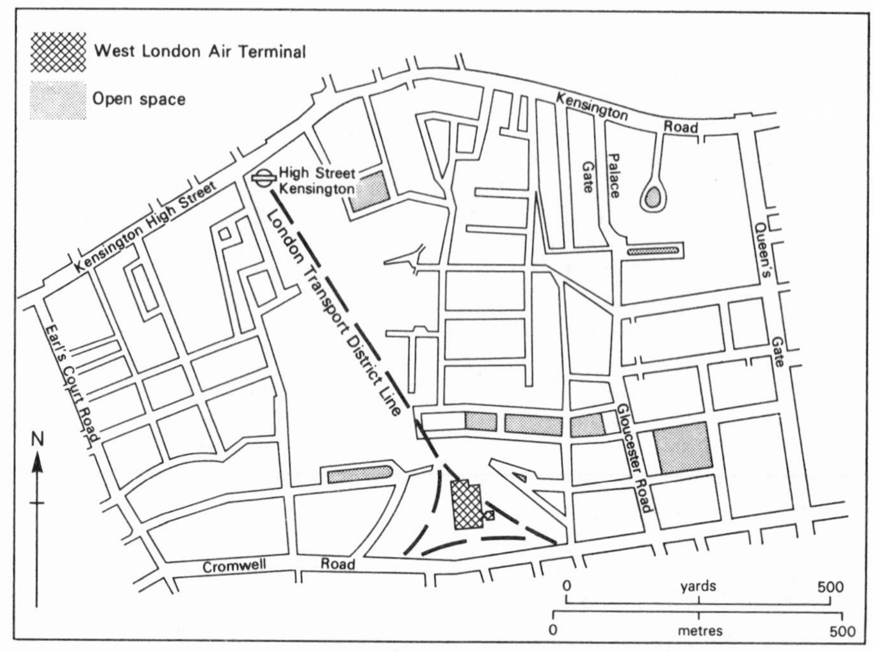

Figure 10 KENSINGTON ENVIRONMENTAL STUDY AREA

some of the more important conflicts lay. Before studying this, it will be helpful to consider the Kensington and Pimlico schemes because they clearly show some of the policy problems in which the Barnsbury scheme later became embroiled.

2 THE KENSINGTON STUDY

In 1964 the Chief Architect of the LCC (who was responsible for planning at that time) and the Chief Engineer were instructed 'to investigate the practicability and possible extent of environmental control in selected areas.'[1] Mr Jordan (an officer in the Engineer's Department), was placed in charge of a team which also included an architect and a planner. An area of Kensington (see Figure 10), covering 225 acres, and with a population of nearly 15 000, which suffered a considerable measure of environmental disruption from motor traffic, was chosen for detailed appraisal.

After the institution of the GLC, the work continued under the same leadership until its completion in July 1965.

The principal conclusion of the team was that traffic within the area could be reduced by using environmental management techniques, but that as a result traffic on the roads bounding the study area would increase. They

[1] GLC (1966), *Kensington Environmental Management Study*, p5.

did not consider that this necessarily precluded the introduction of such measures, although the traffic effects would be sufficiently important, they felt, to justify a revision of improvement priorities on the main roads in that part of London. As a secondary means of improving the environment, they suggested the use of parking control to limit car commuter traffic and to eliminate parking in undesirable locations. Mention was also made of a possible north–south road on the line of the District underground railway which, they felt, divided the area socially as well as physically.[1]

The Planning and Communications and the Highways and Traffic committees of the GLC considered these proposals and put forward a joint report to the Council in December 1965. This report stated that the study 'provided valuable information and that other similar studies in areas of different character should be undertaken.' While the officers responsible for the study apparently had not expected their proposals to be implemented, the joint report nevertheless considered that they should be used as a basis for discussion with the Royal Borough of Kensington and Chelsea 'to see what further steps could be taken.'[2]

It is worthy of note that around this time there was a considerable amount of interest in the future of Kensington generally. In December 1965, for example, the West London Architectural Society completed an independent study of Kensington which embraced aspects of townscape quality and amenity along with the effects of parking and traffic on them. Also, 1966 saw the start of a long debate on redevelopment proposals for the parts of Kensington High Street which formed the northern boundary to the GLC's study area.

It was apparent, therefore, that the GLC's Kensington study could provide a basis for implementing environmental improvement in Kensington, and in October of 1966 a GLC councillor, Mr Robert Vigars (then Opposition spokesman on traffic matters) asked what consideration had been given to this. The reply of the chairman of the Planning and Communications Committee, Mrs Jane Phillips, was far from encouraging. She interpreted the main conclusion of the report as being that 'improvement to the environment could only be made as a long-term policy but that a more limited improvement could be achieved by parking control alone.' Environmental management appeared to be excluded in the short term because of the lack of capacity on the peripheral routes to take the diverted traffic. In reply to Mr Vigars's request for immediate implementation of the Kensington study proposals she said that such action would be 'tantamount to control by congestion which [she was] not prepared to accept as a positive policy.' The only action which was envisaged was the introduction of the Inner London Planning Area (ILPA) regulations (which included the study area), and this together with urban clearways and other measures on the main routes was to provide the 'climate' for the London boroughs to introduce environmental schemes in 'individual areas.'[3]

[1] GLC (1966), pp5, 17.
[2] GLC *Minutes*, 14 December 1965, p886.
[3] GLC *Minutes*, 4 October 1966, p478.

Thus the GLC at that stage saw its role in environmental management as one of encouraging the introduction of parking control and of carrying out measures to improve traffic flow on the roads for which it was responsible. It viewed the devising and implementation of environmental schemes as primarily a borough responsibility, but implicitly recognised that its policy of not allowing increased traffic congestion meant that this could be no more than a long-term responsibility.

This was a situation in which the GLC could have adopted a useful advisory role for the boroughs in developing standards and techniques for the implementation of environmental schemes, i.e. playing a role similar to that of the Ministries of Housing and Transport, but more directly related to London problems. However, the GLC's decision in December 1965[1] (reiterated in the published report[2]) to undertake other similar studies was abandoned, apparently because of an increasing work load on the primary road proposals. Consequently, despite the willingness of Mr Jordan to specialise in this kind of work, no further studies were undertaken by the GLC.

3 PIMLICO

The Pimlico scheme covered a smaller area than the other two schemes. It consisted of 30 acres of mid-nineteenth century, predominantly residential development near Victoria (see Figure 11) with a population of about 5500. The street pattern was such that it was often convenient for drivers to take short cuts through the area, particularly at peak hours when the peripheral main roads were congested. The resulting traffic was a hazard to drivers and pedestrians which found expression in letters of complaint to the local press and the City of Westminster's Engineer's Department from Pimlico residents during the early and mid-1960s. In particular, the layout of streets on a 'grid-iron' pattern meant a large number of cross-roads at at which it was difficult to establish traffic priority. It was suggested that drivers could be 'lulled into a false sense of security and think that the way ahead was clear'[3] and traffic volumes were never sufficiently great by engineering and financial criteria to justify the installation of traffic lights.

The complaints of residents had stimulated some preliminary ideas from the officers who began serious investigations in 1965 to see what could be done. The creation of the new Westminster City Council probably gave a fillip to the desire for a form of traffic management that was related to local problems in a more sophisticated way than traffic lights, and ideas on environmental management were emerging in the technical press which would meet the need.

Having been agreed upon within the Engineer's Department, the approach was approved by the Traffic, Town Planning and Car Parking

[1] GLC *Minutes*, 14 December 1965, p866. [2] GLC (1966), p3.

[3] Westminster CC (October 1968), *Pimlico Precinct*, p3.

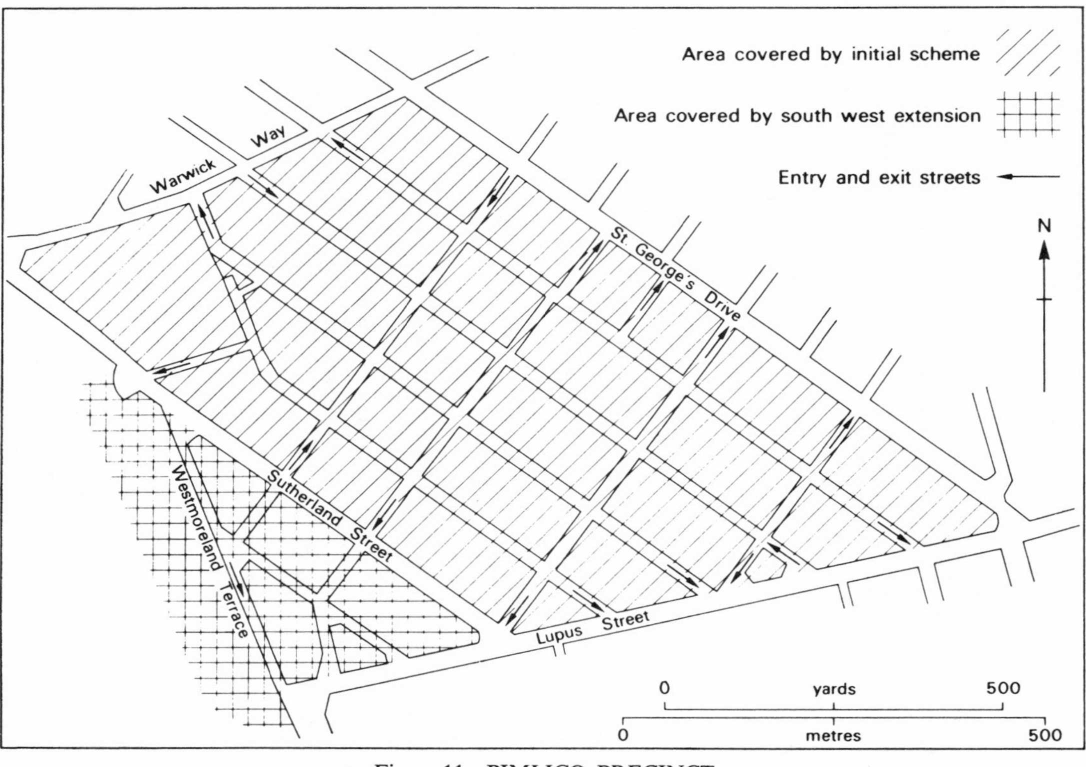

Figure 11 PIMLICO PRECINCT

committees in February 1966, and the following month the Council decided in principle to adopt a scheme that would reduce through traffic in the Pimlico area and improve general amenities.[1] After this, progress was relatively swift and unhampered by disagreements. During the next year the detailed design was completed and approval was sought from New Scotland Yard and informally from the GLC's Highways and Transportation Department.

Problems did arise, however, over the financing of the scheme. In their initial report of the Council in March 1966, Westminster's Traffic Committee pointed out that if the works proposed were accepted by the GLC as a traffic management scheme, the City's expenditure would be reimbursable, but that since a proportion was for improving local amenities, the cost of these particular works would have to be met by the City. They reported in November 1966 that the GLC considered that the scheme was basically designed to improve local amenities and that a contribution of only £8500 would be made towards the cost of works necessary at junctions with major roads. Even this, however, would be subject to an appropriate grant being made to the GLC by the MOT.[2]

Thus at this point the City thought that it would have to meet £30 500 of the total cost of £39 000 and this amount had been allocated on the estimates for the year 1967–68. The Traffic Committee, however, together with the other spending committees, were anxious to make financial cuts to hold down rate levels for that year and it recommended that the Pimlico precinct should be deferred for a year.[3] This delay was avoided, however, by the chairman of the Traffic Committee, Alderman Sandford, who persuaded his Committee to revoke this recommendation.[4]

The traffic scheme was finally implemented on 16 April 1967 (although tree planting and other amenity works followed later).

The GLC's contribution towards the cost of the scheme was not, however, forthcoming.[5] This was due, at least initially, to the MOT's refusal to make any grant to the GLC for this purpose, although the MOT nevertheless regarded the scheme as a worthy project.[6] The Westminster City Council was therefore left to meet the full cost of the scheme.

The City Engineer (Mr F J Cave) in his report on the precinct published in October 1968, described the scheme as a success, and this conclusion was publicly endorsed by the GLC in November (see page 313). There was little or no adverse reaction to the scheme from the public, and a resident Member of Parliament thought that the area was now much safer, particularly for children. He said that the scheme had 'abolished the death penalty for a child's error of judgement.'[7]

[1] Westminster CC *Minutes*, 17 March 1966.
[2] *Ibid.*
[3] Westminster CC *Minutes*, 2 February 1967.
[4] *Westminster and Pimlico News*, 10 February 1967.
[5] *Pimlico Precinct*, p3 (revised passage).
[6] Westminster CC *Minutes*, 4 May 1967.
[7] Letter in *Westminster and Pimlico News*, 21 April 1967.

One environmental problem not solved by the princinct scheme, however, was the parking of cars, particularly by all-day commuters. This was largely dealt with by the introduction of a parking control scheme in November 1968 as part of ILPA (described in Case Study *Q*).

Despite the achnowledged success of the initial scheme, extensions to it proposed in the Pimlico Report were not implemented quickly. The western extension came three years later in 1970 but no mention had then been made of the proposed eastern extension (see Figure 11). This latter scheme was dropped after the GLC raised objections to its traffic implications for Pimlico as a whole.[1]

4 BARNSBURY

Introduction

Barnsbury is an area of north central London within the borough of Islington developed in the mid-nineteenth century as a residential suburb of good quality. Over the years, as the wealthy moved to houses further from central London, the ageing properties became the homes of poorer sections of the community and succumbed to considerable infiltration by small industrial and commercial concerns. Increasingly too, the area suffered from the intrusion of heavy traffic so common in inner city suburbs, disturbing the life of the area, and lacked adequate open space and school provision. But unlike many other areas in inner London with similar deficiencies, Barnsbury was laid out with streets and squares of fine scale, including buildings of considerable architectural merit.

Inevitably, it was soon realised that a good and potentially attractive home could be had in Barnsbury much cheaper than for comparable property in the more select inner residential districts such as South Kensington or Chelsea. In the 1960s the solid 'working-class' character of Barnsbury began to change as houses were bought up and renovated by 'middle-class professionals.' This change is represented statistically by the rise from 4 to 8% between the 1961 and 1966 censuses of the proportion of Barnsbury households in the 'professional and management' group.[2]

The newcomers brought with them an awareness of Barnsbury's potential as an attractive place in which to live and they were keen to ensure that this potential was realised. The first important move was the formation in August 1964 of the Barnsbury Association which intended to promote future planning and development of the area which paid regard to its special architectural qualities.

Accordingly, the BA opposed a proposal by the GLC to compulsorily acquire and demolish some residential property in Bewdley Street.[3] At the

[1] Interview with Westminster City Council officers.
[2] *Barnsbury Environmental Study*, joint study team of MOHLG, GLC and LB Islington, July 1968, p7.
[3] Originally an LCC proposal.

public inquiry into this proposal held in June 1965 by the Minister of Housing and Local Government, the Association argued that redevelopment should not be tackled in this piecemeal fashion. It was described as 'contrary to good planning principles and should only be allowed within the framework of a plan for the whole neighbourhood.'[1]

In December of the same year Mr Richard Crossman, the Minister of Housing and Local Government, approved the compulsory purchase order but at the same time commissioned a planning and environmental study of the whole of Barnsbury to be carried out jointly by a team of officers of the GLC, the new London Borough of Islington, and the Ministry itself. The resulting study received much attention because it was expected to be the first major attempt at attacking the problems of a 'twilight area' in a comprehensive manner. This research, however, is concerned primarily with the traffic (i.e. environmental management) proposals for Barnsbury, and attempts to show how these influenced and were themselves changed by various parts of the system.

The Barnsbury environmental study

While approving the GLC's Bewdley Street compulsory purchase order, the Minister's decision to commission a study of Barnsbury appeared to be a direct response to the BA's plea for a comprehensive approach to the planning of their area. But it must also be remembered that the MOHLG had already been showing a positive interest in the problems facing older urban areas generally. They had already commissioned the Deeplish and Halliwell studies previously mentioned and Barnsbury might simply have been seen as a next step in developing ideas on environmental planning, because it was larger in area and population, and with a wider range of problems.

To whatever degree the BA was instrumental in Mr Crossman's final decision, it had good reason to be satisfied, especially with his statement of intent that interested parties should be consulted during the formulation of the plan. The Association had expressed a willingness at the inquiry to participate in the formulation of any comprehensive plan for Barnsbury and had demonstrated that they had considerable professional resources at their disposal for this purpose. Their inquiry case, for example, was backed up by the production of a planning report drawn up by David Wager, an architect and a founder member of the BA.[2]

Public participation in planning was, of course, a very new idea at that time, but the Ministry's interest in it appeared more than casual. In January 1966 Mr Crossman sent a letter to the BA promising that the joint study team, who were to carry out the study, would consult them.

By February 1966 a Steering Committee composed of senior officials of the GLC, the Islington Borough Council (IBC), the MOHLG and the

[1] Barnsbury Environmental Study, *Interim Report*, August 1966, p1.

[2] D Wager (1965), *A Planning Report on Barnsbury*, prepared for the BA.

MOT had constituted the joint study team and drawn up its working brief. The study team itself was led by a MOHLG planner and included officers of MOHLG, IBC and the GLC. The work was divided into two parts. The first (Phase I) was to be a 'quick probe study to examine the feasibility of creating an environmental area in Barnsbury.' This was to be followed by a fuller study (Phase II) which could be used as a basis for detailed planning and the implementation of both short- and long-term environmental improvements.[1]

Phase I of the study, however, turned out to be rather less worthwhile than had been intended. Criticisms were made at all levels both of the Interim Report (on Phase I) and hence implicitly of the joint Steering Committee and study team who were responsible for it. First, the BA became disillusioned about the Ministry's promise of consultation.The quick probe study was to have taken no more than three months (from February 1966) and although the study team had produced a draft report by June, the Steering Committee withheld its issue to the BA.[2] Nevertheless a copy was obtained, and the Association submitted comments to the study team.

The Interim Report then went to the Highways and Planning committees of the GLC and IBC who approved the traffic management proposals contained in it. In November, key members of the BA met the Minister (then Anthony Greenwood) to press for effective citizen participation and then, just before Christmas, they received a copy of the Interim Report and were asked to give their comments within two weeks. In terms of their ideas on the meaning of public participation, the Association was understandably disappointed and felt that Mr Crossman's promise of consultation had not been carried out. They and eleven other local societies wrote a joint letter to the chairman of the Steering Committee complaining that two weeks was too short a time for intelligent and considered comments. They also decided to commission Peter Hills, a planning consultant and member of the former Buchanan *Traffic in Towns* team, to appraise the Interim Report.

In March 1967, before Mr Hills' comments appeared, the second major criticism arose, concerned this time not with lack of opportunities for public participation, but with the integrity of the Steering Committee. It came in the form of an article in the *Spectator* in which Patrick Hutber openly accused them of cutting out parts of the draft Interim Report which, although important for the study, conflicted with certain existing policies and proposals to which the IBC and GLC were committed.[3] Other people involved in the issue confirmed that the published Interim Report 'merely represented what the Steering Committee would allow.'[4] This was a serious charge which, although substantiated by quotations from both the draft and published Interim Reports, was swiftly denied by Mr Christopher

[1] Terms of reference of the study team, *Barnsbury Environmental Study Report*, p61.
[2] Internal records of the BA; by kind permission of the Hon Secretary.
[3] The *Spectator*, 3 March 1967, 'The Barnsbury Scandal.'
[4] Interviews.

Higgins, who at that time was chairman of the GLC's Planning and Communications Committee.[1] He claimed that the MOHLG planner who headed the study team that drew up the first draft also sat on the Steering Committee which altered it and that consequently what Mr Hutber had called 'censorship' was simply 'sub-editing.' Mr Higgins was supported by IBC's Assistant Town Clerk and Public Relations Officer in a letter to the *Spectator* the following week asking Mr Hutber to 'publicly withdraw his allegations.'[2]

Alongside Mr Higgins's letter was one from Tom Blyth, chairman of the BA, who welcomed Mr Hutber's article but supported his comments on the lack of consultation rather than his attack on the Steering Committee. Nevertheless, the tension generated by the *Spectator* controversy was sufficient to persuade the Steering Committee to invite the BA to meet them. The Association duly sent a deputation.

On 26 May 1967 another article by Mr Hutber appeared in the *Spectator* commenting on this meeting which he had also attended. It seemed that the Committee were 'genuinely surprised that the BA did not regard the opportunity to comment on an already published report as the consultation they had been promised by the Ministry of Housing.'[3] But the meeting also secured an offer from the Steering Committee to institute 'genuine consultation' (Hutber's words).

By this time the third, and perhaps most effective, criticism had appeared in the form of Peter Hills' appraisal of the Interim Report, which was as substantial as the Report itself and strongly attacked its technical content.[4] 'At this stage,' Mr Hutber wrote, 'the BA decided to fire all its guns. It dispatched Mr Hills' comments with a series of open letters, to every authority in sight, disassociating itself entirely from the censored Interim Report and calling for the appointment of an independent assessor.' Once these criticisms and activities were made public it was perhaps inevitable that the Steering Committee should respond, and the situation may also have been instrumental in bringing official discredit to the Interim Report as a result of which, the BA was given to understand, it was dropped in June.[5]

Meanwhile the joint team had continued to work on Phase II of the Barnsbury study, but this time they interpreted the BA's role in the participation exercise as nearer to that eventually offered by the Steering Committee. Between June and September 1967 under the new leadership of Chris Whittacker (an architect/planner at MOHLG) the study team held four meetings with the BA to discuss housing, parks, and traffic. The BA itself also secured a further meeting with Anthony Greenwood and with the Steering Committee, who assured them that Mr Whittacker would be

[1] The *Spectator*, 10 March 1967, Letters.
[2] The *Spectator*, 17 March 1967, Letters.
[3] The *Spectator*, 'Barnsbury Again,' 26 May 1967.
[4] P J Hills (1967), *An Appraisal of the Barnsbury Environmental Study Interim Report* (produced in April by the BA).
[5] Records of the BA.

empowered to provide them with a copy of the final Barnsbury report.

The Association, anticipating that the Report would appear by the end of 1967, mounted an exhibition in Barnsbury to stimulate public interest which was attended by 1000 people. The study team had in fact completed their work by January 1968 and, while the report was being drafted, were considering how to get the views of a wider range of residents. They also decided on a public exhibition which was held in Barnsbury during the Easter school holidays after four months of preparation. Just how representative an impression of views was obtained from the 1150 Barnsbury residents who attended the exhibition is impossible to say, but the GLC stated soon after that the Report was being redrafted in view of the comments received.[1] One officer involved, however, thought that the Report had been substantially completed before the exhibition and that only post-consultation 'trimmings' had been added.

To whatever extent the BA and members of the public generally influenced the Final Report, the Association at least was disillusioned by the amount of consultation it had received during the two-year study period. They had succeeded in meeting both the study team and its Steering Committee on several occasions during the preparation of Phase II and perhaps they were unreasonably optimistic in expecting more. It was not until March 1968, after all, with the appointment of the Skeffington Committee[2] that the Ministry decided to examine the concept of public participation in planning with any vigour, let alone commit itself to how it should work in practice.

In any event the BA now turned its whole attention to getting the Study Report published (it eventually appeared in October 1968) and action taken on its proposals.

Implementation of environmental management in Barnsbury

Two environmental management schemes were put forward for Barnsbury by the joint study team. The first, contained in the Interim Report, was approved by the GLC and IBC late in 1966. It contained specific proposals for the creation of one-way streets and the imposition of waiting restrictions which would canalise through traffic onto a limited number of routes. This scheme, so the GLC claimed, would probably have been implemented had it not been for difficulties over securing an MOT grant for some of the works involved.[3] Certainly it was put forward as a firm interim proposal in November 1966, to be implemented before the full Report of the joint study team was complete.[4]

[1] GLC *Minutes*, 25 June 1968, p316.

[2] The Skeffington Committee was appointed in March 1968 'to consider and report on the best methods, including publicity, of securing the participation of the public at the *formative stage* [our italics] in the making of development plans for their area,' MOHLG/ Scottish Development Department/Welsh Office, *People and Planning*, HMSO, 1969.

[3] Records of the BA.

[4] GLC *Press Release 421*, 3 November 1966.

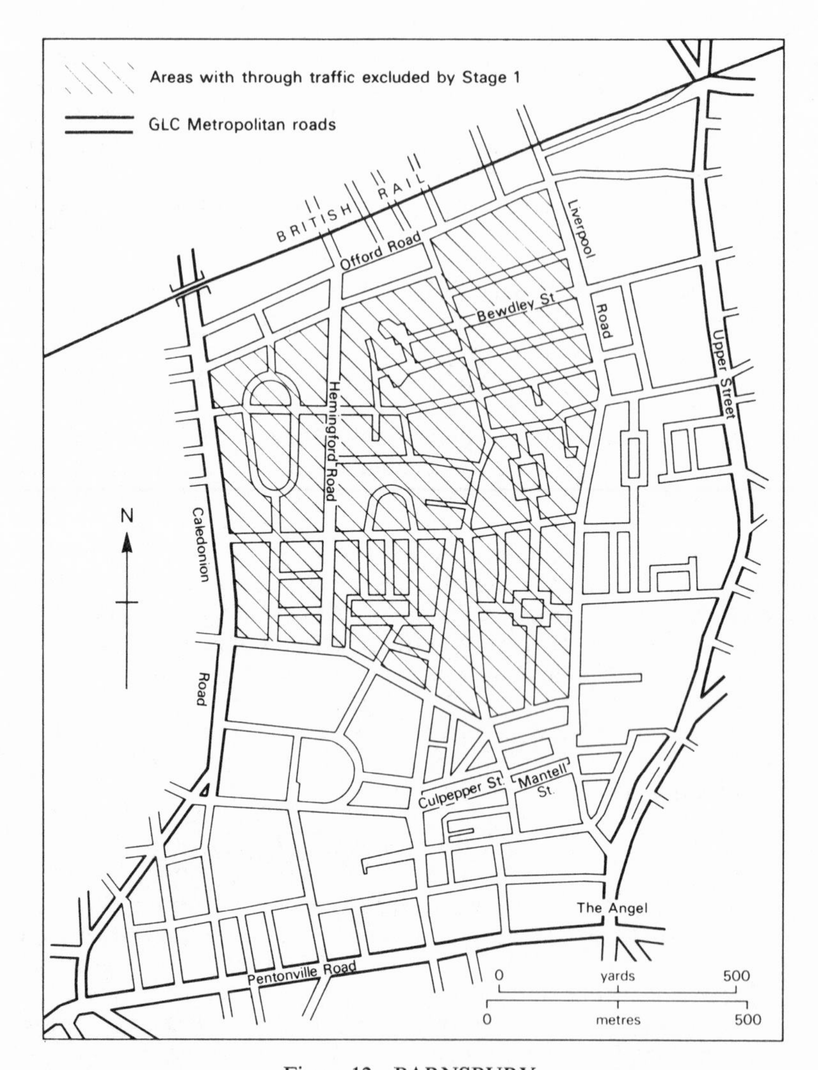

Figure 12 BARNSBURY

The second scheme, which appeared in the Final Report as a revision of the interim proposals, envisaged more effective canalisation of through traffic onto fewer roads in order to create larger environmental areas (free of through traffic) between them. Apart from the suggestion of a new link road on the line of Culpepper and Mantell Streets (see Figure 12) and the possible closure to traffic of many Barnsbury streets,[1] no specific measures were described for implementing this objective.

[1] *Barnsbury Report*, Fig.6.18.

Thus by October 1968 when the Final Report appeared there were still no firm environmental management proposals which could be immediately implemented, except, of course, for the discredited Interim Report scheme. Nevertheless, the publicity given to Barnsbury had ensured that both the GLC and IBC would give consideration to the implementation of an environmental management scheme in the light of the objectives contained in the Final Report.

Barnsbury had been receiving close attention in IBC since the local elections in May 1968. The BA had grown increasingly impatient with the lack of results from the joint study team (it had taken two years from the 'quick probe study' to the study team's exhibition held in April 1968, and the Final Report was not yet in sight) and decided to field three independent candidates. They were all elected and as non-party members of the Highways Committee their concern was largely (but not wholly) that of seeing the Barnsbury Report published and action taken on its proposals, and indeed this was the platform on which they stood for the elections.[1]

This considerably strengthened the BA's hand by giving them a direct link with the Town Hall. Further strength was given by John Szemerey, the Highways Committee chairman of the new Conservative-controlled council, who saw environmental management as a 'vital part of planning for the motor-car in urban areas.' Accordingly, he quickly pushed a policy of environmental planning for the whole borough, backed up by a document produced by the Borough Engineer in consultation with the Borough Architect, on the hierarchy of roads and possible environmental areas for the whole of Islington.[2] The Highways Committee felt a need for completing the draft borough structure plan before proceeding with environmental improvements for the whole borough, but nevertheless saw Barnsbury as fitting neatly into their new policy framework and providing a starting point for the implementation of environmental management.

The Borough Engineer drew up a pilot traffic management scheme (in collaboration with the Borough Architect) and this was approved by the Highways Committee on 14 November 1968. A few days later he wrote to the GLC's Traffic Commissioner and Director of Transportation, Peter Stott, saying that the Barnsbury study team had suggested a pilot traffic management scheme to assess costs and benefits, and that his council wished to implement this as soon as possible, using temporary signs and bollards for closing off streets and diverting traffic. He also said that he wanted informal consultations with the GLC *before* the traffic order-making stage.[3]

At least two meetings took place (with New Scotland Yard's Traffic Branch also represented) at which there was considerable disagreement

[1] Councillors Messrs Martin Reynolds, Tom Blyth and Mrs Brenda Thompson; in addition the chairman of the Committee, Mr John Szemerey, was also a member for Barnsbury Ward.

[2] LB Islington (1968), *Policy Paper No.5.*

[3] Records of the BA.

over the scheme. Apart from a clash of views over various design points, the GLC's representative indicated his dislike of the experimental nature of the scheme. The Borough Engineer, thinking the implication was that the GLC would favour a more permanent scheme, suggested that the cost of this should be met by the GLC on a reimbursable basis as previously outlined by the GLC's Treasurer.[1] Moreover, he felt that the GLC's observations were inconsistent with both the Barnsbury Report[2] and a document entitled *Barnsbury Environmental Study—Suggested Short-term Action* sent to IBC by the GLC Planning Department. It thus appeared as if the GLC planners and traffic engineers were not aware of each other's work. Both, however, should have known that the GLC's Planning and Transportation Committee had already instructed appropriate officers to report to the Central Area Board (a subcommittee of the Planning and Transportation Committee) on the possibilities of implementing certain traffic measures in Barnsbury. These included, amongst other things, a 'low cost' traffic management scheme in Barnsbury and 'measures to limit through traffic in the area.'[3] This, in essence at least, was precisely what the Islington Engineer's scheme had set out to include.

The GLC traffic engineers were apparently having difficulty in accepting the validity of experimental traffic management schemes, and their reply to Islington can only be described as diversionary: they spoke, on the one hand, of the necessity of improving the Angel intersection before any environmental management scheme for Barnsbury could be recommended (see A1 in London, Case Study *K*), and on the other, of the need for 'detailed investigations and designs' in order to assess the advantages and disadvantages of the two schemes then available.[4] They also spoke of more limited traffic management measures to which the GLC would have no objection provided that the traffic implications were satisfactory.

In response to this pressure the Islington Engineer produced a more limited scheme covering a smaller area, but this was rejected by his own Highways Committee. He wrote again to Mr Stott saying that his committee still considered his November 1968 scheme to be the best available and rejected the GLC's suggestion that it would overload the peripheral roads (including the Angel intersection), and were of the opinion that smaller alternative schemes would not solve the problem. He therefore urged Mr Stott to submit the original scheme to the GLC's Planning and Transportation Committee and to make the necessary traffic orders.

While this dialogue was in progress the BA continued to apply pressure on the GLC, particularly Neil Thorne (chairman of the GLC's Central Area Board) and Robert Vigars (chairman of the Planning and Transporta-

[1] Records of the BA.
[2] See *Barnsbury Report* (section on short-term possibilities), p83.
[3] GLC *Minutes*, 22 October 1968, p549. Answer to question by Councillor Rose given by Robert Vigars, chairman of the Planning and Transportation Committee.
[4] One was the 1966 Interim Report scheme which was generally thought to be dead, the other was the borough's scheme, November 1968.

tion Committee). They supported the IBC November 1968 scheme and so identified themselves closely with the IBC politicians. They were concerned with the GLC's apparent lack of interest in Barnsbury as evidenced by the GLC's failure to react to approaches made by the BA and IBC suggesting a joint body to implement the Barnsbury Report. Also the GLC had not sent a representative to a public meeting organised by the BA on 5 December 1968.

Councillor Szemerey supported these direct approaches to the GLC politicians, particularly as he realised that the GLC's statement about the need to improve the Angel intersection could mean a delay of perhaps ten years to any environmental scheme in Barnsbury. On 23 February 1969, he wrote to one of the Barnsbury Independent members saying he thought the GLC's resistance was softening partly because of his committee's point-blank refusal to accept compromise schemes and partly because of the pressure being applied by letters from himself and the BA. A few days later the BA sent a strongly worded letter to Neil Thorne which provoked a long reply intended to clarify the position, but which seemed to confirm the GLC's viewpoints which were causing the rift. However, a chink in the GLC's armour appeared at a meeting at County Hall on 19 March. This was attended by the three Independent Barnsbury Ward IBC members, Neil Thorne, and officers of the GLC's Highways and Transportation, Planning, and Director General's departments. Here it was stated that a joint report was being produced by GLC and IBC officers which would go to the Central Area Board (Neil Thorne's committee) in mid-May. No difficulty was foreseen but the Board's approval was necessary so that the scheme could go to the Planning and Transportation Committee meetings later in May.

Neil Thorne, on 29 April,[1] wrote to one of the Barnsbury Ward IBC members saying that the GLC still considered the 1966 Interim Report scheme the best, particularly in view of the GLC's responsibility as overall traffic authority to take account of the effect of traffic management schemes on neighbouring districts. The next day he attended a public meeting[2] with Councillor Szemerey and other members and officers from the GLC and IBC. David Wager (the architect who had produced the planning report on Barnsbury back in 1965) gave a detailed critique of the various alternative environmental management schemes for Barnsbury. These were his own; the 1966 Interim Report scheme (which he pointed out had only been made available for discussion after its approval by the GLC and IBC, and of which nothing had been heard from that time until recently); the *Barnsbury Report* scheme; and IBC's scheme of November 1968 which he said elevated amenity above other aims and which the GLC had rejected mainly on the grounds that it would overload the peripheral roads, particularly the Angel.

Two weeks after that meeting, the Central Area Board, chaired by Neil Thorne, 'decided that the GLC should play its part in creating traffic-free residential areas in Barnsbury,'[3] and that after considering the alternatives

[1] Records of the BA. [2] *Ibid.* [3] *Ibid.*

the necessary orders should be made for the IBC scheme. On 16 June, the Planning and Transportation Committee approved the scheme subject to reservations about the possibility of altering it if need be, and Neil Thorne wrote to the BA saying he now awaited formal submission of the Borough Engineer's proposals.

These decisions seemed to have a profound significance for the whole future of environmental management schemes in London since they were finally made despite the GLC's traffic engineers' insistence that traffic diverted from residential streets for amenity reasons should not be allowed to overload the main traffic routes.[1]

The next day IBC's Policy Committee decided to appoint a team leader in the Planning Department responsible for environmental planning, and a firm of engineering consultants to design a fully worked out traffic management scheme for Barnsbury. These appointments were made at the Policy Committee meeting on 29 July, where it was stated that in view of the lack of action on the part of the GLC the borough must take the lead in the field of environmental improvement.[2] To this end a joint steering group composed of IBC officers and members was established although its brief included housing, planning, and parks, as well as traffic.

It therefore appeared that Islington Council were taking environmental improvement much more seriously than the GLC and they were certainly anxious to see the Barnsbury traffic scheme in operation. Even so, this took many months from the time of the GLC's approval. The scheme had to be designed and approved both by IBC and by the police before the necessary detailed approval and traffic orders could be obtained from the GLC. In designing the scheme, which they felt should be implemented in two stages, Islington's consultant engineers felt that more permanent structures than oil drums and planks, which had originally been suggested, were necessary to withstand heavy traffic and to avoid abuse. The IBC engineer in charge of the scheme later maintained that these structures (such as railings fixed in properly levelled and drained paving) were still 'experimental' in the sense that they could easily be removed within a day, but that the GLC had satisfied themselves that Stage I would be unlikely to require major alteration once it was implemented. Nevertheless, it was to be experimental for eighteen months, this being the maximum statutory duration[3].

Finally, when the process of approval and order-making was complete, IBC held a public meeting to describe its environmental management scheme a few days prior to its implementation on 'B Day' (as it was called) on 15 March 1970.

At last, then, more than four years after the setting up of the joint study team, Barnsbury saw the first stage of a traffic scheme designed to canalise

[1] See GLC *Minutes*, 24 June 1969.
[2] LB Islington *Minutes*, 29 July 1969.
[3] The scheme was authorised by the GLC under the *Road Traffic Regulation Act 1967*, ch76, s9.

through traffic onto fewer roads in the area. Stage II was to remove through traffic from certain other streets in Barnsbury, particularly Hemingford Road, and was expected to follow after a three-month evaluation of Stage I.

Public and political reaction to the scheme

Although this case study was largely complete by the time Stage I was implemented, subsequent events in Barnsbury put the matter into an entirely different context. Because of their importance these events deserve more detailed consideration than has been possible in this project. But a brief outline is necessary to indicate the broader issues raised and how these were handled.

Immediately after the introduction of Stage I a storm of protest blew up from people who felt that they were suffering from the scheme. Initial complaints were from shopkeepers who said that they had lost much of their passing trade, and from residents in the streets which were carrying increased traffic. Others complained that the scheme hampered easy access for emergency service vehicles and did not appear to be experimental because of the permanent-looking barriers installed. These protests were articulated by a new group set up a week after the scheme came into operation called the Barnsbury Action Group (BAG). Its objective was to get the scheme withdrawn. Petitions were organised and by April, 2000 signatures had been collected supporting this objective. After a demonstration at Islington Town Hall the borough council agreed to receive a deputation to hear the BAG's case. The BAG at the same time made a direct attack on the BA for being concerned only with the interests of its own middle-class members and not at all with the problems of working-class families in Barnsbury.[1] The BA was also criticised by a member of the Barnsbury joint study team for pushing only for the traffic management proposals and not for the Barnsbury Report's proposals as a whole.[2]

During the first few months of the traffic scheme's operation, the local papers were full of letters and articles giving vent to the clash between the BA and the BAG, or at least to the different views they were believed to represent. Increasingly, the BAG's specific objections to the traffic scheme gave way to arguments about the social problems they believed it had aggravated. Through their close association with a voluntary housing aid centre in Barnsbury, the BAG were concerned about the harassment of tenants by landlords wishing to sell their properties for owner occupation. This had been taking place in Barnsbury for some time, and more particularly after the LCC's policy of piecemeal demolition and redevelopment had been abandoned following the Bewdley Street inquiry in 1965. But the

[1] It was later pointed out by John Ferris (see below) that the BA had a membership of about 900 while the area covered by the *Barnsbury Report* had a resident population of 35 000.

[2] *Islington Gazette*, 17 March 1970, letter from Mr Peter Brown.

BAG (and others in the area) believed that the traffic scheme, together with some street improvements which the borough was also carrying out, had exacerbated the problem of harassment by inflating property values in the streets from which through traffic had been removed. The BAG also complained that in improving the appearance of streets before many people had decent housing conditions, the Council had got its priorities wrong. These arguments were put to Islington's Public Services Committee in June 1970, together with the specific objections to the traffic scheme already mentioned.

At a meeting on 23 June, IBC considered a report on the operation of Stage I of the traffic scheme. The Council decided that there was no need for major changes to Stage I and that it should be allowed 'a further period to settle down,' but no decision was made about the implementation of Stage II. It was clear, therefore, that by this time the Council recognised the strength and persistance of opposition to the scheme.

Some time later, certain members of the BAG became dissatisfied with their concentration on the traffic scheme issue (particularly as nothing had been achieved on this front) and formed a tenants association to counteract the spread of harassment and to press the Council for improved housing conditions. As John Ferris (whose research in Barnsbury provided much information for this section) has said: 'The direct relationship between the traffic scheme and the operation of the local housing market . . . was too tenuous and abstract to have much appeal to the tenants as a distinct group.'[1]

Meanwhile IBC pursued consideration of Stage II of the traffic scheme. Consultations were held with the police and the GLC but after strong objections from the police the scheme was considerably altered. The revised proposals did not, for example, include the removal of through traffic from Hemingford Road, a proposal to which the police had particularly objected. The modified proposals were approved by the IBC and the GLC and implemented on 28 March 1971, just over a year after the initial scheme.

In February 1971 Islington's Public Services Committee requested a report on the scheme from the Borough Engineer in time for the GLC to give consideration to any further orders that would be required when the existing ones (for both Stage I and its modifications) expired in September 1971. While this report was being prepared, however, the borough council elections in May brought Labour back in control at Islington. In their election manifesto they stated a firm belief in environmental management but said that 'the Barnsbury scheme illustrates the need to do this in a fair and equitable way.' They promised specifically to 'rethink the Barnsbury traffic management scheme and all others from first principles with the fullest possible consultation and we will not hesitate to radically alter or scrap any scheme which does not measure up to our criteria.'[2]

[1] J Ferris (1972), *Participation in Urban Planning: The Barnsbury Case*, LSE Occasional Papers on Social Administration, p48.
[2] Islington Labour Party *Manifesto*, April 1971, pp10–11.

The Borough Engineer's report, which was considered by the new Public Services Committee on 10 June 1971 said that the Barnsbury scheme was consistent with the Council's existing objectives of concentrating heavy and through traffic onto major roads and excluding such traffic from residential areas and minor roads. The GLC had, however, to consider what steps to take in September 1971 when the experimental orders expired, and two alternatives were put forward.

1 The abandonment of the traffic scheme and a reversal to conditions as existing prior to March 1970.
2 To make the scheme permanent subject to incidental modifications as required for the emergency services. . . .[1]

Despite the report's description of the impact of the traffic scheme, in terms of both traffic flows and environment, the Public Services Committee wanted a more thorough investigation before taking any decision. The council therefore asked the GLC to extend the experimental orders for a further six months to enable this to be carried out. In the event, it was found that experimental traffic orders could not be extended and so a p rmanent order was made which could in any case, the GLC pointed out, be modified or revoked at any time!

Consequently, a working party of nine Islington members was set up to review the Barnsbury scheme and traffic management generally who, in March 1972, produced a report which examined in detail two items of their terms of reference. These were:

1 To review as a matter of extreme urgency, the Barnsbury experimental traffic management scheme and make recommendations to the Public Services, Town Planning and Development and Policy committees.
2 To examine the evidence which is available to support representations being made to place a limitation on traffic in this part of central London and other similar areas. . . .[2]

The Working Party invited the views of thirty-four amenity, trade and other organisations of whom about half responded. It appeared from the comments received that there was very little support for retaining the traffic scheme in its existing form, but there was also little support for reverting to the original (i.e. before March 1970) situation of uncontrolled traffic movements through Barnsbury. Concern was again expressed at the social implications of the scheme by the BAG and also by the Islington Poverty Action Group. Most of the organisations thought either that the scheme should be extended to exclude through traffic from the entire area

[1] *Report* of Borough Engineer and Surveyor to Public Services Committee of London Borough of Islington, 10 June 1971, p2.

[2] LB Islington, *Barnsbury Environmental Traffic Management Review*, Report of Traffic Management Working Party, March 1972, p3.

of Barnsbury bounded by Upper Street, Pentonville Road and Caledonian Road, or that (in the case of the BAG for example) there were no streets in Islington suitable for taking heavy increases in traffic. Two organisations said they felt the only way of securing environmental management was to reduce the total amount of traffic in central London. The Islington Society, for example, said: 'If the GLC were to implement their (central London) parking policy effectively there would be no necessity for their insistence that traffic in Barnsbury cannot be reduced but only canalised on to 'better suited streets within the area' which are themselves residential.[1]

The Report's evaluation of the traffic scheme covered in considerable detail such aspects as: changes in traffic flow, the numbers of people affected, safety, noise, vibration, pollution, accessibility, social and economic effects and the provision of a bus service through Barnsbury.[2]

After making studies of house prices and harassment the Working Party concluded that it was 'more than likely that the scheme by making the area more attractive has aggravated the conflict . . . between tenants and would be owner-occupiers.'[3] As far as the effects of traffic were concerned, however, they felt that the benefits and disbenefits were fairly evenly balanced.

A study was also made of the broader policy context of the Barnsbury scheme, partly to investigate the claim of the Islington Society (and others) that total traffic could and should be reduced. The Working Party did not agree with this, however, and concluded this section of their report as follows:

1 It is unlikely that any significant additional capacity can be gained from the secondary road network in the immediate future (i.e. Caledonian Road, Pentonville Road and Upper Street). Traffic cannot be simply transferred to the secondary network because this would lead to congestion to the detriment of public transport and essential traffic. In any event current GLC policy would inhibit this approach.
2 A tougher parking policy is an objective which should be pursued. However . . . [this] . . . would have no more than a marginal effect on traffic flows.
3 Environmental management schemes must inevitably be compromises. . . .[4]

Having dealt with the effects of the Barnsbury scheme and its relation to questions of broad traffic policy, the Working Party examined various alternative courses of action open to the Council. These were either to abandon the scheme altogether or to modify it in one or more of several ways. They made no specific recommendations, however, and at the time of writing (December 1972) the Council had taken no further decision on the scheme.

[1] LB Islington (1972), pxii.
[2] LB Islington (1972), p9.
[3] LB Islington (1972), p23.
[4] LB Islington (1972), p28.

Whatever the rights and wrongs of the Barnsbury scheme, then, it did succeed in bringing to the surface not only many practical difficulties in implementing environmental management but also the problems of public participation in planning, of class conflict, of inequities in the operation of the housing market and of the difficulties of dividing these issues between the two levels of local government in London.

5 ANALYSIS

The Kensington study, which had been initiated by the LCC and completed by the GLC, remained on the shelf. The GLC, however, had thought it sufficiently worthwhile to commit itself to carrying out further similar studies. This commitment, however, was never fulfilled. One reason may have been the GLC's growing preoccupation with the motorway proposals. But the problem of excluding through traffic from residential areas where the peripheral roads were already overloaded, which the Kensington study had emphasised, was probably the most important factor. The GLC concluded that environmental management was unacceptable where it was likely to increase congestion and further studies would probably have done little more than confirm the importance of this problem.

In contrast, the Pimlico scheme was blessed with more favourable circumstances. It was initiated, designed and implemented within Westminster City Engineer's Department, it concerned a much smaller area with a simple 'grid-iron' street pattern, and the peripheral roads had sufficient spare traffic capacity to accommodate the through traffic which was excluded from the area. It is interesting to note, however, that after the introduction of the scheme no significant changes in traffic volumes occurred on the roads peripheral to it. The implementation process was not hampered by any major disagreements either with the GLC, the police or within the City council. After its implementation, there were no significant adverse reactions to the scheme from local interests. The scheme was thus a success in terms of the local government system and it also became a success in terms of improving the environment and road safety in Pimlico. This prompted Robert Vigars (as chairman of the GLC's Planning and Transportation Committee) to say that the scheme was 'another example of the successful co-operation of the GLC with the London borough councils. I hope both Westminster and other boroughs will now submit further schemes for approval. I would like to see the whole of London treated eventually in this way.'[1]

Thus by the time the Barnsbury study was completed in 1968 the context in which environmental management could be carried out in London had been clarified in three important respects: first, the GLC's policy of not approving schemes which increased traffic congestion on already overloaded roads had been established by the Kensington study; second,

[1] GLC *Press Release*, 18 November 1968.

the GLC's statement on the success of Pimlico made it clear that they saw environmental management as primarily a borough responsibility; and third, financial responsibility was apparently to rest entirely with the boroughs. What still remained to be seen was whether the two levels of local government could co-operate successfully within the context laid down by the GLC to implement environmental management on a wider scale.

The Barnsbury scheme became in this sense a test case since it covered an area of comparable size and complexity of streets to the Kensington scheme and was (unlike that scheme) enthusiastically promoted by a local pressure group. It was also a test case in terms of its broader involvement with the future planning of Barnsbury as a whole, but this case study has not examined this question in depth.

At the time of writing, the environmental management scheme was virtually the only part of the Barnsbury Report's proposals which had come to fruition, although the LCC's policy of piecemeal redevelopment in the area had given way to one of rehabilitation of existing buildings. But the Report, prepared jointly by officers of the MOHLG, MOT, GLC and IBC, at least put environmental management in the broader context of area improvement.

The BA, whose efforts had begun the process in 1965, pressed for direct involvement in the joint study team's work and later for the implementation of the scheme drawn up by IBC. The BA and IBC became closely aligned over this scheme and pressed the GLC for its approval. The GLC at first objected to the experimental nature of IBC's scheme and also said that no action could be taken until the peripheral roads (and particularly the Angel intersection) had been 'improved' to take the diverted traffic. It thus appeared that the scheme would meet the same fate as the Kensington scheme. But continued pressure both from IBC and the BA succeeded eventually in getting the GLC to approve Stage I on an experimental basis.

The introduction of Stage I gave rise to much broader issues in Barnsbury. It acted as a catalyst for the involvement of many more people and interests in the neighbourhood than those represented by the BA. Other groups such as the BAG brought into question the borough council's priorities in an area where bad housing conditions were widespread, and complained that the traffic scheme had aggravated the problem of harassment of tenants by making houses more attractive to would-be owner occupiers and landlords seeking to realise their capital. To what extent this complaint was justified became a matter for continuing debate, but there can be little doubt that the traffic scheme acted as a focus for latent conflicts between the established 'working-class' population of Barnsbury and the 'middle-class' newcomers. Moreover, there was no doubt that the scheme had removed through traffic from some streets in Barnsbury at the expense of increased traffic on others, and this would have most likely provoked bitter complaints from those whose environment had deteriorated, regardless of any social differences between the streets in question. A study carried out by Mrs Enid Wistrich confirmed that similar problems had occurred with Camden borough council's attempts to introduce an environmental management scheme at Primrose Hill in 1970.[1]

Adverse public reaction to the Barnsbury scheme apparently took the Conservative-controlled borough council by surprise, particularly since they had received so much co-operation from the BA in pursuing the environmental management policy when first elected in 1968. By the time Labour regained control in 1971 it had become clear that any further action in Barnsbury would have to take full account of the sensitive situation which had developed. The members' Working Party which was set up to review the Barnsbury scheme thus found that the council was in a difficult position. Detailed comments from various organisations with an interest in the area showed that there would be strong opposition if attempts were made to revoke the scheme, or modify it, or indeed to retain it. The one solution that might have been acceptable, namely the extension of the scheme to exclude through traffic from Barnsbury as a whole, appeared to be impossible while the GLC maintained its policy of allowing no further traffic on the peripheral secondary roads. This difficulty was reflected in the Working Party Report, which made no specific recommendations, and on which, at the time of writing, no further decisions had been taken.

6 CONCLUSIONS: THE ROLES OF THE BODIES INVOLVED

The Ministry of Housing and Local Government

The Ministry displayed a keen interest in environmental planning in the mid-1960s and responded to the BA's case at the Bewdley Street inquiry for the comprehensive planning of Barnsbury. They also became interested in the question of public participation in the planning process although the Barnsbury joint study team never really satisfied the BA's demands in this respect.

The Ministry, however, having commissioned the study and constituted the Steering Committee, declared the end of their active involvement when the Study Report was published in 1968. The Report stated that it would be 'for the two local authorities to consider and act upon the proposals in the Report as they think fit.'[2] In retrospect this was unfortunate as the Ministry might well have been able to help overcome the difficulties which later arose between IBC and GLC. They might also have been able to secure more effective action on the Report's proposals as a whole rather than simply the traffic scheme. Nevertheless, the Report made some sug-

[1] E Wistrich (1972), *Local Government Reorganisation: The First Years of Camden*, pp255–60.
[2] MOHLG (1968), *Barnsbury Environmental Study Report*, p92.

gestions as to how its proposals might be implemented such as an area-based organisation, perhaps linked with existing area-based social services, to co-ordinate the many bodies which could become involved. Also mentioned was the need for pilot schemes to assess costs and benefits before proceeding on a large scale.[1]

The Ministry of Transport

The MOT was represented on the joint study team but played no further part in the implementation of the Barnsbury scheme. This was regrettable because although the MOT had already decided not to contribute towards the cost of environmental management schemes (i.e. with the Pimlico scheme) they might have experienced at first hand the crucial problem of diverting traffic onto Principal roads (for which they provided 75% grants towards the cost of schemes). The apparent dependence of environmental management on Principal road 'improvements' (such as that proposed for the Angel intersection) might have provided the Ministry with a clearer picture of where investment priorities should lie.

The Metropolitan Police

Although the police had no ultimate power in the field of traffic management, in practice their statutory right to consultation gave them a loud voice in the decision-making process. For example, it was largely the strength of their objections which led to the rejection of Stage II of IBC's Barnsbury scheme.

Local pressure groups

The BA chiefly represented middle-class newcomers who saw a need for, and initiated action to promote, the application of comprehensive environmental planning as put forward by Professor Buchanan in his report *Traffic in Towns*. It was mainly due to the BA's advocacy at the Bewdley Street inquiry that the joint study team was set up. They were also extremely willing to participate in the study team's work and had considerable expertise to offer, as evidenced by the 1965 Wager Report. Debate on the role and nature of public participation in planning had at that time, of course, hardly begun, but the BA nevertheless went some way towards clarifying the issues involved. The BA's role became increasingly political in character in urging the authorities to implement environmental management measures. With the strong interest also being taken by IBC's Highways Committee, on which the BA was represented, most of the pressure was directed towards the GLC, and eventually produced results. John Ferris has said that 'the major achievement of the BA (was) the way in

[1] MOHLG (1968), pp84–8.

which they gained official acceptance of what they defined as the major problems facing the area.'[1]

But when Stage I of the Barnsbury traffic scheme was implemented it became clear that others in the area defined its major problems in quite different terms. Other groups, particularly the BAG, immediately launched a campaign to get the scheme withdrawn, and the BA was strongly criticised for pressing their own interests onto the community as a whole.

The London boroughs

None of the boroughs involved in the three schemes examined in this case study (Kensington and Chelsea, Westminster and Islington) seriously challenged the GLC's policy of rejecting environmental management schemes which seemed likely to increase traffic congestion on roads that were already overloaded. Consequently, Kensington and Chelsea seemed content for the GLC's Kensington study to remain on the shelf. But Westminster City Council continued to work within the constraint of the GLC's traffic policy and, no doubt encouraged by their success with the Pimlico scheme, later gained the GLC's acceptance of a large scheme for Queen's Park in the northern part of the City.[2]

Islington council pursued the Barnsbury scheme vigorously and, with the help of the BA, finally managed to persuade the GLC to override their officers' objections about the likely traffic effects on the peripheral roads. But they were somewhat taken aback by the adverse public reaction when Stage I was implemented, and found that the problem of environmental management was likely to be one of gaining acceptance by the public rather than GLC approval.

The Greater London Council

The Kensington study and the Pimlico scheme together led the GLC to clarify their role in environmental management in relation to that of the boroughs. This role was to ease traffic conditions on main roads so that through traffic could be excluded from residential areas without causing additional congestion, and to make the initiation, designing, implementation and financing of environmental management schemes a borough responsibility. The GLC's role would solely be that of vetting schemes and making the necessary traffic orders.

The implementation of, and public reaction to, the Barnsbury scheme did not significantly alter the GLC's attitude. The decision to make environmental management primarily a borough responsibility did not mean, however, that the GLC was unwilling to discuss in detail the design aspects of schemes. It also did not mean that the GLC took no interest in environmental improvement. They were, after all, represented on the

[1] Ferris (1971).
[2] See *Official Architecture and Planning*, February 1968.

Barnsbury joint study team. Although the GLC did not fulfill their commitment to carry out further studies similar to the Kensington study, they later promoted more general studies into problems of environmental improvement.[1]

The decision on financial responsibility was perhaps unfortunate from the point of view of the GLC's objective of encouraging the introduction of environmental management throughout London. Some form of financial commitment might have acted as a positive incentive for the boroughs to draw up schemes.

The GLC confirmed that responsibility for environmental schemes should rest with the boroughs in the GLDP which was published in 1969. The Written Statement, for example, said: 'This . . . planning work will unfold mainly when the boroughs . . . get to grips with detailed environmental planning within their areas.'[2] The GLC's policy with regard to congested Principal roads, however, seemed to limit the possibilities for environmental management which the boroughs could put forward. The Kensington study remained on the shelf largely because of its expected adverse effects on traffic congestion, and the Barnsbury scheme seemed likely to founder for the same reason. The fact that the GLC eventually agreed to Stage I after continued pressure from IBC and the BA, meant either that they reached the conclusion that the scheme would not cause any additional congestion or that they were prepared to accept some; but this vital matter was never clarified. In any event the GLC's policy remained firm enough to rule out the possibility (as far as IBC's Working Party was concerned) of extending the Barnsbury scheme to include the whole area between the peripheral Principal roads, namely Caledonian Road, Pentonville Road and Upper Street. Moreover, the GLC had at the time of writing given IBC no firm commitment that they would approve such proposals even when the traffic capacity of the crucial Angel intersection had been increased (see A1 in London, Case Study *K*).

By the time the GLDP was published in 1969, the role of the GLC in environmental management thus appeared to be twofold. On the one hand they were prepared to make the necessary traffic orders (for which they had the sole power as traffic authority for London) only when they were satisfied that no serious increase in congestion would result. On the other hand they were to provide the 'climate' for environmental management schemes to be introduced by creating sufficient extra capacity on Principal roads to make room for through traffic diverted from environmental areas.

This dual role, however, imposed a strict limitation on the extent to which the boroughs could implement environmental management schemes in their areas. Virtually all that could be done was to channel through traffic onto fewer local (i.e. borough) roads, but this inevitably meant, as was so clearly the case in Barnsbury, that environmental improvements in

[1] For example, studies of North-East London (1970) and Greenwich (1971) carried out for the GLC by Colin Buchanan and Partners.
[2] GLC (1969), *GLDP Written Statement*, para2.10.

one street would be offset by environmental losses in another. Moreover, the provision of extra Principal road capacity seemed to be a long-term objective to be achieved as and when investment in primary and secondary roads was carried out. In the *GLDP Report of Studies*, for example, it was said that motorways would be needed 'if the remainder of the [road] system is to be capable of management to preserve the environment and meet travel needs,' and that the improvement of the environment generally would depend on 'carefully devised policies combining management measures and capital improvements. . . .'[1] Similarly in the *GLDP Written Statement* it was said that 'the primary (motorway) network has a very broad mesh and cannot be relied upon by itself to bring about the full range of environmental improvements. It will need to be accompanied by improvements to the secondary network, by the delineation of environmental areas, and by management measures for the control of traffic.'[2] The possibility of short-term measures to enable environmental management schemes to be introduced appeared (in the GLDP) to have been ruled out. Although in 1966 the GLC had regarded such short-term measures as the ILPA parking regulations and 'clearway' restrictions as providing the 'climate' for the introduction of environmental schemes, by 1972 most of these had been implemented in central London and yet there were still no more than a handful of environmental management schemes.

Finally, then, environmental management in London, although a well-established part of both GLC and borough policy, has taken a subordinate position to the maintenance of traffic flow on Principal roads, certainly as far as the GLC was concerned. Moreover, the definition of responsibilities and powers between the two levels of authority has created a virtual stalemate with regard to the implementation of environmental management schemes. The GLC has the powers to make the necessary traffic orders but regards the implementation of schemes as a borough responsibility. The boroughs on the other hand, having been given this responsibility, have found that they have no powers to carry them out.

[1] GLC (1969), *GLDP Report of Studies*, paras6.239–6.242.
[2] GLC (1969), *GLDP Written Statement*, para2.10.

Case Study H

IMPROVING THE RAIL APPROACHES TO CANNON STREET AND CHARING CROSS

INTRODUCTION

The most important terminal railway stations on the Southern Region's (SR) South-Eastern Division are Charing Cross and Cannon Street (the others being Holborn Viaduct and Blackfriars). All the services from these two main terminals pass through London Bridge station and what is known as Borough Market Junction before separating to serve south-east London and Kent (Figure 13). The maximum capacity of the whole system is largely determined by the capacity of Borough Market Junction, a fact which explains the considerable peak-hour operating problems that have been experienced on these lines for seventy years or more.

The Borough Market Junction bottleneck has been the subject of many suggestions and proposals for increasing capacity, and also the focus for widespread complaints from the thousands of commuters who travel through it each day in overcrowded trains. This case study sets out to show how the problem developed and what factors led, at the end of 1971, to the prospect of at least a partial solution to it.

The bodies involved in the Borough Market issue since 1965 have been mainly British Rail (BR), as the body responsible for the planning and operation of the railway services; the Greater London Council (GLC), as the strategic planning authority for London and (since the Transport (London) Act 1969) transport planning authority for London; the Department of the Environment (DOE) (and formerly the Ministry of Transport (MOT)) as the grant aid authority for capital investment schemes and (since the 1968 Transport Act) unremunerative services, as arbiter on the GLC's statutory plans for London, and as controller of BR's investment plans. Also involved were the Greater London Transport Group (GLTG), set up in 1970 and concerned with co-ordinating the plans of the GLC, London Transport (LT) and BR, and the various regional planning agencies for the South-East—the South-East Economic Planning Council (SEEPC), the South-East Joint Planning Team (SEJPT), and the Standing Conference on London and South-East Regional Planning (SCLSERP)—who were concerned with the capacity of the rail system as it affected the future distribution of population and employment in London and the South-East. Finally, various groups representing the rail commuters, and the local authorities of the areas where they lived, particularly Kent, became involved in the Borough Market Junction and related issues.

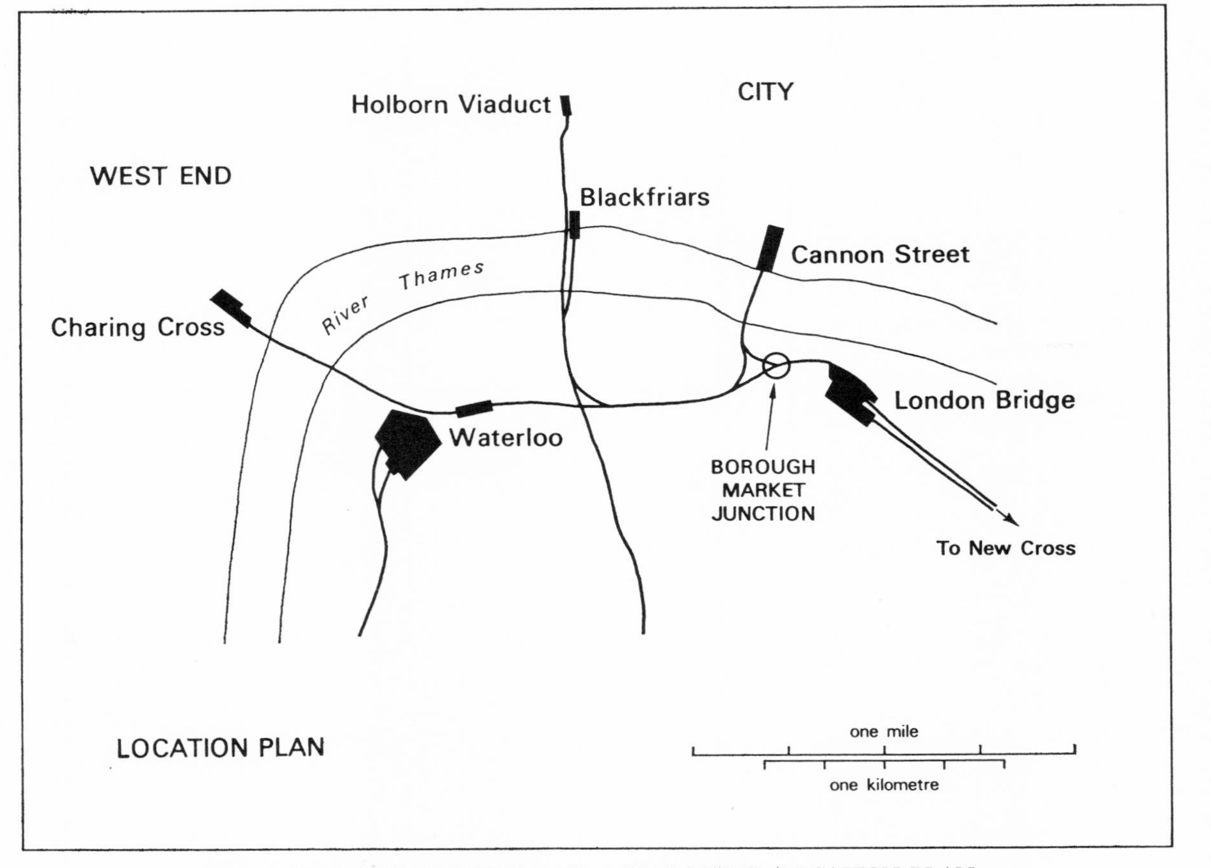

Figure 13 SOUTH-EASTERN RAIL APPROACHES: LOCATION PLAN

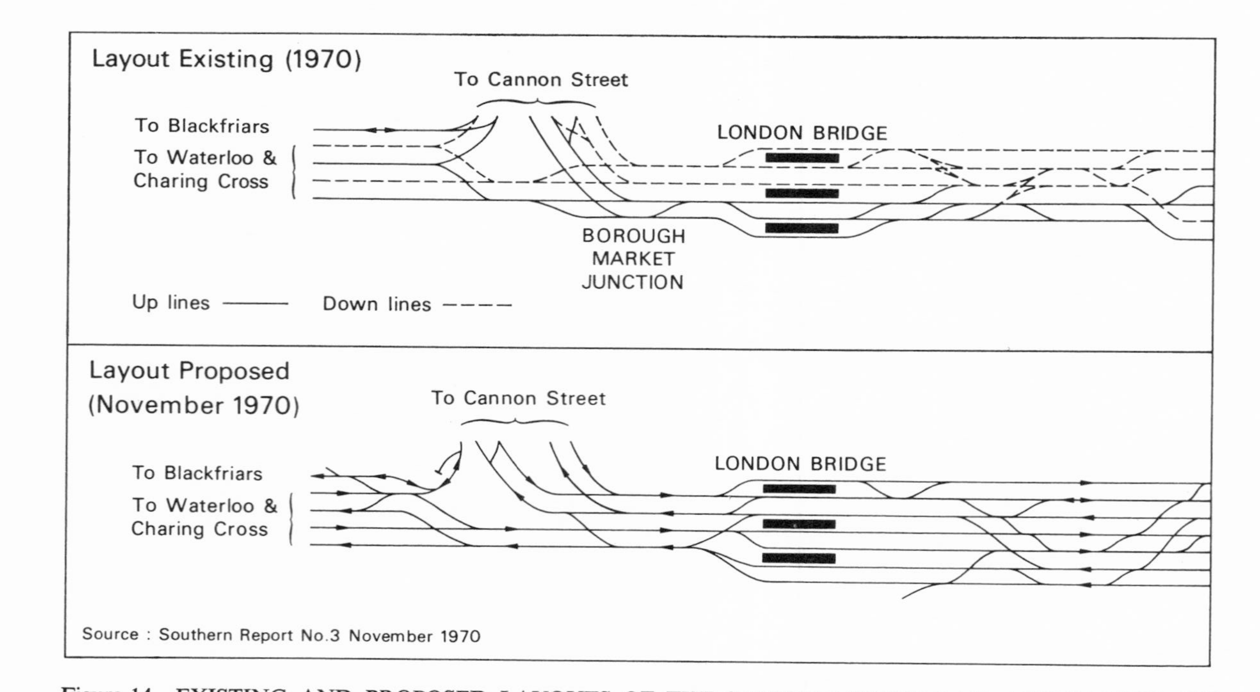

Figure 14 EXISTING AND PROPOSED LAYOUTS OF THE SOUTH-EASTERN RAIL APPROACHES, 1970
(*continued below*)

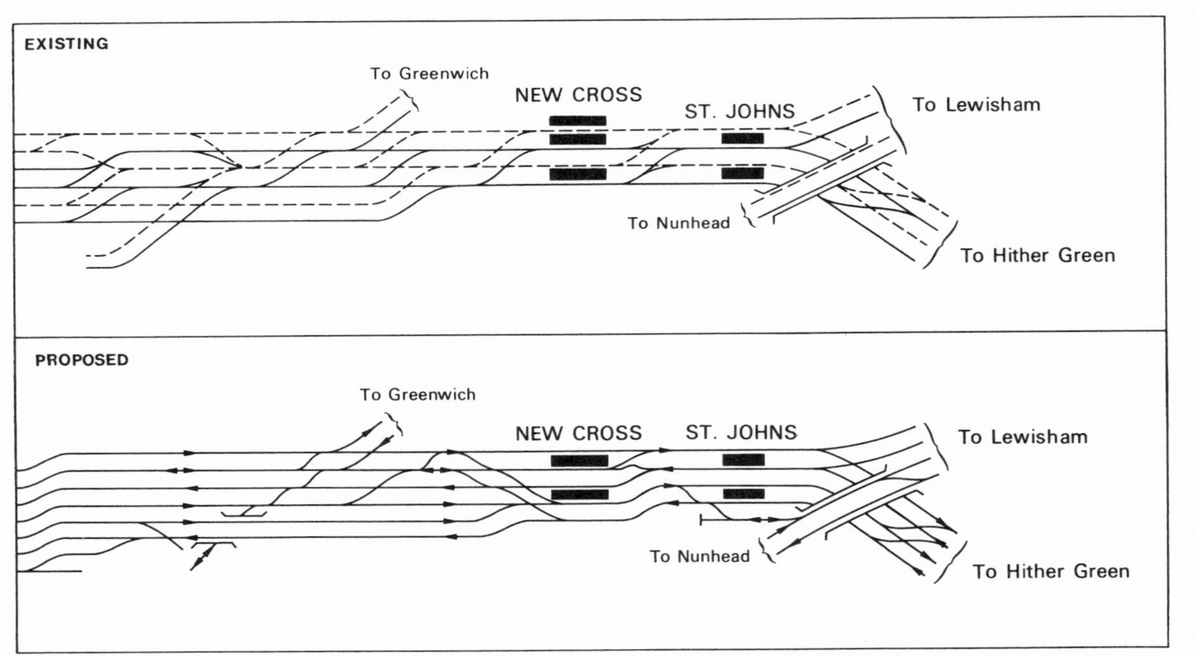

Figure 14 EXISTING AND PROPOSED LAYOUTS OF THE SOUTH-EASTERN RAIL APPROACHES, 1970

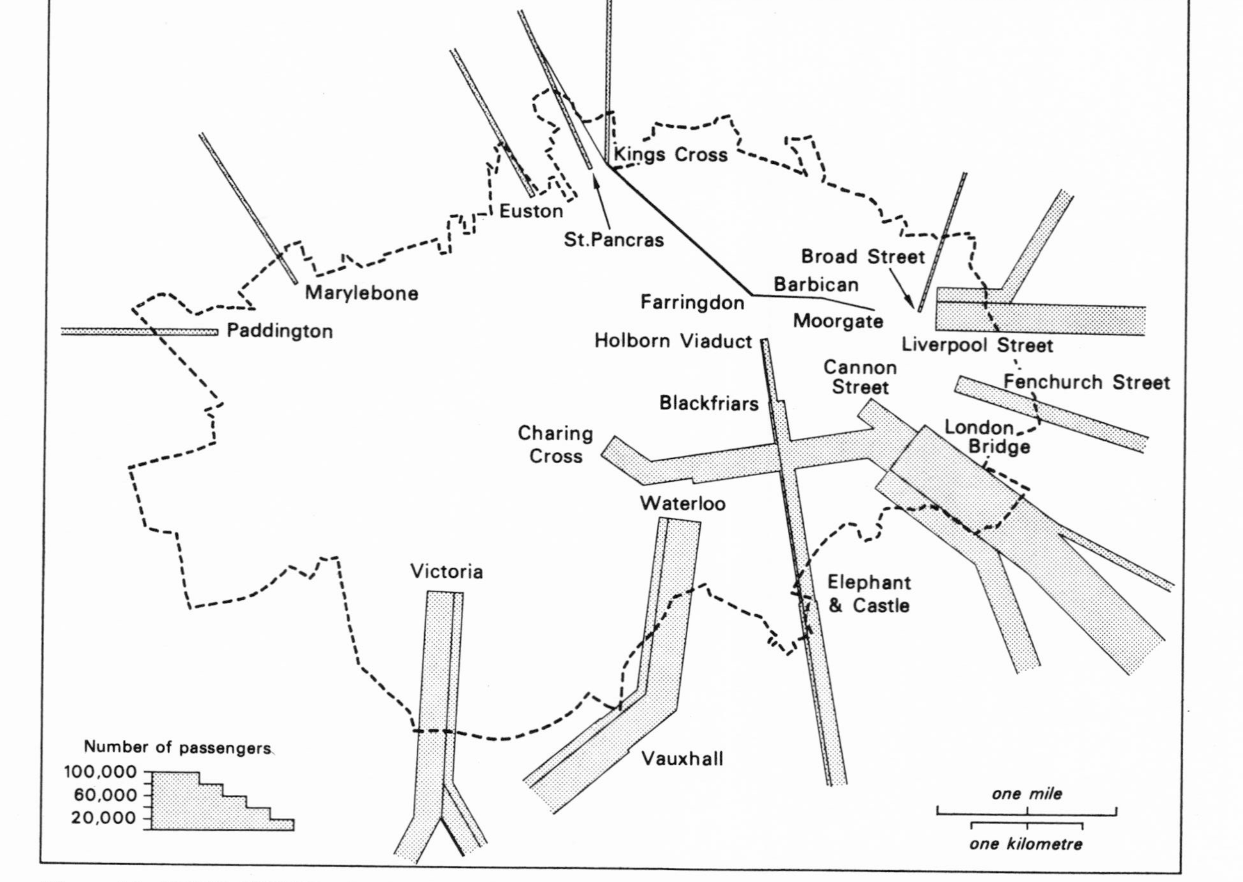

Figure 15 PEAK PERIOD (0700–0959 HOURS) PASSENGER FLOWS INTO CENTRAL LONDON, 1969

HISTORICAL BACKGROUND

The early railway companies operating south of the Thames all had a strong desire to serve both the City and the West End. The least successful in this respect was perhaps the London and South-Western Railway whose one terminal, Waterloo, did not directly serve either—though the Waterloo–Bank underground link later constructed by the Southern Railway remedied this situation to a large extent. The London, Brighton and South Coast Railway served two terminals, Victoria and London Bridge, and the London, Chatham and Dover Railway served Victoria, and Holborn Viaduct. But the South-Eastern Railway operated from Charing Cross and Cannon Street which were (and still are) the most convenient terminals for the West End and City respectively.

The distribution of services between the West End and City terminals, however, brought with it a complicated operating problem, particularly in the case of the South-Eastern Division since all the trains had to be funnelled through Borough Market Junction. During the nineteenth century there were successive alterations and additions to terminals and the approaches to them in order to cope with rapidly increasing passenger traffic, but the junction was physically difficult to expand because Southwark Cathedral and the Borough Market itself were situated close by the railway viaduct.

Originally, Cannon Street was the more important of the two South-Eastern terminals, a fact which is reflected in the design of the track layout. Cannon Street had eight platforms and four tracks through Borough Market while Charing Cross had six platforms and only two tracks through Borough Market. In the early days with steam operation, in order to minimise the number of 'light engine' movements in the peak hours, trains were run into Charing Cross and then reversed into Cannon Street using the triangle at Borough Market, to be ready for the outward journey again (see Figure 13). (If trains were not reversed in this way, additional engines had to be coupled onto the trains for the outward journey.) In 1904, twenty-four down trains (and almost as many up) passed through London Bridge between 5 and 6 p.m. and all but a few of these were reversed into Cannon Street.[1] A widening scheme completed in 1902 was undertaken to ease the chaotic situation that had developed, but the side of the triangle carrying all the Charing Cross trains remained double track and this merged with the four Cannon Street tracks on 'flat' junctions (i.e. involving crossovers and thus conflicting train movements).

By 1902 Cannon Street was handling 13.5 million passengers per year and Charing Cross 10.2 million.[2] Traffic continued to grow, particularly after the First World War and delays arising from the Borough Market bottleneck increased. But no further widening was carried out, and it was

[1] H P White (1963), *A Regional History of the Railways of Great Britain*, vol3, *Greater London*, p27. (Trains have always been described as 'up' *to* London.)
[2] White (1963), p29.

left to the Southern Railway, formed in 1923, to cope with the situation.

Over the years, particularly since the First World War, the relative importance of the two terminal stations altered considerably, with Charing Cross becoming more heavily used than Cannon Street. White has attributed this change to the 'westward spread of commerce and more frequent journey from the suburbs to the West End for shopping or theatre-going.'[1] But the important factor with regard to the limited capacity of Borough Market Junction is the continuing importance of Cannon Street for commuters to the City. Table 23 shows the passenger arrivals in the morning peak period at Cannon Street and Charing Cross (South-Eastern) for 1951, 1966, 1969 and 1971 (see also Figure 15).

DIVISION	1951	1966 (% CHANGE FROM 1951)	1969 (% CHANGE FROM 1966)	1971 (% CHANGE FROM 1969)
Cannon Street	31.2	40.2	39.5	40.9
Charing Cross	40.9	40.5	41.0	45.1
Waterloo (SE)	6.5	8.2	9.0	10.0
London Bridge (SE)	18.5	20.6	18.4	16.7
South-Eastern (Total)	97.1	109.5 (+12.8)	107.9 (−1.5)	112.7 (+4.4)
Central and South-West	180.7	197.7 (+ 9.5)	202.2 (+2.3)	202.6 (+0.01)
Total (Southern Region)	277.8	307.2 (+10.6)	310.1 (+1.0)	315.3 (+1.6)

Table 23 PEAK PERIOD (0700–0959 HOURS) PASSENGER ARRIVALS AT SOUTHERN REGION CENTRAL AREA STATIONS, 1951–71 (000)[2]

Notes

1 Electrification of London–Kent coast services 1959–62
2 Electrification of London–Bournemouth service 1967
3 The opening of the Victoria Line early in 1969 has led to an increase in the number of passengers using that station
4 South-Eastern division services arriving at Victoria (which do not travel over the 'south-eastern approaches' lines) are included in the Central and South West totals
5 Arrivals at Vauxhall station are not included

DEVELOPMENT OF MEASURES TO MITIGATE THE BOROUGH MARKET JUNCTION PROBLEM

The general picture until the mid-1960s was one of constantly increasing

[1] White (1963), p30.
[2] BR Board (1970), *Proof of Evidence, E12/7*, 1972, *Paper S30/76*, GLDP Inquiry Stages 1 and 3; and letter from BR Board dated 20 June 1972.

passenger demand, at least at peak times of the day, on the Charing Cross, Cannon Street and London Bridge lines. Since the nineteenth-century additions and alterations to track and station layouts referred to earlier, there has been a continuous search for methods of handling the increasing peak-hour demand which would avoid the need for physical alterations to Borough Market Junction itself. Some of the measures taken are described in the following paragraphs.

The first major breakthrough in train operations came with the Southern Railway's electrification programme before the Second World War, accompanied by the replacement of 'semaphore' with colour-light signals on many lines. Although many of the longer-distance services (for example to Hastings and some Kent coast destinations) remained steam operated, the electrification and signalling schemes succeeded in greatly increasing the capacity of the system and the reliability of services.

After the nationalisation of the railways in 1947 some double-deck trains were introduced on the South-Eastern Division commuter services in an attempt to provide more seats with the same number of trains, and thus to minimise the number of trains and crews under-used outside the peak periods. This train did not succeed in this purpose, however, partly because of boarding and alighting problems (entailing longer stops at stations) and partly because reduced standing room offset the gains in seating capacity compared with the conventional stock.

In February 1952 BR announced the introduction of new ten-car trains on the lines between Gillingham and Cannon Street and Charing Cross which provided 945 seats compared with 772 seats in the eight-car trains. The terminal and other station platforms were lengthened accordingly.[1] These longer trains had been introduced on to all the peak-hour services into Cannot Street and Charing Cross by 1957.[2]

By 1960 steam operation into the two terminals had been eliminated. While this only marginally increased the effective capacity of Borough Market Junction, it significantly improved the ability to recover lost time when delays occurred, thereby improving reliability. The Kent coast steam services were electrified and the Hastings services were operated by diesel-electric stock. (This was chosen in preference to diesel-mechanical propulsion because of its superior performance and thus greater ability to merge with electric stock on the crucial inner London approaches.)

None of these developments, however, succeeded in eliminating the frequent delays on the south-eastern approaches. Indeed these schemes may be regarded as having postponed the need for major physical alterations to the junction. Some of BR's management did believe, however, that specific investment at Borough Market was necessary. In February 1958, SR's general manager (Mr C P Hopkins) in response to criticisms in the *Evening News* of peak-hour travel on the south-eastern lines explained the

[1] *The Times*, 23 February 1952.
[2] London County Council, *Administrative County of London Plan First Review, 1960, Report*, p78.

problems of operating this section. He said that the only complete solution would be 'not to tinker expensively with individual bottlenecks' but to provide a pair of extra tracks all the way from Charing Cross and Cannon Street to Lewisham plus extra terminal platforms 'at enormous cost.' He suggested that as this investment would be for peak-hour commuters they should in fairness bear the cost through greatly augmented fares. Why, he argued, should general fares revenue be used to provide facilities for one hour of the day for one section of the community? Staggered working hours could, he thought, provide a much better solution.[1] Mr Hopkins' views were reiterated in April 1962 by the South-Eastern Division's line traffic manager, Mr T Bolland. Commenting on the final stages of the Kent lines modernisation, he said that the money invested in the previous five years had not increased the ability of the London termini to receive more trains. Cannon Street and Charing Cross, he said, were running to capacity and that could only be increased by spending millions of pounds which could not be justified. He too felt that staggering of working hours, even by only half an hour, was the only answer to the peak problem.[2]

Despite these statements, however, schemes were devised to squeeze still further capacity out of the junction. In October 1964 a new timetable due to come into operation the following June was announced by BR which would enable nine extra trains to be run into Charing Cross and Cannon Street during the peak hour. This was made possible by running ten existing trains non-stop through London Bridge and thus creating more train paths. It did, of course, mean that passengers using London Bridge station (either as a destination or for interchange) would have fewer trains to choose from.

Even more productive, though costing nearly £½ million, was a scheme announced in January 1966 to push an extra twenty-five rush-hour trains (at least 20 000 seats) through Borough Market Junction. This was to be effected partly by running more trains non-stop through London Bridge and partly by reducing the number of empty trains being returned through the junction during the peak times. This latter measure was made possible by running more trains into Charing Cross and Cannon Street and then retaining them north of the junction on new electrified sidings. Mr David McKenna, then general manager of the SR, pointed out that the proposed £½ million investment (which also included minor track and signalling alterations to increase capacity elsewhere on the Southern commuter network) would bring the commuting capacity of the SR to the limit, despite the £95 million which had already been spent on modernisation over the previous twenty years. Beyond that investment, which was due to be completed about mid-1967, further capacity would only be possible with major works to remodel Borough Market Junction and the approach section between London Bridge, New Cross and St Johns. These works were estimated to cost from about £10 to 15 million. Mr McKenna also

[1] *Railway Gazette*, 21 February 1958.
[2] *The Times*, 4 April 1962.

said that the immediate (£½ million) scheme, whilst allowing more people to commute in the peak hour, would not necessarily mean any increase in comfort or reliability. 'The more you fill up the lines,' he said, 'the more difficult it is to get reliable and punctual trains.'[1]

The proposed scheme received a 'luke warm' welcome from the Travellers' Associations Joint Committee (representing a number of commuter groups using the SR commuter services) who said that the proposed extra trains would only keep pace with rising passenger demand, that time-keeping might worsen and that the £10–15 million scheme would come too late.

Thus it seemed that both BR and the users of its commuter services into London shared a pessimistic view about the possibility of improvements in peak-hour travelling conditions, unless the Government were prepared to finance the substantial investment required. And even this would not eliminate the problem: as Mr McKenna pointed out a year later, capital investment of the sort required, i.e. for the two peak hours or half hours each day, and the provision of extra trains to make use of the extra track capacity gained, would worsen the finances of the railways. Higher fares to cover the costs would probably divert passengers onto the roads, but he thought expenditure on public transport might be better for the life of Londoners than expenditure on roads.[2]

The completion, in July 1967 as planned, of the £½ million scheme and the retimetabling to include the extra peak-hour trains, despite still further possible technical developments, apparently marked the attainment of a threshold of capacity after more than thirty years of improvements to the system, which only major investment could overcome. Thenceforward the issue was one of what kind of major scheme was required, how much it would cost, whether it was justified, and if so, how it was to be financed.

But by the mid-1960s the problem was beginning to be considered from a different angle: the implications of limited commuting capacity to central London were being actively considered in the context of future development in the South-East region. The South-East Study, prepared by the Ministry of Housing and Local Government in 1964, predicted that the number of jobs in central London would increase by 20 000 per year between 1961 and 1971.[3] This growth, it was recognised, would pose commuting problems since sufficient additional housing would not be provided in central London, or even inner London. Moreover, although many BR lines had capacity which could be readily expanded, this was not the case on the SR lines and it was difficult to match the supply of new housing land with the uneven pattern of spare rail capacity. BR estimated that with an investment of £100 million (including £30 million on the Southern) together with reshaping services, they could carry an extra 400 000 commuters to central London, 250 000 more than the predicted increase to 1971. To achieve this it would be necessary to run more trains from greater

[1] *The Times*, 12 January 1966.
[2] *The Times*, 12 January 1967.
[3] MOHLG, *The South-East Study, 1961–81*, HMSO, 1964.

distances beyond London non-stop to central London (i.e. without stopping at inner London stations such as New Cross and London Bridge.) This would mean that commuters would have less choice of termini. Moreover, LT considered that extra tube lines would be required to distribute commuters in central London.

The South-East Study took into account the distribution of spare rail commuting capacity is drawing up proposals for housing allocation in the Home Counties over the period 1961–81.[1] Unfortunately, however, the specific implications for rail development were not described, and BR was therefore faced with the prospect of, and responsibility for, increased rail commuting to central London overall, and the crucial question of Borough Market Junction could not be avoided. When the £½ million investment already described was announced early in 1966, Mr McKenna indicated that future schemes of a more extensive nature were already being planned by BR. He wanted to see a spread of offices outward from central London to cut the growth in peak-hour commuting, but otherwise expenditure over £10 million would be required on the south-eastern approaches. The plans included signalling, track and other works. The colour light signals introduced before the war were obsolete and while they were satisfactory for mixed steam and electric operation, they were not able to provide for the efficiency possible with all-electric operation. Major works would be required to remodel Borough Market Junction and to enlarge the track capacity from there to New Cross, with the construction of a new flyover between St Johns and London Bridge to simplify traffic separation. Provision of extra platforms at the London terminals was also envisaged. The result, however, was not expected to enable more than about twenty extra peak-hour trains to operate into London.

Four draft schemes for the enlargement of the south-eastern approaches were reported to have been produced for study by 1966, varying in scale and sophistication.[2] But despite these plans, the need for such elaborate measures was still being doubted. Some experts, according to the magazine *Modern Railways*, felt that the need for large-scale works would be overtaken by technical developments in the field of automatic train control and signalling: a 5–10% 'economic return' was claimed for investment of this sort.[3]

A more specific challenge to BR's plans came in 1967 when the Sevenoaks Season Ticket Holder's Association (SSTHA) produced alternative plans for expanding the capacity of the south-eastern approaches which were claimed to involve an investment of £4 million as opposed to BR's £10–15 million. The main feature of the SSTHA proposal was the sorting of Cannon Street and Charing Cross trains before they reached London Bridge station, thus greatly reducing the number of conflicting movements at Borough Market Junction. Also, one track through London Bridge

[1] MOHLG (1964), pp44–6 and Table VI, p86.
[2] *Modern Railways*, March, pp156–7.
[3] *Modern Railways*, March 1966, pp156–7.

would carry reversible flows, being used by 'up' trains during the morning peak and by 'down' trains in the evening. The pre-channelling of traffic would be achieved by the construction of a new flyover at Bermondsey and two additional track connections at St Johns and Petts Wood. A 'considerable proportion' of the estimated £4 million investment would be for the replacement of signalling which was in any case due for renewal.[1] It was expected that these proposals would enable ninety-six trains per hour to be run into Cannon Street and Charing Cross compared with (at that time) sixty trains per hour, giving an estimated 36 000 extra seats per hour.

Some exchange of views took place between Mr McKenna and the co-author of this proposal, Mr J H Whittacker. SR later issued a policy document which indicated that consideration was being given to increasing the capacity of the approaches to Victoria as an alternative to improving the south-eastern approaches to Cannon Street and Charing Cross. 'This would have involved the diversion of at least the majority of services to Charing Cross from beyond Orpington to Victoria.'[2] This idea was probably influenced by the fact that the Victoria Line, which was to be opened in 1969, would make Victoria considerably more convenient as a terminal for West End destinations than previously (see page 202).

In February 1968 a meeting was held (at the invitation of SR) between the authors of the SSTHA scheme and SR's Planning Officer who made it clear that he considered the scheme too optimistic about the capabilities of Charing Cross and Cannon Street, and invited ideas for a cheaper solution to the Borough Market problem which might produce smaller gains in capacity. The SSTHA accordingly submitted some suggestions in November 1968, but these did not give rise to debate with SR as the earlier proposal had done.

In December 1968 BR announced a proposal to introduce a peak-hour surcharge of from 10 to 20% which would be used to finance £100 million investment in order to achieve reliability and punctuality on the London commuter system. Commenting on the proposal, *The Times* said that it marked a radical change in BR's thinking after years of fruitless appeals for staggered working hours. Mr Lance Ibbotson (who had succeeded Mr McKenna as SR general manager) commented that season tickets were cheaper than ordinary fares, but the commuter should pay the costs he incurs. The £100 million included new trains (£21 million), track alterations and additions (£14 million), new signalling (£5 million), and plans which were being drawn up to improve bottlenecks such as Borough Market (£60 million).[3] It is difficult to see what became of this £100 million proposal since most of the works envisaged were absorbed into later invest-

[1] P T Banford and J H Whittacker, *A Study of the Borough Market Junction Bottleneck*, SSTHA and Sevenoaks Rail Travellers' Association Joint Committee (April 1967). pp1, 2.

[2] Letter received from Sevenoaks Rail Travellers' Association, 18 October 1971.

[3] *The Times*, 12 December 1968.

ment plans, but certainly fares have increased overall since 1968, and season tickets have been more than proportionately increased. The Transport Act 1968 also brought with it the possibility of specific grants for the unremunerative London commuter services as a whole which enabled fare increases to be kept below the level that would otherwise have been required. Moreover, the criteria for capital investment in the railways through the infrastructure grants introduced by that Act have subsequently been amended to include much of the work envisaged in the £100 million programme (see page 82).

BR also pursued the concept of peak-hour pricing by introducing an experiment at Waterloo. The aim was to encourage commuters to travel outside the peak times by reimbursing part of their fare if they arrived outside the critical period, but this only succeeded in diverting 2% of travellers from the peak. It was considered a waste of money and 'light years away' from being able to make savings in operating costs. It was thought that peak pricing might be feasible on a large scale, but only if a break-even financial situation was achieved first.[1]

By the end of the 1960s, however, the regional planning context had become important in the south-eastern approaches issue because changing trends in population and employment distribution were recognised. The first signs of change came in November 1966 with a report by the SCLSERP on employment data which had just become available from the 1961 census. The report said:

> Had this census data been available when the South-East Study (1964) was prepared, significantly different conclusions about the trends in the region and proposals to meet them might have been made.

Certainly the whole picture of commuting to central London appeared in a new light:

> The employment increase in the City of London and the five central metropolitan boroughs was only 55 000 (1951–61), not 160 000 as previously estimated. There was an increase of the order of 50 000 in the City of London, while the increases and decreases in the five central boroughs more or less cancelled each other out.[2]

In 1967 the SEEPC produced *A Strategy for the South-East* which showed that the total amount of commuting to central London had been decreasing after reaching a peak in 1962. BR's share had increased to 1964 and then shown a decline (though not a steady one) to 1966.[3] The SEEPC

[1] Interview with officers of the BR Board.

[2] SCLSERP, *Population and Employment in the Conference Area*, LRP 721, 23 November 1966, p1.

[3] SEEPC (1967), *A Strategy for the South-East*, table 13, p98.

welcomed what appeared to be a slight downward trend in central London employment, which might reduce the pressures on central London, but it pointed out that: 'There may well be special factors affecting the figures over the last few years and further statistics will have to be collected before we can be sure that this is a significant trend.'[1]

Rail commuting, however, was becoming more 'peaked,' that is, concentrated into shorter periods each morning and evening. Also the reversal of the trend of growth in Greater London's resident population to one of decline,[2] and the increase of growth beyond the Green Belt meant that rail-commuting journeys to central London were getting longer. The SEEPC's strategy for future regional development envisaged a stable population for Greater London of around 8 million (the 1961–64 level) and large increases beyond the Green Belt (from 20 to 25% between 1964 and 1981). Employment growth was envisaged in the outer parts of Greater London as well as in certain areas beyond the Green Belt, but not to any great extent in central London. A better match was therefore sought in the future between homes and work places which, amongst other things, would ease the problems of tidal flow commuting. But also investment in the railways for commuters (which might have to be justified in social benefit rather than financial terms) was thought to be required. Importance was attached to plans for extensions and improvements to both the LT and BR systems, particularly in the South-Eastern Division of BR.[3]

It was not long after the SEEPC's Report appeared that a further regional study was commissioned jointly by the Government, the SCLSERP and the SEEPC. This was carried out by 'a multi-professional team provided jointly by Government departments, local planning authorities and the Planning Council, and headed by Dr Wilfred Burns, Chief Planner of the Ministry of Housing and Local Government.'[4] The report of this SEJPT was published in 1970 entitled *Strategic Plan for the South-East*. The SEJPT was in a better position to see the trends in population and employment which were only just developing at the time of the SEEPC's 1967 study.

Central London employment had increased in the decade to 1961 by 80 000 but between 1961 and 1966 it fell by 65 000 (5%). In this latter period employment in the rest of Greater London had increased by 4% (130 000).[5] The population of Greater London steadily declined over the period between 1961 and 1969 (from 7 980 400 to 7 703 400)[6] while the remainder of the South-East region experienced a steady increase (from

[1] SEEPC (1967), p48–9.

[2] The resident population of Greater London declined by 600 000 between 1951– and 1961. This trend, however, was expected to be reversed by 1981 (table A7). SEEPC (1967), p47.

[3] SEEPC (1967), pp5, 8, 13, 35, 37.

[4] SEJPT (1970), *Strategic Plan for the South-East*, pix.

[5] SEJPT (1970), p13.

[6] SEJPT (1970), p10, table 2.5. This decline continued to between 7.43 and 7.38 million by 1971 according to the preliminary results of the 1971 census.

4 517 600 to 5 253 000 in the outer metropolitan area, and from 3 847 700 to 4 338 200 in the outer South-East).

The SEJPT expected that in 1981, these trends would have created an increase in the numbers travelling to Greater London to work, but a decrease in the numbers travelling to work in central London from within Greater London. This was expected to produce overall a small decrease in the numbers arriving at the central London termini. More specific predictions were made concerning the relationship of commuting to line capacity: namely that commuting would decrease on the South-Eastern and Central divisions, would increase on the least heavily used lines (for example into Euston, Paddington and King's Cross), and would remain about the same on the Liverpool Street and Fenchurch Street services. Thus a better relation between rail commuting and rail capacity was expected in 1981 than in 1970. Looking ahead to 1991, the trend of improved commuting conditions expected by 1981 was expected to continue in both of the alternative regional strategies tested. Indeed the transport implications of the two strategies were not considered to be sufficiently different to influence the choice. Nevertheless, the SEJPT pointed to the fact that, despite increases in the number of peak-hour trains introduced on the Southern Region in 1967, considerable overcrowding remained. The problem had been aggravated by the increased peaking of commuter travel to central London which reflected the fact that manufacturing workers (who usually travel earlier) had given way to office workers.[1]

Examination of the regional situation in the late 1960s appeared, therefore, to have put the south-eastern approaches problem (and rail commuting generally) into a new perspective. If the predictions (particularly those of the SEJPT) were accepted, the problem for the future became one of providing not for more commuters to central London but for longer-distance commuting as population moved further away from the centre and the amount of commuting from the inner suburbs declined. Improvements to the south-eastern approaches could therefore be seen as providing more comfort and reliability for existing commuters rather than meeting increases in commuter demand. This was substantiated in BR's evidence to the GLDP Inquiry in 1971 (see below). There remained, however, the possibility of a further sharpening of the peak, which could undermine the effectiveness of any gains in track capacity.

This, then, was the regional context when BR's plans for improving reliability on the south-eastern section were being prepared by a project team set up by SR in 1968. The details were finalised by technical departments in discussion with operating departments of the SR during 1969. They were then approved by the SR Board before going to the BR Board who carried out a cost-benefit study. This showed, to the Board's satisfaction, that the scheme was justified purely on the time saved to commuters using the lines. The BR Board felt that to be realistic, the cost-benefit study should have used a higher value of time for rail commuters than that used

[1] SEJPT (1970), pp48–9, 54, 71.

for 'optional' road users by the DOE in justifying road schemes. But the DOE had ruled that the same value should be placed on each.

BR's close involvement in the work of the SEJPT meant that when the major part of the Transport (London) Act 1969 was implemented (in January 1970) and the GLTG was set up to co-ordinate BR, LT and GLC plans, BR had fairly firm plans for the south-eastern approaches. GLTG discussions thus began relatively late in the process but a number of schemes were discussed in the first six months of its existence.[1]

To what extent GLTG influenced the thinking and the plans of the constituent bodies is not clear, but the GLC decided to make no financial contribution to any BR scheme for the south-eastern approaches, a decision which BR felt limited the usefulness of co-ordination through GLTG. This was particularly so since the GLC were actively pursuing (with LT) the Fleet Line tube scheme, for which they were prepared to meet 25% of the cost. Although it had been thought that the Fleet Line (when extended to New Cross and Lewisham) would relieve the peak-hour problem on BR's South-Eastern Division,[2] BR themselves were sceptical of its potential in this respect (Case Study *C*). They believed that the improvement of the south-eastern approaches themselves would clear more congestion and bring a greater return (in terms of social benefit) on investment. It was thought that the Fleet Line would not make much impact on the south-eastern lines, where the distances travelled were much greater: for example, commuters were already having to stand on trains from Chatham and beyond. Moreover, although passengers might transfer to the Fleet Line on the inward journey, say at Lewisham, they would not be prepared to travel out to Lewisham in the evening rush hour to squeeze onto already filled trains.

In July 1970 the GLC considered a joint report of the Policy and Resources, Environmental Planning and Strategic Planning committees on LT's Fleet Line and Heathrow link proposals, and BR proposals for investment in the south-eastern approaches.

BR proposed three levels of investment totalling £18 million 'to provide for different patterns of train arrivals at the central London termini.' The first level, £7½ million, was for essential resignalling to enable the existing peak-hour service to be maintained, though it would also improve reliability. The second level, £3 million, was for works to enable more long-distance and less short-distance trains to be run, to meet the travel patterns expected by 1981. The works included 'track and signalling alterations to the approaches to London Bridge station, the provision of a new flyover at St Johns . . . to eliminate the present conflict of movement at Borough

[1] See *HC Debates* 25 April 1970, col1026. Reply to question by Mr Hunt MP.

[2] LT said in 1965, for example: 'If the (Fleet) line were extended to take over one of the SR suburban branches, important relief would be given to the south eastern section of SR between New Cross, Borough Market Junction and the terminals at Cannon Street and Charing Cross.' *Select Committee on the Nationalised Industries* (1965), volII, app7, para8c.

Market Junction, and additional engineering and signalling works in Kent.'[1] The third level, £7½ million, was for works to increase the number of South-Eastern Division train arrivals at Victoria.

The GLC's comments on BR's proposal give some indication of the account which had been taken (before the GLTG discussion) of the regional picture in its preparation, and of the GLC's view of the proposal in the context of the expected 1981 situation, and is therefore worth reproducing in full.

> Source and scale of traffic—When the proposals were prepared in 1969 it was estimated that the level of employment in central London would fall by 170 000 by 1981 but that additional traffic could arise from housing developments at Thamesmead and Kidbrooke. The effect of this would be to reduce the number of arrivals during the morning peak period of three hours (7 a.m. to 9.59 a.m.) from 136 000 to 110 000 passengers. Taking into account the changing make-up of employment in central London and the increasing proportion of white-collar workers, who arrive during the morning peak hour (8.15 a.m. to 9.14 a.m.), it was forecast that between 1968 and 1981 the number of passengers arriving at the main-line termini from the South-East Division during the morning peak hour would fall from 84 000 to 74 000. It was on this latter figure that the second and third levels of investment were prepared. Population and employment forecasts continue to be refined and the latest view is that, although precise new figures are not yet available, the original forecasts may have been unduly low. The population of South-East England is increasing and job opportunities are failing to match the increase. At the same time central London is facing an increasing shortage of labour. It was previously reckoned that long-distance commuting to central London would increase but that it would be offset by a greater fall in short-distance commuting. It could be that the increase in long-distance commuting will be even higher than forecast, with the result that the total number of arrivals at the central termini could be as high, or nearly as high, in 1981 as now.
>
> The figures of 84 000 and 74 000 passengers arriving during the morning peak hour are thus regarded as high and low estimates, equally credible. The number of train arrivals planned for the 1981 morning peak hour, 102, is not hard and fast and could be increased by perhaps three within the same works expenditure.
>
> Strategic planning implications—Since the proposals are but improvements to an existing facility, the planning benefits are limited but are, nevertheless, significant. They include support towards the maintenance of central London as an area of high employment whilst, in providing more attractive services from the South-East, the proposals will be of assistance to this area of higher than average unemployment. Specific benefits will be in the support of Woolwich as a strategic centre and in

[1] GLC *Minutes*, 7 July 1970, p431.

the provision of improved public transport for Kidbrooke, Thamesmead and other new riverside developments.

The Report concluded that as the council had 'no financial commitment' in the proposals its views should relate 'solely to the planning and transportation aspects.' It was felt that the proposals were in accord with the Council's 'transport strategy and its general strategy for south-east London' and as such were to be 'commended.' The Council decided to approve the Fleet Line and Heathrow link proposals and to contribute 25% of their cost, and 'subject to there being no capital commitment by the Council' to support the BR proposals.

BR's firm proposals for resignalling and track modifications on the approaches to London Bridge (i.e. the first two levels of investment discussed by the GLC in July 1970) were publicly announced in November 1970. In a report handed out to nearly a quarter of a million passengers[1] it was stated that it was *not* intended to run more trains, but to improve timekeeping (see below). The main feature of the proposals were to sort out the Charing Cross and Cannon Street trains before they reached London Bridge (see Figure 14) by the construction of a new flyover and extensive alterations to the track layout between St Johns and London Bridge. In addition, a new signal box at London Bridge to replace fifteen existing boxes would control 147 miles of track between the London termini and outer London stations.

According to the SR planning office, the origin of the firm idea of prechannelling the trains before they reached London Bridge was the project team which had been set up in 1968 to consider signalling on this section, although the concept had been put forward earlier. (It was mentioned, for example, in the long-term possibilities put forward by Mr McKenna in 1966, see page 330.) According to the SSTHA, however (renamed the Sevenoaks Rail Travellers Association in 1970), the specific proposals contained in SR's November 1970 Report were 'strikingly similar' to those set out in their letter to the SR in November 1968.[2]

The context of the proposal announced in November 1970 in terms of BR's overall investment plans for the London commuter network, and their assessment of the future prospects for population and employment distribution, were clarified in their evidence to the GLDP Inquiry published in January 1971. The BR Board had based its forward planning on data from the SEJPT: 'To whom they gave assistance on matters of rail transport.' They had also taken account of GLC forecasts for Greater London. As 'a normal commercial expedient', however, the Board 'assessed different levels of commuting as a sensitivity check on the investment programme which they believed necessary to meet the future demand.'[3] That is, the Board checked the existing rail capacity against estimated future demand

[1] BR Board *Southern Region Report No.3*, issued November 1970.
[2] Letter received from Sevenoaks Rail Travellers' Association dated 18 October 1971.
[3] BR Board (1970), *Proof of Evidence, E12/7*, p15, GLDP Inquiry Stage 1.

and also what additional investment would be required to meet any further increases in commuting. The Board summarised the broad implications of the available data as follows:

> Based on this data, the major changes in commuting in the future to 1981—which represents the general timescale of planning—are conditioned by an expected fall of between 120 000 and 170 000 in the number of jobs in central London, and a progressive effective migration of population outwards from the centre. The fall in jobs entails, other things being equal, a fall in commuting; the outward movement involves an even greater participation by the Board in commuter movement.

The Board went on to clarify its future role by saying that:

> While there is a reduction in the forecast of the numbers of commuters to central London from within the GLC area, in order to cater adequately for the additional longer-distance commuters an increase will be required in the train services provided. This is necessary since a higher quality of service with adequate seating capacity needs to be provided for the longer-distance commuter.

More specifically, it was estimated that future peak-hour loadings would require 'particular attention' to be paid to the 'relief of congestion on the rail approaches to London Bridge, Charing Cross, Cannon Street, Victoria, Waterloo and Liverpool Street stations.'[1]

In drawing up its future investment requirements for the London commuter network as a whole two separate evaluations were undertaken by the BR Board 'relating respectively to a *progressive* level and to an *intermediate* position between this higher level and the current level of investment in the area which is at the rate of about £16 million annually.' The south-eastern approaches scheme already described formed part of both these levels.

The intermediate level was seen as permitting the continued provision of existing services 'with such marginal improvements in quality as would be given in the ordinary course of replacement' whilst the progressive level was considered to produce both financial and social benefits. The south-eastern approaches scheme was unlikely to produce a significant financial return on the investment required, but, as the BR Board pointed out, a social benefit study had been applied to determine whether infrastructure grants were justified.[2] As already noted, the south-eastern approaches scheme was considered to be justified in view of the time saved by the commuters.

[1] BR Board (1971), pp16, 21–2.
[2] BR Board (1971), pp23–5.

Although the BR Board investment plans were submitted to the DOE for grant approval in the form of two alternative packages, the DOE confined its consideration (at least before the outcome of the GLDP Inquiry) to individual schemes which were considered to have a high priority. The south-eastern approaches scheme (including resignalling, track alterations and a new flyover at St Johns) turned out to be one of these and on 8 November 1971 the DOE announced its approval of a 75% grant towards the total cost which was estimated at £14 million.[1] The scheme was considered to be a major improvement to the SR rail system:

> It will help to relieve the current congestion on the south-eastern approaches to London and produce considerable improvement in the reliability of services, saving journey time for existing passengers and also relieving road congestion if commuters switch to railways. It will make room for a possible rearrangement of schedules to help overcrowding problems, particularly on the lines from Kent.

Work began almost immediately after the DOE's decision and was expected to be completed by 1976.[2]

It was clear that the scheme was not seen (or justified) as providing more commuting capacity, but as a means of improving timekeeping and comfort. An important question, therefore, was whether the scheme would be able to cope in the long-term if the population and employment forecasts made by the SEJPT and others proved to be incorrect and rail commuting to central London on the South-Eastern Division increased.

One possibility was that the new scheme, although its objective was greater reliability, could allow more trains to be run by 'overtimetabling.' This in effect would mean scheduling more trains than could be run reliably, and is a technique used, for example, by LT on the busiest sections of the District Line. The introduction of new rolling stock with power-operated doors (begun in 1972) could also help to increase capacity by cutting down the length of time spent at stations.

Large increases in capacity could not, however, be gained through these changes, and certainly not in conjunction with a high degree of reliability. In the event of increasing commuter demand on the South-Eastern section, BR thought that the 1968 plans for diverting trains from Charing Cross to Victoria could be revived. This would not in itself be without its operating problems but would probably be easier than increasing the physical capacity of the south-eastern approaches.[3]

These reserve plans, if they became necessary, would almost certainly produce protests from commuters. When the idea was first mooted by BR

[1] 1971 prices as opposed to 1969 prices used when the plans were being drawn up by BR and considered by the GLC in 1970.

[2] DOE *Press Release 347M*, 8 November 1971.

[3] Interview with BR Board officers.

in 1968, widespread concern led to the setting up of a Working Party by the Travellers Association Joint Committee, at the request of the Kent County Council, to examine its implications for commuting on the South-Eastern Division. The chairman of the Working Party was Mr J M Whittacker, co-author of the SSTHA's 1967 report on Borough Market Junction (and chairman of the Travellers' Association Joint Committee). Many bodies were represented including six urban district and borough councils in Kent, eight commuter associations, the Hayes (Kent) Village Association, the National Council on Inland Transport and the Railway Invigoration Society.[1] The report concluded that the forecast decline in central London employment by 1981 was unrealistic and that considerable investment (including the south-eastern approaches scheme) would be required to accommodate sizeable increases in rail commuting from Kent. The diversion of some Charing Cross trains to Victoria was considered to be inconvenient for the majority of those affected and would be unlikely to relieve the south-eastern approaches sufficiently to accommodate expected increases in commuting, particularly in view of the GLC's new development at Thamesmead and Kidbrooke (see Case Study *A*).

In their evidence to the GLDP Inquiry, BR also recognised that altering the terminals used by SR services would bring considerable inconvenience to passengers and operating problems.

> From the railway operating point of view, the most easily worked pattern of service would be one where the whole of the traffic from one originating area was dealt with at one London terminal, as is largely the case with Waterloo. . . . Unfortunately this ideal is difficult to attain, as there is a requirement to serve both the West End and the City from each originating area. If this were not so, many passengers would be taken to terminals much further away from their final destination in London. Quite apart from the justifiable public outcry such a policy would cause, it would place an insupportable burden on LT . . . the construction of the LT Victoria Line tube, however, has made Victoria more acceptable for a larger number of people. An increasing number of trains would, in consequence, be routed there if extra line capacity were made available, thus to some extent, equating the pressure on the terminals, but these trains would have to come from a variety of originating areas; this arrangement therefore, while enabling some increase in capacity to be given will do nothing to simplify the train operating pattern.[2]

Whether or not the south-eastern approaches scheme as approved in 1971 will secure permanent improvements in commuting conditions, then, remains a matter for further debate and the proof of the passage of time. It is clear, however, that this debate must extend far beyond the railway

[1] London Commuter Terminals Working Party, *Report on Rail Commuting To and From Kent*, June 1971, pvi.

[2] BR Board (1970), *Proof of Evidence, E12/7*, p48, GLDP Inquiry Stage 1.

operating context, and beyond the context of planning in the Greater London conurbation. The capacity and operating problems presented by bottlenecks such as Borough Market Junction figure importantly and inextricably in the question of population and employment distribution throughout South-East England.

ANALYSIS

Electrification of the Southern Railway's suburban lines in the 1930s enabled and encouraged a large increase in commuting to central London, particularly after the Second World War. But commuting increased on the South-Eastern Division to a greater extent than could comfortably be accommodated. The result was overcrowding at peak hours and, as more trains were run to meet the rising demand, unreliable timekeeping and severe operating difficulties at the Borough Market Junction bottleneck. Successive measures were effective in squeezing out the last drops of capacity but did little to improve comfort and reliability.

In July 1967, when timetabling allowed a few extra peak-hour trains to be run through Borough Market Junction, a capacity threshold appeared to have been reached which could only be overcome by expensive physical alterations. The need for major improvements had been recognised for many years, not least by the thousands of dissatisfied commuters and the railwaymen who operated the overloaded lines. But the unprofitable nature of investment required solely to ease conditions in the two short peak-periods of the day had proved a major stumbling block. The financial difficulties of BR in the post-war period and the statutory obligation to break even set by the 1962 Transport Act meant that priority was given to schemes such as the modernisation of the Kent coast lines which were capable of producing worthwhile revenue increases. Periodic appeals by BR for Government aid towards the improvement of Borough Market Junction were not successful.

Dissatisfaction with travelling conditions on the South-Eastern Division had led to the formation of several commuter associations two of whom, in 1968, prepared a plan for the improvement of Borough Market Junction. They believed that their scheme would bring a large increase in capacity and would be substantially cheaper than current BR schemes under consideration. Although BR showed an interest in these ideas, they were also considering other plans to divert trains to Victoria.

By this time, however, important changes in commuting patterns to central London were becoming clear. The SEEPC's *Strategy for the South-East*, produced in 1967, had drawn attention to the fact that commuting from the inner suburbs was declining while that from the outer suburbs and beyond Greater London was growing. Commuting to central London on BR services as a whole had shown a decline since 1964. Towards the end of the 1960s the SEJPT confirmed these trends and expected them to continue. Consequently BR, who were then developing an investment strategy for the London commuter lines, began to place more emphasis on improving reliability and comfort rather than increasing overall peak-hour capacity.

The GLC became directly involved in the question of improvements in 1970 when three levels of investment drawn up by BR were discussed by the GLTG. The scheme announced by BR in November 1970 was based on the first two levels of investment for essential resignalling and track works to enable more long-distance (and less inner-suburban) trains to be run. It was aimed at greater reliability rather than increasing overall capacity although it provided for modest gains in capacity in order to ease overcrowding on the longer-distance services. This, the GLC considered, was in accordance with both their transport strategy and general planning strategy for south-east London. The scheme held the prospect of some savings in labour costs (through signalling improvements) and BR also considered that the higher standard of service achieved would help to justify increased fares.[1] But despite these possible financial gains to BR the investment required (more than £10 million) could only be fully justified if the social benefits were taken into account. These were mainly the value of time saved by commuters and increased comfort, but an easing of the daily headache of operating so many trains through Borough Market Junction could also be regarded as a major benefit.

If the scheme was to proceed it therefore seemed likely that a substantial portion of the cost would have to be met by the community rather than the railway, i.e. through a grant from central government or the GLC rather than by BR. In the autumn of 1971 the DOE reviewed the criteria for grant aid for capital investment in public transport to include (amongst other things) new and improved track and signalling. As a result, almost the entire south-eastern approaches scheme became eligible for a 75% Government grant. BR had, by this time, submitted a social cost-benefit study which concluded that the scheme was justified in terms of time saved to commuters alone. Combined with this was the argument that the improvements were an important part of the strategy for maintaining and improving the London commuter network. The GLC supported this and added that improvements were necessary to improve living conditions in south-east London.[2]

The DOE's approval in November 1971 of a 75% grant for the scheme indicated an acceptance of its merit and high priority in social benefit terms, but approval was also made as part of a general drive to inject more money into public transport.[3]

[1] This point was made at the GLDP Inquiry, BR Board (1970), *Proof of Evidence, E12/7*, p25.

[2] See BR Board (1970), *Proof of Evidence, E12/7*, particularly pp22, 34, GLDP Inquiry Stage 1; and GLC *Minutes*, 7 July 1970, p431.

[3] Between July 1970 and December 1971 the DOE authorised £84 million in grant aid for public transport improvements estimated to cost about £125 million. At least £64 million was grant aid for the London area. DOE *Press Release 624M*, 20 December 1971.

CONCLUSIONS

The south-eastern approaches problem may be seen as one of rail operation, of transport planning and co-ordination in London and, more broadly, of regional development. From the rail operating point of view, BR's internal structure proved capable of initiating, designing and implementing the several schemes which succeeded in gaining more peak-hour capacity at Borough Market Junction. All the post-1945 schemes were implemented close to their target completion dates, which is in sharp contrast to the many road schemes in London delayed by lengthy planning and consultation procedures.

But the measures taken (such as the lengthening of trains and retimetabling) were not sufficient to eliminate peak-hour overcrowding and delays. BR were well aware that significant and permanent improvements required large-scale investment. Pressure for this came from BR's hard-pressed operating staff and from the commuters themselves who were becoming increasingly well organised and vociferous in their demands for better travelling conditions. They were represented, for example, by the SSTHA and the Sevenoaks Travellers' Association Joint Committee, who not only sought improvements but also drew up technical solutions for achieving them. The concept of pre-channelling trains through London Bridge, for example, although recognised by BR at least by 1966, was first developed into a specific scheme by the two associations. Their ideas may well have influenced the scheme finally adopted by BR.

The major if not the only problem preventing the go-ahead for major investment was lack of finance for schemes that only brought benefits during peak hours and from which there was little prospect of any large financial return to BR. Alternatives were considered such as staggered working hours and a peak-hour surcharge to spread the commuting peak, but experiments had failed to produce worth-while results. Moreover, the decline of commuting from the inner suburbs and the growth of commuting from the outer suburbs and beyond Greater London did not reduce the need for major investment.

BR's financial obligation compelled them to concentrate on profitable investment schemes unless a Government grant was forthcoming. But the fact that BR did press for grant aid on the south-eastern approaches and developed major schemes as part of its investment strategy indicated more than a purely commercial approach, and perhaps also an expectation that a grant would eventually be forthcoming.

The Transport (London) Act 1969 empowered the GLC to make grants to BR and thus introduced an alternative possible source of aid. But the GLC decided to support BR's proposals on the firm condition that no financial contribution would be made. This decision may have reflected an unwillingness to make a grant towards a project that would to a large extent benefit people living (and therefore paying rates) outside London. It was also consistent with the view, expressed on other occasions, that

Greater London funds should be devoted first to those transport sectors for which the GLC had direct administrative responsibility, namely roads and LT.

It is possible that BR derived some benefit from the GLTG discussions in as much as they clarified the future patterns of commuting, but liaison with the SEJPT had already done much in this respect. The GLTG discussions probably also enabled the GLC more fully to understand BR's operating and financial constraints, and more clearly to see the likely planning and transport implications of the proposed BR investment. But GLTG did not take any initiative by laying down its requirements or firm preferences for improvements or by suggesting alternative investment strategies.

If, as it appears, the GLC's involvement as transport planning authority through the 1969 Act did little to speed the long-awaited decision, the value of transport planning responsibilities without corresponding financial responsibilities must be open to question. But it must be remembered that BR's plans for the south-eastern approaches were already well advanced, both in terms of their design and their social and economic justification by the time the GLC became directly involved. Perhaps grant aid to BR would have been more favourably considered had the scheme been initiated and developed through GLTG. Whatever factors influenced the GLC's decision, the result was that the powers to make grants to BR under the Transport (London) Act 1969 were unused and a go-ahead for the south-eastern approaches scheme depended, as before, on a grant from central government.

The regional implications of the south-eastern approaches problem are equally important as its implications for London, and the machinery for dealing with them perhaps gives greater cause for concern. The wide residential catchment for central London workers and the 'captive' nature of the commuter travel market means that interests need to be represented on such an issue from well beyond the Greater London boundary. The Working Party on the London rail termini set up by the Sevenoaks Travellers' Association Joint Committee at the request of Kent County Council was indicative of the widespread dependence on and concern for BR policy.

The three regional studies for South-East England and especially that produced in 1970, clearly influenced BR's plans for investment in the commuter network, and for the south-eastern approaches in particular. But although the regional plans attempted to deal with the problems of the South-East as a whole, there was no statutory machinery for implementing them. BR's influence over planning decisions that might affect, for example, the distribution of population and employment, depended on the importance which the planning authorities (i.e. the GLC and the adjacent county authorities) attached to rail commuting problems. In their evidence to the GLDP Inquiry, the BR Board commented on their involvement in regional planning in the following terms:

> BR Board plan to continue the process of improving London's railways to meet the increasing and changing demands on them. By advocating appropriate planning action in the South-East they will continue to try to influence demand to areas where it can be most adequately and economically catered for.[1]

Ultimate responsibility for the co-ordination and implementation of regional policies rests with the DOE, and it could be argued that the approval of both the SEJPT regional plan and grant aid for the south-eastern approaches was an example of this responsibility being carried out. But is central control sufficiently direct to ensure that individual development decisions are consistent with broad regional policy without intricate machinery and lengthy procedures? Unless the local planning authorities act in accordance with regional plans the population and employment forecasts could easily be proved inaccurate.

The south-eastern approaches problem will probably be considerably eased by the £14 million scheme due for completion in 1976, and it may be helped in the longer term if the population and employment forecasts prove correct. Yet the uneasy feeling persists that in the absence of controls capable of balancing development with rail capacity, the commuters' captivity may become even more oppressive than hitherto. If it is considered that rail investment considerations would put regional development in a straight-jacket, it might be easier to accept the cost of improving rail commuting conditions, however unprofitable for BR itself.

[1] BR Board (1970); *Proof of Evidence, E12/7*, p22.

Case Study J

MONORAILS AND OTHER NEW SYSTEMS IN LONDON

In their Manifesto for the Greater London Council (GLC) elections in April 1967 the Conservative Party laid down six transport policies, one of which was to 'urgently study new technical solutions for improving public transport.' The Manifesto saw the situation concerning new systems thus:

> One of these (new solutions) is the new and exciting adaptation of the monorail concept for the central congested area of London. By replacing the buses by high-speed transport above the streets, road capacity is substantially increased and the way opened for a noiseless, fumeless, efficient, reliable and speedy public transport system. This is part of the modern approach to make life safer and more pleasant by keeping pedestrians separate from traffic.[1]

This document was produced at a time when ideas for new forms of transport were becoming fashionable. Indeed, some major studies were being undertaken.[2] Examples of monorails in Germany and Japan and in World Fairs and Expositions had caught sufficient attention for a clause to be inserted in the Development Plan Regulations in 1965 whereby any scheme containing a monorail proposal would be referred to the GLC.[3]

THE WATERS REPORT

The approach of *Let's Get London Moving* was directly derived from a pamphlet published immediately after the manifesto (and before the elections) by a young architect, Brian Waters, who had studied monorails in Europe and America and attempted to apply his ideas to London.[4] He claimed that of all the pressures for change, that for increasing mobility was the greatest, and that it could only be satisfied by increasing the capacity of the whole urban transport system, not just the roads alone. He believed, however, that monorails had advantages in only three situations:

[1] Conservative Central Office (1967), *Let's Get London Moving*, pp7–9.
[2] E.g. De Leuw, Cather and Partners (1967), *Manchester Rapid Transit Study*; for the San Francisco Bay Area Rapid Transit Studies see T J Lambie (1965), US Mass Transportation Projects, *Tr Eng & Control*, 7, 5.
[3] *Statutory Instrument 679*, 1965, Regulation 3.
[4] B Waters (March 1967), *Get Our Cities Moving* Conservative Political Centre pamphlet 362). He was also one of Mr Heath's transport advisers during this period.

1 Over difficult terrain.
2 When there are strong travel demands between two points which are not directly served by public transport (e.g. a city centre–airport link).
3 When surface and underground facilities have reached saturation usage and cannot substantially be developed (he gave London as an example).

He also acknowledged problems of building a fixed structure in a changing environment and problems of interchange with other systems but claimed that a monorail system 'can make an exciting contribution to the environment.' It had the important advantages of a comparatively low capital cost, rapid construction, and 'silent, fumeless operation.'[1]

When Waters came to apply his ideas to central London, he saw the monorail as the only means of providing extra transport capacity for distributing traffic within what he called the Central Congested Area (CCA), stretching from Earls Court to the Angel and Camden Town to the Elephant and Castle. He felt that the provision of four loop routes would cover the CCA enabling the majority of buses to be withdrawn to provide extra road capacity, that they would allow easy operation (each loop would be separate, avoiding switching procedures which are very complex with monorails) and could be arranged in order to complement the predominantly east–west lines of the tube system.[2]

He believed that the four loops (totalling 43 miles) could be built in five years. He recommended a suspended type of monorail (available under licence in Great Britain)[3] with three stops per mile, and estimated the total cost at £53 million (£3 million for wayside structures, £1 million per mile for beams and columns, trains, signalling and maintenance facilities, and the remainder for fees and interest charges). No allowance was made for interchange or car park facilities or for adapting existing streets and buildings to accommodate the monorail structure. He believed that eventually a first-floor level of pedestrian ways, shops and other facilities, all related to the monorail, could be created by redevelopment or adapting existing buildings.

In a foreword to this study, Mr Plummer (then leader of the GLC Opposition) said: 'By what is, in effect, lifting the buses off the street, more road space should be available and at the same time the service could be made efficient, reliable and speedy. His solution also complies with our accepted target of pedestrian separation from traffic.' He promised urgent examination of the technical and amenity aspects of central London monorails if the Conservatives were returned to County Hall.[4] A spokesman for

[1] Waters (1967), pp22–3.
[2] Waters (1967), pp25–34.
[3] The Safege system which is available in England under licence from Taylor Woodrow and English Electric Ltd. The straddle-type of monorail (Alweg) is less suitable for urban situations because it cannot negotiate tight turns.
[4] Waters (1967), p5.

Conservative Central Office said: 'If the officials say "yes" to the monorail there will be an enormous drive to get some of it up before the end of the three years. If we could have the visual symbol of a monorail running down the middle of Oxford Street, and if people found it convenient to travel in, it would really help at the next election.'[1]

THE GLC'S STUDY

After the Conservatives' victory on 13 April 1967, the monorail study was soon proceeded with. The officers' report on monorails was requested at the first council meeting on 2 May and it appeared late in June.[2] The report was described as 'a preliminary assessment' and dealt only with heavy elevated systems, namely the Safege and Alweg monorails mentioned by Waters, steel or rubber-wheeled elevated trams or trains, and the Westinghouse Expressway (an elevated guided bus system) because they were either operational or tested prototype forms. The report examined six cities in which new systems had been studied. In five of these conventional two-rail, steel and rubber-tyred systems were eventually recommended.[3] In the sixth, Seattle, a monorail had been built to link the World Fair of 1962 with the city centre, and had been retained. It was well used and businessmen operating nearby thought it good for trade, but residents disliked it from the point of view of amenity.

Realising that these results might not all have applied to London, the report tested these systems against eight criteria to establish practical problems and opportunities. The results were as follows:

(*a*) *System description*. The monorails require good clearance above all other vehicles, and thus would be suspended from portal frame structures; sites for stations and storage areas would also be needed.

(*b*) *Route coverage*. For convenience Waters's routes were examined; the bus routes it would replace were three times as dense.

(*c*) *Transport characteristics*. Compared with existing systems these would be as follows:

SYSTEM	HEADWAY	SPEED	FREQUENCY OF STOPS	IN ONE DIRECTION PASSENGER CAPACITY
Tube	2 min	29 m.p.h.	*c* 1800 ft	30 000
Bus	2 min*	8 m.p.h.	*c* 880 ft	1 800*
Monorail	2 min	15–20 m.p.h.	*c* 1800 ft	9 000

* i.e. for each group of 2–4 routes at any stop

[1] The *Guardian*, 15 April 1967.
[2] GLC Department of Highways and Transportation (1967), *Monorails In London*.
[3] In San Francisco and Manchester, the reasons were general operational, economic, and amenity advantages; in Los Angeles and Boston because they were reckoned to be cheaper; in Washington because 'its monuments, shrines and open spaces have to be preserved' (report published in October 1967).

(*d*) *Physical feasibility*. When Waters's routes were examined in detail, many problems came to light: tight radii at junctions which the route would have to negotiate, requiring demolition of property; foundation difficulties where major service pipes and cables, underground railway tunnels or pedestrian concourses were encountered; problems of passing over existing elevated railways; reduction of street or pavement capacity by supporting columns.

(*e*) *Environmental effects*. As photomontages in the report demonstrated, the elevated systems would dominate the 43 miles of streets through which they would run; they would certainly not be noiseless,[1] probably not vibration-free, would considerably reduce daylight, would invade privacy at first- and second-floor levels, and would ruin many of central London's pavement-level views.

(*f*) *Costs*. Capital and operating costs could only be hinted at without further work, but the Safege system implied expenditures of the order of from £64 to 80 million for construction, rolling stock and signalling, £8–10 million for relocating services, further unspecified large sums for about 100 stations and 9 or 10 interchanges, and £1–1.5 million annually for operations.

(*g*) *Traffic demand*. Virtually no data was available; special analysis of London Traffic Survey data and surveys of BR and bus passengers might be required.

(*h*) *Operating policy*. Fares, levels of service, relationship with parking policies and other modes of transport were not examined, but it did not seem likely that all the buses could be replaced by the coarser monorail network although some street capacity might be released for use by car and lorry traffic or pedestrians.

The report concluded[2] that because of their lack of flexibility, unproven operation, unlikely cost advantage, and great visual intrusion (particularly into London's conservation areas) the 'heavy' monorail forms were not obviously more suitable for central London distribution than existing systems;[3] only a detailed and comprehensive feasibility study could verify this, and would presuppose a 'close assessment of the pattern of demand;' some of the lighter monorail systems as yet operationally unproven might be more suitable (being cheaper to construct and less intrusive) or alternatively new technical and operational development of the buses together with possible general traffic restraint might prove as effective.

This report was considered by the Highways and Traffic Committee on 14 July 1967, and the Members' enthusiasm must have been greatly moder-

[1] Despite Mr Waters's claim that there would be no engine noise, some tyre and coupling noise would be unavoidable.

[2] GLC (1967), foreword and p39.

[3] The Manchester study established the same conclusions with regard to a suburban-cum-airport link, although the Tokyo–Haneda airport line was successful. *Municipal Review*, May 1972, pp120–1.

ated, for the outcome was that 'we have instructed the officers to report further on an investigation to obtain the information on travel demand that would be necessary for an assessment of any new means of transportation in central London and the priority to be accorded to the investigation and the provision for any new system.'

Soon afterwards Labour Opposition members raised questions in Council asking whether this implied that the idea was a gimmick, an unreality on which too much time and trouble had been spent.[1] By October there were hints of disenchantment in an answer to a question about the suitability of a German monorail that had been built at Expo '67 in Montreal and the 1965 Transport Fair at Munich: 'the success of these systems in providing a one-way circuit serving a limited number of points at a fair is no indication of equal success in central London with a very diffuse travel pattern.'[2]

The officers' assessment continued through the winter and spring of 1967–68 but was then abandoned when the Government decided to set up a Joint Transport Research Committee (JTRC) and a supporting officers' group (Transport Research Assessment Group (TRAG)). The GLC's Highways and Traffic Committee decided that although they would provide assistance no further work would be carried out at County Hall because it could provide a comparatively small contribution to the wider problem, and there was a need to curtail GLC expenditure. Individual projects in central London would provide some 'additional knowledge in connection with the Council's immediate objectives,' for instance the plans for developing Covent Garden and Piccadilly Circus.

Thus the onus of research was passed to central government, private firms and private groups (for instance the Hornsey College of Art Study Group).[3] The JTRC (representing the Ministries of Transport and Technology, the National Research and Development Corporation, BR Board and Atomic Energy Authority) pressed ahead with several projects such as the tracked hovercraft, the Speedaway pedestrian conveyer, and Cabtrack.[4] Private research into the feasibility of a light monorail system also helped to maintain interest in the application of new technology to solve central London's transport problems. Both heavy and light monorails were also suggested for the Heathrow airport–central London link,[5] but once again conventional trains have been preferred.

[1] GLC *Minutes*, 18 July 1967, pp449, 458–9.
[2] GLC *Minutes*, 24 October 1967, pp586–7.
[3] See Case Study *A*.
[4] A length of experimental track for the hovercraft was built at Earith near Cambridge (*Observer*, 22 September 1969; 20 March 1970; and 12 April 1970). The Speedaway pedestrian conveyor was being developed jointly by the NRDC, Dunlop Rubber Co and Battelle Institute of Geneva (see the *Guardian*, 22 March 1967 and 22 November 1968; *Observer*, 24 December 1967, 17 November 1968 and 22 November 1968).
[5] The former in Transport Co-ordinating Council for London studies of the Safege system (GLC *Minutes*, 7 November 1967, p638) and the latter with reference to the Urba system (GLC *Minutes*, 17 December 1968, p717).

THE MINI-RAIL

Although the GLC did not follow up the idea of investigating light monorail systems or 'mini-rails'—similar to cable cars but running on beams—a Swiss company, Habegger, produced an operational version which has been used at Expositions; and an example in Britain runs through Butlin's pleasure gardens at Blackpool. Towards the end of 1967 an independent investigation of its potential application to London appeared.[1] This was produced by an architect/planner and an engineer whose interest had been aroused by their collaboration on another project.[2] They believed that a prerequisite of environmental improvement was the segregation (i.e. removal of conflict) of through movement and local movement, and that a mini-rail to provide the latter could be built into new or existing buildings. They believed that this would bring a new coherence to the form and function of streets, which were still being redeveloped piecemeal. This latter idea was also cherished by Waters.

The mini-rails would have a much lighter column and beam structure than the 'heavy' systems studied by the GLC. They were also intended to run mainly above pavements and thus at lower headrooms (about 9 feet). They could certainly run through buildings (such as department stores and major office blocks)[3] but it is doubtful whether they would have sufficient capacity at peak times to serve the major traffic generators such as Oxford Street or major rail termini. Also, unless buses were to be withdrawn and major ground-floor shopping and entertainment displays were brought up to first-floor level, it is extremely doubtful whether any notable modification of the urban form or activities would occur.

The JTRC working through the Urban Transport Technology Group at the Royal Aeronautical Establishment at Farnborough has assessed the possibilities of using a guided cab system (Cabtrack) on a light mini-rail structure in central London. It was estimated that a two-way network at 550-yard intervals, with 240 stations (which would mean an average walk of about 190 yards) would cost £210 million to build. It was admitted, however, that considerable amenity problems were involved,[4] and in 1971 it was decided not to build a test track.

The draft proposals for the redevelopment of Covent Garden and the developers' brief for Piccadilly Circus both left open the possibility of

[1] D Wager and W Frischmann, *West End Mini-Rail* (report published by Construction Publications Ltd, December 1967). See also an article in *The Consulting Engineer*, 1 January 1968.

[2] David Wager had worked for the London borough of Haringey and conceived the idea of linking the Alexandra Palace recreation centre (then projected by the GLC) with a redeveloped Wood Green town centre (and perhaps ultimately with the Lee Valley Regional Park and Hampstead Heath); Wilem Frischmann had undertaken structural engineering consultancy work on this project.

[3] As they did in pavilions at Expo '67 in Montreal and Expo '70 at Osaka.

[4] The *Guardian*, 27 August 1970; and GLC Department of Planning and Transportation *Research Memo 156*, May 1969.

including a new movement system, and the Director of TRAG became interested. A Working Party involving officers of the GLC, the Covent Garden Joint Development Team and Westminster City Council was set up, with assistance from London Transport (LT) and the Institute of Transport. It reported in 1971 after two years' work.[1]

The Working Party believed that there was a gap between walking and the current forms of vehicular transport and attempted to design a system to fill the gap. This turned out to be an automatic small-cab system working on short headways and short stops, automatically guided along an elevated network of tracks. They believed that the system could be operational in ten years, initially running through newly developed areas, but that penetration into existing urban fabric, much of which was designated as conservation areas, would be more difficult.

A system of $5\frac{1}{2}$ miles of track would cost from £4.7 to 6.1 million depending on whether it was implemented as a supplementary mode of travel or more as a replacement for the bus services. Its working deficit would lie between £60 000 and £150 000 in these cases but after considering resulting financial losses to LT's existing services the net annual loss would be from £500 000 to £560 000. In addition, interest charges of from £470 000 to £610 000 would be payable. Thus the system would only be viable with both an infrastructure (capital) grant and an operating subsidy, and 'its realisation would need to be founded on its contribution to broader planning problems' (paragraph 1.1.11).

Although the members of the Working Party served as individuals, the fact remains that officers of central, metropolitan and local government met to develop new ideas about the design and operation of novel urban transport systems.

CONCLUSIONS

The Conservatives' interest in, and enthusiasm for, monorails as an example of a new form of transport foundered upon realisation of the problems of technical operation, of interchange with existing systems, of cost and of amenity. New systems appeared to be attractive because of their very novelty and because they were attributed with greater speed, cleanliness and greater comfort than existing means of transport, but these assumptions were made without operational experience. The Conservatives, however, continued to be attracted by new systems and introduced an experimental hydrofoil service on the Thames between Greenwich and Tower Pier during 1972. Also, Peter Walker expressed the view that Government would 'tend to grow particularly active when the pace of technical development is so swift that the market by itself is unable to respond sufficiently forcefully' and instanced the preparation of roads for guidance systems for electric cars.[2]

[1] Westminster City Council for the Working Party (1971), *An Aid to Pedestrian Movement.*

[2] P Walker (1968) *Transport Policy* (Conservative Political Centre No. 403) pp5–6.

The reality of the monorail's practical problems and attendant costs in the London situation came rapidly to GLC members, but the interest shown in later developments indicated a continuing belief that these problems could be overcome. The appeal of new systems may well have been linked with a feeling of helplessness at the apparently intractable problems of improving bus and rail services.

The GLC's officers, and the transport operators, were at once more aware of these problems and more sceptical about new systems (see Case Study *A*). This may help to explain the extended period over which the travel demand was assessed and the feeling of relief generated by the committee report which recommended that the onus should remain with central government. Interest continued in Cabtrack and the Westminster system but as transport policy broadened, the role visualised for new systems diminished.[1]

A choice has to be made, however, about the share of resources devoted to adapting and improving existing systems of transport and that committed to developing new ones. Throughout the world, governments have been loth to spend money in large quantities on transport research: one of Peter Walker's own Ministers complained in 1970 of Britain's record in this respect.[2] Indeed, successive Ministers of Transport have been blamed for failing to support ventures such as hovercraft, hydrofoils, and rotary internal combustion engines. Projects are often researched too slowly and on too meagre a scale, or not implemented experimentally. Yet a change of policy and the application of research on a similar scale to that devoted to new weapons, new aeroplanes or nuclear power applications could probably verify the technical, economic and environmental feasibility of new forms of urban transport within a very few years. Any contribution to the transport problems of the world's greatest urban areas would be a boon indeed, yet for instance in 1970 only 0.7% of British public-sector research was devoted to transport.[3] This does not seem consonant with the scale of the problems or the possible returns from a successful solution. Indeed, in 1972, one of the British study groups for the United Nations Conference on the Human Environment reported:

> The implication from our evidence is that the balance which appears to have been in favour of road transport is changing rapidly . . . it would imply . . . the development without preconceived prejudices, of fixed-track systems . . . there is growing concern to adjust transport patterns in favour of more efficient modes. The Government must urgently re-examine its transport philosophy.[4]

[1] See GLC (1971), *Paper 487, Public Transport Alternatives*, GLDP Inquiry Stage 1.
[2] Mr John Peyton at the Institute of Transport, Minister of Transport *Press Release 604*, 4 November 1970.
[3] While transport represents 11% of annual capital investment, Ministry of Transport *Press Release 604*, 4 November 1970.
[4] *Sinews for Survival* (HMSO), paras175–6.

The GLC has preferred to broaden the front of its transport policy to take in the restraint of road traffic, improvements for bus operation and the extension of the tube system. The first two of these policies included an experimental scheme to close Oxford Street to general traffic, allowing only buses and taxis to use the carriageway, thus making the street more pleasant for pedestrians for whom the pavements were widened.[1] This was a very long step from the idea, held by the same party in control at County Hall five years earlier, of the 'visual symbol of a monorail running down the middle of Oxford Street.'

[1] GLC *Minutes*, 4 July 1972, p327.

Case Study K

THE A1 ROAD IN LONDON

INTRODUCTION

Any view of London's transport system, and any system of government devised to manage and improve it, must recognise the extremely important role of the city's main roads. These, broadly speaking, are the roads which by accident or design have developed as part of the city's fabric and become established as the major carriers of vehicular traffic. More precise definition of what constitutes a main road is not easy, however, and various criteria could be used varying from the volume of traffic carried to its physical design or even appearance. Moreover, the majority of main roads in London serve many other functions apart from enabling traffic to pass through. They often have residential, commercial and other uses fronting onto them and have numerous connections to other streets, all of which gives rise to intense activity of local vehicular and pedestrian traffic.

In 1965 responsibility for London's main roads was divided between the Ministry of Transport (MOT), the Greater London Council (GLC) and the borough councils. The establishment of three types of highway authority control did not mean, of course, the establishment of three separate networks of roads. All roads are linked to one another, and traffic pays no heed to demarcation lines of administrative responsibility. Consequently, for major schemes of improvement, management or even maintenance, there is an inescapable need for co-ordination between the authorities responsible for adjacent sections of road. The extent of co-ordination required will, moreover, depend on the extent to which traffic crosses administrative boundaries.

As a continuous route subject to all three types of control, the A1 between the North Circular Road and the City of London provides a suitable subject for a study of the co-ordination process (see Figure 16). The choice of the A1 was also influenced by the fact that firm proposals were currently being handled by the new system of London government.

In addition to the question of co-ordination of the road's traffic function, the A1 provides an opportunity to examine the way in which the road has been seen as part of the total transport system and as part of the communities through which it passes. The multiple functions of the A1, as with the majority of London's main roads, inevitably creates conflicts of interest between the pedestrian, the resident, the shopkeeper, the lorry

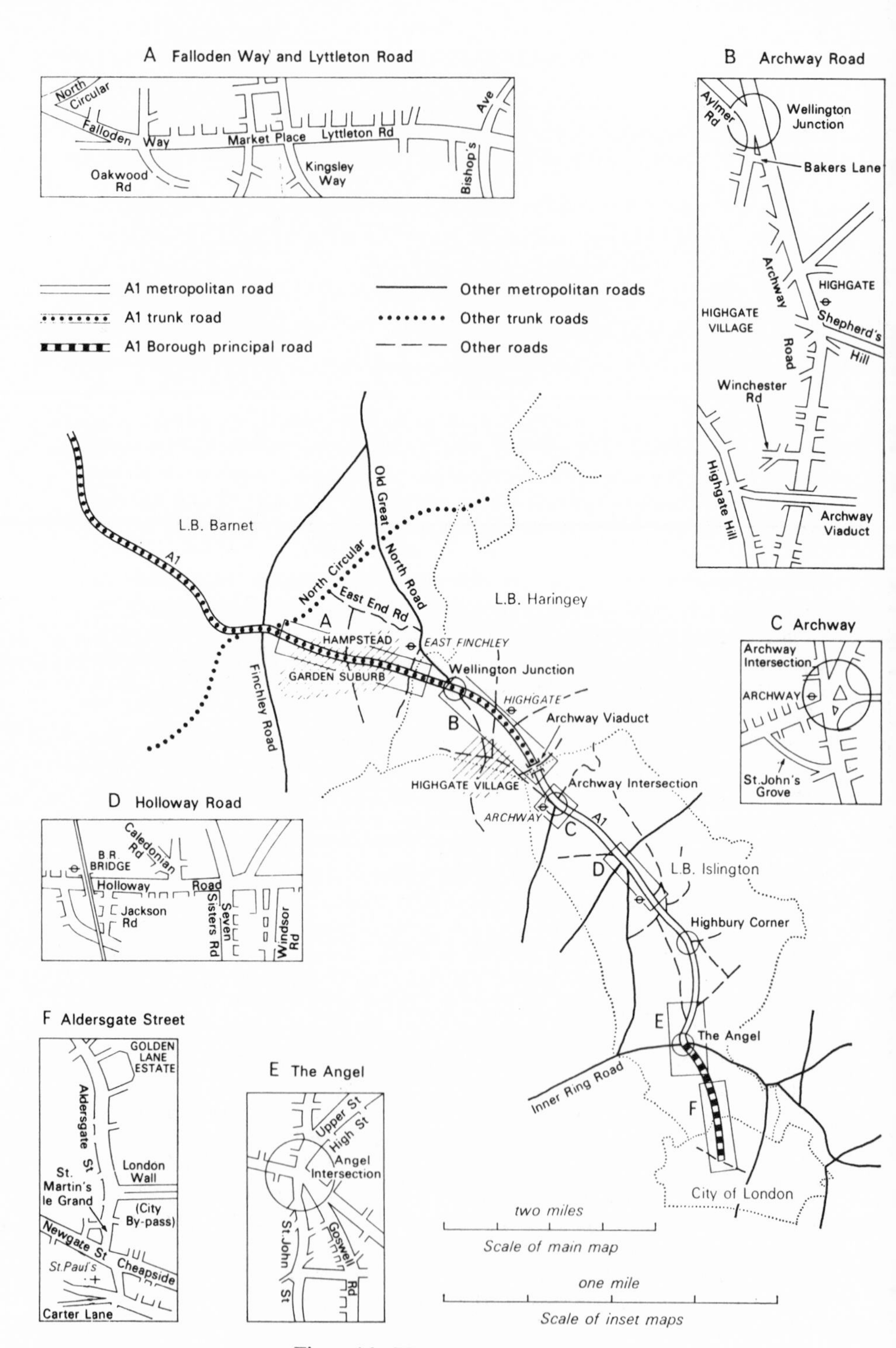

Figure 16 THE A1 IN LONDON

driver, the motorist and others. The effectiveness of the organisational system will therefore depend to a large degree on whether it takes account of and fairly represents these widely differing and often conflicting interests.

The case study is divided into sections, each dealing with various proposals to improve the A1 for traffic between its junction with the North Circular Road and Cheapside. The sections are:

1 *North Circular to Wellington Junction* which comprises Falloden Way, Lyttleton Road and Aylmer Road.
2 *Archway Road* including Wellington Junction, and the Archway Road itself from this junction to the Archway viaduct (which marks the limit of the Department of the Environment (DOE) responsibility and is the Haringey–Islington borough boundary).
3 *Archway to the Angel* which includes that part of the Archway Road from the Archway viaduct to the Archway intersection, the intersection itself, the road south of there to the Angel (Holloway Road, Highbury Corner, Upper Street and Islington High Street), and the Angel intersection itself.
4 *The Angel to St Paul's* which includes Goswell Road, Aldersgate Street and St Martin's Le Grand.

This whole length of the A1 in London has never been the subject of any single detailed proposal for wholesale widening or other works. Nor has it in recent years been regarded as a major artery in the same sense as some of the other radial roads into the centre of London (such as the Western or Eastern Avenues). But it has the historic significance of being the Great North Road and, like many of the main radial roads (e.g. A2, A3, A4, A5) it has some coherence as a route (even if only that afforded by signposting). The danger must be avoided, nevertheless, of regarding a numbered route as an entity which is clearly distinguished either in appearance or function from the whole road network of which it forms a part. We shall be concerned with the extent to which this may be true in the case of the A1, but it is not the reason for selecting the A1 for this case study.

As a background to the study Table 24 lists the more important road plans in London since 1900 and the place each has given to the A1 in the total road network. The bodies involved in the A1 at present are as follows.

The Department of the Environment

The DOE incorporates the former MOT and is similarly responsible as highway authority for the 'national' system of Trunk roads and motorways, which includes the A1 into London as far as the boundary between the boroughs of Islington and Haringey at Archway bridge (the former London County Council (LCC) boundary, see Figure 16). The DOE can

	PLAN	REFERENCE
1	*Report of the London Traffic Branch of the Board of Trade* (HMSO 1910)	Shown on plan as main route throughout (old A1 north of Wellington Junction)
2	*Arterial Roads in Greater London* (Annual Reports on the administration of the Road Improvement Fund, MOT; HMSO 1923, 1924)	Showed 17-mile Barnet By-Pass (now A1) as a 'contemplated extension.' Remainder of A1 route shown as an existing main road as far as the Angel
3	*Greater London Regional Planning Committee Second Report* (1933)	Included in main road network but no proposals for improvement
4	*Highway Development Survey (Greater London)* (HMSO 1937, Bressey Plan)	Barnet By-Pass shown as an 'existing arterial road.' South of Wellington Junction A1 shown as a Principal route into central London (along with nine others). Many proposals for improvement of roads in inner London but none on A1
5	*The County of London Plan* (Foreshaw and Abercrombie, prepared for LCC, 1943)	Shows A1 in LCC area as no more than subarterial status. (Compared with nine other main routes into London, several of which penetrated to central London)
6	*Administrative County of London Development Plan* (LCC 1951)	*20-year improvement programme:* Shows A1 as principal traffic route and Highbury Corner and Angel intersections as priorities for improvement. '*Ultimate*' *Road Plan* shows A1 as far as Angel as 'main radial route' and lists Highbury Corner, Angel and terminal intersection with Cheapside as priorities for improvement
7	*Middlesex County Initial Development Plan* (approved) (1956)	Widening shown diagrammatically North Circular to LCC boundary (Archway). Widening safeguarded from this time
8	*LCC Development Plan* (approved) (1955)	Widening shown diagrammatically from LCC boundary (Archway) to Archway intersection and safeguarded from this time
9	*Report of the Committee on London Roads* (Cmnd 812, HMSO 1959, The Nugent Committee)	Shows A1 as main traffic route, Angel and Cheapside junctions and link from Cheapside to Carter Lane included in both £120 million and £200 million 20-year programmes for improvement

10 *London Traffic Survey* VolII (GLC 1966)	*'1981A' Road Plan* shows present A1 route as far as Highbury Corner as 'high-class road' and remainder to Carter Lane as 'Trunk or Principal' route *'1981B' Road Plan*, A1 from North Circular to Archway (including Archway intersection) for improvements; Holloway Road sections near junctions with Seven Sisters Road and Caledonian Road—for improvement. Angel intersection for improvement
11 *Greater London Development Plan* (GLC 1969)	A1 from North Circular to Cheapside shown as secondary road

Table 24 REFERENCES TO THE PRESENT A1 ROUTE IN VARIOUS LONDON PLANS AND REPORTS FROM 1900

Sources: GLC (1970) *Research Report No.11. London Road Plans, 1900–1970;* and DOE (1971) *Paper B636*, GLDP Inquiry Stage 1

appoint either the borough councils or the GLC as agents for carrying out highway works and maintenance. The DOE pays 100% of the cost of any Trunk road work including a commission for work undertaken on an agency basis by a local authority.

The remaining section of the A1 from Archway bridge to Cheapside is a Principal road for which the DOE pays 75% grant for any schemes excluding maintenance. All schemes on the A1 thus require the approval of the the DOE.[1]

The Greater London Council

The section of the A1 from Archway bridge to the Angel intersection with the Inner Ring Route is a Metropolitan road, for which the GLC is the highway authority. The borough council (Islington) may undertake work on an agency basis for the GLC, or the GLC has the power to carry a scheme through to implementation itself.

As traffic authority for London the GLC is responsible for traffic control and regulation on all roads including, with the Minister's consent, Trunk roads. The GLC also has the power of direction over planning applications concerning land adjoining Metropolitan roads, with the purpose of attempt-

[1] Unless, of course, the local authority wished to meet the entire cost of a Principal road scheme itself. This is unlikely to occur but not impossible. For example the new London Bridge was paid for entirely from the funds of the Bridge House Estates Trust, despite being the carrier of a Principal road.

ing to plan new developments consistent with future road and traffic plans as far as access and traffic generation are concerned.[1] The GLC's fundamental planning function is as strategic planning authority for Greater London.

The GLC had to pay particular regard to London's future road system in drawing up the Greater London Development Plan (GLDP) for London[2] and must pursue policies aimed at providing 'integrated, efficient and economic transport facilities and services for London.'[3]

The borough councils

The boroughs of Barnet, Haringey and Islington may each become involved as agents for the DOE or the GLC in the designing or implementation of schemes on the A1 road or its maintenance. The boroughs are also the local planning and highway authorities for other than Trunk or Metropolitan roads ajoining the A1 and have a statutory right to consultation by both the DOE and the GLC before any works of improvement are carried out on the A1 in their areas.

Islington Borough Council is highway authority for the A1 south of the Angel to the borough boundary and the City of London is the highway authority for the remaining section to Cheapside, though schemes on these sections require the approval of the GLC and the DOE for grant purposes.

The police and London Transport

The statutory consultation procedures extend to both the police and London Transport (LT) as traffic regulation enforcement and bus operating bodies respectively, and also to the statutory undertakers (such as the London Electricity Board and the General Post Office) whose services are located beneath or near the road.

1 THE NORTH CIRCULAR ROAD TO WELLINGTON JUNCTION

The present A1 road north of Wellington Junction to the Greater London boundary and beyond to South Mimms was originally known (and constructed) as the Barnet By-Pass. It was built during the 1920s to relieve the old Great North Road of traffic and to provide a by-pass route for the shopping and residential areas of East Finchley, North Finchley, Whetstone and Barnet, through which the Great North Road passed. The 1¾-mile section of the Barnet By-Pass from where it joins the Great North Road at Wellington Junction to the North Circular Road was designated

[1] A corridor of land 220 feet either side of the centre of each Metropolitan road. *London Government Act 1963*, ch33, 24 (6). (See possible amendments to this provision described on page 109).

[2] *London Government Act 1963*, ch33, s25 (3).

[3] *Transport (London) Act 1969*, ch35, s1.

as a Trunk road in the Trunk Roads Act, 1936. Prior to that date there were no Trunk roads. The route was known as the Barnet By-Pass and was numbered A555 until 1953 when it was renumbered A1 and the old Great North Road became the A1000.[1] This section is taken for the purposes of this study as representative of the Trunk road portion of the A1 in London.[2]

It was completed in 1928, by which time the majority of Hampstead Garden Suburb was developed both to the north and to the south, and was envisaged by Sir Raymond Unwin (the Garden Suburb's architect) as a 'good through road' linking the Finchley and Great North roads, and he planned it as part of the second major phase of the Suburb—the part now adjoining the road to the north.[3] The MOT had acquired land fronting Falloden Way during the 1920s for future widening purposes.

The road in 1971 was largely as it was originally built in the 1920s, but the volume of traffic which it carried was considerably greater than was originally expected. Apart from some piecemeal widening[4] the road was still predominantly a 30-foot carriageway width. In 1968 this section was overloaded[5] by as much as 70% during the morning peak hour,[6] but this fact is only one illustration of the traffic problem which had been developing since the road was constructed. The MOT, whose duty it had been since 1936 to safeguard the free flow and safety of traffic on the national system of Trunk roads, from an early date was thinking of widening the road to take increased volumes of traffic.

Formal announcement of the intention to widen the road came with the publication of the first Middlesex County Development Plan in 1956 which showed the widening proposal diagrammatically. A similar provision was made in the first quinquennial review of that plan which was published in 1963 and approved in 1965. There were no objections to the widening of the A1 in either case, but nor were there any detailed design proposals.

In 1962 Mr Ernest Marples (then Minister of Transport) put forward the idea of a 'lorry route' from the M1 in north-west London to the London docks of which much of the A1 formed a part.

By 1965 the Hampstead Garden Suburb residents (who were, by and large, both wealthy and articulate) were becoming aware of the possible threat posed to their environment by the proposed widening. Although there existed a very strong Residents' Association for the Garden Suburb,

[1] Information from DOE. Letter dated 31 December 1971.

[2] North of the North Circular Road there are no further London boroughs involved and the road is built to a varying but generally high standard for traffic.

[3] Inspector's report on Falloden Way Inquiry, 16 September–20 October 1969, MOT 1969 (unpublished).

[4] E.g. the extreme eastern portion was widened to a four-lane dual carriageway in 1956–57 by the former Hornsey Borough Council as agents for the MOT. Information from DOE in letter dated 31 December 1971.

[5] According to criteria set down in the MOT handbook *Roads in Urban Areas*, HMSO 1966.

[6] Inspector's report, MOT 1969 (see page 363).

people directly affected (i.e. those living alongside the A1) became dissatisfied with its efforts on this particular issue. Consequently a new group was formed by local traders, individuals and local tenant associations as well as the Residents' Association called the Hampstead Garden Suburb Lorry Route Joint Action Committee. A member of the Residents' Association was appointed as its chairman.

After vociferous opposition, both from the Action Committee and from Highgate residents, the lorry route proposal was dropped, but the Ministry's intention to widen the A1 for general traffic purposes remained. The preparation of the detailed scheme for Falloden Way–Aylmer Road was begun by the former Middlesex County Council in 1959 and was continued by the GLC, both authorities acting as agents for the MOT.

The GLC's scheme was published in November 1966 and provided for the widening to dual three-lane standard the entire section of the road from Wellington Junction to the North Circular. Most of it could be implemented using land that was already part of the highway, i.e. the existing very wide verges and footpaths. The exception to this was a $\frac{1}{4}$-mile length between Oakwood Road and Market Place where frontage residential properties lay much closer to the existing carriageway. The scheme involved cutting back the front gardens of these properties to accommodate the wider carriageway and realigned footpaths. The scheme also involved the loss of trees which lined the road for much of its length and would have had a severe effect on the Market Place where the wide pavements would become very narrow, particularly if separate bus lay-bys were to be retained.

The necessary MOT compulsory purchase orders together with two side-roads orders, although concerned with a small part of the total scheme, became the focus for wide-ranging objections to it. The public inquiry into the orders which was held in the autumn of 1969 thus turned out to be a somewhat lengthy examination of the Ministry's case for the whole widening scheme.[1] Most of the opposition was united under the Lorry Route Joint Action Committee who raised a considerable sum of money[2] both to prepare evidence and to engage a QC to present their case. Opposition was mainly confined to the environmental effects of the widening scheme, which would have brought the carriageway to within 13 feet of some of the homes fronting onto the road. The Action Committee was also concerned about the run-down of shopping in the Market Place which they believed to be largely due to heavy traffic.[3] The objectors' case was strengthened by the fact that the whole of the Garden Suburb had been

[1] The objectors were notified of the Minister's decision to hold an inquiry 20 months before it began on 16 September 1969. It lasted for three weeks.

[2] Reported as about £7000, The *Guardian*, 24 February 1971. The Committee hired an engineer, Professor Christie, as expert witness. They had hoped to engage Professor Colin Buchanan who had to decline because of his commitments as consultant to the GLC.

[3] Later on, for example, both Boots and Woolworth closed their stores in the Market Place.

designated a Conservation Area by Barnet Borough Council.[1] Barnet Council itself had no broad objections to the scheme, but urged the Minister to consider the amenities of the area before making his decision. Haringey on the other hand (in whose area a tiny part of the scheme in question fell) argued at the inquiry that a decision to go ahead with the widening of Falloden Way would prejudice the outcome of the study then being undertaken on the Archway Road (see page 369).

The inspector at the inquiry, Mr G S McIntyre, was more impressed with the Ministry's case for the widening scheme than with the objectors' arguments against it and therefore recommended that the Minister should make the necessary orders. He argued that Unwin's through road was simply being brought up to date within limits which the Garden Suburb authorities had approved nearly fifty years earlier. He was satisfied that the scheme was sound on planning grounds because one of the Middlesex County Council's former planning officers had given evidence in support of it on behalf of the GLC. He thought that since the scheme was included in the approved development plans, and the GLC as the 'appropriate planning authority' supported the scheme, the National Trust[2] had no cause for concern about the 'architectural integrity' of the suburb.

Shortly after the inquiry was concluded, the former Ministries of Housing and Local Government and Transport were merged into the DOE. Peter Walker, who was appointed first Secretary of State for the Environment, thus had to make a decision which otherwise would have fallen to the Minister of Transport. The merging of the two Ministries reflected an awareness of the inseparability of transport planning from land use and regional planning and also of the need to take full account of the environmental effects of a scheme. It was the environmental considerations with which Peter Walker was particularly concerned in this case and which led him to reject this inspector's recommendations. Nevertheless, he was 'also aware of his statutory responsibilities to keep under review the national system of routes for through traffic and improve that system as he may consider necessary for the safety and convenience of all road users.'[3]

The time lag between the inquiry and Mr Walker's decision (sixteen months) perhaps reflected the difficulty in reconciling his two apparently conflicting responsibilities. But there was a further difficulty in that the Lorry Route Committee had complained that the inquiry had not been conducted in an impartial manner. The DOE (according to the Committee) had been very anxious that justice should be seen to be done, and this meant that Mr Walker's decision would have to be broadly acceptable to the

[1] Under the *Civic Amenities Act 1967*, ch69, s1. The council also set up a Hampstead Garden Suburb Conservation Area Advisory Committee.

[2] NB. The reference in the Inspector's report to the 'National Trust' may have been an error, probably in place of the 'Hampstead Garden Suburb Trust' which has continuing responsibility for the protection and development of the suburb. The Trust contributed a considerable sum for the objectors' case to be fully represented at the inquiry.

[3] Letter from DOE to objectors, borough councils and others involved in the inquiry dated 25 February 1971.

objectors. Outright acceptance of the inspector's recommendation to approve the orders would clearly not have met the Committee's charge of partiality while a new inquiry would have been expensive and likely to discredit both the DOE and the inspector.

Mr Walker's decision, announced in February 1971, seemed to both reconcile the conflicting environmental and traffic interests and to avoid further criticism of the inquiry.[1] He refused to approve the orders and decided that further study was necessary. He was careful to point out, however, that this did not necessarily mean the end of any widening proposals, as this further extract from the letter quoted above shows:

> The Secretary of State . . . wishes to ensure that any adverse effect of the degree that would arise with the proposed scheme on property closely adjoining the road would be incurred only if there is no other way to deal adequately with the traffic needs of this length of road and which will not at the same time create still greater problems. The Secretary of State is not yet satisfied in this respect and has accordingly decided that it would be wrong to proceed at present with the improvements as planned; he proposes instead to have further investigations made.

Shortly after this decision, the DOE took two further steps. The first was to appoint Barnet Borough Council (who had acted already as agents for maintenance of the road) as agents to carry out *short-term* improvements within the existing highway limits. Thus a direct result of Mr Walker's decision was increased involvement of Barnet Borough in the process of improving the A1 for traffic. The second was to ask a firm of private consultants, who had by that time completed a study of the Archway Road in Haringey, to carry out an appraisal of the *long-term* possibilities.

In November 1971, nine months after Mr Walker's decision, Barnet Borough Council approved a scheme for the 'immediate improvement' of the Aylmer Road–Falloden Way section which had been prepared by the Borough Engineer's Department after consultations with the DOE and their consultants. In January 1972 Mr Peyton (Minister for Transport Industries) announced that he had accepted Barnet council's proposals and that the work (estimated to cost about £1 million) would start in the spring of 1972 with the Borough acting as agents for the DOE.[2]

In drawing up the scheme, the Borough Engineer's Department had considered the urgent need for repairs to the road, whose foundations and surface were breaking up under the pressure of heavy traffic. It was felt that reconstruction of the road to its existing width was inappropriate partly because three-lane main roads had become widely regarded as dangerous and partly because any eventual provision of dual carriageways would

[1] He also decided to allow certain of the objectors to claim costs incurred at the inquiry by an adjournment which had been made by the inspector because of the intervention of other commitments before the completion of the inquiry proceedings.

[2] DOE *Press Release*, 25 January 1972.

involve further reconstruction of the road base.[1] The approved scheme included the strengthening of the carriageway and widening from three to four lanes, except on the narrow Falloden Way length which was to be marked out to provide two westbound lanes and one eastbound lane. Occasional lay-bys were to be provided to allow access and parking along the whole of the widened section.

Three signal-controlled intersections (with Northway, Kingsley Way and The Bishop's Avenue) would be further widened to give three lanes entering the junction and two lanes leaving, thus allowing a separate lane for right-turning traffic. New pedestrian crossings were included at these intersections. The new four-lane road would not have a continuous dividing barrier but central islands were to be provided at intervals. This was thought to make it easier for pedestrians to cross and also less visually disruptive. Most of the existing trees would be retained, though some would be lost at the widened intersections.

The Joint Action Committee (which had decided to remain in being until the whole question was resolved) were opposed to this scheme, partly because they believed it would attract more unwanted traffic but also because it prejudiced the long-term decision on the width and design of the road through the Garden Suburb.

Criticism was also levelled at the Hampstead Garden Suburb Trust 'for failing to grasp the A1 nettle' by a member of Barnet Council's Conservation Area Advisory Committee, Mr Maurice Pickering. The Trust had commissioned a planning study for the future of the Suburb from Shankland Cox and Associates from which consideration of the A1 routing was excluded. Mr Pickering believed it was 'plain to everyone that the A1 needs rerouting.' He envisaged a dual carriageway following East End Road from East Finchley station to the North Circular.[2] The Borough Planning Officer and his Committee, however, expressed no major objections to the Engineer's scheme. The Council itself had had no strong views either way about the widening of the route as a whole either before, during or after the public inquiry. They were reluctant to see the A1 causing any further environmental disruption of the Garden Suburb, but on the other hand could see no alternative to the A1 passing through the middle of it. The Ministry's role of maintaining the 'national' road system was appreciated and the location of ultimate responsibility with the Minister was accepted.[3]

[1] Interviews with Barnet Borough Engineer's Department officers.

[2] *Building Design*, 7 January 1972. Shankland Cox and Associates had previously asserted (in November 1970) that widening to dual two-lane carriageways, possibly in cutting, was the maximum compatible with conservation of the suburb. They had come under strong attack at a public meeting from the Joint Action Committee who felt this was prejudicial to the Minister's decision on the public inquiry. *The Times*, 12 November 1970.

[3] In its evidence to the GLDP Inquiry on secondary roads, Barnet Council said that in its view the A1 should remain primarily a traffic route and that future redevelopment must have regard to this predominant function. *Proof of Evidence, E12/16*, p2, GLDP Inquiry Stage 1.

Both Barnet Council and the local pressure groups had studied possible alternative schemes to alleviate the environmental conflict, including putting the road into a tunnel through the Suburb itself. These were discussed at the inquiry but rejected either because of cost (in the case of the tunnel idea)[1] or because their effect would be simply to shift the environmental problems elsewhere. To those involved, this was one of the most baffling aspects of Mr Walker's decision on the inquiry: what alternatives were there left to consider which could produce a more satisfactory long-term result?

The task of finding out became the job, in September 1971, of the engineering and planning Consultants[2] appointed by the DOE. Although at the time of writing no results of this study were available, one alternative in particular to further wholesale widening was expected to be examined, namely the possibility of gaining extra traffic capacity by the widening of intersections only. GLC evidence to the GLDP Inquiry suggested that 'improvements' to the 'secondary network' of roads (of which the A1 formed part) should be concentrated at intersections and in town centres.[3] This shifting of emphasis away from widening whole lengths of road seemed likely also to prompt a re-examination of the Consultants' study (completed in 1969) on the widening scheme for the adjoining Archway Road, to which we now turn our attention.

2 ARCHWAY ROAD

The Archway Road like the Falloden Way (Barnet By-Pass) section of the A1 was itself originally built as a by-pass (to Highgate village). That was in 1830, however, and development rapidly spread along either side of the new road. From the early 1920s to the 1960s various tentative proposals were put forward for widening the carriageway to accommodate the steadily increasing volume of traffic. With the more rapid growth of road traffic in the 1950s the need for action seemed more urgent.

In 1962 as part of his proposed 'lorry route' from the M1 to the docks, Mr Ernest Marples announced a scheme for routing A1 traffic southbound along Archway Road and northbound up Highgate Hill and through Highgate village. This had also been suggested by a local group, the Archway Road Association, as a means of avoiding the need to widen Archway Road itself.[4] But the proposal produced a great outcry from Highgate residents in the form of the Save Highgate Campaign. The LCC, while supporting in principle the idea of a signposted lorry route with 'clearway'

[1] The GLC estimated that the cost of putting the road in tunnel would be up to £24 million, compared with the £1.5 million MOT scheme. The *Guardian* 21 September 1969.

[2] Messrs Scott, Wilson, Kirkpatrick and Partners, Consulting Engineers in association with Messrs Hugh Wilson and Lewis Womersley, Planning Consultants. *DOE Press Notice 100M*, 7 September 1971.

[3] See particularly GLC *Papers B387* (1970); and *B463* (1971), GLDP Inquiry Stage 1.

[4] LCC *Minutes*, 3 November 1972, p881.

restrictions, were also concerned about the use of Highgate Hill for heavy traffic. They recommended that the scheme should be postponed until more detailed information became available from the London Traffic Survey (LTS) which was being mounted at the time. In May 1963 the LCC reported that advance information from the LTS showed that the volume of A1 traffic to the docks was 'relatively small'[1] and as already noted, the lorry route plan was eventually dropped.

From 1962 onwards the Archway Road and other sections of the A1 became the subject of piecemeal schemes aimed at increasing its traffic-carrying capacity. The A1 and its traffic were repeatedly the subject of debate and attention. For example, in November 1965 LT suggested the Holloway Road–Archway Road as a priority for the urban clearway programme[2] and in the same month Sir Graham Rowlandson asked a question at a GLC meeting about a traffic jam which had held up his car in Holloway Road and about measures the Council were taking to solve the congestion problem.[3]

One measure which the GLC took was designed to 'ease the flow of traffic and improve safety for drivers and pedestrians at the busy junction of the A1 and A1000 at the Wellington Hotel.' They introduced an experimental traffic management scheme in February 1966 which provided for a one-way flow of traffic along Bakers Lane (see Figure 16) thus in effect turning the junction into a triangular-shaped roundabout of which The Wellington hotel formed the central island. Haringey Borough Council undertook the work as agents for the GLC.[4]

Other schemes planned for the A1 south of the Archway viaduct are dealt with later; the remainder of this section concentrates on the widening proposals between the Wellington Junction (subject to the scheme just discussed) and the Archway viaduct, the limit of the DOE's responsibility.

In 1966 the Highgate Society was established largely by former 'Save Highgate Campaign' members and although they were to become a civic society with broader concerns than traffic in Highgate, one of their first activities was to carry out a survey of road communications in the area. Their objective was to have through traffic excluded from Highgate village. It was in doing this that they unearthed the MOT plans for widening the Archway Road between Wellington Junction and Archway viaduct. This scheme was being designed on an agency basis for the Ministry by the Borough Engineer and Surveyor's Department of the newly created Haringey Borough Council, though the former Metropolitan Borough of Hornsey had also prepared sketch proposals for the Ministry.

[1] LCC *Minutes*, 21 May 1963, p391.
[2] GLC *Minutes*, 2 November 1965, p719.
[3] GLC *Minutes*, 30 November 1965, p768.
[4] GLC *Press Release 215*, 15 February 1966. Under the *Road Traffic Regulation Act 1967*, (ch 76) s6, the GLC may, with the consent of the Secretary of State for the Environment, undertake traffic management schemes on Trunk roads.

The widening was approved in principle by Haringey Council in 1967 and their officers then continued to develop the scheme in more detail. But as the scheme progressed, so did opposition to it. The Highgate Society criticised the MOT plan on the grounds that neighbouring residential streets would suffer increased traffic and that little or no provision had been made for 'landscaping' the Archway Road itself. They pressed for alternative proposals including side-road closures in line with Buchanan's 'environmental area' principles.

A similar view was also growing within Haringey Council (whose Engineer felt that the MOT was imposing cost constraints which would not allow the best scheme to be devised) but both member and officer level representations to the MOT in 1967 failed to have the plans reconsidered. Councillor McIntosh, then vice-chairman of Haringey's Planning Committee, attempted to mount a wider campaign of opposition. In January 1968 the Highgate Ward Labour Party (of which he was chairman) issued a statement to the local press calling upon residents in the Highgate area to:

> Unite in protest against the violation of the basic principles of urban planning and of Government policy [which were] expressed in the Buchanan Report. We invite all interested bodies and individuals to join in a campaign against the present proposals and in favour of practical alternatives which are more in line with progressive social planning policies.[1]

Following a meeting in Highgate in March 1968 the Archway Road Campaign (ARC) was formed, representing a number of local residents' groups and with the backing of four political parties. It was chaired initially by Walter Bor[2] and Councillor McIntosh was its vice-chairman. Although in the same month Haringey Council merely noted the MOT's making of a draft highway order for the Archway Road scheme, Councillor McIntosh quickly gained the support of both his Labour colleagues and some Opposition members.

The borough elections in May brought the Conservatives into control at Haringey but the two main parties continued to be united in opposing the scheme. The new chairman (Councillor Douglas Smith) and vice-chairman (Councillor Brian Falk) of the Planning Committee and two Labour members met representatives of the ARC and formulated an agreed strategy.

The Borough's policy was set out in a Planning Committee report accepted in June 1968.[3] It was decided to make 'strong representations'

[1] *Hornsey Journal*, 26 January 1968.

[2] Walter Bor was City Planning Officer of Liverpool and had been a member of the Planning Advisory Group set up by the Ministry of Housing and Local Government to report on the future of Development Plans.

[3] L B Haringey *Minutes*, 18 June 1968, para78.

to the Ministers of Transport and Housing and Local Government for a joint public inquiry to be held into the 'whole concept of the Archway Road scheme.' Other policy decisions were to consider comprehensive redevelopment along the Archway Road and to improve and preserve existing amenities in the area. An amendment to the Planning Committee's report was moved by councillors Falk and Butler (Opposition leader on the committee) to the effect that as agents for the MOT on the Archway Road scheme Haringey Council were being directed to contravene standards laid down by the Ministry itself.[1] The amendment continued:

> As the impact of the proposed road works on the lives of Borough residents has been ignored, as the basic survey statistics have not been obtained, and as no participation by the public has occurred, or is proposed, this Council considers it must further stress that the Archway Road reconstruction should be open to a wider and public discussion of the type soon to be mandatory under legislation.

Throughout the remainder of 1968 the ARC, with the support of the MP for Hornsey, Mr Hugh Rossi, and Haringey Council campaigned for a wide-ranging inquiry into the scheme. A delegation of Haringey officers and members in August 1968 found the MOT still reluctant to reconsider the Archway Road plans and further representations were made by the Council and the ARC in November, backed by a petition organised by the Highgate Society. In December the Minister of Housing and Local Government announced that he was unable to support the proposal for a joint public inquiry with the MOT, but at the same time the Minister of Transport (then Richard Marsh) took the unusual step of appointing two firms of consultants (Scott Wilson, Kirkpatrick and Partners and Hugh Wilson, Lewis Womersley and Partners) to look respectively into the traffic and planning aspects of the proposal. The aim was an independent report on what had developed into a two-sided issue between Haringey Council and organised local voluntary groups on the one hand, and the MOT on the other, though Haringey Council was invited to nominate officers to take part in the direction of the study. The Minister's decision was regarded by the ARC and those Haringey councillors most closely involved as a considerable victory.

During the year which it took the Consultants to undertake the study (1969) another local group—the Shepherds Hill Association (SHA)—was formed to represent residents on the opposite side of the Archway Road to Highgate, and this group was to introduce a new element into the conflict. Its immediate action was to oppose compulsory purchase orders which had been served on properties fronting the Archway Road between Winchester Road and the Archway intersection, which was the subject of a GLC widening scheme and outside the Consultants' terms of reference. The

[1] A reference to the Ministry's road design standards for local authorities: MOT (1966), *Roads in Urban Areas*.

ARC was also amongst objectors to these orders and a public inquiry was held in March 1969.

The ARC took this opportunity to present their case against the Ministry's widening proposals which they said incorporated inadequate design standards and would increase traffic in the neighbouring residential areas. The SHA, represented by their chairman Mr George Stern, went further, however, and argued that *any* widening scheme would have an adverse effect on neighbouring properties and amenities. Mr Stern also questioned the traffic data on which the Ministry based its assumption that the Archway Road needed to be widened. It was this broader opposition to the widening concept which later in 1969 led to a head-on clash between the ARC and the SHA.

The compulsory purchase order was approved by the Minister of Transport just two months after the public inquiry. This led both the ARC and the SHA to question the role of the Consultants' study of the Trunk section of Archway Road, as it appeared that various sections were being considered in isolation. The local MP, Mr Hugh Rossi, took up the matter and in July presented a petition to the Minister of Transport on behalf of his constituents seeking an annulment of the compulsory purchase order since the traffic data on which the Ministry's case was based were being reviewed by the Consultants.[1] At a public meeting held in July the ARC repeated this view and criticised the Minister's approval of the compulsory purchase order as high-handed, and Councillor Falk pledged his support for the campaign.

Replying to Mr Rossi six months later, the Minister firmly refused to annul the compulsory purchase order and justified this decision on the basis of the inspector's report on the March 1969 inquiry. Mr Stern, of the SHA, commented, 'it will be remembered that this inquiry was strictly limited in scope, and objections were confined to property holders immediately affected. This ruled out any serious protest by the amenity associations concerned such as our own.'[2]

Nevertheless the Minister gave the GLC the necessary powers to proceed with the compulsory acquisition of the Archway Road properties in September 1969,[3] whilst further developments lent weight to the argument that the A1 was being handled piecemeal: October saw the opening of the GLC's new Archway intersection scheme which had taken two years and £1 660 000 to complete,[4] and the public inquiry into the widening of the Falloden Way section was being held at this time.

While this debate continued, the Consultants had been assessing the future traffic demands on the Archway Road, the need for increasing its capacity, the feasibility of grade-separated junctions and the effects on the

[1] *Hansard HC Debates*, 25 July 1969, col2234.
[2] *Hornsey Journal*, 23 January 1970.
[3] GLC *Minutes*, 7 July 1970. The compulsory purchase order powers were acquired by the GLC on 9 September 1969.
[4] GLC *Minutes*, 10 February 1970, p126.

adjacent environment, particularly the Highgate Conservation Area.[1] While accepting the Ministry's contention that additional traffic capacity should be provided, they rejected schemes incorporating grade-separated interchanges (estimated to cost £5 million) and the Ministry's original £2.5 million scheme. Their recommended scheme had a similar traffic capacity to the Ministry's scheme[2] but because of additional access roads, pedestrian subways and other safety and environmental provisions was to cost £1 million more (a total of £3.5 million). It also involved the closure of certain side roads to reduce the amount of traffic using residential streets.

The Consultants had held meetings in April 1969 with Haringey officers and members and with representatives of the various local groups. In October 1969 they discussed alternative schemes which they had considered at a further private meeting with the ARC, the SHA and members of the Haringey Planning Committee. A confidential report of this meeting prepared by Mr McIntosh (of the ARC) was leaked to the press at the beginning of November, as a result of which the major division of opinion between the SHA and ARC became apparent. The ARC felt that (together with Haringey Council) they had had considerable success in getting the MOT to appoint independent consultants. They thought the Consultants' recommended scheme went a long way towards meeting their criticisms and was well worth supporting. In a letter to the local press Mr McIntosh and other members of the ARC complained that the breach of confidence on his report:

> . . . may have given the impression of a split between two groups of residents. In fact, the individual responsible has deliberately fostered the idea that a struggle is going on between 'wideners' and 'anti-wideners.' The real issue is rather different. It is whether the accepted need for a pleasanter environment on and around the main road should be met, with traffic properly controlled in a scheme that may or may not involve some degree of widening, or whether it should be frustrated by a few who want nothing done at all.[3]

Mr Stern (chairman of the SHA), however, felt that the ARC had sold out to the Ministry. The leak to the press was, he felt, fully justified because Highgate residents needed to be warned of the increased traffic that would result from the Consultants' scheme. He said that many Highgate village people were supporting the Archway Road widening in an attempt to secure a reduction of traffic in their residential streets, 'but they are making a big mistake. There will be more traffic in the village than ever'.[4]

[1] Scott Wilson, Kirkpatrick and Partners; Hugh Wilson, Lewis Womersley and Partners (1969), *Archway Road Study*, p2.

[2] Both schemes provided for dual three-lane carriageways. The Consultants felt that this was a reasonable compromise for the 'widely fluctuating demand' on the Archway Road.

[3] *Hornsey Journal*, 7 November 1969.

[4] *Ibid.*

The differences between the ARC and the SHA were, however, at least partially healed later in November and the two groups met to consider immediate action. The ARC considered that the next steps in the campaign should be to stop the GLC from starting work on the Archway–Winchester Road widening, to secure the publication of the Consultants' report on Archway Road and the results of the Hampstead Garden Suburb inquiry, and to press for a full-scale inquiry into the need for widening the A1 from Archway to the North Circular. Impetus was given to this last point by a joint complaint to the Minister of Transport by Mr Rossi (MP for Hornsey) and Mrs Margaret Thatcher (MP for Finchley) that he was playing off one community against another. Their letter read:

> Complaints have been received by us from our constituents that representatives of your department have suggested that the extent of the road widening in Hampstead Garden Suburb must be determined by what is done to the Archway Road, and to the Archway Road by what is done in the Hampstead Garden Suburb.[1]

In his reply, the Minister (Mr Fred Mulley) said:

> While we do not accept that the case for widening Archway Road is wholly dependent on the improvement of Aylmer Road–Falloden Way we nevertheless realise that there is bound to be an interaction between the two. You can therefore rest assured that we will not consider one scheme in isolation from the other.[2]

It was clear, however, that the widening of the two adjoining stretches of the A1 had not been considered sufficiently interlinked to make them the subject of a single inquiry.

Following the publication of the Consultants' report on the Archway Road, in February 1970 the MOT asked Haringey Council for their views and those of local groups and individuals to be submitted by the end of April 1970. A group of Haringey members were appointed for the purpose who met the Consultants and held discussions with the ARC, the SHA and a further new group—The North Highgate Group—which consisted of a 'splinter group' from ARC set up to fight the increased traffic that would result in certain residential streets if the Consultants' plan was implemented. The outcome of these consultations were considered, together with an officer's report on the Consultants' study, by the Haringey Planning Committee on 7 April 1970, and a consolidated report was prepared for submission to the Ministry.[3] The Planning Committee expressed 'very serious concern' over the data in the Consultant's study which showed

[1] *Hornsey Journal*, 30 January 1970.
[2] *Ibid.*
[3] LB Haringey *Minutes*, 7 April 1970, p626.

'continued and comparatively unrestrained traffic growth in the conurbation' and called upon the Ministries and the GLC to hold 'wide-ranging inquiries into the planning and transportation studies of London.' (It is not clear what they had in mind at this point since the mammoth GLDP Inquiry had already been announced in December 1969.) Doubts were also expressed about the Consultants' planning bases and their prediction of future traffic demand. Yet despite these apparently fundamental doubts, the Committee's report went on to make a series of detailed points concerning pedestrian facilities, landscaping and associated traffic management schemes, and to make suggestions for improving upon the Consultants' scheme. Thus, although they rejected the scheme as still inadequate, this action implied that they accepted its objectives in principle.

Before considering this report, however, Haringey Council had held a public meeting on 22 April to receive comments on the proposals. This was attended by over 500 people. The Borough Planning Officer, Mr David Frith, stated firmly that he thought the road should be widened because peak-hour traffic conditions on it were 'grotesque.'[1] Mr McIntosh (chairman of ARC) said the Consultants' scheme came nearest to what ARC wanted. Despite considerable discussion over the details of the scheme, the general view of the meeting appeared to be that the Archway Road decision should await the outcome of the GLDP Inquiry. A representative of the SHA for example said:

> We believe that the whole A1 widening scheme and the projected traffic growth must be considered at the public inquiry into the GLDP. A purely local inquiry will not produce the right answers to the problem.[2]

Councillor Falk promised that a report of the meeting would be put to the Council with the Planning Committee's recommendation to reject the plan, and to call for a wider-ranging inquiry into such matters as public transport, parking, traffic growth and the highway system south of the Archway Road. The SHA complained, however, that Councillor Falk had refused to accept a motion from their representative at the meeting urging Haringey Council to resist any road plan until the GLDP Inquiry had examined the projected traffic growth, the contribution that public transport could make, and the future of the A1 as a whole.[3] When the Planning Committee's report was considered in Council, however, Councillor Falk persuaded the Council, after a long debate, to accept the Consultants' report as a 'welcome improvement' on the original MOT scheme.[4] The Council decided that the Consultants' scheme should not be rejected

[1] *Evening Standard*, 23 April 1970.

[2] *Camden News*, 24 April 1970.

[3] *Hornsey Journal*, 24 April 1970.

[4] Councillor Falk had already unsuccessfully pursued this in the Planning Committee. We are grateful to Mr D W D Southron who has undertaken research on the political process in Haringey (London School of Economics, Greater London Group, 1971–72 unpublished) for this and other information used in this study.

altogether since it might create the opportunity for substantial environmental improvements including the redevelopment of frontage properties on the Archway Road.

The GLC entered the scene in November 1970 when it approved the Consultants' recommendations in principle. In December, Peter Walker (Secretary of State for the newly-formed DOE) decided that the detailed planning of the Archway Road scheme should proceed. The Consultants' proposed widening to dual three-lane carriageways was accepted by the DOE, though the proposal that Church Road should carry diverted traffic (which had given rise to the formation of the North Highgate Group) was to be 'examined further.'[1] (For instance the DOE asked Haringey's Borough Engineer for suggestions on the problem.)[2]

At the time of writing (1972) the scheme was still not developed sufficiently to be published as a draft proposal under the Highways Act 1959. When this does appear the matter will once again be open to the objection and inquiry procedures which were avoided or at least delayed by the MOT's appointment of the Consultants in 1968. Local pressure continued, however. In February 1971 a joint meeting of the ARC, SHA and Highgate Society was held together with the North Highgate Group and yet another recently formed group—the Miltons Area Improvement Campaign. It was unanimously decided that 'nothing was to be gained by standing aside when they could put pressure on the Government to provide the best possible road scheme.'[3] The Highgate Society also submitted evidence to Stage 2 of the GLDP Inquiry claiming that if the Consultants' forecast of a doubling of road traffic between 1969 and 1981 was fulfilled, it would mean the destruction of Highgate even if the Archway Road was widened.[4]

3 FROM THE ARCHWAY TO THE ANGEL

Unlike the two DOE Trunk road sections dealt with above, the GLC section of the A1 from the Archway viaduct to the Angel intersection has not been the subject of any major widening proposals. Rather, it has been the subject of a longstanding general policy of piecemeal widening as and when circumstances allow, together with schemes to increase the capacity of intersections. This policy probably pre-dates the Second World War although it has never been explicitly stated in any statutory development plan. The whole route was, however, shown in the County of London Development Plan as a Principal Traffic Route (see Table 24), and various statements by the LCC in the early 1960s confirmed the general intentions.

[1] DOE *Press Release 701*, 21 December 1970.

[2] Interview with Borough Engineer, 16 July 1971.

[3] *Hornsey Journal*, 12 February 1971. It should be noted, however, that the chairman of the SHA Mr G Stern was not present at this meeting. He maintained firm opposition to any widening before the examination of the A1 road as a whole in the context of the GLDP.

[4] Highgate Society (1971), *Proof of Evidence*, *E27/102*, GLDP Inquiry Stage 2.

To see how this policy has been operated and modified over the years it is necessary to examine in some detail how various piecemeal schemes have been pursued, beginning with schemes which were implemented, or begun, by the LCC.

In 1951 the County of London Development Plan specified Highbury Corner and the Angel intersection as priorities for 'improvement' (see again Table 24). In July 1956, the year after the Development Plan was approved, the Minister of Transport approved a 75% grant for a scheme to build a roundabout at Highbury Corner at an estimated total cost of £109 000.[1] The scheme was completed by 1959 for about £8000 less than the estimated cost.[2]

The Angel intersection was shown as part of the 'inner circular route' and programmed for 'improvement' in the period 1960–72. The intersection had frontage development on all four corners which had to be demolished if the road scheme was to proceed. Moreover, the buildings involved were of a substantially higher value than those which had been required for the Highbury Corner roundabout.[3] The LCC began to acquire property at the Angel in October 1959, when it paid £90 000 for the former Angel Inn, the building which lent its name to the intersection. J Lyons, the catering company, who then owned the building, wanted to sell out to the LCC because the early programming of the road scheme meant that modernisation would not be worthwhile.[4] The LCC acquired further properties at the Angel between 1963 and 1965 bringing the total spent to £216 000,[5] and announced that the intersection scheme was in the building programme for 1968–69.[6]

Also in the last five years of its existence, the LCC pursued some minor schemes in line with its policy of piecemeal widening of Holloway Road. In 1960 the Town Planning Committee reported that widening of a third of a mile section (between Hercules Street and Jackson Road) had been included in the list of minor schemes for 1960–61. The estimated cost for grant purposes was £100 000.[7]

In October 1962, the Council confirmed its policy by approving 'in principle' the widening of Holloway Road between Jackson Road and Windsor Road. This scheme included, but was only slightly longer than the Jackson Road–Hercules Street section already approved but which had not been carried out as expected in 1961. The estimated cost of the widening had also increased to £250 000. This included £72 000 for the diversion

[1] LCC *Minutes*, 17 July 1956.
[2] LCC *Minutes*, 2 December 1958.
[3] Property and works (other than road works) were estimated in 1956 to cost £43 000 for the Highbury Corner scheme, LCC *Minutes*, 17 July 1956.
[4] LCC *Minutes*, 6 October 1969, p577–8.
[5] LCC *Minutes*, 10 March 1964, p273; 10 March 1965, p1272.
[6] LCC *Minutes*, 5 May 1964, p424.
[7] LCC *Minutes*, 25 October 1960, p618. In view of the small cost of this scheme it is clear that the widening mainly referred to the carriageway (at the expense of the footways) rather than the road as a whole.

of statutory undertakers' services which, it was said, would have to be carried out quickly if the scheme was to proceed in the year 1963–64.[1] These works were later found to be more expensive and a revised estimate of £106 000 was approved in January 1963.[2] A year later the widening scheme (Jackson Road to Windsor Road) came before the Council again and it was explained that it would provide for a carriageway 75 feet wide, mainly by reducing the width of the footway.[3] The estimated cost of the scheme rose steadily and by February 1965 had reached about £300 000, or three times the estimate for the slightly smaller scheme approved in October 1960.[4]

Meanwhile, the LCC had decided to widen a short adjoining stretch south of Jackson Road which had become possible through BR's decision to reconstruct their railway overbridge at this point. In July 1961 it was reported that for an additional cost of about £39 000 the new railway bridge could be constructed to allow three lanes of traffic in each direction. The Council at the same time reaffirmed its policy of widening Holloway Road as 'opportunities' occurred.[5] This scheme also turned out to be more expensive than when it was approved (£112 000 compared with £39 000). The carriageway on this small section was to be widened to 65 feet as opposed to the 75 feet proposed for the adjacent section.[6]

The largest schemes on the A1 with which the LCC were concerned, however, were the widening of Archway Road and a major reconstruction of the Archway intersection. The LCC approved a major scheme for the Archway intersection in December 1962 which had an estimated cost of £1 430 000 (of which property accounted for £1 150 000). It was explained that it was not possible for traffic to avoid congestion at the intersection by using other streets. A flyover or underpass had been considered impractical because of the gradients in the vicinity. The approved scheme was for a large roundabout which, it was felt, would bring a:

> welcome increase in the capacity of the intersection and ultimately, when all the streets leading into the intersection have been widened, as proposed, the capacity of the intersection will *approach* the aggregate capacity of the feeder roads [our italics].[7]

The 'agreed road programme' envisaged that the cleared site would be available for the works to begin in July 1967, though the Minister of Transport asked the LCC to bring the scheme forward in view of the A1's inclusion in the suggested lorry route from M1 to the docks. The Council

[1] LCC *Minutes*, 16 October 1962, p766.
[2] LCC *Minutes*, 22 January 1963, p43.
[3] LCC *Minutes*, 28 January 1964, pp22–3.
[4] LCC *Minutes*, 10 March 1964, p275; 1 December 1964, p1015; 2 February 1965, p1128.
[5] LCC *Minutes*, 18–19 July 1961, p526.
[6] LCC *Minutes*, 28 January 1964, p23.
[7] LCC *Minutes*, 11 December 1962, pp1060–1.

said that the scheme could not be brought forward as a whole because of the time required to purchase the properties, but in order 'to meet as far as possible the MOT's request' it was hoped that part of the roundabout could be built before the rest.[1] The MOT, however, wanted to introduce an experimental one-way scheme using nearby residential streets aimed at 'increasing the capacity' of all the roads leading into the Archway intersection. Representations from local interests, expressing concern about the use of such streets for one-way traffic, and the LCC's view that clearway arrangements in Holloway Road should be considered first, did not persuade the Ministry to drop their interim scheme.[2] The major intersection scheme was approved by the MOT for grant purposes in May 1964,[3] and by this time the interim scheme had not been introduced.

The other major scheme, the widening of Archway Road from the intersection to the county boundary (at Archway viaduct), was approved in principle by the LCC in February 1964.[4] It was announced the following May that the scheme was programmed to start in 1968–69 together with the Angel and Archway intersection schemes. The LCC entered into an agreement with the MOT (in October 1964) to continue the widening scheme beyond the county boundary onto the Trunk road section as far as Winchester Road (a distance of about 200 yards). This agreement was intended to 'co-ordinate the improvements' with the MOT's proposed widening of Archway Road further north as far as Southwood Avenue (near Shepherds Hill), and in particular to avoid constructional difficulties of terminating the widening at the Archway viaduct itself.[5]

Thus in 1965 the new GLC inherited from the LCC four specific proposals to increase the traffic-carrying capacity of the road. These were: the short length of widening between Archway intersection and Winchester Road just mentioned; the Archway intersection scheme; the short length of widening in Holloway Road in conjunction with the railway bridge reconstruction, and the roundabout at the Angel intersection. The implementation of these four schemes ran into various difficulties after 1965 which delayed their expected completion dates, and it is necessary to examine them in turn in order to see how they were handled after the GLC had assumed responsibility.

The Archway Road widening scheme proved both more difficult and more expensive to carry out than the LCC had originally thought. A revised scheme was approved by the GLC in May 1966 when it was estimated that the total cost would be £644 000.[6] By October 1967, although the estimated starting date was still (as the LCC had expected) in the year

1 LCC *Minutes*, 11 December 1962, pp1060–1.
2 LCC *Minutes*, 19 November 1963, p754.
3 LCC *Minutes*, 5 May 1964, p144. The scheme was part of a £74 million programme which included such schemes as Westway, Wandsworth Bridge approaches and part of the East Cross Route.
4 LCC *Minutes*, 11 February 1964, p180.
5 LCC *Minutes*, 20 October 1964, p886, and interview with GLC officers.
6 GLC *Minutes*, 17 May 1966, p279.

1968–69, the cost of the scheme had risen to £1 094 000.[1] The expected completion date was July 1970 (a construction programme of two years). By February 1968 it was discovered that instability of the very high and steep embankments near the Archway bridge required further changes in the road design which would bring the total cost of the scheme (including property) to £1 399 000. The starting date was also put back from July 1968 to March 1969 due to difficulties which the MOT was having in acquiring properties required on the short Trunk road section north of Archway bridge.[2] By the end of 1968 the starting date had been postponed again—to December 1969—probably because of the impending public inquiry into the compulsory purchase order for properties required (see page 369 above).[3] Two months later the starting date was further put back to July 1970,[4] and finally in November 1969 the date was expected to be March 1971, nearly three years later than the original programme.[5] In February 1970 the GLC reported that some starting dates, 'though not necessarily this one' had been delayed because of lengthy consultation, public inquiry and compulsory purchase order procedures. It was also reported that construction would take longer than the two years originally envisaged and the completion date was put at September 1973.[6]

Although some preliminary works had been begun by August 1971, the GLC announced the commencement of the widening itself in November 1971 and completion was expected thirty months after that, i.e. May 1974. The scheme was justified as follows:

> Even though the DOE has postponed the widening of the A1 (Archway Road) further on, the GLC has decided to go ahead with work on this particular stretch because the existing three-lane road on a steep hill is inadequate for traffic and a danger to drivers and pedestrians.
>
> The widened road will have dual three-lane carriageways and a continuous central reserve.[7]

As already mentioned, this scheme in particular gave rise to criticism from local interests, the main point at issue being the GLC's apparent disregard of the future of other sections of the A1. For example, in November 1969 Mr Neil Thorne, Chairman of the GLC's Central Area Board, declined to comment on a suggestion made to the local press by a Mr John Harvey that the A1 should be dealt with from the North Circular to Highbury Corner 'in one fell swoop.'[8] In March 1970 Mr Thorne denied

[1] GLC *Minutes*, 10 October 1967, p562. The cost estimates did not, of course, include the cost of the short section of Trunk road included in the scheme.
[2] GLC *Minutes*, 27 February 1968, pp134–5.
[3] GLC *Minutes*, 17 December 1968, p714.
[4] GLC *Minutes*, 11 February 1969, p103.
[5] GLC *Minutes*, 4 November 1969, pp593–4, reply to Question in Council.
[6] GLC *Minutes*, 10 February 1970, p126.
[7] GLC *Press Release 478*, 2 November 1971, '£1 million facelift for Archway Road.'
[8] GLC *Minutes*, 4 November 1969, pp593–4, Question in Council.

that there were any further plans to widen Holloway Road and contended that although it formed part of the A1 with the Archway Road, the functions of the two roads were different. He also said: 'traffic in Holloway Road is likely to drop when the Ringways are built.' He was answering criticisms by the SHA that the GLC's Archway Road widening scheme was a precursor to major but as yet unannounced widening schemes on the rest of the A1.[1] A year later Mr Thorne (in reply to a question in Council) said that the widening scheme would 'bring about considerable traffic and environmental benefits irrespective of the decision on the A1 further north,'[2] although he gave no factual statement as to what these benefits were likely to be.

In April 1971 the matter was raised in Parliament by Mr M O'Halloran, MP for Islington North, who suggested that the GLC's widening scheme for Archway Road should be halted. He pointed out that the A1 widening through Hampstead Garden Suburb to dual three-lane standard had been stopped; that it had been put back several years on Archway Road north of Winchester Road; and that the GLC had suggested that the widening of Holloway Road was not necessary. Yet, he said, the GLC wanted to start widening the small section between Archway roundabout and Winchester Road.

In his reply, Mr Michael Heseltine (Parliamentary Under-Secretary for Local Government and Development) said that widening farther north in Archway Road would not start before 1974–75, but that the roundabout to Winchester Road section was proceeding later that year as a joint project of the GLC and the DOE. 'It would be quite unthinkable,' he said, 'having gone through all the statutory processes and, in terms of house clearance, started work, for there to be any possibility of the Secretary of State intervening.' When asked if there were any plans for Holloway Road, Mr Heseltine said: 'This is a matter for the GLC.'[3]

Mr George Stern, chairman of the SHA, commented to the local press that the scheme for Archway Road was 'a fantastic waste of public funds and should be stopped. Clearly nobody knows what they are doing on Archway Road, and it is time for an inquiry to look into the whole A1 widening, to consider whether the scheme is needed.'[4]

The following August the SHA received confirmation from Mr Heseltine that the Secretary of State for the Environment was not prepared to halt the widening scheme on which the GLC had already started work. The widening, he was reported to have said, was a 'necessary adjunct to the Archway intersection scheme' and would 'complete the improvements of this important junction.'[5] The Association was dissatisfied with the decision

[1] *Islington Gazette*, 20 March 1970, and earlier statement to same effect, *Islington Gazette*, 24 September 1969.
[2] GLC *Minutes*, 23 March 1971, p170.
[3] *Hansard HC Debates*, 28 April 1971, cols594–8; and *Hornsey Journal*, 7 May 1971.
[4] *Hornsey Journal*, 7 May 1971.
[5] *Hornsey Journal*, 13 August 1971.

and said that the scheme was a 'foot in the door' for future widening along the A1 from Islington to Hampstead Garden Suburb.

The Archway intersection itself was, as previously mentioned, the subject of two schemes: an experimental traffic management scheme and, later, the construction of a large roundabout with pedestrian subways. In November 1965 the GLC reported that, on various 'optimistic assumptions' that procedural delays would not occur, the traffic management scheme would be introduced the following January. The assumptions indeed proved to be optimistic, however, and the scheme did not begin until August 1966. It involved the creation of a one-way gyratory system using adjoining residential streets, one of which (St John's Grove) was 'completely reconstructed, with improved street lighting, to take the extra traffic.' The GLC stated that the scheme 'should help to relieve congestion at the difficult five-way junction . . . until the impending major reconstruction scheme is completed.'[1] The GLC subsequently received complaints from residents in the area about noise due to the increased traffic, particularly in St John's Grove, but the situation was regarded as temporary until the completion of the major scheme.[2]

The latter scheme ran more or less to the timetable which the LCC had set for it in December 1962, although there was some uncertainty at times. The estimated completion dates ran as follows:[3]

December 1962 (LCC estimate), July 1969.
October 1967 (GLC estimate), January 1969.
October 1968 (GLC estimate), May 1969.
December 1968 (GLC estimate), February 1969.
Actual completion date, 8 October 1969.

The cost of the scheme increased from an estimated £1 150 000 in 1962[4] to a final £1 660 000.[5] Announcing the impending completion of the scheme Mr Thorne said: 'the residents of St John's Grove have had to put up with a great deal during the past few years, and I am pleased that the improvements at Archway will enable us to remove heavy through traffic from this residential street.'[6]

The Holloway Road widening including the reconstruction of the railway bridge was, in comparison, a small scheme, its total cost being less than £200 000. Its implementation, however, was not any the faster for that. It was one of several London road projects deferred by the MOT for six months from September 1965 (when the target date was expected to be June 1967). Further delays arose from BR's decision to revise the design

[1] GLC *Press Release 356*, 9 August 1966.
[2] GLC *Minutes*, 22 October 1968, p548.
[3] GLC *Minutes*, 28 February 1967, p171; 10 October 1967, p557; 22 October 1968 p548; 17 December 1968, p548; and GLC *Press Release, 515* 8 October 1969.
[4] GLC *Minutes*, 28 February 1967, p171.
[5] GLC *Minutes*, 10 February 1970, p126.
[6] GLC *Press Release 210*, 22 April 1969.

of their new bridge.[1] The combined effect was a two and a half-year delay. Subsequent construction difficulties meant that work was still in progress in September 1971, more than four years after the original target date.

The major scheme at the Angel intersection perhaps suffered the most delay of all, and its design and implementation affected the whole future of shopping and commercial activities in the locality. As already noted, the LCC after 1959 bought up some of the properties affected. From 1965 onwards industrial and commercial undertakings in the area served purchase notices on the GLC indicating the 'blight' caused by the impending road scheme.[2] The scheme itself, however, became the subject of lengthy debate.

In 1963 a proposal was included in the forward roads programme for 1968–69, but this was deferred in 1965 pending a decision on the route of Eastern Avenue into London along the Regent's canal.[3] This route would have affected the role of the Angel intersection but it was abandoned in 1967 in favour of an alternative route along Hackney Road. Meanwhile, the new Islington Borough Council produced its own ideas for the Angel as local planning authority. After discussions with the GLC in 1968 it was felt that neither scheme was 'necessarily the best answer to the highways, planning and civic design problems.' Towards the end of 1968 a meeting of Islington and GLC members decided to set up a joint officers Working Party to make 'further detailed appraisal of several alternatives within agreed fundamental principles.' These principles were:

1 Any scheme should be capable of staged construction.
2 It should satisfy immediate and long-term traffic conditions.
3 It should be at the minimum cost consistent with the achievement of these aims.
4 It should secure satisfactory land use and redevelopment.

'Other principles should include:'

5 The need to provide an integrated solution properly related to its environment and to the roads programme as a whole, with full consideration of the preservation of interesting features of the existing environment.

The setting up of the joint Working Party and contacts which were made with amenity bodies and other interests in the area can be seen in the context of a GLC statement in January 1969:

[1] GLC *Minutes*, 13 December 1966, p696.
[2] GLC *Minutes*, 15 November 1966, p626; 27 February 1968, p134; 25 July 1969, p391.
[3] This and the majority of information on the early history of the Angel scheme is summarised in GLC *Minutes*, 28 January 1969, pp57–8.

> The need for a major improvement (at the Angel) has, of course, increased with the passage of time. The improvement is included in the 1971 roads preparation programme and great efforts are being made to reach an agreed solution.[1]

The GLC considered a report of the Working Party in June 1969 which concluded that authorisation should be sought to proceed with a two-stage scheme at the Angel. The first stage was to be a roundabout at ground level, implemented as soon as possible at the 'lowest possible expense'. The second stage included the addition of an east–west underpass at an extra cost of £1 500 000. The first stage was in the 1971 programme subject to the approval of Islington Borough Council.[2]

The remodelling of the intersection, however, became closely bound up with comprehensive redevelopment plans for the area, and a process of public participation on the whole issue was mounted jointly by the GLC, Islington Borough Council and Star (Great Britain) Holdings Ltd, a development company who had entered into negotiations with the Borough for a major commercial redevelopment adjacent to the junction. A public exhibition was held in the old Lyons building which was attended by over 6000 people during three weeks in November and December 1970. Comments were invited on the suggested redevelopment and road proposals, in particular as to which side of St John Street (south of the Angel) should be demolished for road widening.[3]

On 1 April 1971 the GLC announced that revised road proposals, taking account of the views expressed at the exhibition, had been approved for consultation purposes. Islington Borough Council approved the scheme on 26 October 1971.[4] The GLC approved the road scheme on 14 December 1971 at an estimated cost of £7 630 000. It consisted of a large roundabout with pedestrian subways and bus lay-bys. Islington High Street (part of the A1) was to be widened as far as Liverpool Road and the eventual provision of an east–west underpass was allowed for in the design 'should this prove necessary.' A short bus-only lane was also included from Upper Street southbound into Islington High Street. Despite the 'fundamental principles' laid down for the joint officers Working Party in January 1968, the redevelopment proposals for the area had apparently become separated from the roads issue and the Council considered that the scheme was 'justified in its own right, with or without major redevelopment in the area, and [would] attract the traffic now by-passing the intersection back onto the secondary-road system with a consequent improvement in the surrounding areas.'[5] Mr Thorne, announcing the scheme before the Council's decision, said:

[1] GLC *Minutes*, 28 January 1969, pp57–8.
[2] GLC *Minutes*, 24 June 1969, p391.
[3] GLC *Press Release 614*, 29 December 1970; and GLC pamphlet, *Angel News*.
[4] GLC *Press Release 127*, 1 April 1971; and *Camden Journal*, 5 November 1971.
[5] GLC *Minutes*, 14 December 1971, p665.

> For forty years there have been proposals for road improvements at the Angel. We are delighted that a scheme is getting underway at last. . . . Now that the uncertainty is ended, the Borough Council can consider the future of the surrounding area in the light of firm road plans.[1]

After the exhibition at the Angel had made clear to the public what was intended, however, opposition began to mount during 1971. The Islington Society, for example, seeing the GLC's arguments for the scheme, expressed regret that they had not opposed earlier the widening schemes in Holloway Road and at Archway. In June 1971 the Society produced a joint report with five other societies[2] condemning the Angel road plan as being self-defeating because of the amount of additional traffic that it would generate. This move was prompted by similar assertions about new major road building in inner London made during the previous month by the London Motorway Action Group and the London Amenity and Transport Association at the GLDP Inquiry.[3] It was claimed, however, that the Borough Council took little or no account of the points raised in the joint document when approving the GLC's scheme the following October.[4]

Before going on to consider the final section of the A1, from the Angel to the City, the general handling of the four schemes on the GLC section since 1965 provides an opportunity to recap on what has necessarily been a lengthy and complex story.

Although at the time of writing no further definite schemes were programmed, the whole of the remaining sections of the road under the GLC's responsibility were safeguarded for eventual widening to provide a carriageway at least 70 feet wide which meant that any new frontage development was to be set back to a new building line.[5] The four GLC schemes described came to the fore either as a result of the high priority attached to them (the Archway and Angel intersections, for example, had both been notorious traffic bottlenecks for many years), or because of opportunities that had arisen (the LCC and the GLC, for example, had seen BR's decision to reconstruct the Holloway Road railway bridge as an opportunity to widen the road in that vicinity).[6]

The statutory division of powers allowed a good deal of flexibility between the GLC and (in this case) Islington Borough Council in the preparation and implementatjon of schemes. The GLC could initiate schemes and either carry out the work itself or arrange for the Borough to carry it out

[1] GLC *Press Release*, 8 December 1971.

[2] These were: The Angel Association; The Barnsbury Association; The Canonbury Society; The Finsbury Society; The Liverpool Road Association.

[3] The Islington Society *et al.* (1971), *The Angel*, document submitted to GLC, IBC and other interested bodies in June 1971, p4.

[4] *Camden Journal*, 5 November 1971, letter from Islington Society.

[5] Interview with GLC officer involved in planning of central area roads.

[6] GLC *Minutes*, 3 May 1966, p210; and *MOT Press Release 404*, 16 July 1970 which reads: 'A decision by the BR Board to rebuild the bridge has provided the opportunity for the GLC to widen the road under and adjacent to the bridge from 45 to 70 feet.'

as its agent. There were no hard and fast rules on the agency arrangements operated by the GLC. Islington had on occasion undertaken quite major works on an agency basis for the GLC (e.g. in City Road) but the Holloway Road widening scheme referred to was carried out entirely by the GLC itself.[1] This may have been due to the fact that the scheme was prepared in conjunction with BR[2] though this need not necessarily have precluded Islington from carrying out the road works involved.

As far as working relationships between Islington and the GLC were concerned there appeared to be little in the way of conflict. Borough views tended to concentrate on considerations of local access and environmental implications of schemes whereas the GLC was concerned primarily with the traffic implications. But the individuals involved in the schemes in both camps seemed aware and tolerant of the others' problems and point of view. Conflicts of view which did arise were regarded by the officers involved as not only inevitable but desirable expressions of different interests.

In noting the generally amicable and workable relationship between the Islington Council and the GLC, however, it is important to realise also that in fundamental outlook there was little difference between individual officers. All apparently accepted the long-standing proposal to widen the A1 to increase its traffic capacity throughout, and regarded the achievement of this objective as extremely difficult in practice because of the amount of property involved. Widening was very slow if one had to await rebuilding to a set-back line determined in years past, or extremely costly if one decided to acquire and demolish the properties at one fell swoop before their economic life had expired. There did not seem to be any official support for the view expressed by the SHA and later the Islington Society that large-scale road widening might not be appropriate at such an inner London location. The GLC's secondary road policy for example (that secondary road 'improvements' would be concentrated at intersections) was drawn up as a guide to investment priority for secondary roads rather than a move to abandon eventual wholesale widening of roads like Holloway Road and Upper Street, Islington.

Seen in the context of the eventual widening of the A1 to dual two- or three-lane standard from the Angel to the North Circular Road, the implementation delays to the four schemes described were not of any great significance. The widening of the north end of Holloway Road between the Archway intersection and Tufnell Park Road, costing £3 million, was excluded from the GLC's list of schemes for the DOE's 1972–78 preparation programme because although 'very desirable' there was 'no special reason for preference.'[3] The remainder of Holloway Road was envisaged

[1] To be precise, the GLC let the contracts for the work. Islington did become involved in the temporary diversions and traffic management necessary in the area during construction. But the GLC were entirely responsible for the widening itself.

[2] The GLC concurred with the LCC's earlier decision to pay BR the extra costs involved in providing a bridge which would span the widened road. MOT *Press Release*, 16 July 1970.

[3] GLC *Minutes*, 9 February 1971, p92.

by an Islington official as being ten or fifteen years away from final 'upgrading' and the Highbury to Angel stretch as more than twenty years away. Moreover it has already been noted that some time would elapse before a final decision was taken on the widening to dual three-lanes of the Archway Road and Falloden Way sections.

Although procedural delays were prominent in the handling of the four GLC schemes, the gradual remodelling of this stretch of the A1 was almost free of any outside opposition—certainly in comparison with the explosive public reaction to the road proposals affecting Highgate and Hampstead Garden Suburb. This was probably a clear reflection of the social differences and degree of articulate representation north and south of Archway but it may also have had something to do with the GLC's pursuance of individual piecemeal schemes (which may diffuse potential opposition) as opposed to the MOT's two large and relatively comprehensive proposals. There was a limited amount of concern expressed about the Archway intersection and Archway Road schemes but this was largely related to temporary disruption (albeit for nearly three years in the case of the intersection) before completion of the final schemes.[1] Opposition to the Angel scheme came relatively late in the implementation process.

4 FROM THE ANGEL TO ST PAUL'S

The A1 classification begins (or ends) where Aldersgate meets Cheapside and Newgate Street near St Paul's Cathedral. South of the Angel, the A1 consists of Goswell Road and Aldersgate Street and, being a borough Principal road, responsibility for this section is divided between Islington Borough Council and the City of London.

According to a senior Islington official, the A1 route only had traffic significance north of the Angel. From there traffic was distributed mainly by the so-called 'Inner Ring Route.' South of the Angel, he contended, the A1 route was simply a matter of convenience in numbering. Islington apparently had no schemes in mind on Goswell Road, although the GLC intended to divert traffic from its northernmost end into Spencer Street and St John Street as part of the Angel scheme. This was seen by Islington officers as a GLC matter. Nevertheless new frontage development on the Goswell Road continued to be subjected to safeguarding lines for eventual widening. One example of this safeguarding policy in operation was the setting back of buildings fronting Goswell Road and Aldersgate Street in the Golden Lane estate development carried out in the 1960s. In July 1960 the LCC said, in approving the road widening at this point, that: 'The increase in carriageway area and the improved alignment which will result from the widening will assist the flow of traffic on this busy thoroughfare.'[2]

[1] GLC *Minutes*, 20 June 1967, p389; 22 October 1968, p548; 7 July 1970, p423; 9 February 1971, p55 respectively.
[2] LCC *Minutes*, 19 July 1960, p526.

The City of London similarly wanted to widen Aldersgate Street. In 1963, for example, it was decided to widen a 210-yard stretch to provide a carriageway of between 40 and 46 feet, although the ultimate intention was to widen Aldersgate Street to provide a 48-feet carriageway throughout.[1] More recent schemes were aimed at providing a 'City By-Pass' of which the London Wall dual carriageway (passing through the Barbican redevelopment) formed a part. One such scheme was the building of a large roundabout at the intersection of London Wall and Aldersgate Street.[2] Another was the creation of a one-way system at the southern end of Aldersgate Street where it joined Newgate Street. This was seen as 'a further step in the plan to provide a high capacity northern by-pass of the congested central area of the City.'[3] Thus the City of London appeared to be more concerned with widening Aldersgate Street as part of its by-pass scheme than as part of an improved A1 route to the north.

5 CONCLUSIONS

The objectives of the various authorities relating to the A1 in London were, as we have seen, broadly similar, though they varied as to their emphasis. The clarity of these objectives also varied. Perhaps the clearest view was expressed by the DOE in its letter of decision on the Falloden Way inquiry, i.e. that of protecting the traffic interests on the system of national (Trunk) roads and of ensuring that this did not have serious adverse environmental effects. The GLC's objectives were, if one cast about to seek them, very similar in their dual emphasis of traffic and environment, although the best indicator in this respect was GLDP documentation relating to the secondary road network in general rather than statements about the A1 in particular. Much more significant was the implicit acceptance of the need to increase the traffic capacity of the road, even where circumstances made this a difficult and lengthy task, such as on parts of Holloway Road.

The boroughs presented no unified set of objectives. Barnet seemed to fully accept the DOE's role on the Falloden Way section. Haringey on the other hand became concerned about the effects of the Archway Road widening on properties adjoining the road and on residential streets in the area. They were also concerned about the possible prejudicial effects of widening the Falloden Way section before the question of their own (Archway Road) section was settled, and they appeared at the inquiry to say so. Islington presented a less coherent view of what they wanted to achieve on the A1, but on the other hand were not presented with comprehensive schemes for the section in their area. Their approval of the Archway and

[1] LCC *Minutes*, 7 May 1963, p305.

[2] DOE *Press Notice 670*, 10 December 1970. A special feature of the scheme was that the proposed London Museum would be built on the central island.

[3] DOE *Press Notice 445*, 2 December 1971.

Angel schemes implied an acceptance of the GLC's desire to increase traffic capacity as and when this became possible. Moreover in 1968 they had produced a road hierarchy for the Borough which include the A1 as a major route (see Case Study *G*). Islington officers, however, believed that the importance of the A1 route diminished sharply at the Angel, where it joined the Inner Ring Route, and they had no immediate desire to widen it south of that point (i.e. Goswell Road). The City of London clearly had the objective of increasing the traffic capacity of Aldersgate Street but seemed to view this as of importance to the City rather than to the A1 route as a whole.

The fact that each body had broadly similar objectives did not in itself, however, ensure co-ordinated planning. Division of responsibility for the road meant that joint objectives had to be co-ordinated between the different bodies, unless there was no real need for different sections of the road to be planned in relation to one another. The main onus inevitably fell on the GLC as strategic planning authority for deciding what degree of co-ordination was necessary, and carrying it out.

The first question that arises is what, if anything, was gained by the DOE's involvement on the A1 in London? The A1 Trunk road was regarded as part of the national system on which it was vital to 'deal adequately with the traffic needs.' Yet it was the responsibility of the GLC to decide the relative roles of roads in London, and in the GLDP the A1 received not primary but secondary road status. It was not explained how the road could be of national importance while being of only secondary importance to London. Furthermore, inside the North Circular (which is also a DOE responsibility) the A1 Trunk road is an administrative cul-de-sac. The value of the Trunk section as part of a major network could therefore only be seen if it was closely co-ordinated with the adjoining roads for which the GLC was responsible.

The DOE considered the A1 inside the North Circular for widening in two sections, each between two major junctions, which were handled separately. The initial schemes were prepared by separate bodies and the decisions on them were made at different times. One was the subject of a public inquiry after which the scheme was rejected and independent consultants appointed, while the other was the subject of a consultants' report first, and was likely to come to inquiry at some later stage. The only common link was that for both sections the DOE (or MOT) had appointed consultants in response to objections on environmental grounds and that the same consultants were employed on both sections. On the Falloden Way section a more limited widening was proceeded with which would raise its traffic standard above that of the Archway Road. This was said to be required as an immediate measure for safety reasons.

Length for length, the DOE undoubtedly made considerable efforts to strike the right balance (which is political) between traffic and the environment. But there was little sign that the DOE, and still less the GLC, were determined to make sure that the standard on one length would be compatible with that on adjoining lengths.[1] The situation existed where the Falloden Way section was being widened largely to dual-two standard, the DOE Archway Road section was being designed to dual-three standard but would not be implemented (if at all) until several years later, while the remaining half mile of Archway Road was being widened to dual-three standard by the GLC with a grant from the DOE.

One conclusion is inevitable. Either the amount of traffic varies between the North Circular and Archway justifying different standards of road at different times, or co-ordinated planning was not successful. If co-ordination was lacking, was this wholly or partly due to the division of responsibility between the GLC and DOE? There is no evidence to suggest that given full control the GLC would definitely have handled the matter any better. Indeed the GLC's pursuance of much smaller piecemeal schemes on the Metropolitan road section suggests that its handling might have been rather worse. It is possible, however, that GLC responsibility for the A1 from the North Circular to the Angel would have encouraged a more co-ordinated approach, simply by concentrating responsibility for the whole road with a single body.

The remaining justification for continued DOE responsibility was one of financial arrangements. No reason was proffered, however, why these arrangements should not be changed so as to permit the transfer of responsibility from the DOE to the GLC. The present arrangements are described in Chapter 3 and their inadequacies are discussed in Chapters 6 and 7.

The second question is to what extent the division of responsibility for the Principal road section (from Archway to Cheapside) is justified. The whole of this stretch was classified as a secondary road in the GLDP, but this classification was not related to specific objectives for the road. Both Islington Borough Council and the GLC saw the major traffic function of the A1 terminating at the Angel. That, for example, was where the firm intention to widen to 70 feet ceased. But further south the City of London was widening Aldersgate Street and providing for greater traffic capacity at the intersections with London Wall and Cheapside.

If indeed the traffic function of the A1 route diminishes sharply at the Angel there is some logic to end GLC responsibility for it there also. In that case the piecemeal widening at the City end (and the continued safeguard on Goswell Road operated by Islington Borough Council) would have to be justified by its benefits to the immediate locality.

The third question which lies behind what has already been discussed, is whether it is valid to consider (in planning terms) the A1 as a whole from the City to the North Circular and beyond, or conversely whether

[1] This does not necessarily mean that the traffic capacity would be the same; one could conceive of a route progressively increasing in capacity as flows converge onto it towards the city centre, or one which successively decreased in size either as traffic flows into London dispersed or to reflect an increasing degree of traffic restraint towards the centre.

consideration of individual schemes of differing standards along its length is justified. If a piecemeal approach is justified because of the different levels of traffic and varying functions of the road, is the institutional system adequate to distinguish these differences and relate them to the road network (and indeed the transport system) as a whole?

The Case Study produced no evidence that the route had been considered as a whole for planning purposes except in the most general terms. There had certainly never been any inquiry into the widening of the route as a whole. The evaluation of different schemes (i.e. to establish their priority, scale and design) was only carried out on the DOE lengths by their Consultants. Their studies, for example, attempted to see the future design of the road in relation to the demands that would arise in the long term with and without the proposed motorways. They also saw it as necessary to take account of changes in the strategy for secondary roads which emerged at the GLDP Inquiry, both for the Falloden Way study which they were about to undertake and for reviewing their earlier study of Archway Road.

There was no evidence, however, that the GLC officers related their intentions for their section of the road to the strategy that was put forward at the GLDP Inquiry. The GLC schemes fell into two categories: those inherited from the LCC (i.e. Archway Road, the Archway intersection, Holloway Road railway bridge widening and the Angel) and those dependent on the application of planning control to safeguard widening lines. The inherited schemes mostly carried with them a heavy commitment in terms of property acquired and design work completed, but the 'safeguarding' provisions were merely a matter of ensuring conformity of redevelopments to a long-term widening objective.

While the GLC's piecemeal approach to increasing the traffic standard of the A1 would be justified if each scheme was related both to specific local objectives and to an overall strategy for secondary roads, such relationships were not demonstrated. The evolving secondary roads policy had little or no influence on the design and phasing of the schemes which the GLC was carrying out, except in as much as it gave (because of its generality) a virtual *carte blanche* approach to any scheme which would increase traffic capacity. Certainly, considerations of pedestrian traffic, local shopping needs, residential environment and public transport never received sufficient weight to alter the emphasis on providing for more motor traffic. In this situation the widened half-mile section of Archway Road and the planned Angel intersection scheme could stand only as witness to the inflexibility of the planning system rather than as contributions to an explicitly defined future role for the A1 in London.

It appears then that the justification for any of the schemes described was never more than a firm belief that roads such as the A1 should be widened wherever possible to meet a growth in the volume of vehicular traffic. That such a growth might not, or need not, occur became the subject of much debate at the GLDP Inquiry, but this proposition played no part in determining the future of the A1. Certainly officers in the GLC and Islington Borough Council regarded the eventual widening of the entire A1 as an inevitable and agreed policy (and to the extent that the entire route was safeguarded for this purpose they were right) although the safeguarding which had been operated by the LCC had never been specifically ratified by them or the GLC. Thus they believed that it was just a question of acquiring the necessary properties and going through the necessary but time-consuming planning procedures.

The unquestioned acceptance of traffic growth also helps to explain the otherwise unscrupulous process which Dr Peter Levin described in a letter to *New Society*, an edited version of which was published at the time of the Falloden Way inquiry:[1]

> The Ministry is . . . arguing that simply because the *capacity* of other sections has been increased, the present scheme must go through.
>
> In one other section in particular—the Archway Road—widening has not yet begun: an inquiry into that proposal may yet be held. But at the Hampstead Garden Suburb inquiry, the Ministry is saying that the Archway Road *will* be widened, and that the traffic it will attract will necessitate the widening of the HGS section. Thus the present proposal is said to possess merit simply by virtue of conforming to an intention elsewhere that is yet to receive legal sanction.
>
> Of course, once the HGS section is widened, the traffic it attracts will strengthen the case for widening Archway Road. So the Ministry's argument amounts to a self-fulfilling prophecy: there are plans to widen Archway Road, therefore the HGS section needs to be widened, and then Archway Road will *have* to be widened.

While, during the course of this study, much evidence was found of officers involved in highway planning accepting the rightness and inevitability of the widening of the A1, it should also be said that the approach of the various politicians involved was considerably more changeable. Peter Walker, for example, was perfectly willing to postpone the widening to dual-three lanes of the Falloden Way section while alternative possibilities were considered. Haringey councillors were similarly prepared to oppose the Archway Road widening until a scheme had been produced which satisfied local interests. GLC councillors on the other hand often pursued the GLC's road schemes with vigour although it was difficult to see whether they were aware of the overall picture. Mr Neil Thorne, chairman of the GLC's Central Area Board stated, for example, that the GLC did not intend to widen the section of Holloway Road to the south of the Archway intersection, but in a GLDP Inquiry Background Paper, the widening of Holloway Road was included in a list of possible road schemes after the 'five to eight year programme from 1971–72.'[2] In commenting on this to

[1] *New Society*, 24 September 1969.

[2] GLC (1971), *Paper B458*, p92, GLDP Inquiry Stage 1 (quoted from GLC *Minutes*, of 9 February 1971).

the local press, a GLC spokesman was reported to have said: 'It [the widening of Holloway Road] is still only a germ in a planner's mind, but we want to carry out improvements when the cash is available.'[1] He believed a greater priority for the GLC would be to improve the traffic flow between the Archway intersection and Tufnell Park (not part of the A1).

Mr G Stern, chairman of the SHA, made the following comment to the GLDP Inquiry on these apparently conflicting statements from different quarters of the GLC:

> It would seem that the GLC is widening Holloway Road on Tuesdays and Thursdays when they are trying to gain support for the pointless widening of Archway Road, and are not widening it on Mondays, Wednesdays and Fridays when they are trying to quieten local people who are concerned about their district.[2]

Mr Stern's cynicism, whether justified or not, clearly stemmed from the difficulty he experienced in finding out what exactly the GLC intended to do on the A1 and when. Precisely the same difficulty was experienced in compiling this case study.

One further point must be made concerning the nature of objections to the A1 road schemes. It appeared that the most vociferous and articulate opposition came from middle- or upper-class groups who were concerned about the environmental effects of the DOE widening schemes. South of Archway there were far fewer people living beside the A1 who fell into this category and few groups emerged to fight the various proposals. The exceptions were the Islington Society and the Angel Association. But it also appeared that piecemeal schemes (even quite large ones as at the Archway) were far less likely to produce large-scale opposition than the relatively comprehensive schemes put forward by the DOE.

[1] *Islington Gazette*, 7 December 1971.
[2] SHA (1971), *Paper S27/327*, GLDP Inquiry Stage 2.

Case Study L

WALKING IN LONDON

INTRODUCTION

At one time the traffic on city streets consisted almost entirely of people on foot. In the narrow, winding streets of the mediaeval city any wheeled traffic of necessity took second place. In those days, however, distances within the city could easily be traversed on foot. As the cities grew beyond the purely pedestrian scale and as urban activities became more specialised, particularly in the late eighteenth and nineteenth centuries, people began to be dependent on wheeled traffic—horse-drawn carts, carriages and (later) the horse buses. But as the quantity of horse-drawn traffic increased, so did the need for disciplined use of the streets and a clear demarcation of the 'carriageway' and 'footway.' The precursor of the raised kerb and pavement, and, incidentally, a much more effective means of keeping vehicles in their place, was the row of iron bollards at regular intervals. But the streets were not paved until the eighteenth century, beginning with the footways which carried far more people than the carriageways.

London was the first British city to outgrow the scale of universally convenient pedestrian travel and, as it did so, the traffic (which itself partly enabled the growth) also grew, as did the conflict between pedestrians and vehicles. Gradually the work of the municipal engineer became more and more concerned with facilitating the passage of vehicles along city streets; the provision of a clearly defined carriageway with sturdy paving was required, together with proper drainage and street lighting.

Thus the role of the engineer developed not according to the overall transport needs, but to meet those problems whose solution needed to be *engineered*. Vehicles were (and still are) much less versatile, and potentially far more dangerous when moving than people on foot, and so demanded greater application of the engineer's skills. The footway was always, in terms of cost and construction, less important than the carriageway. Though the characteristics of movement on foot did not change through the generations, both the number and the speed of vehicles increased dramatically, generating obvious and often spectacular problems of congestion and danger. It is perhaps not surprising, then, that the needs of vehicles came to be regarded as more important than those of pedestrians. The aim of the highway engineer, as expressed by several nineteenth-century commissions of inquiry, was to provide for the former without the slaughter of the latter.

Recently there has, however, been a reaction to what is now regarded as the traditional approach to highway engineering, partly through the development of the planning profession and the awakening of public awareness of the quality of the urban environment, and more attention has been paid to the needs of people on foot. Residential areas in the post-war new towns, for example, were often planned with footpath systems segregated from the roads. In the town centres, the 'pedestrian shopping precinct' from which all vehicles were excluded became standard practice. In existing towns, areas of comprehensive redevelopment[1] enabled pedestrians to be physically separated from vehicular traffic, the Barbican and Elephant and Castle redevelopment schemes being well-known examples in London.

By the early 1960s, the concept of pedestrian and vehicular segregation was being explored as a method of achieving environmental and safety improvements in conventional streets. Impetus was given to this line of thinking by the publication of the Buchanan Report[2] and the creation during the 1960s of many pedestrians-only shopping streets in Europe.[3] Consequently most plans for new or redeveloped town centres include the provision of pedestrian-only areas.[4]

Pedestrian travel is not, of course, simply confined to residential areas or to shopping centres, and certainly not to redevelopment areas. It is a mode of travel in its own right as well as being an essential part of travel involving the use of vehicles. Planning for the pedestrian is therefore, in this sense, no different in concept from planning for the motor vehicle.

This case study examines the institutional arrangements for managing and planning pedestrian movement in London. It concentrates, however, on pedestrians in existing streets of conventional piecemeal development, not least because this aspect of pedestrian planning has usually received less attention than the planning of 'showpiece' pedestrian facilities in areas of new development such as Covent Garden and Piccadilly Circus. Moreover, planning for the pedestrian (indeed, all traffic) within the constraints of existing street patterns poses altogether different and often more difficult problems in terms of institutional co-ordination.

All three levels of government are involved in planning for pedestrians in London, according to the division of the relevant powers and responsibilities in the various highways, traffic and planning Acts (see Chapter 2). The Department of the Environment (DOE), apart from its functions with

[1] The 1947 Town and Country Planning Act enabled local planning authorities to designate, purchase, demolish and rebuild whole areas to a comprehensive and statutorily approved plan.

[2] C D Buchanan (1963), *Traffic in Towns.*

[3] See A A Wood (1966), *Foot Streets in Four Cities*, for a description of pedestrian shopping streets in Düsseldorf, Essen, Cologne and Copenhagen. See also J G Gray (1965), *Pedestrian Shopping Streets in Europe*, Pedestrians' Association for Road Safety.

[4] E.g. Southend (where part has already been implemented in the Victoria Circus scheme), Hornchurch (L B Havering) and plans for Bromley and Wood Green. The latter two will allow buses and service vehicles to use the shopping street but a substantial degree of freedom for the pedestrian will be obtained by widening the pavements.

regard to Trunk roads, has had overall responsibility for pedestrian crossings in London although this function was transferred to the Greater London Council (GLC) (except on Trunk roads) with the implementation of Section 32 of the Transport (London) Act 1969. In addition, the DOE may indicate broad policy or give advice to local authorities on pedestrian matters, for example through circulars and design bulletins. As traffic authority for London, the GLC is the main executive body concerned with pedestrians, particularly on roads for which it is also the highway authority (i.e. Metropolitan roads). But the boroughs also have major executive functions as highway and local planning authorities. They can, moreover, initiate highway or traffic schemes even though GLC or DOE approval or finance may be necessary.

The police are closely involved in any scheme affecting pedestrians (as with other traffic) since they are responsible for enforcing any consequent orders or regulations. They have a statutory right to consultation over any scheme which involves such enforcement.

Although not statutorily involved, London Transport (LT) inevitably has an interest in any scheme to pedestrianise or limit vehicular movement in streets used by buses. Traders and residents, both individually and in association, also have an interest.

This case study is set out in two parts. The first covers the general situation regarding pedestrian travel as a part of London's transport system. There appeared to be no major plan or policy issue in which the interests of pedestrians became crucial; there were only special instances where the interests of pedestrians were represented, for example in the comprehensive redevelopment areas already mentioned, and in some new developments such as Thamesmead (see Case Study *A*).

The next part of the study deals with two of these special (although important) instances, namely proposals to turn Bond Street and Carnaby Street in London's West End into pedestrian-only streets.

WALKING AS A MODE OF TRAVEL

Various policies and proposals for the control of vehicular traffic have been discussed elsewhere (see Case Studies *G*, *M* and *Q*). This section is concerned with general policies for the pedestrian; not those to deal with the special problems arising in redevelopment schemes, new development, interchanges or particular points of high pedestrian activity, but for the pedestrian as an element of road traffic sharing London's streets with vehicular traffic.

Central government has been involved to the extent of giving certain guidance and setting the legislative framework within which local authorities formulate traffic policy. In a White Paper published in 1967, the Minister of Transport (then Barbara Castle) announced that urban local authorities *outside* Greater London would be asked to prepare short-term 'traffic and transport plans.' Amongst other things these plans would have to 'hold the scale between the needs of people on foot and those using vehicles.' She also said that existing legislation did 'not have sufficient concern for people on foot in towns,' and proposed legislation to place on local authorities 'a duty to use their powers in order to secure convenient and safe movement of pedestrians as well as wheeled traffic.'[1] This move, however, was to bring other authorities into line with the GLC in this respect. The London Government Act 1963 had already conferred on the GLC the general duty 'to secure the expeditious, convenient and safe movement of vehicular and other traffic (including foot passengers)' whilst having due regard to access requirements, amenities and any other relevant matters.[2] The specific mention of 'foot passengers' was a clear indication of the Government's wish to see them receive equal consideration with other traffic in matters of traffic control.

Further mention of pedestrians came in a White Paper, *Transport in London*, published in July 1968, which pointed to inadequacies of the system for dealing with pedestrians. Criticism was, however, confined to the difficulties of exploiting opportunities for pedestrian–vehicular segregation in areas of redevelopment.[3] The only specific proposal concerning pedestrians was to give the GLC responsibility for the siting and control of pedestrian crossings within a quota fixed by the Ministry.[4] Close control had been kept by the Ministry over pedestrian-crossing provisions, partly to avoid a repetition of the situation after the Second World War when the number of crossings was said to be so great that drivers paid little head to them. Criteria for the provision of pedestrian crossings have been developed by the DOE, taking account of existing vehicle and pedestrian flows.[5]

Other guidelines to local authorities from the Ministry of Transport (MOT) (and DOE) have concentrated on technical matters of design and layout. Criteria have been established, for example, for the provision of pedestrian subways or bridges in order to help local authorities to choose the facility most suited to local circumstances.[6]

Guidance on many aspects of road design and layout was given in a MOT booklet published in 1966, but this devoted no more than seven of its ninety-two pages to pedestrians and footways, the remainder dealing with vehicles and carriageway designs.[7] This document, however, which remains a basic source of information in engineering departments, limited its

[1] MOT (1967), *Public Transport and Traffic*, Cmnd 3481, paras116, 122. This provision was enacted by the *Transport Act 1968*, ch73, s133, amending the *Road Traffic Regulation Act 1967*, ch76, s84 (1).

[2] Ch33 (1963), s9 (2). This duty was repeated in the *Road Traffic Regulation Act 1967*, ch76, s84 (1), as amended by s133 of the Transport Act 1968.

[3] MOT (1968), *Transport in London*, Cmnd 3686, para33.

[4] Cmnd 3686, para63, proposal No.58. Enacted by *Transport (London) Act 1969*, ch35, s32.

[5] J T Duff (1970), *Engineering for Road Safety*, Public Works and Municipal Services Congress 1970, paper 15.

[6] MOT (1969), *Criteria for the Provision of Pedestrian Subways or Bridges*, Technical Memorandum No.H8/69.

[7] MOT (1966), *Roads in Urban Areas*.

advice to the design requirements in any particular situation of conflict between pedestrians and vehicles, and was of little help in determining policies to influence the nature or extent of that conflict. Later documents have been more forthcoming in this respect, for example a DOE circular issued in 1971 dealt with considerations in determining priorities between buses and pedestrians in pedestrianised streets.[1]

Whatever role Government plays in pedestrian planning, local authorities are better placed to determine and implement particular policies. In London it might be argued that the boroughs are more suited to this task than the GLC. But in the Greater London Development Plan (GLDP) the GLC stressed that they also had a role to play. The Written Statement's brief section on pedestrians began:

> London's roads are for pedestrians as well as traffic. For the pedestrians this situation has become progressively more difficult over the years, facing them with conditions of discomfort and potential danger. It is particularly important therefore that planning *at all levels* should keep their special needs in mind . . . [our italic].[2]

The GLDP's policies for pedestrians, however, were of a general nature and consisted largely of statements of expected benefits from building the proposed 'primary' and 'secondary' roads:

> The strategy of establishing a network of primary routes is intended to ensure that no significant increase will be necessary in the mileage of secondary roads and thus no further disruption of the environment through which they pass. The level of use will be such as to avoid the creation of new barriers to local movement on foot and in vehicles.[3]

Moreover, the Council put forward no specific policy for pedestrian travel, other than the provision of pedestrian and vehicular segregation in large-scale developments (paragraph 5.48) and 'wherever possible' when improving the road system in central London. Emphasis was on the problems of vehicular traffic:

> . . . the extent of segregation which can be achieved is bound to be limited for many years to come. . . . Planning must therefore aim to make conditions more tolerable for pedestrians. Road layouts, traffic management schemes, and the design of interchanges should all be devised with the needs and limitations of the pedestrian *in mind* . . . (paragraph 5.49) [our italics].

In a later document the GLC amplified its policy for 'secondary' roads and

[1] DOE (1971), *Circular Roads 58/71.*
[2] GLC (1969), *GLDP Written Statement*, para5.47.
[3] GLC (1969), *GLDP Written Statement*, para5.25.

said that these 'should border environmental districts or areas' the layout of which could 'make it safe and simple for the pedestrians to move to the centres of attraction—to the schools, the shops, the offices, the open spaces. . . .' The difficulty, as the Council recognised, was that 'many of today's main traffic routes are themselves centres of attraction for pedestrians.' The policy for overcoming this was a long-term programme of finding new routes for secondary roads or changing the nature of development alongside them.[1]

The Council was cautious in its approach to the problem of pedestrians wishing to cross the secondary roads. It ruled out the universal provision of bridges or subways on grounds of cost. 'The use of signals' they said, 'is the key to the problem. Not only can pedestrians cross under their protection at intersections but the intermittent flow they induce can provide gaps for pedestrians to cross at refuges at points between intersections. . . . For this reason the use of signals on the system at intersections is to be preferred to free-flow devices. . . .' They concluded, however, that 'some restrictions must . . . be accepted by the pedestrian.' Provision of crossing facilities 'should improve his safe movement but jay walking will tend to be even more hazardous than it is now.'[2]

In its suggested revisions to the Written Statement of the GLDP, the GLC said that the boroughs should prepare local plans 'consistent with the general strategy for both (secondary) roads and the environment within which they function' specifying amongst other things pedestrian routes. Since they have no traffic powers the boroughs, of course, can do no more than initiate schemes for pedestrians or criticise those put forward by the GLC or the DOE in the hope of modifying them. At the time of writing none of the borough Development Plans was complete and policies for pedestrians (apart from those of a very general nature, or relating to specific schemes) had not apparently been formulated.

It is thus difficult to illustrate how in practice pedestrian interests are represented in the institutional system, but we now turn to some scattered examples of pedestrian involvement.

Some examples

First, Table 25 sets out extracts from a number of GLC or DOE official press statements relating to highway improvement or traffic management schemes. Two points are clear from this collection: every scheme was supported by claims to increase pedestrian safety, but in most cases there was no specific mention of greater convenience; and all but two of the schemes quoted (GLC numbers 533 and 98) were supported by the specific claim of benefits to vehicular traffic as well as to pedestrians.

Second, during 1970 there was a considerable amount of correspondence

[1] GLC (1970), *A Secondary Roads Policy* (revised after consultation), p3.
[2] GLC (1970), pp10, 11.

PRESS RELEASE REFERENCE	SCHEME REFERRED TO (TITLE)	EXTRACT SENTENCE(S) RELATING TO PEDESTRIANS (OUR ITALICS)
GLC, 23 August 1966 (No.361)	Footbridge over Leytonstone High Road	Crossing the road by footbridge may take a little longer but it will be *safer* and *traffic will be able to flow more freely*
GLC, 11 August 1970 (No.406)	Plans to improve Rayners Lane area, Harrow	After consultation with the police and road user organisations, an amended traffic management scheme . . . has been approved. . . . The proposals aroused considerable interest because of the beneficial effect they will have on pedestrian *safety*
GLC, 18 November 1970 (No.533)	Improved conditions for pedestrians in Kingsbury Road	These (traffic) lights will be provided at the end of a busy shopping parade and will greatly improve *safety conditions* for pedestrians including shoppers and schoolchildren
DOE, 31 December 1970 (No.718)	Three new pedestrian subways at Croydon	The main subway . . . will replace a busy pedestrian crossing. The removal of this crossing will not only make conditions *safer for pedestrians* but will also *improve traffic flow*
GLC, 5 February 1971 (No.49)	New traffic management scheme for Putney High Street	On Sunday 14 February, the first steps towards implementing a traffic management scheme designed to *reduce congestion* and improve pedestrian *safety* in Putney High Street will be taken, the Joint Traffic Executive for Greater London announced today
GLC, 12 February 1971 (No.60)	Pedestrian subway at Barking station	The subway would be built through a railway arch under East Street. This would considerably ease the traffic delays in peak hours caused by pedestrians crossing East Street to the station. Mr Bernard Brook-Partridge, chairman of the (North-East Area) Board, said: 'This area near the station has a very poor *accident* record'

GLC, 1 April 1971 (No.131)	Pelican crossing for pedestrians at Stanmore station	Heavy flows of traffic along the road and large numbers of pedestrians using the (uncontrolled zebra) crossing mean *long delays for both.* Mr Harold Mote, chairman of the (West Area) Board, said: 'Not only will a Pelican crossing *reduce delays and congestion for traffic* but it will mean greater *safety* for pedestrians'
GLC, 2 April 1971 (No.134)	Safety improvements in Craven Park Road	Pedestrian-controlled traffic lights at this point will greatly improve *safety for pedestrians* and will also *reduce traffic delays*
DOE, 5 April 1971 (No.192)	As above	The subway, which will replace the existing pedestrian crossing will make conditions *safer for pedestrians* and *improve traffic flow*
GLC, 23 February 1972 (No.98)	Pelican crossing for Shooters Hill Road	A Pelican crossing is to be provided . . . following a request from local residents. . . . A signal-controlled pedestrian crossing here should greatly improve pedestrian *safety and convenience* and should not cause serious delays to traffic on this busy route

Table 25 REFERENCES TO PEDESTRIANS IN SOME LONDON ROAD AND TRAFFIC SCHEMES

in *The Times* about pedestrians' conflict with vehicles turning at junctions. Two of the writers said:

> Following a furious encounter with a motorist at the corner of Conduit Street, I insisted that he come with me to Saville Row police station just around the corner. Nobody there had ever heard of Section 47 of the Highway Code (which reads: 'When turning at a road junction, give way to pedestrians who are crossing') and it was only after a considerable search that a copy of the Highway Code was found.

> Some time ago after dodging a vehicle at traffic lights, I asked a nearby policeman the legal position in those circumstances. The reply was: 'It's a question of using your loaf.'[1]

The third case is that of Fleet Street. A MOT committee on the design of urban roads reported in 1946 that safety would be materially advanced if regulations were introduced making it illegal to cross the road within 100 yards of a pedestrian crossing.[2] Two experiments were initiated by MOT in line with this finding. In 1965 an experiment was carried out in three London boroughs (Haringey, Ealing and Westminster) in which pedestrians were compelled to cross only at points provided every 100 yards. The results were apparently disappointing. Delays to pedestrians and vehicles increased, enforcement became extremely difficult while the accident record was not significantly improved. The second attempt was carried out by the City of London in 1966 to cut down the accidents on four particularly dangerous streets, one of which was Fleet Street. Here red lines were painted on the kerbs between pedestrian crossings and pedestrians were liable to fines of up to £20 if they crossed them. The experiment lasted no more than three months during which the City of London Police found enforcement impossible. It was reported that 5000 pedestrians had been warned during the experiment (none was actually prosecuted) but a police census showed that the lines were being ignored by between 3000 and 4000 pedestrians each day.[3]

The fourth example, the East Cross Route, forms the eastern side of the proposed Motorway Box (Ringway 1) and is a 'special road' without frontage access or footways, its use being limited to motor vehicles. The degree to which this major road has divided the locality through which it runs can be indicated by the number and convenience of pedestrian links which existed before and after its construction.

The motorway comprises the Blackwall tunnel and its northern and southern approaches. The northern approach[4] has five pedestrian subways fairly evenly spaced over its length of 1.4 miles. It is difficult to compare this with the situation before construction because the new route

[1] Letters to *The Times*, 26 October 1970.
[2] MOT (1946), *The Design and Layout of Roads in Built-up Areas.*
[3] The *Guardian*, 11 November 1968.
[4] That is, the part described in a GLC pamphlet published in 1971 entitled *The East Cross Route: Blackwall Tunnel Northern Approach.*

followed closely that of an existing conventional road which pedestrians had the opportunity of crossing at will. There were, however, about fifteen cross-streets providing access at junctions alone between the development on either side of the route.

The southern approach to the tunnel, approximately 1.7 miles long, has eight places at which pedestrians can cross by underpass or footbridge, compared with about fourteen cross-streets before the new road was built. However, only the southernmost mile has development on either side, and here the number of pedestrian crossing places has been reduced to seven from a minimum of ten.

Many of the new pedestrian facilities are less convenient than the former crossings at ground level. For example, a new footbridge on the southern approach has increased by 2.75 times the distance on foot between two points on either side of the motorway.[1]

PEDESTRIANS-ONLY SHOPPING STREETS

In places of intense pedestrian activity and conflict with vehicles the restriction or banning of wheeled traffic can bring about immense benefits for the safety and convenience of those on foot. The environmental benefits that can be achieved in shopping streets when vehicles are excluded have been demonstrated in several British towns and cities, of which perhaps the best-known examples are Norwich and Leeds. There are numerous examples throughout Europe where central shopping streets have been turned into pedestrian-only streets.[2] The delights of traffic-free streets have, of course, been on permanent display for centuries in Venice, for example, and in many other towns such as Zadar, Split and Dubrovnic on the Yugoslav Adriatic coast. The antithesis is to be found in major shopping streets such as London's Oxford Street described by Buchanan as 'the most uncivilised street in Europe' and by Henry Barnes[3] as simply 'a disaster.' (But see Case Study *M* on the Oxford Street experiment introduced in November 1972.)

In London, although there are examples of purpose-built traffic-free areas,[4] few attempts have been made to close shopping streets to vehicles. Two examples, Bond Street and Carnaby Street, are described below.

Bond Street

Severe traffic congestion led to the implementation in 1962 of major traffic management measures in the Mayfair area.[5] These included the

[1] GLC (1971), *Blackwall Tunnel: Southern Approach.*

[2] For example: Amsterdam, Brussels, Copenhagen, Paris, Cologne, Hanover, Kiel, Essen, Düsseldorf, Rotterdam, Stuttgart, Salzburg.

[3] Henry Barnes: former Traffic Commissioner of New York City.

[4] For example, Burlington Arcade off Piccadilly; Hornchurch and Romford suburban town centres.

[5] Bounded by Park Lane, Oxford Street, Regent Street and Piccadilly.

making of Bond Street[1] into a one-way street between Oxford Street and Piccadilly. This work was carried out by the MOT's London Traffic Management Unit (LTMU) in conjunction with the City of Westminster, and was designed with the sole objective of easing the passage of wheeled traffic through the area. As a result, congestion in Bond Street probably became less than at any time during the previous 100 years.[2] But in speeding the traffic, the scheme had the effect of increasing the maximum flow from 1230 to 2000 vehicles per hour or more.[3] The convenience of the pedestrian, and the quality of the environment generally had thus only improved to the extent that the free flow of vehicles contributed to this.

It is often said that congested traffic conditions have an adverse effect on the environment, yet in a narrow street such as Bond Street, crossing from shop to shop may often be safer and easier (although not pleasant because of fumes and noise) when the flow of vehicles is slow or intermittent. On the pavement, too, it can be more unpleasant to have cars and lorries passing at 30 m.p.h. only a few feet away than when they are slowed to walking pace by congestion. This is particularly true when pedestrian densities are high. In Bond Street, for example, a maximum flow of 2470 pedestrians per hour was recorded along one side of the street where the pavement was less than 5 feet wide. In these circumstances many people necessarily walked in the carriageway.[4]

In 1963 the London County Council decided to safeguard the ultimate widening of Bond Street to an overall width of 70 feet by establishing a line to which new buildings would be set back, stretching along the southern part of New Bond Street and the entire length of Old Bond Street. If it was to be achieved, it would have involved the demolition of several buildings listed by the Ministry of Housing and Local Government as of architectural or historic interest and the 'smoothing-out' of properties fronting Bond Street.[5] The intention, of course, was to provide for increased vehicular traffic flow.

It was in the same year that Buchanan first voiced the idea that Bond Street was an obvious example of a street from which traffic should be excluded for environmental reasons.[6] The idea was taken up not by either of the local authorities (Westminster City Council and the GLC) but by a *Daily Mail* staff reporter, Peter Lewis, who in June 1966 commissioned two of Professor Buchanan's team at Imperial College, Peter Hills and David Briggs, to carry out a feasibility study. Completed in July 1966, the

[1] In this study 'Bond Street' refers to the entire length between Oxford Street and Piccadilly consisting of New Bond Street and Old Bond Street.

[2] A member of the Bond Street Association said that the congestion of hansom cabs in Victorian days made the street itself something of a social centre, with people stepping into each other's cabs for a leisurely chat while the flow of vehicles was halted.

[3] Westminster CC (1967), *Bond Street Study*, pp2–3.

[4] Westminster CC (1967), p3.

[5] In 1969 the City Council designated the whole of the surrounding area as a Conservation Area under the Civic Amenities Act 1967.

[6] C D Buchanan (1963), *Traffic in Towns*, para134.

study discussed the existing problems of traffic and pedestrian movement in the area and proposed closing Bond Street to all traffic for part of the day.[1] This was to be achieved in three stages. The first stage was to make a full study of traffic in the area to assess the effects of any traffic scheme. Stage II was to discourage through traffic (i.e. vehicles having no business in the street) by the erection of two barriers and a complementary one-way system. The third stage was to close Bond Street to all vehicles during the busy part of the day. It was estimated that even with the implementation of Stage II, noise levels would be reduced by two-thirds and crossing the road would become considerably easier.

The report was distributed to all interested authorities (MOT, GLC, Westminster City Council, the police, LT Board); it was presented by Peter Hills to the Bond Street Association (a body primarily representing the commercial interests in the street); and it was discussed at a joint meeting of GLC and Westminster City Council traffic and planning officers. Soon afterwards Peter Lewis began a press campaign that continued for several days in which several prominent architects as well as Buchanan expressed support for the idea.[2] Buchanan also raised the issue at the fifth world meeting of the International Road Federation held in London shortly afterwards, and on 21 September Barbara Castle (then Minister of Transport), speaking at a conference of the Association of Municipal Corporations, mentioned the need to introduce legislation enabling the exclusion of traffic from shopping streets for reasons of amenity.[3] A week later Mr Algernon Asprey, President of the Bond Street Association, informed the GLC that at a special meeting his association had 'unanimously agreed that the use of the street as a through traffic route must cease.' Thus with support for the idea at both ministerial and 'grass roots' levels, the decision-making process was narrowed down to the local authorities concerned.

Response at County Hall was rapid; on 3 October the chairmen of the GLC Planning and Highways committees discussed the proposals contained in the report with Peter Hills and Peter Lewis.[4] However, in reply to a Question in Council the following day, Mrs Jane Phillips, chairman of the Highways Committee, said: 'It is clearly impossible for me to risk causing chaos in this important area. . . .'[5] Her main arguments were, first, that no scheme could be undertaken without a thorough traffic study of the whole Mayfair area, and that the GLC staff capable of doing this were already fully occupied that year. Second, she considered it 'common

[1] P J Hills and D A Briggs (August 1966), 'Bond Street,' Imperial College (unpublished).
[2] *Daily Mail*, 19 September 1966.
[3] *Daily Mail*, 22 September 1966, Mrs Castle apparently was considering the change in legislation because a similar scheme put forward by Leeds City Council for traffic-free shopping streets had had to be refused for lack of powers. Leeds had overcome its problem through a Private Member's Bill which had received Royal assent a month previously.
[4] Peter Hills' personal records.
[5] GLC *Minutes*, 4 October 1966, pp490–1.

sense' that traffic shut out of Bond Street would have to be accommodated on other roads which could not take any extra load. She hoped to offer many pedestrian precinct schemes in the future but hoped that 'everyone (would) be patient a little longer' while overall problems were tackled.

The Conservative opposition at County Hall launched an immediate attack on this attitude spearheaded by Mr Robert Vigars, spokesman on planning and transport. On 1 November he tabled a motion calling for a report on the effects of closing Bond Street to traffic, which was also signed by Mr Desmond Plummer and Mr Horace Cutler.[1]

In December a joint report of the Highways and Traffic and Planning and Communications committees pointed out that the traffic assessment shown to be necessary by the Hills–Briggs Report could not be carried out immediately because of Christmas traffic. The report gave two views, however, which were claimed to obviate the need for a thorough survey. The first repeated the argument made by Jane Phillips two months previously, namely that 'transfer of Bond Street's considerable traffic load would cause serious extra congestion in the area' and in the surrounding main roads.[2] The second point was that it was already known that most traffic in Bond Street had business there or in other parts of Mayfair so that closure would inconvenience local traffic movements.[3]

Meanwhile the Bond Street issue was receiving attention by Westminster City Council, whose Highways and Traffic Committee had instructed the City Engineer to carry out a survey of traffic conditions 'with the aim of formulating a scheme for the elimination of vehicular traffic in the street.'[4]

In May 1967 Robert Vigars, who was now chairman of the Highways and Traffic Committee in the newly elected Conservative GLC, explained to Peter Lewis that further action on Bond Street awaited the appearance of the Westminster City Engineer's Report. The City Council considered the Report in July 1967 and the City Engineer's two main recommendations were approved. The first was the introduction of simple traffic management measures to reduce the amount of traffic using the section of Bond Street between Bruton Street and Grafton Street. The second was to review the situation in six months to see if new north–south routes could be provided 'thus enabling Bond Street to be given over largely to pedestrians'[5] (thus by implication the Westminster officers also accepted that there would be overspill traffic).

The scheme was submitted to the GLC the same month[6] but progress was slow. By 24 October Robert Vigars was only able to report that following technical discussions (involving officers of the GLC, Westminster

[1] GLC *Minutes*, 1 November 1966, p598.

[2] She had given the same answer earlier in the year to questions about experimental closures of Oxford Street and Regent Street. See GLC *Minutes*, 25 January 1966, p10.

[3] GLC *Minutes*, 13 December 1966, p725.

[4] Westminster City Engineer's Report E239/67, *Bond Street Study*, June 1967, p1.

[5] Westminster CC (1967), *Bond Street Study*, p4.

[6] Also consultation took place with the police, Bond Street and Mayfair Associations.

City Council and the police) 'the question of an investigation over a wider area (was) being considered' to examine the effects of diverting traffic from Bond Street.[1] Westminster's City Engineer, however, believed that sufficient information had been collected to proceed with an experiment to reduce traffic in Bond Street. In a Report to the Highways and Traffic Committee in November 1967 he said that 'the practicability of this . . . can probably only be tested by bringing it into operation.'[2] The following February, the same Committee considered the GLC's formal comments on their Report. The GLC had said that while useful, the Report did 'not cover in sufficient detail the matter with which the GLC and Commissioner of Police are most concerned, namely the impact of the displaced traffic on main peripheral roads.' The GLC considered that 'even more help could be given to the Mayfair area overall, including Bond Street, by a different traffic scheme,' although because their staff was engaged on other matters they could not explore this further without the aid of Westminster's officers. They added that traders in the area (not just in Bond Street) might raise objections to the scheme.

Westminster City Council was clearly frustrated by the GLC's attitude. Local interests had been informed and discussions had taken place between City Council officers and the Bond Street and Mayfair Associations as a result of which general agreement had been reached on the need to reduce traffic in the street. The City Council was therefore prepared to proceed with an experiment with this objective. The points of disagreement with the GLC were made clear in the Highways Committee Report to the City Council in March 1968:

> We have no reason to depart from our original view that the first phase of the proposed scheme could be put into operation quickly with the minimum of expense and would show whether or not consequential difficulties arose elsewhere . . . the traffic investigation which was carried out was in far greater detail than any previous investigation of which we are aware prior to the introduction of other extensive traffic management schemes by the former LTMU.

The Committee did not feel that further studies would reveal any additional information of significance. The GLC was duly informed that Westminster was 'regrettably' unable to provide assistance for further studies and wished 'to see a scheme based on its own study introduced as soon as possible.'[3]

Action at County Hall continued to be conspicuous by its absence, until the *Evening Standard* saw a 'ray of light and hope' in a statement by

[1] GLC *Minutes*, 24 October 1967, p586 (reply to Question in Council); Westminster CC *Minutes*, 27 July 1967.
[2] Westminster CC *Report of City Engineer to Highways and Traffic Committee*, 7 November 1967.
[3] Westminster CC *Minutes*, 14 March 1968.

Robert Vigars on 28 November 1968 which read, 'we must use traffic management not just to ease congestion of the motor vehicle, but also to create amenity for London's pedestrians, shoppers and residents.' This statement was prompted by the appearance of a traffic management scheme produced by the GLC's engineers which was intended to 'improve traffic circulation in the Mayfair area, while improving the environment in the shopping area of Bond Street.'[1] But after nearly two years of inaction, scepticism was growing about Mr Vigars's sincerity, or at least his ability to influence the work of his own officers. The *Evening Standard* reporter said that 'the number of proposals for traffic-free streets that must have ground to a halt in the traffic engineers' office at County Hall probably equals the number of times London politicians have made speeches supporting them.'[2] In December, representatives of the London Amenity and Transport Association (an umbrella group for local civic societies throughout London) held a meeting with Mr Vigars 'to remind him of his zeal in Opposition days with special reference to pedestrianising Bond Street.'[3]

The GLC traffic management proposals consisted largely of a rationalisation of the 1962 LTMU scheme. They were not entirely traffic-oriented but neither were they aimed at the specific objective of eliminating vehicles in Bond Street, which was the main feature of those drawn up by Hills and Briggs and Westminster City Council. Through traffic was to be discouraged by the creation of a modified system of one-way streets, reversing the existing flow in the southern section of Bond Street between Grafton Street and Piccadilly. The removal of the need to use this section by through traffic was thought to provide the 'possibility' of closing it to vehicles altogether for part of the day.[4] Like Westminster City Council's earlier Report, TMS 107 was intended for consultation purposes. Westminster's Highways and Traffic Committee considered the report in February 1969 and made a number of observations on the traffic implications. In particular the ability of the proposals to reduce traffic volumes in Bond Street was doubted. The cost of the scheme (£100 000) was also thought to be too great for an experimental scheme and Westminster City Council's own proposals were considered to be a far better proposition in this respect. The Town Planning Committee also considered the report the following day, but neither committee was prepared to comment on the broader amenity issues until the views of local associations were available.[5]

In March, Peter Hills and David Briggs sent their comments on TMS 107 to the GLC and Westminster City Council.[6] They thought that it

[1] GLC (1968) *Traffic Management Scheme for Mayfair including Bond Street*. Report No.TMS 107, p1.

[2] *Evening Standard*, 29 November 1968.

[3] P J Hills (1968), 'Bond Street—A History of Civic Inaction' (unpublished).

[4] GLC (1968), *TMS 107*, p2, para3.6.

[5] Westminster CC *Minutes*, 13 March 1969 (H and T Report, 11 February 1969).

[6] P J Hills and D A Briggs (March 1969), 'Comments on Mayfair Traffic Management Scheme TMS 107' (unpublished). It was also reported that the Bond Street and Mayfair

represented 'an encouraging step in the right direction' but made the following criticism amongst others:

1 Pedestrianisation of Bond Street should be undertaken on a proper experimental basis and not simply talked of (as in TMS 107) as a 'possibility.'
2 The scheme made no proposals for physically ensuring that the assigned traffic flows would actually occur, or (if they did occur) for preventing increases in traffic beyond these levels.

They suggested two means of overcoming this latter problem: narrowing the carriageway between intersections (by 'selective widening' of the footways); and introducing the two traffic barriers suggested in their original proposals (one of which had also been a feature of Westminster City Engineer's proposals).

The GLC also consulted the police, the Grosvenor Estate, the Bond Street and Mayfair Associations, LT, Westminster Chamber of Commerce, motoring organisations and other bodies interested or affected in the proposals.[1] In October 1969 the GLC Planning and Transportation Committee reported that after 'prolonged consultation' with Westminster City Council they had approved a further traffic management scheme for the improvement of amenity and traffic conditions in Mayfair. The scheme was intended to achieve the eventual removal of traffic from Old Bond Street and the southern part of New Bond Street (as suggested in TMS 107) but because of the traders' fears of loss of business it was to be implemented in three stages, each of which would be studied before proceeding to the next.[2]

Five months later in March 1970 the same committee announced that the first stage (a traffic gyratory system not involving Bond Street, and agreed earlier as a separate scheme with Westminster City Council) should be implemented by October 1970. The GLC believed that this stage alone would improve amenity in the area.[3] It was in fact not until 30 January the following year that this first step was taken although Robert Vigars said he hoped that all three stages would be completed by the end of 1972 with the erection of a barrier across New Bond Street (i.e. the one included in the original Westminster City Council scheme). After that, he said, it would be possible to turn the section of the street between the barrier and Piccadilly into a pedestrian-only street.

In October 1971 Simon Jenkins of the *Evening Standard* tackled the GLC on its hesitancy in introducing pedestrian-only streets to central

Associations and the City of Westminster Chamber of Commerce concurred with Westminster City Council's views on TMS 107. See Westminster CC *Minutes*, 24 April 1969.

1 GLC *Press Release 91*, 14 February 1969.

2 GLC *Minutes*, 21 October 1969, p582.

3 GLC *Minutes*, 10 March 1969, p244.

London. He pointed out that the original eighteen-month time scale for pedestrianising the southern part of Bond Street was 'looking a bit thin.' He reported the chairman of the GLC's Central Area Board, Mr Neil Thorne, as saying:

> We have got a little behindhand . . . the Government restricted expenditure on those schemes so we are spacing the phasing out . . ., we don't want to force anything on the traders. We haven't tried to sell them the scheme. Besides, here in Britain we tend to move more slowly than they do in the Continent. We have to give everyone time to object.[1]

Nevertheless the second stage of the Mayfair Traffic Scheme was announced the following week. It was brought into operation in November and consisted of a number of adjustments to traffic movements in Mayfair which the GLC claimed would 'in themselves reduce traffic in Bond Street south of Conduit Street. A careful watch will be kept on their effect on residential amenity, vehicles, and pedestrians before it is decided to introduce the third stage.'[2]

Consultation carried out by Westminster City Council during 1972 revealed some measure of discontent with Stage II, particularly about increased traffic which their counts had shown in some surrounding streets. Opposition was also expressed to the introduction of Stage III which involved the erection of a barrier in Bond Street to prohibit through traffic. In fact a majority of the bodies consulted were against Stage III. Nevertheless, in view of the success of the scheme in reducing traffic in Bond Street, Westminster's Highways Committee decided that Stage III should proceed for an experimental period of six months, subject to possible modifications.[3] No detailed proposals had then been drawn up for the exclusion of traffic from Bond Street altogether so that this objective (a feature common to the original Westminster City Council and GLC intentions) still seemed a long way from being achieved.

Carnaby Street

In April 1967 the GLC invited the London boroughs to prepare schemes for environmental improvement in selected areas, and at the same time put forward for consultation a proposal to close Carnaby Street to vehicular traffic between 11 a.m. and 8 p.m. At that time Carnaby Street was rapidly achieving enormous popularity for its fashionable boutiques which attracted a large number of foreign and British tourists.

The object of the GLC's proposal was 'to try out how far conditions can be made pleasanter and safer in shopping streets in the London area by

[1] *Evening Standard*, 19 October 1971.
[2] Joint Traffic Executive for Greater London, *News Release 469*, 27 October 1971.
[3] Westminster CC Highways Committee *Minutes*, 28 March 1972 (item No.4). It was implemented towards the end of 1972.

"pedestrianisation".'[1] There was little doubt that closure to vehicles would make Carnaby Street safer and more pleasant for shoppers on foot. A survey carried out by Westminster City Council showed that between 8 a.m. and 7 p.m. the street was used by 15 000 pedestrians but only 2000 vehicles (of which a mere 390 stopped).

The scheme provided for deliveries to the shops outside the hours of closure to traffic (11 a.m. to 8 p.m.), which would be effected by removable posts at either end of the street. The cost of the scheme was estimated to be about £1500.

Westminster City Council welcomed the GLC's proposal and agreed to co-operate in implementing it as an experiment, initially for twelve months. The GLC, incidentally, were not informed of this decision until 4 July 1967, nearly a month after the matter appeared on the agenda of their traffic management subcommittee. Consultations took place during the remainder of 1967 between the GLC and businesses in the area and in March the following year it was decided to proceed with the scheme. But local redevelopment schemes and work on electric cables under the street prevented implementation throughout 1968.

Unabashed, in December 1968, while answering a Question in Council, Neil Thorne said he hoped that the Carnaby Street scheme would proceed in 1969–70 if finances were available.[2] Such caution was rare for schemes costing as little as £1500! Meanwhile Westminster's City Engineer saw a possible alternative (albeit a temporary one) to the GLC's lengthy procedure. A Report to the Highways Committee said:

> While the City Engineer has no further information on the action being taken by the GLC to make a Traffic Order to implement the Carnaby Street proposals, he would draw attention to the Traffic Directions made by the Commissioner of Police for the Christmas shopping and winter sales periods. . . . Paragraph 7 of these Regulations reads: *Closed Streets*. The following streets (or parts of streets) may at the discretion of the Senior Police Officer on duty be closed to vehicular traffic when pedestrian concentration makes this course desirable: Carnaby Street, Great Marlborough Street (southern arm), Granton Street (between Newburgh and Carnaby Streets), Fouberts Place (between Kingly and Carnaby Streets).'[3]

These streets were precisely those included in the GLC's proposal and, as the City Engineer pointed out, if the police implemented the Direction, it would bring the pedestrian precinct into operation (but without the barriers and signs necessary for a full experimental scheme). In fact the police did not use these powers.

[1] GLC (1967), *Traffic Management Scheme for Carnaby Street in the City Westminster*, TMS, No.58, p1.

[2] Question in Council, GLC *Minutes*, 17 December 1968, p716.

[3] Westminster CC *Report of City Engineer to Highways Committee* (for information) 17 December 1968.

For nearly two years the public heard nothing more of the Carnaby Street proposal until in November 1970 the GLC announced, as though unaware of what had already taken place, that they had put into motion informal consultations with businesses in the Carnaby Street area.[1] This time fears were expressed by a group of traders that closure to vehicles would adversely affect their business, although almost all had apparently supported the proposal when it had first been put to them more than three years earlier.[2] In February 1971, the GLC proposed to begin the statutory implementation process.[3] The scheme was approved by the Central Area Board (a subcommittee of the GLC Environmental Planning Committee) in August 1971, although the chairman (Mr Thorne) agreed to a request from the traders that implementation should be deferred until after the summer.[4] The Carnaby Street scheme was finally implemented on an experimental basis on 27 March 1972.[5]

CONCLUSIONS

Positive policies for pedestrian movement have been lacking in London as elsewhere.[6] It is rare that pedestrian interests are totally ignored by the highway and traffic authorities, but consideration of them has been limited in two important respects. First, facilities for pedestrians have been dependent on measures to deal with vehicular traffic. The needs of the latter have been the main determinant of traffic and highway schemes and the satisfaction of these needs has constrained the extent of provision for the pedestrian. It is difficult to find an example in London where a road 'improvement' scheme has been abandoned because of the greater inconvenience it would cause to pedestrian movement.

Second, in almost every example examined in the general part of this case study, where pedestrians have been considered, it has been from the point of view of their *safety* and not of their *convenience*. Yet 'to secure the expeditious, convenient and safe movement of vehicular and other traffic (including foot passengers)'[7] has always been a general duty of the GLC.

Interviews with officers both of the boroughs and the GLC confirmed that their predominant concern was with congestion of vehicular traffic and its adverse effects on pedestrian safety and, in many cases, the environment. In view of the inevitable inconvenience to pedestrians caused by schemes

[1] GLC *Press Release 543*, 23 November 1970.

[2] *Evening Standard*, 7 December 1970.

[3] GLC *Press Release 55*, 11 February 1971.

[4] GLC *Minutes*, 2 November 1971, pp542–3, Questions in Council.

[5] GLC *Press Release 154*, 25 March 1972.

[6] Though interest has been shown elsewhere in creating a network of pedestrian streets instead of isolated examples, for example Gloucester, Glasgow and Bolton. R H King and R M Eagland (1971), 'Gloucester's Traffic and Transport Plan—Fair Treatment for the Pedestrian,' *Tr Eng and Control* 12, 9, pp456–9; J Armour, paper to Institute of Highway Engineers Conference, April 1971; and R H Ogden, 'Town Centre Precinct for Bolton,' *Surveyor*, 8 August 1969, pp26–31.

[7] *London Government Act 1963*, ch33, s9 (2).

designed to aid the flow of vehicles, it is surprising that their interests were not better represented. A more positive approach to walking as a mode of travel was undoubtedly hindered by a noticeable lack of information about pedestrian movement and the factors affecting it. Moreover, few attempts were being made to collect such information. This lack is not peculiar to London; a GLC witness at the GLCP Inquiry pointed out that:

> All of the major conurbation transport studies that conducted a home interview included walking as a mode for the journey to work but not for other purposes . . . the only conurbation study to my knowledge that considered walk trips in the forecast year is that conducted in Tyneside.[1]

With some exceptions, such as the campaign to close Bond Street to vehicles, there was little evidence that organisations or individuals had brought strong pressure to bear on the GLC or the boroughs. The Pedestrians' Association for Road Safety, for example, voiced no serious objection to the GLDP statements on pedestrians described earlier in this study, although their evidence suggested that greater priority should be given to peedstrians: 'This Association asks for adequate facilities to be provided for pedestrians whose needs and safety should not be subordinated to the demand for increased traffic flows.'[2]

The Bond Street and Carnaby Street examples not only illustrate some of these general conclusions but point to a marked reluctance on the part of the GLC in particular to grapple with the problems of streets where intense pedestrian activity occurs, even on an experimental basis. In the case of Bond Street, Buchanan's suggestion of closing the street to traffic came only a year after the LTMU's scheme had been implemented to improve vehicle flows. Although one could not expect the attitude of all the bodies involved to change overnight, the Hills and Briggs study and Lewis's press campaign in 1966 rapidly gained support from members of the public and some experts. Lewis's concern was for improving London's environment generally; it was an accident of history Bond Street should become the 'test case' of pedestrianisation in London.

Support for an experiment to reduce traffic was expressed by the Bond Street Association, by Westminster City Council and others, including (implicitly at least) the Minister of Transport who wanted to introduce legislation to enable local authorities to close streets to vehicles specifically for amenity purposes. Responsibility, however, rested with the GLC as traffic authority and they quickly rejected the idea. They thought that closure of Bond Street would inconvenience local movement but their main concern, shared also by the police, was that it would cause extra congestion on the surrounding main roads. The Conservative opposition

[1] GLC (1971), paper prepared by B V Martin, 'Walk Trips,' *Paper S12/254*, p1, GLDP Inquiry Stage 1.
[2] The Pedestrians' Association for Road Safety (1971), *Proof of Evidence of G C Jenkins, E12/35* GLDP Inquiry Stage 1.

at County Hall at the time criticised this approach and promised positive action if they gained control at the following elections in Spring 1967. Yet after three years in power, their 1970 election manifesto declared that 'we shall proceed as quickly as we can with the experiment aimed at turning Bond Street and Carnaby Street into London's first traffic-free shopping streets.'[1] Even so, at the end of 1972 Bond Street was still open to traffic throughout its length, and the Carnaby Street experiment was implemented in March 1972, five years after the GLC themselves had first proposed the scheme.

The protracted process of implementation was mainly due to the extremely cautious approach of the GLC. Despite the Conservatives' open support for the scheme, they appeared unable, once in power, to overcome the resistance (supported by the police) of their officers to the idea. The latter first of all (in 1966) rejected the Hills and Briggs proposal, and later sought gradual traffic changes after extensive studies of the whole area. This contrasted with the desire of Westminster City Council for a more experimental approach. In the case of Carnaby Street the GLC's concern was not so much with the traffic implications of pedestrianisation, for it was a much less heavily used traffic route, but with the possible adverse reactions of local traders. Although the scheme was only experimental, the GLC took five years to complete consultations and to make the statutory orders.

A brief experiment had been carried out, however, in Marylebone High Street (also in Westminster) where traffic was excluded from 10 a.m. to 2 p.m. on four Saturdays in January 1971. Bad weather may have prevented the full benefits from being realised but in any case the GLC reported that some traders in the street were 'unhappy about the scheme.' There is little evidence from other pedestrian-street schemes to show that the GLC's fears were well-founded although difficulties may be greater in the larger cities. In Norwich it was found that 'most of the traffic directed from London Street just disappeared, an experience confirmed in Strøget (Copenhagen) where in a similar situation over 60% of the traffic displaced did not reappear in the surrounding area.'[2]

A further important conclusion from experience of pedestrian shopping streets elsewhere was that business turnover usually increased. Increases of about 20% were reported in the Leeds precinct. A paper prepared for the Organisation for Economic Co-operation and Development said that:

> In Vienna shop owners reported a 25–50% increase in business in the first week after the traffic ban went into effect. In Norwich, all but two of the shops in the exclusion area did more business, some experiencing increase in sales of 10% or more. In Essen the increase in trade has been reported to be between 15 and 35% depending on the type of shop; in Rouen, between 10 and 15%.[3]

[1] Conservative Central Office (1970), *Towards a Greater London.*

[2] F Berry (1972), 'Inquiry into Pedestrian Precincts,' *Municipal Review*, 510, pp162–3.

[3] C K Orski (1971), *Car-Free Zones and Traffic Restraints*, OECD, Department of Urban Affairs.

The important point is that these conclusions, as to both the traffic and business turnover implications of pedestrian shopping streets, were based on the results of practical experiments, whereas the views of the GLC were not.

Westminster City Council, although concerned about consultation of local interests, were prepared to proceed with experimental schemes. They took the initiative in carrying out a traffic study in the Bond Street area, as suggested in the Hills and Briggs Report. They were sceptical about the value of the further detailed study demanded by the GLC and considered that a low-cost experimental scheme would be the best way of assessing the traffic implications. After lengthy discussions with the GLC, Westminster agreed to implement the phased scheme. They also supported from the start the GLC's proposal to close Carnaby Street to traffic, but again, with ultimate power resting with the GLC, there appeared to be little they could do to speed the process.

To summarise, this study has three main conclusions. First, the interests of pedestrians are poorly represented in the present institutional system in London; in as much as they are recognised the concern is almost always with their safety rather than their convenience. The lack of any major decision or policy that would have demonstrated, through a detailed case study, how the general needs of pedestrians are handled by the system is itself a significant finding. Amenity and transport user groups have been slow to recognise this gap in the institutional system; even the Pedestrians' Association for Road Safety appeared rooted in its original concern for purely safety matters. But major policy matters should not, in any case, be left to voluntary pressure groups.

Second, bearing in mind that the major problems of pedestrian movement arise from conflict with motor-vehicles, any firm policy for the encouragement of walking as a mode of travel will require a greater concern for the *convenience* of pedestrians. Indeed, there is little evidence to show that the GLC in this respect have fulfilled their statutory duty as traffic authority for London.

Third, while existing legislation does *enable* local highway and planning authorities (including the GLC and the London boroughs) to plan positively for the safety, convenience and encouragement of pedestrian movement, it has not in itself been sufficient to promote this in practical terms of schemes on the ground or even a significant number of proposals. The lengthy deliberations over the Bond Street and Carnaby Street proposals showed that even in particular places of intense pedestrian activity with the special characteristics of tourist attractions, the interests of motor traffic tend to prevail. It appears that what is lacking is not so much the scope of statutory powers and responsibilities, but the will of the local authorities in London, and particularly the GLC, to do anything which would encourage the use of legs rather than wheels for the purpose of getting about.

Case Study M

BUS PRIORITY SCHEMES

THE EXAMPLES OF TOTTENHAM HIGH ROAD AND PICCADILLY BUS LANES

INTRODUCTION

The concept of priorities for public transport in city streets is not new: European tram systems have been assisted by special arrangements of both lanes and signals to combat the rising tide of other traffic.[1] During the 1960s too, Continental cities were more active than British cities in introducing lanes for buses only. By 1970 there were 83 lanes in Paris, 35 in Milan and considerable numbers in Marseilles, Strasbourg, Liège, Stockholm and elsewhere. At the same time there were some 20 to 30 schemes in the whole of Britain (with 12 to 20 more in preparation) but only 3 in London. The British schemes were small (the longest, of 1000 yards, was in Reading) and isolated.[2]

The various bodies involved in providing priority schemes for public transport in London have certain clearly defined roles to play although they may become involved in wider considerations or take varying attitudes. The Ministry of Transport (MOT) has given some lead to experiments and policies to help public transport (one of the four main objectives for the Traffic and Transport Plans required under Circular 1/68).

The Greater London Council (GLC) as overall traffic authority in London has to approve any bus priority scheme and to process it legally and check it financially even if a London borough acts as their agent. Their powers under the 1967 Road Traffic Regulation Act permit them to designate bus lanes.[3] More recently their responsibility for London Transport (LT) might be expected to bring more direct concern for public transport problems.

LT as bus operators could be expected to welcome any scheme which facilitated bus movements more than general traffic flow, since congestion

[1] See B H Harbour, 'Problems of Traffic Flow: Preferential Treatment for Public Transport,' *Rev de l'Un Int des Tr Pub*, XII (1) 3/1963, Brussels. Segregation of public transport from other traffic was suggested for Britain over thirty years ago (see *The Times*, 6 December 1940, p4).

[2] *Working Group on Bus Demonstration Projects*. Report to Minister of Transport February 1970 and T Constantine and K P Young, 'Bus Priority Schemes,' *Traffic Engineering and Control*, January 1969, pp466–9 and May 1969, pp36–9.

[3] Ch76, 1967, s6 and schedule.

was a major cause of irregularities of their bus operations and they had suffered extra mileage in traffic management schemes. In their annual reports they continually pressed for bus lanes as an aid to services.[1] A senior officer has used passenger flow figures to demonstrate that at peak hours buses are twelve times as efficient as cars in terms of road space, and even averaged over a 24-hour day, 7-day week they are three times as efficient.[2]

The London boroughs whether or not they actively promote bus lane schemes are involved because of concern for local traffic movement and possible conflict with access to premises; the boroughs could also act as the GLC's agents in devising, discussing, publicising, and implementing schemes.

The Metropolitan Police are responsible for supervising and enforcing bus priority schemes since instructions from the Home Office have not so far included this task amongst those that may be handled by traffic wardens. Difficulties of enforcement have arisen where schemes become too complicated or when the main enforcement effort is required at peak times.

THE LONDON SITUATION

Despite the attention paid to the severe traffic problems in London by the London Traffic Management Unit (LTMU) within the MOT there was no effort paid to the particular problems of buses until 1965; indeed in many traffic management schemes buses were disproportionately hampered in diversions. The financial and operational problems of LT became more evident through the inquiries of the Select Committee on Nationalised Industries which examined LT during the first half of 1965.[3] Following this the Minister of Transport on 8 August requested the GLC to set up a Working Party of representatives of the GLC, LT and the Metropolitan Police to suggest measures to improve London's bus services.

The Working Party, which reported in November the same year,[4] suggested three avenues of action:

1 The improvement of bus services, e.g. by restructuring long bus routes into shorter loops operating from major centres.
2 The increased effectiveness of general traffic management measures, e.g. by owner instead of driver-liability for minor traffic offences.
3 Special aspects of traffic management to help buses.

Under the latter heading they examined bus-only lanes specifically; lanes with the general traffic flow were thought to entail 'serious practical diffi-

[1] E.g. LT Executive *Annual Report*, 1970, p14.
[2] E R Ellen, 'Ways of Helping Buses in Urban Areas,' *Rev de L'UITP*, XVIII, 4/1969, pp289–314.
[3] *Hansard HC Papers 313–1*, 1964–65.
[4] GLC *Minutes*, 2 November 1965, pp710–22.

culties; whilst there is no scope for immediate action, the idea warrants further study in the light of experience abroad.' Bus lanes against-the-flow were valuable 'in saving long detours and preserving attractive bus stops.' Few streets were considered to be wide enough to accept such lanes, and only one project was known to be programmed, in Tottenham High Road, to be introduced by October 1966. The report commented that 'this one case, approximately half a mile long, is the only one which has become a practical proposition during some five years of active traffic management in London.' In fact this scheme was not implemented until April 1970.

In the intervening period discussions between the GLC and LT continued, and short bus lanes (with the main flow) were introduced along Park Lane and Vauxhall bridge in February 1968 and Brixton Road in June 1969.[1] Meanwhile the MOT had attempted to promote measures to help public transport within the general Traffic and Transport Plans requested (under circular 1/68) of local authorities with populations over 50 000, and reinforced this with a letter to Town Clerks of those authorities in October 1969 to increase the response.

In January 1969 the Ministry set up a working group to select a range of demonstration projects to cover all three aspects mentioned in the GLC report, with a view to assessing the effects of each project by means of 'before and after' studies which would be widely publicised. Three of the eleven projects proposed by the group in their report of February 1970 were in London: the Tottenham scheme, another contra-flow lane in Seven Sisters Road, Holloway,[2] and a system of intensive traffic and parking surveillance along a complete bus route, the E3 from Greenford to Chiswick via Acton. The Tottenham High Road scheme, the first contra-flow lane proposed for London, provides many points to indicate the nature of the problems involved during the early days of the priority policies.

A BRIEF HISTORY OF THE TOTTENHAM SCHEME

A one-way traffic system incorporating a bus lane had been evolved between Tottenham Borough Council and the MOT's LTMU before the reorganisation of London government, whereby southbound traffic would be diverted about 1300 yards along two minor roads (Chestnut Road and Broad Lane) and the High Road itself would become one-way only (northbound) between these junctions, with a separate lane in the southbound direction for buses. This would reduce traffic delays at the five-way Ward's Corner junction by simplifying turning movements, and give buses a

[1] GLC *Press Release 96*, 19 February 1968; and *107*, 20 February 1969. The Park Lane scheme was modified because the previous scheme showed no benefit to buses. It ended 155 yards short of the crucial junction and motorists prevented buses from moving quickly down the inside lane. The second scheme was better but subject to substantial contravention by motorists. For a review see E R Ellen (1969).

[2] It was hoped that the Seven Sisters lane would be introduced in 1971 but the scheme was later abandoned.

considerable time-saving especially in the morning peak period. In June 1965 the Borough Engineer recommended the Highways and Public Works Committee of the new London borough (Haringey) to accept this scheme; they agreed and the Council ratified this decision.[1]

Discussion of the scheme and local press publicity led to fears by local traders on the eastern side of the High Road that there would be no effective access to their shops for motorists,[2] and by residents in the proposed one-way streets that they would suffer considerable loss of amenity. They formed the High Road Diversion Protest Committee and sent representatives to explain their objections to a Highways Committee meeting. Subsequently the Council decided to defer judgement on the scheme pending further discussions with the GLC.[3] Meanwhile, however, the GLC were considering the report of the Working Party on LT mentioned above, which expressed the hope that the scheme would be implemented by October of the following year, and at the end of November 1965 a report was produced by the Department of Highways and Transportation formalising the LTMU proposals.[4]

At this time both officers and members at Haringey became increasingly concerned with the local implications of the scheme and on 7 February 1966 the Council felt that it could only approve the traffic scheme if the bus lane was excluded and if the residential High Cross Road one-way link was only included until Chestnut Road could be improved.[5] In June the Borough Engineer and a local Councillor, Mrs Protheroe, visited the GLC to express these views. On 15 July a letter was received from the Clerk to the GLC to the effect that the scheme should be implemented in full, and later in the same month a press release was issued explaining that the GLC proposed to introduce it as an experiment. It said the likely improvement in traffic conditions and the need to maintain bus access to the hospital, the Town Hall, and the Technical College overrode the Borough's considerations.[6]

This caused considerable concern at Haringey and in September the Town Clerk was asked to protest most strongly at this treatment and to invite the Minister of Transport and the Chairman of the GLC's Highways and Traffic Committee to see for themselves the problems involved.[7] The site visit took place on 20 October when the Minister was represented by Mr Stephen Swingler, Parliamentary Private Secretary, and the GLC by Ted Castle, the vice-chairman of the Highways and Traffic Committee. As a result of this meeting the Borough was informed the following day

[1] LB Haringey, *Minute 159*, 18 June 1965.

[2] Contra-flow lanes pose a greater problem in this respect than with the flow-lanes because they must operate all day long, particularly if they involve physically separate carriageways.

[3] LB Haringey *Minute 2308*, 27 September 1965.

[4] GLC *Minutes*, 2 November 1965, p718; *Report TMS (6)*; and *Press Release*, 1 December 1965.

[5] LB Haringey *Minute 3659*, 15 January 1966.

[6] GLC *Press Release 349*, 28 July 1966.

[7] LB Haringey *Minute 942*, 19 September 1966.

that the Ministry and the GLC were both of the opinion that the whole scheme should proceed, but on a strictly experimental basis. Haringey's Highways and Public Works Committee agreed that it was willing to act as the Ministry's agent on these terms, and the GLC Highways and Traffic Committee hoped that the scheme would now be introduced by September 1967.[1]

At this point it seemed that the project would proceed, but one final episode was to come: on 5 December 1966 the Highways and Public Works Committee's agreement came before the Haringey Council for ratification but after debate they refused to do this and proposed instead to send a delegation to the MOT to restate their case.[2] The Ministry replied two weeks later that it would be inappropriate to receive a delegation over this matter and that they intended to appoint the GLC as agents for the scheme; the GLC also informed Haringey that they had agreed to this proposal. Early in the new year the leader of the Haringey Council and the chairman of the Highways Committee met and agreed to have the refusal rescinded if the GLC would circularise all residents in the area with a statement pointing out that the Borough Council were acting as agents in this scheme and that it was strictly experimental. This was accepted by the Ministry in February 1967.

Thus the main parties in the scheme had returned to the point reached in mid-1965, and despite their worries about local effects, the Borough Council had gained no extra concessions for local circumstances, and no extra control over the implementation of the scheme.

In late 1965 the GLC had estimated that implementation would take eleven months; a year later they had reduced this to nine months. They were soon to be shown to be very optimistic. During the spring and summer of 1967 the Borough Engineer's Department at Haringey undertook traffic counts to ascertain the current traffic situation and began design studies in consultation with the Ministry, the GLC, LT and the Metropolitan Police. Outline estimates of cost were produced in August. The MOT formally appointed Haringey's agency to implement the scheme in January 1968; draft tender documents and draft traffic orders were prepared in May and June; more detailed estimates were ready in June, when the GLC costed the scheme at £227 000 to be shared between the Ministry (£202 000) and the GLC (£25 000).

In December tender documents were sent to five contractors, and returned in February 1969. The tender was approved and the contractor appointed in April and work actually began in August. In January 1970 the GLC sent out 5000 circulars publicising the scheme to local residents and made the necessary traffic orders. The general traffic diversions came into force in February.[3] Local works on a major sewer delayed the operation of the bus lane for a further nine weeks, but it was finally introduced in April.

[1] GLC *Minutes*, 13 December 1966, p724.
[2] LB Haringey *Minute 1538*, 5 December 1966.
[3] GLC *Press Release 24*, 19 January 1970.

The lane was a success in speeding bus traffic and the adverse effects on other traffic and frontages was minimal (indeed two traffic policemen were rendered unnecessary). And so, after a meeting at Tottenham Town Hall between Department of the Environment (DOE) and Borough officers, residents and traders to discuss pedestrian and loading facilities, the scheme was made permanent in April 1972 (although further amendments were possible).[1] Later Mr Vigars, the chairman of the GLC's Environmental Planning Committee, remarked: 'Tottenham is a particularly successful one, and the indication is that contra-flow lanes are particularly successful because they are self-enforcing.'[2]

This bus lane, a local improvement and no sizeable scheme in the context of a decade of rigorous traffic management, took almost six years to translate into reality, after which time there were only three other lanes in London. After a further two and a half years, however (autumn 1972), a further twenty-five had been approved, six had been implemented and it was hoped that several more would be on the ground by the end of the year. During 1971 and 1972 a proposal for a contra-flow lane in Piccadilly was debated: an examination of the way in which this more prominent and perhaps more ambitious scheme was handled indicates the considerable changes since the Tottenham scheme.

PICCADILLY BUS LANE

In April 1971 the bus unit within the GLC's Traffic Operations Group and the Department of Planning and Transportation produced a report suggesting a contra-flow bus lane westbound along Piccadilly to restore four bus routes, which had been diverted into Pall Mall by a traffic order made under police powers as an experiment in 1961 and later made permanent. The diversion had added 900 yards to the bus routes and reduced their custom.[3] The proposed bus-only lane would be separated from the three to four eastbound lanes by a 4-foot kerbed strip from which loading and unloading for the shops would be allowed, except at junctions. The cab ranks in the centre of Piccadilly would be removed and only replaced in part in other streets. Buses using the lane from Shaftesbury Avenue would enter by a lane cut through the main island at Piccadilly Circus alongside the Eros statue. The initial cost of the scheme was estimated at £60 000 and operating savings to be at £50 000 annually.

The GLC decided to publicise the proposal widely, including local traders and the public as a whole by means of explanatory leaflets and an open meeting. Mr Thorne, chairman of the Environmental Planning Committee's Central Area Board, said 'we are in favour of bus lanes wherever possible. This is the most important so far to come before the

[1] GLC *Press Release 22*, 18 January 1971; and *129*, 1 April 1971.
[2] *Observer*, 6 December 1971.
[3] Departmental Report, *TMS 125A*, B L Allen and S L M Hockaday.

Council.'[1] In the light of this statement and Piccadilly's prominent location it is not surprising that this was considered something of a test case by all concerned. The first public meeting was held on 29 July in a very crowded St James's Church Hall. Alderman Sandford, chairman of the Highways Committee of Westminster City Council, said that his Council was neutral about the scheme, but concerned about the extra problems for pedestrians at the Circus and about access to premises on the southern side. Westminster Councillor John Beveridge later stated 'the GLC have introduced this scheme against the advice and wishes of the Council and its technical officers. Traffic conditions in Piccadilly are already difficult and complex and the introduction of the bus-only lane can only aggravate the position. Surely Piccadilly is the last place for experiments of this kind.'[2] Mr Ellen, Director of Transportation Planning for the LT Executive, however, was enthusiastic about the scheme, believing that the diversion of buses in 1961 had cost LT at least 500 000 passengers annually, and possibly three times as many. He estimated benefits at £78 000 annually, split equally between savings in operating costs and passenger time.

The Piccadilly and St James's Association (of traders) were more or less evenly divided over the scheme. Ten of the major businesses were unequivocally against it and employed consultants (a surveyor and a traffic engineer) to make their case; they claimed that difficulties of goods delivery in particular, but also of refuse collection and fuel-oil delivery, pedestrian access, and disbenefits to other traffic in Piccadilly and elsewhere would more than offset the claimed benefits. They were supported by the vicar of St James's, whose church lies on the south side.[3] The press coverage spoke of a battle between 'the carriage trade' and the Rolls Royce, and the bus.[4]

The GLC attempted to seek opinions by distributing 8000 illustrated informative leaflets with reply-paid postcards; later 2000 more were distributed by the AA and the RAC.[5] The GLC received 746 replies with a slight majority in favour,[6] and convened another public meeting 'to report back' on 26 January 1972 in the larger Criterion Restaurant, together with a two-day exhibition of the scheme. Mr Ellen again represented LT Executive, adding to his previous points that benefits were now calculated as £38 000 savings in annual operating costs (assuming that route 506 continued to serve Pall Mall) and £47 000 in passenger time. Alderman Sandford of Westminster City Council emphasised his claim that traffic congestion would result over a considerable area, and that delays for eastbound traffic could be estimated at £16 000 annually. Mr J M Thomson, chairman of the London Amenity and Transport Association, who had

[1] GLC *Press Release 237*, 9 June 1971.
[2] *Municipal Engineering*, January 1972, p128.
[3] Statements by K M Sanders and C A Lea, and Notes of Meeting, 29 July 1971.
[4] For example the *Guardian*, 30 July 1971; and *The Sunday Times*, 12 September 1971.
[5] GLC *Press Release 344*, 30 July 1971.
[6] The *Guardian*, 1 January 1972; and GLC *Press Release 582*, 30 December 1971.

been invited by the GLC to speak in favour of the scheme along with Mr Ellen, pointed out that since there were fifteen traffic lanes entering the Circus but only eight leaving it, the removal of one inward lane for the bus scheme would hardly be likely to increase congestion overall. The traders were represented by Mr G Dobry, QC, who complained that none of their objections at the first meeting had been taken into account.[1] After a heated discussion between speakers both for and against the scheme, Mr Thorne (of the GLC) again invited written comments.

It was hoped to make a decision by the end of February but more time was needed to digest the response, and in the meantime a lively press correspondence ensued.[2] The Central Area Board recommended in March that the scheme should proceed experimentally (i.e. subject to review after six months' operation) at a cost of £91 000 against an estimated annual saving of £83 000. Further discussions were to be held with the traders over loading problems and it was hoped that the scheme might be in operation by the end of 1972.[3] Within a few weeks the DOE had agreed to give a 75% grant (£64 275 of £85 700) under its newly extended grant aid rules (see below).[4] Thus, in contrast to the lengthy deliberations over the Tottenham scheme, the more expensive and prominent Piccadilly scheme seemed likely to be implemented within two years of the proposal being mooted, despite considerable and publicised controversy. The very different handling of these two schemes may be attributed to considerable changes of attitude and policy, particularly by the GLC, coupled with certain institutional changes. But before dealing with these points in detail it will be helpful to examine some of the external pressures for change that were exerted on the GLC and other bodies. These can be classified as the influence on the DOE, operating experience with the early lanes in London and elsewhere, studies undertaken by the London Borough of Camden, pressure group activities and criticism by professionals in the transport field, and others.

THE INFLUENCE OF THE DOE

A significant pressure for change was the desire of the DOE to see better support for public transport, as evidenced by their demonstration projects begun in 1970. In 1971 and 1972 their policy was continued in word and deed. In April 1971 bus priority schemes were made eligible for 50% grant (75% in the case of Principal roads) as long as the claiming authority spent at least £5000 annually on such work; a year later this was increased to 75% for all schemes.[5] The Minister emphasised that because of local

[1] Notes of Meeting and *Buses both Ways in Piccadilly?* (1972) by the Association of Stores.

[2] GLC *Press Release 93*, 2 February 1972; and Letters to *The Times* 25 January, 25 February, 28 February and 1 March 1972.

[3] GLC *Press Release 126*, 13 March 1972; and *Minutes*, 21 March 1972, pp166–7.

[4] DOE *Press Release 538*, 4 May 1972.

[5] DOE *Press Release 248*, 26 April 1971; and *538M*, 4 May 1972.

knowledge, local authorities have an inescapable responsibility; he offered the financial aid of the Department to anyone wanting to undertake new priority or bus-only schemes.[1] Later in the year the DOE advised that where pedestrian streets are required, public transport and service vehicles should still have access.[2] In 1972 sufficient bus lanes were envisaged to require a Departmental circular to ensure a standard system of traffic signs.[3] Also the first evaluation report was produced on the Leicester demonstration project showing that worthwhile reductions of delays could be obtained by bus-actuated priorities at signal-controlled junctions.[4]

OPERATING EXPERIENCE WITH THE EARLY LANES IN LONDON

By the time of the Greater London Development Plan (GLDP) Inquiry the first five lanes had been operating for one or two years, and questions by objectors and the Panel elicited information from the GLC about their effects: the Vauxhall bridge lane was saving passengers between 1.5 and 3.7 minutes per journey; that on Albert Embankment 1.6 minutes and in Brixton Road 2.5 minutes. In Tottenham, passengers were over 2 minutes better off on the morning peak journey and more than 1 minute in the evening compared with the previous situation, while evidence from the intermediate period when road works precluded the operation of the bus lane showed that while buses had to follow the detour taken by general traffic in the management scheme, time losses were almost a minute for buses compared to the previous situation.[5] These results helped to confirm the tangible benefits experienced elsewhere. Only the Park Lane scheme showed dubious results, mainly because of some encroachment into the lane by general traffic.[6]

EXPERIENCE ELSEWHERE

Probably the most notable bus priority scheme was at Reading, where a 1000-yard contra-flow lane was established in 1968 and 1970 in order to allow a trolley-bus route to continue while other traffic was made one-way. An MOT–Borough Council study showed that this produced time savings of 14% in one direction and 10% in the other.[7] The success of this scheme led to four other lanes and two bus-only streets being implemented on a

[1] DOE *Press Release 83M*, 3 September 1971; and *164M*, 23 September 1971; Mr John Peyton, Minister for Transport Industries.

[2] *Circular Roads 58/71*; DOE *Press Release 447M*, 30 November 1971.

[3] DOE *Press Release 51M*, 17 January 1972. These incorporate international signs.

[4] DOE Division PUPS (1972), *Summary Report No.1 on Bus Demonstration Project: Bus Priority at Traffic Signals, Leicester.*

[5] GLC *Press Release 107*, 20 February 1969; and LT Executive (October 1971) *Paper S12/305*, GLDP Inquiry Stage 1. See also DOE (nd) *Bus Demonstration Project Summary Report No.2, Tottenham.*

[6] GLC (1972), *Paper S27/376*, para3.4, GLDP Inquiry Stage 2.

[7] T Bendixson (1970), 'Results of Reading's Bus Lane Experiment,' *Tr Eng and Control*, 8, 70, pp188–9.

total of 2 miles of road. As a result, the buses ran more mileage, avoided 'bunching' and attracted 4% more passengers and revenue in 1969–70, and 6% in 1970–71, while most undertakings were losing 3% annually. Such an increase, Bendixson claimed, would bring LT from £4.6 to 6.9 millions annually.[1] Yet the chairman of the GLC's Environmental Planning Committee declined to have the officers undertake an evaluation of the Reading scheme because it 'is so small by London standards that it has little relevance.'[2]

In the autumn of 1972 a study by the Transport and Road Research Laboratory of ten lanes in Dublin, Paris, Marseilles, Reading, London and Manchester found that the average journey time was reduced by 2 minutes.[3] In Dublin where in addition thirty extra buses were added along a main commuter route and fares reduced by 1p, patronage rose by 13%; in Marseilles traffic rose by 4% on routes with lanes, while dropping by 5% elsewhere. The study also showed that lanes were best sited at junctions to facilitate the bus to re-enter the traffic flow and to help passengers to change from bus to bus. (Most bus-only lanes in London have stopped short of junctions so as not to reduce capacity for other traffic.) At the same time reserved busways were one of the major elements in the transport system proposed for south Hampshire in its draft structure plan.[4]

STUDIES BY THE BOROUGH OF CAMDEN

The London Borough of Camden followed up this evidence at the GLDP Inquiry with much more detailed evidence on the primary and secondary roads including the inability of the GLC's proposals to improve bus operation when traffic demand would rise faster than the network could be adapted.[5] In particular they undertook a study of the advantages and disadvantages of a segregated system over a ten-mile network of bus routes in central London.[6]

The study concluded that bus speeds would be increased from 8 to 11 or 12 m.p.h. (including stops); that other traffic speeds would be decreased from 12 to about 9 m.p.h.; that bus travel would increase by about 10%; and that other traffic would be decreased by about 7%. Making two alternative assumptions—that the scheme would cover only the study area (one-sixth of the central area) and that it would cover the whole of the central area—the results shown in Table 26 were obtained. The figures show remarkable

[1] T Bendixson, the *Guardian*, 9 November 1970 and 19 July 1971.
[2] GLC *Minutes*, 7 March 1972, p128.
[3] TRRL Report, *LR 448* (1972), *Priority to Buses as Part of the Traffic Management* by Dr F V Webster.
[4] South Hampshire Advisory Plan Committee (1972), *Draft Document for Participation and Consultation.*
[5] LB Camden (1971), *Proof of Evidence, E27/104*; and Papers *S27/221* and *S27/224*, GLDP Inquiry Stage 2.
[6] LB Camden (1972), *Buses in Camden S27/223*, GLDP Inquiry Stage 2, esp chs4–6, tables 16 and 17.

(£000)	SEGREGATION ONLY IN STUDY AREA		SEGREGATION THROUGHOUT CENTRAL AREA	
	BENEFITS	LOSSES	BENEFITS	LOSSES
Savings in travelling and waiting time for existing passengers	424		502	
Revenue and savings in travelling time for generated passengers	71		71	
Reduced costs to bus operators	335		335	
Losses due to slower-speed of other traffic		580		398
Restrained traffic		20		23
Total	830	600	908	421
Net benefit	230		487	
Cost without physical separation	80		80	
Rate of return p.a.	288%		608%	
Cost with physical separation	130		130	
Rate of return p.a.	177%		374%	

Table 26 CAMDEN BUS LANE STUDY, 1972: ECONOMIC EVALUATION

rates of return; as Camden's Chief Traffic Engineer, Mr Lane, said, 'there can be few transport investments which would have such a dramatic effect,' particularly since the scheme would cost 'only as much as 11 yards of Ringway 1.'[1]

The report was discussed on four days of the GLDP Inquiry, and caused great interest in the technical and general press. The GLC officers responded with a detailed twenty-five-page comment on the Camden study,[2] criticising the general approach, the practical difficulties (loading and unloading, pedestrian movement, and enforcement of segregation and construction), effects on other traffic (claiming that they had been underestimated) the gains to passengers and LT (claiming that they had been overestimated) and the economic evaluation. The GLC said that net benefits might be nearer £290 000 than £230 000 but that the costs would be nearer £320 000 than £80 000. Seven bus lane schemes in the study were being examined by the Bus Unit, and the GLC hoped that after considering them in the light of the Camden study there would be 'significant gains for bus passengers and LT without some of the more serious disadvantages.'

The LT Executive also produced a commentary,[3] prefacing it with the remark that the Camden proposals were to their knowledge 'of a different

[1] *Evening Standard*, 15 December 1971.
[2] GLC *Minutes*, 21 March 1972, pp165–6; and *Press Release 133*, 15 March 1972.
[3] LT Executive (1972), *Paper S27/363*, GLDP Inquiry Stage 2.

order from any previously suggested.' They were of the opinion that 'facilities of this sort could bring substantial benefit if applied over, say, about 100 to 159 miles of road carrying the most intensive bus services. Nothing short of such far-reaching measures is likely to bring any significant improvement.'

Camden also requested the GLC's Environmental Planning Committee to consider the report[1] which they did in March 1972.[2] The Committee endorsed their officers' comments, preferring to identify and remedy the worst congestion points. They said, 'we have therefore decided that we are unable to implement the Borough Council's proposals in full, but that a limited experiment, in those parts of the study area where the Council's own studies indicate the feasibility of separate bus lanes, should be mounted quickly. We have also agreed to study further with the Borough Council the remaining routes in the area.' Mr Brew, the chairman of the Committee, later commented that the proposals 'would undoubtedly be good for buses in the area but we think it would lead to hardship and inconvenience to some people and businesses in Camden. It would also cause very considerable congestion in surrounding districts, affecting other bus routes.'[3] Later LT commented 'welcome though the GLC's limited introduction of short lengths of bus lanes has been it is clear that the far more drastic introduction of continuous lengths of reversed track and bus-only streets will be required.'[4]

CRITICS AND PRESSURE GROUPS

Initially the Government, and later and more particularly, the GLC, received strong criticism in the national and London press and in several municipal, political, planning and transport journals for failing to pursue adequate policies to assist buses.[5] Other critics also had an influence at the GLDP Inquiry and elsewhere; for example, the London Amenity and Transport Association pressed for the rapid introduction of a comprehensive system of bus priorities in its evidence to the GLDP Inquiry.[6] In the following two years the Association produced several statements pressing for a bolder approach from the GLC and, like Camden, for a network of bus priorities rather than isolated ones. They also pressed the GLC to abandon the idea that the pre-existing capacity for general traffic was inviolable when introducing bus lanes.[7] There was renewed enthusiasm, too, of the GLC Labour members in 1970–71 for helping public transport;

[1] Question in Council, GLC *Minutes*, 25 January 1972.
[2] GLC *Minutes*, 21 March 1972, pp165–6; and *Press Release 133*, 15 March 1972.
[3] *Municipal Engineering*, 1 January 1972, p129.
[4] LT Executive (1972), *Annual Report and Accounts for 1971*, p7.
[5] An editorial in the *Guardian* (12 February 1969), for example, called the London experiments 'derisory.'
[6] LATA/LMAG (1971), *Proof of Evidence, E12/20*, pp220–1, GLDP Inquiry Stage 1.
[7] In papers commenting on the GLC's Green Papers on LT and Traffic and the Environment, on the GLC's Strategy for LT, and on two sets of proposals for fares increases.

while some members were pressing for free fares, one member especially, Mr O'Connor, constantly questioned Robert Vigars and Richard Brew, chairmen of the Environmental Planning Committee during that period, about the progress of bus lane schemes.[1]

EVOLUTION OF GLC POLICY

Until the takeover of LT and the development of the Bus Unit (see below) the GLC did not have much faith in bus lanes as a means of helping buses; general traffic management measures were held to be more effective.[2] Even when the Unit and consultants were beginning to yield numerous proposals the tone was little more sanguine:

> Some are impractical and others would be difficult and expensive to introduce with relatively low benefit. Experience of the schemes already introduced shows that many of the proposals are likely to present insoluble problems of enforcement. Many of London's roads are too narrow to permit the reservation of a whole traffic lane for buses only without detriment to essential commercial and other traffic.[3]

In their evidence to the GLDP Inquiry (E12/1) the GLC's view of the role of the bus in a congested situation was chiefly that of fighting a rearguard action against declining demand. Although they stated the principle that 'the maintenance of good bus services lies in effective management of the general traffic by the Council and of the bus operations by the LT Executive' (paragraph 4.3.14), they saw the chief means of achieving this as the improvement of the primary and secondary road networks and wider parking controls. Specific measures to help buses (such as separate lanes, signal priorities and bus-only turns) were said to have only 'limited value' (paragraph 8.5.6). Their evidence continued (paragraph 8.5.17):

> A number of bus lanes have been installed in London with varying degrees of success, the main disadvantage being that even though the road capacity may not be reduced the queues of ordinary traffic excluded from the bus lane are longer and can block intersections further back, thus generating more congestion. Generally it appears that the number of single bus lanes that are worth introducing on existing roads will be quite limited—possibly twenty to forty in all—and though useful, they will not significantly improve the overall running of buses. There may well be more scope for introducing them in new traffic management and road improvement schemes.[4]

[1] GLC *Minutes*, Motion, 1 December 1970; Questions in Council, 4 May 1971, 2 November 1971, 30 November 1971 (two), 25 January 1972 and 7 March 1972.
[2] GLC *Press Release 102*, 20 February 1969.
[3] GLC *Minutes*, 1 December 1970, p664.
[4] GLC (1970), *Proof of Evidence, E12/1*, pp77, 125, 127, GLDP Inquiry Stage 1.

This was scarcely an optimistic elaboration of the basic statement in the Plan itself: 'when the roads are under heavy pressure, no longer can buses be expected to be sufficiently flexible to run good services without some special provision.'[1] The GLC were unwilling to reduce the amount of space for general traffic; on the Albert Embankment, for example, traffic islands were made smaller and lanes narrower to avoid this. The influence of the police was considerable:

> Our policy, which has been thrashed out with the GLC, is to say 'if you are going to introduce a bus lane then we should like you to provide traffic management measures as well so that as far as possible the remaining traffic has as much space or capacity as before.'[2]

After Camden Borough Council had given their evidence to the GLDP Inquiry the GLC said that they 'were also examining the use of bus lanes as a means of traffic restraint' although it was restated that 'the gains for buses must be set against the loss for other road vehicles including commercial vehicles and the problems that could arise for frontagers and pedestrians.'[3]

At the beginning of 1972 Mr Horace Cutler, chairman of the Policy and Resources Committee, declared that it was to be 'the year of the bus'[4] and certainly a considerable number of individual bus lane schemes were devised during the year. The GLC also reviewed London's traffic issues in *Traffic and the Environment: A Paper For Discussion*, and asked what degree of freedom and priority should be given to buses. Some comments were familiar: 'nearly all the problems come at junctions and the benefit to be gained by long lengths of road set aside for buses away from junctions is not great.' Others were new: 'the priority intended for buses in Oxford Street is the most striking proposal so far . . . it might well save as much as a million bus passenger hours a year . . .' and 'the Council is studying the likely effects of using bus lanes in a systematic way, as deliberate chokes to traffic flow in a ring around central London.' The Council summarised their approach as tackling the bus problem 'as a whole over a wide area with definite priority where action is needed most. What is in hand is far reaching but is being progressed step by step at a pace that allows people to change and particular problems to be dealt with as they arise.'[5]

The scheme for Oxford Street was significant for three reasons. First, helping buses was one of three main objectives, the other two being to improve conditions for pedestrians and to reduce accidents; it differed from bus lane schemes in that the carriageway over a half-mile length was narrowed (i.e. by providing wider footways) and all traffic excluded from

[1] GLC (1969), *GLDP Written Statement*, para5.64.
[2] *Hansard HC Papers 107 (xviii)*, 1971–72, p420, Q1932.
[3] GLC (1972), *Paper S27/376*, p3, GLDP Inquiry Stage 2.
[4] *London Transport Magazine*, No.25, 10 January 1972.
[5] GLC (1972), *Traffic and the Environment*, paras6.1–6.7, pp23–5.

this section except buses, taxis, bicycles and service vehicles for nine hours of the day. Second, the scheme significantly reduced the amount of road space for general traffic in the area and thus was almost certain to cause extra traffic delays, at least in the short term. Third, despite its novelty (to London at least) the scheme was implemented more rapidly than most of the more conventional bus lanes. It was the subject of a major report by the GLC's consultants, approved for consultation purposes by the GLC in June 1972, and was implemented as an experiment during November the same year.

THE BUS UNIT

The stated objectives of the Bus Unit set up within the Traffic Branch of the GLC's Planning and Transportation Department were[1] (our italic):

1 To *evaluate* LT delay points and bus lane proposals and to search for additional lanes; to initiate executive work within the Traffic Branch's Area Teams.
2 To *monitor* the DOE's demonstration projects (the E3 route scheme, a computer control system for Route 11, and the Tottenham High Road contra-flow lane).
3 To *ensure* that all new traffic management schemes help buses so far as is reasonable.
4 To *investigate* with the Area Teams the traffic and highways implications of the bus reshaping plan.
5 To *consider* the introduction of traffic management measures to improve bus flow (e.g. signal priorities, banned right turns, bus cages, etc.).

The Unit was reported to have three main criteria for installing bus lanes: the buses must be frequent enough and crowded enough to merit a lane to themselves; the lane must be able to be enforced by the police; and the lane must cause 'no significant disbenefit' to other vehicles or pedestrians.[2]

Proposals from LT, the general public or from other sources rapidly overloaded the small Unit's capacity, and from November 1970 consultants were employed, working within guidelines set down by the Unit. In the first year B Colquhoun and Partners examined 18 proposals of which 5 were rejected and 10 resulted in firm projects for discussion, and by November 1971 they had 70 sites under examination.[3] A procedure became established whereby the Unit or their consultants drew up proposals for a lane after agreeing the basis of it with LT. These were confidentially discussed with the London boroughs and the Metropolitan Police before going before the Environmental Planning Committee and its area boards for approval, either as an experimental or a permanent scheme. The GLC

[1] GLC (1972), *Paper S27/376*, app*A*, GLDP Inquiry Stage 2.
[2] *Municipal Engineering*, 18 February 1972, p295.
[3] GLC *Press Releases 454*, 18 October 1971; and *88*, 16 February 1972.

had also agreed with LT which sections of their 1700-mile network of bus routes suffered the worst from traffic congestion and, having whittled these down from 135 to 52 miles of route, Colquhoun's attempted to devise suitable 'packages' of traffic management proposals to improve conditions. Meanwhile a second firm of consultants, W S Atkins and Partners, had been asked to undertake studies of 10 sectors comprising a ring of inner suburbs 2 to 6 miles from the centre, encompassing what in pre-traffic management days used to be called 'the glue-pot ring,' to see whether comprehensive traffic engineering techniques could be applied over large areas to greater benefit, particularly for bus passengers, than by introducing individual schemes. By November 1972 this had resulted in a proposal for a pilot study covering nearly 4 square miles of north Battersea including 6 or 7 bus lanes, at an estimated cost of £44 000. The scheme would be eligible for 25% infrastructure grant from the DOE. At that time the practical results of this growing volume of interest and work were 11 lanes in operation, and this total was expected to rise to 20 by the end of 1972 and to 35 by April 1973.[1]

Of the 45 lanes approved or under discussion by November 1972, 4 were contra-flow and 1 a bus-only street (see Table 27). They ranged from 35 metres to 785 metres in length (Tottenham High Road was still the longest continuous lane at 780 metres); 36 allowed cyclists to use the lane, and 24 allowed taxis; they carried between 26 and 140 buses an hour. Some were very cheap, costing only £2000 or £3000 to install, whereas Buckingham Palace Road and Piccadilly cost over £70 000. The most startling thing about these bus lanes is their great savings in operating costs and passenger time, and their low capital costs, compared with major road and rail schemes.

Another remarkable fact about them is the variety of control styles for with-flow lanes; contra-flow lanes by their nature operate twenty-four hours a day. The periods of control varied according to local traffic conditions: there were 5 different periods to cover the morning peak, 4 for the evening peak, and 5 for those lanes covering both peaks. This was the situation only a year after protracted discussions between the police and the traffic authorities to attempt to reduce the proliferation of categories of traffic control.[2]

LT run buses on 1700 miles of road, many of these comprising the GLC's secondary network, and the Executive identified points on the network where delays of 5 minutes or more frequently occur (see Figure 17 which shows those in central London and the inner suburbs).[3] It will be seen that all of these occur on the secondary roads, and nearly all at major junctions, some in principal shopping streets. LT had also suggested some 45 places where bus lanes could be provided. In Greater London, the 45 lanes that had been approved or were under discussion only partly coin-

[1] GLC *Minutes*, 14 November 1972, p528.
[2] LBA *Minutes*, 26 November 1969, pp95–6; and 17 March 1971, p18.
[3] LT Executive (1971), *Paper S12/295*, GLDP Inquiry Stage 1.

	LOCATION[a]	LENGTH IN METRES	NUMBER OF ROUTES	BUSES PER HOUR	HOURS AND DAYS OF OPERATION	TIME SAVED (MIN)	VALUE TO LT AND PUBLIC (£p.a.)	COST (£)	DATE APPROVED FOR CONSUL-TATION	DATE IMPLE-MENTED (*ESTIMATED)
1	Tottenham High Road	780	8	62	24 hours, 7 days	2.5–1.25	Unquantified	227 000	6/65	4/70
2	Park Lane	165	12	140	1600–1900, Mon–Fri	0.5	Unquantified	1 500	—	2/68[e]
3	Vauxhall bridge[b]	250	8	96	1600–1900, Mon–Fri	3.5	34 000	1 500	—	2/68
4	Brixton Road	320	7	105	0700–0930, Mon–Fri	2.0	16 600	1 000	—	6/69
5	Albert Embankment	293	6	51	0800–1000, Mon–Fri	1.0	16 400	2 100	6/70	5/71
6	Upper St Islington	285	10	130	0800–1100, Mon–Fri	3.5	35 000	3 500	3/72	8/72
7	Seven Sisters Road	343	7	79	1630–1900, Mon–Fri	5.0	12 000	2 750	1/72	8/72
8	Buckingham Palace Road	560	2	26	24 hours, 7 days	5.0 peak	26 000	80 000	—	—
9	Vauxhall Bridge Road	675	7	61	1300–1900, Mon–Fri	6.3 peak	39 500	11 600	12/71	7/72
10	Gloucester Place	230	7	117	1630–1830, Mon–Fri	1.0	5 000	2 200	12/71	8/72
11	Westminster Bridge Road	137	4	58	0800–1830, Mon–Sat	0.8	4 000	2 200	12/71	5/72
12	Camberwell Green	150	10	70	24 hours, 7 days	1.5 peak	15 000	23 000	12/71	8/72
13	Shoreditch High Street	210	12	110	0800–1000, Mon–Fri	0.7	6 600	4 300	2/72	7/72
14	Bishopsgate	150	9	88	0800–1000, Mon–Fri	1.5	10 000	6 000	7/72	1/73
15	Piccadilly	440	6	86	24 hours, 7 days	3.5	87 000	73 000	3/72	5/73*
16	Theobalds Road	168	4	65	0830–1030* } Mon–Fri	0.5	7 500	3 345	7/72	12/72
17	Bloomsbury Way	215	6	95	1600–1830 } Mon–Fri	0.6	9 400	4 000	7/72	12/72
18	Camberwell Church Street	190	5	72	1600–1830, Mon–Fri	1.2	6 650	3 300	7/72	4/73*
19	East India Dock Road	310	6	52	0800–1000, Mon–Fri	3.0	16 200	2 900	7/72	11/72
20	London Bridge–Borough High Street[c]	230	12	—	0730–1800, Mon–Fri	3.0	—	—	7/72	—
21	Kingsland Road (Sbd)	270	6	69	0800–1000, Mon–Fri	0.5	2 400	3 250	7/72	12/72
22	Stamford Hill	320	6	50	0730–0900/1630–1830, Mon–Fri	0.5	4 750	3 700	—	4/73*
23	Stoke Newington Road	202	5	66	0730–0930, Mon–Fri	0.8	5 750	8 950	7/72	4/73*
24	Kingsland High Street	248	5	66	0730–0930, Mon–Fri	0.8	5 750	8 950	7/72	4/73*
25	Kingsland Road (Nbd)	166	6	76	1630–1830, Mon–Fri	0.5	4 000	1 500	—	4/73*
26	Park Road–Baker Street–Portman Square	785	9	90	0830–1030/1630–1830, Mon–Fri	2.0	31 000	8 300	4/72	—
27	Croydon High Street	250	6	47	1630–1830, Mon–Fri	1.5	7 700	3 450	4/72	—
28	Lewisham High Street (A), Lewisham hospital	110	8	70	0730–0930, Mon–Fri	0.7	7 800	6 900	—	3/73
29	Lewisham High Street (B), Lewisham clock tower	60	6	59	0730–0930, Mon–Fri	0.7	7 800	6 900	8/72	3/73
30	Lewisham Way	335	8	56	0800–1000, Mon–Fri	0.9	18 200	7 500	—	—
31	Parkfield Road Lewisham	140	2	36	0800–1000, Mon–Fri	3.6	18 200	7 500	—	—
32	Kensington Gore (E Bnd)	215	3	50	0800–1000/1600–1830, Mon–Fri	0.8	13 750	4 200	9/72	12/72
33	Kensington Road (W Bnd)	430	5	78	1600–1830, Mon–Fri	3.1	29 000	9 100	—	4/73*
34	Camden High Street	195	8	130	1630–1830, Mon–Fri	1.0	12 000	4 300	10/72	—
35	Hampstead Road	35	6	130	1630–1830, Mon–Fri	1.0	12 000	4 300	10/72	—
36	High Holborn	150	5	70	1600–1800/0830–1030, Mon–Fri	0.7	6 500	2 350	10/72	—
37	Trafalgar Square	80	9	90	24 hours, 7 days	0.6	16 000	8 000	—	—
38	High Street, Bromley	180	8	62	1630–1830, Mon–Fri	0.4	1 900	7 200	10/72	—
39	Brighton Road, Croydon	450	8	60	0800–0930, Mon–Fri	1.6	4 700	2 400	10/72	—
40	Camberwell New Road	285	4	38	0800–1000/1600–1830, Mon–Fri	1.5	12 900	6 800	11/72	—
41	Holborn viaduct	190	4	49	0830–1030/1600–1800, Mon–Fri	0.5	4 400	6 050	11/72	—
42	Kensington High Street	425	7	90	0800–1000/1600–1830, Mon–Fri	1.5	36 000	11 500	11/72	—
43	Kensington Road (Knightsbridge)	450	4	60	1600–1830, Mon–Fri	1.5	10 800	7 400	11/72	—
44	Shaftesbury Avenue	195	8	90	24 hours, 7 days	0.7	11 600	5 000	11/72	—
45	Wandsworth Road[d]	466	4	37	0730–0930, Mon–Fri	3.0	—	—	11/72	—

Table 27 BUS LANES IN LONDON, 1965–72[f]

cided with either LT's suggestions (17 of 47) or the known congestion points (19 of 126), even taking a generous definition of 'coincide' to include all lanes on sections of road within the vicinity of the offending junction.

ANALYSIS AND CONCLUSIONS

The MOT originated the Tottenham scheme through the LTMU but were rather tardy in processing it, and did not wish to become involved; in December 1966 they were willing for the GLC to act as agents for the scheme but were content to let the protracted negotiations between Haringey and the GLC take their course before appointing the Borough as agents in January 1968. After exhorting local authorities to help public transport through the demonstration projects in February 1970 and by improving the grant aid provisions in 1971–72, they were content to leave subsequent schemes to the new transport planning system, although they responded quickly to the approval of the Piccadilly scheme by offering a 75% grant within two months. The DOE's commitment to helping public transport was made clear by Mr Eldon Griffiths, Parliamentary Under-Secretary of State, who in September 1972 said: 'We are pro-bus because only the bus can preserve civilised life in our towns. . . .'[1]

LT increasingly pressed for the more rapid and widespread introduction of bus priority measures. Their concern in Tottenham was to prevent losses that would occur if services were diverted; in Piccadilly to recoup some that had already occurred. The transfer of policy responsibility to the GLC gave them direct access to an elected body and much closer contact with the professional traffic engineers, which helped mutual understanding of both policy and operational problems. Had the traffic and transport responsibilities remained separate it is doubtful whether this would have occurred even if LT had established a bus priorities unit. The Piccadilly scheme also gave LT a chance to enlist public support for their needs more widely than their Annual Reports normally allow, and they took it in the public meetings and through advertising space in buses and tubes, whereas they had not always had a good reputation for their consultative procedures (see Case Study *N*).

The Metropolitan Police had three main concerns: that the schemes should operate safely, that they should not significantly reduce the capacity for general traffic and that they should be able to be enforced. Experience

[1] DOE *Press Release 1048M*, 25 September 1972.

Notes and Sources to Table 27

a All the lanes are with the main traffic flow except numbers 1, 8, 12, and 15 which were against it, and 37 which is a short bus-only street. Number 7 should not be confused with an abortive contra-flow lane that was to be a DOE demonstration project in 1970–71.

b Lane suspended April 1972 during widening of bridge; it is hoped to reinstate the lane on nearside of eastbound carriageway.

c Scheme withdrawn by Central Area Board.

d Scheme withdrawn by GLC Bus Unit.

e Repositioned 8/69.

f For comparison the Oxford Street scheme was 970 metres long, carried a total of 400 buses per hour, cost £35 000 (together with measures to widen pavements, etc.) and gave an annual estimated benefit of £475 000. It was approved for consultation in June 1972 and implemented in November the same year.

Sources: GLC Minutes and Press Releases; *Quarterly Bulletin*, No.21; and information from the Bus Unit, 9 April 1973.

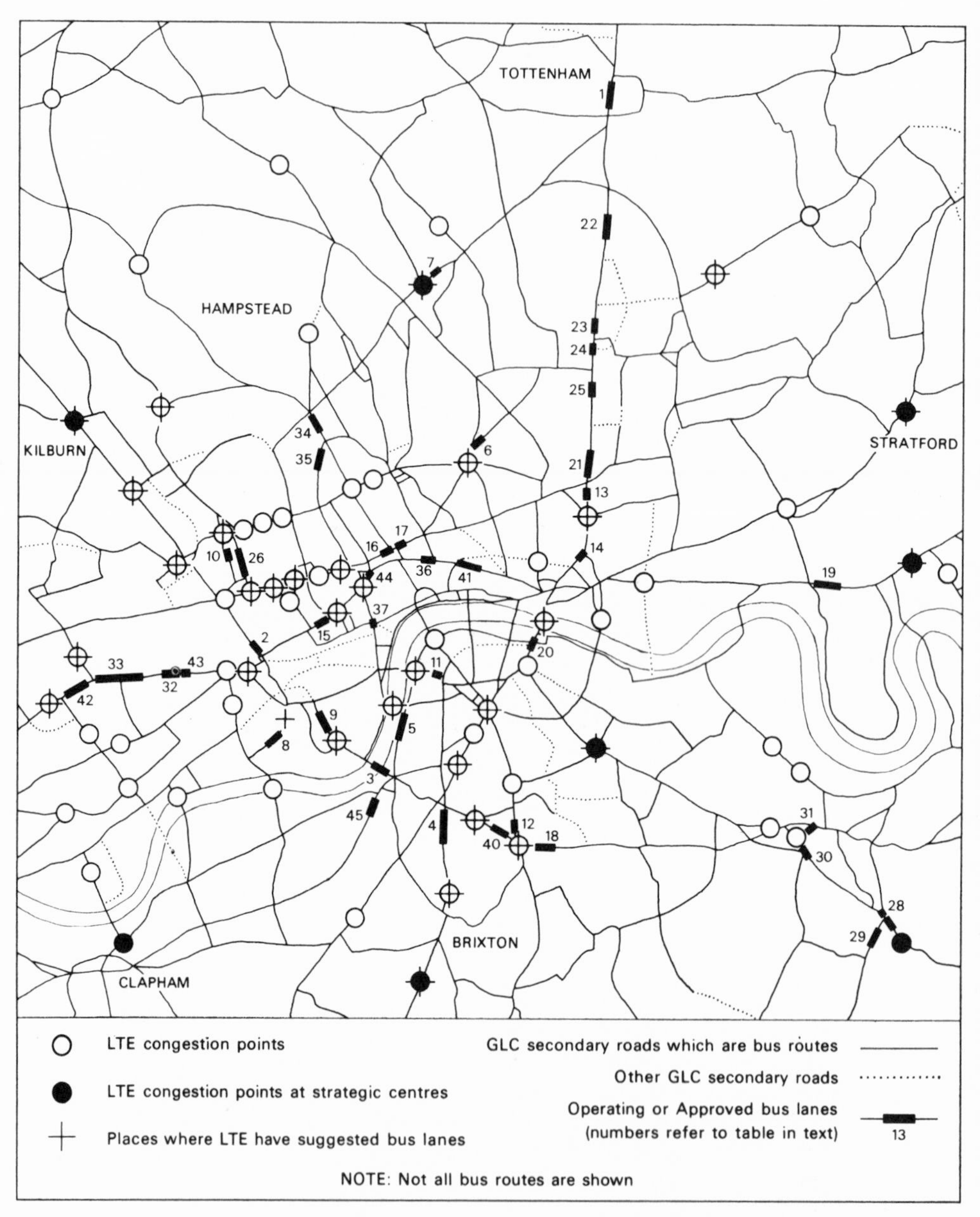

Figure 17 BUS PRIORITIES IN CENTRAL AND INNER LONDON

with existing lanes shows that contra-flow lanes are self-enforcing to a great degree even with regard to loading and access to premises across the bus lane. With-flow lanes, demarcated usually only by painted lines, presented more difficulty. The police were very stringent in their design requirements for the early lanes but technical and administration novelties quickly became accepted procedures, indeed more acceptance and flexibility has occurred (*vide* the wide range of operating times).

The London Boroughs varied in their response: Camden wished to go further with bus priorities as a means of making public transport more attractive and of restraining general traffic than the GLC would allow, and devoted most of their transport planning resources to the study in 1971. Wandsworth and some of the other inner London boroughs were also beginning to favour Camden's approach. Westminster, however, believed that the Piccadilly bus lane would increase congestion, but did not demonstrate that this would occur, and both they and Haringey were concerned to represent and to be seen to represent the interests of the local residents' and shopkeepers' groups. The City of London Corporation was the only authority to speak against bus lanes in principle, claiming that the traffic displaced from the stretches where lanes were sited would impede buses in the intervening stretches. They believed that proper lay-bys for buses at bus stops would provide better value, although this measure was seen by some as a means of giving priority to other traffic, not buses.[1]

The residents' and shopkeepers' groups in the Tottenham and Piccadilly cases represented people who believed that their interests would be adversely affected. Experience in Britain and elsewhere, however, confirmed the MOT's view that these local fears were often exaggerated.[2] The importance of the Piccadilly lane in one of the capital's major tourist and shopping streets, and the form of consultation procedure chosen by the GLC, allowed other non-local amenity groups to become involved, including the London Amenity and Transport Association who welcomed the opportunity to put the strategic case for bus priority schemes.

The GLC, as already explained, were under several major external pressures to take up the idea of bus priorities, and especially bus lanes, with vigour. They also had to vindicate themselves as a competent transport planning authority in the eyes of the DOE, and, at least during the GLDP Inquiry, in the eyes of informed sections of the public and the press. Having begun a programme of injecting capital into the underground system in 1970 and 1971, and become increasingly concerned with traffic restraint, it was not surprising that the Policy and Resources Committee should have given some priority to bus management schemes to further improve their record on public transport.

An overriding concern of the Council was still that bus priority schemes should not substantially reduce general traffic capacity and this was one of

1 City of London Comments on GLC's Green Paper reported in *Evening Standard*, 19 October 1972.

2 MOT TPP Division (1969), *Traffic Management and Parking, A Manual.*

the major remaining obstacles to introducing a bus priority network rather than isolated schemes. The fact that one of the boroughs, Camden, was the first body to examine such a scheme was perhaps indicative of inertia on the part of the GLC, similar to that found in other policy areas (see Case Studies *F*, *G*, and *L*). But the Oxford Street experimental scheme and perhaps the A10 'chain' of bus lanes (numbers 22–5 on Table 27 and Figure 17) represented an apparent change of attitude. With regard to the Oxford Street scheme, for example, the GLC's consultants claimed that it would be successful only if general traffic in the area was thereby significantly restrained.

The pressure to produce and process schemes soon exceeded the Bus Unit's capacity and by 1972 the bulk of the work was being done by consultants at a cost of £130 000 in 1972–73 with a forward commitment of £106 000 for 1973–74.[1] Progress, then, had accelerated (as can be seen by comparing the two years taken to process the Piccadilly scheme with the six for Tottenham); the administrative methods were established, basic design parameters devised and the consultation procedures more or less formalised with the other authorities. Compare the public consultation and participation procedures for the two sample projects: in Tottenham, only elected members were involved until an *ad hoc* pressure group was formed; the Piccadilly scheme was advertised through the press and local radio, and on public transport, while public opinion was sought through 8000 prepaid postcards and two major public meetings; moreover, interested groups were invited to present their cases. Most bus lane schemes have not required that scale of effort, but public participation procedures appeared to make the minimum period from initiation to operation about two years, according to the GLC.[2]

To enable schemes to be implemented more quickly, the GLC's decision in early 1972 to introduce bus lanes with experimental traffic orders considerably reduced the consultation procedures. The Oxford Street experiment, for example, was discussed only with LT, Westminster City Council and the police in June 1972 and was implemented five months later. The GLC's experience over Piccadilly may well prove a salutory one, however, in confirming the view of the MOT's demonstration project group that 'local authorities would be surprised at the public support they would receive if they showed that they were in earnest about public transport.'

To summarise, the evolution of this policy in the hands of the GLC is an excellent example of gradualism in local government politics and administration. Perhaps the single most important influence was the GLC's assumption of responsibility for LT and transport planning in January 1970. Without this it is doubtful whether progress with bus priorities would have been as fast despite the favourable situation created by the DOE by exhortation and grant aid. Probably, the Bus Unit and its consultants would not have been established, LT would not have had the power or traffic

[1] GLC *Minutes*, 14 November 1971, pp527–8.
[2] GLC *Minutes*, 2 November 1971, p528.

experience to initiate suitable schemes, the DOE would not have been close enough to the ground to exert direct influence, and the pressure from boroughs in favour of such schemes like Camden and Wandsworth would have been diffused and consequently less effective.

Despite making 1972 'the year of the bus,' the GLC remained extremely conservative in their approach to bus priority measures, but nevertheless they were moving with the tide of accepted 'enlightened' policy, individual schemes were showing benefits, and the consultation procedures with other agencies and the public seemed to work well, if slowly. In the light of these accelerating changes, it seems likely that this limited success could foreshadow greater achievement in the future.

Case Study N

ALTERATIONS TO SERVICES

1 INTRODUCTION

Since the early 1950s, falling passenger demand has made it increasingly difficult for public transport undertakings, in London as elsewhere, to maintain financial equilibrium, let alone profitability. In order to lower costs, bus and rail services have been progressively reduced (or withdrawn) or altered in pattern, reflecting the uneven distribution of both demand and costs in time and place and hence profitability. Cuts have been concentrated on the most unprofitable and least used services.

It is notoriously difficult, however, to define in any one situation what operating, capital and other overhead costs are incurred and what revenues are earned, because many of the cost elements in the second and third categories are shared. Public transport fares cannot, therefore, be fixed so accurately as to reflect the costs of individual journeys, even if this were desirable. Consequently, regardless of whether total revenues are more or less than total costs, some services 'cross-subsidise' others. A certain amount of such cross-subsidisation within a public transport system is usually regarded by operators as inevitable and, up to a point, acceptable. But there are often 'weak links' in the system where costs so far exceed revenues (however narrowly defined the former, or widely defined the latter) that operators seek to remove them or reduce the burdens. This is particularly so in a situation of falling passenger demand.

How are grossly unprofitable services dealt with in London? Do the operators continue to operate them because they feel that they fulfil a social need? Do they try to cut their costs, or raise fares, or both? Do they try to stimulate new traffic to help the service pay its way? Or do they seek to withdraw the service unless someone pays them to keep it going? Decisions about alterations to established public transport services have to take account of operational and social as well as financial factors, and the institutional system can be judged according to how well the interests of the community and the operator are represented within it.

Invariably London Transport (LT) or British Rail (BR) as the transport operators are the initiators of alterations to services since they are motivated by the need to maximise revenues and minimise costs. Both undertakings are required by statute to pay their way,[1] a requirement which is qualified with provisions as to the length of the accounting period and

[1] *Transport Act 1968*, ch73, s41; and *Transport (London) Act 1969*, ch35, s7; for BR and LT respectively.

powers for the Government or local authorities to pay grants.[1] In the case of LT this requirement must be reconciled with a requirement to provide such public passenger transport services as best meets the needs 'for the time being' of Greater London.[2]

The Transport Users' Consultative Committee (TUCC) for London is the statutory body concerned with hardship arising out of rail closures (either BR or LT) and is required to hear objections to closure proposals and to report to the Secretary of State for the Environment.[3] The LT Passengers' Committee is the consumer body for LT services set up by the Greater London Council (GLC) after it was given control of LT policy, and may deal with both suggestions and complaints about the level of services. Its responsibility is confined to the GLC area and does not include rail closures or fares and charges.[4]

The Department of the Environment (DOE) is involved in permanent rail closures for it is the Secretary of State who must take the final decision if objections are raised. In doing so he must take account of any report on hardship by the TUCC and he can request information on any aspect of operation from LT or BR. If rejecting the proposal, and if satisfied that the line is making a loss, he may provide a grant for its continued operation.[5]

The GLC are involved as transport authority for London and have a statutory duty to develop and promote an 'integrated, efficient and economic' transport system.[6] They also set the overall financial target for LT's operations.[7] BR (and, of course, LT) must notify the GLC about a proposed rail closure and the Secretary of State for the Environment must consult them before deciding on a rail closure in Greater London.[8]

All local authorities, including the GLC, have the power to pay grants for unprofitable services in their areas[9] and to that extent may become involved. It is, of course, also open to local authorities, as representatives of local populace, to make representations about proposed changes in services either to the operators, the consumer bodies, or indeed, if it is felt that political pressure must go farther than the formal channels of representation, to the GLC and the DOE.

Private bus services cannot be operated within Greater London except with the approval of LT who have taken over the licensing functions formerly held by the Metropolitan Traffic Commissioner.[10]

[1] 1968, ch73, s39 (Government grants to BR); and 1969, ch35, s3. (GLC grants to BR or LT.)

[2] *Transport* (*London*) *Act 1969*, ch35, s5.

[3] *Transport Act 1962*, ch46, s56.

[4] *Transport* (*London*) *Act 1969*, ch35, s14.

[5] *Transport* (*London*) *Act 1969*, ch35, s26 for LT lines (Transport Act 1968 for BR).

[6] *Transport* (*London*) *Act 1969*, ch35, ss1, 2.

[7] *Transport* (*London*) *Act 1969*, ch35, s7.

[8] *Transport* (*London*) *Act 1969*, ch35, s25.

[9] The GLC may also make grants for services outside its area. While there are no specific provisions for grants to unremunerative bus services in London, the *Local Government Act 1948*, ch26, s136, can be construed for this purpose with the Minister's consent.

[10] *Transport* (*London*) *Act 1969*, ch35, s24, amending the *Transport Act 1960*, ch16, s119 ff. Moves were made in 1971 to alter the licensing arrangements laid down in 1930 in

The legislative and policy background against which decisions about unprofitable services are made in London is described in Chapter 3. This case study describes how in practice the institutional system has dealt with a loss-making rail service on both LT and BR, an LT bus withdrawal and with a local bus reorganisation.

2 EPPING–ONGAR RAILWAY CLOSURE

The electrification of the Central Line of the Underground system beyond Epping to Ongar was planned during the 1930s as part of the London Passenger Transport Board's drive to serve (and stimulate) development in the rapidly spreading outer suburbs. Electrification proceeded only as far as Epping before the Green Belt legislation[1] brought speculative residential development beyond Debden to an abrupt halt. Consequently the stations beyond Debden serve a very much smaller population than was envisaged by the pre-war tube builders.

The section from Epping to Ongar was operated by BR and later by LT as a steam-hauled shuttle service until 1957, when electrification to Ongar was completed. At the time there was some discussion as to whether the line should be closed completely, but LT hoped for a build-up of traffic on the line and claimed that electrification would reduce the annual operating losses by £20 000.[2] The operation of Epping–Ongar trains independently from the rest of the Central Line was a survival from steam days: a separate electricity generator at Epping dictated a maximum of two four-car trains (or one eight-car train) running at the same time, and passenger demand has never justified the same frequency of service which the line south of Epping enjoys. After settling this dilemma LT seemed content to run the line for more than a decade. Indeed, during the mid-1960s investment was made in new track, signalling, resurfaced station forecourts and other improvements.

The first attempt by LT to reduce financial losses on the line was the cutting in 1966 of certain services to Blake Hall, one of the intermediate stations, including the withdrawal of all trains on Sundays. This move was not an uncommon one[3] but the Epping and Ongar Rural District Council regarded it as the 'thin end of the wedge' and tried unsuccessfully to per-

order to stimulate the adaption of public transport services to new demand situations. (See, for example, DOE *Release 164M*, 23 September 1971.) John Hibbs, and others, have put forward proposals for abolishing quantity licensing altogether on the thesis that private operation could hardly do worse than the statutory operators. (See, for example, John Hibbs (1971), *Transport for Passengers* (2nd edn) Hobart Paper No.23; and G J Ponsonby (1969), *Transport Policy: Co-ordination Through Competition*, Hobart Paper No.49.)

[1] *Green Belt (London and Home Counties) Act 1938*, ch93.

[2] *The Times*, 4 November 1957.

[3] In 1972 a total of fifteen LT stations were closed on Sundays, nine of which were also closed on Saturdays. For one of these, Roding Valley, also on the Central Line, Chigwell Urban District Council for a time in 1970 paid a grant to LT to retain its weekend services.

suade LT to restore the service. In November 1969, the wedge was driven further when LT announced its intention to close the whole Epping–Ongar section on Sundays from 1 February 1970. The news of LT's intention provoked more reaction amongst local residents than the Sunday closure of Blake Hall had done and a deputation was quickly sent to meet Sir Maurice Holmes (then chairman of the LT Board) consisting of the two local Members of Parliament (for Chigwell and Epping) and representatives of the local authorities. At this meeting, a petition signed by nearly 2000 residents in the locality was presented to Sir Maurice, who agreed to a postponement of the Sunday closing while LT deliberated whether to close the line completely.

By the end of July 1970 the LT Executive (as it had then become):

> . . . had decided to go ahead with the statutory procedure which is necessary to enable a full and independent inquiry to be carried out as to the hardships or degree of hardship which might be caused if the . . . line were closed.[1]

When making public this intention, LT stated that objections had to be lodged with the TUCC for London before 6 October 1970, otherwise closure would take effect from 2 November. In the event the TUCC received a substantial number of objections and so the closure was made the subject of a public inquiry to be decided by the Secretary of State for the Environment.

Meanwhile a group of GLC Labour (Opposition) councillors led by Mr Ellis Hillman requested the preparation by the Policy and Resources Committee of a report on the line—a request which under GLC standing orders must be passed without debate. When it appeared in October 1970, the report concentrated on a description of the line, the loss which it was making ('about £90 000 p.a.') and the closure procedure which LT had initiated. It cautiously concluded that 'in the light of the procedure now under way, we thought it inappropriate to attempt any judgement on the proposal at this stage.'[2]

Attention was therefore focused on the objections that were made to the TUCC at the public inquiry which took place on 20 January 1971. The local authorities directly concerned had had no talks with LT about the future of the line apart from the meeting over the Sunday closing issue, but the formal notice of closure produced objections from all of them: four parish councils, Epping and Ongar Rural District Council (EORDC) and Essex County Council. These six authorities decided at a meeting called by the EORDC to combine their strength in a Joint Committee. The Joint Committee also included the two local MPs and (later) a representative of each of the local voluntary action groups which had been set up in 1969 to fight the Sunday closure. The Committee's aims were simple: to lodge the

[1] Letter received from a senior official of LT, dated 27 July 1971.
[2] GLC *Minutes*, 6 October 1970, p532.

constituent members' objections, to prepare a case and to engage and brief counsel to present this evidence at the inquiry. It was 'serviced' by officers of the EORDC, the other councils agreeing to share the costs.

The case which was prepared set out to identify the hardship which would result from closure of the railway. One of the EORDC officers involved said that there was 'a lot of feeling' that the TUCC's powers should not be limited to the investigation of hardship. Although, for example, there was no doubt that the Epping–Ongar railway operated at a loss, there may have been scope for questioning the size of the loss. However, the Committee did not attempt to make any representations for the broadening of the TUCC's brief. In fact its contact with the TUCC was on a strictly formal basis, discussions prior to the public inquiry being confined to questions of procedure.

To assess the extent of the hardship which would be likely to result from closure, the Committee carried out a census of the use of the line. A principal finding was that since this section of the Central Line was used largely as a feeder to the rest of the Underground system, it was unrealistic to assess its function in isolation. For example, it was found that almost 90% of the 800 passengers who used the line daily travelled to destinations beyond Epping, and a substantial proportion of these travelled to the City or the West End. Of all passengers, 70% used the line for journeys to and from work, 20% for school trips, and 10% for social and other trips (such as shopping and personal business). The second major finding was that a majority of the users of the line would find it difficult to travel by any other means. The survey showed that 60% of adult users did not have the use of a car. Moreover, London Country Bus Services Ltd (the company running the two bus routes serving the locality) readily made clear that it was proving difficult, because of staff shortages, to maintain the present scheduled bus services, let alone any additional buses which would be required to cater for ex-railway passengers. A further consideration was that any extra bus services would be unlikely to be profitable. The majority (59%) of the railway's users travelled during the peak hours (on this line 7–8.30 a.m. and 4–7 p.m.), a demand situation that was satisfied by the provision of one extra train in service, but which would require five or six additional buses and crews, which would be idle at off-peak times.

In addition to this quantifiable evidence of hardship, regular users of the line drew up many instances of personal difficulties that would arise if the railway was closed. It was part of the Joint Committee's case, but it was brought out forcibly by the two voluntary local opposition groups, one representing residents at North Weald, the other at Ongar. The latter, called the Epping–Ongar Rail Transport Users' Committee (EORTUC) was the more active of the two and in its first year of existence mounted an impressive campaign including petitions, posters and placards, and the sending of delegations to LT and the GLC. The Joint Committee had avoided this kind of activity and indeed considered it to be the proper role of the voluntary groups. On 16 September 1970 the EORTUC held a public meeting in Ongar which aimed to encourage individual users of the line to send objections to the TUCC. Impressed by the attendance of 750 people, the Joint Committee invited representatives from the EORTUC and the North Weald Rail Closure Committee to attend their meetings. Co-operation between the Joint Committee and the users' groups, however, was little more than a courteous acknowledgement of each other's role in the general opposition to the proposed rail closure. The TUCC received separate objections from these organisations, and indeed many from other organisations[1] and individuals which brought the total to well over 600.

The EORTUC's encouragement to as many people as possible to speak about their own particular case of hardship resulted in the inquiry (for which the TUCC had originally set aside one morning) continuing until four o'clock in the afternoon. At that point the chairman, Major-General Sir Lancelot Cutforth, decided that he had heard sufficient evidence to be able to report to the Secretary of State for the Environment that 'closure of the railway would cause severe hardship to the communities it serves.'[2] Thus the ball passed into the DOE's court. Although the Joint Committee saw no point in taking further action now that the formal channels of objection had been exhausted, the EORTUC continued to canvass support for their campaign, and to make direct representations to the Secretary of State. The GLC decided that as they would be consulted by the Secretary of State before he made his decision, they would make no judgement before then.[3]

The Secretary of State (Mr Peter Walker) was faced with an inevitably difficult decision. If he consented to the closure of the line he would knowingly inflict hardship on the communities which it served—hardship which would be difficult to alleviate. It had become common practice since the 1962 Act to provide for additional bus services as a condition of a rail closure, but there was clear evidence in this case from the bus company that it would be difficult to provide a satisfactory alternative to the railway. If, however, he ruled that the line should stay open, knowing that it would make a loss, he would be expected to authorise a Government grant. This would by implication be inconsistent with his Government's policy as exemplified by their recent decision to eliminate grants to BR's London commuter services.[4]

Two alternatives to closure were possible. First, attempts could be made to reduce the operating loss on the line; the DOE explored this possibility and requested information on operating costs from LT. If a grant was to be paid, it was clearly important to know what cost elements were to be covered. In fact the Ongar line appeared to offer considerable scope for

[1] These included the Inner London Education Authority, who had a school for the mentally handicapped at Ongar; industrial concerns adjoining the Central Line at Debden; the local Traders Council; three schools and two hospitals in the locality; and the National Council on Inland Transport.

[2] TUCC *Press Statement*, 5 April 1971.

[3] GLC *Minutes*, Question in Council, 9 February 1971, p59.

[4] A decision announced by the Chancellor of the Exchequer on 27 October 1970.

further reduction of operating costs[1] including the removal of permanent station staff and the introduction of 'one train on the line' working which although reducing peak services, would bring savings in train operating staff and signalling costs. Second, and depending on the first, the necessary grant could be met either wholly or partly by the local authorities. Although probably beyond the resources of the EORDC, both the GLC and Essex County Council had powers and resources to pay a grant for the line.

The GLC, no doubt concerned at the possible repercussions of a rail closure in its first year of policy responsibility for LT, had deferred LT's public announcement (of the closure proposal) until it had confirmed that the County Council were not immediately willing to pay a grant for the line. The GLC's concern, however, did not extend to making their own grant for the line, a move which would have conflicted with their own established policy of withholding operating subsidies.[2] The local authorities thus declined to commit themselves to a grant for the Epping–Ongar line at least until Whitehall's policy had become clear. LT was eager to get a clear-cut decision on the closure proposal as they were 'testing the temperature of the water' concerning possible grants for most of its unprofitable services.[3] The DOE for its part took a similar attitude: it wanted some indication of the scope for reducing the cost (and hence the losses) of operating the line and also of the likelihood of local government contributions to an operating grant. The DOE asked LT to arrange an informal meeting with Essex County Council with this second purpose in mind, but LT demurred, feeling that the Government should handle the matter themselves.

Meanwhile, the EORTUC continued their campaign, increasingly using environmental arguments. For example, they issued posters emphasising the benefits of country living on the one hand, and the necessity for city dwellers to have a direct link with the countryside on the other. This latter point was appreciated by Tower Hamlets Borough Council who, in July 1971, pledged their support for the retention of the line.[4]

In April 1972, just over a year after the TUCC inquiry, the Secretary of State for the Environment refused to allow LT to close the Epping–Ongar line because of the ensuing hardship. No concurrent decision was made about financial assistance but LT announced that 'in view of the Secretary of State's decision, we shall now be applying for a grant to meet the heavy losses which would otherwise have to be met by passengers on other parts of the Underground.'[5]

The future of the line, however, was still not assured. Not only was the source of possible grants still unsettled, but such grants would be subject

[1] A view confirmed by a senior LT official in 1971.

[2] See, for example, the statement by Desmond Plummer (leader of the GLC) 9 July 1968 (*Press release 410*). The GLC decided specifically not to assist the line financially in February 1972. *Minutes*, 22 February 1972, p111.

[3] Interview with a senior LT official.

[4] LB Tower Hamlets *Minutes*, 3 July 1971.

[5] LT *Press Notice 336*, 13 March 1972.

to review after some years.[1] The EORTUC, therefore, while feeling that its campaign had had a critical influence on the Secretary of State's decision, opposed the payment of grants to LT. Not only did they question the scale of the losses reported by LT but they wanted the service actively promoted so that it would become fully viable. On this latter point LT agreed to investigate suggestions raised at a public 'rail victory meeting' held by EORTUC in May 1972. In the short term, at least, LT pressed for financial assistance but at the time of writing (August 1972), no agreement had been reached with either the DOE or any of the local authorities concerned.

3 'SHOPPERS BUS' EXPERIMENT

The LT bus route 151 used to run Mondays to Saturdays from Morden Station via Sutton and Carshalton Beeches to Belmont, and a Sunday service was provided by route 213A between Sutton and Belmont. Outside the rush hour passenger loadings fell to a low level creating substantial operating losses.[2] Between the morning and evening peaks each bus was often carrying only five or six people.

In January 1970 the London Borough of Sutton received from LT a Notice of Intent to revise bus services in the area, including a proposal to withdraw the 151 and 213A routes because of the considerable losses which they were making.[3] Other routes remained between Morden and Sutton[4] (though not travelling via North Cheam) but the Sutton–Carshalton Beeches–Belmont section was left with only a peak-hour service on Mondays to Fridays operated by the route 213 which terminated at other times at Sutton.

The effect of the proposed withdrawal would be to leave more than 200 acres of residential development without a regular bus or rail service within a half-mile walk. This appeared to involve the breaking of LT's own criterion of a reasonable network which was that 'there should be no substantial numbers of people more than half a mile from public transport in built-up areas.'[5]

Sutton Borough Council informed LT that they objected to the proposal to withdraw the 151 and 213A and referred the matter to the Transport Facilities Conference, a group set up in September 1966 to co-ordinate transport facilities for residents in the London boroughs of Sutton and Merton and the Borough of Epsom and Ewell (across the GLC boundary).[6]

[1] *Transport (London) Act 1969*, ch35, s26 (1).

[2] The heaviest costs are incurred by the provision of the peak service. The crew's wages and most of the expenses of operating the vehicles have to be met whether or not the service is continued outside the peak times.

[3] LT *Notice of Intent*, No.70/16.

[4] Routes 80, 80A, 154, 164, 164A as well as a BR Service.

[5] LT *Memorandum for the London Transport Passengers Committee. Policy as Regards Level of Service Provided*, 7 April 1970, p3. See also *Report from the Select Committee on Nationalised Industries, London Transport*, volI, 1965, para228.

[6] A Standing Conference was set up prior to the 1965 London government reforms and consisted then of representatives of the boroughs of Epsom and Ewell, Lambeth,

In addition, the Council sought the support of local MPs, the members of the GLC for Sutton and the Director General of the GLC. The Conference discussed the Notice of Intent and expressed 'profound regret that there had been no consultations with the Borough Councils concerned . . . prior to its issue.' It also wanted:

> . . . a broader interpretation of section 23 (3) of the Transport (London) Act 1969 than that indicated to the Conference by representatives of LT which sought to limit consultations to routing of services, terminal points, points of taking up and setting down, or points where vehicles might turn at terminal points.[1]

A week later Sutton Council wrote to LT disputing their interpretation of their duty to consult London borough councils before varying bus services, and pointing out that 'full and frank discussions' before Notices of Intent were issued would help LT's problems to be understood more fully. At the same time the Council asked the LT Passengers' Committee to take up this matter (see section 5).

During March 1970 a Sutton councillor sent two petitions together containing 3642 signatures to Sir Richard Way, chairman of the LT Executive, asking him to reconsider the closure proposal. In reply, Sir Richard said that LT's decision had been made after very careful consideration and that the number of people who would be inconvenienced was very small. Buses were on average only one-third full even at peak times while off-peak loadings fell to seven or less. The average load on Sundays was three or four passengers. He suggested that if the Borough Council thought that the service was a social necessity, they could make a grant to cover the operating loss of about £120 per week (£6000 p.a.). The service withdrawal took effect from 18 April. Two days later, Sutton Council considered the possibility of making a grant for different levels of service on the route, but decided to take no action.

Although no further efforts were made to restore the Sutton–Belmont services, Sutton Council's Principal Chief Officer asked the London Boroughs' Association (LBA) to consider the desirability of amending section 23 of the 1969 Act to bring the social effects of bus alterations within the statutory consultation procedures of LT. Camden Borough made similar representations to the LBA. After discussions in October 1970 between LBA representatives and GLC members, the general question of consultation was raised by the GLC with both LT and the LTPC.[2]

After the withdrawal of the 151 and 213A the LTPC, who had received ten letters of complaint from individual passengers, suggested to LT on its

Mitcham, Sutton and Cheam, and Wimbledon and the urban districts of Carshalton, and Merton and Morden.

[1] Report of meeting of Transport Facilities Conference held 10 February 1970, in letter from Sutton Borough Council, 29 July 1971.

[2] LBA *Minutes* (Works Committee Report), 14 June 1971, p43.

own initiative that a restricted service could be provided between Sutton and Belmont on the 151 route. LT agreed to operate, initially for a three-month period, a one-man-operated bus to serve (in particular) the three hospitals in the area and the needs of those without a car. This became known as the 'shoppers bus experiment.' The experiment was carried out in such a way that operating costs were kept to an absolute minimum and that they could easily be related to takings. One single-decker one-man-operated bus was operated at a low frequency only between the peak hours using a driver from another route. It was given considerable publicity: 15 000 leaflets were distributed in the area of which 4800 were delivered on a door-to-door basis along the route itself. This was augmented by an advertisement in the local papers and notices on other buses in the area, and in the streets.

The 'shoppers' bus' began operation between Sutton and Belmont via Carshalton Beeches on 10 October 1970. It lasted longer than the three-month experiment period (eighteen weeks), but loadings were consistently poor (averaging about seven per trip) and the bus was finally withdrawn on 10 April 1971. One factor which may have worked against its success was that the route was without a service (except in peak hours) from April to October 1970. This was sufficient time for people in the area to make other arrangements for travel (such as buying a moped or arranging a lift with a neighbour to the shops). Even the publicity given to the experimental bus (which was considerable) would be unlikely to induce people to reverse decisions of this sort. LT reported to the LTPC that the net loss of the experiment was £556. No further attempts were made to restore the service either by the Borough Council, LTPC or local residents.

4 PARLIAMENT HILL BUS SERVICE REORGANISATION

Not only has LT been faced with a steadily declining number of passengers on its bus services since about 1952 but the services themselves have become unreliable due to traffic congestion, staff shortage and the heavy peaking of demand. To combat these four major problems LT produced its *Bus Reshaping Plan* in September 1966 which proposed four main courses of action:

1 Routes must be shortened.
2 One-man-operation must be extended throughout the fleet.
3 More standing accommodation must be provided on short routes.
4 New methods of fare collection must be worked out.[1]

It was in line with this philosophy of restructuring bus operations to meet changing circumstances that LT decided, in October 1969, to alter the pattern of services running from the terminus at Parliament Hill Fields. The proposals were also said to reflect a changed pattern of demand result-

[1] LT, *Bus Reshaping Plan*, September 1966.

ing from the opening of the Victoria Line in March 1969 (which gave a more rapid connection between Kings Cross and the West End).[1]

Prior to 24 January 1970 three services ran from Parliament Hill Fields. Routes 63 and 214 ran to Kings Cross (route 63 via Camden Town) and route 163 ran to Westminster and across the river. Traffic and staff problems led to an unreliable service and the loadings (at least at off-peak times) were insufficient to support good frequencies on all three routes between Parliament Hill Fields and Camden Town. LT therefore decided to concentrate its resources over this section onto route 214, to increase its frequency to match that achieved with all three routes, and to reroute it through Camden Town. Route 63 was withdrawn between Parliament Hill and King's Cross and route 163 was withdrawn altogether. Passengers to the West End were expected to change at Camden Town onto either a bus from the west side of Hampstead Heath or onto the Northern Line, or to change at Kings Cross onto the new Victoria Line.

The interesting aspect of these changes from the point of view of this study is the controversy which surrounded LT's action, and in particular the 'imperial fuss' over the withdrawal of the 163.[2] Rumours had been in the air for some time before LT made any official announcements about the proposed changes. One Camden borough councillor who used the 163 route regularly brought the matter to the notice of his Council's Finance and General Purposes Committee early in November 1969. The Council at that time had received no formal notification from LT, nor had any consultations taken place. Following representations by residents and local groups and articles in the local press, the Council asked LT to explain their reasons for the rumoured service alterations at a public meeting. LT declined this but met a deputation from the Council on 12 January 1970 when the rationale behind the move was explained, i.e. to provide a better service within the context of persistent operating difficulties, falling passenger demand, and the requirement of LT to pay its way.

Meanwhile a group of residents in the locality had formed the Parliament Hill Bus Users Group (PHBUG). One of their members organised a petition opposing the 63 and 163 cuts which was signed by 1500 residents and presented to Camden Council on 7 January. PHBUG representatives also met LT officials but nothing was resolved. LT's first official confirmation of the proposals came on 9 January—just fifteen days before the changes were due to take place. The PHBUG contacted their local MP, Mr Kenneth Robinson, who had already shown interest in the matter. He had written four times during December 1969 to Sir Maurice Holmes (Chairman of the then LT Board) but had received no reply until 6 January when Sir Richard Way (Chairman of the new LT Executive) explained the proposals but said that they would have to go ahead as planned. Mr Robinson then suggested to the PHBUG that a telegram be sent to the newly created LTPC asking them to restrain LT from making the cuts.

[1] *The Times*, 25 March 1970.
[2] Remark of a senior LT official.

The LTPC secretary replied two weeks later that his Committee had not met but that the matter would be considered by them. This delay ruled out any hope of LT being restrained from making the changes on 24 January. Four members of the PHBUG therefore decided to act on their own initiative and applied to the High Court for an injunction to restrain LT from going ahead with the cuts. They arrived at the court on 23 January only to hear that LT had not had sufficient time to prepare evidence and that the hearing would be adjourned for two weeks. LT had, however, made preparations for the bus service alterations which duly took place on 24 January. During the two-week adjournment, Camden Council became co-plaintiffs in the action, a move which added much-needed strength to the case as doubts had been expressed about the rights of four individual residents to apply for an injunction.

In proceeding with the service alterations, LT had anticipated correctly the court's finding on 12 February that their action was lawful, and the consequent refusal of the injunction. Of the three judges, only Lord Justice Sacks expressed some dissent from the court's general opinion that to reinstate the services would cause more chaos than such a move was worth.

Camden Council were still dissatisfied with the way LT had handled the matter and lodged an appeal on the grounds that the statutory consultation procedures laid down in section 23 of the Transport (London) Act 1969 had not been complied with.[1] The appeal was dismissed, however, and LT's view was upheld that the Act's provisions related only to the traffic implications of service alterations and not to the convenience of the travelling public.[2]

Camden Council also approached the LBA with a view to recovering some of the legal costs, as the LBA had also received representations about inadequacies in LT's consultation procedures from Ealing and Hackney Councils and from the Transport Facilities Conference (see pages 443–4).[3] Subsequently in October 1970 the LBA and GLC members met to consider improving procedures, and the GLC in turn held discussions with LT and the chairman of the LTPC. The LBA hoped that these discussions would produce a new procedure whereby: 'the strategic implications of alterations to services [were] dealt with at GLC–LBA level, together with the possibility of a local borough organisation to consider local implications.'[4]

The LTPC were also concerned about LT's consultation procedures.

[1] The gist of section 23 is: 'Where it is proposed . . . to provide (or) to vary a bus service . . . then, before deciding on . . . any variation affecting the route of that service (or terminals, picking up, setting down, and turning points) the Executive shall . . . consult with the GLC, with the Commissioner of Police concerned, with any of the councils of the London boroughs or the Common Council of the City of London . . . and with any other person whom it appears proper to the Executive for them to consult.'

[2] *The Times* (Law Report), 25 March 1970. Court of Appeal, Sinfield and Others *v* LT Executive, 24 March 1970.

[3] LBA *Minutes*, 29 April 1970, p32; 17 March 1971, p17; 14 June 1971, p43.

[4] LBA *Minutes*, 17 March 1971, p17.

They had been shocked to learn that the Parliament Hill changes were made public so shortly before they were carried out and had later received complaints 'from several sources and in various connections' about the lack of consultation.[1] The Committee asked LT preferably to give at least three months' notice to local authorities of major changes in passenger services and this, according to the Committee, worked 'moderately well' for a time.

On 6 July 1971, however, the GLC decided as part of a wider policy package drawn up for LT to formalise this procedure and direct the Executive as follows:

> Before making any major variations of route or withdrawals of service, the Executive (shall), so far as practicable, give no less than three months' notice of their proposals to the Council, the London borough councils concerned or other local authorities whose areas are affected by the changes proposed and (shall) take into consideration any representations received from those authorities within twenty-eight days of their being notified by the Executive.[2]

The Parliament Hill affair was the first major issue to be raised with the LTPC[3] who continued to be concerned about the matter long after the initial controversy had subsided. Although they did not attempt to prevent the service changes taking place, the LTPC heard personal representations by Kenneth Robinson (the local MP), Councillor Roger Robinson (of Camden) and Mrs Barbara Beck (secretary of PHBUG) that the 163 service should be reinstated. Subsequently the Committee asked LT 'to examine the situation arising from the withdrawal of the 163 and 63 bus routes with a view to improving the service between Parliament Hill Fields and the West End.'[4]

LT replied in May 1970 that after re-examining the position they were sure that the new arrangement was an improvement for the majority of passengers, but Councillor Robinson and Mrs Beck still submitted that a through service from Parliament Hill Fields to the West End was required. The LTPC reaction was similar to that over the 151 withdrawal and they asked LT to consider a reduced through service. Some time elapsed before LT reported (in January 1971) that such a service would be uneconomic and that they were not prepared to provide it at the expense of other facilities. The LTPC, however, were sufficiently concerned to refer the matter to their General Purposes subcommittee who felt that an independent survey was required. Lengthy discussions were held with the GLC who had the powers to provide both manpower and accommodation to carry out what-

[1] LTPC *Annual Report*, 1970, p4. These complaints presumably included one from Sutton Council concerning the withdrawal of the 151—see section 3.

[2] GLC *Minutes*, 6 July 1971, p348. The direction was actually made on 20 July 1971.

[3] The Committee became operative on 1 January 1970, twenty-four days before the bus changes were implemented.

[4] Letter received from LTPC, 9 September 1971.

ever appeared 'to be requisite for the proper discharge of (the Committee's) functions.'[1] A survey based on a questionnaire designed by a statistician member of the PHBUG was eventually carried out in September 1971. (The PHBUG had originally intended to carry out the survey themselves but were prevented from doing so by lack of money.) The survey report concluded that the potential demand for a through service to the West End by people using the 214 amounted to about 260 passengers a day. After consideration of the report by LT and the PHBUG the Committee decided that the present services were adequate and made no further representations on the matter.[2]

A further side issue of the Parliament Hill bus reshaping scheme was the extra cost to passengers previously making through journeys, arising from LT's fare structure. Fares are tapered with the length of the journey so that a journey made by two buses (or bus and tube) is usually more expensive than a single through journey. Passengers to the West End from Parliament Hill are therefore not only inconvenienced by having to change at Camden Town or Kings Cross but also by having to pay more for their journey. In view of the fact that the reshaping plan would give rise to the need for more changing, the LTPC recommended that tickets should be inter-available. More specifically for the Parliament Hill users, the Committee studied the interchange arrangements at Camden Town and were instrumental in getting an additional bus stop provided to avoid the need for passengers to cross a main road when changing buses.

5 BROAD STREET–RICHMOND LINE

The BR London commuter network has been established largely in its present form for 70 to 100 years, although the pattern of services—the frequency, routing, cost and comfort—continues to alter and evolve. The Broad Street to Richmond line has seen considerable changes:

> From 1860 to 1910 this route, in whole or in part, was one of London's principal arteries for passenger traffic . . . but while passengers are still carried over much of it, they create but minor cross-eddies in the great rivers of present day passenger flow.[3]

The main commuter flows are, of course, radial in pattern whereas the Broad Street–Richmond line forms a mainly orbital route through north London. The line consequently became the subject of some debate at the

[1] *Transport (London) Act 1969*, ch35, s14 (4).
[2] GLC (December 1971), *Parliament Hill Fields Bus Stop Survey*, TSN 14 and letter received from LTPC, 16 March 1972.
[3] H P White (1963), *A Regional History of the Railways of Great Britain*, volIII, *Greater London*, p74. White was speaking of the North London Railway of which the present Broad Street–Richmond line formed a part.

GLDP Inquiry as some objectors believed it might provide an alternative to the GLC's proposed orbital motorways.[1]

The decline in traffic—or rather passenger traffic since the line remains a vital cross-London link for freight traffic—which the line has suffered in the past fifty years has been due largely to competition from the Underground and, of course, the car and by the early 1960s the economic viability of the line was in doubt. White said in 1963 that:

> Because there are no marked diurnal peaks on the Broad Street–Richmond service, it was reputedly among the most profitable in London, though in March 1962 the London Midland Region [of BR] claimed to be incurring substantial operating losses.[2]

Doubts about the future of the line and a controversy about its possible closures were growing several months before the appearance in April 1963 of the Beeching Report[3] which recommended the line for closure with scores of others. This was not an official proposal to close the line as BR were quick to point out,[4] but neither was there any official indication that the future of the line was assured. This perpetuated a controversy which still continues. Opposition to the threat of closure began in 1962 and in April 1963 a meeting of protest was held at the House of Commons which was attended by over 300 residents and the mayors of five metropolitan boroughs affected as well as local MPs. At a debate on the matter in the House of Commons initiated by Mr Lawrence Pavitt (MP for Willesden West) support was also expressed from over sixty organisations, schools, trade unions, three transport user groups, and industries with local interests including Messrs Guinness and Heinz—who had 'more than fifty-seven reasons for supporting the protest!' In view of the scale of concern, Mr Marples (then Minister of Transport) replied to the debate himself, but he considered that the TUCC established by the Transport Act 1962 provided adequate safeguards in dealing with rail closures, including the Broad Street–Richmond services.[5]

At this time there were at least three committees fighting the closure threat who between them had produced substantial documentary evidence on the importance of the local passenger services. The spearhead of action was, however, the Broad Street–Richmond Line Joint Committee, a group organised by individuals affected and with representatives from the metropolitan boroughs. They pointed out, for example, that unlike most commuter lines in London it carried substantial weekend traffic—mainly family outings to Kew Gardens and Richmond. The objectors gained tem-

[1] See particularly evidence of R Calvert, for National Council on Inland Transport. *Paper S12/125*, GLDP Inquiry Stage 1.
[2] White (1963), p81.
[3] BR Board (1963), *The Reshaping of British Railways*.
[4] E.g. see *Railway Magazine*, August 1963, p587.
[5] *Hansard HC Debates* 17 May 1963, cols1777–90.

porary relief with an announcement by BR in October 1963 that a decision on whether to put up a formal closure proposal would not be made for six months. Perhaps in anticipation of BR's decision, a group of objectors from Hampstead produced a report claiming that the social costs imposed on the community if the line was closed would amount to £578 000 p.a. It concluded that as BR were claiming to make an annual loss of only £69 000, the line's closure could not be justified.[1] The six months passed, however, with no decision from BR. In July 1964 three MPs tabled a motion in the House of Commons calling for an end to the uncertainty.[2]

A lapse of over a year prompted the MP for Richmond, Mr Royle, to initiate a further debate in Parliament. In reply Mr Swingler (then Joint Parliamentary Secretary to the MOT) said that a decision was expected from BR within 'a month or so.'[3] He also said that if BR decided to put up a closure proposal, and if it was found that this conflicted with future transport plans under consideration for the London area (he was referring apparently to the London Traffic Survey (LTS) then being carried out by the London County Council (LCC)), then the Minister would ask BR to withdraw the proposal.[4] In February 1965, BR announced that it was considering alternatives to withdrawing the line's passenger services and would not put up a closure proposal until this examination was completed. The following June Mr Swingler again said in Parliament that BR had made no firm decision. This time, however, he referred to the Labour Government's policy of taking social effects into account when considering rail closures. He said that 'those who understand the significance of the Government's transport policy would realise that the service represented by the line was going to continue.'[5] The MOT he said, was awaiting proposals from BR as to how the policy principles were going to be applied.

Although 1962–65 was a period in which local feeling over the rumoured closure of the line ran high, it was also a period of considerable activity on the part of BR in an attempt to improve the economic health of the line. A revised timetable came into operation in January 1963 giving a regular-interval service of 20 minutes (30 minutes on winter Sundays and 15 minutes on summer Sundays) and cutting the total journey time by 5 minutes. The aim was to give a better service and to make better use of rolling stock.[6] In July the same year 'travelling porters'[7] were introduced on the trains replacing sixteen or seventeen station porters. These obvious

[1] Save the Broad Street–Richmond Line (Hampstead) Committee (30 April 1964), *Hampstead and the Broad Street–Richmond Line*. The calculations were said to be based on the methods used by C D Foster and M E Beesley in their social cost-benefit study of the Victoria Line (see Case Study *C*).

[2] The *Guardian*, 4 July 1964.

[3] *Hansard*, 11 December 1964.

[4] *Hansard*, 11 December 1964. As pointed out earlier (pages 96 and 188) the LTS only dealt with public transport in Phase III, after 1966.

[5] *Hansard*, 4 June 1965, col2233.

[6] *Railway Magazine*, 1963, p140.

[7] Further economies were made when these too were removed after experience had shown that the guard was able to cope with the odd door that was left open.

efforts to improve the service and to cut costs[1] did not, however, allay the fears of users of the line that closure was a real possibility. In June 1965 the Joint Committee reported that it and affiliated committees had virtually exhausted the possibilities for complaint and protest, but that BR had still made no decision. The Committee wanted a deputation from all the London boroughs affected to press BR to lift the threat to the line and to clarify its future role.[2]

On 21 June 1965 Mr Fraser, then Minister of Transport, announced that the service would not be withdrawn,[3] and this appeared to be a starting point from which BR planned to make further improvements to the line. In 1966 BR initiated a plan to publicise and improve the image of the line. In the short term, obsolete platform buildings (most of them were over 100 years old) were to be replaced by new lightweight shelters, and new signs and lighting were to be provided. In the longer term the booking halls were to be remodelled to facilitate one-man-operation and to incorporate automatic ticket machines.[4]

To publicise the line BR sought the help of both the GLC and the borough councils through whose areas the line passed. Shortly before its demise the LCC had thought it 'highly desirable' that the line should be better known and used. The GLC likewise supported the publicity drive and gave BR both 'encouragement and material support' by financing a series of local newspaper advertisements and by arranging with the Inner London Education Authority to distribute publicity material.[5] Some of the boroughs affected agreed to contribute towards the costs and to provide sites for posters.[6] Camden, for example, was glad to promote the line to attract people off the roads, whilst the GLC felt the campaign would help to promote its policies for making the best use of highways and public transport.[7]

By 1971 most of the twenty stations on the line had undergone physical improvements of some kind and some of the better-used ones had already been converted to one-man-operation and had automatic ticket machines installed. But even this continuing investment did not dispel the cloud of uncertainty that hung over the line. A request in Parliament by Geoffrey Finsberg, MP, for a Government undertaking that the line would not be closed received a 'categorical "no"' from Mr Eldon Griffiths, MP, Under-Secretary of State for Transport Industries.[8] A GLC councillor, Mr Ellis

[1] A reported loss in 1961 of £200 000 was apparently substantially reduced. *Railway Magazine*, August 1963, p587; and *Railway World*, June 1967, p233.

[2] LB Camden *Minutes* (Planning and Development Committe Report), 16 June 1965.

[3] *The Times*, 22 June 1965.

[4] *Railway World*, June 1967, p236.

[5] GLC *Minutes* (reply to Question in Council), 13 December 1966, p698.

[6] In 1967 Camden Council received sanction from the MOHLG to make a grant of £700 to BR, in addition to a grant of £2400 made by the GLC, for newspaper publicity as part of the promotional campaign. Letter received from Camden's Town Clerk, 23 September 1971.

[7] LB Camden *Minutes* (General Purposes Committee), 15 February 1967.

[8] *Hansard*, 19 February 1971.

Hillman, pursued the matter with questions in Council in February and June 1971 while a colleague, Mr George Tremlett (who had also been involved in the early campaign to keep the line open), was pressing a suggestion that the line should be incorporated into the LT Underground network.[1] Also in June 1971 the London Passenger Action Confederation (a voluntary organisation for promoting better public transport in London) convened a meeting at which a committee was formed to examine ways of boosting the use of the line.

There remained, however, some confusion as to why the line was thought to be threatened with closure. As in the early 1960s, BR were quite firm that the Broad Street–Richmond services were not proposed for withdrawal.[2] Without any official closure proposal neither the GLC nor the TUCC for London would become formally involved in the issue. The chairman of the GLC's Policy and Resources Committee said that the Council would make its views on the line known if and when BR put up a formal closure proposal.[3] BR, moreover, reported to the GLDP Inquiry that passenger usage of the line had increased from 227 000 weekly in 1968 to 233 000 in 1969 and 248 000 in 1970 (increases of 2.6% and 6.4% respectively) as a result of publicity, the face-lifting exercises and growing road congestion.[4] But the TUCC for London said that BR were still losing about £300 000 p.a. on the line and that if a grant was not forthcoming 'it is possible that its closure may be proposed.'[5]

6 CONCLUSIONS

The four examples of service alterations have to be judged in the context of the broader legislative and policy situation with regard to unprofitable parts of the public transport system. This is described more fully in Chapter 3 and its implications are discussed in Chapter 6 but some basic points bear repeating.

First, the days when urban transport undertakings were lucrative have long since passed (if they ever existed at all) and both BR and LT have sought to contain their losses by cutting their most unprofitable services, particularly after being clearly obliged under the 1962 Act to pay their way. Second, the 1968 and 1969 Acts reinforced this obligation, but at the same time removed their obligation to operate grossly unremunerative services, unless the MOT or (DOE) or local authorities paid them grants to do so on account of social needs.

[1] This suggestion was also put to LT in 1965. At that time Mr A Bull (for LT) said that the line was 'an integral part of the BR system with . . . heavy freight working. We believe it would be difficult, if not unpractical, for LT to take it over.' *The Select Committee on Nationalised Industries (1965) London Transport*, volII, Q1231, 5 May 1965.

[2] Confirmed with BR Board, 28 June 1971.

[3] GLC *Minutes* (reply to Question in Council) 23 May 1971, p105.

[4] BR Board (1972), *Paper S30/76*, GLDP Inquiry Stage 2.

[5] Letter received from TUCC for London, 9 July 1971. See also similar statement by chairman of GLC Policy and Resources Committee, GLC *Minutes*, 7 March 1972 p135.

In this context, how well did the system handle the four cases examined here? This question may best be tackled by discussing in turn each of the bodies involved. The DOE was involved only with the Epping–Ongar and Broad Street–Richmond services. It took more than a year after the TUCC's inquiry for the DOE to decide not to allow LT to close down the Epping–Ongar line. Apart from any internal inefficiencies within the DOE this was due to investigations into the size of the annual loss which LT claimed the line was sustaining, and the possibility of other authorities contributing a share of the grant for the retention of the line. The DOE appeared as unwilling as the GLC and Essex County Council to commit themselves to paying the full grant, at least before the attitude of the other authorities was established. The decision announced in March 1972 was otherwise relatively straightforward, the TUCC having submitted clear evidence that hardship would arise from the line's closure. At the time of writing, however, no decision had been taken regarding a grant and so LT, contrary to the intentions of the 1969 Act, had continued to operate the line at a loss.

The Broad Street–Richmond passenger services have a longer history. Although the future of the line was discussed in Parliament on a number of occasions during the 1960s, this led to no direct action on the part of the Minister, who evidently believed that the TUCC for London would ensure that any closure proposal would receive a fair hearing. After the 1968 Act the line attracted a grant together with others in the London 'pool' network and BR made it increasingly plain that removal of such grants might lead to a firm closure proposal. One question which was not raised, however, was whether a decision by the Government on an individual closure proposal (or indeed on the social grants for the London network) would pay adequate regard to the GLC's overall transport policy. The GLC's policy, however, appeared too broad to aid decisions over specific services. The GLDP for example stated that it was the Council's policy to improve public transport 'in all possible ways' and yet the GLC specifically rejected the principle of paying grants to both LT and BR to retain unprofitable services.

The gap between broad policy and individual services was clear in all four cases studied. After an initial flurry of enthusiasm for promoting the Broad Street–Richmond services in 1966–67 (which was in any case inherited from the LCC) the GLC consistently refused to express any view on the line's role in London's transport system. The possibility of orbital rail services (involving the Broad Street–Richmond line) was examined but from the economic viewpoint rather than those of social need or the future structure of the city. This indifference to the potential of the line may have been at least partly engendered by the fact that the decision on a proposal to withdraw the services was a DOE, not a GLC, responsibility.

Although entirely outside Greater London, the future of the Epping–Ongar line met a similar disinterest from the GLC. Little consideration was given to aspects such as the impact of closure on road traffic, or the role of the line as part of north-east London's rail system. Despite their responsibility for LT and their general duty to maintain a transport system which 'best meets the needs of Londoners,' the GLC seemed reluctant to take any part in the wider issue. They clearly did not welcome the publicity attached to LT's proposal, but neither did they wish to pay a grant for the line's retention—or even to examine the need for such a grant (for example because of its role of supplying central London with labour, and Londoners with access to the countryside).

LT's attitude was dominated by their obligation (under the 1969 Act) to maintain financial viability and by proposing closure of the Epping–Ongar line were 'testing the temperature of the water' as regards the possibility of attracting social grants. But LT also showed little interest in discovering whether the financial position of the line could be improved. Little attempt had been made, for example, to reduce operating costs *before* the closure was proposed. Nor had any special efforts been made to exploit the line's potential (for example the link it provides between central and east London and the beautiful countryside of west Essex) by even the experimental introduction of cheap day return tickets from inner London stations.[1]

The 151 and 163 bus withdrawals similarly failed to prompt any of the parties involved to consider the relationship between individual services and the general 'level of service' operated by LT. The withdrawal of the 151 demonstrated that the 'half-mile walk' criterion adopted by LT for defining a reasonable network of routes was not one which LT was prepared to maintain regardless of cost. The usefulness of such a criterion was thus thrown open to question. The definition of an 'adequate level of service,' however, was not simply drawn up as a guide for LT's operating managers. The GLC has a statutory duty to consider levels of service together with LT's financial performance when determining policy not only for LT, but for the whole conurbation transport system.[2] The 'half-mile walk' criterion would act as a guide for the GLC's purposes only if it applied independently of financial performance. As soon as this standard begins to be eroded (and the withdrawal of the 151 is only one example of what has been happening steadily in all the outer London suburbs) the GLC can no longer look upon it as a guide to the level of service being maintained within the overall financial policy which they impose on LT. The GLC must seek a better criterion for level of service which takes account of social as well as financial considerations or at least monitor plans for actual route and service modifications to see where LT's criterion is breaking down.

As early as 1965, however, the GLC's newly appointed Director of Transportation indicated that he felt the half-mile criterion was unrealistic in outer London where 'it means a lot of buses.'[3] In the years that have elapsed since then, there does not appear to have been any attempt by LT

[1] This had been tried with some success on LT's Metropolitan Line to Amersham.

[2] *Transport (London) Act 1969*, ch35, s28.

[3] *Report from the Select Committee on Nationalised Industries. London Transport*, volII, 1965, Q1483 (of Mr P F Stott).

or the GLC to arrive at more realistic criteria for 'adequate levels of service.' Consequently, although LT are continually pruning and altering their services (particularly in outer London) to meet falling demand and to keep their operations within the financial limits set first by the Government and since 1969 by the GLC, there is nothing to suggest that the GLC is sufficiently aware of these changes for them to act as positive feed-back on general planning and transport policies.

In some respects, however, the GLC's assumption of responsibility for LT policy brought improvements in the procedures for service alterations, in particular by directing LT to consult with borough councils affected over proposed bus service withdrawals. It is interesting to note that the limited scope of section 23 of the Transport (London) Act 1969 (dealing with LT's obligation to consult local authorities) was effectively extended by a GLC direction made under powers contained in section 11 of the same Act.

LT was the initiator of the two bus service alterations as well as the Epping–Ongar closure proposal. The 151 was undoubtedly a victim of a situation which is common in the outer suburban areas: a low intensity of demand is eroded by the growth in private car use to the point at which a regular conventional bus service is no longer profitable. LT, although accepting a large degree of cross-subsidisation throughout its system believed that the cost of a service used by a handful of people should not be borne by the users of the rest of the system.

The withdrawal of the 163 was also motivated by falling passenger demand, but was part of a package of service alterations in the Parliament Hill area. Accepting the philosophy of the bus reshaping plan, LT was able to justify this package (when pressed by Camden Council and the LTPC to do so). Those responsible for designing the changes were confident that between Parliament Hill and Camden Town the modified and more frequent 214 service provided a better facility than the three routes which it replaced. Whether or not this view was shared by the passengers there can be little doubt that LT handled the changeover insensitively. No attempts were made to gain the passengers' support for or even their views on the service alterations. One senior LT official thought that, particularly in view of the public agitation about services in the area prior to the changeover, his colleagues who had been responsible were 'asking for it.' A judgement on LT's decision to go ahead with the alterations before the court case was heard and in spite of the fierce complaints from passengers, depends on one's priorities—the convenience of LT's internal management or its responsibility and accountability to its customers. This issue, the 151 withdrawal and the Epping–Ongar proposal all point to a general lack of concern for the consumer on the part of the LT Executive.

Quite apart from any inconvenience caused to the travelling public (or the councils which represent them), a further regrettable aspect of LT's scant consultation of other bodies on service withdrawal was that no monitoring of changes in the level of service could be fed directly to those concerned with transport planning as a whole—namely the boroughs and particularly the GLC. It is difficult to see how the GLC could consider overall planning and transport policies if they were unaware of the progressive reduction of bus services being made as passenger demand declined. The procedure adopted at least in part by LT in April 1970 (and formalised and strengthened by the GLC's directive in July 1971) only partly filled this gap.

The most striking aspect of the Broad Street–Richmond line issue was the uncertainty which began in 1962 and which is still unresolved; an uncertainty which was only temporarily dispelled by the Minister of Transport in 1965. BR apparently remain unable to reassure the public or the local authorities by committing themselves to the indefinite retention of the Broad Street–Richmond services. But it is unreasonable to expect BR to give assurances about services which consistently fail to cover their costs, since the Transport Act 1968 placed responsibility for such services squarely on the shoulders of the DOE. The BR Board made its position clear to the GLDP Inquiry:

> From 1 February 1973 (when the government grant aid for the London commuter services will be completely withdrawn) . . . the Board will have to aim for a London commuter network which pays for itself; including provision for renewal. In addition to any fare increases needed to offset inflation, the Board will need to make good the loss of the revenue grants by increasing fares and/or reducing the level of service provided.[1]

Assurances about the line therefore depended on assurances from the Government about social grants for services in the London area. All four of the issues involved one or more of the London boroughs or, in the case of the Epping–Ongar line, the county, rural district and parish councils. In the latter case, the EORDC co-operated with the parish councils affected to object to the closure of the line. But their case was confined to the question of hardship arising from closure, i.e. matters within the TUCC's brief. None of the councils involved (including Essex County Council) were prepared to commit themselves to pay a grant to LT for the line's retention, at least before it became known whether or not the DOE would make such a grant. As already stated, the DOE likewise awaited the local authorities' decision! The decision by Tower Hamlets Council to support the campaign against closure, however, showed a broader concern for the line's future.

Similarly, with regard to the 151 bus route, Sutton Borough Council, although concerned at the loss of the off-peak service on an entire route in their borough, were not sufficiently concerned to set aside perhaps £1000 or more from their rate income to maintain it. No doubt this attitude recognised that there was little evidence of widespread distress amongst

[1] BR Board (1971), *Proof of Evidence, E12/7*, p41, GLDP Inquiry Stage 1.

local residents. The Transport Facilities Conference (of which Sutton Council was a member) acted as a catalyst for the interchange of ideas and views between the boroughs, LT and the LTPC, but evoked little response from the GLC.

Camden Borough Council was concerned with the 163 issue and in particular with LT's consultation procedures (or rather lack of them) in such cases. With Sutton and other boroughs they were instrumental in moving the LTPC to persuade LT to consult more fully with local authorities over proposed bus service changes. Camden, again with the support of several other boroughs, was also concerned about the future of the Broad Street–Richmond services. The co-operation over publicity for the line between five boroughs, the GLC and BR was an example of how different authorities may combine to promote a common facility despite differing reasons for doing so. Although valuable, this was an inexpensive and somewhat indirect course of action. But while the London boroughs expressed clear concern for specific services in their areas there was little evidence of concern for the matters of broad policy which largely determine the future of unremunerative services. In contrast, the GLC tended to take the reverse attitude, being concerned with broad policy but taking little interest in the implications for individual services of which the network is comprised. The operators were in theory better placed to *understand* both levels, but not to influence overall policy.

The LTPC, which played a major role in both the 151 and 163 issues, seemed, in the words of a senior LT official, to be 'a fairly lively body.' They were quick to respond to representation about the 151 withdrawal and to initiate the 'shoppers' bus' experiment, though some of this enthusiasm may have been due to the fact that the LTPC was at that time a newly constituted body. The Parliament Hill affair was more significant for the LTPC who became both sympathetic to the users' complaints and active in urging LT to improve the Parliament Hill links with the West End. The Committee was shocked to learn of the short notice LT had given to users about the cuts and of the absence of consultation with Camden Council. It was largely as a result of this experience that the LTPC persuaded LT to adopt a more open and public-minded approach to service changes. But although formalised in the GLC's direction to LT in July 1971, the consultation procedures now adopted are confined to local authorities concerned. It remains possible for LT to inform the local authorities without informing the public—a situation which could prove unsatisfactory should a local council not be as concerned for the mobility of its populace as Sutton and Camden.

The LTPC, moreover, were not simply concerned with LT's procedures and continued to seek ways of overcoming the Parliament Hill complaints despite LT's assertion that the new 214 service was better than the three routes which it replaced. Indeed, the Committee pursued the matter (by carrying out an independent bus stop survey with the aid of the GLC) after the complaints from local residents had subsided.

The PHBUG's earlier disenchantment with the LTPC's commitment to formal procedures arose in the heat of the battle over the 163 and could be regarded as a product of circumstances rather than as a fundamental criticism of the Committee: it was constituted less than a month before the bus changes took place, and (more importantly) the situation should never have arisen where bus services were cut without the public and the local authorities having been forewarned.

As a body to protect and represent consumer interests the TUCC for London appears less successful than the LTPC. It was not involved in the Broad Street–Richmond issue, for example, simply because no formal closure had been put forward by BR. With regard to the Epping–Ongar line the TUCC's brief was confined to reporting on hardship to the Secretary of State. Their evidence, as it transpired, was sufficient to persuade Peter Walker that the line should stay open, but it left major problems for him to solve. The TUCC made no investigation, for example, of the accuracy of LT's estimates of operating losses, of policies for minimising these losses, or for attracting more custom to the line. Wider powers for the TUCC could have brought these matters into the arena of public debate and thus helped to allay the impression that the fate of the line was being deliberately decided behind closed doors.

It has been suggested that the TUCCs are less effective bodies than, for example, voluntary pressure groups, but during the period of this study the TUCC for London had the same chairman as the LTPC which, as we have seen, was active. The inadequacies of this TUCC appear to be the result of the very narrow terms of reference left to it by the 1969 Act rather than any incapacity of the group itself.

Voluntary groups did, however, play a major role in all the issues except that of the 151 bus service. The Parliament Hill group, although not successful in retaining the 163 to the West End, set the pace with regard to improving LT's consultation procedures. The PHBUG itself appeared to run out of steam when their particular battle over the 163 was lost, but continued to express their belief that London's public transport system was inadequate; their secretary later became a founder member of a London-wide group to promote its improvement (the London Passenger Action Confederation). The Broad Street–Richmond line, although never the subject of a firm closure proposal, attracted the attention of a number of voluntary groups over the years. Uncertainty over the future of the line was clearly sufficient to provoke widespread concern and indicated that this can be as much a source of hardship as an actual closure. The groups continued to exert pressure on BR and the GLC to promote better use of the line as a positive way of safeguarding its future. The Epping–Ongar group (EORTUC) similarly explored every possible argument in favour of the line's retention and maintained an almost continuous barrage of letters to the local press, posters, demonstrations and petitions for more than two years. Their efforts were clearly instrumental in the Secretary of State's decision to refuse closure. The fact that there were important questions (such as the accuracy of the LT's estimates of loss) which LT was not obliged to answer and which were outside the TUCC's terms of reference remained a source of bitter complaint for the group. As with the Broad Street–Richmond line groups, they continued to press for better use of their line because they believed that grant aid provides at best an uncertain future.

Finally, the areas which produced active pressure groups were, by and large, those with residents able to make known their problems and suggestions to the authorities in loud and coherent voices. Yet bus service withdrawals and frequency reductions are being made steadily throughout the London suburbs to match filling passenger demand. In areas not so well endowed with articulate people as, for example, Parliament Hill, who is to speak for those who suffer hardship? As one LT official put it: 'a withdrawal in Poplar similar to the 163 would provoke as much if not more anger at the bus stop, but this might never reach the ears of 55 Broadway.'

Case Study P

OPERATION MOONDROP: AN EXPERIMENT IN OUT-OF-HOURS DELIVERIES OF GOODS[1]

INTRODUCTION

This is a study of an experiment that failed: an experiment to deliver goods out of normal shop-opening hours, so that the distributors could avoid the problems of growing traffic congestion, and at the same time help to relieve the congestion. The scheme was sponsored by the Greater London Council (GLC) as strategic traffic authority, with a major interest in achieving the second of these objectives, and the National Economic Development Council for the Distributive Trades[2] whose interest lay more in the first objective of achieving efficient distribution. Also involved were the trade federations (Traders' Road Transport Association (TRTA) Road Haulage Association and later the Freight Transport Association (FTA)). They undertook the detailed organisation and most of the participation in the scheme, and were intended to be the main beneficiaries through easier, quicker and cheaper operation. The Metropolitan Police gave advice on traffic aspects.

During the 1960s the growth of traffic congestion and the rising costs associated with delays began to worry the operators in the goods distribution industry and the major food manufacturers who distributed their own products. The extra distribution costs ultimately meant higher product prices, and the social cost of road congestion (to which the goods vehicles added) in terms of obstruction, noise, fumes and mutual delay was recognised as a large and growing problem. The problem was aggravated by two factors: limitations by retailers on the periods when they were willing to accept goods, and growing traffic regulations. Many stores did not like deliveries on their busy days (Friday and Saturday), their early closing day, before 10 a.m., during the lunch break (1 to 2 p.m.) or after 4 p.m.[3] This reduced the wholesaler's delivery schedule to three days a week and concentrated it within a five-hour day. The spread of traffic controls through bans or time limitations on parking and loading meant

[1] Much of the information for this study was gained from interviews with officers of the GLC, NEDO, and *The London Grocery Out of Hours Delivery Experiment: Comprehensive Report* (GLC Policy Memorandum No.29, August 1969).

[2] GLC *Minutes*, 9 July 1968, p392.

[3] Survey of thirty-six firms in 1966 by SPD Ltd (Unilever's transport subsidiary), reported in *DTEDC Newsletter*, No.5, July 1967.

further difficulties, particularly where there was no off-street shop access. The rapid spread of peak-hour clearway controls introduced by the Ministry of Transport (MOT) and the GLC, which affected twenty of London's twenty-nine major shopping centres, meant that early morning and evening deliveries were also restricted.

After much discussion, the Food Manufacturers' Federation managed to initiate a pilot experiment in out-of-hours deliveries from May to October 1966. Twelve manufacturers delivered goods to thirty London branches of Tesco supermarkets between 6 and 10 p.m. on Monday evenings. This experiment showed that there were average gains in travel speed of about 20%, and off-loading was achieved more quickly at the stores, usually without any waiting. It proved uneconomic, however, because the costs of the extra staff time involved outweighed the time savings, but eleven of the twelve manufacturers expressed a willingness to join in a permanent scheme on a four or five nights-a-week basis, with a regular night shift (rather than overtime payments as in the pilot experiment). This obviously meant a scheme with much greater geographical coverage and participation from retailers.

THE BIRTH OF THE NEW EXPERIMENT

There the matter rested for some months, although it was being considered by the Economic Development Committee ('Little Neddy') for the Distributive Trades which had been established at the National Economic Development Office (NEDO). In March 1967 officers of the GLC met members of the DTEDC and of the food manufacture and road haulage industries to discuss matters affecting them in the preliminary draft of the Greater London Development Plan. The latter had been increasingly worried about the rising cost effects of traffic congestion and the growth in traffic regulation,[1] and after suggestions made at this meeting about a possible new experiment on a large scale which might lead to a permanent scheme, another meeting was arranged in May at County Hall. This was held under the auspices of the Freight Group of the Transport Co-ordinating Council for London, set up by Barbara Castle in 1966.

The Freight Group included representatives of the TRTA, the Road Haulage Association, the Port of London Authority, the Transport Holding Company, British Rail and the GLC. At this meeting Mr Joyce, the TRTA representative, said that his organisation could not undertake a large scheme involving a wide sample of suppliers and retailers, both geographically and functionally. Mr Beckham, manager of SPD Ltd, the Unilever transport subsidiary, mentioned that he had experienced en-

[1] A MOT Report (June 1967), *The Better Use of Town Roads*, had suggested that short of road pricing, kerbside controls could be used to improve the efficiency of goods delivery by co-ordinating loads onto fewer vehicles and trips, and make more effective use of the roads by diverting goods deliveries to off-peak times (paragraphs 3.4.2, 3.4.8, and 3.5).

couraging cost savings in the past from out-of-hours deliveries, and thought that retailers could benefit from increased efficiency and from lower stock-holding.

It was hoped to begin the experiment in October 1967, and the project was to be guided by a Steering Group of twenty-seven people chaired by J D C Churchill, of the GLC's Policy Group (Transportation Department). The contacting of participants, detailed organisation and scheduling, and other day-to-day matters were to be handled by an Action Group of nine people chaired by Mr Beckham.

It was decided to operate the scheme for four nights a week (to avoid the busy Fridays) and to deliver from 6 to 10 p.m. (so that retailers need not employ an extra shift) and London was divided into four sectors each corresponding to one evening (north-west, Monday; south-west, Tuesday; north-east, Wednesday; south-east, Thursday). The experiment began with 21 distributors and manufacturers and 11 retailers, involving 6 warehouses, 93 shops and from 70 to 80 vehicles. The three companies carrying the largest loads (SPD, Nestles, and Proctor and Gamble) scheduled their first shops and predetermined a route for their deliveries ('drops'). All other medium-size companies scheduled only their first drop and adjusted their route to suit their loadings. The GLC operated a telephone information service to notify participants of delivery concellations or closure of outlets. Drivers and warehousemen completed log sheets to enable the scheme to be evaluated (see below).

In the early meetings of the Action and Steering Groups it was stressed that the experiment must succeed as the backing of the Minister of Transport herself had been obtained. The NEDO encouraged forward publicity in the national and trade press and the GLC arranged a large reception in July 1967 to launch the scheme, at which Mrs Castle said that she was pleased to see London acting as a pacemaker and innovator in such experiments and also to see TCCL, her own creation, producing something 'really practical and tangible.' Liaison had been achieved with the retail trade unions[1] and the Metropolitan Police. Already, however, there had been some reluctance to join the scheme particularly amongst retailers (for instance, from meetings it seemed unlikely that it could be extended to department stores) but also amongst suppliers. Tate and Lyle, who handled 20% of the total goods involved in the proposal, decided that they could not participate.

THE SCHEME IN OPERATION

The scheme started in January 1968 and after a few weeks three problems were immediately apparent: the whole level of operation was too low (leaving vehicles and drivers and store staff under-used); drivers were still having to queue on arrival at stores, despite the attempts at scheduling;

[1] The Transport and General Workers Union, and the Union of Shop Distributive and Allied Workers.

and the limited number of outlets meant long drives averaging over 14 miles between drops, whereas it had been hoped to achieve an average of 4 miles.[1] These problems could have been at least partly overcome if more retailers and suppliers had been involved.

The Action Group held meetings in February and March and followed up individual large firms in April. But despite some enthusiastic comments nobody joined; indeed, three further suppliers withdrew.

The Action Group then tried to encourage other stores affected by the clearway proposals to join, but again to no avail. It did suggest, however, that there might be a prospect of extending the scheme to early morning deliveries, which would enable suppliers to use a two-shift system, while retailers with a small staff could manage without employing further personnel.[2] It was also suggested that the scheme might be extended to restaurants, hotels, chemists and launderettes.[3] Before these ideas could be pursued, Tesco and Finefare announced that as a result of their own costing, they had decided to withdraw from the scheme.[4] Since they controlled over half the shops involved the Action Group decided to end the experiment on 27 June.

AFTERMATH

The Action Group had hopes of running a smaller scheme with a greater degree of flexibility, and at the same time its chairman (Mr Taylor, succeeding Mr Beckham at SPD) sent a questionnaire to eight major supermarket chains and their store managers and to twenty-one suppliers seeking their opinions.[5]

	EXTEND IN GLC AREA		EXTEND NATIONALLY	
	YES	NO	YES	NO
Eight supermarkets	4	2	3	3
Twenty-one suppliers	7	8	5	7

As the table shows[6] there was no outstanding support for an extension of the experiment and the Action Group decided fully to evaluate the experimental scheme and then wind up its activities.

EVALUATION OF THE EXPERIMENT

The scheme was not an economic success: analysis of the completed returns showed that suppliers were operating at only 59% of capacity and

[1] Steering Group *Minutes*, 11 July 1967.
[2] It must be remembered that Selective Employment Tax was in force at the time.
[3] Action Group *Minutes*, 13 May 1968; *Grocers Gazette*, 9 March 1969, *The Financial Times*, 5 March 1968; the *Guardian*, 15 April 1968.
[4] Tesco's losses for example were estimated to be running at the rate of £25 000 p.a.
[5] Action Group *Minutes*, 5 September 1968; TCCL *Freight Group paper*, No.51/68.
[6] *Minutes* of Steering Group, 5 April 1968.

retailers at 53% and that their delivery costs were 133% and 200% of daytime costs respectively. This seriously affected confidence in the scheme. The suppliers had additional problems in that each of the four sectors of London had a different workload (being much heavier in the north-west and south-east) and the limited number of retail outlets participating caused 'bunching' of delivery vehicles. The GLC commented that 'possibly Operation Moondrop was planned on too rigid a basis; the scheme attempted to submit the highly complex system of wholesale distribution to a fixed pattern. Such a pattern may evolve, but from our experience on this scheme it seems doubtful whether it can be imposed.'[1] As with the problem of staggered working hours there was a dilemma between a need for great flexibility and very precise and reliable scheduling. As the FTA later commented 'the overall picture presented was that the detailed co-operation necessary to achieve a system of reasonable and economical night deliveries was most unlikely to be obtained, particularly from shopkeepers who are much more numerous and usually in a smaller way of business than distributors.'[2]

Nevertheless the scheme had two direct benefits. First, 'firms are now aware that the GLC is willing to work with them as a partner . . . and that it takes seriously its freight transportation role.'[3] Despite comments that TCCL acted only as a 'talking shop,' since its demise members of the freight trade have asked for a similar group to be set up under the aegis of the Greater London Transport Group. Second, wholesalers' and retailers' relationships have improved and some firms continued with 'moondrop' deliveries using their own delivery fleet (Tesco) and with outside suppliers (Pricerite). Large firms like these can economically use staff for shelving and pricing goods during the evening. Many suppliers have improved their daytime deliveries also by means of an appointments system.[4]

THE ROLE OF OUT-OF-HOURS DELIVERIES AND TRENDS IN GOODS DISTRIBUTION

Four developments may encourage limited developments in out-of-hours deliveries: the growth of automated or otherwise rationalised goods handling; the introduction of daytime traffic bans in shopping streets; the controlled routing and parking of lorries; and the longer-term possibility of road pricing. A Swedish firm have developed a system of containers which are placed into a retailer's lockable 'night safe' (Combitainer) and a similar system (Nightpak) has been designed by a subsidiary of National Carriers Ltd: this could overcome the smaller retailer's problems of providing staff to meet evening deliveries. Other methods might be to use smaller

[1] *GLC Policy Memo 29* and *Minutes*, 9 July 1968, pp392–3.
[2] FTA (1971), Research Report No.1: *Designing for Deliveries*, app1, p19.
[3] GLC *Minutes*, 9 July 1968, p393, and interviews.
[4] R J Banister (1968), *Economist Intelligence Unit Marketing Review*; and 'Night Deliveries,' *Freight Management*, June 1970, pp68–83.

vehicles for the whole delivery trip or to have a 'break of bulk' point on the edge of town centres or elsewhere. The GLC and the operators' groups decided, for example, to investigate alternative systems of servicing the town centre at Thamesmead.[1]

Some wholesalers are now handling their own goods on a bulk load basis in the evenings. This would certainly seem capable of extension to all multiple and co-operative group stores who could use their own warehouses instead of having numerous small direct deliveries from the manufacturers.

In Paris a complex system of controls for the movement, parking of and servicing by large vehicles has been instituted to cover a central 'green zone' and a wider area with different degrees of control for three size categories of vehicle. Paris is also experimenting with two 'break-of-bulk' depots. As Robertson has pointed out, the French haulage industry has responded flexibly to these controls but they tend to have been used to keep the streets freer during the daytime for the private motorist, and he was opposed to such rapid and radical changes in London because of their effects both on the haulage industry and traffic generally. He believed that a new primary road system was the best means of segregating heavy traffic.[2] In London many retailers have overcome clearway regulations, which have proved less of a problem than formerly feared; small retailers in any case seem 'prepared to take their chances rather than undertake evening deliveries.'[3]

The growth in popularity of pedestrian precincts is now influencing local authorities in London and elsewhere to ban vehicles in shopping streets permanently or for part of the day (see Case Study *L*). If, as in many existing shopping centres, servicing can only be achieved from the pavement, then this can often be done only at night or early in the morning; Continental cities have successfully adopted such schemes.[4] The introduction of a scheme of road pricing would very probably encourage both the transfer of deliveries to times before or after the normal working day and better organisation of distribution arrangements to achieve more fully-laden vehicles making fewer trips. Finally, the introduction of any scheme to stagger shopping hours such as that discussed for Oxford Street would appear to facilitate the easier introduction of evening deliveries.

CONCLUSIONS

As an experiment in cutting distribution costs and easing traffic congestion Operation Moondrop was not a success. With hindsight one could criticise

[1] J S Moulder (1971), 'Heavy Vehicles in Town Centres,' *Qtly Bull GLC Int Unit* (15), pp9–14.
[2] J J S Robertson (1971), 'Urban Traffic Policy for Goods Vehicles,' *Qtly Bull GLC Int Unit* (17), pp27–36.
[3] GLC *Policy Memo*, No.29.
[4] Institute of Food Distribution Seminar, *Servicing Shops*, 27 April 1971, including Metra Consulting Group paper, *The Problem of Supplying the Shops*; and Distributive Trades EDC (1971), *The Future Pattern of Shopping*, pp6, 25–6, 40.

some aspects of the GLC's handling of the experiment as sponsor and co-ordinator. First, the Steering Group was a very unwieldy body having three times the membership of the Action Group. Second, the GLC and NEDO were rather self-effacing in their publicity: the potential benefits of the scheme to the goods suppliers and distributors were obvious but the GLC might have made more effort to persuade retailers of the more indirect benefits for them. The GLC could, for example, have promoted Mr Beckham's idea that a more regular and reliable system of deliveries achieved out of normal hours could decrease the size of stocks and the costs of holding them. Better publicity might have helped retailers to overcome the feeling that 'delivery is the responsibility of the manufacturer and [that] it is for him to overcome the problems without in any way disturbing the established routine at distributive premises.' Third, the GLC could have promoted a more comprehensive experiment involving staggered shop hours, controlled access and parking, pedestrianisation and improved servicing facilities (accesses, waiting bays, etc.).

Nevertheless, as a genuinely experimental venture the GLC must take much of the credit for initiating and conducting Moondrop. It could hardly have been organised under the former London government system where none of the institutions had the resources to mobilise it, except the London County Council who did not have the statutory responsibilities to do so. It would have been particularly difficult to evoke enough voluntary multi-lateral co-operation within the food trade itself. The MOT and the Department of the Environment latterly began to show more interest in research in the commercial road traffic field but were content to leave the GLC to make the running in this case. It is rather ironic that on one of the relatively few occasions when the GLC succeeded in promoting an experiment of strategic importance to London (and potentially other conurbations) its benefits should have been so limited. Nevertheless it is significant in itself that the GLC took an interest in the concept of Moondrop and had the incentive and ability to involve and co-ordinate private industry, still a rare event in transport and land-use administration. That it was undertaken at all was wholly to the GLC's credit; with the eyes of experience one would now attempt to handle it on a larger scale and as part of a wider transport policy.

Case Study Q

THE IMPLEMENTATION OF THE GLC'S INNER LONDON PARKING AREA POLICY

1 INTRODUCTION

The early history of parking control

Uncontrolled parking has been recognised as a major cause of traffic congestion for many years; in 1929 a Royal Commission on London's Traffic said: 'The streets are intended for movement of all kinds and not for the purpose of parking cars.'[1] As car usage grew after the Second World War this condemnation became more general but the powers available to control parking on the streets were very limited and inflexible, amounting basically to a blanket restriction or no restriction at all. The London and Home Counties' Traffic Advisory Committee (LHCTAC) in their 1951 report *London Traffic Congestion* recommended that more off-street parking space (including some under the London squares) should be provided to allow cars to be cleared off the streets, but also advised an experiment in metered parking. A Working Party set up by the LHCTAC repeated this idea in 1953,[2] with the aim that parking control should not only aid traffic flow, but also make efficient use of scarce street space in central London, and that this should be done by favouring the short-term parker.

Powers to provide metered parking spaces were included in the Road Traffic Act 1956. The first scheme to use these powers, for 647 meters, was introduced by Westminster City Council in July 1958 in north-west Mayfair. Its success (easier parking and access to buildings, higher traffic speeds despite greater flows) led to its extension to the whole of Mayfair and parts of Holborn and Marylebone, and (later) to Saturday mornings as well as weekdays. By December 1960 there were 4600 meters in central London and schemes in three suburban town centres (Woolwich, Kingston and Croydon). In 1961 a further 5700 were installed and provincial towns began to emulate London.[3] In 1963 the Buchanan Report appeared; although its main concern was the long-term policy of reorganising the urban fabric and road structure to accommodate the car, it emphasised

[1] *Royal Commission on Traffic, First Report*, July 1929.
[2] MOT (1953), *Report on Car Parking in the Inner Area of London.*
[3] LHCTAC (1959), *Thirty-fourth Annual Report*, '*London Traffic*,' pp12–13; and MOT (1963), *Parking: the Next Stage*, p15.

the importance of parking control as a short-term policy for limiting traffic in town centres.[1]

During the same year the Ministry of Transport (MOT) attempted to assess how meter schemes were working and to suggest amendments which would allow them to be more effective and to be extended. The Report stated, in order of priority, that parking controls should:

a Ensure that moving traffic can proceed smoothly and safely.
b Release kerbside space where it is needed for loading and unloading goods and for picking up and setting down passengers.
c Indicate clearly and precisely where vehicles may or may not be parked.
d Give priority as necessary for the short-term parker.[2]

The Ministry believed that traffic movement in general had been improved, and that of buses in particular: traffic speeds had increased by 16% in the West End and the mileage of scheduled bus services lost because of traffic congestion had fallen by 18% between 1960 and 1961.[3] But difficulties had arisen, including:

1 'Meter feeding' (the insertion of extra money to secure a long stay).
2 'Musical meters' (motorists exchanging meter spaces to the same end).
3 Congestion on Saturday morning (there was originally no meter control at weekends).
4 Congestion around the fringes of control zones, as motorists attempted to avoid paying for parking.
5 Lack of parking space for residents' cars in control zones.

The report concluded that solutions to the first two lay in making the use of space more efficient by adjusting meter charges upwards to balance supply and demand; and in acquiring more space by reducing the amount of kerb given over to loading bays, which appeared to be under used. It proposed to extend meter control to Saturday mornings and to extend the control area both around central London and in the suburbs; and recommended a further look at residents' problems, and the possibility of including schemes for specially licensed residents' parking areas.[4] Nevertheless, the overall effectiveness of parking meters as a traffic management tool was shown by the rapid growth in their use, and by the time the new government of London came into being there were at least 15 000 metered spaces in Greater London and 26 000 in the country as a whole.[5]

[1] *Traffic in Towns*, HMSO, 1963, paras452–4; and accompanying Steering Group ('Crowther') Report, para34.
[2] MOT (1963), *Parking: The Next Stage*, HMSO, esp pp8, 21.
[3] MOT (1963), p19.
[4] In fact the Minister invited local authorities to prepare schemes, *Parking: The Next Stage* (1963), p38.
[5] AA statistics, the *Guardian*, 31 August 1964.

The authorities involved

The GLC's policy for the control of on-street parking soon became one of the main arms of their traffic and transport programme, involving a great deal of liaison and co-operation with other bodies. It affected and was influenced by the policies of the GLC and other bodies in several other fields such as off-street parking, highways and traffic management, public transport operation and law enforcement, and cannot therefore be viewed in isolation.

As a strategic planning authority the GLC was required to include in its development plan 'a statement of policy as to the provision of public and private car parks throughout Greater London.' The plan also had to lay down standards for provision of parking in new development as part of its system of standard controls.[1] The responsibility 'to secure the provision of suitable and adequate parking facilities on and off the highway,' which was exercised by the Minister of Transport before 1965,[2] was nominally shared between him, the GLC and the boroughs.[3] Moreover until 1969, when the condition was removed, the GLC could only act in a borough with the consent of that borough's council.[4] The GLC later pioneered legislation to allow prepayment for parking spaces in order to make special provision for residents or other groups of people[5] and this was consolidated in the Transport Act 1968.[6] The GLC have powers over the design, pricing, maintenance and suspension and revocation of parking schemes but they, and any London borough making an application for a new or modified scheme had to undergo a long and complex process before the necessary orders could be made.[7]

The London boroughs will be expected to apply Greater London Development Plan (GLDP) standards (when these are approved) for off-street parking in processing planning applications for new development, and refer schemes containing large public car parks to the GLC.[8] The boroughs act as the GLC's agents in designing and implementing new on-street parking schemes and since 1971 have undertaken the follow-up of defaulters of excess-charge payments. They may also take the initiative in suggesting new schemes.

The boroughs are empowered to act as executives for the GLC in the

[1] *Town and Country Planning (Development Plans for Greater London) Regulations and Amendment SI No.48*, 1966; and 1968 *No.815*, sII (O) & (M).

[2] S81 of the *Road Traffic Act 1960*, ch16.

[3] S84 of the 1967 Act.

[4] S3(13) of the *London Government Act 1963*, ch33; and *Road Traffic Regulation Act 1967*, ch76, s35 and sch4; *Transport (London) Act 1969* ch35, s35.

[5] *Greater London Council (General Powers) Act 1967*, chxx, s26.

[6] *Transport Act 1968*, ch73, s127.

[7] S36–7 of the 1967 Act, and SI 729 London Authorities' Traffic Procedure Regulations 1972.

[8] That is, a car park for more than fifty cars. *Town and Country Planning (Local Planning Authorities in Greater London) Regulations 1965* (SI 679), issued in relation to s24 (6) of the London Government Act 1963.

licensing and regulating of the use of off-street car parks open to the public in areas designated by the GLC; as explained below these powers have not yet been taken up.[1] The boroughs' interests are represented by their Association in such matters as discussing new legislation, regulations or other issues of wide interest (e.g. the scale of payments to the police for traffic wardens).

The police have to be consulted by any authority applying for a parking order; they are concerned chiefly with its enforceability and its effect on traffic.[2] The bulk of parking control offences involve parking at prohibited places, over-staying the allotted time at a meter, failure to pay fines, and those such as obstruction and parking without lights which pre-dated parking control. The enforcement may be carried out by police constables but, because of the great demands on limited manpower, police forces in London, as elsewhere, have increasingly relied upon fixed penalty 'tickets' for parking offences[3] and the use of traffic wardens.[4]

The operators of public road services are also considerably affected by the action of the traffic and parking authority[5] because the imposition of parking control and its associated waiting restrictions can help ease congestion. It has been customary for London Transport (LT) to be consulted when new parking zones or radical alterations to existing zones have been proposed. Originally it was intended that any surplus revenue from parking schemes should be used for the provision of off-street parking, but in 1968 the options were extended to the improvement of highways or public transport services. At the same time the GLC has to take into account the ease of movement of public service vehicles in exercising its role as traffic authority.[6]

The next section of this case study surveys the strategic role of the GLC and the changing objectives of parking control, and section 3 examines some problems handled by the system in implementing parking schemes. Section 4 covers operational problems—finance, enforcement and the follow-up of defaulters.

2 THE ROLE OF THE STRATEGIC AUTHORITY AND THE OBJECTIVES OF PARKING CONTROL

Soon after its assumption of office the first GLC had to consider the priorities established in the MOT Report *Parking: The Next Stage*. In July 1965 the Minister of Transport requested the GLC, the LT Board and the Metropolitan Police to work jointly upon proposals for helping bus

[1] *Transport (London) Act 1969*, ch35, s36.
[2] S84C (1) of 1967 Act and SI 729 of 1972.
[3] *Road Traffic Regulation Act 1967*, ch76, s80.
[4] Ch76, s81; and *Transport Act 1968*, ch73, s131.
[5] See GLC *Minutes*, 2 November 1965, pp710–22 (Report of Working Party on London Transport Bus Services and Traffic Management); and *LT Annual Reports*, 1960–70.
[6] S127 (6) of the Transport Act 1968 amending s44 (3) of the *Road Traffic Regulation Act 1967*, and s130 (3) amending s84 (1).

services through traffic management. A Working Party was established and suggested, amongst other things, that the central London meter zone should be extended to cover the notorious 'glue-pot ring' of congested radial roads in inner London and also the main suburban centres of outer London. This, it was said, would not in itself ensure improvements but 'should help, in that denial of free street parking space tilts the bus–car balance in favour of the bus.' The report listed twelve inner and fourteen outer London parking control schemes under consideration by the boroughs and the GLC, which on the most optimistic assumptions (e.g. no fiscal, staffing, legal or administrative restrictions or hold-ups) could be in operation by early 1967.[1]

A matter of weeks after this Report the Minister met GLC representatives and asked them what parking measures could be taken in the short term, particularly to aid peak-hour problems and to restrict the car commuter, and what legislative changes they could recommend. The GLC considered and accepted a major policy report in February 1966, although enforcement had yet to be discussed with the police and implementation with the boroughs.[2]

To combat increasing traffic and parking pressure, the Report (which will be called the 'ILPA Report') proposed a major extension of the central London parking zone (of about 8 square miles supervised by 400–500 wardens) to an area of 40 square miles for which it was estimated that

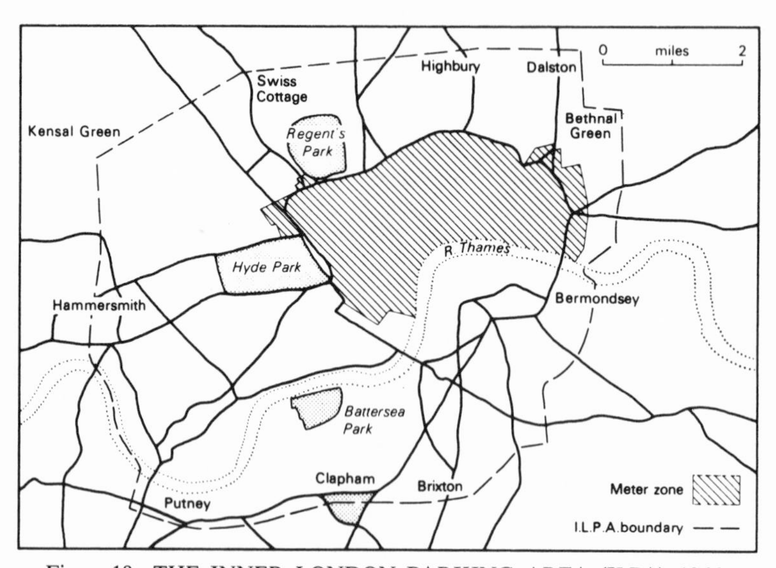

Figure 18 THE INNER LONDON PARKING AREA (ILPA), 1966

[1] GLC *Minutes*, 2 November 1965, pp710–22.

[2] *Parking in Central London*, March 1966; reprint of GLC *Minutes*, 22 February 1966, pp114–24.

	CENTRAL LONDON (10 SQ. MILES)			REMAINDER OF ILPA (30 SQ. MILES)			REMAINDER OF INNER LONDON (12 BOROUGHS EXCL. C. AREA) (110 SQ. MLS.)	
(000 SPACES)	1962 (1)	1966 (2)	1971 (3)	1961 (4)	1966 (5)	1971 (6)	1968 (7)	1971 (8)
Controlled (meter)	10	15	21	—	—	12	—	—
Resident	—	—	7	—	—	26	—	—
Uncontrolled	53	40	2	210	192	134	688	680
Total on-street	63	55	30	210	192	172	688	680
Residential	—	13	17	—	78	—	159	180
Non-residential	41	47	53	—	63	—	108	120
Public	25	28	30	—	10	—	15	20
Total off-street	74	88	100	—	151	—	282	320
GRAND TOTAL	137	143	130	—	342	—	970	10C0

Table 28 CONTROLLED PARKING IN CENTRAL AND INNER LONDON, 1961–71

Notes
a Cols1 and 7 from table 6.28, Col2 from table 6.4, *GLDP Report of Studies* (1969)
b Col5 from GLDP, *Proof E12/1*, table 8.1 (1970)
c Cols3, 4, 6 and 8 from GLC (1972), *Traffic and the Environment*, pp9, 12, 31

2000 wardens would be required to cover its 200 000 parking spaces (see Figure 18 and Table 28). This area, referred to as the Inner London Parking Area (ILPA), had a resident population of about 1.4 million and covered:

> the principal shopping and office districts of inner London and their more purely residential fringes. This area would include the main congested junctions around central London, as well as a number of inner rail and tube stations which attract car movement through these junctions (paragraph 11).

The ILPA Report emphasised that 'the main purpose of our traffic and parking policies must be to increase mobility wherever possible' but pointed out that 'it would be wrong, however, to take measures which would make the use of private cars for some purposes less attractive, except as part of an integral policy providing also for improving the attractiveness of the alternative' (public transport) (paragraphs 4, 6). The report also proposed improvements to the rail and tube networks and interchanges, to bus and taxi services, and suggested a staggered pattern of work and shopping hours.

Four principles were set out for allocating parking space on the streets, which gave some idea of the GLC's priorities:

1 In the interests of safety and traffic movement, street corners and other critical points should be kept clear of standing vehicles by restrictions on both waiting and loading.
2 Suitable kerbside lengths, including the full length of main roads where practicable and loading gaps in side-roads should, by waiting restrictions, be kept clear of parked vehicles.
3 Spaces for the expected short-term parking demand should be provided in groups near centres of attraction and in smaller numbers elsewhere, with parking meters enforcing time limits (up to two or five hours) and collecting charges.
4 All-day parking should be permitted in any remaining kerbside space, under arrangements giving preference to residents.

Besides reiterating the objectives and priorities contained in the report of the Ministry, the ILPA Report raised two new matters of principle and set out some new operational objectives necessary for such a large scheme to be administered indirectly through the City of London and eleven London boroughs. The matters of principle were special provision for residents in preference to any other long-term parkers, and the deliberate restriction of the long-term parker on an unprecedented scale with a view to transferring some to places where parking pressure was slight and others onto public transport. The Report stated 'some 75 000 all-day non-resident on-street parkers will have to pay instead of parking free, and most of them will be shifted too—some by a long way' (paragraph 39).

On the principle that each zone might take fifteen months to survey, design and put into operation, the Report looked for completion of ILPA by the end of 1968. This was a mammoth task, involving a scheme five times the size of the meter zone then existing in central London, which had taken eight years to establish.

The Report suggested that a complementary policy for off-street parking would be needed if the objectives of restricting car commuting and the efficient use of parking space were to be met, and recommended that the 'price mechanism' should be brought to bear on both public and private car parks, and that the GLC and other government agencies could provide a lead in this respect with their own parks (paragraphs 34, 35). Standards for parking provision in new schemes, it said, would be announced after a survey of traffic generated by businesses in central London had been completed.

Concerning legal changes, the ILPA Report pointed out that some changes in the scale of parking charges would be necessary to maintain a viable supply–demand balance, that new legislation might be needed to legalise residents' parking, that owner rather than driver liability for parking offences might be considered (which could mean a new change both in vehicle licensing methods and court procedures) and that some minor procedural improvements could be made in the processing of schemes. The Report suggested that the GLC might be given concurrent enforcement powers with the police (paragraphs 28, 29, 32).

The Council approved the ILPA policy and began negotiations with the boroughs, stressing that it had the support of the MOT and needed the co-operation of the boroughs.[1] It was soon obvious that the process of implementation was going to be longer and more complicated than expected; problems arose over the principle of payment of provision for residents, the programming of schemes, and the quality of public transport in certain parts of ILPA[2] (see section 3). In 1966, 1967, and 1968, only 2, 0, and 5 inner and 0, 4, and 2 outer zones respectively became operational. The GLC warned that 'in default of speedy action from the boroughs it might be necessary for the Council to undertake the preparation of the schemes itself.'[3]

In July 1967 a MOT Working Party looking at methods of restraining traffic in towns estimated that there were about 30 000 regular car commuters to central London. It recommended *faute de mieux* that 'the most promising method . . . at least for the shorter term would be to intensify control over the location, amount and use of parking space.' In a White Paper later that year the Ministry stated 'local authorities' powers to

[1] GLC (1966), *Traffic Management in London, 1965–66*, p29 (Report of Highways and Transportation Department). The Minister (then Barbara Castle) herself endorsed the policy at a conference on 21 March 1966 and in a White Paper, *Transport Policy* (July 1966), Cmnd 3057, para52.

[2] For example, GLC *Minutes*, 21 June 1966, p293; 28 February 1967, p140; 14 March 1967, pp193–4, 197–8.

[3] GLC (1967), *The Work of the Highways and Traffic Committee, 1966–67*, pp28–9.

control parking have so far usually been regarded as a way of reducing the amount of obstruction caused to moving traffic by vehicles parked on the highway, or to share out scarce parking space. . . .' This, however, foreshadowed wider powers in the 1968 Transport Act and the encouragement of a more definite role for parking control as part of comprehensive transport plans.[1]

From a survey of parking spaces in central London in 1967, J M Thomson estimated the number of regular car commuters to central London to be 35 000 and said of them:

> They represent a tiny fraction of workers in the centre, about 2%. They occupy over a quarter of total parking space all day. Nearly half of them park in the streets. A few of them add a heavy load of illegal parking at meter sites, but most of them obtain free parking. It is known from other surveys that most of them drive in alone in their cars. They are a tiny minority of Londoners yet they contribute far more to the traffic and parking problems of the city, in relation to their numbers, than any other comparable group of people.[2]

In May 1968 the GLC produced a report entitled *A Parking Policy for London* which it described as 'a comprehensive policy relating on- and off-street parking to road network capacity, land use, the density of development and socio-economic needs.' Accepting the 1966 strategy for on-street parking control in inner and outer London, the report proposed that as much off-street parking space as possible should be available to the public for business, commercial, shopping, or, 'if the Council desired it,' commuting purposes, at a charge that 'ensured efficient use.' The GLC showed concern about private off-street parking over which it had 'no means of exercising an effective management policy,' because 'as off-street parking is increased and on-street parking is reduced, the proportion of the total parking space which the Council has power to control . . . will be reduced.'[3] The GLC also realised that the development control standards for parking space in new schemes which had been exercised by the London County Council and other counties, whereby developers had to provide a specified *minimum* number of parking spaces related to the floorspace of a scheme, had encouraged car commuting. It was therefore proposed that private non-residential parking should be limited to a specified *maximum* number of spaces related to certain operational purposes (business visits and deliveries).[4] This meant a considerable reduction in the number of

[1] MOT (1967), *The Better Use of Town Roads*, paras1.2, 8.2, 8.3, 10.1, 10.4; and *Public Transport and Traffic*, Cmnd 3481, paras124–5; see also *Roads Circular 1/68: Traffic and Transport Plans.*

[2] J M Thomson (1968), *Some Characteristics of Motorists in Central London*, LSE Greater London Paper, No.13, p50.

[3] The distinction had been suggested earlier by the Ministry of Housing and Local Government in their Planning Bulletin No.7, *Parking in Town Centres*, HMSO, 1965.

[4] GLC *Minutes*, 7 May 1968, pp258–64.

	INITIAL DEVELOPMENT PLAN (PRE-1968) (MIN. PROVISION)	GLC PROPOSALS MAY 1968 (MAX. PROVISION)	GLDP STANDARDS 1969 (MAX. PROVISION)
Shops			
Central	2.5	5.0	5.0–12.0
Inner	—	2.5–5.0	2.0– 8.0
Outer	0.5	0.5–2.0 to 3.5	0.4– 2.0
Offices			
Central	2.0	15.0	5.0–12.0
Inner	—	2.0–15.0	2.0– 8.0
Outer	—	0.5–1.0 to 8.0	0.4– 2.0
Industry			
Central and Inner	—	1.25 } decreasing with scale	Not fixed (each case upon its merits)
Outer	—	0.25 } decreasing with scale	

Table 29 STANDARDS FOR PARKING SPACE IN NEW DEVELOPMENT (THOUSANDS OF SQUARE FEET PER SPACE)

spaces provided as shown in Table 29. To accommodate boroughs' claims of widely varying conditions the limits of the proposed ranges were broadened slightly in the GLDP and standards for industrial premises were dropped altogether.

About the time that the London policy report was published, the Government requested cuts in public spending. As a result, the GLC decided to reduce the Highways and Traffic Committee's budget, and the Home Office asked the Metropolitan Police to hold traffic warden strength at the January 1968 level (i.e. to do no more than replace losses). It had been hoped to introduce 8 new zones in 1968–69 and GLC approval had been given to a 1969–70 programme of 29 zones in ILPA and 35 in the outer areas requiring 2000 wardens. By reorganising existing manpower, 5 zones were introduced in 1968–69.[1] Extreme pressure was applied professionally and politically and the Home Office eventually allocated a further 635 wardens for 1969–70, sufficient to cope with the 4 zones which became operational. Five more zones were introduced in 1970 and 7 in the first part of 1971 (see Figure 20).[2] To add to their problems, the GLC were advised by the Metropolitan Police that the spread of controlled parking, clearways and other traffic management measures was putting a considerable strain on enforcement (see section 4).

Despite the slow progress of ILPA, by March 1969, when the preliminary

[1] GLC *Minutes*, 22 March 1968, pp189–90; and 25 March 1969.

[2] *Metropolitan Police Reports*, 1968–70; and paper by Deputy Assistant Commissioner Candy to British Parking Association Conference, July 1971, app*B*.

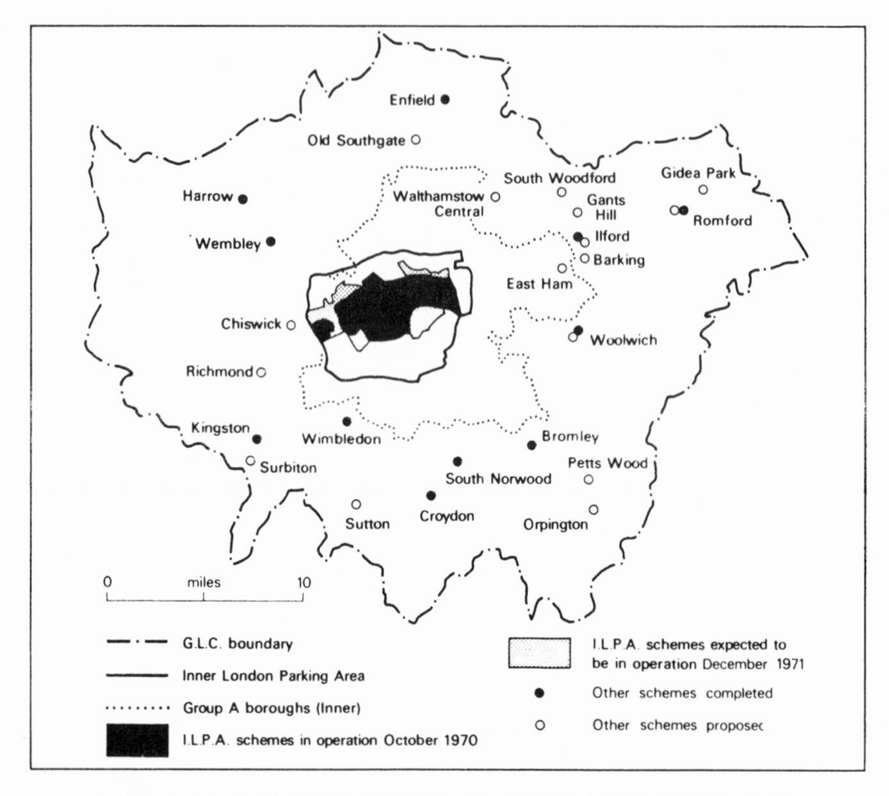

Figure 19 ON-STREET PARKING CONTROL IN LONDON, 1970

drafts of the GLDP were circulated, the GLC was standing firmly by parking control as a means of diverting those commuting by car to the central area to public transport.[1] The GLDP Statement itself (published in September) went further (paragraph 5.33):

> Even with a much higher expenditure on roads than the plan can contemplate it would not be possible to meet future traffic demands in full. Some restraint on the use of private cars is therefore needed. . . . The control of parking is at present the best means of applying restraint and is likely to be so for the forseeable future.[2]

In October 1969 the GLC produced a pamphlet consolidating their on-street, off-street, and development control policies. They pleaded for better enforcement including making the owner rather than the driver of a

[1] GLC *Minutes*, 25 March 1969, p212.
[2] See also GLC (1969), *Report of the Department of Highways and Transportation*, 1968–69, para1.3.2.

vehicle liable for offences. The delays in the ILPA programme were also pointed out, and the Council stated that it hoped to complete ILPA and the 'more urgent' outer London shopping centre zones by 1974, i.e. six years later than the target (1968) set in the original ILPA Report.[1]

By mid-1970 the new zones being implemented were beginning to extend into primarily residential areas in Kensington, Chelsea and Hammersmith and were being planned for Camden, Lambeth and Southwark. This

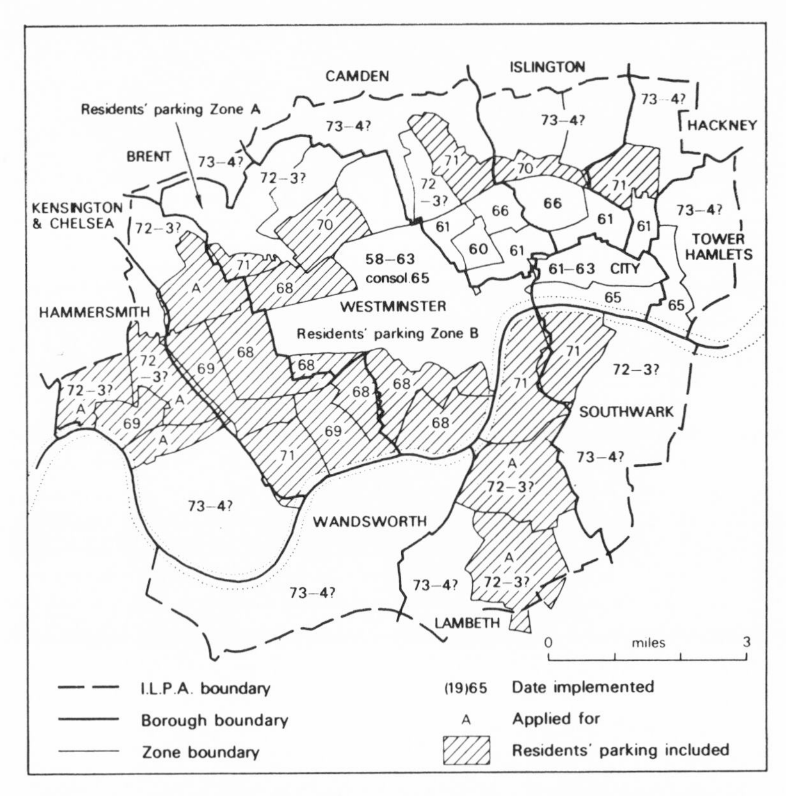

Figure 20 THE DEVELOPMENT OF ILPA AND RESPARK, 1966–71

brought a need to appraise the balance between special provision for residents and the needs of the short-term parker near shops and other facilities (see section 3).

In their evidence to the GLDP Inquiry the Council made great play of the need for a traffic restraint policy and of the practicability of using parking control. About a quarter of ILPA had been completed in terms of parking spaces (see Figure 20 and Table 28) but the Council was tentative about a completion date, saying that this '*could* be effected by 1975'

[1] GLC (1969), *Parking Policy in London*, esp pp6, 8, 9, 11.

(our italics). Their evidence stated that experience elsewhere had shown that isolated zones had little restraint effect and suggested that this might influence the priorities for introducing new zones. Moreover, if the road building programme was extended into the 1990s, fewer parking spaces would be needed in the shorter-term to cope with the terminating traffic.[1]

In supplementary documents the GLC pointed out that experience in implementing control zones had shown that a higher proportion of kerb space was 'lost' to prohibited parking areas than had been allowed for in previous estimates, and that 20% fewer spaces might be available (i.e. 153 000 on-street spaces in ILPA rather than the 192 000 estimated in 1966); a high proportion of spaces would be reserved for residents; and moreover 'the provision achieved will be open to manipulation downwards for restraint purposes, which could reduce the figure further.'[2] As an allied restraint measure, the GLC were undertaking a feasibility study in Westminster of their powers to license public off-street car parking. They believed it would 'best be achieved in areas where effective control of on-street parking was already operative.'[3]

Some papers requested by the GLDP Inquiry Panel helped to elucidate possible future lines of action. One[4] pointed out that by the end of 1971 control of street parking in the central area would be virtually complete (except for some 2000 spaces on the fringes and another 2000 in the Royal Parks[5]), ILPA would be 40% complete, and nine strategic centres would be covered by controls. However, 40% of parking supply was within private non-residential property, of which two-thirds was used by car commuters, over which the GLC had no control. In order to make restraint more effective, it would be necessary to adopt measures such as converting some of this space to public parking where its use could be controlled by licences.

Adoption by the boroughs of the GLC's proposed standards for off-street parking in new development would also reduce the rate of provision, although the number who by mid-1971 had either undertaken comprehensive appraisals of their parking needs, or had adopted the development control standards was small.

Another paper[6] examined how effective parking control could be as a method of traffic restraint. Parking control had been criticised because it was not effective for restraining through traffic or commercial vehicle trips. Nevertheless, it bore strongly on work and peak trips 'for which control is most strongly justified,' and it had already helped to arrest

[1] GLC (1969), *Proof of Evidence*, *E12/1*, s8.3, GLDP Inquiry Stage 1.

[2] GLC (1969), *Paper S12/186*, paras9, 10, GLDP Inquiry Stage 1.

[3] GLC (1972), *Paper S12/245*, paras 3–5, GLDP Inquiry Stage 1.

[4] GLC (1972), *Paper B483 Future Assessment and Development of Parking as a Means of Restraint*, GLDP Inquiry Stage 1.

[5] These were the responsibility of the Minister of Housing and Construction and it had irked the GLC and Westminster ever since 1965 that these were not controlled.

[6] GLC (1971), *Paper B479 The Effectiveness of Parking Control as a means of Traffic Restraint*, GLDP Inquiry Stage 1.

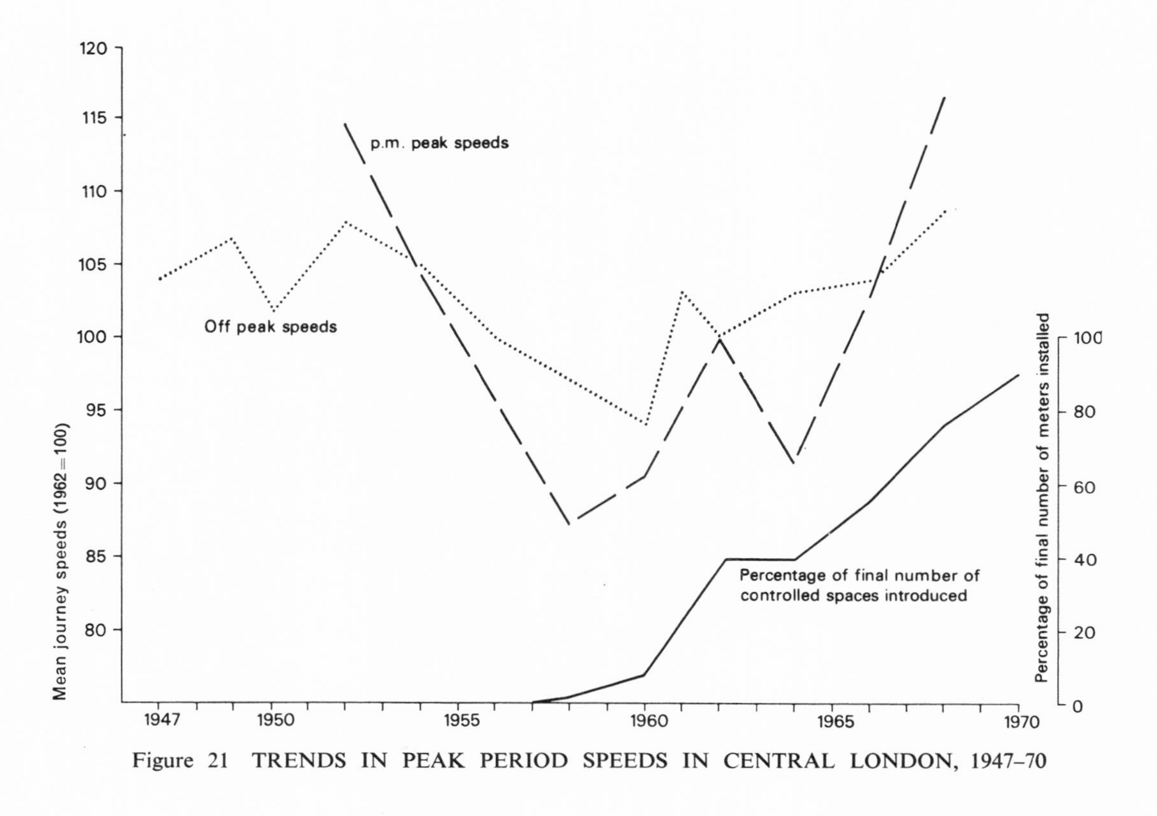

Figure 21 TRENDS IN PEAK PERIOD SPEEDS IN CENTRAL LONDON, 1947–70

traffic growth and improve traffic speeds in the central area (Figure 21). The paper also assessed what could be done to reduce the central area parking supply to help achieve the estimated degree of restraint required. Using six different measures, it was considered possible to reduce the total number of spaces from 170 500 (the number estimated in the GLDP for 1981) to 118 000 which might reduce peak-hour traffic flows by one-third.

Just after the end of the Inquiry the GLC produced a discussion paper called *Traffic and the Environment* which said: 'It is impossible to escape the conclusion that in the short term the problems of traffic and the environment can only be attacked effectively by direct measures to restrain the use of motor-cars.'[1] The GLC believed that effective methods of restraint should:

1 Control journeys causing most traffic and environmental nuisance.
2 Limit those car journeys which easily transfer to public transport.
3 Limit the less important journeys.
4 Restrict as few journeys as possible whilst achieving the desired effect.
5 Be thought fair and reasonable.
6 Be administered and enforced without too much diffculty.[2]

The paper continued (paragraph 3.8):

> The present parking control policies unfortunately do not score highly against these criteria. Public car parks operated in such a way as to encourage peak-hour travel fail to satisfy the first two criteria. Lack of control over the use of private parking under offices and the general inability to deal with through traffic mean that none of the first five criteria is satisfied. The difficulties of enforcing on-street parking control lead to the sixth not being met.

Two immediate policy changes were suggested: that keeper liability for parking offences should be made legal (see section 4) and that public off-street parking should be licensed in the central area, with a price structure designed to discourage long-term parking. Allied to strict control of the provision of new off-street parking, this could restrict the growth in control area parking space up until 1981 to 15% in total and 8% for non-residential, compared with 21% and 16% on current policies. Longer-term possibilities were also discussed—a tax on private non-residential off-street parking space, incentives for its conversion to other uses, supplementary licensing for weekday travel in the central area, or full road pricing, which had been widely discussed before and during the Inquiry.[3]

[1] GLC (1972), *Traffic and the Environment*, esp pp7–18, 27–36. Quotation from paragraph 2.11.

[2] GLC (1972), para3.7.

[3] For example, MOT (1967), *The Better use of Town Roads*; G Maycock (1972), *Implementation of Traffic Restraint* (DOE/TRRL Report No.LR422); *Papers S12/64, 117,*

Thus from tiny beginnings parking control had become a major element of London's traffic policy within ten years. In the first seven years of the GLC's existence it evolved from a means of 'tidying up the street system, of clearing away parked cars where they were in the way of moving traffic and of making the streets safer' through a stage of 'rationing the road space for the various types of user' to a point where the GLC were beginning to use it for a much wider restraint on the use of the car.[1] During this time the GLC as strategic authority needed to devise broad guide-lines to fill out the policy framework which was hurriedly adopted in 1966 and 1968. The officers and members of the GLC had to sell the concept of ILPA to eleven London boroughs and the City of London, seven of whom had no experience of controlled parking by 1966, and to guide them to implement quickly a massive, co-ordinated, and as far as possible uniform programme of zones. The borough councils, of course, had to represent their local problems and interests. How this situation worked out is discussed in the next section.

3 IMPLEMENTING ILPA: MAKING UP THE COAT OF MANY COLOURS

In this section the boroughs' attitudes to implementation are examined, concentrating on problems that arose over the principle of payment, arrangements for residents to park, programming and procedure, reconciling schemes to meet local needs (i.e. the principle of flexibility) within the GLC's strategic guidelines (i.e. the principle of uniformity), and the operation of public transport.

The GLC were aware of their dependence upon the London boroughs as agents for the quick and trouble-free implementation of their ILPA policy and discussions at officer and member level proceeded quickly after the scheme was announced.[2] By 1968 the Highways Committee could report, 'the long arguments, negotiations, and hammering out of ideas appears to have resulted in workable schemes.'[3]

Acceptance of the principle of payment for parking

Although it had always been held in law that no one has a right to park on the highway, the main problem in persuading the boroughs to accept ILPA was the principle of payment for parking hitherto available free of charge. The boroughs who had previous experience of metered parking where congestion was acute (Westminster, the City of London, Kensington and

209 and *B613*, GLDP Inquiry Stage 1; counsel for the GLC said at the Inquiry that its view 'had not nearly reached the point where any such system could play its part in the plan we now present,' *Transcript*, day 53, p17.

[1] See GLC (1972), *Traffic and the Environment*, para3.1.

[2] GLC *Minutes*, 21 June 1966, p293.

[3] GLC (1968), *The Work of the Highways Committee, 1967–68*, p18.

Chelsea, and Camden in particular) welcomed the scheme,[1] whereas Southwark, for example, agreed to undertake survey work 'without committing the Council to the form of control proposed by the GLC,' and Wandsworth said, 'whilst we are prepared to accept that all these measures may be necessary in the congested areas of London, we are far from satisfied that they are necessary or appropriate in Wandsworth.'[2]

The most intransigent borough was Hackney, whose complaints were based mainly on their belief that it was not right to charge for parking when public transport facilities were inadequate.[3] The Council at first refused to co-operate, but when the GLC threatened to introduce its own scheme, Hackney produced a scheme with free parking, time-controlled by discs. This, however, was unacceptable to the GLC because it breached the principle of payment accepted by adjoining boroughs. It was also disliked by both the GLC and the police because it would be less flexible and more difficult to enforce. Hackney considered appealing to the MOT but eventually some reconciliation was achieved in 1968, when they agreed to introduce short-term meter and resident parking schemes, but to leave open the question of free long-term parking.[4]

Resident's parking

The introduction of parking control brought difficulties for residents of competing for space either with short-term parkers at high rates, or with commuters. There was also the problem of the 'pyjama brigade'—those drivers who had to rise to feed their meters at 8.30 a.m. for such extra time as the meters would allow them.

In 1963 the MOT's opinion was that 'the only real answer' which would avoid the appearance of giving people the right to garage their cars on the public highway, was 'the provision of sufficient off-street parking.'[5] In 1964 the advisory officers of the London Boroughs' Committee (later the London Boroughs' Association (LBA)) went further and proposed that a condition of licensing a car should be the availability of an off-street garage.[6] The Ministry rejected G J Roth's idea for a 'householder's meter' which would be rented from the local authority and sub-let when not in use,[7] on the grounds that it ensured neither optimum usage, nor that space

[1] *Council Minutes*: Kensington and Chelsea, 3 May 1966; Camden, 12 February 1969; Westminster, 16 June 1966.
[2] *Council Minutes*: Southwark, 11 May 1966; Wandsworth, 4 May 1966 and 25 July 1968.
[3] Other boroughs made the point less forcibly. *Council Minutes*: Hackney, 22 February 1967; Wandsworth, 4 May 1967; Tower Hamlets, 22 April 1969; 16 September 1970; Lambeth, 29 March 1969.
[4] LB Hackney *Minutes*: 25 May 1966; 22 February, 25 April, 25 May, 27 September and 26 December 1967; 28 February and 29 September 1968.
[5] MOT (1963), *Parking: The Next Stage*, sV.
[6] LBA *Minutes*, 5 November 1965; the *Guardian*, 5 November 1965; *Evening Standard*, 4 November 1965.
[7] G J Roth (1965), *Paying for Parking*, CUP: Hobart Paper 33, pp41–5; 'Parking Where You Live,' the *Guardian*, 10 December 1962; *Daily Telegraph*, 16 July 1968.

would always be available for residents, nor that payment would be made. They concluded that the best solution might be some form of special licence or badge to park in specially designated areas; ten-hour meters might be an interim measure.

The Metropolitan Borough of Kensington took up Mr Marples's invitation to prepare parking schemes including provision for residents and in December 1963 proposed a scheme of free short-term parking (in preference to meters) combined with a residents' licensing system costing 10*s* (50p) per week or £26 a year, for an area around Kensington High Street tube station.[1] A member of the Council said 'the object . . . is to protect the interests of residents. We are seeking, by this plan, to keep out the commuters who are filling the streets as they are driven out of the West End and Westminster.' A similar scheme was prepared by Chelsea Metropolitan Borough. The MOT, however, objected to these proposals on two counts: that control of parking so close to the central area must be by meters, and that no legislation was available for any form of season ticket or other means of prepayment. The new Borough Council of Kensington and Chelsea thought that prepayment was vital to the future of (residents') parking control and asked the GLC to approve the scheme and press the Ministry for legislation.

When instead the GLC included similar proposals for the whole of ILPA in the 1966 report, the first major British city to do so, hopes of legislation were raised, but pressure of Government business prevented its consideration.[2] Through the LBA, the boroughs of Westminster, Kensington and Chelsea, and Camden requested the GLC to include a clause in their current General Powers Bill, and this was duly approved.[3] Kensington and Chelsea had awaited the legislation before introducing schemes but Westminster had put in some ten-hour meters as a temporary measure to be replaced later by residents' spaces. The first residents' parking zone in both boroughs came into effect in January 1968 in the East Chelsea and Belgravia areas respectively. There were considerable objections from residents' and ratepayers' associations at having to pay for something that had hitherto been free and the boroughs were at pains to emphasise that in return residents should be reasonably assured of finding a space. Experience quickly showed that this was so. One problem, however, was the definition of a 'resident:' Kensington and Chelsea adopted 'one whose usual abode is in the zone;' neither they nor Westminster included shopkeepers within this scope, because many were in effect commuters.[4] The success of these zones[5] led to their rapid extension within these two boroughs, and to Hammersmith in 1969, Islington and Camden in 1970,

[1] The *Guardian*, 5 December 1963.
[2] R B Kensington and Chelsea *Minutes*, 24 June 1965.
[3] LBA *Minutes*, 25 January 1967; Westminster CC *Minutes*, 3 October 1967.
[4] *Minutes*: Westminster, 4 December 1968; Kensington and Chelsea, 22 March 1966.
[5] Westminster CC *Minutes*, 24 October 1968; and interview with Kensington and Chelsea's Director of Technical Services.

	2-HOUR METERS (%)	4-HOUR METERS (%)	RESIDENTS (%)
Westminster			
1 Belgravia–Knightsbridge (1968)	16	22	62
2 South Paddington (1968)	23	25	52
As extended and amended (1969)	19	18	63
3 Pimlico (1968)	17	20	63
As amended (1969)	16	13	71
4 Lisson Grove (1970)	16	19	65
Kensington and Chelsea			
1 Knightsbridge–East Chelsea (1968)	24	11	65
2 Kensington High Street (1968)	19	7	74
3 Southern (1969)	9	15	76
4 Earls Court (1969)	8	7	85
5 South-western (1971)	12	6	82
6 Ladbroke Grove (1972)	13	7	80
Hackney no.3 zone	30	25	45
Islington no.3 zone (1970)	29	34	37
Camden no.1 zone (Camden Town East) (1971)	24	11	65
Hammersmith zone no.1, amendment 2 (1970)	8	7	69*
Southwark (1971)	36	15	49

Table 30 ALLOCATION OF PARKING SPACES BY TYPE

Note: * Plus 16% long-term, all-comers parking

and Hackney, Southwark and Lambeth in 1971 (see Table 30 and Figure 19).

As the number of residents' parking zones grew an unforeseen problem arose: would permits for one zone be available for use in another? Since there is no time limit on residents' parking spaces there is a risk of replacing long-distance by short-distance car commuting within or between zones. Neither the GLC nor Westminster reports of 1966 mentioned the problem. Interavailability was limited by borough boundaries, by different charging methods and by various pricing systems (see Table 31). In Westminster it was decided to make permits available in two blocks of zones (*A* and *B*) divided by Oxford Street–Bayswater Road. In May 1971, 11 086 Westminster residents held permits and were using monthly cards or season tickets thus:[1]

[1] Letter from City Engineer, 4 August 1971; Westminster CC *Report E138/70*.

	TICKETS OR TOKENS (£)			SEASON TICKETS (£)		
	DAILY	WEEKLY	MONTHLY	3-MONTHLY	6-MONTHLY	ANNUAL
Westminster present	0.12½			7.50	14.00	18.00
Westminster proposed	0.15					
Kensington and Chelsea	0.15			7.50	13.00	26.00
Hammersmith						4.40
Camden	0.10		1.00			12.00
Islington present				9.00		35.00
Islington proposed	0.12½			7.50		26.00
Southwark		0.12½	0.50			6.00
Lambeth			0.50	1.50		6.00
Tower Hamlets	0.5					
Hackney	0.2½		0.50		2.50	5.00

Table 31 RESIDENTS' ON-STREET PARKING CHARGES, 1971

	CARDS	QUARTERLY SEASONS	YEARLY SEASONS	SPACES
Zone *A* (south)	3190	1466	1865	4671
Zone *B* (north)	2024	1426	1115	4332
Total	5214	2892	2980	9003

Within each borough the consideration must be what degree of freedom can be allowed without encouraging too much traffic. Westminster believed that intrazonal commuting had begun to occur but not on a major scale (the current arrangements allow trips of up to 3 miles). It might, however, grow to affect significantly the availability of space for other residents' use.[1] The GLC have suggested that if this became a problem the size of the zones might be reduced, but an easier and earlier step would be to reduce the degree of interavailability.[2]

In areas of greatest pressure the local authorities have considered extending special arrangements for residents to off-street car parks. In Westminster's case this has first meant special contracts in Council-owned car parks: for example, in the Harley Street garage residents may park 24 hours a day, 7 days a week for £30 per quarter, or £15 per quarter overnight only; Camden with a greater proportion of speculative car parking has arranged a special rate with National Car Parks, their main contractor.[3] In 1971 the GLC suggested that this should remain a borough responsibility and should be linked to off-street licensing because of 'the high degree of local variation.'[4]

By comparison, in the more recent zones introduced in the outer parts of ILPA, where pressure is lower, new arrangements were evolved. In their Fulham zone Hammersmith Council introduced a new form of control; this had local areas of high traffic attraction (the shopping centres and tube stations, Fulham Football Club stadium, etc.) where short-term meters were needed, surrounded by high-density residential development where a residents' permit scheme was needed to control the parking situation. In the rest of the area, however, pressure was lower and parking permits were issued for residents who may park in designated areas free of both charge and time limits.[5] By comparison in North Paddington, Westminster thought it necessary to maintain the principle of payment, but considered opening long-term parking to all comers at a low charge.[6]

Originally the GLC recommended that about 40% of permitted parking space should be allocated to residents: in fact the average in zones intro-

[1] Westminster CC (1969), *Parking Policy: A Reassessment*, para10.8; letter from City Engineer, 4 August 1971.
[2] GLC (1971), *Paper B479*, p8, GLDP Inquiry Stage 1.
[3] *Council Minutes*, Camden 22 July 1970; GLC, 21 July 1970, p478; letter from Westminster City Engineer 4 August 1971.
[4] GLC (1971), *Paper B483*, p10, GLDP Inquiry Stage 1.
[5] Information from interviews.
[6] Westminster CC (1969), *Parking Policy: A Reassessment*, para2.09.

duced by mid-1971 was 47%.[1] In the latest zones residents were allocated up to 80% (see Table 30) and earlier zones were being amended to increase the proportion by reducing short- and medium-term meter space or the amount of yellow line waiting restriction (for instance in South Paddington and Pimlico). Westminster were reluctant to do this in the case of Mayfair and Marylebone because this would displace too many short-term meters but were considering Victoria.[2] Islington and Camden stated that they put the needs of residents before any other category of parker.

By the end of 1970 there were 26 200 residents' spaces in ILPA. The GLC foresaw that residents parking would increase from 23% to 31% of the total space on central area streets, and from 15% to 50% in the rest of ILPA, by 1981.[3]

Priorities, the rate of introduction of schemes, and (as is shown later in this section) methods of payment and levels of charge varied from borough to borough, and not with any determined relationship to demand. Each borough made clear that this matter was close to its heart because of the direct effects upon its ratepayers, the principle of flexibility undoubtedly predominated over uniformity.

Programming and procedure

As we have seen the only overt and prolonged clash over the basic principle of ILPA came with Hackney and this was not settled until September 1968, but there was a distinct lack of enthusiasm in those boroughs on the fringes of ILPA and especially south of the river where the extent of central-city activities and very high parking pressure was limited. Westminster City Council who rigorously maintained two economic principles with which the GLC accorded (namely that charges should be arranged so that demand is related to supply, and that so far as possible parking revenue should cover parking costs) and who produced the most comprehensive parking plans,[4] had commented that the timetable for ILPA was 'unrealistic, arbitrary.' They would not initially commit themselves to any programme outside the Belgravia zones, and said that progress 'should be related to parking densities . . . which in turn will be governed by other factors including car ownership.'[5]

The survey and design of zones implied immediate recruitment, diversion of manpower, and/or employment of consultants.[6] Lambeth estimated that they would need four extra staff and that their ultimate

[1] GLC (1971), *Paper S12/186*, para10, GLDP Inquiry Stage 1.
[2] *Evening Standard*, 11 November 1970; Westminster CC (1970), *Residents Parking in the Central Area*, Report to Council E138/70.
[3] GLC (1972), *Traffic and the Environment*, table 1.
[4] *Future Parking Policy* (1966); and *Parking Policy: A Reassessment* (1969).
[5] Westminster CC *Minutes*, 16 June 1966.
[6] Southwark employed Freeman Fox, Wilbur Smith and Associates to undertake a survey for them, and Islington appointed F R Bullen and Partners to survey and design their zones. *Minutes*: Islington, 3 January 1967; Southwark, 16 February 1966.

expenditure would be £500 000 for equipment and £150 000 annually. When, however, the extent of the Government's restriction on spending was known, the Highways Committee instructed the Borough Engineer not to recruit staff, to give the design of the zones 'second place to essential work,' and told the GLC that their timetable for seven Lambeth zones by October 1968 was no longer valid. The Clerk to the GLC wrote to Lambeth commenting that compared with public transport improvements, 'imposing parking control in the area is a process capable of swift and unhindered execution,' and that 'it was time the ILPA was removed from the area of debate to that of action.'[1]

In fact the first Lambeth zone programmed originally for February 1967 did not go into operation until January 1971. Several other boroughs were slow to undertake the survey procedure. Hammersmith suffered delays over Government approval of loan sanction for implementing the Broadway zone.[2] The Kensington programme was delayed for six months while prepayment powers were obtained. The 1968 standstill on traffic warden recruitment was blamed for delays to zones in Hammersmith, Kensington and Westminster.

The boroughs imparted some share of the blame to the GLC, but criticised them more for taking a long time to process schemes. They complained that it took a long while to agree the content of schemes, and sometimes even longer for the GLC to prepare the orders and have them approved by the MOT (later the DOE).[3] Worse still, there was no special means for the GLC to approve minor changes in schemes: whether produced by the boroughs or the Council itself, even small alterations had to undergo the same lengthy process. As the modifications accumulated this became important:[4]

1965	4	1968	29
1966	55	1969	35
1967	11	1970 (January–September)	14

After representations by several boroughs, including Westminster, the LBA pressed for machinery to shorten this operation.[5] The new regulations devised by the DOE, GLC and LBA which give the GLC power to decide on new parking schemes or modifications proposed by the boroughs or its own officers, with or without a local public inquiry, could shorten the process once the authorities have become familiar with the procedures.[6]

The original proposals for the Kensington High Street area brought forth 1300 objections and consequently the scheme was completely re-

[1] LB Lambeth *Minutes*, 29 March 1967, 20 September 1967.

[2] The *Guardian*, 29 August 1967; and LB Hammersmith *Minutes*, 16 October 1968.

[3] For example, LB Islington *Minutes*, 15 November 1969.

[4] Letter from GLC, 3 September 1971.

[5] RB Kensington and Chelsea *Minutes*, 27 January, 22 July, 28 October 1970; Westminster CC *Minutes*, 15 May 1967; and LBA *Minutes*, 13 October 1971, pp72–4.

[6] *The London Authorities' Traffic Orders (Procedure) Regulations*, 1972, *SI No.729*.

designed. As control became more common there was greater acceptance of the principles of parking control by shopkeepers and by residents, so that the first scheme in any borough tended to be the most difficult. Equally important, however, the councils and their officers became more experienced in the process of taking local needs into account in the design and the publicity–participation process. For example, in Hammersmith the

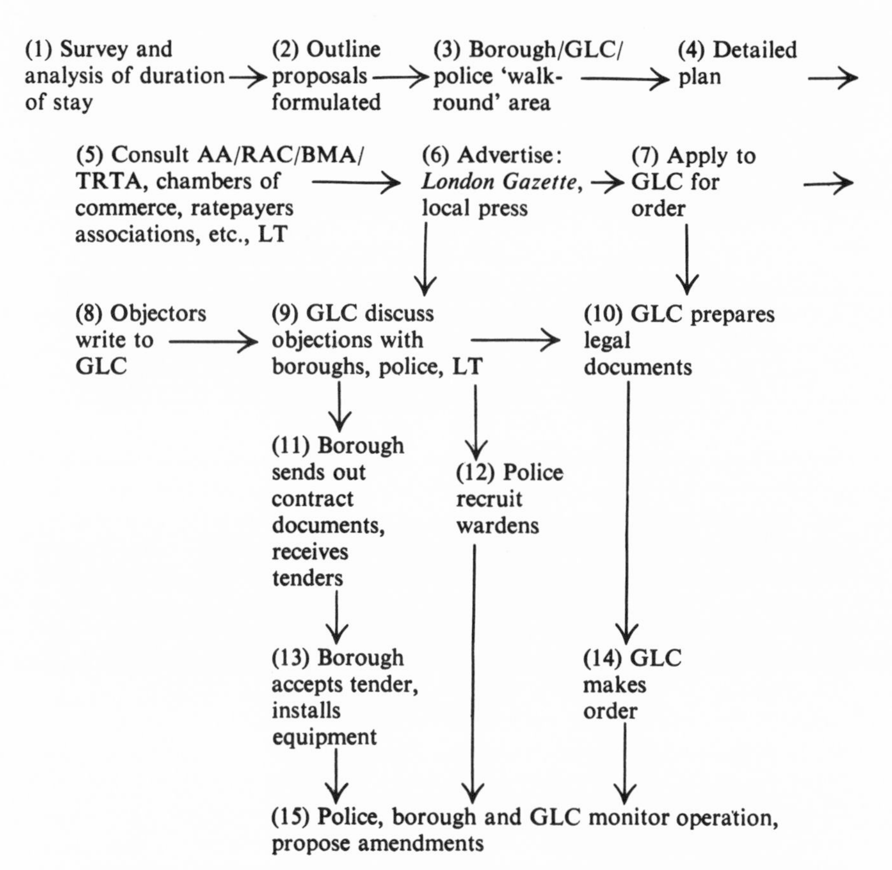

Figure 22 THE PROCESS OF IMPLEMENTING PARKING CONTROL

first extension to the Broadway scheme was prepared without any leaflet distribution or local public meetings and 200 objections resulted. In the case of the second extension a public meeting attended by 300 people was held to discuss the proposals before consulting local groups or requesting the GLC to make an order (stage 5 in Figure 22). Subsequently, there were only 12 objections. When preparing the Fulham zone every household (40 000) received an explanatory leaflet before the public meeting. Similar procedures in Lambeth led to ratepayers' groups actually writing letters of congratulation to the Council![1]

Problems of designing and equipping the zones—uniformity versus flexibility

In 1966 the GLC set a minimum number of operational rules besides the four priorities set out on page 474. They fixed a minimum price for residents of 5p a day and suggested that meter prices should be fixed so as to ensure about one in seven being free at any one time. They also suggested that the sign system, control periods and exemptions (doctors, disabled drivers, etc.) should be as uniform as possible but left the allocation of space and fixing of charges to be tailored to local situations and needs.[2] The requirements for uniformity also suited the police because they desired as simple a system as possible for both the public and their own wardens or constables.

The police have a statutory right to be consulted about new schemes but in practice were very closely involved in the whole process. They helped to decide where to permit parking, so that it would be safe, would not be detrimental to traffic or access and would be enforceable (stage 3 in Figure 22).[3] They influenced the allocation of spaces, mainly to ensure that short-term demand (which gave rise to illegal parking that was difficult to prevent) could be satisfied. They checked the details of the orders, and suggested amendments on the basis of past experience.

The police have increasingly shifted the burden of traffic enforcement, and more particularly parking enforcement, to traffic wardens (Table 32, item 9). As a result the training manuals for traffic wardens have grown considerably in complexity. Partly to aid the motorist in comprehending regulations and partly to aid the enforcing officers and wardens, the police were in favour of as wide a standardisation of regulation as possible; they participated in a Working Party which proposed a reduction from fifty-seven to twenty types.[4] The concern of each borough to tailor its parking schemes to local circumstances conflicted directly with this aim. They introduced new periods of control such as Saturday afternoon, different times of control such as mornings only (to prevent commuters, or for residents or for all comers), controls for amenity,[5] night-time control, or control for street cleansing.[6] There were, moreover, variations in charge and methods of control (permits, tokens, money, discs).

The determination of the size of a new area for controlled parking and the selection of its boundaries is crucial in introducing parking control. In his book *Parking Motor Vehicles* John Brierley said that an area 'should be

[1] Information from interviews with officers of Kensington & Chelsea, Lambeth and Hammersmith.

[2] GLC (1966), *Parking Policy in Central London*, para14.

[3] See GLC (1971), *Paper S12/186*, GLDP Inquiry Stage 1.

[4] LBA *Minutes*, 26 November 1969, pp95–6, and 17 March 1971, p18.

[5] As in the case of Havering's scheme for Gidea Park (see Case Study *F*).

[6] See Haringey Corporation Act 1971, ch51.

	1965	1966	1967	1968	1969	1970	5 YEARS CHANGE
1 Fixed penalty tickets (000)	228	272	390	604	811	887[a]	+290%
2 Change from previous year (%)	—	+19	+69	+31	+34	+10	
3 Excess charges (000)	291	325	392	446	500	454	+56%
4 Change (%)	—	+12	+21	+14	+12	−9	
5 Total of (1) and (3)	519	597	841	1049	1311	1341	+160%
6 Parking offences (000) in control zones (part of 1)	n.a.	90	118	226	339	371	+313%
7 6 (as a % of 1)	—	33	26	37	42	42	
8 Other offences in control zones	n.a.	182	341	377	472	516	+185%
9 Percentage of (8) dealt with by traffic wardens	n.a.	43	66	76	78	87	
Fixed penalty tickets							
10 Paid (%)	61	57	53	45	43	45	
11 Excused or lapsed (%)	23	24	21	29	32	32	
12 Legal proceedings (%)	3	3	3	1	1	1	
13 Outstanding at end of year (%)	14	17	24	24	24	22	
Excess charges							
14 Paid (%)	n.a.	67	66	60	60	60	
15 Excused or lapsed (%)	n.a.	18	18	19	23	25	
16 Legal proceedings (%)	n.a.	2	2	2	1	2	
17 Outstanding (%)	n.a.	13	14	19	18	14	
18 Nos. of traffic wardens (GLC area)	463	698	1247	1221	1394	1585[b]	+228%
19 No. of meters in GLC area (000)	17	16	20	24	28	31	+82%

Table 32 PARKING ENFORCEMENT IN LONDON, 1965–70

Notes
[a] By 1971 this figure had reached 1 019 000
[b] By 1972 this figure had grown to 2056

large enough to ensure that there will be a sufficient demand for short-term parking and that the congestion caused by parked cars will not be transferred to another area on the fringe of the zone.'[1] The situation in central London is particularly difficult from this point of view since there

[1] J Brierley (1962), *Parking Motor Vehicles.*

is almost continuous parking pressure over a very large area. Westminster in their 1966 Report said (paragraph 2.18):

> If the area of a new controlled parking scheme is too small the metered parking places tend to be under-used while surrounding uncontrolled streets become saturated with parked cars. This is clearly indicated in the existing Hyde Park Ward zone and the adjoining streets in South Paddington. The boundaries of any new areas of control must therefore be carefully selected, wherever possible using main traffic routes as boundaries. Where the proposed area of control abuts on the boundary with another local authority, it will be desirable to advise that authority at an early stage of the Council's proposals so that, if possible, a common policy can be agreed on such matters as the method of control and charges.

In fact the zone size in London varies from under a half to over 1 square mile. It is apparent from Figure 19 that two initial constraints were operating on the design of zones within ILPA, namely the existing controlled areas and the local administrative boundaries. Another conditioning factor appears to have been the strength of the individual boroughs' staff. Kensington and Chelsea said that one of their zones was the largest individual scheme ever processed by a local authority in this country, and they attributed some delays to the sheer size and complexity of the tasks involved. Westminster could not 'digest' the whole of the St John's Wood area at one attempt.[1]

Meter charges and methods of residents' parking control vary throughout ILPA. Before the ILPA policy several boroughs had meters for short-, medium- and long-term parking, but prices varied. As costs have increased, charges have been raised (though not in direct proportion), but a price gradient with the highest charges in central London has been maintained.

One of the needs in residents' parking schemes is a means of paying in advance. In 1966 the GLC saw 'distinct advantages' in using ticket machines, and Kensington and Chelsea decided to use them. Westminster saw no advantages in the system, however, and after conducting experiments found that each machine was as expensive as twenty meters but covered fewer than twenty spaces; that they could hold large quantities of money and so were a security risk; that the tickets were small and difficult to identify which slowed down supervision; and that drivers might have to walk a considerable distance to reach a machine.

Westminster therefore commissioned an office equipment company to design a different system. They produced a 'token' system consisting of a monthly transparent plastic calender, adhesive backed, to which was attached the resident's permit and a daily ticket. There were several advantages: the driver only paid for space he used; no on-street equipment other than signs was needed; no money had to be stored; and the capital

[1] Information from interviews.

costs were lower as the estimates[1] in the table show. The idea of simplifying prepayment by a season ticket system was soon adopted by Kensington and Chelsea. Westminster followed suit, but eschewed the annual season ticket because it was more liable to fraud by transfer to non-residents upon the sale of the car.[2] The token system was adopted by Islington, and the ticket machine system by Camden and Hammersmith. Season tickets were adopted by Brent, Hackney, Lambeth and Southwark as well as the five boroughs just mentioned.[3]

ZONE	ESTIMATES (£000) MACHINES	TOKEN SYSTEM
Belgravia	89	34
Knightsbridge	42	19
South Paddington	126	63

Commenting on the difference between the Westminster token and the Kensington ticket machine methods for residents' parking where the same principle and comparable scales of charge held good, the Commissioner of the Metropolitan Police said 'simplicity and uniformity in regulation is important if parking is to be properly controlled by traffic wardens using the fixed-penalty procedure.'[4]

The level of residents' charges is also variable: the 1966 GLC Report suggested a minimum of 5p (1*s*) per day. Westminster undertook a detailed costing exercise and in their 1966 Report calculated that a breakeven figure would be nearly 20p (4*s*) per day if three-quarters of the total parking spaces were allocated to residents and used to 75% capacity. They concluded, 'we cannot envisage that the charge can ever be less than 12½p (2*s* 6*d*) per day, and in order to avoid heavy deficits on the parking meter account, which would seriously prejudice the Council's ability to build off-street car parks, it may well have to be more.'[5] Kensington and Chelsea also proposed a 2*s* 6*d* charge and the GLC accepted this.

Other boroughs in ILPA, however, questioned this, particularly Hammersmith. While agreeing to co-operate they doubted the validity even of the proposed 1*s* minimum charge. They proposed a scheme, with ticket machines for short- and medium-term parking, and residents parking either free or at a very nominal charge.[6] The GLC assured the borough that they only required a scheme to conform to broad principles and would not insist on a minimum residents' charge. If the scheme was generally satis-

[1] Thomas de La Rue and Co, *Interim Report on the Westminster Residents Parking Scheme*; and 'Residents Parking—Three Solutions Evaluated,' *Traffic Eng and Control* (1969), pp395–7.

[2] Westminster CC (1969), *Parking Policy: A Reassessment*, para5.02.

[3] Letter from GLC, 3 September 1971.

[4] Metropolitan Police, *Annual Report*, 1968, p72.

[5] Westminster CC (1966), *Parking Policy*, para2.17.

[6] Hammersmith *Minutes*, 16 March and 7 December 1966; 18 January, 12 April, 12 July 1967.

factory, 'the Borough Council would have freedom to adjust the charges at anytime if they so desired, and the GLC would not themselves take any action as regards those charges.'[1] The nominal fee was later raised. As Table 31 shows all the boroughs around the fringe of ILPA, except Islington, opted for much lower rates of charge than Kensington and Chelsea, and Westminster. For ease of purchase and the better relation of residents' parking to off-street charges, both Kensington and Chelsea, and Westminster, raised their residents' charges to 15p (3*s*) daily.[2]

Effects on public transport

LT expressed an interest in the general policy of parking control for three reasons: the relatively minor matter of the siting of bus stops; the prospect of quicker bus operation as part of an improved general traffic flow; and, more importantly, the use of parking control as a means of traffic restraint. They were very keen to see the 1965 Joint Working Party (see Bus Lane Case Study *M*) proposals for expanding the original area of meter control and making the main radial routes peak-period clearways,[3] but subsequent LT annual reports reflected their dissatisfaction with progress: 'ILPA should be implemented as a matter of urgency' (1967); 'the Board . . . have stressed the need to maintain the programme' (1968).

The Board had no formal liaison with the local authorities designing the ILPA schemes. The Operations Group of the Transport Co-ordinating Council for London established in February 1966 which might have acted as a link proved to be very weak, and practically ceased to function after its chairman Sir Alex Samuels resigned in 1967.

The Borough of Hackney was particularly concerned to see public transport improved *before* parking control was introduced, but other inner boroughs did not link these two policy issues, until the question of traffic restraint was discussed at the GLDP Inquiry.

The GLC, of course, was taking a cautious approach to traffic restraint measures. The 1967 MOT Report, *The Better Use of Town Roads*, concluded that parking control was the best means of restraint applicable to London. The GLC made no comment, but while negotiating the transfer of LT, insisted that the extension and improved enforcement of parking control was also essential.[4] LT's evidence to the GLDP Inquiry suggested that if the GLC's parking policy:

> is pursued to the extent that the volume of traffic on the roads used by buses is significantly lower in relation to capacity than experienced

[1] Hammersmith *Minutes*, 1 November 1967 and 13 March 1968.
[2] *Council Minutes*: Kensington and Chelsea, 18 March 1969; Westminster, 1 December 1969.
[3] GLC *Minutes*, 2 November 1965, pp710–22.
[4] GLC *Minutes*, 9 July 1968, p383; 17 December 1968, p710; 21 October 1969, p572; 4 November 1969, p613.

today, this will bring a major benefit in time-saving and improved reliability of service to both bus passengers and those private motorists using the roads; will reduce bus costs by permitting higher speeds, and so help to keep fares down, and will result in more *people* travelling by road more quickly. In today's road conditions such measures are urgent.[1]

Successive documents (the Green Paper on *The Future of London Transport* in July 1971, and *Traffic and the Environment* a year later) and two major policy statements on LT in the autumn of 1971 and 1972 saw public transport operation set in the context of a road system on which parking was heavily controlled. The GLC's view had changed sufficiently for them to say 'an essential part of the balanced strategy is that the public transport undertaking should be placed in a relatively favourable position . . . this means the creation of conditions of controlled competition by parking policies and general parking policies for road use.'[2] The chairman of the LT Executive, Sir Richard Way, welcomed this change of heart and suggested that parking space should be reduced as much as 40% to give a really efficient bus service.[3]

4 THE PROBLEMS OF OPERATION

Enforcement and the role of the police

Responsibility for enforcing the parking and associated waiting regulations fell mainly to the Metropolitan Police through constables and, increasingly, traffic wardens. Four boroughs employed parking attendants[4] who supervised meters but not yellow-line waiting restrictions. The cost of the warden force, 2056 strong by March 1972, was just short of £4 million, and was shared between the police and the local authorities.[5]

The enforcement task had two main parts. The first was the identification 'on the street' of illegal parking and deliberate overstaying of time limits by 'meter feeding.' This was dealt with either by applying a fixed penalty notice, or alternatively the vehicle can be towed away. Wardens also affixed excess charge notices to vehicles that overstayed the period for which the driver had initially paid.

If the excess charge was not paid the local authority had to take action (since April 1971, see below). The fixed penalty (currently £2) could be paid to a court within 21 days; if this was not done the Central Ticket Office had the task of identifying and prosecuting the driver usually

[1] LT (1970), *Proof of Evidence, E12/2*, GLDP Inquiry Stage 1, p6.
[2] GLC *Minutes*, 6 July 1971, p340.
[3] *Evening News*, 10 January 1973.
[4] Greenwich, Kingston, Croydon and Bromley.
[5] *Expenditure Committee* (Environment and Home Office Subcommittee) *Minutes of Evidence* (memorandum from Metropolitan Police) *Hansard HC Papers 107 (xviii)*, 1971–72, Q1961, p423.

through the registered keeper of the vehicle. This, the second major task of 'follow up' had to be done by police constables.

The main concerns of the police have been ensuring adequate warden and constable manpower for both these tasks, and pressing for changes in the law and procedures to cope with the growing problem of tracing defaulters. 'At this moment of time the success of parking control depends . . . upon the extent to which physical presence is an essential factor in supervision' said Deputy Assistant Commissioner Candy to the 1971 British Parking Association conference.[1]

In 1966 the GLC admitted that 'the on-street arrangements (in ILPA) will work only as well as drivers abide by the rules. Enforcement is therefore of crucial importance.' Proposals for quadrupling the labour force had been discussed with the police, but even at that time staffing was 150–250 below an establishment of 651.[2] During the year an energetic recruiting campaign was undertaken but the numbers rose only to 700, one constraint being the lack of accommodation for wardens in new control areas. Recruitment was better in 1967 with an increased number of women (61% compared with 37% in 1966, a proportion that has since been maintained).

As already mentioned, in 1968 the Home Office, on the insistance of the Treasury, directed that manpower be held at the January 1968 level of about 1250 wardens in order to limit expenditure. This led to immediate protests from the boroughs individually, the LBA and from the GLC, at both officer and member level, because it meant delaying the implementation of ILPA and some outer zones. The chairman of the GLC's Highways Committee, Robert Vigars, commented that it 'threatened our progress.' The police went to great lengths to redeploy staff and to limit their use outside control zones.[3] Eventually the Home Office agreed to increase the allowance for the next financial year (1969–70) by 500 wardens, still far short of the GLC's aspirations, but in the event new zones were processed more slowly than expected and:

> The introduction of a controlled parking zone has never had to be delayed because of inability to complement it. There have, however, been some close calls: there was serious under-complementing up to 1965 and delay in the completion of a new traffic warden centre made it necessary in 1970 to ask for the introduction of a zone to be delayed for four months. In the event, however, the centre was ready before the zone.[4]

Since 1969 the warden system has been given a proper career structure and better pay, and despite higher entry standards recruitment has improved

[1] Paper on *The Metropolitan Police's Attitude To and Involvement With Parking Policy* July 1971.

[2] *Parking Policy in Central London* (1966), paras25–8.

[3] GLC *Minutes*, 22 March 1968, p189, 25 March 1969, p236; LBA *Minutes*, 6 March 1968, p19; Metropolitan Police, *Annual Report*, 1968, p17.

[4] *Hansard HC Papers 107* (*xviii*) (1971–72), p413.

(probably aided by the state of the national and London labour markets). To some extent the rate at which future zones can be introduced will depend on three factors:

1 How many wardens are deployed outside zones (25% in 1972).
2 How many are allocated to duties other than attending parking.
3 Whether more economic methods of enforcement can be found (for instance experiments with a mobile warden squad are being used in isolated control areas outside ILPA and 'swoop squads' have been used to raise general levels of compliance with the law through sporadic enforcement in suburban centres.[1]

When the early timetables for completing ILPA were given, no estimates of the likely enforcement manpower were made, but police witnesses before the House of Commons Expenditure Committee thought that 3200 would be needed to man ILPA and the scattered outer suburban zones, then envisaged. This increase of 60% over the 1972 complement would hold good only as long as no new major duties were added, such as enforcing bus lanes, controlling overnight lorry parking[2] or other possible developments such as lorry routes, supplementary licensing, or overnight residents' parking control. The police also drew attention to two other on-street enforcement problems: one was the difficulty of defining 'loading' (for which waiting is allowed for twenty minutes on a yellow line), and the second was the problem of meter feeding. They believed that the former accounted for the apparently low 'productivity of traffic wardens,' while the latter prevented the turnover of parked cars.[3] The only feasible solution produced by the police for the latter seemed to be either the use of plain clothes officers to enforce meter schemes, or a more ruthless tow-away policy. The GLC have suggested that time limits at meters could be abolished if meter prices could be set at a level that ensured turnover.[4]

As car ownership increased and parking control extended, the number of drivers parking illegally or exceeding the time limits grew even faster. Between 1965 and 1971 the number of fixed-penalty tickets quadrupled to over 1 million, and between 1965 and 1970 excess charges grew by 60% to about half that number (Table 32 items 1 and 3). Not surprisingly, the Metropolitan Police became hard pressed to process the tickets, even with the aid of a computer installed at the Central Ticket Office. Indeed at one stage they had to limit the criteria for issuing fixed-penalty tickets in order that the Office could cope.[5]

Even more important, however, the proportion of drivers paying their

[1] *Hansard HC Papers 107* (*xviii*), 1971–72, p414; the *Guardian*, 2 December 1970.
[2] *Hansard HC Papers 107* (*xviii*), 1971–72, p414, Q1990–1, 2013–9.
[3] *Hansard HC Papers 107* (*xviii*), 1971–72, p418–19; Westminster CC (1970), *Report E138/70*, p8.
[4] GLC (1972), *Paper B479*, p15, GLDP Inquiry Stage 1.
[5] Metropolitan Police *Annual Report*, 1968, pp72–4; letter received from Kensington and Chelsea Director of Technical Services, 1 September 1971.

dues within the prescribed time dropped as the numbers increased, and this has meant a growing burden of follow-up work. As the following figures show, between 1966 and 1971 fewer people paid their fines, and more paid late. The number of tickets which lapsed (because follow-up could not be completed in time) or were excused (e.g. foreign tourists, or diplomats) continued to grow. The former—a measure of 'failure' of the system—grew by about 130% in the five-year period from 1966 to 1971 (see table).[1] By 1971, 23% of the excess charges also had to be 'written off.'

FIXED PENALTY NOTICES (%)	1966		1971	
Paid within twenty-one days	35	66	16	56
Paid late	31		40	
Excused	19		19	
Written off	10		23	
Summonsed	5		2	

Follow-up of fixed penalties was formerly carried out by sending a letter to the licensee of the car to discover the identity of the offending driver, followed by personal inquiries by a police constable. If this failed, court procedures were instituted. Apart from the fact that follow-up and legal proceedings involved costs far exceeding the 50p excess charge or the £2 penalty, they involved the use of skilled manpower which the police felt could not reasonably be sustained. In April 1970 the Commissioner therefore proposed to cease processing excess-charge notices from 1 October 1970 leaving this task to the boroughs, who received the income.[2] The boroughs reluctantly agreed to the takeover, but protested that this could not be achieved so quickly and 1 April 1971 was settled as a compromise date; in return the boroughs' contribution to Metropolitan Police costs was reduced.[3]

Tickets of persistent offenders were given 'special accelerated treatment' but these cases were a small part of the problem.[4] The danger that the increased failure rate was bringing the whole system into disrepute was recognised by both the police and the GLC. To overcome this the police have been pressing since 1967 in firmer and more definite terms for a change in the law to make the keeper of a vehicle rather than the driver responsible for illegal parking actions.[5]

The GLC supported this more strongly from 1971 onwards while recognising that they, as licensing authority, might have to alter their licensing procedure, partly because each vehicle would have to display its

[1] *Hansard HC Papers 107 (xviii)*, 1971–72.

[2] Metropolitan Police *Annual Report*, 1968, p17.

[3] LBA *Minutes*, 15 June 1970, p52; 29 July 1970, p64.

[4] *Evening Standard*, the *Guardian*, 15 September 1971 and 23 February 1972. 3700 vehicles in a trial period accounted for 30% of the 161 000 unpaid tickets.

[5] Metropolitan Police, *Annual Reports*, 1967, pp12–13; 1968, pp17, 75; 1969, pp15, 63; 1970, pp15, 60; *Hansard HC Papers 107 (vii)*, 1971–72, pp126, 131; *(xviii)* pp417–18, 423–5, 431; GLC (1972), *Traffic and the Environment*, pp9–10.

owner's name; also court procedures would have to be changed.[1] Commenting on the effects of British Rail fare increases as an additional pressure to use the car the GLC said in 1970 'there is no doubt that pressure will build up on the weak points in the existing control machinery. There is need for a strengthening of the system over the whole field of enforcement, especially in owner liability.'[2]

The MOT took note of this concern over liability and other enforcement matters and appointed a firm of consultants to investigate the possibilities. The consultants' findings remained confidential,[3] and the MOT/DOE remained of the opinion that there were substantial difficulties (e.g. over taxis and hire cars). The precedent of owner liability exists in acts governing possession of drugs,[4] and the system is in use in some states in Australia and America. In addition to owner liability the GLC in 1971 suggested three further possibilities

1 Fines should be higher, more than covering administrative costs; a new single fixed penalty was needed nationally.
2 Payment of fines could be linked to licence renewal (in conjunction with owner liability).
3 Licence renewal could be denied to persistent offenders.[5]

The latter point relates to a GLC engineer's comment that the enforcement situation 'is not going to get better until people think of parking where they should not as an anti-social act.'[6]

Finance

In 1970 the Commissioner of the Metropolitan Police commented: 'The marked improvement in parking discipline following the introduction of parking schemes enforced by the fixed penalty system has tended to divert attention from the high and continually rising costs of enforcement, both in money and manpower.' This, he said, was occurring to the point where it had 'low overall effectiveness in relation to the cost of the large resources involved.'[7]

In the early days of meter parking it was thought that parking control would be relatively cheap and profitable, but both capital and running costs have turned out to be quite high. Between 1966 and 1969 they grew from 54% to 75% of income (Table 33). A meter costs £40, a ticket machine

[1] GLC *Minutes*, 6 July 1971, p331, 341; *Parking Policy in Central London*, 1966, para29; and *Parking Policy in London*, 1969, p8.
[2] *Sunday Times*, 13 December 1970.
[3] P Anderson and Co, *Operational Research on Enforcement of Parking and Waiting controls*.
[4] *Hansard HC Papers 107 (xviii)*, 1971–72, p433.
[5] GLC (1972), *B479*, p20; and *B483*, p11, GLDP Inquiry Stage 1.
[6] *The Sunday Times*, 5 April 1970.
[7] *Evening Standard*, 14 July 1971.

about £300; at high borrowing rates loan charges on a meter scheme therefore became quite significant (Table 33A). Even conversions for decimalisation were expensive; for example Camden's bill was £5500, and that of Kensington and Chelsea was £6500 for its ticket machines alone. Meters and ticket machines are also liable to vandalism or theft. Westminster estimated a loss of £30 000 in 1969 (two-thirds from lost revenue, one-third in repairs); Islington lost £5000 in the first three months of 1971 and as a result was considering some other form of control.

(A) *Annual costs in Westminster* (£000) (Westminster 1966, 1969 Reports)

	METER PARKING 1966	METER PARKING 1969	RESIDENTS' PARKING	1969
Direct costs				
Traffic wardens	24.85	36.00	Traffic wardens	14.44
Maintenance	4.83	5.00	Tokens	6.13
Loan charges	5.78	10.85		
Total	35.46	51.85		20.57
Indirect costs				
Signs, etc.	0.74	0.85		0.37
Administration	10.00	8.00		6.00
Total	10.74	8.85		6.37
TOTAL ALL COSTS	46.21	60.70		26.94
AVERAGE INCOME	n.a.	88.00		25.88

(B) *Some examples of costs* (£000) (Borough Minutes)

	BOROUGH CAP. COST	GLC CAP. COST	EST. INCOME p.a.	EST. EXPEND. p.a.
Westminster				
Belgravia–Knightsbridge	53	4	176	185
South Paddington	76	3	218	235
Pimlico	38	1	113	124
Lisson Grove	32	2	n.a.	n.a.
Hackney				
Zone 3	21	1	26	31
Kensington				
Zones 1–4	—	—	230	2
Zones 5+6	—	—	775	75
Kensington east Chelsea zone				
Meters	—	—	104	77
Respark—tickets	—	—	20	16
Respark—seasons	—	—	42	22
Total	—	—	166	115

(C) *Financial data for years ending 31 March* (£000) (GLC Annual Abstract of Statistics, vols1–4)

		1966	1967	1968	1969
Greater London	(*a*) Income	1275	1353	1509	1966
	(*b*) Expenditure	689	815	1175	1472
	(*c*) Surplus	586	538	334	494
	(*d*) Applied to parking	726	574	381	299
Westminster	(*c*) Surplus	993	1688	293	364
	(*d*) Applied to parking	957	1440	293	240
12 ILPA boro's	(*c*) Surplus	n.a.	n.a.	348	510
Other boroughs	(*c*) Surplus/deficit	n.a.	n.a.	−15	−16

Table 33 SOME FINANCIAL ASPECTS OF PARKING CONTROL

Note: Where *d* is greater than *c* deficits have been rate-borne. 'ILPA boro's' is not the same definition as GLC's 'inner boroughs'

Enforcement and follow-up labour comprises 75% of all annual costs and slightly more for residents' zones (Table 33A). Westminster paid £463 000 to the Metropolitan Police in 1968–69 as their contribution towards the cost of wardens. Basic salaries for wardens increased by 74% between 1965 and 1971. Thus the gap between costs and income was becoming increasingly narrow as Table 33C shows. Westminster had the majority of the income and surplus, as the following figures[1] show:

1958–70 (£M)

	INCOME	EXPENDITURE	PARKING INVESTMENT
Greater London	9.3	6.4	2.4
Of which Westminster	7.2	4.6	2.0

Originally all surpluses on the parking account were to be applied to off-street parking;[2] under the 1968 Transport Act[3] this was widened to allow them also to be put towards highway or public transport improvements. The motoring organisations regarded this as a political sell-out,[4] but in fact virtually all surpluses went to car parking and in Westminster, which received 80% of all surpluses in Greater London (£609 000 in 1970–71), the chairman of the Highways Committee stated categorically that they would continue to devote the whole of the net income to off-street parking. Other boroughs with long-standing political motivations for improving public transport (such as Tower Hamlets, Hackney, and Southwark) might have desired different priorities if they had achieved surpluses. Although in

[1] RAC figures, *Evening Standard*, 23 February 1971.
[2] *Road Traffic Regulation Act 1967*, ch76, s44 (3)d.
[3] *Transport Act 1968*, ch73, s127 (6).
[4] Especially the RAC; see the *Guardian*, 9 March 1965 and 24 February 1971; *The Times*, 19 October 1969; and *Evening Standard*, 23 February 1971.

1966 the GLC promised to discuss the allocation of surplus revenues,[1] they have never suggested that any borough should take a particular line. The Metropolitan Police have not entered into questions of pricing, although they have viewed higher charges as only a partial contribution to restraint.[2]

This does raise the question of whether the GLC should be involved in ILPA's finances particularly as these are likely to become increasingly adverse. Hammersmith for a time felt that they should subsidise their residents' parking; Westminster and to a slightly lesser degree Camden and Kensington & Chelsea were very keen to see the overall parking account break even and were willing to increase short-term charges to almost any level to maintain the 85% usage rate, whereas some outer boroughs remained opposed to the concept of charging. The GLC was consistently of the opinion that charges were a matter for the individual borough in the light of local circumstances.[3]

5 CONCLUSIONS

The practical benefits of ILPA have been to make controlled streets safer and more orderly; to enable traffic to move more freely;[4] to give drivers a reasonable chance of finding a parking place, particularly residents; to hold down the growth of traffic. Research into other effects, however, is only just beginning[5] and the effects on the ILPA policy of, for example, long-distance traffic, heavy vehicles, and off-peak passenger use of buses have not so far been quantified. There is also only limited experience of the precise effects of pricing as a means of control. The mere fact of control where formerly there was none was a sufficient regulation for a few years but the ILPA scheme will need overall financial management (including the relationship of charges for on-street and off-street parking) in the longer term, certainly if time limits at meters, and consequently excess charges, are to be abolished. *Ad hoc* increases in meter prices agreed after application from individual boroughs, as at present, will not be enough. J M Thomson in evidence submitted to the GLDP Inquiry estimated that prices might reach from 20p to 35p per hour in inner London and from 40p to 60p per hour in the central area by 1981.[6]

The scale and comprehensiveness of the on-street parking control measures undertaken by the GLC have not been matched by any other

[1] *Parking Policy in Central London* (1966), para31.
[2] *Hansard HC Papers 107 (xviii)*, 1971–72, p435.
[3] *Parking Policy in Central London* (1966), paras16, 18.
[4] See P W Munt (1971), 'Road Traffic in Greater London: Results of Speed and Flow Studies 1968–70,' *GLC Intelligence Unit Quarterly Bulletin* (16), pp3–14.
[5] T May (1972), 'Parking Control for Restraint in Greater London,' *GLC Intelligence Unit Quarterly Bulletin* (19), pp30–42.
[6] London Amenity and Transport Association/London Motorway Action Group (1971), *Proof of Evidence, E12/20*, s3.6, GLDP Inquiry Stage 1—similar prices were assumed by the South-East Strategic Plan Joint Study Team (1971), *Studies*, vol3, HMSO.

city in the world. New York has expanded its meter provision but has continued to encourage the building of off-street space; its only traffic restraint policies have been localised proposals for closing streets to traffic in a limited area of Lower Manhattan.[1] Paris only accepted parking meters in 1971 after many years of pressure from the Prefect of Police and fruitless attempts to enforce a disc system. Rome extended parking control and traffic management over the whole central area in 1972 but this was reported to have created problems in the adjacent suburbs. Tokyo planned to reintroduce meters after the failure of an earlier experiment.[2]

Although other British cities have adopted parking control, few have yet adopted policies for manipulating parking as a means of traffic restraint. None has had powers over off-street parking comparable to those of the GLC although Glasgow and Manchester have pressed for them.[3]

The relatively rapid and effective implementation of the original idea of ILPA and the subsequent widening of its scope can be cited as a successful product of the two-tier system of local government in London. The GLC played its proper (and intended) role of strategic authority having been urged by the Minister of Transport to produce a scheme quickly, but without binding its new partners, the boroughs, too tightly. While it may be possible, with hindsight, to criticise the lack of research and consultation procedures, it must be remembered that at the time there was no experience of widespread on-street parking control. Within this system the role of central government is limited to that of overseer and legislator. The DOE said as much at the GLDP Inquiry:

> Traffic management is primarily the responsibility of local government. It is for the local authorities to determine what level of restraint is appropriate to their areas and how best to achieve this level in practice with regard to local circumstances. The Government's role is to ensure that local traffic authorities are in a position to exercise their responsibilities.[4]

Elsewhere the DOE expressed the belief that parking controls provided the only practical means of traffic restraint 'for the next five years,' while 'thereafter it may be possible to introduce more sophisticated controls such as road pricing through an off-vehicle metering system.'[5]

[1] *The Times*, 22 April 1969.
[2] *The Sunday Times*, 28 August 1971.
[3] Papers of BPA conference 1972 reproduced in *Journal*, Institute of Highway Engineers, volXIX, I, January 1972, *passim*; R Hodgen (1970), 'Traffic Restraint Policy,' *Tr Eng and Control*, pp199–201.
[4] DOE (1971), *Methods of Traffic Restraint; Paper B625*, GLDP Inquiry Stage 1, para11.
[5] *Restraint of the Motor-Car*, Memo M4 to Expenditure Committee (1971–72) (Home Office and Environment Subcommittee), also submitted to Stage 2 of GLDP Inquiry as paper *S27/359*.

The GLC has described its role in parking as that of 'policy maker.'[1] An important question is whether the basic principles of the ILPA policy set by the GLC in 1966 have stood the test of time. In a letter to Lambeth Council in 1967 the GLC outlined these principles which dealt with the order of priority in allocating parking space (short-term first, commuters last); special provision for residents and uniformity in the design of signs and markings. They listed the variable details as the scale of provision of each type of parking, the method of operating residents' parking, details of waiting and loading restrictions, zone boundaries, rates of payment for meters, programming of implementation and provision of public and resident off-street parking. The principle of uniformity did not extend far beyond the general layout of zones, the use of wardens for enforcement, and design of signs. In the main, the exercise of local flexibility has been paramount, but it was unlikely that it would have been practical politics to have it otherwise, and that the scheme could have achieved its present state without it. Thus the GLC has managed to retain the essential elements of the scheme while accommodating local needs, including variations in actual parking demand, technical preferences for managing the zones, and current political views.

The GLC's interest in uniformity was to ensure that any parking policy 'bit' equally in different zones in the same borough or between boroughs; the police on the other hand were also concerned for a certain degree of uniformity to make the wardens' job manageable, and to make the system as simple as possible for drivers to understand. One problem resulting from the considerable flexibility, for example, in pricing and control systems is the increasing difficulty for the public in understanding the ramifying regulations. For example, in 1972 John Gorst, MP for North Hendon, sought to discover what the current situation was. He learnt that he would need:

> five documents, one published by the Stationery Office for the Minister of Transport, and four issued by the GLC. In all, the regulations run to 67 pages, with 826 pages of schedules; and there are 76 amending orders running to another 749 pages. A conscientious MP determined never to commit a parking offence outside his own house would need to spend £12.84.

Accordingly Gorst wrote to the DOE, 'it is impossible for the general public to know what rules they are breaking or what they have to observe.'[2]

The process of implementation was to some extent inadequate, both in administrative and legal terms, and regarding public consultation. The order-making procedure did not differentiate between matters of major or minor importance or between the relatively great impact of a new zone and

[1] *Hansard HC Papers 107 (xviii)*, 1971–72, pp121, 130.

[2] *The Times*, 12 October 1972. Since that time, the 1972 regulations have come into effect.

the relatively minor impact of a modification. Hopefully, new legislation will improve this and by specifying consultation procedures will overcome some of the snags caused in the past by sustained objections from particular interest groups. Through experience of parking control the public has made objections rather less emotively and more thoughtfully.

One of the most marked features of the role of the boroughs is that their views of parking control have mostly been seen in terms of local problems such as street congestion, untidy parking, double-parked unloading and lack of space for residents. Westminster were an exception in that they quickly adopted a wider view of the policy as a means of restraint on car commuting to the central area. The one feature which made ILPA at first acceptable and in some cases positively attractive to the boroughs was the feature of residents' parking, for this enabled the councils to offer something positive to their ratepayers and electorate in return for the extra restrictions and costs incurred. It gave residents a better chance of finding a space at a price lower than that in off-street car parks or private lock-up garages.

The other main aspect of parking policy is concerned with surveillance and enforcement. The problem of enforcement appeared to be universal, with rising numbers of unpunished offences and unpaid fines. In 1971, New York police issued 4 million summonses and 'meter maids' another million: more than half were unpaid and 110 000 cars were towed away. In Tokyo parking controls are blatantly flouted despite the fact that fines may reach £35. Several cities have been driven to fairly desperate enforcement methods: in Denver and Paris offenders are likely to have a large frame ('the Denver shoe') locked onto one of the wheels; in Tokyo plastic parking tickets are padlocked to wing mirrors or windscreen wipers; in Mexico City the licence plates are removed. In West Germany a 'sinner's index' ensures that persistent traffic offenders are not allowed to renew their licences immediately. In Britain as a whole, according to Home Office statistics, the 'failure rate' on excess-charge and fixed-penalty notices rose from 8 to 16% and from 10 to 21% respectively between 1966 and 1969.

The Metropolitan Police have become increasingly worried about the growing failure both of surveillance and follow-up procedures (in July–December 1972, 23% of issued fines were unpaid, numbering 127 000). Extra manpower will probably be required to improve the rigour and frequency of observation on the street, changes in regulations regarding waiting and meter feeding could also help. Although running very near to manpower limits at times, the police have usually recruited sufficient wardens to man the zones being processed, but not to follow up all the defaulters. The police have pressed for heavier fines[1] and for changes in the law, notably for keeper liability. Although their claim has been supported by the GLC, the Government has appeared reluctant to introduce the necessary legislation.

The liaison bodies between the police and the GLC (Joint Traffic

[1] H Hunt, Assistant Commissioner, Traffic; the *Guardian* 9 January 1973.

Executive (JTE)) and the JTE and the boroughs (through ALBES) co-operated well on executive matters, but links with wider transport policy discussions were very tenuous: GLTG, for example, which included the transport operators (who would benefit from traffic restraint measures) did not include the police. The JTE has given the police a direct contact with GLC officers which, as one senior officer put it, 'we are learning how to handle.'

Thus the future problems of ILPA are very much those of management: in particular the development of on-street parking control as an element of overall parking and restraint policies, and the legal, technical and practical problems of enforcement. The inception and implementation of the ILPA policy may, however, be regarded as an example of successful co-operation between the two tiers of local government in London.

Chapter 4

LONDON'S TRANSPORT PROBLEMS

1 THE NATURE OF THE PROBLEM

There is at least one topic on which the people of virtually every major city in the world could agree, namely that travelling from one place to another is often more difficult than they would like. Each city has its own particular transport problems but invariably they are found to be both serious and apparently intractable. London is certainly no exception.

To find a universally acceptable definition of 'the transport problem' is a difficult task since each person has differing needs and circumstances and hence a particular view of what is inadequate or intolerable. The institutions and groups concerned with city planning and administration also have their own conceptions of the transport problem, and these may or may not coincide with those of individual citizens. We know, of course, that Londoners are far from satisfied with the city's transport system, or at least with many parts of it. They expect, and are often prepared to pay for, various kinds of service and facility to meet a variety of transport needs, which appear to them to be reasonable. At the same time, they do not expect these services and facilities to interfere too seriously with their living environment. Some of their expectations may be unreasonable in relation to what is economically practicable or acceptable to the community as a whole, but these cannot be ignored since without expectation there can be no measure of dissatisfaction.

The findings of the previous chapters have led us to a view of what are the most persistent and widespread problems in London. The aim here is to put these into some sort of perspective before moving on in the following chapters to appraise how the institutional system tackles them at present and to suggest how it might be better equipped to tackle them in the future.

Despite its deficiencies, the contribution made by London's transport system to the economic, social and physical environment is in general thought to be superior to that found in Paris, Tokyo and New York by many who have experienced those other giant cities. But this offers little comfort to Londoners who have to cope with the particular problems of their own city.

One way of describing these problems would be to set out Londoners' own conception of them. Opinion research on such complex subjects is full of pitfalls and results are open to varying interpretations. Moreover, little definitive work has been carried out in this field, but some information

	GLC AREA (%)	OUTER METROPOLITAN AREA (%)	ALL (%)
Giving more help to old people	65	68	66
Building more new homes	59	51	55
Providing more recreational opportunities for young people	30	36	33
Improving secondary education	30	28	29
Controlling air pollution	26	31	28
Improving primary education	23	26	25
Improving the bus service	25	20	23
Reducing noise	18	23	20
Improving the railways and underground	15	9	13
Building new motorways inside London	9	8	8
Number of people	1102	775	1877

Table 34 PREFERENCES FOR PUBLIC SPENDING*

Note: * P Willmott and M Young, 'How Urgent are London's Motorways?' *New Society*, 10 December 1970. Article extracted from wider work being undertaken by the authors at the Institute of Community Studies into social attitudes

elicited in recent surveys may help to put London's transport deficiencies in perspective. Perhaps a good first question to ask is how much importance Londoners place on transport as compared with other aspects of city life. A random sample of 2000 adults living in the Greater London Council (GLC) and outer metropolitan areas were asked in 1970 which three of a number of choices for public spending they considered most important. (They were not asked to place these in order of priority so that the total responses add up to 300%.) The results of the survey are given in Table 34.

According to this survey the needs of old people and housing are considered the most important of the options presented. Education and recreational facilities were also mostly ranked above the other options which relate directly or indirectly (i.e. noise and pollution) to transport problems. These results must be treated with caution (as Willmott and Young recognise) partly because only one question was asked which was neither qualified nor expressed in alternative ways. (The question was: 'Here is a list of things that the Government and local councils have to spend money on. You may think all these things important. But if you had to decide, which three things would you put at the top for spending money on?') Also the options for spending were selected by the authors; 'there may have been other things, even more important to people, that were left out.' In relation to the low scoring of urban motorways the authors felt that this might have been accounted for by people's ignorance of the current proposals and their implications.

In another sample survey, carried out for the British Road Federation in late 1969,[1] only 59% claimed awareness of the Greater London Development Plan (GLDP) and of these only 38% were aware that Ringways were being proposed whilst hardly any had a clear idea even in general terms of the routes, type of construction, housing loss, cost, etc. In the same survey, however, questions were asked about the likely importance of issues at the forthcoming GLC elections in April 1970. When asked if there were any issues of importance, 31% replied 'no' and 20% 'don't know.' The remaining 49% who answered 'yes' made the following choices (the figures are percentages of the total): housing, 21; rents, 11; roads, 9; taxation/cost of living, 8; education, 8; transport, 7; rates, 5; others, 17. The separate listing of roads and transport is somewhat confusing and may disguise some double counting, but in any case transport issues are indicated to be on a par with the other issues except housing, which stands out as the area of greatest concern. (This is interesting since the widest powers and responsibilities for housing lie not with the GLC but with the London boroughs.)

2 DEFICIENCIES IN THE TRANSPORT SYSTEM

Environment

Practically every form of motorised transport creates noise, vibration, visual intrusion and, in the case of combustion engines, exhaust fumes. Near airports, and beneath the flight-path approaches to them, air traffic is often the major source of excessive noise. It has been calculated, for example, that 137 000 residents near Heathrow airport are eligible for grants from the British Airports Authority for sound-proofing.[2] Much wider areas, particularly in west London, are affected to a lesser degree, but aircraft noise is much more difficult to avoid than that created by ground transport since buildings of ordinary construction do not provide an effective shield. Thus, both indoor and outdoor spaces are more vulnerable to aircraft noise than to ground sources of noise such as road traffic.

Railways in urban areas can also cause a serious noise problem unless they are below ground; the degree of disturbance depends on the speed of trains, their frequency, their motive power and on the form of surrounding development. They can also be visually intrusive, particularly when elevated, as is the case with much of the network in south London. The view of Southwark cathedral from the Charing Cross railway line, for example, is unfortunately not matched by the view from the cathedral itself. Another problem is sometimes said to be the divisive effects railways

[1] Research Services Ltd for the BRF, *Roads in London: The Public View*, BRF 1970.
[2] *GLDP Report of Studies*, para6.158.

have on communities, where they constitute barriers to local movement.[1]

The most ubiquitous environmental disturbance in London is that caused by road traffic. Unlike trains, road vehicles (apart from buses) are not confined to particular routes, and consequently their side effects are felt to a greater or lesser degree in almost every corner of the metropolis. The motor cycle is one of the noisiest vehicles but generally it is large vehicles such as buses and heavy lorries which are the loudest, exude the most exhaust pollution and intrude most into the city scene. In practice, however, it is the smaller vehicles which are the source of most environmental disruption because there are far more of them. To the effects of the vehicles themselves can be added the preponderance, especially on main roads, of traffic signals, parking meters, car parks, petrol filling stations, and car sales sites with their attendent advertising, which rarely enhance London's appearance.

The most intrusive roads are four-, six- or eight-lane motorways[2] such as Westway and the M1 which run radially into London. The volume of traffic carried may be 70 000 vehicles or more per day (depending on the number of lanes). It is impossible to conceal motorway structures in existing towns and cities and they radically alter the scale and appearance of the areas through which they pass, though tunnelling or the suitable redevelopment of land adjoining them can help to reduce their intrusiveness. The quality of the environment also tends to suffer where a new road is known to be planned but has not actually been built, because of consequent lack of maintenance or improvement of the urban fabric; the area is 'blighted,' and property values depressed.

At present, however, there are comparatively few motorways in London (15.6 miles in April 1969)[3] and the most serious problems are on the main roads which serve and pass through most of London's major shopping and employment areas and have virtually continuous frontage development. In London, there are approximately 1000 miles of roads classified as Principal and these are the main carriers of traffic,[4] with volumes of perhaps 20 000 or more vehicles per day. As with the railways, the often disturbing environmental conditions on roads which have for many years carried large volumes of traffic of all kinds (horse-drawn vehicles and trams also brought serious problems of odour, dust and noise) may be tacitly accepted as an inevitable part of city life. It is impossible to say how much suffering is caused by heavy traffic but it is certainly more widespread than the occasional outbursts of protests in critical situations or from articulate communities indicate. It has been reported, for example,

[1] The GLC, for example, has cited the divisiveness of existing railway lines in London as one justification for the building of major new roads alongside them. *GLDP Statement*, para2.11; and GLDP *Proof of Evidence*, *E12/1*, paras6.3.1, 6.6.3, and figs 6.7–6.9.

[2] Motorways are roads specially designed (under the Special Roads Act 1949) for the high-speed movement of motor traffic segregated from the ordinary road network, with a limited number of free-flow intersections and without frontage development.

[3] GLC (1971), *Annual Abstract of Statistics*, vol4, 1969.

[4] GLC (1970), *Secondary Roads Policy* (revised), table 4.

that certain sections of the Archway and West India Docks Roads have much higher noise levels than Westway;[1] yet public protests on these roads have been small compared with the anger aroused by the opening of Westway.

Property values might give a better indication of the nuisance of road traffic but though it is generally believed that values are adversely affected there has so far been little authoritative research in this field. The publication *Houseowner* gave examples in 1971 of houses backing on to the M1 at Mill Hill which cost £10 000 compared with £12 000 for similar houses on the other side of the road.[2]

As road traffic has increased, many roads, particularly in central and inner London, which were built for purely residential use now bear the brunt of traffic trying to avoid the congested parts of the main road network. This practice (commonly referred to as the use of 'rat runs') has led to widespread deterioration in the quality of residential areas and, as in the cases of Barnsbury, Pimlico and Kensington (see Case Study *G*), has given rise to pressures for schemes aimed at restricting traffic flows to the established main roads. In some instances the use of residential streets as traffic routes has actually been deliberately increased by traffic management schemes. On other roads which serve purely local traffic, environmental disturbance is small though there may be accident risks at badly designed junctions and intrusion of parked vehicles.

There has been, particularly since the mid-1960s, a growing if sometimes ill-defined desire in central and local government, the media, and local groups to secure a balance of policy which aims to maintain or improve the quality of the environment. Both proponents and opponents of the GLDP motorways proposals, for example, had the same aim of reducing traffic in residential areas, although they disagreed as to the means of achieving this. The number of voluntary pressure groups concerned with protecting the environment has increased dramatically since the war and one of their major concerns has been with the impact of motor traffic in urban areas. But the need to safeguard and improve the environment has also found recognition at the institutional level. There is now, for example, a major Government department to serve this general aim, and an Environmental Planning Committee within the GLC.[3]

Road Accidents

Apart from accidents in the home, the motor vehicle is the largest single cause of personal injury and death. The number and severity of road accidents in London, however, has not increased in proportion to the growth in motor traffic. During the 1960s, as Table 35 shows, the number

[1] *The Sunday Times*, 9 August 1970.
[2] Reported in the *Guardian*, 8 June 1971.
[3] See also T Aldous (1972), *Battle for the Environment*, ch1 and 2.

of accidents has shown a slight downward trend. Although the factors influencing the number and severity of road accidents are by no means fully understood, the design of the road, the speed and volume of traffic and the number of conflicting movements (vehicle to vehicle and vehicle to pedestrian) are probably the most significant. The worst periods of the day for accidents are the peak periods, particularly in the evening.[1]

Pedestrians usually account for roughly half the number of people killed and a quarter of personal injuries. Children and old people are particularly vulnerable. The accident rate to children under 15 years old is more than twice that of people between 15 and 65, while the rate to those over 65 is about one and a half times that of the middle age group.[2] The Metropolitan Police said in 1969 that the chance of a child aged 5 becoming a pedestrian casualty before his or her 15th birthday is on average about 1 in 18. 'If the child lives in inner London the chance is as high as 1 in 14.'[3]

Comparisons of accident rates (per million vehicles) by year or between London and other cities may indicate the success of safety measures or indeed transport policies. But these statistics give no real measure of the suffering caused by road accidents. They do not indicate the losses to the bereaved, relatives, employers, employees, customers and acquaintances. Measurements of loss of earnings and production and cost of hospitalisation for injury accidents also grossly understate the problem (Table 35).

YEAR	DEATHS	SERIOUS INJURIES	SLIGHT INJURIES	TOTAL
1960	912 (+11.8)	12 023 (+5.2)	61 206 (+2.5)	74 141 (+3.0)
1961	852 (− 6.6)	11 817 (−1.7)	59 931 (−2.1)	72 600 (−2.1)
1962	802 (− 5.9)	11 069 (−6.3)	58 366 (−2.6)	70 237 (−3.3)
1963	767 (− 4.4)	11 280 (+1.9)	61 679 (+5.7)	73 716 (+5.0)
1964	906 (+18.1)	12 008 (+6.5)	65 557 (+6.3)	78 471 (+6.4)
1965	873 (− 3.6)	12 441 (+3.6)	68 723 (+4.8)	82 037 (+4.5)
1966	898 (+ 2.9)	11 760 (−5.5)	66 139 (−3.8)	78 797 (−3.9)
1967	792 (−11.8)	10 839 (−7.8)	59 827 (−9.5)	71 458 (−9.3)
1968	710 (−10.4)	10 528 (−2.9)	60 007 (+0.3)	71 245 (−0.3)
1969	744 (+ 4.8)	11 314 (+7.5)	59 674 (−0.6)	71 732 (+0.7)
1970	809 (+ 8.7)	10 745 (−5.0)	61 080 (+2.4)	72 634 (+1.3)

Table 35 DEATHS AND INJURIES DUE TO ROAD ACCIDENTS IN THE METROPOLITAN POLICE DISTRICT, 1960–70 (PERCENTAGE CHANGE FROM PREVIOUS YEAR GIVEN IN BRACKETS)

Source: Reports of the Commissioner of Police for the Metropolis, 1960–70

[1] See, for example, *Report of the Commissioner of Police of the Metropolis for the year 1968*, Cmnd 4060 (1969), p66.

[2] GLC (1969), *GLDP Report of Studies*, para6.137.

[3] *Report of the Commissioner of Police of the Metropolis for the year 1969*, Cmnd 4355 (1970), p59.

Pedestrians

The daily activities of people are dependent on walking, whether to local shops, to work, to and from bus stops, railway stations or parking places. Pedestrian movement is therefore a basic part of the city's transport system. In a large city like London, distances between trip ends can be so large that walking can cover only a fairly small part. The homes of the majority of people who work, shop or are otherwise engaged in the central area lie beyond walking distance, and some vehicle is needed to get them there. But elsewhere in London, and indeed for movement *within* the central area, walking plays a large role. It has been shown, in fact, that the majority of all trips take place on foot or by bicycle.[1] As regards work trips, the London Transportation Study showed that 18% were made on foot, compared with, for example, 5% in St Louis, Missouri, USA.[2] A survey in Southwark showed that more than half of all leisure trips were made on foot. Most people walked on shopping trips under three-quarters of a mile.[3]

The source of most difficulties for the pedestrian is his conflict with motor traffic; he is vulnerable to its dangerous and unpleasant aspects. In the Metropolitan Police district in 1970, 436 pedestrians were killed (53% of all road deaths in that year), 4223 seriously injured and 14 763 slightly injured.[4] Pedestrians also suffer exposure to noise and fumes, delay in crossing roads, and inconvenience in being obliged to use subways, bridges, ramps and steps. The speed, noise and bulk of large vehicles can also be particularly intimidating to nervous and elderly people and young children. The effects of motor traffic are specially offensive to the pedestrian in shopping streets and other centres of activity. As Case Study *L* showed, this can be reflected in shopping turnover figures, which tend to increase when streets are closed to motor vehicles.

Not all pedestrian difficulties arise from direct conflict with motor traffic. In certain areas, particularly the lower density outer suburbs, the dispersed nature of development can result in a lack of facilities such as shops or entertainment within easy walking distance of the home or work place. This may effectively exclude walking as a means of getting about. Even for the journey to work, travelling to the station by car may be more attractive than walking, bringing environmental problems of parking near the station.

Further problems arise from pedestrians' vulnerability to bad weather, excessive gradients, steps and poor pavement surfaces. Difficulties of orientation can also be a particular problem, it seems, in newly redeveloped areas.[5]

[1] GLC (1968), *GLDP Draft Statement*, p79.

[2] London Transportation Study (1), table 6.33 and paras6.91–6.94.

[3] LB Southwark (1970), *Recreation in Southwark*, tables 52.2 and 53.18 (b).

[4] *Report of the Commissioner of Police for the Metropolis, 1970*, Cmnd 4680 (1971), app3, table 5.

[5] The Elephant and Castle redevelopment area has been cited as a particularly bad example. See O Marriott (1967) *The Property Boom* (Pan Books, 1969 edn), pp263–6.

Cyclists

As with the pedestrian, many problems for the cyclist lie in his relation to motor traffic. There are few cycle-ways in London and the cyclist must share the carriageway with motor vehicles, but while he may suffer delay through congestion, he probably does so to a lesser extent than other vehicle users. On roads marked out with relatively narrow traffic lanes (on Cromwell Road in Kensington, for example) lack of space may force the cyclist into the gutter.[1] He may have difficulty in changing lanes, or in turning right where he is in competition with the faster vehicles on the road. His relatively low speed may also mean that he is intimidated by the impatience or inconsiderateness of drivers. At junctions designed for the free flow of vehicular traffic such as Hyde Park Corner or Parliament Square, there is scarcely any way in which the cyclist can be assured of his safety other than by dismounting and using pedestrian crossing places. Many places also lack special parking facilities for bicycles, and where facilities are provided at stations, charges can be prohibitive (20p per day at some British Rail stations).

There is even less information about cyclists in London than about pedestrians, though it is known that cycle traffic has declined sharply over the post-war period. The number of cycle trips in London is estimated to have declined from 3.76 million in 1952 to 0.61 million in 1968.[2] The reasons for this decline have not been investigated but the problems and dangers of cycling are undoubtedly a contributory cause.

Particularly in the outer suburbs many local journeys to work, school, station, shops and friends could be made conveniently by bicycle, particularly in areas poorly served by the bus system. Specific provision for cyclists is planned at Thamesmead where a segregated cyclepath system, the most comprehensive form of provision, is envisaged (see Case Study *A*).

Road congestion

Each morning and evening when people are travelling to and from work the transport system in London is used most intensively. Roads become more congested than at other times of the day and movement by all classes of road users becomes much slower than at other times. Although this is a readily observed phenomenon, there has been little research into the precise implications of road congestion or (apart from central London) into the incidence of delay by time and place or the factors which influence it. It is consequently difficult to judge how serious a problem road delays are, and who are the road users most affected. A survey in 1971 on com-

[1] Traffic management schemes have often aggravated this problem especially at junctions by 'squeezing in' extra lanes.

[2] Derived from police census data and included in GLDP Inquiry Stage 1, *Paper S12/163* (LMAG–LATA).

muters' opinions about their daily journeys to work[1] found that the most satisfied were those who normally travelled to work by car—90% said they were satisfied (see Table 36). This apparently high degree of satisfaction may be partly explained by the fact that the car tends to be used for the journey to work more extensively in the less congested areas of London.

In contrast, only 47% of commuters by bus were found (by the same survey) to be satisfied with their journey to work. This must be largely a reflection of the unreliability of bus services which in peak hours at least is largely attributable to congestion. Bus passengers are often subjected to long waits for buses held up *en route* and then to further delays caused by congestion once they are on the bus.

	ALL	CAR	BUS	BR	LT RAIL
Very satisfied	33	57	13	24	24
Fairly satisfied	43	33	44	51	50
Neither satisfied nor dissatisfied	7	4	13	7	6
Not very satisfied	11	4	19	12	14
Not at all satisfied	6	2	11	5	6

Table 36 SUMMARY FROM ORC OPINION POLL, 1971: SATISFACTION WITH JOURNEY TO WORK IN LONDON (PERCENTAGES)

Note: This is a summary of replies to the question: 'How satisfied are you with the method of transport you normally use for your journey to work?'

Road congestion is not, however, wholly confined to the weekday rush hours; it occurs at other times, for example, near major recreation areas or airports. Accidents and breakdowns too can cause widespread disruption to the flow of vehicles. In central London, there is evidence that congestion has become fairly uniform throughout the daylight hours as traffic has reached a saturation level during the rush hours but has continued to increase during the off-peak hours.[2]

The location and extent of delays to road traffic vary considerably from day to day. This makes it difficult to predict how long a journey will take, particularly for bus users. This means either that the time allowed for a journey must be suitably greater than the average journey time or that late arrival at one's destination must be accepted from time to time.

[1] Opinion Research Centre Poll carried out for the *Evening Standard*, LT and BR into commuter attitudes (unpublished). Reported in the *Evening Standard*, 25 October to 5 November 1971.

[2] See, for example, GLC (1970), *Proof of Evidence, E12/1*, para2.8.2, GLDP Inquiry Stage 1; LB Camden (1971), *Buses in Camden, Paper S27/22*, s2.6 and fig 5, GLDP Inquiry Stage 2.

Public transport

Railway services are similarly overloaded at peak times particularly on some longer-distance BR services and on the Underground. Delays occur and passengers regularly have to travel without a seat and suffer the unpleasantness and indignity of extreme overcrowding. The problem of discomfort on the railways is emphasised by the fact that approximately two-thirds of London Transport and BR rail journeys in London are made during the peak periods. Moreover, rail journeys are often long ones —on average twice as long as those by car. At peak times, too, station concourses, lifts, escalators, subways and platforms are crowded and further delays and discomfort occur.

The case study on the south-eastern approaches (*H*) drew attention to lateness and overcrowding on BR services in that area. Figures produced by BR for the GLDP Inquiry showed that in 1970 during the morning peak period (7–9.59 a.m.) more than 10% of all arrivals at the Southern termini were over 5 minutes late. Other lines, (notably those into Liverpool Street and longer-distance commuter lines into Euston and King's Cross) showed a similar timekeeping record in 1969, although the number of trains was small compared with the Southern Region.[1] In 1971, the majority of trains arriving in central London during the morning peak hour (8.15–9.14) had standing passengers and the average load factor (passengers as a percentage of seats) was higher than 120 on some of the longer-distance trains.[2]

Despite these facts, and the readily observable conditions on the railways at peak times, the survey of commuter attitudes referred to above found that about three-quarters of rail commuters were satisfied with their method of travel to work. It was pointed out, however (from discussions with groups of commuters carried out before the survey was undertaken), that:

> Many of the major decisions a commuter takes about where he lives, his work place and his general life-style are partly based on his ability to travel between work and home. The cost and quality of this journey are factors in his decision and to this extent he feels he has committed himself to the mode he has chosen. So in a way he would be questioning his own judgement if he was not satisfied with his method of commuting. He has to justify his original decision.[3]

An indication of concern about the problems of peak travel to central London, particularly by rail, is given by the repeated calls for the staggering of working hours (see Case Study *B*), though admittedly this has often been seen as a help to the rail operators' problems referred to later as well

[1] BR Board (1970), *Proof of Evidence, E12/7*, table 4, GLDP Inquiry Stage 1.
[2] BR Board (1972), *Paper S30/76* (Amendment 1), GLDP Inquiry Stage 3.
[3] *Evening Standard*, 26 October 1971.

as a means of making commuting more agreeable. The overcrowding on certain tube lines in central London has also been a major argument in support of the new Victoria and Fleet lines (see Case Study *C*).

In contrast to peak congestion which affects all modes of travel, off-peak problems are largely confined to public transport passengers. Services are less frequent, which means (unless a reliable schedule is adhered to) longer and less predictable journey times, particularly where interchange is involved. In outer London and at night bus and train services are often so sparse that people without cars have to walk, cycle or use taxis instead. For those on shift work, this can be a serious problem and the social life of people without access to cars may also be restricted.

Some indication of dissatisfaction with public transport in London is given by the BRF opinion survey referred to near the beginning of this chapter. Table 37 suggests that unreliability of public transport services is the major deterrent to their use. The survey did not attempt to compare attitudes to different forms of public transport, but since the railways are in

REASONS GIVEN FOR NOT MAKING MORE USE OF PUBLIC TRANSPORT SERVICE	PUBLIC TRANSPORT IN ITS PRESENT FORM	PUBLIC TRANSPORT IN AN IMPROVED FORM (MORE REGULAR SERVICE)	A MORE RELIABLE BUS SERVICE
Unreliable service	55	3	4
Too expensive	26	20	13
Waiting time too long	16	3	1
Uncomfortable	10	3	3
Journey inconvenient	9	11	7
Prefer private transport	8	30	27
Journey time too long	7	2	2
Would not use it more	6	10	8
Won't get better	5	12	21
Never uses it	4	9	8
Other	14	11	14
Don't know	2	2	4

Table 37 BRF SURVEY, 1969: REASONS GIVEN FOR NOT USING PUBLIC TRANSPORT MORE

Notes: Answers are given in percentage terms; the base of the percentage is the number of respondents who answered 'No' to the question: 'Instead of having the new roads (the GLC's motorways) would you be prepared to use public transport more in (a) its present form? (b) an improved form? By that I mean a more regular service?' Or (as appropriate): 'Again, as an alternative to the new roads, would you be prepared to use buses more if the volume of cars could be reduced, thus allowing the buses to be more reliable?'

Some respondents gave more than one reason.

The figures given are those contained in the BRF Report but the form of the table has been slightly altered.

general far more reliable than the buses, it is fairly safe to assume that this particular cause of dissatisfaction related especially to the latter. Bus services, because they tend to be used for shorter trips, need to be reliable, particularly in the off-peak periods and in the outer districts where services are infrequent, yet in London they often are not. Punctuality is not so important, of course, when service frequencies are high, but few bus services in London are scheduled at intervals of less than 5 minutes, and operating difficulties can easily give rise to a 10 or 15 minute wait. To the bus passenger it is irrelevant whether this is caused by infrequency or unreliability.

A survey was carried out by the Consumers' Association in 1968 of bus passengers at 108 bus stops in different parts of London—'from the bustle of Oxford Street to the tranquillity of Valentine's Park.'[1] The figures below show that 'nearly one-third of people at bus stops got a bus in under a minute, and three-quarters got a bus in less than 5 minutes. But one in twenty-five gave up altogether' (see table). It was found that people had

WAITING TIME (MINUTES)	PERCENTAGE OF PEOPLE WAITING THIS LONG
0–1	32
1–5	44
5–10	15
10–15	3
15–20	1
20 or more	1
Went away	4
	100

to wait slightly longer at weekends than on weekdays but there was no significant difference in waiting times between peak and off-peak times. Although the percentage waiting more than 10 minutes was only 5–9%, this result—if it is representative of the 1500 million bus passengers each year—indicates a considerable problem in terms of frustration and inconvenience, especially if one allows for the number of people who never appeared at the bus stop at all, because of previous experiences of long delays.

There are several other public transport problems which should be mentioned. In certain places, bus stops are inconveniently sited in relation to 'passenger generators' such as Piccadilly Circus and Victoria station. Bus stops often have no shelters. On the railways many stations are unattractive, some may only be described as dilapidated, lacking in amenities and having poor interchange facilities (such as narrow, long subways, stairways, poor sign posting, inadequate lighting and shelter).

[1] Consumers' Association magazine *Which?*, September 1968. Survey carried out in May and July 1968.

Parking

Motorists experience considerable difficulty in finding convenient parking spaces, particularly in areas where activities are concentrated. In central London and the suburban centres especially, shoppers, commuters, shopkeepers, residents and van drivers all compete for the same scarce parking spaces. Thus, in central London, because of on-street parking controls, parking all day can be difficult, though short-term parking is easier (see Case Study *Q*). Off-street spaces are scarce in some areas and many of these are reserved for private use. Parking at home can be difficult, too, where there is little provision for parking off the street, for instance in the high-density residential areas of inner London. Motorists find that the difficulty of finding a space in on-street control areas can (because of time limits on meters) bear little relation to the amount they are prepared to pay. Prices for on- and off-street parking are often unrelated to each other. In areas not subject to parking control, short-stay parkers and residents often find that spaces are taken up by commuters' cars during the working day. This problem prevails around some railway stations in the suburbs where no special 'park and ride' provision is made (see Case Study *F*).

Dependence on travel

One aspect of life in large towns and cities is that the use of motorised forms of transport, sometimes for quite long journeys, is difficult to avoid. The majority of those working in central London must (because of the separation of homes and workplaces) commute several miles or more. For most people the choice of home and work locations is constrained by a whole host of factors not all related to the ease or cost of travel between them.[1]

Major locational decisions, once made, are often not easily changed. Consequently, reductions or withdrawals of public transport services may bring hardship in the short term and relocation of jobs or homes in the long term (see Case Study *N* with reference to the Broad Street–Richmond and Epping–Ongar services). Similarly, passengers can find themselves having to make adjustments to their style of life when fares are increased, particularly if the increases are well above the general rise in prices and incomes. Further dissatisfaction will inevitably arise if the fare increase is accompanied by a deterioration in service. (In the same way, but not necessarily to the same degree, motorists become dissatisfied if motor taxes are increased while the problems of parking and road congestion merely get worse.) In certain outer areas (e.g. parts of Stanmore and Emerson Park) the availability of public transport is so poor that people are dependent on car travel and may be virtually immobilised if they

[1] For example, house prices or rent levels, house types, family circumstances, community ties, the availability of suitable schools, shops, entertainments and other facilities, and all these things in relation to income and income expectations.

cannot afford or are not able to own a car. In such areas, a household may need two cars to satisfy its travel needs. At the other end of the scale, living in central London makes car travel difficult and relatively expensive, because of congestion and parking charges; but most activities are within easy reach on foot or by good public transport.

3 THE NATURE AND RELATIONSHIP OF MAJOR FACTORS AFFECTING THE TRANSPORT SYSTEM

To the Londoner who has daily experience of the problems and frustrations of the transport system, there are a host of questions which it seems reasonable to ask. Why, for example, are not more new roads built to relieve traffic congestion? Why, despite fare increases, are not extra trains provided to ease the overcrowding at peak hours? Why are there so few pedestrian crossings in some roads? Why are heavy lorries allowed to come into the centre of London? Why aren't more buses provided at off-peak times? and so on. In other words, why are London's transport facilities failing to meet the demands made of them? Unfortunately, there is no simple answer to this question. First, the different methods of travel are often closely related to one another so that a solution to one problem tends to have repercussions elsewhere—hence the use of the term transport *system*. Building a new railway, for example, may affect the pattern of road traffic including buses, and hence the problem of road congestion, while this in turn may affect decisions concerning new roads or parking facilities. Second, and equally important, are the reciprocal relationships which exist between the transport system and the activities which it serves. The relationships between the various elements of the transport system and, more widely, the urban system are often both subtle and complex and the current state of knowledge does not allow full comprehension, let alone manipulation of them. The next part of this chapter attempts to clarify some of these relationships under four headings: the spatial, social, operational, and economic aspects of transport.[1]

Spatial aspects

There is a reciprocal relationship between the structure of urban activities and the transport facilities which enable them to function. On the one hand the pattern of movement is determined by the density to which land is used and the degree to which activities are separated or mixed. On the other hand, these spatial relationships are influenced by the space requirements of the transport system itself. For example, it would be impossible for the hundreds of thousands of people who work in offices tightly packed together in the relatively small central area of London to live five, ten, or thirty miles away as they do without the use of highly concentrated (i.e.

[1] We concentrate here on passenger travel. The movement of goods is a problem of a very different nature.

spatially efficient) forms of travel such as railways. Different modes of transport have widely varying space requirements in relation to the function they perform, and the amount of space required is therefore one measure of the efficiency of each mode. Spatial efficiency of transport is of crucial importance in built-up areas because the supply of land is relatively fixed and transport facilities therefore compete for land with the very activities which they serve. Moreover, this competition can be considered unfair or unequal in a number of ways. The peaking of demand for transport facilities can make it difficult to justify new facilities which would be underused for most of the working day and at weekends. Also the extension of roads or surface railways requires continuous corridors of land whereas the expansion of other activities can take place on sites physically unrelated to one another.

	PARKING SPACE AT WORK OR SHOPPING DESTINATION (SQ. FT.)	APPROXIMATE SPACE PER PERSON FOR TRANSIT (WORK AND SHOPPING TRIPS)* (SQ. FT.)	CAPACITY IN USE (WORK AND SHOPPING TRIPS) (PERSONS)
Pedestrian	—	6 at 3 m.p.h.	1
Pedal cycle	10–12	36 at 15 m.p.h.	1
Bus	—	13–11 at 20 m.p.h.	55–65
Car	Min 42		
	Max 250	450–225 at 20 m.p.h.	1–2

Table 38 COMPARISON OF SPACE REQUIREMENTS OF FOUR MODES OF ROAD PASSENGER TRAVEL FOR WORK AND SHOPPING TRIPS

Note: * Assumes three times mode unit area at speeds stated

Source: Incorporating work by Paul Ritter (1964), p65

Some theoretical work has been undertaken to compare the spatial efficiency of modes. Detailed analysis has tended to concentrate on vehicular modes of travel,[1] while more comprehensive analysis (i.e. including walking and cycling) has mostly been of a general nature.[2] Table 38, while not based entirely on empirical research, serves as an example of varying transport space requirements. The car uses more space per person carried than any other mode of travel, and when occupied by one person only it can require well over ten times the space required (per person) for a pedal cycle or a well-filled bus. LT, in its comments to the GLDP Inquiry, had this to say:

[1] See, for example, J R Mayer, J E Kain and M Wohl (1963), *The Urban Transport Problem.*

[2] See, for example, P Ritter (1964), *Planning for Man and Motor.*

> In the height of the traffic peak, buses are at least twelve times more efficient than private cars in the use of road space, measured by the numbers of people carried. Annual traffic at cordon points on the road approaches to central London between 0700 and 1000 hours on Mondays to Fridays show between 1959 and 1969 an increase in cars entering the central area of 15 200 and a decrease in buses of 1200; but that the 14 000 additional vehicles carried 49 200 fewer people. Over the ten years, because of the transfer from bus to car, a rise in vehicular traffic volume of 16% (taking one bus as equal to three cars for this purpose) has been accompanied by a fall in people carried by road of 16%. These figures justify giving priority to buses on the roads, even at some inconvenience to private car traffic.[1]

Studies have also been made by R J Smeed of theoretical towns with working populations ranging from 10 000 to 5 million to determine the spatial relationships between workplace and transportation needs according to different modes of travel.[2] He assumed for this purpose that the transport routes would be located where required, that a 1.5 car occupancy rate would operate, that space per worker was 100 square feet and that car parking required 200 square feet per space at ground level and 29 square feet (of ground space) in a sixteen storey multi-level car park. Smeed's calculations do not include shopping, social or commercial trips which would in practice inflate the demand for transport space. Table 39 shows Smeed's calculations for town centres with a working population of 100 000 and 1 million. It illustrates the devastating spatial effect of universal private car usage and shows that the *proportion* of the central area devoted to roads and parking increases with the size of the town.

Smeed and Buchanan[3] and others have arrived at the conclusion that, because of this spatial effect, full motorisation in the larger towns and cities is not feasible without extensive use of multi-level development. Los Angeles is often cited as an example of a city where immense efforts have been made by the provision of roads and car parks to satisfy the appetite of the car for city space. Yet even there, more than half the journeys to work (in the centre) in the early 1960s were made by public transport.[4] It is clear that the motor-car is by far the most space-consuming mode of transport. Buses and trains require far less space in relation to their carrying capacity and (in the case of railways) speed, whilst walking and cycling are the most economical of space. The quickest way to move 10 000 people at one time from Charing Cross to Leicester Square is to let them walk: put them in cars and most of them could never arrive.

These simple facts have important implications for both land use and

[1] LT (1970), *Proof of Evidence, E12/2*, para21, GLDP Inquiry Stage 1.

[2] R J Smeed *The Traffic Problem in Towns*, Manchester Statistical Society, 1961, pp27–33.

[3] C D Buchanan (1963), *Traffic in Towns*, HMSO, p94.

[4] P Johnson-Marshall (1966), *Rebuilding Cities*, p58.

COMMUTERS' TRANSPORT IN CENTRAL AREA	TYPE OF PARKING	WORKING POPULATION IN TOWN CENTRE: 100 000				1 MILLION			
		RADIUS OF CENTRAL AREA (MILES)	PERCENTAGE OF GROUND AREA DEVOTED TO			RADIUS OF CENTRAL AREA (MILES)	PERCENTAGE OF GROUND AREA DEVOTED TO		
			CARRIAGE WAY	PARKING	WORK		CARRIAGE WAY	PARKING	WORK
Urban railway	—	0.34	0.6	0	99.4	1.08	2.0	0	98.0
Bus on narrow urban streets	—	0.35	4.0	0	96.0	1.15	13.0	0	87.0
Car on urban motorway	Multi-level	0.37	6.0	11.0	83.0	1.25	17.0	10.0	73.0
Car on urban motorway	Ground level	0.53	4.0	55.0	41.0	1.75	13.0	50.0	37.0
Car on narrow urban streets	Multi-level	0.52	26.0	8.0	66.0	1.79	60.0	5.0	35.0
Car on narrow urban streets	Ground level	0.57	19.0	47.0	34.0	2.24	47.0	30.0	23.0

Table 39 COMPARISON OF LAND USES IN CENTRAL AREAS OF TWO THEORETICAL TOWNS ACCORDING TO MODE OF TRAVEL TO WORK

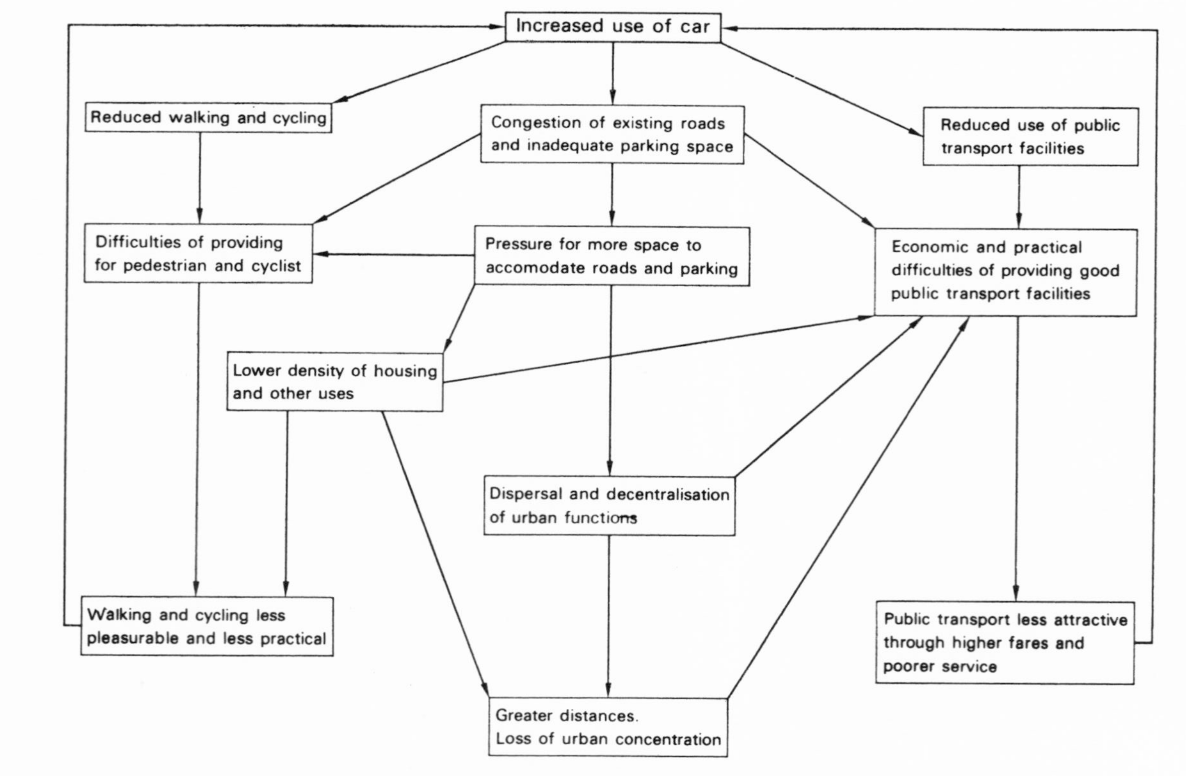

Figure 23 SOME EFFECTS OF INCREASED USE OF THE CAR

transport planning. If the space used for transport increases (as a result of growth either in total travel or in travel by car) then for a given population the overall density of land use will be lowered and the degree of concentration will be reduced. Some important effects of increased use of the private car on urban form are shown in diagrammatic form in Figure 23. It is this reciprocal effect between transport and urban structure that makes it so important to plan land use and transport together.

There is, however, little information on the kind of urban forms best suited to different modes or different patterns of travel. Some general comments can be made, however, in respect of three scales of planning. At the regional scale, the role of transport is to provide links between separate villages, towns and cities. The size and interdependence of these settlements, and the distances between them, are some of the factors that will determine the demand for transport in the region. In turn the quality of transport facilities will influence their degree of interdependence and growth.

Concern at the regional scale, then, is principally with inter-urban travel. One of the prime aims of the new towns was to produce communities with a high degree of 'self-containment' for employment, social and recreational purposes, i.e. that did not generate heavy flows of traffic into London. More recently, the South-East Joint Planning Team tried to relate future population growth in the South-East to the available (or readily provided) capacity of the region's roads and railways. The expansion of urban development in south Hampshire, at Milton Keynes, Northampton, Wellingborough, in the Blackwater Valley and in south Essex was intended to create 'counter magnets' to London on an even larger scale.[1] Ray Thomas has stressed that the post-war new towns have a small percentage of people living in them but working elsewhere; they therefore stand in strong contrast to towns such as Southend and the Medway Towns, many of whose population work in London thus generating considerable inter-urban travel at peak times.[2]

At the other two scales—crudely, city and local—the principal relationship between activity and transport patterns is concerned with intra-urban travel (the larger the town, the greater the proportion of intra-urban trips in total travel). Recently, some consideration has been given to the possibility of restructuring urban land use as a way of alleviating transport problems (see, for example, Case Study *D*, Development at Stations), though this involves a long process of modifying the existing structure by controlling new development and redevelopment. At the local scale, the relationship between urban structure and transport focuses more on the detailed arrangement and design of buildings and the use to which they are put. An illustration of this relationship is provided by Runcorn New Town which is planned to accommodate 100 000 people around a segregated

[1] SEJPT (1970), *Strategic Plan for the South-East; A Framework*, HMSO.
[2] See R Thomas (1969), *London's New Towns* (PEP Broadsheet No.510), for an examination of this concept of self-containment.

busway system as an alternative to the roads for general traffic. 'The presence of the Busway is such that it can be detected in the design of almost everything constructed within the new town, whether it be a factory estate, a housing area or a shopping centre.'[1] In order to encourage use of the busway the industrial estates have been arranged so that communal parking places are usually farther away from the factories than the busway stops (i.e. outside individual factory curtilages). In the layout of the residential areas, stops are sited to be as convenient as private garages and most houses are well under 500 yards away from the nearest busway stop. The shopping and community centres for each housing area are arranged around bus stops forming a natural focus for pedestrian activity and the most convenient picking up and setting down points for passengers. As far as possible these stops and the footpaths leading to them are under cover. By this means it is hoped to serve 50% of all internal movement in the town by bus.

Although a new town situation is very different from that of existing built-up areas in a vast city like London, the Runcorn example does draw attention to the design implications of planning for the use of a particular mode of travel. It provides an interesting comparison, for example, with the transport considerations used in the design of Thamesmead (see Case Study *A*) and suggests an alternative to planning layouts and building designs in redevelopment areas which encourage the use of the car. The design of urban areas at the local scale is not only relevant to the operational requirements of bus or rail systems. The density of development and the degree of mixture of land uses will also greatly influence the ability to make journeys on foot or by pedal cycle, and hence the demand for motorised travel whether public or private.

Social Aspects

The mobility of the population is related to the different characteristics of each mode of travel. Walking, for example, is practical only for short trips while cycling is reserved for the fit and healthy; the railways in London provide mainly for radial trips; buses are a universal mode of transport. Use of the car is restricted to those who can afford to buy one, or have one by virtue of their job, and who are able to drive. Statistics indicate that about 40% of the population (of both Greater London and England and Wales) is either under driving age or over 65.[2] Public transport for journeys beyond walking distance is therefore necessary if large sections of the population are not to be virtually immobile.

The spatial conflict between the car and urban structure is again important in the social context since the land-use pattern most suited to car travel is low density and dispersed. Public transport requires higher densi-

[1] Runcorn Development Corporation and Crosville Motor Services Ltd (1972), *Runcorn Busway booklet.*

[2] Based on tables from the 1966 Sample Census.

ties and concentrations of development, and walking requires a mixture of land uses in order to keep distances between activities short. Thus, as more provision is made for the car, the other modes of travel become less effective. Travel by car also adversely affects public transport by reducing the number of revenue-paying passengers, especially in off-peak hours when the marginal cost of carrying them is very low. It seems undeniable, then, that the mobility of a large part of the population depends on modes whose needs are in direct conflict with those of the private car. Even when every *household* can afford a car, provision for the cars at the expense of the other modes can deprive over half the *population* of efficient transport, and it will be many years before all London households can afford a car.

London has by no means reached the position of some American cities where so much traffic has been drawn away from the buses and trains that those services have virtually disappeared, and the roads are severely congested in spite of huge road-building programmes; the poor, the elderly, housewives and children in one-car families have to put up with expensive, infrequent or non-existent public transport and thus become members of a newly identified group—'the transportation poor.' In Los Angeles, for example, ownership of a car is often the prerequisite for being able to get a job.[1] In England similar signs are beginning to appear in rural areas where railway services no longer exist and bus services are under continual threat because they cannot be operated without operating subsidies.[2] London's services are generally much better than this, but there are some low-density areas where bus routes are sparse and services infrequent, and housewives rely on the car being available.

Operational aspects

Since the relative use of various modes of travel (the 'modal split') is of great importance to the physical form of the city and to its transport problems, what are the factors that influence the modal split?

Of those determining which journeys can be made on foot and bicycle, distance is probably the most important. A study in Gothenburg in Sweden found that the willingness to walk decreases constantly from 300–400 metres, and virtually ceases at about 1000 metres,[3] though the Southwark survey referred to earlier found that people often walked somewhat greater distances for leisure and shopping purposes. No such observations have been made of cycling.

In London, buses tend to be used for shorter journeys than the car, while the railways cater for the longest trips. This reflects how the time dis-

[1] See State of California Business and Transportation Agency (1970), *Los Angeles Transportation—Employment Project Interim Final Report*, esp pp4–8, 41–8.
[2] See, for example, articles by D Gray in the *Guardian*, 2 and 3 February 1970.
[3] O Lovemark (1970), 'Study of Accepted Distances by Pedestrians; Study of 8000 Interviews Carried out in Central Business District of Gothenburg,' Sweden 1965, *Proceedings of the Second Technology Assessment Review*, OECD.

advantage of the railways relative to the car *diminishes* as the trip length increases (through walking, waiting and interchange times), whereas the time disadvantage of the stage bus (because of frequent stops) *increases* relative to the private car[1] and the railway. Table 40 shows the average length of journeys to work by motorised transport in London (shown separately for workers in car-owning and non car-owning households).

Different average trip lengths are to be found for other purposes, although in general the *relationship* between the modes is the same. Other activities tend to be more dispersed in time and space so that it is not so easy for buses and trains to cater for them: shopping trips, although concentrated in directional flows and traditionally the preserve of public transport, may be undertaken by car if bulky or heavy goods have to be carried.

	CAR-OWNING HOUSEHOLDS (MILES)	NON CAR-OWNING HOUSEHOLDS (MILES)
Car	4.4	4.5*
Bus	2.8	2.7
LT rail	7.1	5.7
BR	9.7	7.9
All modes (excluding walking and cycling)	4.9	4.0

Table 40[2] AVERAGE LENGTH OF JOURNEY TO WORK IN LONDON

*Note:** Includes both drivers and passengers

The railway's inherent advantage lies in the fact that it uses a segregated track and is, therefore, unlike the bus or car, free from interruption by other traffic. Average speeds of 25 m.p.h. including stopping times are fairly common throughout the system while road traffic speeds often drop below 15 m.p.h. particularly in central London. Scheduled speeds for buses in 1970 were 8 m.p.h. in the central area and 12 m.p.h. elsewhere, though these were often not achieved.[3] Proposals for bus lanes and automated guidance systems for vehicles are an attempt to obtain the value of segregated or regimented flow conditions.

Direction can also be an important influence on the mode of travel chosen. In London the easiest journeys are generally those in a radial direction since most of London's main roads and railways converge on the centre. For many journeys (though not necessarily work journeys or others

[1] It is usually found that the speed of buses is about 3 m.p.h. slower than that of other road traffic. For example, LB Camden (1971), *Buses in Camden: a Study of Bus Segregation in the Centre of London, Paper S27/223*, pp16, 29, GLDP Inquiry Stage 2.

[2] GLC (1970), *Proof of Evidence, E12/1*, table 2.16, p40, GLDP Inquiry Stage 1.

[3] GLC (1970), *Proof of Evidence, E12/1*, para7.6.2, GLDP Inquiry Stage 1.

which are made frequently) which do not relate to the pattern of roads or bus routes, the car shows its particular advantage of door-to-door travel without interchange, and freedom of route.

The time of day when journeys are made is also important because of the peaking of travel demand. Congestion on the roads (quite apart from shortages of parking space) makes the railway the quickest mode at peak times especially for longer journeys, but when roads are not congested, the balance swings more in favour of the car. Other factors also fluctuate with the time of day as we have already seen; in particular the comfort, availability and reliability of public transport services and the predictability of journey times—especially on the roads. Age, health and disability can greatly influence choice of mode: not everyone can drive a car; not everyone can walk or cycle.

Economic aspects

Another factor determining the choice of mode is price. Consideration of the transport system as a whole, moreover, requires an understanding of the costs of a journey both to the traveller and to the rest of the community.

Transport (including walking) like air, water and shelter, is essential to everyone. As societies become more specialised, transport becomes increasingly important. Most people have an unavoidable need to make regular journeys to work, to shop, to find entertainment and recreation, to visit friends and to attend to personal matters. Everyone is also dependent on transport for the supply of goods and services. With the exception of walking, no one mode of transport is absolutely essential, but the size of the city, and consequently the length of many journeys, makes some form of vehicular transport essential for most people. The various vehicular modes are in competition with one another, and thereby the transport 'market' reveals its major imperfection. This is that public and private transport, even when offering a broadly comparable service in terms of journey time and convenience, are paid for in entirely different ways.

Private transport is paid for largely in lump sums. Once the purchase price of a car, road tax and insurance have been met the motorist is virtually free to use any road at any time for any purpose, subject of course to traffic regulations and parking controls. Petrol tax is roughly related to journey distance, but a tank of petrol will take the motorist in any direction at any time of the day, and petrol usually accounts for much less than half of the total cost of running a car.[1] The fixed payments are spread over the total distance travelled before the next payment has to be made; it is therefore in the motorist's financial interest to make as many of his journeys as possible by car. As the motorist pays virtually the same wherever and whenever he travels, he has no financial incentive to relate the use of

[1] The GLC, for example, have said that petrol costs for a 1000 cc car running 10 000 miles p.a. account for one-quarter of total costs. GLC (1971), *Paper B486*, p44, GLDP Inquiry Stage 1.

his car to the cost of providing the roads on which he is driving. Therefore, if (as has probably been the case for many years) the total revenue from motor and fuel tax covers the total cost of providing and maintaining roads,[1] then motorists pay too much when driving on country lanes which are cheap to provide, and too little when driving on congested urban roads which are comparatively expensive.

The indirect methods of payment for private motoring result in the costs as perceived by the motorist being well below the actual costs of the journey he makes. A study carried out of 100 families in the Newcastle-under-Lyme area[2] found that car owners consistently underestimated the cost of car

BUS

Operating cost: 2.0p per passenger mile

FARES	STANDARD AND INNER ZONES	
1 mile	2.5p	Average 2.5p per mile
2 miles	5.0p	
3 miles	7.5p	
4 miles	10.0p	

(Red Arrow 4p flat rate)

Source: LT Executive

RAIL

Operating cost: 1.5p per passenger mile (LT)

	SINGLE			QUARTERLY SEASON*		
FARES (PENCE)	LT STANDARD	LT INNER	BR	LT STANDARD	LT INNER	BR
2 miles	5	5	7	4.7	4.8	5.2
5 miles	10	15	11	7.8	8.9	8.2
10 miles	20	20	19	13.0	14.0	13.9
20 miles	30	30	36	21.4	22.0	23.1

Table 41 OPERATING COSTS AND FARE STRUCTURES OF BUS AND RAIL SERVICES IN LONDON, 1970

* Based on 250 return trips p.a.

Note: The LT inner zone is that bounded by the Circle Line. The standard zone covers the rest of the system

[1] The BRF estimated that in 1969 road user taxes (fuel tax, licence duties, purchase tax on vehicles) totalled £1582 million whereas £533 million was spent by central government and local authorities on roads. This expenditure did not include road maintenance, policing and other non-construction costs.

[2] C S Riley (1970), 'A Motivational Inquiry into Car Use,' *Tr Eng and Control*, 12, pp192–3. It was noted that a complementary survey carried out for the MOT produced identical findings.

travel, largely because they ignored vehicle depreciation costs. The study concluded that 'from the gross underestimates which were made regarding cost per mile and the very few occasions on which depreciation was mentioned, it would seem that motorists try to forget many of the costs of car ownership.' It found that 'car owners are relatively indifferent to the costs of car ownership. Once bought, the car is something to be used . . . and used very intensively.'

Payment for public transport services is, and always has been, organised on an entirely different basis and more closely related not only to the total cost of providing the services but also to the cost of individual journeys. This is particularly so with fares paid for each journey on a graduated scale according to distance travelled but much less so, of course, where flat fares, season tickets or other methods of payment are used. Generally speaking, however, the public transport user is more aware of the cost to himself of each individual journey than is the car user.

Table 41 gives as an example bus and rail operation costs and fares on LT and BR services in 1970, and shows the proximity between fares and average costs per passenger mile. Public transport fares also include an element of capital costs, the actual proportion depending on grants for capital investment and the extent of revenue from other sources (e.g. advertising).

So far only the demand for travel and some of the factors which influence it have been discussed; it is equally important to examine the supply of transport facilities. It has been suggested that virtually all the problems of London's transport system (such as those described in the first section of this chapter) stem from an imbalance between the supply of facilities and the demand for them. It is certainly true that more people attempt to use the railways in peak hours than the railway services can comfortably accommodate, and similarly that more *vehicles* squeeze onto the available roads than would be necessary for rapid and even flow, safety and so on. With most consumer goods when demand increases, supply is increased to satisfy that demand or, if extra supply is limited for some reason, prices are increased so that demand is limited. What is it about urban transport which has excluded it from all but the crudest forms of control by the price mechanism? The key problem is the shortage of space in built-up areas and the fact that transport competes for this space with the very facilities it serves. The more intensive other activities become (e.g. towards the city centre) the greater the opportunity costs of using the space occupied by them for transport. Once a road or railway reaches capacity it becomes extremely costly to expand—even for a few extra people (see reference to Borough Market Junction, Case Study *H*).

The demand for travel has, however, not been limited by price at the very places and times where it is most costly to satisfy, because the marginal cost of providing extra capacity has not been charged. LT calculated in 1970 that it cost them 25p per passenger mile to put on an extra bus at peak times whilst they received only 2½p per passenger mile in fares

(fares are related to average cost, not marginal cost, see Table 41).[1] Yet according to an earlier study every passenger mile they lose to the car represents a net loss to the community of about 25p because of the extra congestion costs created.[2]

Many factors have worked against a closer relation of transport prices to transport costs: successive governments have attempted to hold fares at a reasonable (i.e. politically acceptable) level, if necessary by subsidy; free use of the roads has been accepted as an inalienable right; fares have been standardised as between different routes and even between buses and trains for various reasons including simplicity in use of the system and social equitability; cheap fares have been used to encourage development in certain areas (e.g. workmen's fares to Walthamstow and clerk's fares on the Great Northern Line in the nineteenth century, season ticket promotion to the North Kent and Sussex coasts in the 1930s and to Buckinghamshire and Berkshire in recent years).

There is, however, a further major gap between the price of transport facilities and their costs if social costs are included. Social costs are imposed by travellers on other members of the community (apart from the transport authorities), in other words the 'external costs' of transport. Economists distinguish two main kinds of social cost in transport. The first is congestion cost. As the amount of traffic on a road increases and it becomes congested, each vehicle contributes to the delay and wasted fuel, loss of passenger time, etc., of the other vehicles on the road and so creates a cost which, it has been argued, should be included in the price paid by the road user.[3]

Second, there are the environmental costs caused by the use of transport facilities, particularly roads. If, for example, when an aircraft flew over London at night each person disturbed by its noise were to be paid 1p by the airlines in compensation for their loss of sleep, then the cost of night air travel might become so prohibitive as to be eliminated altogether. But the nuisance caused by aircraft and vehicles is not paid for in this way: the noise, dirt and fumes from cars, buses, trains and aeroplanes are created without any cost to those making the journey but they are suffered by the community as a whole.

There may be a third element of social cost where people transfer from buses or trains to the car. If (as has often been the case) a community has developed on the basis of (for example) a bus service then passengers who desert that bus service may leave behind a cost for the remaining passengers to pay, either in the form of higher fares or poorer service, or as a cost to the community as a whole if the service has to be maintained through a subsidy.

[1] National Board for Prices and Incomes, *Report No. 159 London Transport Fares* (1970), Cmnd 4540, p13.
[2] National Board for Prices and Incomes, *Report No.112, Proposals by the London Transport Board for Fares Increases* (1969), Cmnd 4036, app3.
[3] See, for example, G Roth (1967), *Paying for Roads.*

	WOOD GREEN STATION		TURNPIKE LANE STATION	
	ON	OFF	ON	OFF
LT bus				
0815–0915	757	1980	1666	2553
1715–1815	1970	688	1874	961
LT tube				
0815–0915	3194	455	3512	413
1215–1315	250	220	200	240
1715–1815	579	2993	627	4735

Table 42 PASSENGER FLOWS AT TWO SUBURBAN INTERCHANGES

Source: LT Executive Survey, 1969

Before leaving the subject of supply and demand it is important to emphasise that imbalance between the two occurs mainly at certain times and places on the transport system, due to the uneven distribution of demand for transport. Demand is higher near centres of activity such as central London and suburban town centres so that transport facilities are more heavily used as one approaches these areas. The biggest differences, however, arise from the peaking of demand by time of day, related mainly to the journey to work. Transport systems (highways, bus services, and railways) are designed on the basis of sufficient capacity to cope with the demand during peak hours. This 'lumpiness' of demand requiring the use of expensive resources, fixed equipment, rolling stock and staff is of crucial significance for the economic efficiency of the transport system as a whole and particularly public transport services. The main problem arises from the fact that massive amounts of capital equipment (roads, railways and

	1956	1961	1966	1971	% CHANGE 56/71 TOTAL	(av p.a.)	% CHANGE 66/71 TOTAL	(av p.a.)
1 Peak a.m.	7140	6420	6220	5460	−24	(−1.6)	−13	(−2.4)
2 0930–1600	—	4140	4010	3465	−31	(−2.0)	−14	(−2.7)
3 Peak p.m.	7210	6540	6240	5467	−24	(−1.6)	−12	(−2.5)
4 Early evening	4100	3600	2950	2450	−40	(−2.7)	−17	(−3.5)
5 Late evening	3960	3080	2870	2330	−41	(−2.7)	−19	(−3.8)
6 (2) as % of (3)	69	63	64	63				
7 (4) as % of (3)	57	48	47	45				

Table 43 NUMBER OF LT BUSES IN SERVICE BY TIME OF DAY, 1956–71

Source: LT data (see also Table 11)

	1949	1962	1967	1969	% CHANGE 49–69	% CHANGE 62–69
LT buses	180	153	124	105	−42	−31
LT tubes	418	318	308	314	−25	−1

Table 44 PRODUCTIVITY OF LT OPERATING STAFF, 1949–69 (000 PASSENGER MILES PER MEMBER OF OPERATING STAFF)

Sources: R Thomas (1968): and LT *Annual Report and Accounts* (1969)

vehicles of all sorts) and labour (which accounts for roughly three-quarters of the total costs of public transport provision) are grossly under-used outside the two to four hours of the peak periods. Moreover, many peak-hour flows are unidirectional—for example, into central London in the morning and out again in the evening, and on both road and rail only a limited amount of traffic management is possible to provide 'reversible' lanes or tracks. Table 42 illustrates this 'tidal' nature of peak traffic at two suburban bus–underground interchanges on the LT system. Tables 11 and 43 show that only about 45% and 60% of LT rail rolling stock and buses respectively are in service between the peaks and in the evening respectively as compared with the maximum utilisation that occurs in the evening peak period. The number of buses in service has been steadily reduced but proportionately more so during the day time and evening off-peak periods. The number of buses operating in the evenings was only 45% of the peak service in 1971 compared with 57% in 1956.

Between 1951 and 1967 the number of passengers on LT buses declined by 59% in off-peak periods compared with 32% in the peak. On the tubes peak travel increased by 11% while off-peak travel fell by 24%.[1] This decline in off-peak use of public transport means that the costs of running the system, which are largely determined by the cost of maintaining the peak services, have to be met (in so far as they are met from passenger revenues) from a declining number of passengers. The main reason for this off-peak decline in demand has been the increasing ownership and use of cars but television has also been a major factor and has eroded the number going to cinemas, theatres, spectator sports and other communal events. Since the capacity of the system is determined by the peak, it is available for use in the off-peak (even if underused) at little extra cost. Moreover, there is a need to maintain a fairly regular service throughout the day if worthwhile passenger loadings are to be attracted. Individual buses or trains which are uneconomic cannot in many cases be withdrawn without disproportionate repercussions on the economy of the route as a whole. Consequently services have not been reduced proportionately to the fall in passengers. This is reflected in the productivity of LT's labour force which fell by about 40% on the buses and 25% on the tubes between 1949 and 1969 (see Table 44).

[1] R Thomas (1968), *Journeys to Work* (Planning XXXIV, No.504), table 1, p346.

POLICY OPTIONS FOR TACKLING LONDON'S TRANSPORT PROBLEM

The choices open in practice to policy makers do not always include the full range of those theoretically available. There is an obvious necessity to keep within the limits of financial and other resources and within the limits of technological feasibility. There are also political constraints such as the willingness of the public to accept particular measures. This section outlines the main policy options for tackling the transport problem in London under the following heads:

Land-use plans
Road building
Traffic management
Parking controls
Pricing and regulation of vehicles
Development of urban railways
Development of bus transport
Operating subsidies
Fares
Technical innovation.

Land-use plans

Since the function of transport is to link activities, the pattern of land use can be considered a basic 'input' of the transport system. Land-use planning is not concerned solely with planning transport but the two cannot be pursued in isolation. The basis of land-use planning is the control of the form, density and type of development and this can be applied at the regional, city and local scales. Land-use policies in London must begin with the city as it stands and the way in which its structure is changing. The most concentrated development occurs in the city centre which is linked by road and rail with other less dense parts of the city. If the city centre is to remain strong there is a strict limit on the amount of access to it which can be allowed by car. There is a simple choice to be made between a dense and diverse city centre served mainly by public transport and one in which activities give way to space for increased access by car. There is very little room for compromise in making this choice since even a relatively small increase in the proportion of travel to and within the centre by car is sufficient to congest the roads and undermine the efficiency of the bus services. 'Between 1955 and 1965 on routes into the central area even during the morning peak, 29 000 extra cars carrying 39 000 people took the place of 1900 buses but occupied five times as much road space. Although the number of passenger road vehicles entering the area rose by 30%, 17% fewer people came by road.'[1] Thomas has shown that between 1952 and

[1] MOT (1968), *Transport in London*, Cmnd 3686, para37.

1967 road traffic (in vehicle units entering central London) rose by almost 50% while travellers fell by 20% resulting in a fall in the efficiency of road use to 54% of the 1952 level.[1]

If the rail and bus systems are to maintain a sufficient level of passenger use to keep unit costs to a level which can reasonably be met from fare revenues, they must be able to collect passengers from relatively dense suburban areas concentrated in corridor fashion along the bus routes and around the railway stations. A decision to maintain the importance of the city centre therefore implies a decision to maintain a structure for the rest of the city which is based on a mainly radial public transport system. The detailed form and density of the residential areas will depend on a host of factors including the 'thresholds' of service provision either in terms of the frequency of service or the type of vehicle. For instance, minibuses, single-deck buses, double-deck buses and eight- and twelve-car trains all require different levels of traffic generation to support them. In drawing up a structure plan for the city as a whole similar decisions have to be made regarding many suburban town centres. If shopping, employment and other facilities are maintained (or provided) in these centres they may retain a degree of local self-containment. This can reduce the base load of travel to the city centre as well as providing a focus for community life other than the city centre. The strength of suburban centres does, however, depend on the maintenance of good public transport access to them. A higher degree of private car access to them is possible than to the city centre but the nature of conflict between concentrated development and car access is the same. The difference is one of scale rather than one of kind.

The alternative to a concentrated city centre with a diverse range of activities is either to allow a general dispersal of employment and other facilities (to suburban centres of similar size and specialised function or to scattered sites throughout the city) or selective dispersal. Gains in space could either be used to allow an increase in accessibility by private car (by loosening the density of the remaining functions) or to develop housing. Again, there is a similar choice to be made with regard to the suburban centres. Efforts could be made to increase densities along roads leading to town centres and to the stations on the main radial railway system. This would facilitate the provision of an effective public transport system. Alternatively densities could be lowered and smaller centres created in order to maximise the provision for travel by private car, though some form of public transport will always be necessary if a substantial proportion of the suburban population is not to be relatively immobile. This latter choice would mean either the outward spread of London or the accommodation of some of its population beyond the Green Belt.

A further choice is whether land uses should be zoned in homogeneous units or mixed. One of the early aims of planning was to segregate industry from residential areas. This has evolved into a planning philosophy which seeks to designate a dominant function to each area and then to control

[1] Thomas (1968), pp335–419.

development so as to eliminate 'non-conforming' uses particularly when comprehensive redevelopment occurs. Now that industry is considerably less noxious than it used to be and an increasing proportion of employment is in non-manufacturing businesses (e.g. in service industry and office employment), the original reasons for strict zoning have largely disappeared. The importance for transport is that, other things being equal, predominant-use zoning increases the average distance between homes and other activities. While these increases may be small—to be measured perhaps in hundreds of yards rather than miles—they can radically influence the extent to which journeys can be made on foot or by bicycle. (These modes as we have seen are particularly sensitive to distance.) Zoning therefore may increase the base load of demand for vehicular transport while mixed development can reduce it.

Road building

In existing built-up areas the main purpose of road building, and the one to which most road-building policies have so far been directed, is to provide for an increase in road capacity which mainly allows for a greater amount of travel by car. Exceptions to this are where new roads are required for access to redevelopment areas (such as London's dockland) or new development (such as Thamesmead). There may also be circumstances in which a new road caters mainly for commercial traffic or buses or replaces a road which is given over to pedestrians.

Building roads in London becomes progressively more costly towards the centre. Construction and especially property acquisition costs generally

PROPOSAL	COSTS PROPERTY (£M)	WORKS (£M)	TOTAL (£M)	APPROX AREA OF LAND REQUIRED (ACRES)	APPROX AVERAGE COST OF LAND (WITH PROPERTY) PER ACRE (£)
Ringway 1	144	336	480	1048	137 405
Ringway 2	85	334	419	1227	69 275
Ringway 3	26	180	206	2800	9 285
Radials	55	236	291	1095	50 230
Total	310	1086	1396	6170	—

Table 45 COSTS OF GLDP MOTORWAY PROPOSALS 1970

Source: GLDP Inquiry, *Proof E12/1*, table 6.5

Note: The East Cross Route, the Dover Radial route Parkway East and the Chiswick interchange are not included. The figures make no allowance for land or property beyond that required for the highways themselves

increase with the density of development. Table 45, for example, shows the relatively high cost of the two inner ringways proposed in the GLDP (Ringways 1 and 2) compared with Ringway 3 and the radial motorways. It is also more difficult or more costly to avoid the adverse environmental effects of new or enlarged roads in the inner parts of the city. New roads rarely improve the immediate environment through which they pass. Environmental problems can be overcome or minimised by tunnelling or cut-and-cover-construction or by the redevelopment in a suitable way of the areas adjacent to the new roads, but these measures are invariably costly. A committee set up by the Department of the Environment (DOE) to investigate urban motorways concluded that they have been built 'on the cheap' because environmental treatment has not been carried out, or because owners of property adversely affected have not been adequately compensated[1] and there has been a great deal of public dissatisfaction about this.

There is a number of alternative methods of providing for an increase in road capacity, and choices will depend on the speed, volume and direction of traffic and the length and purpose of journeys involved. Where large increases in capacity are required urban motorways can be the cheapest way of providing for them. Their capacity will depend on the number of lanes and the speed of traffic on them. They are meant to serve mainly longer-distance traffic because their design requires relatively few intersections. Their ability to increase the overall speed or the number of intra-urban trips depends, however, on their relationship with the existing road network on which all journeys begin and end. In London the provision of even four-lane motorways will usually require the simultaneous expansion of capacity on the existing roads to enable traffic to enter and leave the motorways. The larger the increase in capacity provided on new motorways, the larger the increases on the existing roads will need to be. If this complementary capacity is not provided the motorways themselves will not operate to their full capacity and the accesses to them will be congested.

New roads, however, do not have to be built to motorway standards. Non-motorway roads are less damaging to the environment because tighter curves, steeper gradients, the absence of 'hard shoulders' and smaller interchanges make it easier to fit them into the existing urban structure. They can also (with frequent links with existing roads) serve shorter-distance trips.

Whatever form they take, there are several possibilities for the pattern of the road network. Geometric patterns have sometimes been proposed such as a grid pattern (which is often preferred in traffic engineering terms) or a ring and radial pattern (as proposed in the GLDP). Increased access to the city centre by car would require the provision of new or widened radial routes, while inter-suburban car movement would require increased capacity in an orbital direction as well.

Policies aimed at the dispersal of activities or lower densities in order to

[1] *The Times*, 29 November 1971.

facilitate travel by car require the provision of new road capacity. Conversely the provision of new roads, particularly orbital (or inter-suburban) ones can encourage the dispersal of activities away from concentrated centres and established radial public transport routes. The maintenance of a strong city centre and the dispersal of activities elsewhere in the city underlay the London proposals for a ring and radial system of motorways outside the central area.[1]

An alternative to building new roads is to increase the capacity of existing ones, although the gains in capacity may be smaller in relation to the costs incurred. Whole lengths of road can be increased by providing extra lanes at signal-controlled junctions (as proposed on the A1—see Case Study *K*), roundabouts (e.g. Wandsworth bridge southern approach, the Angel), flyovers or underpasses (e.g. Old Kent Road, Euston Road). These methods are invariably costly and environmentally damaging, particularly where frontage properties are involved. Increasing the capacity of existing main roads is particularly damaging in shopping centres where the conflict between local activities (particularly pedestrian movement) and traffic passing through is inevitably heightened.

A third alternative is to build new small-scale (i.e. non-motorway) roads in selected locations in order to facilitate more journeys by car in particular localities. Such roads could also be built to divert traffic out of shopping and residential areas in order to improve their environment without substantially increasing the total amount of traffic. But this can be done only if traffic management or other measures are taken to secure the environmental gains on the 'relieved' routes. In London many plans for town centre redevelopment incorporate new 'by-pass' roads and the creation of pedestrian or bus only shopping precincts. Examples are Putney, Kingston, Wood Green, Bromley, Lewisham, Greenwich and Harrow, but the opportunities for building such relief roads which do not create environmental problems of their own will be limited, particularly in inner and central London. The important question is whether the gains in environment in one place will be offset by losses in another.

Any of the roadbuilding options described will, if they are designed to increase the amount of vehicular traffic, make conditions more difficult and possibly more dangerous for pedestrians and cyclists unless special provision is made for them. Segregation from motor traffic is the only sure way of improving the safety of pedestrians and cyclists but this is difficult or costly to achieve without at the same time inconveniencing them with subways or bridges. Provision for increased motor traffic will also probably result in a greater number of road casualties. New roads and traffic management schemes which reduce the number of conflicting traffic movements can help to reduce the accident *rate* but consequent increases in

[1] See J Hillman (ed) (1971), *Planning in London*, pp79–85. John Blake criticised the GLDP for proposing to concentrate development in strategic town centres without improving access to them, while proposing the ring and radial motorway system to provide for projected dispersed movement patterns.

total traffic can lead to a greater *number* of accidents. The GLC has said that its motorway proposals could reduce the death rate on the roads in London from twenty-one in 1962 to nineteen in 1981 per year for each daily million vehicle miles.[1] The same proposals, however, were expected to provide for more than double the 1962 level of traffic. The effects on the total number of road deaths could therefore be as follows:

	DAILY MILLION VEHICLE MILES	ANNUAL FATALITIES PER DAILY MVM	TOTAL DEATHS PER ANNUM (APPROX)
1962 (without motorways)	23.4	21	490
1981 (with motorways)	50.0 (projected)	19	950

Traffic management

Measures to control and order the movement of road traffic can be applied to achieve a variety of purposes. The earlier and simpler forms such as the 'rule of the road,' designated stopping places for buses, traffic signals, speed limits and pedestrian crossings were primarily aimed at safer and more orderly movement of traffic, but with increasing volumes of traffic in urban areas emphasis shifted to methods of easing congestion. Notable in London were the series of schemes carried out mainly in the central area by the London Traffic Management Unit in the early 1960s. These included the creation of one-way flows using parallel streets (the Tottenham Court Road–Gower Street and Baker Street–Gloucester Place schemes are well known examples) or the turning of squares into (in effect) large roundabouts (Russell Square and Parliament Square for instance).

One-way streets are now common throughout central and inner London and in many suburban centres and their ability to produce further capacity increase is probably limited. The effectiveness of some schemes genuinely to increase road capacity rather than merely ease the flow of traffic or shift congestion from one place to another has also been called into doubt.[2] Moreover, such schemes have usually led to considerable deterioration of the environment by deliberately routing traffic through previously quiet streets. Buses have also suffered from extra mileage and diversion away from main passenger-generating activities.

Other measures to improve the flow of vehicular traffic include the banning of turning movements, prohibition of parking on main roads at peak hours (e.g. the 200 miles of 'clearways,' as they are known, introduced in 1967–68), box junctions, 'green wave' signals, reversible traffic lanes (e.g. Albert Bridge) and signal-controlled rather than zebra crossings for pedestrians. A significant development in recent years has been the linking of traffic signals over a whole area to a centralised computer-control centre. This has been introduced in west central London and

[1] GLC (1970), *Proof of Evidence, E12/1*, p172, GLDP Inquiry Stage 1.

[2] J M Thomson (1968), *Journal of Transport Economics and Policy*, January, May, September 1968 (volII, Nos.1–3).

Glasgow and has apparently succeeded in reducing both congestion and accidents.[1] This method of traffic control might be the only way of making any significant future contributions to street capacity short of road building.

Measures designed to aid traffic flow, however, usually have adverse effects on pedestrian convenience by reducing the number of opportunities for crossing the road or by making this action hazardous because of faster flowing traffic. Cyclists are also adversely affected when traffic is speeded up, particularly at multi-lane or free-flow junctions. Environmental conditions are worsened by more traffic. Advantages for motor traffic must therefore be set against these adverse effects but traffic management can be employed in their interests too.

Pedestrian movement can be helped by the introduction of longer 'green time' when traffic signals change and greater provision of crossings of various kinds. Pavements can also be widened making it easier to cross the road and more pleasant to walk alongside it. Since the capacity of roads is largely determined by the capacity of intersections, roads could in many cases be made narrower between them. The provision of traffic islands is also an important way of making pedestrian movement safer and more convenient although they have often been removed to provide more traffic space. Certain streets, such as shopping streets, can be closed to traffic altogether either for the whole or part of the day.

Measures specifically designed to help cyclists are rare in London but separate paths and traffic signals for them are fairly common in the new towns and some foreign cities, e.g. Amsterdam and Copenhagen. Opportunities for such measures in London may be limited but cycling can be made easier by the provision of adequate nearside lane widths, the maintenance of a smooth carriageway right up to the gutter, and the elimination of free-flow intersections.

Other fields of traffic management which are still very underdeveloped are those aimed at environmental improvement and giving priority to public transport. Traffic can be discouraged or prevented from entering certain streets or areas in order to improve the environment (and safety). Once this has been done play streets may be introduced. The parking of lorries in residential streets can be banned and special lorry parks provided (e.g. the pilot scheme in Tower Hamlets).[2] The removal of 'through' traffic from environmental areas onto predetermined routes will present three choices where the receiving roads operate at or near capacity:

1 The total volume of traffic can be reduced. (This may be achieved by positive measures of traffic restraint or, as the Pimlico scheme suggested, traffic may simply 'evaporate.')
2 Extra traffic capacity can be provided.
3 Any additional congestion that occurs can be accepted.

[1] *Traffic Engineering and Control*, vol9, No. 10, February 1968, pp496–8, 503.
[2] GLC *Minutes*, 4 July 1972, pp327–9.

The environment and safety can also be improved by measures to limit the speed of traffic. Slip roads on some German urban motorways, for example, are cobbled or ribbed for this purpose. It is possible in minor roads to lay ramps across the carriageway to deter drivers from speeding. These 'sleeping policemen,' as they are sometimes called, may be found in some private residential estates in London, Blackheath for example.

Traffic management designed to give public transport priority over other traffic has been introduced on a limited scale in many cities particularly in Europe, Paris having the most examples. English examples are less numerous though many are under consideration including latterly in London (see Case Study *M*). The provision of segregated lanes both with the flow of traffic and against it has been the most tried method of freeing the bus from congestion. There is considerable scope for the development of other measures to produce the same effect and various possibilities are the subject of studies in many cities. These include the phasing of traffic signals to favour bus routes rather than other roads (as in Bitterne Road, Southampton), the creation of bus-only streets (as in Reading), and the provision of cab-controlled traffic signals (as in Leicester) and bus-only right turns. Using any or a combination of these and other methods, networks of bus priority routes might be developed rather than individual isolated schemes as has been the case so far. Bus priority measures may often require a reduction of road capacity for other traffic (this will be particularly true with bus lanes and at congested junctions). The choices presented are much the same as those mentioned with regard to the creation of environmental areas, with the addition that priority measures, if they succeed in improving the overall quality of bus services, can themselves facilitate a reduction in overall traffic by attracting journeys from cars to buses.

Parking

Control of parking on the street began for the purpose of securing more orderly traffic flow conditions and access to premises but developed into a way of rationing scarce space as the number of cars increased (see Case Study *Q*). It is at present the main method consciously used to limit road traffic. Its effectiveness as a means of traffic restraint is, however, dependent on how directly the amount of traffic in an area relates to the amount of parking. Parking controls restrain trip ends, not vehicle miles, so they could encourage more through (longer) trips in control areas, and more commercial vehicle trips.

On-street parking is virtually unrestricted in the outer suburban areas although pressure for parking space has led to the introduction of meters at town centres and parking restrictions around stations (e.g. Gidea Park station). Free parking is also allowed in many areas which are subject to time limits (not more than a certain period during the day, as at many shopping centres) or bans on main roads and near junctions. There is an inherent conflict between local traders, who like to have sufficient and cheap parking nearby to attract custom, people driving through (for whom main road parking restrictions aid traffic flow) and lorry drivers wishing to deliver to premises and local residents.

Meter control is one of the easiest ways of rationing on-street parking spaces and has been widely used in London, particularly the central area, but enforcement can be a difficult problem. The principle of paying for parking appears to have been accepted where parking demand is sufficiently high to require some limitation, but meter *time* limits are more readily disregarded when demand is great. Overstaying at meters and meter feeding constitute the main enforcement task. Meter control is, however, fairly flexible and a number of alternative policies are possible. Time limits can be standardised (at present there are both long-stay and short-stay meters) or they can be abolished altogether. The reason for time limits was to discriminate against the all day parker (particularly the car commuter) in favour of shoppers and other short-stay users. They have probably, however, contributed in central London to the gradual 'filling in' of the traffic peaks on the roads as the turnover of parking space has increased. Meter charges can be varied according to the demand for parking from one area to another and can be raised progressively to limit demand so as to maintain a sufficient proportion of available space for newcomers (usually considered to be 15%). Adopting this policy and abolishing time limits might greatly ease the enforcement problem. Other than for enforcement there is no evidence as to whether discrimination by price is any better than time limits as a means of traffic restraint. It is possible, however, that raising charges as demand increases would turn the current overall losses on the parking account into a useful source of revenue. Another important consideration, however, as with road pricing, area licencing or toll systems, is to keep the number of price brackets fairly simple for the motorist to remember.

A further development of on-street control has been the special provision for residents parking in meter control areas (as described in Case Study *Q*). Usually a charge has been made to cover administrative costs of issuing the special permits but, as with meters, charges could be raised deliberately to restrain demand. If time limits at meters were abolished, residents could use meters along with other parkers. The decision to provide special (and especially cheaper) spaces for residents could be seen as a social rather than an economic policy.

Off-street parking falls into two categories, public and private. As with meters, the use of public spaces is fairly easily controlled by price and/or time and the GLC has unique powers to do this by a system of licensing under the Transport (London) Act 1969. The control of private off-street parking poses quite different problems. The provision of extra spaces can be required or limited by planning controls. The use of private off-street space, however, cannot yet be controlled and parking restraint policies will therefore be limited in their effectiveness depending on the proportion of spaces which are privately operated. Again the total traffic generation depends not simply on the number of spaces but on their turnover in use.

Special mention should be made of parking at stations. The provision of off-street space for 'park-and-ride' commuters can ease the problem of all-day parking on local streets near stations. It can also be used (together with pricing policies) as a way of encouraging motorists to drive to the station and complete their journey by train, thus reducing traffic (see Case Study *F*).

Pricing and regulation of vehicles

Some of the shortcomings of the present methods of paying for private car use have already been discussed, but vehicle and fuel tax can be used for various governmental purposes. Purchase tax can influence the level of car ownership. Although the purchase of the first car in a household may often be regarded as simply a socially necessary progression from the cycle and motor cycle, the purchase of further cars is probably much more sensitive to the extent of capital outlay required.

Purchase tax and licence duties may be used to discriminate in favour of vehicles with particularly desirable design features such as exhaust control equipment, safety devices and quiet engines. A considerable stimulus to the development of electric vehicles, for example, might be given by making them exempt from tax. A current example of the influence of differential taxation is the relatively low tax on diesel oil which has led to the change-over from petrol to diesel propulsion of almost the entire fleet of London taxis. Vehicle duties and fuel taxes have so far been channelled to the Exchequer but they could be transferred to local authority revenues.[1] This could give local authorities a vested interest in vehicle ownership and use in their areas, but at the same time would provide them with a useful source of income which could be used, for example, to provide bus services.

The most interesting and potentially effective tax, however, is the congestion tax. This has not yet been applied anywhere but has been widely discussed. Its aim would be to charge directly for the use of road space by both time and place, instead of the present indirect fuel and road tax. The means for doing this has been developed by the Road Research Laboratory involving the use of meters located either on or off the vehicle which are triggered by detector loops set in the road surface. Charges would be clocked up and paid for in the same way as electricity and gas charges are at present. The charges made could be varied according to the levels of traffic demand and supply of road space, thus making it possible to greatly reduce congestion even in the most dense parts of the city. Road pricing (as it is called) has virtually reached the limit of initial technical development and now awaits the introduction of a practical experiment.

Other methods of charging for the use of road space such as tolls and area licences for use in certain areas and at certain times of the day would

[1] *The Future Shape of Local Government Finance*, Cmnd 4741, 1971, app2.

probably be less effective in reducing congestion since they would be much less flexible.[1] Tolls are easy to administer and enforce but can themselves give rise to congestion at collection points. Area licences might pose enforcement problems and give rise to traffic pressure outside the control area. Both might provide, however, a political stepping stone towards a system of comprehensive road pricing.

Although road pricing has mostly been discussed as a method of reducing congestion and achieving more equitable road taxation, it could also be used to achieve environmental objectives such as limiting the use of cars in areas of architectural merit, or relating traffic flows to the 'environmental capacity' of streets,[2] and the levels of charge could reflect the varying cost of adverse environmental effects, which would have to be socially or politically determined. The long- and short-term effects of road pricing on land prices, land use, densities, public transport and road investment have not been thoroughly investigated, nor have its social implications. On the one hand, for example, the high cost of car use in densely built areas might encourage urban sprawl and the dispersal of activities, but on the other hand the elimination of congestion could allow the development of a sufficiently attractive public transport system to retain the relative advantages of urban concentration.

Other instruments of control over vehicles include the regulation of vehicle sizes, weights, and design features for greater safety and to control pollution. The setting of such standards is a national matter (although the enforcement of them may be delegated locally). One problem is that standards designed to set maximum limits tend to become the norm: they tend to encourage what is tolerable rather than what is desirable. A good example is the size and weight limits on commercial vehicles which were designed to prevent larger vehicles from coming onto the roads but which have nevertheless allowed a large increase in the average size and weight.

Development of urban railways

London has a very extensive network of railways both for passenger and freight use, although the former has a very strong radial emphasis. There may therefore be relatively little scope for the construction of entirely new lines (see Case Study *C*). London's railways (or many of them) became unprofitable by about 1930 and the construction of new lines came to a virtual standstill until 1960. Investment in new and improved rolling stock and other capital equipment slowed down to such an extent that the quality of service was barely maintained, let alone improved. But although the railways became unprofitable, the dependence of London on them

[1] GLC (1972), *Traffic and the Environment* (Discussion Paper), pp14–17.

[2] This is a generalised measure consisting of noise, pollution, pedestrian delay and other factors in different kinds of street, suggested initially by Professor Buchanan (as he then was) in *Traffic in Towns* and developed by his colleagues at Imperial College, London.

increased because of their role in carrying people to and from the central area, with its growing labour market.

The role of the railway system largely depends on the city structure which it is intended to maintain or develop, particularly the function of the city centre. If it is to continue to carry out its present task investment will be required both to make up the back log of replacement necessary and perhaps to improve the quality of the system overall. It will also be necessary to maintain the radial structure of the railway system and it has already been emphasized that the city structure necessary to support radial lines is fundamentally different from that which would be generated by orbital motorways. The relationship between the railways and city structure also depends on access to stations. Access on foot or by bicycle or feeder bus, for example, requires the concentration of development around stations. Park-and-ride facilities on the other hand can encourage the use of railways for certain journeys even in very low-density and dispersed suburbs.

The capacity and the quality of railway services is dependent on investment in rolling stock, signalling, track and stations. This investment can be paid for out of fares, or by grants to the railway operators from either central or local authorities, or by a mixture of these. The dependence on railways and their efficiency in environmental and spatial terms compared with roads have led to a greater willingness to provide capital grants (and to bring the proportion of grant aid into line with that for roads), particularly since the advent of accounting methods which include social costs and benefits (see Case Studies *C*, *E* and *H*).

Whether new lines and improvements are profitable or not, there is a case for providing capital grants from the community if it is felt that present passengers should not pay for improvements which will benefit future users. The justification in social cost-benefit terms, or even the profitability of railway schemes might be radically altered if stringent policies to restrict the use of private cars were introduced (such as road pricing).

Many problems of both road and rail travel are confined to peak periods. Consequently the staggering of work, shopping and school hours has often been suggested as an alternative to major investment in the transport system (see Case Study *B*). Staggered hours can be achieved in a number of possible ways. Peak-hour fare surcharges might help to divert passengers away from the peak. Employers and others may be pursuaded to alter their hours either voluntarily (though attempts in London have not been particularly successful) or through financial inducements such as rate rebates or a central area employment tax. Conditions stating hours to be worked in new establishments could be attached to planning permissions. Locating employment at or near stations can also bring a measure of staggering (see Case Study *D*).

One very neglected field of public transport development is that of interchanges between different modes. Responsibility for the planning and financing of interchanges is almost inevitably divided between institutions and no agreed basis of sharing cost and responsibility or even of assessing the social benefits of interchange improvements has yet been devised. Nevertheless the time involved in interchange between different modes of public transport can be a considerable proportion of total journey time, and it therefore seems undesirable to improve public transport links without at the same time improving interchange between them.

Development of bus transport

Ways of improving bus operating conditions on the roads have already been discussed. There are, however, further ways of improving the quality of service. Reliability can be aided by the introduction of two-way radio systems bringing drivers in close touch with controllers. This has been introduced experimentally on some LT routes and is already used extensively on Leicester's bus system. More sophisticated electronic location systems are also being developed, for example on London's Route 11. The aim of these measures is to improve reliability and to provide information so that delays can be avoided and the passengers can be informed more readily about them. Radio control might also increase staff morale.

Savings in operating costs can be made by the introduction of one-man operated buses,[1] though simple fare collection methods (such as pre-paid tickets and automatic ticket machines) are required for boarding times to be kept within reasonable limits.

Public transport subsidies

The purpose of subsidies is to meet costs or to make improvements which cannot (or should not) be financed from fares revenue. Capital subsidies are often favoured because they are related to specific schemes and therefore provide no open-ended commitment to prop up financially ailing undertakings. They do, however, discriminate in favour of capital-intensive improvements which may not necessarily be the most desirable. For example, is investment in automatic train control on certain parts of tube system more or less worthwhile than the maintenance of unremunerative but socially desirable outer suburban services? Capital subsidies also discriminate against bus services which have less scope for capital improvement: new buses, however comfortable, will not be appreciated if they do not run on time.

Operating or revenue subsidies have a different function, and different effects on the whole transport system. There is, of course, a good deal of cross-subsidisation within the BR and LT systems because the fares collected do not relate directly to the costs of providing the services. But operating subsidies are usually taken to mean those paid to the transport operators by the community. A number of arguments are put forward in

[1] Although not necessarily complete conversion to one-man operation, see DOE *Working Party Report*, 1972.

support of operating subsidies. Economists argue that since motorists do not pay directly for the use of road space public transport fares should be subsidised, particularly on the buses which are most affected by road congestion, to enable fairer competition between the two.[1] It is also argued that many services while unprofitable are socially necessary. Some believe that public transport can never pay its way in a situation of labour shortage and rising labour costs because it is so labour-intensive, but that nevertheless it should be maintained in order to preserve urban concentration, or to contain the adverse effects of traffic on the environment. Whatever the justification, operating subsidies seem the only way of maintaining efficient public transport services and at the same time keeping fares to a level which does not seriously discourage the use of the system. Larger subsidies could be paid to positively encourage the use of public rather than private transport.

The main argument against operating subsidies (apart from lack of resources) is that they reduce or remove management incentive to maintain and improve operating efficiency and that they stultify technical innovation. This danger can be avoided, however, by paying subsidies for specific purposes (such as maintaining certain routes or services which are identified as unprofitable but considered necessary for social reasons) or relating them to specified levels of service or to the number of passengers or passenger miles carried.

There are a number of possible sources of operating subsidies. They can be paid by central government out of general taxation (in which case they can be seen as a transfer payment from motorists to public transport) or they can be paid out of local taxation (i.e. rates levied by local authorities). Discriminatory taxes can be imposed for this purpose, hotel, central area employment and local purchase taxes being amongst those suggested. Revenues from parking charges (if these were obtained) could also be used. In Copenhagen the transport undertaking receives a subsidy from the profits of the municipal electricity and central heating undertakings. There is a similar arrangement in Vienna, while in some Swedish cities operating subsidies are provided out of local income tax revenue.

Fares

The level of fares and their structure provide a further instrument for influencing the relative use of public and private transport. In London there has invariably been an immediate and predictable decline in passengers each time fares have been increased. Lower fares would attract passengers but the ability to do this would depend on how good an alternative to the car the public services provided. Much depends on the existing situation: 'In most American situations the public alternative is so inferior to the private car that modal choice is regarded as insensitive to the level of

[1] L C Fitch and Associates *Urban Transportation and Public Policy*, pp156, 209; and G Roth (1967), *Paying for Roads: The Economics of Traffic Congestion*, pp79–83.

fares.'[1] The situation in London is quite different where a fairly comprehensive public transport system (including bus services) still exists and where car ownership has not reached American proportions. In any case, reduced fares will only attract significant numbers of passengers from cars if there are restrictions on the use of cars.

Traditionally in London fares have been graduated according to distance (beyond a certain minimum fare) and great efforts have been made to standardise fare scales on different routes, between LT and BR services and even between bus and rail. (This, as noted in Chapter 3, was one of the main concerns of the Transport Tribunal.) In recent years there has been a shift towards more selective pricing on both BR and LT services. The aim of selective pricing is twofold: first, to relate fares more closely to marginal costs (thus reducing the extent of cross-subsidisation between services); second, to increase fare revenues whilst minimising the loss of passengers. Selective pricing may be achieved by charging what the market will bear (for example recent LT increases have concentrated on central London bus services and rail services to the centre, where the car provides less of an alternative than in outer London, while BR have concentrated increases on long-distance services to which commuters are 'captive,' or have charged more for better quality services.

Several other fare structures are possible. Graduated fare scales can be 'coarsened' as has been the trend on LT services in recent years, particularly on the tubes. While this makes fare collection easier (for example by simplifying automatic ticket equipment) fare increases can only be made in sharp jumps. Flat fare systems are common in many cities throughout the world: they greatly ease the task of fare collection and avoiding 'bilkers' because automatic ticket issuing and inspection are greatly simplified. Pre-payment of tickets is also easier. Flat fares are often thought to be impracticable on a comprehensive basis in London because of the long distances involved—to maintain similar fare revenues, a flat fare in London would have to be pitched so high (from 10 to 15p for the buses and from 20 to 25p for the tubes has been suggested) that the short trips which form the bulk of LT's passenger mileage, particularly on the buses, would be severely discouraged. Very low flat fares would involve a subsidy for longer-distance passengers. This would have the advantage of encouraging long-distance trips to be made by public transport (including those which might otherwise contribute the greatest number of car miles to road traffic with their attendant social costs); but, in the long term, it might also encourage the outward movement of population and devalue the distance factor in people's decisions about where to live and work. The effect would be to increase travel (in terms of passenger miles) without producing any equivalent increases in revenue. For a city the size of London, the introduction of a limited number of fare zones might help to overcome these problems.

[1] J M Thomson (1972), paper submitted to OECD on Urban Transport Policy (unpublished).

The most radical alternative is to abolish fares altogether, although experiments elsewhere (Moscow and Rome for example) have not been considered successful. The main argument in favour of a fares-free system is that it avoids the cost of fare collection and that it particularly benefits the poorer members of the community. Some of the arguments against it are that people would get into the habit of making more and longer journeys (thus making the system increasingly costly to run), staff morale would be low and, most of all, it would not of itself be likely to solve the key problem of road congestion.

There are further possibilities such as 'go anywhere' period seasons, cheap or free off-peak tickets, cheap day-return tickets, and tickets valid on both bus and rail systems. Other systems may be developed and in choosing from the list of alternatives a sound knowledge is required of people's travel demands.

Technical innovation

Research into new forms of urban transport has been lacking for much the same reason as investment in existing public transport systems has declined, but there may be considerable scope for the development of entirely new systems (such as automatic taxis, monorails and moving pavements) as well as technological solutions to the problems of more traditional methods of movement (such as vehicle guidance and dial-a-bus). Entirely new vehicular forms are often considered to be difficult to introduce to London because of the scale and nature of the existing urban fabric, the multiplicity of land ownership, the rate of redevelopment and above all attitudes and policies about the environment (see Case Study *J*).

The development of new forms of road vehicle propulsion which are less noisy and polluting could have a marked effect in improving the environment while automatic control of trains and bus monitoring systems (already mentioned) could greatly improve public transport efficiency and reliability.

It is obviously difficult to predict the kind of innovations which are possible, and even less their impact on urban transport and life in general. What is important is that developments which promise to aid the desired direction of change should not be pushed to one side because of institutional inertia or for the sake of protecting existing vested interests.

Chapter 5

THE CHOICES TO BE MADE IN METROPOLITAN TRANSPORT PLANNING

In the previous chapter London's main transport problems and a range of policy options for dealing with them were discussed. Making policy decisions about London's vast and complex transport system, however, is no easy task. Both the problems and the methods of dealing with them are closely related so that almost any action designed to combat one problem will tend to alleviate or aggravate other problems: what may meet the needs of some people will endanger the interests of others; what is appropriate in the long-term may conflict with the satisfaction of short-term needs. Moreover, the transport system is no isolated phenomenon but is shaped by other aspects of the city within which it has developed—such as housing, industry and social services—and it in turn influences the growth and character of these other activities. These relationships and conflicts are illustrated in the following words of a former chairman of Camden's Planning and Communications Committee:

> Planning is in essence a way of balancing our requirements by adopting or rejecting various options that are open to us.
>
> All too often, unfortunately, there is no absolute right nor wrong. All we can hope for is to achieve the right balance. One man's desecration by demolition is another's progress by redevelopment. The ability to move rapidly from place to place by car is often only achieved at the expense of somebody else's amenity. What is acclaimed as the gain of an open space in one area is condemned as the loss of valuable residential land in another.[1]

Because of these complexities and the changes in circumstances and priorities which inevitably occur, activities must be monitored so that policies and proposals can be modified as the need arises. Changes in policy, of course, must be capable of being translated into changes of executive action. In order to cope with all these factors and to reduce uncertainty, public authorities have been moving increasingly towards a more quantitative and comprehensive approach to decision making. But while techniques such as planning programming and budgeting systems can inform and clarify the decision-making process, they cannot remove

[1] Councillor Alan Greengross (1970) in foreword to *Camden Scene: A Planning Survey*, p1.

the ultimate need for value judgements. In answering a question on the Department of the Environment's use of cost-benefit analysis in relation to transport investment decisions, Peter Walker (then Secretary of State for the Environment) said: 'I cannot say that what we are developing . . . is a totally accurate science. It is a question of assessing a range of experience, and trying to come to a sensible conclusion.'[1]

It is important, then, for the extent of concurrence or conflict between different objectives and interests to be understood, even though it is not always possible to quantify the 'trade-offs' involved. The rest of this chapter therefore seeks to make explicit the more important choices that have to be made, and the factors which should be taken into account by those who make them. In short, it seeks to describe institutional objectives for achieving a balanced approach to the transport problem, and to serve as a basis for evaluating, in Chapter 6, the present institutional arrangements. For the sake of continuity the discussion is structured broadly under the headings of the transport problems set out in Chapter 4.

IMPROVING LONDON'S ENVIRONMENT

Major improvements to the environment could be effected if more stringent standards to control the noise and atmospheric pollution caused by vehicles and aircraft were implemented. This would require national legislation and the benefits would accrue to the country as a whole. The choice, therefore, between environmental gains, manufacturers' and operators' profits, and technological feasibility for a given cost is appropriately the responsibility of central government. The principal cause of environmental degradation in London as in other cities, however, is road traffic and much can be done at the metropolitan and local levels to reduce its harmful effects.

There are two key choices to be made, one of a strategic (i.e. metropolitan) character, the other concerned with particular localities. First, a broad decision must be made about the amount of traffic that is desirable or acceptable in environmental terms. The main variable is the amount of movement by car compared with other modes of travel and, as explained in Chapter 4, possibilities exist for influencing the total number, length, and distribution of trips and the means by which they are made. Freight traffic is also capable of being influenced in a similar way. Between the extremes on the one hand of banning cars entirely from built-up areas and on the other of expecting them to provide the universal means of travel, there lies a wide range of possibilities. The choice should vary according to the nature of each area of the city. For example, in the densely developed central and inner parts of the city, it is more appropriate, on environmental grounds, to restrict the amount of vehicular traffic, than in the less dense outer suburbs. It is important also that, when speaking of improvements to

[1] Expenditure Committee (Environment and Home Office Subcommittee), 1971–72, *Minutes of Evidence*, 27 June 1972, *Hansard HC Papers 107 (xxii)*, p500, Q2407.

the environment, policy makers should make explicit whether they aim to improve upon present conditions, or merely to reduce the degree of damage by motor traffic by comparison with what *pro rata* increases in traffic would induce. Thus if it were planned to double the volume of traffic, vehicles might need to be made at least half as noisy if current noise levels were to be improved upon.

The second broad choice concerns the distribution of a given volume of traffic. Traffic may be allowed free movement along all streets, regardless of their environmental characteristics, or measures can be taken to channelise it onto particular routes (e.g. by creating 'environmental areas'). The factors involved can be complex (as Case Study *G* showed). It may sometimes be possible to produce a net environmental gain by transferring traffic from, say, a shopping street to an alternative existing road or by building an entirely new route, but the opportunities within the built-up area of London will be few without large-scale redevelopment. Moreover, where new roads are built the traffic capacity of existing roads must be proportionately reduced if the generation of extra traffic (and thus extra environmental damage) is to be avoided. It is particularly problematical if the traffic excluded from certain areas cannot be directly accommodated on the peripheral roads: it is then a question of deciding whether to tolerate the additional traffic delays (if these in fact arise), or to attempt to reduce the amount of traffic by general restraint measures, or to increase the traffic capacity of the peripheral roads, or to build new ones. These factors are inevitably bound up with strategic transport policy, but the determination of those streets which should or should not carry through traffic (if indeed this is a valid exercise) would seem primarily a local matter. Land use, residential density, pedestrian movement, architectural quality and other matters would need to be considered. Buses may require special consideration, for example, by providing bus-only through routes in environmental areas.

If environmental improvement through a reduction of noise, pollution, and visual intrusion were the primary consideration, policies would probably need to give first priority to travel on foot, then by pedal cycle, bus and train, and lastly by car.

IMPROVING ROAD SAFETY

While the objective of improving road safety has never been in question, policies are often ambiguous in terms of the kind of improvement they are expected to achieve. It may be possible, for example, by building new urban roads to improve upon the accident *rate* (i.e. to reduce the number or severity of accidents per million vehicle or pedestrian miles) but at the same time to produce an increase in the *total* number of road accidents. There are immense difficulties in designing policies to reduce road accidents because of the very large number of controllable variables involved such as traffic volume, speed, flow characteristics, road design and lighting (even disregarding rogue weather conditions) and the very incomplete knowledge of their interaction. But if policies are to accord a high degree of priority to the objective of safety, there are clearly limits to how far one can allow increases in travel by road, and by car in particular. The fabric of the city could in the long term be transformed to incorporate full segregation of pedestrians and vehicles and to improve the safety of vehicular movement, but removing conflict in this way is usually costly both financially and socially, and often unacceptable environmentally. The violent debates over the Bath and York ring roads, for example, and many of the Greater London Council's proposals have centred on these factors, and on the great length of time needed to achieve the transformation.

Pedestrians are the most vulnerable to accidents but, as Case Study *L* showed, providing subways or footbridges for their safety can often only be achieved at the expense of their convenience. Indeed, for pedestrians crossing busy roads, safety and convenience are often inversely related.

IMPROVING TRAVEL ON FOOT AND BY CYCLE

Since distance is a crucial factor for walking and cycling, the disposition and intensity of land use and activities has a major influence on the extent and quality of travel by these modes. Despite London's size, for example, a considerable proportion of its working population still walks or cycles to work. Land-use policies at the regional, metropolitan and borough scales can have an important effect (particularly in the longer term) in encouraging or discouraging these modes of travel. Other important factors, of course, are the safety and attractiveness of streets for walking and cycling, both of which are largely matters of local design. In general it is probably true that roads which are attractive to motor traffic because of their design for safe and rapid vehicular movement are by that very fact unattractive, dangerous or inconvenient for pedestrians and cyclists. Therefore, quite apart from broad considerations of influencing the volume and mode of travel, the scale and design of urban development suitable for motor traffic is usually in direct conflict with that most suited to walking and cycling.

Apart from the environmental and personal advantages of being able to walk or cycle, policies aimed at encouraging these modes can help to ease dependence on either the car or public transport. Such policies are essential if most people are to retain the choice of whether to own a car (and *when* to use it if one already owns or has the use of one), and if hardship caused by expensive public transport facilities and restrictions on the use of the car is to be reduced. Parking restrictions in a suburban centre, for example, are the least troublesome to those who live within comfortable walking distance of the facilities it has to offer. Increasing residential densities around suburban stations is one policy that would allow more people to live within a walk or short bus-ride of the railway thus discouraging the use cars for basic trips to work, school or shop.

REDUCING DELAYS TO ROAD TRAFFIC

Easing traffic congestion, or reducing the frequency with which it occurs, can be tackled by increasing road capacity or by limiting the demand for it. The policies of easing traffic flow by building roads or widening existing ones within London often conflict directly and indirectly with those of improving the quality of the environment, of encouraging pedestrian and cycle travel, and of maintaining or improving the use of public transport (see below) through the generation of extra traffic. These conflicts and the cost of road building obviously vary with the intensity of development so that broadly speaking the obvious benefits of improving traffic flow and the returns for each sum invested diminish towards the centre of the city (i.e. as density increases). Therefore, if responsibility for roads is divided between different parts of the city (as at present) one would expect to find different approaches between the inner and outer authorities.

Policies which provide for widespread increases in traffic flow encourage greater dependence on the car beyond the short term and militate against improving public transport; for example, there may be a gain for bus operation if new or widened roads provide bus lanes or other priorities, but there will be no encouragement for passengers to continue to use or change over to buses.

A further conflict arises, when catering for easier traffic flow, between people making local trips and those involved in longer distances, whose needs are often very different. The creation of an 'urban clearway,' for example, may significantly ease the passage of traffic, but this is gained at the expense of convenient waiting and loading facilities for frontage properties. A clear example in London of this conflict is the Finchley Road–Swiss Cottage area where the local shopping and other facilities front onto the main road from the M1 to the West End. Safety railings erected along the main road make pedestrian movement and the loading of vehicles extremely inconvenient, while local vehicular journeys in the area are made more difficult by a system of one-way streets designed to ease junction problems with the major road. If, on the other hand, the needs of local movement (both vehicular and pedestrian) are given priority over longer-distance traffic, problems may arise with 'essential' commercial traffic and bus services. Although buses cater mainly for local movement, their routes often need to be relatively long, so that efficient operation depends on ease of movement for 'through' traffic. Bus priority measures can, however, reduce this conflict.

The main alternative to increasing road capacity is to limit the amount of traffic. The various policies for achieving this can be categorised as traffic restriction, traffic restraint and traffic avoidance,[1] and may be applied as complementary to road building or as independent measures. Traffic restriction depends partly on physical measures, partly on laws to

[1] To use the terminology developed by J M Thomson in 'Methods of Traffic Limitation in Urban areas' OECD, 1972.

exclude vehicles; traffic restraint uses a wider range of measures, including pricing policies, to discourage the use of vehicles; and traffic avoidance seeks designs for the structure of cities and regions and their public transport systems so as to minimise the future generation of road traffic.

The effects of traffic limitation are clearly the converse of those of increasing traffic and promote objectives for improving the environment, public transport, walking and cycling and reducing the extent of dependence on the cars. What would conflict with policies for limiting traffic (apart from practical difficulties arising from their implementation) is the extent to which people are able to travel by car. But the nature of this conflict is complex and would be related to the particular traffic limitation policies adopted. A long-term policy of land-use planning aimed at reducing the need for car travel would produce relatively few conflicts. But an immediate policy of restraining the car trips currently being made could give rise to more problems particularly in law enforcement but also concerning fairness and benefit. For example, road pricing has been seen by some as a policy which in practice would discriminate against the lower-paid sections of the community while others have argued that it would bring overall benefits to the community, particularly through general improvements to bus services and environmental conditions.

IMPROVING THE QUALITY OF PUBLIC TRANSPORT

In Britain generally and in London it is now agreed that if public transport is to compete successfully with the car and if it is to be accepted as an alternative mode of travel when car travel is restrained or restricted, then its quality must be improved. Indeed it would need some improvement to meet the increased aspirations of existing users in terms of standards of service. A major problem arises, however, in that different groups are almost certain to have different priorities. For the wealthier the quality of public transport is more important (up to a point) than its cost. But for those with lower incomes a lower standard of service would be preferable to expensive fares which make it difficult for them to make even their most important journeys. Thus while transport operators may be required to decide on priorities between fare levels and level of service, equitable policies will depend on broader social considerations outside the normal scope of their responsibility or influence. The evolution of a concessionary fares policy for the elderly and handicapped is one strand of such a wider policy which has so far been accepted in London.

IMPROVING THE QUALITY OF RAIL TRAVEL

Provided that money is available to build and operate extra rolling stock, improving the comfort of rail journeys at peak hours can be fairly easily achieved, though not necessarily in the short term if investment in more track capacity is required. The main problem is financing the capital and operating costs of providing extra trains which are required only during the peak hours of the day. Charging commuters the true cost of providing extra peak-hour services in order to reduce overcrowding could involve a transfer of passengers from rail to road. This would give rise to traffic and environmental problems probably even more costly to solve than the alternative approach of subsidising peak-hour travel from rates, taxes or other sources.

One of the great difficulties in cities like London where employment is concentrated in the centre and the workforce is drawn from a wide catchment area is that the majority of journeys are uni-directional and confined to a few hours of the day. A fundamental choice, therefore, has to be made for the long-term planning of the region whether to seek to rearrange the distribution of homes and workplaces or to accept the provision of transport facilities which are costly either to the individual traveller or to the community as a whole. Recent experience in London has been that the twin forces of job attractions in the centre and house availability in outer London and beyond have stretched the length of the journey to work much faster than jobs and workers have been decentralised to new or expanded towns with a greater balance of houses and workplaces.

There is also a conflict between objectives for improving short-distance and long-distance commuter services. The longer-distance services are generally able to cover their costs from fares more easily than short-distance services and consequently it will generally be in the interests of the railway operators to give them priority. A similar conflict can arise concerning inter-city and freight services which are usually more profitable than commuter services. Thus as far as London is concerned there is a potential conflict of interest between the needs of Greater London and the needs of the remainder of the South-East region, institutionalised as an issue between the GLC and British Rail. This conflict is further reinforced by the need to decide priorities for improving station and interchange facilities. For example, station car parks may be desirable to serve the needs of commuters from the London suburbs, but such a policy conflicts with the railway operators' desire to encourage commuters from outside Greater London to board a train at their nearest station rather than to drive as far as possible into London before 'parking and riding' (see Case Study *F*).

IMPROVING THE BUS SERVICES

Without massive subsidy the quality of bus services in terms of frequency, fares, and to a degree reliability, depends on the number of passengers carried and thus to a very large extent on the basic choice already described between encouraging or reducing travel by car. Moreover, buses are directly affected by road traffic conditions, and their ability to provide a good service depends on a pattern of urban development which is concentrated in 'corridors' or 'nodes' (generating concentrated flows of people) rather than dispersed or low-density arrangements which can only be conveniently served by private transport. Apart, therefore, from the strategic question of modal split, good bus services depend both upon traffic management policies favourable to bus operation and on land-use policies to maintain or create an urban form compatible with bus use. The improvement of bus operation and use is therefore as much a matter for local as for strategic consideration.

IMPROVING OFF-PEAK PUBLIC TRANSPORT SERVICES

To improve public transport outside the peak periods one can, for example, increase the number of buses and trains in service, raise demand by preferential fare structures, encourage staggered hours and increase traffic and parking restraints. The main point is that this objective is an essential corollary to the improvement of peak-hour bus and rail services because it increases the return on the resources employed mainly for a few hours' use. It is also helpful in reducing dependency on the car and conducive to the functioning of a concentrated city, whereas it is an expensive objective in areas where activities are dispersed.

INCREASING THE AVAILABILITY OF PARKING SPACE

The close relationship between parking space and road capacity means that policies for them must be mutually consistent. But while the amount of parking space required depends on the number of trips and their distribution in time and space, control over the amount and use of parking space is in itself an important method of influencing the amount of road traffic. Parking policies should therefore be formulated both as part of strategic transport policy and to influence local travel patterns, but the two levels must be related: the local implications for residents and shopkeepers of car parks at stations, for example, are of equal importance to their strategic implications for the overall balance in the use of railways and roads.

Two examples of the choices that have to be made in deciding on parking policies are, first, the priority to be given to residents, doctors or other groups in the allocation of scarce space and, second, the types of car trip to be restrained by parking control. In consideration of the latter it must be borne in mind that restraint of peak-hour trips by commuters in favour of short-term parking by shoppers, businessmen or other visitors in the off-peak periods may exacerbate the financial difficulties of public transport by increasing the 'peaked' character of passenger demand.

REDUCING DEPENDENCY ON INDIVIDUAL FORMS OF TRANSPORT

It was noted in Chapter 4 that, because at least 50% of the population would always be without the exclusive use of a car, it was an important objective to avoid situations where people are dependent on the car alone for their travel needs. This objective, however, will usually be inconsistent with that of providing for travel by car and of developing more spacious and dispersed patterns of land use.[1] Public transport services can be supported by a specific subsidy, though dependence on subsidised services can itself give rise to problems of uncertainty for passengers. A land-use policy to relate and encourage spines or nodes of higher-density development can minimise the areas where subsidy is necessary and may be able to generate enough passenger traffic along the main routes to cross-subsidise the less heavily-used services, if this is an acceptable management policy.

RELATING LAND USE AND URBAN FORM TO THE TRANSPORT NETWORK

As explained in Chapter 4, there are two major elements in land-use structure: the degree of dispersal or concentration (in terms of density of development and activity) and the amount of mixing or segregation of different land uses. Although London, like most large cities, comprises a wide variety of urban form (dense, mixed suburbs, for example, as well as low-density residential suburbs with clearly segregated industrial, commercial or recreational areas), each form tends to generate and support different patterns of transport demand.

A city with a strong central area, major and minor subcentres and other concentrated employment areas served primarily by public transport, walking and cycling (i.e. the structure of London in the middle of the present century) has a strong base on which to improve its public transport as the city develops. The car encourages and demands travel patterns which are very different. Residential densities can be lower, and need to be if the car is to be environmentally acceptable, while employment, commercial and recreational patterns will tend to disperse over wide areas. The provision of a new major road network in response to such trends suddenly provides a host of new development opportunities which are almost inevitably in direct competition for capital with existing ones.

A basic choice, therefore, has to be made: to provide generously for the motor-car (except in the city centre where it is generally agreed to be impractical) or to limit its use to times of the day and for trip purposes which the existing city structure can accept. A compromise can be made, but this will tend to devalue the advantages of both types of policy.

An indication of the scale and pace of land-use change that new roads and widespread use of the car can generate is given by the pressures that have developed for new industrial estates and distribution depots adjacent to the British inter-urban motorway network, but American examples are more striking. The full effects on urban structure have not been thoroughly

[1] Though mini-bus services may be developed which can partly overcome this problem, e.g. the Dial-a-bus system.

investigated in Britain and certainly not in London, although the local effects on urban fabric and environment have become clearer.[1]

Enough has been said in the foregoing paragraphs to illustrate the complexity of the relationships between the various problems and policy options. One could visualise the relationships between each of the variables as a matrix, each relationship representing two variables which were concurrent with or opposed to each other. But the exercise does not lend itself to easy tabulation and quantification partly because of lack of experience or monitoring of some policies and lack of agreement on the efficacy or effects of others. Nevertheless, it should be clear from what has been said in this chapter that by far the most important and far-reaching choice concerns the use of the motor-car. It is relatively easy to see that its uncontrolled use brings many disadvantages and aggravates many urban problems: it degrades the environment, it undermines the economy and efficiency of public transport, it makes walking and cycling more difficult, dangerous and unpleasant, it is a major cause of accidents on the roads, it demands urban forms which are incompatible in many ways with the majority of existing ones (particularly in the central and inner parts of the city) and it consequently reduces the choices for travel open not only to the majority of the population who do not have the use of a car, but also to car owners themselves.

Against all this, of course, must be set the benefits which the car is able to give to a substantial proportion of the population. The more cars there are, however, the less the individual user can realise his potential benefit: the freedom to drive anywhere must be limited either by competition from others attempting to do the same or by regulations and controls. The problems which the car even in its present numbers has brought to London has led some to suggest that it should be banned entirely from some inner areas of the city. Others suggest that more roads should be built to accommodate more trips by car in London. As the whole of this chapter shows, the choice is not simply concerned with numbers of cars. More important will be decisions about the encouragement or discouragement of car ownership (particularly the acquisition by householders of a second car), and about how cars are used within the city: whose cars, for what purpose, at what time, in what direction, by which route, and at what price. Whatever choice is made will have a significant influence on the life of the city for generations to come. Such decisions are not simple. They must be taken, however, and one of the most fundamental requirements of the government of a great city is that it should have the power and structure to enable it to take them.

[1] For example, LB Camden (1971), *Paper S27/221, Environmental Effects of the Primary Roads*, GLDP Inquiry Stage 2.

Chapter 6

THE ORGANISATION OF TRANSPORT IN LONDON: AN APPRAISAL

The material in the foregoing chapters and case studies makes up a twofold investigation into the subject of transport in London. The first and major part is concerned with the various institutions involved, the development and statutory definitions of their roles and the ways in which these roles have been interpreted in practice. The second part examines the problems of transport, the methods available for tackling them, the choices to be made and the effects of pursuing particular courses of action: these are the concerns of the institutional system, whatever its form. This chapter brings together the results of these two investigations in order to evaluate the performance of the present institutional arrangements. The process of evaluation may be summarised as follows: from the evidence contained in Chapter 3 and the fifteen case studies, the ability of the institutional system to cope with London's major transport problems (Chapter 4) by exercising its powers (outlined in Chapter 2) is assessed on the basis of broad criteria for a balanced approach (discussed in Chapter 5). The role played by the various institutions is considered for each problem area in turn, and at the end of each section an assessment is made of the collective institutional effort, and the extent to which it falls short of a comprehensive and balanced approach. Shortcomings are analysed primarily in terms of statutory powers and responsibilities and institutional structure, and some light is thrown on policies and attitudes adopted.

ENVIRONMENT

The evidence has shown that despite sudden and widespread growth of 'environmental awareness' there are few statutory duties upon public authorities to improve environmental quality through the application of transport policies. In contrast to the Greater London Council's (GLC) explicit duty 'to secure the expeditious, convenient and safe movement of vehicular and other traffic,' the effects on the environment of actions made in the name of that duty have only 'to be taken into account.' The highways legislation virtually ignores the environmental implications of the wide powers it gives to highway authorities for building, widening and altering roads. The highways, traffic and planning Acts do, however, provide a wide choice of measures that may be taken specifically to improve the environment. Thus, while there may be many reasons for supporting the claim that insufficient attention has been paid to improving the environment in London, a lack of powers is not one of them. The significant point about the statutory framework for environmental improvement is that it is a negative one: it allows for improvements to be made but does little to promote them.

Environmental improvement in a large city can be effected through policies to reroute and channelise road traffic, or to limit the amount of traffic in total or in particular areas. Local authorities in London have frequently approved such policies in principle, and then adopted courses or attitudes which impeded their implementation. Pedestrian-only streets and 'environmental areas,' for example, were widely recognised as important ways of achieving local environmental improvements, but the case studies revealed major conflicts which obstructed the implementation of such schemes. The source of the conflicts was the lack of coincidence between the responsibilities and policies of the boroughs and the GLC. The GLC decided in principle that policies concerned with environmental improvement should be the responsibility of the boroughs, although they initiated the Kensington environmental management study and the Carnaby Street and Marylebone High Street pedestrianisation experiments. The evidence collected shows that most of the boroughs made efforts to devise plans for environmental areas, although the degree of exertion varied considerably. But no schemes could be implemented without approval by the GLC as traffic authority. The experience of both Westminster and Islington (in Pimlico and Barnsbury respectively) was that the acceptance of schemes by the GLC depended on the ability of the peripheral roads to take the diverted traffic without unduly increasing delays. The same requirement, which was also often supported by the police, applied to the Bond Street scheme for pedestrianisation. The effect of this clash between environmental and traffic interests varied, but the GLC's final control over traffic matters was in all cases the deciding factor. Their defence of the traffic *status quo* made the progress of environmental management schemes a slow and often bitter process. For example, Camden's evidence at Stage 2 of the Inquiry stated that to prevent widespread bad traffic conditions a complete cover of environmental areas was needed for the borough, similar to the two already implemented in Camden Square and Primrose Hill after very slow legislative and public participation processes.[1] The evidence continued:

> Such a solution will not come about despite lip service to the principles of co-operation (GLC *Evidence E12/1*, paragraph 7.4.3), unless the GLC is prepared to accept: (1) a reduction in the traffic-carrying capacity of the base road network, or (2) a radical investment in secondaries, or (3) a combination of (1) and (2).
>
> Our experience is that there is the greatest reluctance on behalf of the GLC to accept any reduction in the capacity of the network. Indeed we

[1] For more details of the latter see E Wistrich (1972), *Local Government Reorganisation: The First Years of Camden*, pp162–3, 255–62.

find quite the contrary, that the GLC faced with congestion on the secondaries, is inclined to look covetously at other local base roads as a means of obtaining extra capacity via traffic management schemes.[1]

The same conflict, combined with delays in making traffic orders ensured that progress on pedestrianisation schemes was virtually nil. Slow progress, however, was partly attributable also to a rift between stated GLC policy and the proposals the Council advanced. As explained in Chapter 3, the GLC usually claimed that its proposed new or widened roads would bring environmental benefits by providing sufficient extra road capacity to attract traffic out of residential and other local roads. But none of their road schemes included traffic management measures to prevent traffic from using the local roads and thus to ensure that these environmental benefits were in fact secured. Those with the power to act are not always those with the incentive to act, and this appears to have been the case in the issue of local environmental improvements: the boroughs were given the responsibility by the GLC but had no power; the GLC had the power but lacked the will.

Given the particular policies of the GLC, what was the importance of the boroughs' role in initiating, designing and implementing environmental schemes? There was evidence that those boroughs who sought environmental improvements took pains to ensure that the public was at least consulted. In Camden, for example, actions to encourage residents to participate in formulating the Primrose Hill environmental area led to both delay and modification of the original scheme. Islington Borough Council was also concerned to please all parties over the Barnsbury scheme, which had become a focus for class conflicts within the area. Harrow Borough Council had actually abandoned an environmental area scheme because residents said they were prepared to tolerate through traffic in their streets in order to maintain convenient access by car. Westminster's Pimlico scheme was a response to complaints about accidents in the area.

Another important issue was that these local reactions were highly unpredictable, as were the traffic implications of the schemes, and this characteristic warranted an experimental approach. This, too, became a source of conflict between the boroughs and the GLC. For example, a prolonged argument arose over whether streets in Barnsbury should be closed to traffic by the use of temporary barriers or more permanent railings. An experimental approach would have been equally suitable for assessing the effects of closing Bond Street and Carnaby Street to traffic. It was adopted in Marylebone High Street, but some adverse criticism from local traders was sufficient for it to be labelled a failure.

The half-hearted approach to pedestrianisation in London is difficult to understand. Experience from European and provincial cities confirmed that pedestrian-only streets were almost always popular with both traders and shoppers, even if servicing became more difficult. The GLC apparently

[1] LB Camden (1971), *Proof of Evidence, E26/104*, paras6.2.15–6.2.16, GLDP Inquiry Stage 2.

believed that London was a special case where such schemes are difficult to implement. It is certainly true that there have been fewer such schemes in the large cities, but the difficulties of implementation should be weighed against the much larger benefits to be obtained than in smaller cities.

The case of Barnsbury was particularly important. The problems and conflicts which arose in its implementation and in deciding whether to keep, modify or reject the traffic scheme after its experimental period were significant because Barnsbury was regarded by many as the first real test case of implementing environmental area policy in inner-city areas. Because of this, it was perhaps unfortunate that the Ministry of Housing and Local Government (MOHLG), having spent three years studying the problem, should abandon their involvement once their report was published. The important lessons to be learnt from the Barnsbury scheme related more to the difficulties of the implementation process and the social problems to which it drew attention than to the technical aspects of the scheme. All the parties involved could therefore have benefited from continued MOHLG involvement, particularly as initial steps had already been taken towards public participation.

While, however, there was little active promotion of local environmental interests, and such as there was often lacked success, both the institutions and certainly the public showed themselves able and willing to defend environmental interests when these were threatened by another party. The A1 case study, for instance, demonstrated the strength of local opposition when Peter Walker rejected a scheme to widen the road through Hampstead Garden Suburb for which his own Department was responsible, and the local residents and Haringey Council demanded a more environmentally acceptable Archway Road scheme. It also clearly showed that it was the wealthier and already more attractive areas that produced the strongest and most articulate opposition to the road widening scheme.

The GLC defended environmental interests on occasions: they rejected the monorail idea partly for environmental reasons, and insisted upon the road tunnel at Thamesmead in preference to the bridge which would have prejudiced the creation of satisfactory environmental conditions in the new development.

Generally, and perhaps not surprisingly, it was local groups or the boroughs who sought to defend local environmental interests, particularly against road and traffic schemes put forward by the GLC or the Department of the Environment (DOE). There was evidence too, particularly in inner London, that borough planning departments were as apprehensive of the environmentally damaging schemes put forward by their own engineering and highway planning colleagues, as of those put forward by metropolitan or central government. On the whole, however, the representation of environmental interests constituted an emergency service rather than an integral part of the transport planning process.

The use of strategic transport policies to improve the environment is more difficult to evaluate, because policies have been pursued primarily to meet other objectives, although this in itself is an important conclusion. Environmental arguments have been used in support of the GLC's ringway proposals for example, but environmental improvement was not their *raison d'être*. Likewise traffic restraint policies have been pursued primarily for traffic reasons with a secondary interest in helping public transport. Nevertheless it is possible to assess the capability of the present system to meet a different set of priorities. The question of roadbuilding is dealt with later. The other broad policy option is traffic limitation and from what has already been said, such a policy if consistently applied could probably do much to reduce the conflict between the boroughs and the GLC over environmental and pedestrian area schemes. Indeed, such schemes could (by reducing available road space) themselves be used to restrain traffic, in which case the GLC as traffic authority would have a greater incentive to initiate them. In other words both levels of government would have a strong incentive to implement such schemes but their objectives would differ.

To summarise, all the institutions in London and particularly the DOE, GLC and the boroughs subscribed to the need to promote improvements to the environment. Improvements schemes were formulated by planning and sometimes engineering departments but progress in implementation was slow in relation to the size of the task, the importance which the authorities said they attached to the problem, and the energies devoted to meeting other transport objectives.

It has become clear that more rapid improvement of the environment, at least in areas where improvement is most needed, would require either the boroughs to be given wider traffic powers, in order to be able to decide for themselves between traffic and environmental priorities, or the GLC to adopt an approach to its traffic responsibilities which more freely admitted greater priority for environmental improvement. Once the deadlock created by the present arrangement of powers and policies had been broken, it might stimulate a more imaginative approach, at both GLC and borough level, to the promotion of environmental interests rather than simply their defence when threatened.

The boroughs were usually better placed than the GLC to play this role because they were more closely involved with local problems and usually had a greater knowledge of and closer contact with local communities and their representatives. There was, however, plenty of scope for smaller representative units (whether neighbourhood councils or amenity, residents or traders groups) to generate interest in and advise the boroughs on local environmental matters. What was lacking was any regular or formal method of communication between borough and local interests.

ROAD SAFETY

The GLC, the police and most of the London boroughs have staff, and in some cases sections, specifically responsible for monitoring the accident situation and initiating action where required for accident prevention. While the vigour and the competence of road safety sections and committees varied amongst the boroughs, the framework for action was well established. No attempt was made, however, to spell out and act upon the implications of strategic policy for road safety. The quantity of roads and traffic in London is not fixed and can be greatly influenced by strategic policy of which road safety should be an important determinant. There was no evidence that this had been the case in the Greater London Development Plan (GLDP) strategy and its motorway proposals. This plan held no prospect of reducing the number of accidents or fatalities in London: any hoped-for reduction in the accident *rate* would be more than offset by the very large increase in vehicle miles which was planned and which is a major determinant of the number of accidents. If this implication of the plan was understood and accepted it was certainly never made publicly explicit. The GLC's road safety unit was well placed to co-ordinate research findings and to analyse statistical data on accidents, but it appeared to have little influence on broad transport policy within the Council. As with considerations of the environment and pedestrians, the fundamental choice about the volume of road traffic to be provided for was at no point influenced by or reappraised in the light of considerations of road safety.

At the borough level effectiveness in dealing with local 'black spots' was often dependent on the public or the police drawing the attention of the council to a dangerous situation, but there was little evidence of a lack of concern. Because of the lack of knowledge of the relationship between traffic and accidents a few boroughs felt that a more flexible approach to traffic management would aid the formulation of a more positive policy for road safety.

The institutional structure, therefore, seemed well suited to the function of monitoring and dealing with *ad hoc* problems as they arose, but road safety received little priority in the formulation of strategic transport policy. In short, the system was geared to a far greater interest in the prevention of road accidents than in the promotion of road safety.

PEDESTRIANS AND CYCLISTS

In terms of the GLC's duty as traffic authority for London 'to secure the expeditious, convenient and safe movement of vehicular and other traffic (including foot passengers) . . .' pedestrians and cyclists are quite rightly regarded as 'other traffic,' but separate consideration of them is justified partly because their comparative vulnerability demands a different approach to design and management from that for motor traffic, but more importantly because their interests have been sadly neglected. Evidence from both interviews and the case studies emphasised that pedestrian traffic received secondary consideration to the claims of motor traffic. The case study on *Walking in London* concluded that where consideration was given to pedestrians it concerned their safety, not their convenience. The special needs of cyclists were all but totally ignored except in the special situation of Thamesmead.

This neglect of pedestrians' interests or, alternatively, this bias towards motor traffic, was most obvious in the work of the GLC as traffic authority for London: for example, their support of the needs of motor traffic as they saw them, was sufficiently strong to bring the already slow legislative and consultation procedures to a virtual standstill in the case of the Bond Street and Carnaby Street schemes. But it would be wrong to imply that this attitude was peculiar to the GLC; the same bias was found to varying degrees in the boroughs and in the London highways division of the DOE.

Various reasons for the neglect of pedestrians and cyclists have been suggested. First, there is no agreed measure of traffic efficiency but it has usually been regarded as the movement of vehicles rather than of people and goods. It is rare that the benefits and disbenefits of a traffic scheme have been measured in terms of people and goods. The London Traffic Survey's definition of a trip, for example, excluded both pedestrians and cyclists. Second, pedestrian movement is generally far less demanding of precise engineering techniques and standards than vehicular traffic, and consequently it is the needs of the latter which have attracted most attention from engineering departments. The only exceptions have been where the flow of people is so great that design parameters have had to be sought, e.g. for bridges, escalators and subways, pedestrian concourses at railway stations and the like. A third point is that facilities for pedestrians are cheap by comparison with those for vehicles and it is an observable phenomenon that those services of government which receive most consideration are those whose financial demands are greatest.

Case Study *L* showed that the GLC as traffic authority has paid little attention to its statutory duty towards the *convenience* of pedestrians, and this, it is suggested, has contributed to a growing public disenchantment with its traffic policies. The GLC's road policies were not designed to meet the objective of improving pedestrian movement and indeed it was admitted that its secondary road policies would often mean greater inconvenience for pedestrians. The main method of providing for the safety of pedestrians was to move them out of the way of motor traffic and give them new but reduced opportunities for crossing the road. Pedestrian barriers, controlled crossings, subways, bridges and other means of regimenting people on foot were integral parts of secondary road 'improvements.' Moreover, many road schemes made conditions more dangerous for cyclists by providing free-flow turning movements at intersections. The only instance of special provision for cyclists was at Thamesmead, where design concepts were borrowed from the New Towns.

The boroughs and the DOE, where they have been involved in planning roads, have also neglected pedestrians. The highways legislation itself although enabling highway authorities to provide pedestrian (and cycle) facilities is not framed to give incentives for such provision. For example, as noted in Chapter 2, a scheme to widen a carriageway is termed an 'improvement' even if it involves narrowing the footways. Some degree of concern for pedestrians was shown by the boroughs in road or redevelopment schemes for town centres in which creating pedestrian-only (or pedestrian priority) areas in town centres was a major objective. Most of these, however, took second place to schemes designed to cater for longer-distance traffic (the proposed motorways, or schemes to increase the capacity of existing main roads). But while some boroughs pressed the GLC for permission to proceed with town centre schemes, few saw it as part of their role to question the GLC's strategic priorities. Other than in town centres and perhaps with regard to pedestrian movement to primary schools and playspaces, the planning departments of both the GLC and the boroughs had few recognisable concepts, let alone policies of planning new developments so as to maximise the opportunity to walk and cycle to various activities as opposed to using cars or public vehicles.

Pedestrian interests are also poorly represented by pressure groups and voluntary organisations. The Pedestrians' Association for Road Safety for example has concentrated, like the local authorities in London, on pedestrian safety rather than pedestrian convenience. Some middle-class pressure groups are beginning to take a wider interest. But voluntary groups, however active, are no substitute for the exercise of statutory powers and responsibilities by government bodies.

In London, as in other cities, the interests of pedestrians and cyclists have been poorly represented; walking and cycling have long been neglected as a part of the city's transport system and their special needs have been subjugated to the demands of motorised forms of travel. The source of this neglect does not lie in any particular authority or department nor even in inadequate statutory powers but in general attitudes which have persisted throughout the system. It is increasingly being seen by some pressure groups as an issue of 'humanity and urbanity against technology.' Certainly a balance has been lost and needs restoring. 'Traffic' responsibilities have been interpreted in terms of motor traffic the needs of which have received an attention not paralleled by any promotion of the interests of pedestrians and cyclists. As a result of this there has been no positive policy towards travel on foot and by bicycle from either the boroughs, the GLC or central government; schemes to improve pedestrian safety have resulted in a loss of pedestrian convenience and schemes to ease the flow of motor vehicles have worsened conditions for those on foot and on bicycles. Over this issue of conflict with motor traffic the GLC has substantially failed in its statutory duty as traffic authority to provide for the convenience of pedestrians and cyclists. Thus a more balanced approach to transport clearly would require either a change in the attitudes that predominate in the present structure or the creation of some new statutory power to champion the interests of pedestrians and cyclists.

ROAD CONGESTION

As Chapter 5 showed, in tackling the problem of lengthy and often unpredictable traffic delays there are broadly three alternative courses of action: to build new or widen existing roads (i.e. to increase road capacity), to limit traffic, or to leave things as they are. The third alternative has consistently been rejected by central government, the authorities in London and their critics, although the latter have sometimes thought a 'do nothing' solution preferable to some of the policies which have been pursued and proposed. In London, a major part of the resources devoted to transport, particularly since the Second World War, have been aimed at the problem of road congestion. 'Traditional' road building policies were supplemented during the 1960s by major programmes of traffic management. Both approaches have been of great importance since the early 1960s and are dealt with separately, and the pricing and regulation of vehicles is also discussed.

Road planning and construction

Definitions of roads of different types have been notoriously difficult to reach and there has often been much confusion between institutional (i.e. administrative) and functional classifications. In London for example there is the administrative hierarchy of Trunk roads, Metropolitan roads, borough Principal roads and local roads, but these do not entirely correspond to the functional hierarchy of primary, secondary and local roads suggested in the GLDP or to the older engineering definition of trunk roads, *A* and *B* roads later supplemented by motorways used by the Ministry of Transport (MOT). This section deals with the subject of roads in London under three broad functional headings: new major roads (such as those proposed in the GLDP), existing main roads (i.e. present multipurpose roads carrying fairly large volumes of traffic) and purely local roads (including lightly trafficked roads and pedestrian streets).

Major new roads. The largest road planning effort in London since the local government reforms of 1965 has come from the GLC and the DOE and has been directed towards the development of a network of motorway-standard roads. The proposals for this 'primary network' of roads contained in the GLDP came as no surprise: they were, if nothing else, consistent with the London Government Act 1963 which said that the GLDP was 'in particular to give guidance as to the future road system.' Although the wording itself is open to widely differing interpretations it was couched in the Herbert Commission's expectation that one of the principal advantages of a Greater London authority would be to get on with the job of building a comprehensive network of major new roads. Moreover, not only the overall pattern but also many sections of the network were based on schemes which had been discussed or incorporated in plans many years before.

In planning this new network the GLC's hand was considerably strengthened by the fact that the MOT was responsible for Trunk roads in Greater London (except within the old London County Council (LCC) area) and was busy preparing a programme of schemes. The two authorities jointly provided staff specifically for developing the primary road proposals, which included the enlargement of many of the existing Trunk roads (for example the North Circular Road and the A40). The GLDP primary road network consisted of a network that had been devised and tested as an entity, although composed of GLC and DOE roads. This common objective of developing a motorway network for London led to an almost complete absence of conflict between the GLC and MOT (and later on the DOE), despite the potential for differences arising from the somewhat arbitrary division of responsibility between the two bodies. There were differences in some instances, but these were mostly over local environmental problems (for example over the effects of the MOT's proposed extension of the M23 into London) or questions of route capacity or alignment rather than any disagreement over basic aims. In spite of the relative lack of conflict, however, the continued central government responsibility for Trunk roads in the Greater London area has been recognised by both the GLC and the DOE as 'clearly anomalous'[1] but it has had a considerable influence on the transport planning process and needs examination.

There were at least two reasons why the 1963 Act did not accept the Herbert Commission's recommendation, and excluded Trunk roads in Greater London from the GLC's responsibility. The first was a reluctance within central government to entrust the new metropolitan authority with too much power, at least before it had proved itself as a strategic planning authority. Coupled with this may have been internal pressures for the retention of London highway functions within the MOT on a basis analogous if not similar to the Road Construction Units for the other regions established in 1967–68. The second and more important reason was that Trunk road schemes in London (for which the Government meets the entire cost) would become eligible for only 75% grant like other Principal roads if transferred to the GLC. While wishing to have control over the planning and management of these roads, the GLC was unwilling to meet the extra 25% share of the cost of schemes, and generally took the view that they should become responsible only after major schemes had been completed.

What, then, has been the effect of the continued existence of Trunk roads in London? The DOE has in one sense acted as if Trunk roads were entirely a national matter, overriding London considerations. For example, the schemes for the enlargement of the North Circular Road to near-motorway standards were continued independently of the examination of the GLC's transport strategy at the GLDP Inquiry. No separate case was put forward for these schemes: the DOE's acceptance of them as an

[1] DOE (1971), *Paper B624*, GLDP Inquiry Stage 1.

executive function of the London Highways Group was apparently un-trammelled by any considerations of broader policy. But in another sense, the split responsibility for the proposed new motorways compelled the DOE to play a rather schizophrenic role: at the same time as his staff were planning, designing and promoting major road schemes, the Secretary of State had to make, and be seen to make, an impartial judgement on the GLDP in which these schemes were a major element. The influence of the divided responsibility for roads on the planning of London's transport as a whole, which since 1970 has been solely the responsibility of the GLC, must also be considered. Would the GLC have been so ambitious in its motorway plan if it had been responsible for 25% of its total cost? The danger in the present administrative arrangements of at least a distortion of the GLC's investment priorities must be recognised. From 1971 onwards the GLC had pressed the Government for 75% grants towards all capital investment for which they were responsible whether in road, rail or bus facilities, but they had indicated no desire to bring London's Trunk road schemes into line with this.

One further striking aspect of the GLC's attitude towards the GLDP motorway proposals must be highlighted. They were highly impatient with what they considered to be an unduly lengthy period of investigation into the plans. The GLDP was published in mid-1969 and the report of the Inquiry reached the Secretary of State at the end of 1972, making a period of well over four years from publication to a final decision. The motorways, however, would have an enormous, complex and irreversible impact on London and it was in recognition of this that the Minister, Anthony Crosland,[1] established what turned out to be the largest development plan inquiry yet held. Moreover, the GLDP Inquiry enabled wide and disparate views on many aspects of London's problems to be brought into the open and clarified. It gave the opportunity for all parties involved to enhance their knowledge. In view of these benefits, the GLC's complaint about consequential delays seems mistaken and short-sighted. It was hardly extravagant to spend four years evaluating the merits of a plan containing a thirty-year, £2000 million investment programme for roads alone. The GLC, it appeared, were concerned as much with keeping a steady flow of work for its primary road planning staff as with the long-term future of the metropolis.

While the planning of the primary road network was carried out by the GLC with the co-operation of the DOE it is the borough councils (as representatives of local interests) who are most concerned with the effect of these roads in the different parts of London. The GLC consulted the boroughs in drawing up its plan and encountered little initial opposition to the concept of a new major road network. By and large the boroughs saw this as a GLC responsibility and were concerned only that the new roads should be integrated in the best way possible with the local environment and existing road network. Although the motorway plan produced an

[1] At the time he was 'overlord' minister to the MOHLG and the MOT.

enormous wave of public protest, the boroughs (with very few exceptions) did not represent this concern at the first (strategic) stage of the Inquiry. Indeed, some boroughs (e.g. Newham and Harrow) claimed that the motorways would not affect their areas. The implication is clearly either that the primary roads would not have a strategic impact on London's transport system (which was patently untrue) or that the nature of this impact was inadequately explained by the GLC or understood by the boroughs.

At the GLDP Inquiry, only four boroughs (Camden, Croydon, Greenwich and Hounslow) gave any substantial evidence against the motorway plan in principle. It was thus left to a few (though sometimes powerful) voluntary groups and bodies outside local government to challenge the GLDP strategy as a whole. It was not until the 1971 elections, when many boroughs changed from Conservative to Labour control, that they offered any substantial opposition to the motorways, at the second (local) stage of the Inquiry. Up to that time both political parties had supported the concept of new motorways: it was a Labour GLC that approved the 'motorway box' (Ringway 1) and it was the Conservatives who approved the GLDP motorway network. This commitment, moreover, came before the completion of the London Transportation Study, and certainly before any radically different alternatives had been formulated.

It is necessary, however, to see their actions in the context of the mood of the early 1960s and indeed the whole spirit in which the Herbert Commission made its recommendations and the GLC was set up. Most people in positions of responsibility—officers, consultants, and politicians at all levels—believed that major new roads were required in London. At that time criticism was levelled more at the delay in the building of new roads than at the adverse effects which they might have on the city's structure, environment or transport system. Nevertheless, it was a major shortcoming of the planning process that alternatives to the building of major new roads were not considered. The fact that the DOE was also actively planning a large road-building programme within Greater London would in any case have partly constrained the GLC in considering radically different options. It was clear, however, that the GLC themselves believed in a road building solution. Because of this emphasis it was unlikely that the large highway planning groups of the DOE and the GLC could have had sufficient and varied skilled manpower to formulate and evaluate alternative approaches to the transport problem.

Existing main roads. It is the existing main roads in London which pose the most difficult problems because most of them serve several different and competing functions. Almost without exception, for example, London's shopping streets are also the carriers of large volumes of long- and short-distance vehicular and pedestrian traffic. More often than not a road scheme which aims to improve conditions for one set of users at the same time succeeds in making things worse for other users.

As already explained, responsibility for London's main roads is divided between the boroughs, the GLC and the DOE. The question here is not so much why the system has not overcome congestion, unreliability of buses, environmental degradation and other problems to be found on London's main roads, but whether it is capable of tackling them. The role of the GLC is examined first as they were the most important agency as planning authority for London as a whole and as highway authority for Metropolitan roads (which form a large proportion of the main road network). They included this wide network in the GLDP as 'secondary roads' and produced general policy guidelines for investment in them. Perhaps the most significant aspect of their policy was that it was designed mainly to meet the problem of traffic congestion, in particular in the hope that it would enable the primary roads to fulfil their traffic functions. Moreover, longer-distance or 'through' traffic was implicitly regarded as of more importance than local traffic: for example the GLC spoke of the need to take account of 'wider traffic needs' in considering the Bond Street pedestrianisation and Barnsbury environmental area schemes.

Apart from the formulation of general policy, the GLC were also pushing ahead with the implementation on its Metropolitan roads of schemes inherited from the pre-1965 authorities. Examples in inner London were the Archway and Angel schemes on the A1, the enlargement of the 'Inner Ring Route,' the Wandsworth bridge approach, Finchley Road, and West Cromwell Road. The GLC also agreed to schemes on the borough Principal roads. All this work was designed to increase the capacity of the main-road network for vehicular traffic.

More recently, the problems of adverse effects on the environment and on local accessibility were being taken more seriously by the GLC, but it was rare that these considerations took precedence over their desire for increased traffic capacity. Moreover, while the boroughs were often quick to represent local environmental and other interests when these were threatened by GLC or DOE road schemes, they rarely questioned the need for the schemes themselves. Local amenity groups, however, sometimes demanded a fundamental reappraisal of policy as well as defending their own local interests. For example, the GLC decided to drop its plan for a new road through the Greenwich conservation area after opposition from local groups combined with criticism of the scheme by Sir Colin Buchanan in his capacity as consultant to the GLC.

The difficulty of reconciling road widening with local interests was one reason why the GLC had rejected the possibility of providing for a large increase in traffic in London by wholesale widening of the existing main roads as an alternative to building motorways.

How does the GLC's handling of the main-road network compare with that of the boroughs? In general terms it is probably fair to say that the GLC and the boroughs have shared the view that increased traffic capacity on existing roads will help to reduce traffic delays. There were differences over how this capacity should be provided and in what places it was acceptable. But the underlying assumption always seemed to be that, difficult though it might be to achieve, the provision of extra traffic capacity was justified. The GLC undoubtedly played the major role in translating this objective into the formulation and preparation of schemes, but the work was in many cases shared with highway planning sections in the boroughs. Indeed, schemes were put forward by the boroughs themselves for increasing the traffic capacity of both borough Principal roads and Metropolitan roads. Also, prior to the 1969 Act, the boroughs wished to gain control of certain Metropolitan roads. This policy was not due to any basic dislike of the GLC's proposals for these roads but to a desire to gain more control over land-use planning in their areas (i.e. to avoid the referral to the GLC of planning applications within 220 feet of a Metropolitan road).[1] Later a basis for the transfer of borough Principal roads to the GLC under the powers of the 1969 Act was negotiated, and this too related more to the handling of applications for planning permission than to the locus of responsibility for road planning. It remains to be seen how this will work in practice, for example with regard to the safeguarding of road widening lines.

Case Study *K* provides evidence on several aspects of how the planning of London's main roads has been handled, in particular the rather tenuous links that have existed between stated policies and actual schemes, and the extent of co-ordination (or lack of it). The creation of the GLC with its strategic planning responsibilities in 1965 made little difference to the planning of the A1. Most of the widening schemes and widening safeguarding lines had been drawn up many years before by the MOT and the LCC. Some, like the proposed roundabout at the Angel intersection, dated back to the beginning of the century. All were accepted, however, after the London government reforms, by the GLC, the new London boroughs and the MOT.

The preparation of the GLDP provided an opportunity to review the various schemes which had been developed on a piecemeal basis under the old system, but the 'secondary road' policy produced by the GLC in 1970 gave no indication that such a review had been carried out. To the contrary, its statements of policy were so general and contained so many qualifications that virtually any highway scheme would be consistent with it. Thus the stated intention of concentrating investment on the widening of intersections rather than the lengths of road between them did not alter the GLC's decision a year later to proceed with the widening of Archway Road; and the moves towards traffic restraint in the central area did not weaken the GLC's commitment to the long-standing scheme for the Angel. The other authorities involved, the MOT (later the DOE) and the boroughs, also accepted the widening of the A1 and continued with their own schemes without questioning the lack of strategic policy for the road as a whole. Several arguments including the easing of traffic flow and

[1] Greater London Group (1968), *Lessons of the London Government Reforms* (vol4 of Research Studies by the Royal Commission on Local Government in England), p31.

environmental improvements were used in favour of individual schemes, but with the exception of the MOT–DOE Archway Road scheme, no evidence was produced to support the assertions. Indeed it appeared that the highway authorities regarded road widening as a purely executive matter, no more relevant to broad transport policy than the maintenance of street lights and drains.

This divorce of policy from executive action and the apparent immunity of road widening schemes from policy changes meant that co-ordination between the different authorities over the various schemes was largely confined to detailed engineering matters. Moreover, there were no successful attempts to ensure the phased implementation of the widening of the A1 and the prospect for the future continued to be a mixture of hope and uncertainty.

A further disappointing aspect of the handling of the A1 was that the three levels of government played no distinct role in representing different interests: it was difficult for the MOT (and DOE) to represent the interests of 'national' traffic on a road that was accorded only 'secondary' status by the GLC; the GLC as already said made little attempt to interpret the 'metropolitan' function of the A1 in London; and the boroughs did not always represent the local interests of residents and other people affected by the widening schemes. Barnet, for example, expressed no firm views on the MOT scheme for Falloden Way and left the people of Hampstead Garden Suburb to make their own objections at the public inquiry; Haringey pressed for a better Archway Road scheme but Islington made little attempt to safeguard environmental interests threatened by the Archway and Angel schemes. Amenity groups sprang up in the Hampstead and Highgate areas to defend their local interests but received little response when they tried to question the strategic implications of the policy.

Thus the A1 case study illustrates two important features of the present system in London. First, there has been a great momentum behind the roadbuilding philosophy which at all three levels of government has shown itself to be remarkably resistant to change; resistant not only to changes in local government structure but also to changes of stated policy and political control. This, it appears, is a direct reflection of the situation where highway planners and engineers, again at all three levels of government, have remained not only largely separate from their land-use or 'strategic' planning colleagues but have also shown themselves sufficiently influential to be able to resist changes in their traditional role.

Second, the division and particular interpretation of responsibilities for existing main roads has considerably hindered progress towards an effective representation of both local and broader planning interests through the two-tier local government system.

Local roads. The overwhelming proportion of road mileage in London consists of what may be described as local roads, their traffic function being mainly to provide access to premises and for local journeys by vehicle and on foot. Generally speaking, they do not carry large volumes of traffic, though many of them are used as 'rat runs' especially during peak hours. Few roads of this type were included in the GLDP secondary road network, nor would they generally be Principal roads attracting Government grants for schemes. The administration of these roads has been mainly concerned with the routine maintenance of carriageways, drainage and lighting, and the design of new links in redevelopment schemes. There appeared to be few major problems in carrying out this function. Some boroughs, however, particularly in outer London, complained of difficulties in recruiting sufficient staff and consequently were finding it difficult to maintain proper standards of repair.

As far as the planning of local roads was concerned, most boroughs, apart from initiating or implementing traffic management schemes, exercised safeguarding lines for widening as redevelopment of frontage properties allowed. Although this procedure was adopted on many local roads it was nearly always an inheritance from the pre-1965 authorities which in few cases had received reappraisal or even ratification by the borough councils as a conscious policy. It was in fact often the case that widening lines had been established by council officers and had never been subject to the formal consultation and designation procedures set out in the Highways Act 1959. But the most significant features of the widening line policy were its evolution purely as a response to traffic problems and the implicit underlying assumption that widening was both the right answer to the traffic problem and a reasonable solution in the urban situation. Whether or not the first part of the assumption was correct, land use and town-scape had apparently been ignored in most boroughs. There were instances of road widening lines that had been reviewed (for example, Bond Street, see page 402) but few boroughs appeared to have even considered making a comprehensive reappraisal of the widening of local roads as a policy.

As with main road planning, the rather vague acceptance of a long-term widening policy by most of the boroughs meant that only occasional matters of principle arose over the co-ordination of roads which crossed borough boundaries. Agreement between boroughs about the traffic role of particular local roads was usually reached on an *ad hoc* basis.

The scope for the boroughs to influence local traffic flows is limited because local highway schemes will inevitably affect traffic over which the GLC has ultimate responsibility. There were apparently few instances where local road widening schemes had been opposed by the GLC's traffic section, but there was sometimes conflict with the GLC's Historic Buildings Board or with borough planning departments when schemes affected listed buildings or conservation areas.

The most unsatisfactory aspect of the administration of local roads was a general lack of imagination in using highway powers to secure improvements not only for vehicular traffic but also for the environment, road safety and cyclists and pedestrians. For example, it appeared to be standard practice to resurface local roads to their original width and shape without first considering whether the opportunity could be taken to, say, widen pavements or realign kerbs at junctions to make better and safer provision for pedestrians, or to improve the appearance of the street by tree planting. Such consideration was often given in General Improvement Areas by borough planning departments, but the promotion of positive improvements was limited even when opportunities arose from routine maintenance work. There appeared to be no one with the specific task of considering possibilities for improvement.

Amenity societies often made suggestions for local street improvements and would probably be more forthcoming if approached as a matter of course by local councils to give their views. Not all councils have seemed keen on such a dialogue with local residents, though Camden's participation exercise over the Primrose Hill environmental management scheme and Islington's in Barnsbury were examples. Moreover, not every community has the ability to communicate its wishes to its borough council, or even to make representations on schemes initiated by the councils. Indeed evidence from the A1 and environmental management case studies suggested that those streets whose inhabitants lobby hardest for improvements are by no means those which most need them.

This section on London's roads concludes with a consideration of the extent to which the organisation of the road system has fulfilled the intentions behind the 1963 Act and the later recognition embodied in the 1969 Act of the need to integrate all forms of transport in London. Despite the fact that responsibility for new and existing major roads has been divided between the three levels of government, many potential problems of coordination have been avoided by the general predominance of a road-building philosophy to which local, metropolitan and central governments have devoted considerable resources in planning and implementation. It has been this very momentum which has inhibited a more rational and comprehensive approach to the transport problem of which road congestion is only a part. For a fresh approach to have developed it was necessary for road planning to be subsumed within the broader task of transport planning which the 1969 Act placed firmly in the hands of the GLC. In the light of this new function for local government the continued responsibility of the DOE and the London boroughs for many of London's major roads has come to be seen as an administrative anomaly. But, more important, it could be represented as an inhibiting factor in the GLC's consideration of a wider range of transport policies. The power of highway planning departments at all three levels ensured a consistent philosophy but at the same time hindered the practical interpretation and implementation of any policies which required the reduction or modification of their traditional roles. The borough councils and local groups were often concerned to moderate the adverse local effects of new roads but rarely challenged the philosophy of road-building as an element of strategic transport policy. The boroughs, however, were in a good position to seek out and act upon problems concerning purely local roads and often did so. But the problem of drawing a formal distinction between local and main roads remains, and the boroughs need to be able to better represent local interests on roads which because of their wider traffic role must be the responsibility of the metropolitan authority.

Traffic management

Traffic authorities have very wide powers for traffic management which may be used for the purpose of improving general traffic flow, controlling particular classes of traffic, regulating or restricting traffic by time, direction and speed, and improving the environment. In London these powers are concentrated largely in the hands of the GLC, the DOE being responsible for traffic on Trunk roads. The boroughs initiate traffic management schemes and implement them as agencies, but they require GLC approval and processing of the statutory orders. The police play a large part in traffic control but again the orders which they enforce are made by the GLC or, in the case of experimental orders, with the GLC's consent. The comments which they have a statutory right to make on the enforcement aspects of GLC or borough schemes are also very influential. Consequently, responsibility for traffic management in London, whether good, bad or indifferent, falls squarely on the shoulders of the GLC.

In a city the size of London traffic control needs to be fairly comprehensive if the road system is to be used efficiently. The planning, implementation and maintenance of traffic schemes inevitably creates an enormous workload. This has been handled not only by the large executive traffic department at County Hall, but also by traffic departments within the boroughs as agents. Consultants have also been employed by both the boroughs (e.g. by Islington on the Barnsbury traffic scheme) and the GLC (e.g. on bus priority schemes). It was a common complaint amongst the boroughs, however, that traffic work was not being effectively divided, and that the GLC's traffic department was checking their work, both in designing and cost estimating, to a fine degree of detail. Complaints on this score varied in intensity between boroughs—Westminster for example found that the GLC's engineers generally trusted the accuracy of their work particularly if consulted early in the design stages, while some other boroughs with staffing difficulties were glad to have an informed second opinion from the GLC. Evidence from some boroughs and the GLC (particularly about those schemes described in the environmental management and pedestrian Case Studies *G* and *L*) gave strong indications that a great deal of work carried out by the boroughs (or their consultants) was repeated by the GLC for the purpose of checking before agreement was finally reached. Some duplication of work is probably both inevitable and desirable if the GLC as traffic order-making authority is to ensure that schemes are consistent with their traffic policies. The amount and similarity of work carried out at both levels of government, however, indicates either that the boroughs lack the resources to prepare traffic management schemes adequately or that the GLC underestimates their capabilities and duplicates their efforts to a needless degree, or that the GLC has failed to identify and adhere to the strategic aspects of traffic management.

It was also the opinion of some borough engineering departments that the close involvement of the GLC in detailed traffic management work was a major cause of delay in implementing schemes, although the order-making procedures were also considered to be unnecessarily lengthy and complicated, particularly those for relatively minor modifications to schemes.

This situation had clearly affected the morale of staff in the boroughs. The rechecking, and sometimes subsequent modification or rejection of work by the GLC was a source of frustration to officers and might well have contributed to the difficulties of some boroughs in recruiting sufficient trained staff. Even chief officers resented the situation where in practice they had two sets of political masters, one at the GLC and one in their own council.

Not surprisingly it was the more innovatory traffic management work of the boroughs which was subject to most scrutiny and delay at County Hall (for example Westminster's Bond Street scheme which was rejected by the GLC, the scheme for Barnsbury drawn up by Islington with their consultants and Camden's scheme for a network of bus-only lanes). In making these comments, however, it must be pointed out that the relationship between the GLC and the boroughs was comparatively new and some difficulties in defining their relative roles were to be expected. Just as in the early years of the new system the MOT was reluctant to transfer all its traffic and highway powers in London to the GLC, so the GLC might be expected to exercise caution over delegating work to the boroughs.

The boroughs, usually much more familiar with their particular localities than the GLC, nevertheless played an important role in traffic management work. They were better placed than the GLC to anticipate local difficulties in advance of implementation, to adjust the implementation of schemes as local circumstances demanded, and to monitor the effects of schemes on local interests (e.g. traders and residents).

The management of traffic is complicated by the need for supervision and enforcement. These tasks are the responsibility of the police. Although traffic wardens in London have been employed to supervise on-street parking and have taken over certain other traffic functions of the police, the enforcement of traffic law has become an immense and often difficult task. Some traffic schemes are virtually self-enforcing but the GLC have regarded enforcement problems as a major hindrance if not an obstacle to the introduction of measures such as bus-only lanes and bans on lorry parking. For instance, neither they nor the police had any long-term plans for enlarging the warden manpower to cope with such policies.[1]

[1] See *Hansard HC Papers 107* (*vii*), 1971–72, pp121–6 and Case Study *Q*.

A major difficulty was that owners and not drivers were liable for traffic offences. The shortage of police manpower was a major problem and the gradual shift of traffic responsibilities from police constables to traffic wardens would seem a worthwhile and to some extent inexorable trend.

The police often have an intimate knowledge of local traffic conditions, perhaps even more so than the local authorities themselves, and through their close day-to-day involvement on the ground have accumulated considerable experience in traffic matters. This involvement has, however, given rise to certain problems which together justify a reappraisal of the role of the police in traffic matters.

First, as a body under entirely separate control the police may and often do have different priorities from those of the other traffic management agencies (i.e. the boroughs, the GLC and the DOE). When consulted on traffic management schemes, for example, the police have tended to take a practical and short-term view which although of considerable value, has often hindered the promotion of new techniques and reinforced the GLC's reluctance to adopt an experimental approach (see Bond Street, Case Study *L*). Another important point is that when confronted with a situation of quite severe manpower shortage, they have developed their own priorities on the enforcement of schemes. As pointed out in Chapter 3 and the studies on environmental management, Inner London Parking Area (ILPA) and station car parks, the police have given higher priority to the maintenance of traffic flow than the enforcement of schemes aimed at improving the environment. Moreover, the police appear to have exercised little if any discrimination in their control of vehicular traffic: it seemed to matter little whether traffic comprised buses, taxis, lorries, cars or cycles—as long as they were kept moving the police would feel that they had done their job. The view increasingly taken by the GLC that buses should receive priority over other traffic was not reflected in the training of police traffic control officers.

Second, both borough and GLC officers complained that the police, despite their having few powers and little training in the use of traffic management techniques, expressed views on technical matters outside their field of responsibility as well as problems of enforcement. Certainly the police were building up their section dealing with the evaluation of traffic management schemes (see Chapter 3), and this raises the ominous possibility of even more detailed examination of traffic schemes. The use of more sophisticated traffic control techniques and equipment might make jobs in the Traffic Branch of New Scotland Yard more attractive, but these techniques should not be developed and operated independently of the traffic authority.

Day-to-day relationships between the police and both the boroughs and the GLC seemed generally amicable. The Joint Traffic Executive handled schemes and individual policies capably. The evidence from the studies, however, was that it had not proved a productive forum for the discussion of traffic with particular reference to enforcement, against the broadest transport policy background, for instance concerning the long-term repercussions of widespread traffic restraint.

The main obstacle, however, to developing new forms and ways of using traffic management in London, lay in the attitudes of most of the authorities concerned, but particularly the GLC and the police. A dominant belief was that existing levels of vehicular traffic should be accommodated (preferably with a reserve capacity as recommended for new schemes by the former MOT, of up to 20% where this could be achieved), and that schemes should not deliberately restrain traffic by congestion. It obviously became difficult to reconcile this view with schemes to improve pedestrian, environmental, or bus operating conditions which could involve a loss of capacity for general vehicular traffic. On the other hand, there was little evidence in London as to whether and to what extent such action would cause increased congestion in practice. The Pimlico environmental management scheme suggested that no additional congestion would arise, i.e. that trips would be diverted to other routes or not be made at all. In spite of this the GLC and the police were reluctant in the extreme to undertake experimental schemes in order to test the reactions of drivers and other members of the community.

A change in this attitude and an increased willingness to experiment could open up a much wider range of possibilities in the use of traffic management to meet objectives other than that of easing the flow of vehicles. Considerable pressure from professional and lay circles persuaded the GLC in 1972 to introduce the experimental scheme in Oxford Street which was designed to alleviate the appalling conditions for pedestrians and public transport at the expense of road space for general traffic. If this scheme should confirm the experience from provincial and European towns that traffic restriction in certain streets causes little if any extra traffic delay, it could prove to be a turning point in the history of traffic management in London.

As far as traffic management is concerned, then, the concentration of powers in the hands of the GLC has created a powerful structure for tackling this important and complex aspect of transport organisation. The objective of easing traffic flow has been actively pursued and the momentum established by the London Traffic Management Unit in the early 1960s has been maintained. The main problems, however, as already noted, have been the conflict between traffic, environmental and pedestrian interests, and the slow development of techniques to take adequate account of the special needs and potential of certain classes of traffic such as buses and bicycles. Conflict has also arisen between the needs of through traffic and local movement and access. All these problems have been reinforced by the priorities of enforcement held by the police, the spirit of the road traffic acts, and the traditional preoccupation with the flow of vehicles. Of course, traffic management which is designed to meet the objective of reducing traffic delays and increasing traffic flows is plainly difficult if not impossible to reconcile with the other objectives described. The subject requires much more research and practical experimentation. Consequently a change in the direction of policy would be more dependent upon a change of attitude and priorities than upon changes in the structure of traffic powers and responsibilities. Indeed since 1971 the GLC has shown itself capable of applying traffic management to aid bus operation. Two further factors, however, have hindered the development of traffic management in London. One has been the inordinate length of time taken for the making and amending of traffic orders. The other has been the reluctance of the GLC to take a flexible approach to the implementation of experimental schemes. This latter problem is unlikely to be eased while the quantity and pattern of traffic on the roads is regarded as relatively fixed and sacrosanct.

Pricing and regulation of vehicles

Both the characteristics of road vehicles and the use that is made of them are controlled to some extent by pricing and regulation. The operation of most vehicles is not confined to particular areas and standards for controlling noise, fumes and the maximum size and loading of commercial vehicles apply nation-wide. They are the responsibility of the DOE, which is not only the guardian of national policy on environmental matters, but also controls research bodies who help to define the standards. Vehicle and fuel taxation has also been in the hands of central government and is thus also capable of being an instrument of national policy; for example the financial aid to public transport through reduced fuel tax for buses. Taxes on commercial vehicles may also be used to influence the relative use of road and rail, or the size of vehicle in most common use.

This book has not examined in detail how central government is structured to implement national policy in these ways but it has looked at regulations which control the use of vehicles in London. The control of parking by the GLC and the boroughs through pricing, time limits and the rationing of space is dealt with below, but other area-based controls have also been put forward. The GLC, for example, suggested a system of daily supplementary licenses for vehicles entering central London. As with parking controls, the boroughs would need to be involved in fixing boundaries and measuring local effects, but although the discussion of such a policy could be initiated by the GLC, it would almost certainly need the DOE to negotiate new legislation through Parliament to enable such policies to be effected. Likewise the GLC as strategic planning transport and traffic authority for the metropolis could implement a road pricing scheme in London, but the development of the techniques required has naturally fallen to central government because it is a matter of national significance involving, for example, basic alterations to the system of vehicle and full taxation and a reappraisal of common law rights concerning the use of the highway.

An anomaly of the present system is that the GLC issues licences for private vehicles while the police are responsible for licensing and inspecting public vehicles (including taxis) and their drivers. Even since the publication of the Maxwell Stamp Committee's Report,[1] taxis have not received much attention as an element of transport in London despite the very important role they play, particularly in the inner parts of the city. Private hire cars ('mini-cabs') have also been neglected and are not even subject to the same licensing procedures as taxicabs. If these modes of travel were to be more positively integrated into the transport system there would be a need for close involvement between the operators and the GLC, a move which could be hindered under present arrangements by the police responsibilities for taxicabs.

Parking

The GLC have since 1967 had considerable powers to control parking. They can specify standards of provision of parking space in new buildings, which the boroughs are expected to accept and implement, and may design and implement on-street parking control schemes, although the borough's consent was required until 1969. Since 1969 the GLC have also had wide powers to control public off-street parking by licence but have not yet employed them. This leaves the *use* of the existing private non-residential parking a large element outside public control.

As with traffic management, much detailed and executive work is done by the boroughs either as the GLC's agents, or more usually as executives for schemes of their own proposing, but which have been approved by the GLC after consulting at least the police and London Transport (LT). The Metropolitan Police undertake the surveillance of parking on the street and follow up defaulters on parking fines, while leaving borough officials to deal with people who have not paid their excess meter charges. The test of this system is whether it enables parking policy as a whole to meet local parking needs (i.e. the availability of space in particular localities) whilst forming an important element of London's strategic transport policy.

The GLC, who soon recognised that parking and road capacity were related, developed policies for both on- and off-street parking to limit car commuting, particularly in central London. They reversed the LCC's policy of insisting on a minimum number of parking places related to the floorspace of non-residential development, and established a maximum number related to the service traffic generated by the buildings, necessarily a much lower figure. It remains to be seen whether the boroughs will implement these standards; few have yet done so, to the chagrin of the GLC.

[1] Home Office (1970), *Report of the Departmental Committee on the London Taxicab Trade* (Cmnd 4483).

It was shown in Chapter 3 and Case Study *Q* how the control of parking on the streets began as a means of ordering moving and stationary vehicles and allowing access to buildings and bus stops, but came to be seen as a major means of regulating the demand for car use. In this respect, and in the scale of parking control the GLC led the field, and acquired a unique power to extend control to off-street public parking. The formulation of the ILPA policy and the progress made in its implementation, although not as rapid as the original expectations of the GLC, may be regarded as a positive achievement of the two-tier local government system: the 'strategic' authority designing broad policy, and detailed design and implementation being carried out in co-operation with the boroughs. Initially there were differences of view, sometimes over matters of principle such as that of charging for a facility that was previously free. But on the whole the differences were valuable in the sense that they helped an acceptable balance to be struck between local and strategic considerations. The broad principles of ILPA were eventually accepted by the twelve boroughs involved and they were flexible enough to allow the boroughs' views to influence such matters as parking charges, time limits, the proportion of residents' bays and the details of implementation including zone boundaries and public consultation procedures.

Two clear problems with on-street parking control emerged, however, both attributable more to the structure of powers and procedures than to inefficiency or misguided policy. The major difficulty was enforcement. The problems created by the shortage of police manpower and driver rather than owner liability as described in relation to traffic management, apply even more to the expansion and enforcement of on-street parking controls.

The other problem was the lengthy and cumbersome procedure for implementing schemes and particularly for modifying them. The implementation process was sometimes delayed by differences between the GLC and the boroughs and sometimes by public opposition to parking control schemes, although early and informal local consultation was found to alleviate these problems. Modifications to schemes, however, were subject to the same lengthy order-making procedures as initial schemes and the boroughs on occasion had to resubmit a whole new scheme to the GLC. It could take many months even to change a meter space to a residents' bay, or a few two-hour meters to four-hour meters, but the time taken to alter meter charges could take two years or more, by which time, of course inflation had reduced the value of the revenue, and therefore the desired effects of increased restraint or parking availability.

If parking control is to be effective either charges must be kept permanently under review to ensure that meter spaces are always available, or more parking space must be provided. Otherwise, as was often the case in central London, the lack of available spaces makes parking difficult and encourages motorists to park illegally, usually not because of deliberate disregard for the law, but from sheer frustration. Some boroughs seemed unaware that increased meter charges could alleviate this problem by regulating demand and considered the only solution to be the provision of more off-street car parking, which, of course, could maintain or increase traffic generation.

It is clear that the integration of meter charges in total parking policy has not been at all easy and is not yet complete. The GLC's power of control extends only to off-street parking in public use; its standards for provision in new development are not yet statutory. The boroughs may pursue their own policies of off-street provision for private use and (until the GLC takes up its powers under the 1969 Act) public use. Few boroughs, even those within ILPA, made any serious attempt to relate their policies for on- and off-street parking.

Another factor which emerged was that parking policies (or at least views) differed between the boroughs. This was particularly noticeable in suburban town centres where the diversity of approaches was apparently matched and perhaps explained by a lack of interest on the part of the GLC compared with their concern for inner London problems.

It was also clear that the GLC had concentrated on the restraint of car commuters to central London by parking controls and had paid much less attention to the provision of station car parks which could serve as the commuters' alternative. The provision of car parks at stations is, by its very nature, a strategic problem. Clearly the boroughs cannot be expected to handle it individually as the extent, location and management (especially charges) of provision have implications far beyond borough boundaries. The boroughs, however, do need to be closely involved in any schemes because local interests are directly affected.

In one sense the interest of the rail operators in station car parks coincides with that of the community in that persuading motorists to go by train for as much of their journey as possible maximises railway revenue and minimises traffic on the roads. But a problem arises over the provision of station car parks in Greater London, because car parks serving the outer suburbs also tempt motorists to drive in from outside Greater London. It was for this reason in particular that British Rail (BR) had concentrated on provision outside Greater London. The same problem could arise as between inner and outer London. Both BR and LT have pursued their own policies for station car park provision and management. The pattern of provision reflects not only their own commercial considerations but also the fact that they have tended only to use easily available sites, not attempting to provide car parks where difficulties of land acquisition and interference from the local authorities would have arisen.

It is clear that as far as Greater London is concerned, station car park policy (as recognised in the GLDP) should be the responsibility of the GLC as it is a matter of strategic importance which transcends the interests of both the railway operators and the London boroughs. But, as shown in Case Study *F*, there was little interest in station car parks on the part of the GLC, and so the problem of resolving conflicting interests had scarcely arisen, despite claims in policy documents that they were 'encouraging' their provision. The potential conflict, however, between the provision of station car parks in Greater London and BR's policy of avoiding 'rail-heading' is a matter which would require careful negotiation between BR, the GLC and the county authorities concerned. It may be, of course, that station car parks are not considered to be suitable for Greater London and that feeder bus services, cycling and walking should be the main means of access to stations, but the promotion of a positive interchange policy of any sort requires a co-ordination of interests which has been sadly lacking.

The rapid evolution of on-street parking control and particularly ILPA was an example of a strategic policy that was interpreted successfully at a practical level, and also of relatively successful integration of the borough and metropolitan levels of government. The control of off-street parking is at an earlier stage of development, but seems to be a difficult subject for GLC–borough co-operation, perhaps reflecting their differing motives for adopting the policy. As with roads the links between policy statements and the provision of parking facilities were not always explicit. The main problem of on-street parking control was that of enforcement, aggravated, as with other traffic management, by a shortage of police manpower and the difficulty of following up offenders. Also the difficulty of revising meter charges meant that in many areas parking demand had outgrown supply, and thus encouraged the flouting of parking regulations.

The system was least capable of devising and implementing an effective policy for the parking of cars at stations despite the inclusion of this in the GLC's transport strategy. As with other interchange problems, the GLC failed to seriously tackle, let alone overcome, the undoubted difficulties of co-ordinating their own interests and those of LT, BR and the boroughs.

IMPROVING PUBLIC TRANSPORT

Most of the world's major cities have suffered a period of decline in their public transport systems as the use of motor-cars has increased. By the end of the 1960s, however, many authorities had come to recognise the large degree of dependence on public transport, particularly those that wished to maintain a large and thriving central area. They actively began to seek ways of reversing the deciine, of making recompense for past lack of investment and, in many cases, of providing new and additional facilities to improve the passenger and operating conditions of public transport relative to the car. In London the argument is no longer whether public transport should be maintained and improved, but where, how, and to what extent.

In the following paragraphs, therefore, the institutions responsible for public transport are examined not for their ability to administer its gradual reduction (though some cynics have argued that they and their policies have been well suited to this end) but for their capability to improve and integrate bus and rail services with the transport system as a whole.

Railway planning and construction

Unprofitability brought major railway development in London to a sudden end before the Second World War. After a period of virtual stagnation particularly on the Underground and BR suburban systems, it became generally recognised that the full benefits of railways were not reflected in the operators' accounts. This proved a turning point because both BR and LT were able to improve their claims for investment grants by presenting evaluations of projects which took account of social as well as financial costs and benefits. A comparison of the cost-benefit studies for the Victoria, Brixton and Fleet lines (Case Study *C*) showed how criteria for evaluation were gradually extended to take into account passengers' time saved, road congestion avoided and the value of a seat on a train and comfort. The Heathrow link Case Study (*E*) demonstrated how, after only three years, a reconsideration of the criteria for evaluation completely changed the recommendation.

The establishment of Government infrastructure grants by the 1968 Act was largely based on the recognition of the social benefits to be gained from railway improvements and, in 1971, stimulated by pressure from the transport operators, the GLC and the passenger transport authorities, the Government widened the scope of the grants to include major replacements of track, rolling stock, signalling and other equipment.[1] The south-eastern approaches scheme (Case Study *H*) was an example of how an operator's scheme of long-standing priority but low financial return went ahead when the grant basis was changed and passenger time saving included in the economic assessment.

The grant procedures, however, were not simply changed as the economists modified their cost-benefit analysis techniques. They must be seen in the context of an increasing political will at all levels of government to inject more money into public transport. Central government, for example, gave grant approval to certain major rail schemes in London in advance of a decision on the GLDP. Several boroughs in the east and south-east parts of the conurbation pressed strongly for new tube lines to serve their areas. The GLC also took an increasing interest in rail schemes particularly after a few months' experience of its new responsibilities for LT and transport planning in 1970: it urged the Government to pay grants for rail schemes equal to those for roads and, although belatedly, included investment programmes for both BR and LT in the suggested revisions to the GLDP in 1972. The GLC also agreed to pay 25% of the cost of new tube lines in London and strengthened LT's hand in securing Government grants for the Heathrow link and Fleet Line Stage 1 projects. Moreover,

[1] The grants claims were in fact quite slow to build up; for example, in 1969 BR only received £0.35 million.

they supported the claim that large but unquantifiable planning and land-use benefits would accrue to south-east London from the construction of the later stages of the Fleet Line. Support was also given to specific BR schemes such as that for the south-eastern approaches (Case Study *H*), although this was not backed by any financial commitment.

Thus the political and economic climate had turned in favour of investment in railway projects. But it is not enough simply to allow individual schemes to go ahead: a balanced approach requires the priority of different possible schemes, both road and rail, to be judged according to their value to the system as a whole. Just as the 1963 London Government Act aimed to provide a framework for the comprehensive consideration of roads in London, so the intention of the Transport (London) Act 1969 was to extend this framework to embrace the planning of public transport facilities and services. To assess the extent to which this intention has been or could be fulfilled, it is necessary to look at the roles played by the major bodies involved in rail planning—central government, the GLC, BR and LT.

Most of the rail schemes examined in the case studies were, like many of those for new roads, of long standing. They had been evolved over a number of years to meet operators' (and passengers') requirements. Both BR and LT had developed their own schemes within their forward planning departments, though largely independently of one another, and certainly independently of the planning departments of the GLC and the DOE (and MOT), despite the existence of the Transport Co-ordinating Council for London (TCCL) and later the Greater London Transport Group (GLTG) (see below).

Involvement of the GLC in rail schemes noticeably increased after the implementation of the 1969 Act. After two years it was having a significant influence in establishing a flow of investment schemes for LT's Underground system including in many cases the payment of a 25% grant. Although BR schemes were also supported, the GLC steadfastly refused to make any financial contribution towards them. The GLC argued that financial commitment to BR would be unacceptable while their first responsibility was to LT and their resources were already strained. A further reason, however, could have been a belief that they would receive little political benefit from helping the BR system, for which they had no direct administrative responsibility.[1] Moreover, schemes such as that for the south-eastern approaches would bring benefits not only to London's ratepayers, but also to many from well beyond the Greater London boundary (see Case Study *H*).

Despite the GLC's growing interest in rail schemes, rail planning formed a relatively small part of the strategic planning work of its Planning and Transportation Department. It was perhaps inevitable that the long-standing schemes which were both initiated and developed by LT and BR dominated the rail planning side of the picture, but there was little serious

[1] See *Hansard HC Papers 107 (vii)*, 1971–72, p124.

attempt to review these schemes in the light of the other policies drawn up in the GLDP, even the extensive motorway proposals.

The various investment schemes drawn up by LT and BR (including schemes for replacement of existing assets as well as for extensions and improvements) were simply added to the road investment proposals in the GLC's evidence to the GLDP Inquiry and their subsequent revision of the GLDP. There was little indication of the priority that should be attached to each scheme, or even of the specific nature of the individual schemes. This lumping together of three investment 'plans' (roads, BR and LT) drawn up by separate bodies showed a tacit recognition on the part of the GLC that all three systems should be considered together but indicated no commitment to the view that the allocation of investment between road and rail was interdependent. The operators' views as to what rail schemes were necessary may well have been consistent with the GLC's road and traffic policies but, in the absence of a comprehensive review of transport planning, there was no *a priori* reason for this being so.

The major contribution of the GLC to rail planning was made through the TCCL and (after the transfer of LT to the GLC) GLTG, which constituted machinery for joint discussion by the GLC, central government, BR and LT. The TCCL, set up by Barbara Castle, was intended to bring together and co-ordinate the forward planning of road and rail, but although it did have certain limited achievements (such as the formulation and evaluation of alternative plans for the rail link to Heathrow airport—see Case Study *E*) it certainly did not reconsider established plans either for road or rail. The same was true of the first two years of GLTG's operation. Indeed neither of these co-ordinating bodies nor any of the institutions represented on them had what could be described as a large transport planning staff. As the Sharp Report[1] emphasised, there were few professional transport planners (as opposed to highway, civil, traffic, signalling, mechanical and other engineers and land-use planners) and few facilities for training them.

Co-ordination, of course, is a more limited objective than integration and it is unreasonable to attribute a failure to achieve the latter to TCCL and GLTG. Even so, these groups often appeared to fall short of what was expected of them, particularly in the co-ordination of road and rail investment. Difficulties arose, for example, over the different criteria applied to road and rail schemes. There was evidence that the GLC, BR and LT were more anxious to defend their own particular schemes than to arrive at a concensus about all the schemes. Furthermore, BR became sceptical about the value of GLTG once the GLC had decided to make no financial contribution to BR schemes. BR considered that they could not participate in a way that would give real meaning to their operations while the scope of the meetings was constrained by predetermined financial policy. By contrast, the co-ordination of major road schemes by the MOT–DOE and the GLC demonstrated that a considerable degree of collabora-

[1] MOT (1970), *Transport Planning: The Men For The Job.*

tion between two separate authorities can be achieved. In that particular case, however, the two bodies had a unity of purpose which, moreover, was not apparently constrained by the need to prove, or even claim an economic rate of return from the schemes under discussion, as BR and LT had to do.

The role of central government in rail planning has remained a crucial one. The GLC, although responsible for the planning of transport in London, has little power (though it may have considerable influence) over the division of investment between road and rail. This power lies, as it always has done, ultimately with the Government, i.e. the DOE and the Treasury.

The DOE was formed to aid the development of an integrated approach at the national level to all aspects of the environment including transport, and a key feature of the Government's philosophy was that the executive role played by its former constituent Ministries, particularly the MOT, should be greatly reduced. The DOE, however, still retained direct executive control over Trunk roads and overall policy control of BR. Where Trunk roads were concerned, as already noted, the DOE and the GLC had a common aim of developing a high capacity road network for London: close co-ordination was required, but also assured at a working level. The co-ordination of road and rail planning involves more than close working arrangements at a day-to-day level. The philosophies of road, bus and rail planning have developed along separate and often fundamentally different lines and the reconciliation of the different interests involved cannot be simply a matter of stitching together different policies, but involves new relationships and major choices between one policy and another. Despite the high-level membership of GLTG (and TCCL before it) it is still only an advisory body (although stemming directly from the 1969 Act) and as such is a rather weak vehicle for such an important and inherently difficult task. The actual pattern of co-ordination therefore, whether good or bad, has been influenced by the locus of statutory powers in the DOE as well as the limited attempts at overall policy making through GLTG by the GLC.

As explained in Chapter 3, the DOE is involved in co-ordinating road and rail when approving GLC plans, setting criteria for Government grants and examining individual investment proposals from BR, LT and the GLC to see that they are good value for money. This role reflects the need to co-ordinate transport policy and public expenditure at the national level, but there are two objections to the way in which it has operated.

First, it has led to duplication of effort between the DOE and the GLC. The GLC has developed a large planning and transportation department and has devoted huge resources in particular to road planning and research. Yet because of the DOE's role in transport planning, and its direct responsibility for BR, the DOE also has a large establishment which inevitably competes directly with the GLC in recruiting specialist staff, particularly the rare breed of transport planners. In addition, both

BR and LT have staff to carry out long-term planning, albeit specifically from an operator's viewpoint.

Second, the DOE's examination of schemes for eligibility for grant aid (both road and rail) continued as if evaluation of the GLDP was a separate and unrelated activity. The dangers of this approach were anticipated by Richard Marsh, chairman of BR, who said that policies developed in isolation for the various forms of transport would lead to an 'increasingly fearful price' in terms of noise, congestion, pollution and discomfort.[1]

Thus the DOE has had a considerable influence over transport planning in London, and over the relationship between short- and long-term policies. Where Government finance was concerned, however, the DOE's co-ordinating role was itself influenced by the Treasury. The DOE would hold the ultimate co-ordinating position if the separate claims for investment in all parts of the transport system (from BR, the GLC, LT and the DOE itself) were considered as a whole and submitted to the Treasury each year as one transport 'vote' to be considered along with other sectors of public expenditure. But this was not the case. The Treasury considered separately the claim for investment in roads, LT and BR. Moreover these claims all related to different geographical areas: that for roads applied nation-wide, that for BR also covered the nation but isolated the London and South-East 'Pool' area (similar to the metropolitan economic planning region), and only that for LT roughly coincided with the Greater London area. Thus although the recommendations of the DOE may carry increasing weight as comprehensive plans are approved for London and the other conurbations, it is still open to the Treasury to perform its own brand of transport co-ordination.

Railway operation

The existence of two railway systems in London which are to a large extent physically independent of each other poses a difficult co-ordination problem not only for the planning of new investment but also for the determination of levels of service, fares and other aspects of rail operation. This is particularly so because the two systems have been operated by separate bodies and fulfilled different functions. The LT Underground system carries passenger traffic in north and west London whereas the BR surface railway system also carried inter-city and freight movement, as well as a very large volume of long-distance commuters and suburban passenger traffic, particularly in south and east London.

The need for co-ordinating the services of the two systems, at least at a very practical, day-to-day level, has been recognised for many years. One of the functions of both the London Passenger Transport Board (LPTB) and the Transport Tribunal, for example, was to maintain the principle of comparable fares for comparable services on BR and LT lines. There was also the well-established standing liaison group which handled,

[1] The *Guardian*, 24 February 1972; *The Times*, 25 February 1972.

for example, the co-ordination of timetables where the two networks met. But the concept of 'co-ordination' has broadened to one of 'integration' in recognition of the relationship between rail and road transport and also (though to a lesser extent) the effect of transport on urban development. This approach was certainly implicit in the provisions of the Transport (London) Act 1969, and it is from this wider viewpoint that this section looks at the handling of railway operation in London.

Traditionally the planning of railway fares and timetables (train frequencies, routes, speeds, stopping places, etc.) has, like the planning of new lines and capital investment, been carried out by the operators themselves. Despite public criticism of the services operated, this pattern of responsibility was hardly challenged until recent years, due partly perhaps to a general belief that such matters required specialist knowledge and expertise which only the railway operators could provide. What has been challenged, however, is the terms of reference within which railway services have been planned, particularly when changes motivated by commercial objectives (such as fare increases) have conflicted with social objectives.

The subject of railway fares and services, particularly in the London area, has always attracted political interest at the national level and consequently neither BR nor LT have had anything like a free hand in determining their own objectives and priorities. The approach of BR and LT has been conditioned and often constrained both by statutory requirements and by their absence of control or influence over many factors affecting the competitive position of the railways (such as the growth of car use, the building of new roads and the location of new development).

How, then, have the roles played by the controlling authorities (i.e. the MOT and DOE and latterly the GLC with regard to LT) contributed towards an integrated approach to rail operation in London, and to what extent have they determined the social and commercial objectives of the transport operators?

The influence of central government upon rail operation has always been strong, early landmarks of intervention being the grouping of the railways in 1921 and the formation of the LPTB in 1933. The nationalisation of the railways in 1947 was a further step which heralded much closer Government involvement in railway affairs, particularly in financial policy and the related matters of fares and railway closures. The machinery employed to operate the control included the Transport Tribunal and later on the National Board for Prices and Incomes (on fares) and the transport users' consultative committees (which dealt amongst other matters with proposed rail closures). The aim of the Government for the nationalised railway undertakings may be generally described as that of striking a balance between on the one hand the objectives of financial viability and on the other what was considered to be socially (or politically) acceptable in terms of service levels and staffing. In the face of competition from road transport and rising unit costs partly caused by the increasingly 'peaked' nature of passenger demand, the operators' task of maintaining and improving levels of service became increasingly difficult within the financial remit set by the Government, and until the 1968 and 1969 Transport Acts, usually resulted in the payment of Government grants to make up the annual revenue deficits incurred. Moreover these 'topping-up' grants were aimed at restraining fare increases or avoiding rail closures, and only secondarily at the more general issue of levels of services which was regarded by central government as less politically sensitive.

Thus the operators attempted to steer a course between conflicting and ill-defined social and commercial obligations. The 1968 and 1969 Acts for BR and LT respectively clarified the situation considerably. The 1968 Act established that the Government was to be responsible for determining and paying a specific grant for those unprofitable BR services which were socially necessary. As explained in Chapter 3, however, the payment of grants for the London 'pool' commuter services was a reflection of Government policy towards BR unremunerative services as a whole and did not eliminate uncertainty about the future levels of fares or services, nor could it be seen as a policy formulated with specific regard to London's overall transport needs. Despite these shortcomings, the 1968 Act at least enabled BR to adopt a positive commercial approach without raising matters of social conscience or prejudicing its statutory duty to break even. It is, however, difficult to separate commercial from social objectives. For example, there is a social element in the extent to which BR has accepted cross-subsidisation between services in the London area.

A further principle behind the 1968 Act was to enable the levels of service to be determined as far as possible at a regional or local level (through the creation of the passenger transport authorities) and the 1969 Act embodied a similar principle for London. The effect of the 1969 Act was to provide the GLC with powers and responsibilities over public transport services in its area unprecedented for any local authority. It became possible for the GLC as the elected body for London not only to set the financial objectives for LT, which had been the prerogative of Whitehall, but also to become closely involved in the planning of its services. But this new opportunity for transport integration was not complete as it did not extend to BR, whose metropolitan services remained outside GLC control. It was a clear intention of the 1969 Act, however, that the GLC's new responsibilities to promote the integration of transport in London should embrace BR services, and to this end it was empowered to make grants to BR.

In the first two years since the Act, the GLC's practical interpretation of this intention was lacking in two important respects. The first concerns the relative quality of BR and LT services. Certain aspects of both services, particularly their frequency and regularity, have over the years been shaped by and have shaped both travelling habits and the patterns of development in the areas served. It cannot therefore be automatically assumed, for example, either that the frequency of BR's suburban services should be increased to match that of the Underground services, or that the Underground services are super-abundant. Nevertheless there is a need to review differences between the two systems. The GLC were now clearly in a position to carry out such a review in the light of transport needs as a whole, but so far had taken little action in this respect.

Second, the GLC took little interest in individual services—this was as much the case with proposed rail closures as with reductions in number and frequency of BR's inner suburban services. This disinterest was clearly illustrated in the Epping–Ongar and Broad Street–Richmond examples (see Case Study *N*). These were both services whose future was under debate and could therefore have been expected to attract more attention than issues such as apparently routine timetable alterations. The Epping–Ongar case revealed the anomaly of the 1969 Act whereby the continuing DOE responsibility for decisions about LT rail closures enabled and perhaps encouraged the GLC to avoid commitment to a policy for the line. Where the DOE refused permission to close an unremunerative line, it was morally obliged to pay a grant to help its continued operation. Had the GLC given early support to the retention of the Epping–Ongar line they too might have been under a similar obligation. A further factor in the GLC's disinterest could have been that the line lay wholly outside Greater London, although Tower Hamlets Borough Council had considered it sufficiently important to their area to support the case against its closure.

A further point illustrated by the Epping–Ongar case study concerns the narrowness of the TUCC's terms of reference with regard to rail closures: their task is limited to reporting to the Minister on hardship arising from a proposed closure and on alternative ways of alleviating this hardship. The operator's case for closure is excluded from public debate at TUCC inquiries and can only be investigated by the Minister before he makes his decision. This procedure means not only that operators have little incentive to apply imaginative measures to get the best results from a line *before* proposing its closure, but also encourages public distrust of the system. In the case of the Epping–Ongar line the local pressure groups formed to fight the closure proposal believed, with good reason, that the decision on their line was being taken behind closed doors.

As far as the Broad Street–Richmond services were concerned, the GLC supported local efforts initiated jointly by several borough councils as well as voluntary pressure groups to encourage their use. But although BR had never formally proposed the withdrawal of these services, the GLC took no policy decision which could have helped to put an end to the long period of uncertainty. The position on grant aid, however, was much clearer than for the Epping–Ongar line in that from 1968 onwards the services were aided by an annual Government grant. But, again, the GLC saw no reason to offer part of the cost, even though this service operated wholly within their area.

The GLC hesitated to move away from the kind of control over LT formerly exercised by the Government who had concentrated on the financial performance of the undertaking and taken only a sporadic and vague interest in its function within the transport system. This approach, however, was virtually inevitable given the GLC's initial inexperience and its particular policies of financial control, the most important of which was the decision not to pay a revenue subsidy to LT. Meanwhile, as far as BR was concerned, the GLC decided not to pay any form of grant for its London services. The result of this was that attempts to integrate their respective transport responsibilities through the GLTG were abortive; since the Government remained in control of BR's broad financial policy little remained to be discussed. Thus the GLC's refusal to pay revenue subsidies either to LT or BR clearly limited the possibilities for the operators to alter the levels of service or fares except in ways that were consistent with maintaining financial viability. In practice this meant the pruning of unprofitable services (or at least raising doubts about their future) and raising fares and charges to cover the effects of rising unit costs and falling passenger demand.

Towards the end of 1972, however, there were signs that the GLC was beginning to take a closer interest in the transport services operated by LT. Assurances were given, for example, that during 1973 services would not be cut back and that fares would not be increased. At the same time it was recognised that some contribution towards LT's revenue account would be required for the achievement of these objectives. No parallel change of attitude towards BR occurred, although the Government decided to continue its revenue grant for the London and South-East 'pool' services. Thus it was still the case that BR and LT services were determined separately by the Government and the GLC and that they were certainly not the result of any integrated transport strategy for London. In these circumstances widely divergent policies for BR and LT were by no means impossible, and this could give rise to greater inequalities in railway services for residents in different parts of London.

Buses

Any evaluation of how London's bus services have been handled must allow for the major change of responsibility for them brought about by the Transport (London) Act 1969. The first two years of GLC control of LT coincided with a period when the role of bus services was receiving increasing attention from central and local government throughout the country and this complicates the identification of changes resulting from this particular institutional reform. But it is an important fact that the 1969 Act was itself a product of changing attitudes and a recognition that the exclusion of public transport from the strategic planning functions of the GLC was a major shortcoming of the London Government Act 1963.

In one sense it was the particular problems of the bus that had made clear the need for a more comprehensive approach to transport planning and management in London because it shared its operating conditions with traffic generally. In competition with the car, the bus, to an even greater extent than rail transport, had suffered from greatly reduced passenger demand but, unlike rail transport, from deteriorating traffic conditions as well. This had put bus services into a rapid decline: as roads became more congested, bus services became less reliable, which in turn caused more people to take to other forms of travel but especially the car, creating more congestion and an even poorer bus service (see Figure 23) The London government reforms in 1965 had, if anything, further impeded an overall approach to this problem; while the MOT retained its responsibility for the nationalised LT undertaking, its responsibilities for road traffic, which had a direct effect on bus operating conditions, had been mostly transferred to the GLC. Speaking in a House of Commons debate in 1967 on the White Paper concerning transport in London, Barbara Castle had recognised this problem when she said:

> I believe we shall never break out of this vicious circle until public transport becomes much more closely linked with the local authority which is also responsible for planning control, traffic management and parking policies.[1]

The transfer of LT to the GLC under the 1969 Act was clearly consistent with her view.

Thus from the beginning of 1970 when the 1969 Act was implemented, control of London's bus services once again lay with its traffic authority. This change, combined with a growing concern for public transport on the part of the GLC, set the stage for a more integrated approach to the problems of road traffic and bus operation.

Central government nevertheless continued to play an important role through financial and other incentives for the improvement of bus services. The demonstration projects set up by the MOT in 1969 and the earlier GLC Working Group report requested by the MOT (see Case Study *M*) were indicators of the concern of central government for urban bus problems and the value of its exhortative role in tackling them. The introduction of capital grants for new buses, bus terminals and other facilities made it easier for bus undertakings to provide replacements or improvements which were overdue. These grants, however, despite substantial increases in 1971, did not match those for railway projects or Trunk and Principal roads, and they were available only for a specified period whereas those for roads were on a permanent basis. The crucial financial problem of the buses, however, was not so much their capital account but the sorry state of their revenue account. London buses, which before the Second World War subsidised the Underground system, have been losing money since the 1950s and the size of the losses has been increasing. In this problem

[1] *Hansard HC Debates*, 22 February 1967, col1738.

central government gave very little help. From 1970 the only contribution to LT bus revenue from central government was the partial relief on diesel fuel duty, and the 1969 Act had removed the powers of central government to make revenue subsidies to the undertaking as a whole. Although the GLC acquired wide powers to make both capital and revenue grants, it became something of an anomaly that central government could decide between capital and revenue grants as the best means of assisting BR and rural bus services but was precluded by statute from taking the option of revenue assistance to LT services. The significance of this situation is heightened by the fact that the Government, which collects motor tax revenue, is prevented from paying LT a bus subsidy which could well be justified in terms of the direct and deleterious effects of motor traffic on bus operation. The emphasis, however, has been on concentrating responsibility for subsidies with the GLC as overall transport authority, and it would certainly also be anomalous if central government were to decide on bus revenue subsidies independently. This problem is further discussed in Chapter 7.

The reduced involvement of Whitehall in LT's affairs meant that a relationship had to be forged between the new LT Executive and the GLC. The broad nature of this relationship as set out in the 1969 Act itself was clear enough: the Executive was responsible for the day-to-day management and operation of services, and the GLC for laying down broad financial policy and the levels of service required. In practice, however, it was inevitable that difficulties in drawing a precise distinction between the roles of the two bodies would arise. From the start of the GLC was closely involved in the financial side of LT's activities, producing clear decisions on the amount to be set aside for general reserve each year and the maintenance of financial viability without revenue subsidies, and appraising the fare increases designed by LT Executive to achieve these targets in the face of rising costs and falling bus passenger demand.

Much less clear cut was the GLC's role in the determination of levels of service. There is a point at which the effects of day-to-day decisions about alterations to services reveal and have a real bearing on the need for broad policy decisions. If the situation had been relatively static requiring only minor adjustments at the day-to-day level the involvement of the GLC would have needed to be only slight, but this was far from the case with the buses. The fundamental question to be asked, therefore, is whether the GLC's degree of involvement has been adequate for the formulation of a policy for bus services as part of a general and integrated approach to traffic and transport problems.

After two years there was evidence that at a working level both the LT Executive and the GLC had made genuine efforts to define the limits of their respective day-to-day roles in executive and policy matters, and that the standing liaison committee had enabled officers of both authorities to understand better one another's problems. For example, the opportunity the officers of LT now had to explain rather than complain about the difficulties of bus operators meant that they were now able to understand and influence traffic management work at County Hall. Concerning policy, the GLC produced some standards for service provision which were incorporated into the suggested revisions to the GLDP statement, although these could be regarded as minimum standards rather than desirable target levels of service.

Thus there were at least a few signs by 1972 that the GLC had become aware of the role of bus services within the transport system and were beginning to extend their concern from purely financial considerations towards the implications of these for levels of service available to the public. On the other hand, much still depended upon LT's own policies since the GLC were reluctant to take a radically new approach despite the recognised urgency and seriousness of the bus problem. The treatment of LT's bus reshaping plan provided a significant example of their attitude. The plan was drawn up by the former LT Board in 1966 and its aim was to reduce the problems of bus operation caused by staff shortage and traffic congestion in a situation of falling passenger demand. Looked at in isolation (i.e. from the point of view of bus operation rather than transport efficiency) the principles of the plan were sound and appropriate for the role of the LTB at that time. But LT policy was now in the hands of the body which also had responsibility for road building, traffic management and strategic planning, all matters which were beyond the influence of LT when the reshaping plan was drawn up. The GLC, however, made little attempt to examine this plan in the light of their new responsibilities for LT. They ignored the opportunities this offered for achieving more ambitious aims for the future role of the bus as part of the total transport system. One factor may have been a lack of appropriate expertise within the GLC for such an examination to be carried out: the bus unit, for example, which was set up in 1970 within the Traffic and Development branch of the Planning and Transportation Department, by the end of 1971 consisted of seven traffic engineers; this compared with a total of about 500 staff in the executive wing as a whole dealing with roads, traffic management and development control.

To give a more detailed example, the Parliament Hill Fields and 151 bus service withdrawals similarly showed the GLC's acceptance of LT's own policy for operation of the services. In both cases the GLC took little, if any, interest in the effects that changes in services could have on road congestion or any other social factors. While confidence in the Executive's role could itself be seen as a desirable aim, these examples were not isolated instances of reduced bus services; some of the strategic implications of the reshaping plan and other changes were in direct conflict with the GLC's stated aim of maintaining and improving the public transport system.

In contrast to the rather slow and uncertain steps towards a more integrated approach to the planning of London's bus services, there were more encouraging signs that the new relationship between the GLC and the

LT Executive was giving an increasing impetus to the development and implementation of traffic management techniques to assist bus operation. LT certainly recognised that its responsibilities for day-to-day management could do little to solve the problems brought about by traffic congestion and falling passenger demand and became increasingly firm in its request for action on the part of the GLC.

The bus priority case study demonstrated that possible schemes, particularly bus-only lanes, received more favourable consideration by the GLC after January 1970. Traditional forms of traffic management were extended, e.g. in computer-controlled signal systems, in right turns for buses only and in the successful experiment of extending clearway-type control along the E3 bus route.

The GLC also employed consultants to undertake route studies of possible bus priority measures and decided to use its experimental powers to reduce the time taken to implement schemes. It did not, however, approve bus lanes which were thought likely to increase significantly delays to general traffic. A policy was adopted of implementing isolated schemes where traffic conditions and street designs were favourable rather than a network of lanes as suggested by Camden and pressure groups such as the London Amenity and Transport Association. This policy was consistent with the GLC's general traffic policies referred to earlier, but it was criticised by the proponents of more radical bus priority measures for preventing improvements for buses at the very places they were needed most, i.e. heavily congested streets and junctions. If their criticism is valid, it suggests why bus services were not improved sufficiently to start attracting passengers again and so halt the vicious circle to which Barbara Castle referred in 1967. It was attitudes to traffic management and not the locus of responsibilities for bus services which was hindering development.

Setting aside, then, criticisms of the GLC's initially rather weak interpretation of its responsibilities and policies for LT, the actual structure of powers and responsibilities for buses in London seemed capable of integrating operational and strategic needs. At a more local level, however, there was much less evidence of, and less scope for, the co-ordination of bus services with the needs of the communities they served. Perhaps the most striking gap was between the provision of bus services and local land-use planning. This is dealt with more fully below. A further problem was that the boroughs, while often recognising a need to maintain and improve bus services in their areas regarded it as politically unrealistic to pay subsidies to LT for services which invariably operated beyond borough boundaries. This was aggravated in some cases by the ambiguity of the statutory powers which enabled the boroughs to contribute to the cost of LT services.[1] Most boroughs and the London Boroughs' Associa-

[1] The *Local Government Act 1948*, ch 26, s136, had to be invoked for this purpose and at least one borough claimed that this did not empower local authorities to make payments for public transport services.

tion considered public transport subsidies to be the responsibility of the GLC although they had shown little interest in the future of individual bus services, let alone considered specific subsidies.

A further lacuna at the local level was apparent concerning the accountability of LT to the public they were serving. The handling of the Parliament Hill Fields bus service alterations demonstrated an unfortunate lack of concern on the part of LT for their passengers in the area. The new statutory consumer body, the LT Passengers' Committee, took a serious view of the very short notice which had been given about the bus service changes, and persuaded LT to give local authorities at least three months' notice of bus service changes in their areas. In the case of both the Parliament Hill Fields bus services and the withdrawal of the 151 bus in Sutton the LT Passenger's Committee showed a genuine desire to represent fairly the passengers' point of view, not only in addressing LT but also in attempts to influence GLC policy.[1] But it is doubtful whether the Committee, despite its important role in helping to overcome individual difficulties, could ever adequately mitigate public feeling against LT in the face of a general and continuing decline in the quality of bus services which had, after all, become one of the most fundamental aspects of London's transport problem.

The general conclusion to be drawn about public transport is that while the transfer of LT to the GLC and certain other changes, such as the provision of infrastructure grants, have brought visible improvements to LT services and given opportunities to develop transport planning in London on a wider basis, there remain certain major inadequacies in the organisational structure. These mainly relate to the continued separation of public transport planning from the strategic planning process, the arrangements for the planning and operation of BR inner London suburban services and the lack of co-ordination of these with the bus and rail services operated by LT.

For a number of reasons the GLC's responsibility for transport planning (under the 1969 Act) has not so far led to the comprehensive approach to transport planning at the metropolitan level that was intended. Such an approach seems unlikely unless three fundamental conditions are fulfilled: firm responsibilities for BR services in London should lie with the GLC; the present ambiguous and confused system for the payment of public transport grants and subsidies should be overhauled; professional staff should be trained and employed specifically to develop an inter-disciplinary approach to the formulation of transport strategy, and central and metropolitan government departments should be restructured accordingly.

[1] Also, in 1972, the LT Passengers' Committee submitted comments to the GLC on its Green Paper, *Traffic and the Environment*, based on experience of the complaints from the public with which they had to deal.

The incorporation of public transport into the overall picture of transport planning in London has further been hindered by lack of concern by the GLC for changes in the level and quality of bus and rail services. This could be partly overcome by the development of a monitoring system capable of keeping the policy makers informed of the effects of their decisions. At the same time the GLC should be much more specific about the actual services which they consider desirable from a general transport viewpoint, thus becoming more closely responsible for them than at present. This would be particularly beneficial to BR's inner London suburban services which are at present the subject of policies and directives established at the national level, and to London's bus services whose future has had no more than a cursory review despite the fact that a single body is now responsible both for them and for the traffic conditions in which they operate.

Another inadequate aspect of public transport organisation is the representation of consumer interests through the TUCC for London and the LT Passengers' Committee. The TUCC's brief on rail closure proposals which excludes consideration of anything except hardship that would arise is paternalistic in the worst sense. There can be no justification for limiting the scope of public interest and the arguments they may use in defence of their transport services. It is also iniquitous that those who are served by bus rather than rail have no formal channel for appeal against a proposal to withdraw a service. On the other hand, however, consumer bodies do not and cannot be expected to make up for major inadequacies in the organisation of the public transport system.

INTERCHANGES

By its very nature the task of providing for the efficient interchange of passengers between different modes of travel requires the co-ordination of the various authorities involved in transport. Where, as in London, responsibility for roads, car parks, buses, taxis and railways is divided between several different authorities, and the physical network of facilities and services is dense, extensive and complex, the need for co-ordination is correspondingly great. The quality of interchange provision is therefore a useful pointer to the ability of the institutional system as a whole to provide integrated transport facilities. Co-ordination, moreover, can and should be concerned with more than merely overcoming the design problems of individual schemes. Interchange facilities greatly influence the relative quality (and hence the use) of different modes of travel and consequently should form an important element of strategic transport policy.

The public transport operators, BR and LT, have clearly been at the centre of interchange provision in London and much of the initiative for new facilities such as station car parks and major improvements at railway termini has come from them. To some extent they have been able to achieve their aims by making better use of their existing assets, as long as policies have not conflicted with other planning issues. Both LT and BR, for example, built car parks on surplus land at suburban stations to encourage commuters to park-and-ride. Promotion of profitable development at stations, particularly BR's central London termini, was also seen as a way of providing opportunities to secure interchange improvements as well as increased passenger traffic.

This opportunist and consequently rather piecemeal approach by the operators no doubt reflected their overriding concern that each scheme should make a positive contribution to their financial position. The introduction of capital grants for interchanges under the Transport Act 1968 gave some hope of easing this constraint, or at least was intended to do so (see below). In practice the planning and implementation of interchange schemes was subject to yet further constraints deriving from the conflicting interests and priorities of other bodies over whom the operators usually had little influence. The viability of station car parks, for example, was undermined in some cases by the absence of on-street parking restrictions nearby; developments at the central London rail termini often clashed with national office location policy or metropolitan commercial land-use policy. To expect BR and LT to develop a comprehensive programme of interchange schemes that would satisfy both their own and wider transport needs was clearly unrealistic given the practical and financial constraints involved, and it was in recognition of problems of this kind that the Minister of Transport established the TCCL to achieve greater co-ordination in transport planning as a whole. The interchange problem was specifically identified and a group was set up within TCCL to deal with it.

The MOT in this way initiated important steps towards transport co-ordination, but it is ironic that improvements to interchanges were hindered by central government involvement in other ways. One example already mentioned was the system of Office Development Permits in central London operated by the Board of Trade and latterly by the DOE: this thwarted some BR developments which could have financed improvements to central London's congested transport facilities; the ODP system was itself designed partly to ease the growing problem of congestion but the proposed BR developments were not interpreted as having any special merit in this respect.

A more direct influence of central government was the allocation of transport infrastructure grants under the Transport Act 1968, but this was handled in such a way that interchanges received less priority than other public transport improvements. Not only were the grant rates lower than for most other capital schemes (25 or 50% compared with 75%) but the absence of any agreed method of evaluating their full social benefits hindered the planning of new schemes. The Waterloo interchange improvements planned jointly by Lambeth Borough Council and BR foundered because the evaluation technique was ill-suited to demonstrate the full social benefits that would have accrued. Similar difficulties have arisen over the evaluation of road schemes in London but the MOT and the DOE have rarely insisted upon a satisfactory rate of return being demonstrated before approving grants for them.[1]

The GLC was well placed to take a general view of and interest in the interchanges issue. Moreover, its initial involvement through the TCCL machinery was superseded by the more specific responsibilities for promoting the integration of transport given by the Transport (London) Act 1969. The co-ordinating role was duly taken over by the GLTG but again interchanges were accorded no special priority for attention and no counterpart to the TCCL interchanges group was established. The GLDP suggested two broad catagories of interchange improvements but little indication was given as to how these might relate to the overall transport strategy and no firm programme of schemes was included.

The three studies of interchanges (Development at stations, Case Study *D*; Heathrow link, Case Study *E*; Station car parks, Case Study *F*) clearly demonstrated the enormity of the co-ordination problems to which the large number of parties involved and the overlapping financial powers and responsibilities gave rise, but by the same token also demonstrated the pressing need for a strong policy framework. The GLC preferred to place emphasis on individual interchange schemes as opportunities arose and this approach was reflected in the establishment of *ad hoc* working parties, for example those for King's Cross, Victoria and Hammersmith. These bodies played an important role in bringing together the different interests of the transport operators, the boroughs, the GLC and in some cases (e.g. King's Cross) the DOE and other bodies such as the British Airports' Authority, but although differences were highlighted as detailed studies proceeded the results were mostly inconclusive and failed to bring about concerted action. The Piccadilly Line Heathrow extension (which provided improved interchange at the airport) was an exception but in this case the project was able to proceed because of financial benefits to LT.

The opportunity for interchange improvements by development at stations was bedevilled by conflicts between national, metropolitan and local planning interests. The difficulties of providing station car parks within Greater London without interfering with borough car parking policies or obstructing BR's aim of attracting motorists from outside the conurbation to leave their cars at their nearest station have already been described. The uncertain position with regard to national (or South-East England) airports policy also made the problem of in-town air terminals a difficult one to resolve. In these and other ways the case studies showed not only the problems arising from fragmented responsibilities

[1] One example was the West Cross Route scheme (part of Ringway 1) for which a grant was assured by the DOE (subject to the statutory planning procedures) but a cost-benefit analysis was attempted neither before nor after this assurance was given. See also evidence by Messrs Janes, Wardale and Berry of the DOE to House of Commons Expenditure Committee *Hansard HC Papers 107* (*i*), 1971–72.

but also the diverse incentives for action which the various bodies possessed.

The boroughs, not surprisingly, mostly confined their interest to the local effects of individual schemes and usually took two dominant, but sometimes conflcting standpoints. They wanted to promote major interchanges that would boost development and hence rateable values, for example Hammersmith, Westminster (Victoria) and Lambeth (Waterloo). On the other hand, they were concerned about the effects of major developments on local traffic and environmental conditions, for example, Westminster's position on the Victoria transportation centre proposal. Some boroughs also questioned the GLC's involvement in local planning issues. Camden believed, for example, that the GLC had not set out a clear strategy within which the planning of the King's Cross terminal could proceed and was instead attempting to usurp the role of the borough in local planning.

While the outer boroughs in particular were interested in station car parks to the extent that they wanted to remove the nuisance caused by commuters' cars parked on the streets, most did not consider that it was their responsibility to provide even a part of the necessary finance. Moreover, the police were often unwilling or unable to attach any priority to the enforcement of on-street waiting restrictions which would have encouraged the use of car parks. The initiative and success of Havering Council in promoting the Gidea Park scheme was an exceptional and isolated case which did nothing to promote the park-and-ride policy.

The major conclusion about the handling of passenger interchanges in London is that the machinery for transport planning in London has been largely unable to provide the necessary degree of co-ordination. The GLC's wide responsibilities in this sphere have not yet led to any significant moves towards a strategic interchanges policy. Different interests represented by different authorities have at best only been resolved on a piecemeal basis. Consequently, interchange improvements have come about only when they have brought financial benefits to the public transport operators or other sectional interests, but not when the benefits have been dispersed amongst the wider community. A firmer lead could be taken at the metropolitan level, without any changes in statutory responsibilities, but certain features of the present situation have hindered progress. Perhaps the most important has been the overlapping responsibility for finance between the GLC, the DOE, LT and BR, coupled with the generally unfavourable criteria for the evaluation of interchange schemes. But also of key importance has been the separation of BR and LT planning from that of the GLC, a gap which the major co-ordinating group, the GLTG, has been unable fully to bridge. These problems are unlikely to be resolved without the establishment of much clearer lines of responsibility, particularly for the GLC, backed up by sufficient financial powers to translate words into action.

INTEGRATING LAND USE AND TRANSPORT PLANNING

It was argued in Chapters 4 and 5 that relationships between land use and transport are apparent at three levels: regional, metropolitan and local. While it may not always be easy to distinguish clearly between these levels, the regard that has been paid to them in practice is reflected in the different roles adopted or defined by central government, the GLC and the London boroughs.

Regional planning, at least in terms of land use and transport rather than economic planning, developed long after London had grown into what has been described as a 'regional city.'[1] The spate of interest during the 1960s produced three advisory plans for the South-East, the last of which was adopted by the DOE. This followed a period of almost twenty years in which the only guide to regional development was the pioneering Abercrombie Plan of 1944.

Initiative for all these plans came from central government, although their production involved the participation of local authorities and other key bodies such as BR. Co-operation was particularly significant in the South-East Joint Planning Team's preparation of the *Strategic Plan for the South-East*, published in 1970.

A significant feature of this plan was that passenger transport factors appeared to vary little between the alternative strategies examined and thus played a small part in the final choice of plan. The reasons for this were apparently different in the cases of road and rail. The question of road provision in the South-East was assumed in the plan to be dependent on factors such as population, income and car ownership rather than on choices between public and private transport, which might have suggested different solutions. As far as railways were concerned the most important point was the impact of alternative strategies on the pattern and quality of commuting to London, especially central London. Since all the strategies envisaged a growth in commuting by rail from outside Greater London, they all pointed to greater profitability (or at least reduced losses) in the operation of the South-East rail network. They were thus consistent with BR's long-term aims. Understandably, BR was willing and even anxious to play its part in any strategy which gave hope of financial viability for the London and South-East services as a whole, and they certainly incorporated the forecasts of the Strategic Plan in the preparation of their long-term investment plans.[2]

Thus BR's commercial objectives have been consistent with the distribution of homes and workplaces in the South-East that has been envisaged for the future. Moreover, if past experience is to serve as an indicator, BR is likely to play as vital a role in the further outward dispersal of London's population as central and local government.

[1] See, for example, Peter Self (1971), *Metropolitan Planning: The Planning System of Greater London*, Greater London Paper No. 14, LSE, pp35–46.
[2] See BR Board (1970), *Proof of Evidence, E12/7*, GLDP Inquiry Stage 1.

The important question remains, however, to what extent these powerful trends in regional development will alleviate or aggravate problems within Greater London. The secondary importance attached by BR to its inner suburban services because of their declining passenger usage and their unprofitability could reduce the relative quality of travel within inner London, and hence its attractiveness as a place in which to live. Despite this the GLC, although increasingly worried about the decline of population in central and inner London and its associated social and economic problems, had not greatly concerned itself with the planning of BR services.

This brings us to the metropolitan scale of planning and to the question of how far the government system, and the GLC in particular, has recognised and acted upon the structural relationships between transport facilities and the activities they serve.

In Chapter 1 attention was drawn to the way in which the form of Greater London was shaped by the speculative ventures of railway and other public transport companies, a process which continued into the 1930s with the extension of Underground lines north of the river Thames. Although those who promoted these projects probably did not foresee the financial difficulties which would arise, they were certainly well aware that railways were powerful generators of development; their lines encouraged and facilitated the outward spread of residential development but at the same time enabled central London to draw on a larger labour market and to expand and diversify its job opportunities.

The passing of rail and bus undertakings into public ownership and control, however, heralded an era in which the impact of transport upon the structure of London appears to have been almost entirely forgotten, and it was certainly not until the 1960s that moves were made to integrate their planning. Consequently, while it could be seen that London's radial pattern with a large concentration of employment and other activities at the centre had given rise to considerable transport problems related to the peaked demand for travel, solutions to these problems were usually regarded as the responsibility of transport operators themselves. The growing financial problems of the bus and railway undertakings meant, for the most part, that nothing was done.

Such plans as there were to redistribute activities in London were found in practice difficult to operate, or to have little impact on transport conditions, or both. The LCC and the Government, for example, endorsed Abercrombie's proposals for dispersing people and employment from London in order to ease congested conditions at the centre, but as people and jobs vacated the city, others arrived to take their place. There was also the series of attempts by the Government to introduce a comprehensive system of staggered working hours in central London (see Case Study *B*). This was a surrogate aimed at redistributing the timing rather than the location of activities, but proved to be an extremely difficult way of improving transport conditions.

The 1960s, however, saw the emergence of policies which showed greater recognition of the problems which the railways were facing. The payment of both capital and revenue subsidies to BR and LT, for example, could be regarded as Government subsidies for the maintenance of the existing structure of London. Also, as shown in the development at stations case study, there were moves towards patterns of development aimed at easing the railways' financial problems; and these moves were initiated by the railway operators themselves.

The creation of the GLC provided a unique opportunity for the long-term development of transport facilities—road as well as rail—to be planned in conjunction with broad changes in land use over the whole of the conurbation, but this opportunity was barely recognised. The London Transportation Study, which was fundamental to the GLDP, included future land uses as an input to the modelling and transport planning processes, but there was little attempt to predict the land-use changes that would be generated by the transport proposals themselves. In particular, no assessment was made of how the building of the proposed orbital motorways would affect London's predominantly radial structure, even though the North Circular road had already shown a potential for generating development that departed from the established patterns. For example the Brent Cross shopping centre was being built adjacent to a major new road junction (of the North Circular, A1, A41 and A5 roads). It had 3000 free parking spaces to take advantage of its great accessibility by car from north-west London and Hertfordshire, but had only a fraction of the public transport access to be found to the established suburban shopping centres of comparable size.

The Thamesmead and development at stations case studies (*A* and *D*) demonstrated the very minor role which the GLC had played in developing a land-use–transportation strategy, but they also showed that this role had been constrained by the involvement and differing objectives of central government. The GLC had to work within national economic policy concerning new office and industrial development as exercised through the controls applied by the Departments of the Environment and Trade and Industry. The problems for BR's office development proposals at the central London termini have already been discussed. At Thamesmead, the GLC's proposed new industrial development for several years had to take third priority after the Government's designated Development Areas and new and expanding towns; more recently the interpolation of the Intermediate ('Grey') Areas and the growth areas of the *Strategic Plan for the South-East* relegated Thamesmead to fifth position.

A further constraint at Thamesmead was that the GLC had little control over prospective residents (compared, for example, with the considerable influence which new town development corporations have over their newcomers). Thus the size and character of the population and the housing and employment opportunities were not closely related to the problem of rail commuting capacity to central London. It will be purely fortuitous if the general decline in the population of inner London continues so that this problem is not aggravated as the population of Thamesmead expands.

What has so far been said about planning at the metropolitan scale has painted a rather bleak picture of the GLC's role, but it would be wrong to leave the impression that the problems have been confined to London or indeed to any particular authority, central or local; recognition of the need for integrating transport planning with land-use planning, at least at a more sophisticated level than that shown by the railway and other speculators in the past, has universally been slow to find its way into planning practice.

It would also be wrong to imply that no progress at all had been made in this direction. Lady Sharp was very much aware of the problem in her report on the training of transport planners.[1] The suggested revisions to the GLDP put forward by the GLC in 1972 placed a much greater emphasis on linking land use with transport, particularly by suggesting that new development should be concentrated at railway termini, other stations, passenger interchanges and major road junctions. Higher residential densities around suburban stations were also suggested. Only general indications of preferred locations were given and very little was said about priorities, criteria for the evaluation of schemes or methods of implementation, but it was a significant advance on the GLDP of 1969.

It is interesting to note, however, that changing attitudes within the GLC had not a little to do with the initiatives shown by the railway operators, particularly LT which was now under the GLC's control. The development at stations (Case Study *D*) showed that calls from BR to build offices and other facilities at the central London termini were beginning to receive a more sympathetic hearing. Attention was also being paid to the ideas promoted by the LT estates department for intensifying densities around Underground stations. This interest received some stimulus when the increase in land values which followed the opening of the Victoria Line was discovered. The 'new tubes' case study (*C*), however, showed that new lines had mostly been planned to serve areas without good rail services to central London and had not been related to redevelopment and land-use patterns until the discussions that took place over the proposed south-eastern section of the new Fleet Line and a possible line through the docklands. Thus there was plenty of scope for the GLC to develop the integration of land use and transport planning at the metropolitan level.

Finally, what efforts have been made at the local level, either to plan transport facilities so as to influence the pattern of activities, or to shape development as an instrument of transport policy? The local and metropolitan levels are, of course, by no means easy to distinguish and the schemes such as development at stations, air terminals, interchanges, while being of strategic importance also raise many local planning issues.

[1] MOT (1970), *Transport Planning: The Men For The Job.*

This overlap of interests, as already emphasised, has created problems between the GLC and the boroughs where their particular roles have not been clearly defined (e.g. between Camden and the GLC over the King's Cross development). Nevertheless the planning and implementation of development at the local level has tended to be handled in much the same way whether the boroughs or the GLC have been ultimately responsible.

Thamesmead, which was a GLC project, was much larger than schemes normally handled by local authorities but, as a large new settlement on an open site, it provided the opportunity to consider from first principles the desirable pattern of transport and how the form of development could achieve this. Case Study *A* emphasised that little such consideration was given either in the early design stages or later when the initial stages of the new development had been completed and revisions were under consideration. The GLC's Master Plan for Thamesmead was based largely on architectural principles within the dictates of road and parking provision devised (mostly separately) by the highway engineers at County Hall. The siting of the industrial areas, for example, was determined by the engineers' desire to balance road (predominantly car) traffic flows evenly over the network (see Figure 6, page 150). Although the road system was modified to improve bus operation after LT objected to the original pattern, the disposition of housing densities, workplaces and shopping and other facilities remained unchanged.

The majority of local planning issues, of course, have been handled by the London boroughs who are largely responsible for development control, local plans and redevelopment and rehabilitation schemes. At the time of writing none of the boroughs had completed structure plans but individual schemes provided evidence on their approach to transport matters. In the design of major schemes such as town centre redevelopments and public housing projects, the boroughs played a role similar to that of the GLC at Thamesmead. Their specific responsibilities for local roads and parking, and the typical separation of highway planning from planning departments led to the design of schemes being dominated by provision for road traffic, and the car in particular. This is not necessarily a technical criticism of the work produced, but it has meant that important decisions, such as the relative split of public and private transport, have been predetermined by the institutional factors rather than guided by the nature of the problem to be solved.

It is obviously difficult to generalise about the London boroughs from specific examples, but the A1 case study showed that while both Haringey and Islington had actively promoted redevelopment alongside the Archway Road and the Angel intersection respectively, in both cases the schemes envisaged was largely shaped by the road proposals, and the road proposals had come first. On the other hand, parts of the A1, where the safeguarding of widening of lines was exercised, redevelopment preceded the road works. Such has been the acceptance of the need for more roadspace, however, that it has generally been true that road schemes have been held to provide the 'opportunity' for redevelopment, and redevelopment to provide the 'opportunity' for roadbuilding

This approach has not always or even in most cases been balanced by any close involvement of the borough councils with the public transport operators, and there has been no machinery to ensure their co-ordination in plan making or execution. New rail or interchange facilities have usually brought some contact on an *ad hoc* basis (for example, through the working groups for the major rail termini, and Westminster City Council's representations over the new LT station at Pimlico), but the respective planning activities of the boroughs and the transport operators have often passed each other by. This appears to have been true in particular concerning bus services and other aspects where relatively little long-term fixed capital is involved.

LT has usually (but not always) been consulted on borough redevelopment schemes and plans so as to be able to extend or modify their services to new road patterns, but often too late to influence the basic design. Yet the detailed design of a scheme involving the disposition of high- and low-density housing, the arrangement of footpaths, the siting of bus stops and, more importantly, factors such as the relative accessibility to shopping areas by car or bus, may determine whether or not it can support an economically viable and convenient bus service.

The boroughs also have rarely developed land-use policies with the deliberate intention of influencing the length of journeys or the mode used, although highway and parking policies have nevertheless had a considerable influence over patterns of travel. One notable exception has been the practice of locating small play parks, primary schools and certain social services within walking distance of the majority of homes. But on the other hand the trend towards zoning land uses and providing facilities such as shops, secondary schools, hospitals and 'civic centres' in larger units has continued regardless of the consequent increases in journey length and use of motorised transport rather than walking and cycling.

Bus service provision appears to have been treated by the boroughs as a residual activity in which it is LT's responsibility simply to serve passengers who present themselves at bus stops. There has been no formal (and little evidence of informal) machinery whereby the question of how passenger demand arises can influence both borough planning decisions and bus operating decisions. The relationships between transport and land use are very under-researched, but the professional and organisational divisions in the boroughs (which are typical within local authorities generally) will prove to be a major stumbling block wherever a more comprehensive approach is attempted. To give one example, inadequate local housing compels many people to travel further to work than they would prefer, yet housing has always been handled separately from planning. Such issues have rarely, if ever, been raised.

The integration of land use and transport planning poses problems which recent structural changes in both central and local government organisation have been designed to overcome. Indeed, at the metropolitan level in particular, the GLC's statutory responsibilities cover almost every aspect of this complex field of city government. But although there has been some recognition of the interaction between transport facilities, and the activities served, and some effort to exploit the planning possibilities, there is considerable evidence to show that the far-reaching implications and long-term potential of transport and land-use planning have been barely realised.

That the problem is not confined to London but is a general one suggests that its cause is deep-seated. Integrated planning is a relatively new art which needs not only an appropriate organisational environment but also some new political and professional inspiration before it can be fully developed.

There are some practical ways in which this objective can be encouraged in London. First, because the GLC's involvement in the planning of public transport has been slight (although greater in the case of LT for which it has direct financial and policy responsibility), much closer involvement could place a new perspective on its strategic planning activities. This could be greatly aided if the GLC had a much more direct responsibility for BR services in Greater London.

Second, some new co-ordination machinery between the London boroughs and the public transport operators would help to break the virtual silence that has existed between them in the process of plan making, execution, development control and alterations to the pattern of public transport services. In plan making this might be a statutory requirement for consultation throughout the formulation process; for implementation and development control it might involve some means of monitoring schemes involving a specific liaison responsibility for officers of the boroughs and BR and LT.

Third, at both the metropolitan and borough levels, the scope for integrated planning would be widened immensely if the divisions between the land use and highway planning functions (which persist even where departments or committees have been merged) were finally broken down. Lastly, and closely related to this, there are obvious benefits to be gained (and few losses other than a break from tradition) from a merging of professional interests and a development of professional training towards a comprehensive view of land use, transport and related problems.

Chapter 7

A BETTER ORGANISATION FOR TRANSPORT PLANNING AND MANAGEMENT IN LONDON

The purpose of this final chapter is, in the light of the research and analysis contained in the foregoing chapters, to suggest changes in the present institutional arrangements which could stimulate improvement in the planning and operation of transport in London. The aim is not to give a detailed organisational blueprint, but to outline the context within which the changes are put forward and to indicate in general terms their nature and the means by which they could be effected.

The principal conclusion of this book is that the reform of local government structure in London in 1965 and subsequent legislative and institutional changes, including in particular the provisions of the Transport (London) Act 1969, have in the main enabled and promoted major improvements to the planning and management of transport. An equally important conclusion, however, is that the changes so far accomplished have taken London only part of the way towards achieving an integrated and balanced approach to its transport problems.

The proposals put forward in this chapter reflect these two conclusions in that, while they represent a call for substantial reform, their implementation would not mean any departure from the general direction of change already established by legislation and practice since 1960. This general direction has had two main characteristics which future changes should seek to enhance. First, an increasing range of powers and responsibilities for dealing with transport matters in London has been devolved from central to local government, especially for strategic planning at the metropolitan level. Second, at all levels of government there has been an unmistakable and extremely valuable move towards a comprehensive approach in transport and land-use planning, as indeed in other fields of public administration such as social services. The suggested changes represent only a partial step towards the type of institutional structure that may ultimately be required to link the planning and management of all related government functions. For example, particular attention is paid to the need to bring together the different aspects of transport—road and rail, public and private—and the planning of land use and transport as a whole. But eventually, further reforms may be necessary if these are to be judged in relation to other major functions such as housing, education and other social services.

London's transport problems are the result not simply of failure in professional competence or political decision making, although these may be important contributory factors, nor it is believed of any permanent intractability of the transport problems themselves. To a significant extent, London's transport problems are perpetuated and even exacerbated by inadequacies in the institutional system. In particular it has been argued in Chapter 6 that the present system, despite significant improvements, still presents obstacles to the formulation and evaluation of alternative transport strategies, to the integration of transport with other aspects of city planning, to the interpretation of broad policy through executive action (especially in the field of road planning), and to the adequate and balanced representation of varied interests which are frequently in conflict.

In all these respects changes in the structure of powers and responsibilities can act as a prime mover in securing improvements to London's transport system. Structural changes may not in themselves bring about these improvements because to a very large extent fresh thinking and even new skills, both technical and managerial, will need to be acquired and applied. But the right framework within which the latter can evolve is crucial. If there is any truth in the saying 'the job makes the man,' then there may be equal truth in saying that the structure of the institutional system determines the tasks which it is able and willing to carry out.

1 A NEW TRANSPORT GRANT STRUCTURE FOR GREATER LONDON

The effective co-ordination of transport planning demands above all the co-ordination of transport expenditure, yet the concentration of transport planning responsibilities in the hands of the Greater London Council (GLC) through the Transport (London) Act 1969 has not been paralleled by financial responsibilities. Overlapping powers to make transport grants have confused the roles of central and local government and have clearly contributed to the piecemeal approach to transport planning in London. Even at the national level, despite the calls for integration which heralded the creation of the Department of the Environment (DOE), different elements of transport expenditure (road, British Rail (BR), London Transport (LT), etc.) continue to be separately considered. The criteria for evaluating schemes also vary. Quite apart from different fixed rates for capital grants (100% for Trunk roads, 75% for Principal roads, 75% for most railway investment, 50% for new buses, etc.), individual grant claims are drawn up for different geographical areas and the totals of estimated expenditure are considered by the Treasury in relation to all the other items of Government expenditure: Trunk roads in London are lumped together with the national inter-urban motorway programme; Principal roads in London compete with those elsewhere; BR claims (for both revenue and capital grants) relate to the South-East 'pool' area which extends far beyond the Greater London boundary; and LT claims (for capital but not revenue grants) relate to yet another area.

The present system has shown itself open to *ad hoc* manipulation and buck-passing between different levels of government, and has severely restricted the GLC's ability to fulfil the intentions of the 1969 Act. Many of the problems have been recognised for a number of years and in 1972 Peter Walker, then Secretary of State for the Environment, announced his intentions to develop a new structure of Government grants as part of the local government reforms due in 1974. 'It is vital,' he said, 'to take a new look at the whole transportation problem. At present there is a whole range of grants. . . . Hitherto the practice has been to treat [various] fields of activity as self-contained and related to specific projects. I believe that such an approach does not satisfy the need to tackle problems of land use and comprehensive planning.'[1] In a further statement on the subject later in 1972 he said:

> I am anxious to develop a new system of Government finance for transport as a whole. The present system, whereby we give various specific grants for roads, public transport and sundry other matters concerned with transport, results in much fragmented investment. For example, I would argue that we may spend millions of pounds on a road scheme which merely results in moving a traffic jam a mile up the road, thereby not getting the full benefit from the investment.
>
> Now that we have the erstwhile Ministry of Transport and the planning side of the erstwhile Ministry of Housing and Local Government in one Department, I want to develop a total block grant for transport so that we can go to the local authority concerned and say: 'When you have completed an adequate overall transportation strategy we will decide on the quality of that strategy and give you a grant to cover the whole of it, not just a fragmented part.'[2]

The evidence compiled in this book suggests that a new system of Government finance, very similar in approach to that outlined by Peter Walker, is urgently required for Greater London. Indeed, it will be essential if the transport planning responsibilities of the GLC are to replace in practice and not merely in theory the piecemeal approach which the 1969 Act was intended to overcome.

How would the new system work in practice? The GLC would prepare, within the context of a strategic plan for London, alternative investment programmes covering all major aspects of transport expenditure including principal roads, railways (both BR and LT), buses, interchanges, traffic management, parking, programmes of expenditure on capital projects and revenue assistance to public transport and other revenue-earning transport facilities. The alternative levels of expenditure would explicitly reflect different qualities of service overall or different emphases for particular parts of the transport system. The intentions about the extent of provision for travel by car and by public transport, for example, would need to be made clear. The alternative plans would certainly be more

[1] *Hansard HC Debates*, 23 March 1972, cols1699–1700.
[2] *Hansard HC Debates*, 26 June 1972, col1100.

broad-ranging than those considered during the preparation of the Greater London Development Plan (GLDP). Within each level of investment, individual schemes would be arranged in order of priority according to explicit criteria for comparison. Improved methods of evaluation are being devised and can be further developed, for example to avoid the present unacceptable situation where interchanges receive low priority simply because there is no agreed way of assessing the size or value of their social benefits.

The Transport (London) Act 1969 required the GLC to produce transport plans, but responsibility for the BR rail services and for Trunk roads in London would help to ensure a more comprehensive approach. (These matters are dealt with separately below.)

The DOE would be involved in the guidance of studies and techniques used in the plan-making process. The Secretary of State, of course, will approve the GLC's overall strategy (the GLDP or a modified version of it) and the transport plans and programmes drawn up under the 1969 Act. The programme of expenditure (capital and revenue) and the amount of Government grant would be decided on the basis of the agreed strategy and plans. Ceilings of expenditure would be determined by the DOE and approved by the Treasury for periods of possibly three years, and more tentative allocations up to five, ten, and fifteen years; these would be reviewed each year and revised if the GLC (or other transport agencies) were not making expected progress, or if the plan itself required modification, or if cutbacks in public expenditure were planned.

The DOE would be far less involved than hitherto in the evaluation of individual schemes although, in order to ensure that the Government obtained value for money, they would be closely interested in the criteria employed by the GLC. The development of agreed criteria for assessing schemes would make for smoother operation of the system, but the onus should be on the GLC to make clear and justify their preferences within the expenditure programme. Thus while central government would be concerned with priorities as between London and other parts of the country and between transport and other sectors of public expenditure, the GLC would have a strong control over priorities between different aspects of transport within London. A reduction in Government expenditure might affect the block grant for transport investment in London, for example, but it need not affect the priorities within the agreed programme; those schemes with low priority overall would be cut, whether road or rail, capital or revenue.

It is worth noting that the House of Commons Expenditure Committee for the session 1971–72 (which considered the DOE's block grant proposals) recommended that the DOE should have a powerful and detailed role in the scrutiny of individual investment proposals by the new county councils:[1]

[1] Second Report from the Expenditure Committee, *Hansard HC Papers 57*, 1971–72, volI, para146.

> We broadly welcome the proposals for a new grant system, but we recommend that the Department should fix a low 'threshold' in order that the major portions of expenditure will be by way of supplementary payments rather than in the generalised rate support grant allocation, *thus ensuring* detailed scrutiny by the Department [our italics].

This conclusion was apparently based on an acceptance of the DOE's desire to ensure that 'national considerations are brought to bear . . . in the preparation and execution of programmes.'[1] But too great a degree of involvement would undermine one of the key advantages of the block grant system, namely the devolution of responsibility from central to local government. The DOE should certainly be concerned with national issues in the approach and subsequent review of the GLC's transport strategy, but should be involved to the smallest possible extent in the preparation and evaluation of individual schemes within that strategy. The complexities of the evaluation process, however, require that the DOE supervise the methods employed.

The changes required to secure the new grant procedure may be summarised as follows:

1 Greater financial responsibility for the GLC in the preparation of a comprehensive transport programme and in the evaluation of individual schemes.
2 The abolition of the Principal and Trunk road programmes, and BR and LT capital programmes, in as much as they affect Greater London.
3 The abolition of different fixed grant rates for different kinds of investment.
4 The payment of a block grant to the GLC for transport within Greater London.

2 THE TRANSFER OF TRUNK ROADS IN GREATER LONDON TO THE GLC

It has been suggested in earlier chapters of this book (pages 387–8, 572–4) that the role of the DOE with regard to transport planning and the ability of the GLC to fulfil its duty as strategic planning authority would be significantly improved if the latter was responsible for *all* major roads in greater London, both existing and proposed. In line with this it is suggested that Trunk roads in Greater London which are at present the responsibility of the DOE should be brought under the GLC's control. (The question of borough Principal roads is dealt with in section 5 below.)

The aims behind this suggestion have been generally accepted for many years. Continuing central government responsibility for Trunk roads in London was recognised as an anomaly by the promoters of the London Government Bill. In the Committee debates, for example, it was said:

[1] *Hansard HC Papers 57*, 1971–72, volI, para128.

> It may well be that in the course of time entirely different arrangements will be made. . . . As the local authorities are reorganised it may well prove highly unsatisfactory, and indeed, illogical, to leave the trunk roads unchanged.[1]

Two reasons given for not dealing with the problem in the provisions of the 1963 Act were that adequate powers already existed for the transfer of Trunk roads under the Highways Act 1959, and that it was necessary first to carry out 'a comprehensive review' of these roads in London, taking into account the results of the London Traffic Survey (LTS) and the views of the GLC, particularly on the financial implications.

The 1968 White Paper preceding the Transport (London) Act 1969 said:

> It is the Minister of Transport's view that ultimately all important roads—including present trunk roads—in the GLC area . . . should be the responsibility of the GLC.

But despite the fact that the results of the LTS were largely complete and that the GLC agreed in principle to the take-over, the White Paper announced: 'On trunk roads it has not yet proved possible to achieve this.'[2] After a further three years no progress had apparently been made and the DOE stated:

> As far as trunk roads are concerned, the implications of changing the present division of highway responsibility between the GLC and the Secretary of State have not yet been fully examined, and it is not possible to say when the Secretary of State might consider it appropriate to change the highway authority for the present trunk roads in the GLC area.[3]

The main stumbling block to implementing the transfer has been that within the context of the differing grant rates for Trunk and Principal roads and the major proposals for new and widened Trunk roads in London, a heavy additional burden would be placed on GLC resources. The GLC would have been responsible for 25% of the capital cost of any Trunk road schemes incorporated in the GLDP together with maintenance costs. In 1968 it was estimated that this would require expenditure of £5 million annually and the GLC considered that it was not worth taking on this additional burden simply to eliminate an administrative anomaly.[4] The GLC was willing to take on Trunk roads from the Ministry of Transport (MOT) (now DOE) once major works had been completed, thus becoming responsible only for maintenance costs.

[1] House of Commons Standing Committee F, *Official Report*, 12 February 1963, cols163–6.

[2] MOT (1968), *Transport in London*, Cmnd 3686, para59.

[3] DOE (July 1971), *Paper B624*, GLDP Inquiry Stage 1.

[4] GLC *Minutes*, 9 July 1968, p387.

The transfer of Trunk roads in London, consequently, has not been considered worth the effort necessary to overcome the financial problems involved. Moreover, the unity of purpose of the highway planners at County Hall and Whitehall has no doubt prevented the motivation for a transfer that might have arisen if there had been major differences of opinion.

There are a number of reasons, however, for suggesting that much greater importance should have been attached to the elimination of central government highway responsibilities in London. One is that the present arrangements whereby many of the outer London boroughs consult with and undertake agency functions for the DOE in planning, implementing and maintaining Trunk roads in their areas could be avoided. Joint working and consultation between the GLC and the DOE (i.e. through the joint highways planning group) could also be rendered unnecessary. Another is that the DOE have no powers to buy land or houses for rehousing people displaced by Trunk road schemes and they rely on the co-operation of local authorities in this.[1] By far the most important reason, however, is that the present arrangements contain a strong possibility of bias towards highway investment as opposed to other forms of transport investment. This danger was implicitly recognised by Peter Walker in a House of Commons statement:

> . . . sometimes these fixed grants have created a position where local authorities have often given the wrong priorities in their transport investment to enjoy a higher level of grant which is available for a particular facility.[2]

Moreover, DOE commitment to major road schemes in London compromised the Secretary of State's position of impartiality in reaching a decision on the GLDP which incorporated these schemes.

How, then, shall the transfer proceed? The possible methods and implications are discussed below in terms of finance, staffing, boundaries and co-ordination. The GLC as highway (and traffic) authority should become responsible for the present Trunk roads in London. The financial implications of this have no bearing on the logic of this move although they may have an important effect on its political acceptability. They do, however, depend on a number of alternative assumptions. If, as has been suggested in the previous section, a new system of block grants for all transport purposes were introduced for London, the Trunk road anomaly would be easily removed at the same time: the fixed grant rates would be abolished and it would be the responsibility of the GLC to demonstrate their overall requirements for Government aid and to apportion this between road, rail and other investment according to their strategic plan. If the block grant system were not introduced then it would be for the

[1] DOE (1971), *Paper B610*, GLDP Inquiry Stage 1.
[2] *Hansard HC Debates*, 19 July 1972, col854.

GLC (in view of their added commitment to 25% of the cost of current Trunk road schemes) to decide whether the phasing of schemes should be altered to spread the financial load over a longer period of time,[1] whether additional income should be found, or some (or all) of the schemes be abandoned altogether. In making this decision the GLC would be aware of the need to compare the relative costs and benefits rather than the relative rates of grant for all its proposals, including those inherited from the DOE. The deletion of some or all of the Trunk road schemes from the GLDP by the Secretary of State would, of course, reduce the problem.

As far as staff resources are concerned, the functions of the DOE London Highways Division of the London directorate would in large part become the responsibility of the GLC (but see below on the future planning role of the GLC). This would simply further decrease central government involvement in detailed or local planning. Remaining staff at the DOE would be concerned with ensuring that the London roads policy was in accordance with that for the rest of the country and with the remainder of the GLC's transport and land-use plans, and that road schemes gave good value for money.

Finally, the limit of DOE responsibility (i.e. for the inter-urban Trunk roads approaching the metropolis) would need to be defined. It is suggested that the Greater London boundary should form the division between the GLC and DOE highway and traffic responsibilities, or, alternatively, some convenient junction on each road that lay near the boundary. This arrangement would mean that the Trunk road system would not form a continuous network, but there is no reason why a more 'tidy' solution should work any better in practice. The DOE has given network continuity as one criterion for defining the Trunk road system[2] but has given no justification for this. It should be remembered also that not all the present Trunk roads in London link up (see Figure 2). Wherever the division of responsibility occurs there will be a continuing need for co-ordination between the GLC and the DOE. But if, as suggested, it occurred at or near the GLC boundary the London boroughs would no longer be directly involved.

3 TRANSFER OF RESPONSIBILITY FOR BR SERVICES IN LONDON TO THE GLC

During discussions in 1967 and 1968 over the transfer of responsibility for LT, both the Government and the GLC recognised that ideally some way should be found of bringing BR's London services under local rather than

[1] The basis for evaluation should not vary because it has been recognised that, as with Principal road schemes '. . . the proposed investment in trunk roads within Greater London . . . will serve an essentially urban function. . . .' DOE (1971), *Paper B623*, p4, GLDP Inquiry Stage 1.

[2] DOE (1972), *Reshaping of the Trunk Road Network*, Consultation Paper circulated to local authorities in relation to proposed changes in the Trunk Road network to coincide with the reorganisation of local government (outside London) in April 1974, p3.

central government control. This was not effected by the Transport (London) Act 1969 because the BR system posed entirely different and much more difficult problems than did that of LT. The BR network in Greater London is not self contained: it handles inter-city and freight services as well as 'suburban' passenger services and medium-distance 'stopping' services. These services share common operational buildings, equipment, staff and administration. Moreover the London commuter services extend far beyond the Greater London boundary, in some cases up to 100 miles from central London.

Although it was considered impracticable for BR to hand over its London services to LT (or the GLC),[1] the 1969 Act was intended to give the GLC 'a significant role' in BR services over this wider commuter area.[2] The GLC were given powers to make financial contributions to BR, and BR were required to consult the GLC about fares and levels of service, to agree financial objectives with the Minister and the GLC, to be consulted by the GLC in making transport plans, and to take note of such plans in proposing investment. While the leader of the GLC, Sir Desmond Plummer, regarded this as 'a reasonable approach to a very difficult problem,' a joint report of four committees to the GLC at the same time commented that 'some substantial link with the BR commuter services will obviously be required in the long run.'[3]

The research on the operation of the 1969 Act strongly suggests that a far greater involvement of the GLC in BR services is both desirable and necessary. One fundamental problem identified is that the GLC has played a limited role in the planning of BR services, including the development of investment proposals, fare structures, levels of service and possible rail closures; the main limitation has been the GLC's decision, '. . . in the absence of any direct policy control of BR . . .'[4] not to use its powers under the 1969 Act to contribute financially to BR. In answer to a question in Council about the integration of BR and LT services, for example, Horace Cutler (chairman of the GLC's Policy and Resources Committee) said that the Council had decided 'that all the resources [they] could spare should be devoted to getting LT itself right.'[5]

This limited involvement has meant that BR services have not been made an integral part of the GLC's responsibilities for developing a transport strategy for London. This failure is exemplified by the continued piecemeal handling of interchange schemes and the lack of any clear interchanges policy.

There is a further danger under the present arrangements that the

[1] Consideration had also been given in the early 1930s to the possibility of 'hiving off' the main-line suburban services to the London Passenger Transport Board, but the same conclusion was reached. *Hansard HC Papers 107* (*xiv*), 1971–72, p368, Q1731.

[2] MOT (1968), *Transport in London*, Cmnd 3686, para41, p9.

[3] GLC *Press Release 410*, 9 July 1968; *Minutes* 9 July 1968, p383.

[4] *Hansard HC Papers 107* (*vii*), 1971–72, p124.

[5] GLC *Minutes*, 14 December 1971, pp648–9. See also GLC *Press Release 556*, 25 November 1970.

differences in financial objectives and operational criteria for the LT and BR systems could lead to inequitable policies for north and south London respectively. This problem was recognised in 1972 by Peter Stott (Joint Director of the GLC's Department of Planning and Transportation). Giving evidence to the House of Commons Expenditure Committee on urban transport planning he said:

> I suspect that what is very difficult for anyone to sum up is whether the policies of the GLC, that is to say, road, parking and direct policies of LT, will continue to march harmoniously in the next few years with those of the BR Board, who perhaps have other directives from the Government as to what their financial objectives will be, what part the social aim should play and the frequency and type of service they run. This is the problem one must see in the present arrangement. . . .[1]

The problems outlined above stem from the 1969 Act which empowered the GLC to influence BR's operations in the London area but did not place on the GLC any firm responsibility for doing so. The Act failed to provide any tangible incentive for the GLC to devote resources to the BR undertaking. The requirements for liaison and consultation between the GLC and BR have in practice easily become subordinated to financial policies which have left little room for debate between the two bodies. The proposal discussed below is therefore aimed at giving the GLC responsibility for planning and policy control of the BR London services, while avoiding the apparently insurmountable problems of separating the management and operation of the London services from the rest of the BR system.

The GLC should decide and be responsible for the quantity and quality of services operating on BR lines in Greater London. Its policies would cover levels of service (i.e. the capacity, frequency and reliability of the trains and the routes operated), and the quality and efficiency of stations, trains and interchange facilities. Related to this the GLC would decide on fare structures and allocation of revenue subsidies. These policies and capital investment programmes should be drawn up on the basis of a transport strategy for Greater London covering relationships with road, traffic management, parking, interchange and land-use policies and BR's policies for the inter-city passenger and freight services. The strategy itself, of course, would be prepared by the GLC as at present, but BR could be involved as 'planning agents' in developing detailed alternative rail investment schemes.

Thus the GLC would decide the contribution to be made by the BR London services to London's transport system as a whole. It need not, however, be involved in BR's day-to-day management or operational matters except to the extent that these have a direct bearing on the levels of service that could be provided. The BR Board would act (as far as the

[1] *Hansard HC Papers 107* (*vii*), 1971–72, Q767, p139.

London services are concerned) as an executive body operating the services and carrying out alterations and improvements required by the GLC.

Both operating and capital expenditure would be met by the GLC, the amounts being negotiated with the BR Board taking into account elements of shared costs (and benefits) with inter-city, freight or long-distance commuter services.[1] The fares collected from all-London services would be received by the GLC so that in effect the GLC would be buying services from the BR Board who would retain their statutory responsibilities to the Government for financial viability and the safe and efficient operation of services.

A number of important questions deserve further discussion; these include the relationship of BR services within London to those which extend beyond the Greater London boundary, the limit of GLC responsibility, the allocation of Government funds, the financial negotiations that would be required between the GLC and the BR Board, and the maintenance of management incentives for BR.

(a) *Relationship between London and other South-East services*

Broadly speaking the GLC would be responsible for passenger services operating wholly or providing stopping services within Greater London. Other services operated in Greater London, including inter-city, freight and long-distance 'commuter' services running fast to central London, would continue to be the responsibility of BR and the Government. It is possible that these services, which tend to be more profitable than the London suburban services, could be operated on a commercial basis by BR and the present South-East 'pool' arrangements (which allow an element of cross-subsidisation between services) could be abandoned. The difficulties of defining loss-making services which led to the introduction of the pooling system would be greatly reduced once the Greater London services had been isolated, and unremunerative but 'socially necessary' services in the remainder of the South-East could be the subject of specific operating grants like those elsewhere on the BR network.

BR would continue to handle investment and planning matters within Greater London which related to its regional or national services (including inter-city and freight) but a contribution to the cost of improvements which would also benefit the London suburban services may need to be negotiated with the GLC.

In carrying out its responsibilities it would be vital for the GLC to pay

[1] Similar negotiations have already taken place between BR and the provincial Passenger Transport Executives established under the Transport Act 1968. By January 1973 two of five Executives, those for south-east Lancashire, north-east Cheshire (SELNEC) and the West Midlands, had signed contracts for BR to operate commuter services in their areas at a cost of £4.5 million and £3 million a year respectively (see *The Times*, 13 January 1973).

full regard to the regional implications of its BR policies and proposals, and this would be taken into consideration by the DOE in approving the GLC's strategic plans. For example, changing passenger demand between the London and outer services would give the GLC a direct concern in decisions about transport and other matters beyond its boundary and this could be regarded as a desirable further involvement in regional planning.

As at present, the GLC could have powers to contribute financially to BR services outside (or partly outside) Greater London, which meet the needs of London itself.[1]

(b) *The boundary of GLC responsibility*

Basically the GLC should be responsible for BR suburban services within the Greater London area, but the boundary could be extended to convenient stations on the BR network. This is already the case with some LT lines (e.g. Ongar and Amersham). The *Transport in London* White Paper of 1968 said that 'Greater London . . . has no special significance in terms of BR operations,' but in fact the character of BR suburban services in many cases changes at certain key stations just inside or outside the GLC boundary. On the Southern Region, for example, which accounts for the majority of BR's suburban operations, a pattern of services has been established in which longer-distance trains tend to run non-stop from stations on the fringe of the conurbation (such as Dartford, Swanley, Croydon, Epsom, Surbiton and Staines) into central London, while other trains provide stopping services within the conurbation which often terminate at these railheads.

(c) *The allocation of Government funds*

If the proposed new transport grant arrangements were implemented, the GLC itself would become responsible for allocating this income between revenue and capital grants to the BR and LT undertakings, and other elements of transport expenditure. For example, if it were intended to maintain fares and services on the two networks at broadly the present levels, the determination of the size of the GLC's block transport grant would need to allow for the element of the pool area subsidy which relates to Greater London.

The problem would be somewhat more complex if the block grant system were not introduced, since the GLC would have to press the case for grants towards operating losses or investment projects on BR services separately from its other claims on Government resources. Thus the Government would need to decide on two claims for BR services in the

[1] Under section 20 of the Transport Act 1968 the Secretary of State for the Environment can order a Passenger Transport Authority to make operating and financial agreements with the Railways Board concerning services which operate within and up to 25 miles from their boundary.

South-East (one from BR for the outer services and one from the GLC) in place of the one claim for the pool area as at present. This is an argument in favour of the block grant system rather than an objection to placing greater responsibility for BR services with the GLC.

(d) *Financial negotiations between BR and the GLC*

Perhaps the greatest problem of all will be the need for BR and the GLC to reach agreement on the 'price' of services and the sharing of investment costs. This will involve apportioning shared costs between London and other BR services. Techniques for doing this have evolved in recent years as a result of the Transport Act 1968 which required BR to identify its loss-making passenger services and to agree the extent of the loss with the MOT (DOE) for grant purposes. The BR Board employed consultants (Cooper Brothers) who produced a formula for calculating the share of the local services in a line's total costs. This formula has also provided a basis on which financial agreements have been or are being reached between BR and the provincial Passenger Transport Authorities for the Liverpool, Manchester, Birmingham and Tyneside conurbations for suburban rail services.[1] The GLC would be in a relatively strong bargaining position if, as seems likely, the transfer meant relieving BR of responsibility for some of the heaviest loss-making services in the present 'pool' area.

Shared contributions to investment on schemes which benefited both outer and London services would also need to be agreed between the GLC and BR. The schemes themselves would be carried out by BR or their contractors. Where agreement could not be reached between the GLC and BR on the 'price' of services or the sharing of costs of investment schemes which the GLC decided were necessary, the Secretary of State for the Environment would act as arbitrator. Some difficulties might be inevitable, at least until the GLC had acquired some experience of rail service provision and the methods of assessing costs. It would probably, however, be in the interests of both BR and the GLC to reach agreement through their own negotiations, and it would certainly be desirable to avoid as far as possible the involvement of the DOE in individual problems.

(e) *Management incentives for BR*

Some method of ensuring that BR had financial incentives to promote greater efficiency and productivity while maintaining the required standards of service provision is necessary. One possibility would be to negotiate the 'price' of services in advance for a period of time, rather than continuously reviewing them or determining them at the end of each accounting period.

[1] The difficulties of making such agreements should not be underestimated, however, and the London network is far more complex than those of the provincial conurbations. See Tyneside PTA–PTE (1970), *Joint Policy Statement*, p35; and West Midlands PTA–PTE (1971), *Joint Policy Statement*, p3.

Savings in costs during the operation of any one agreement would thus bring financial rewards to BR until the next round of negotiations, and likewise they would have to bear any losses which had begun to occur.[1] A maximum limit on the amount of fares revenue to be paid to the GLC in any one period could also be predetermined, so that any additional revenues collected would accrue to BR, or could be shared.

Enough has been said to indicate that there are major problems to be tackled in the development of a closer involvement of the GLC in BR services. But the approach put forward, which involves the separation of BR's London services in accounting and policy rather than physical or operational terms, provides opportunities for integrated and equitably managed rail services both north and south of the river Thames not practicable within the present institutional arrangements. It was rightly recognised in the drafting of the 1969 Act that 'urban transport is essentially a local rather than national matter.' The bringing of LT under metropolitan rather than national political control has already begun to produce tangible benefits. A similar transfer of responsibilities for the BR London services as suggested would not only provide opportunities for improvement of the BR services themselves, but also for better interchange between them and other transport facilities.

4 NEW ARRANGEMENTS FOR TRAFFIC AND PARKING SUPERVISION AND ENFORCEMENT

With the establishment of traffic warden services in the early 1960s, a trend was started towards relieving police constables of an increasing number of traffic duties. The greater reliance on traffic wardens for traffic supervision and enforcement has been generally welcomed by the police and the public alike. Writing in 1966, Michael Austin[2] quoted the Chief Constable of Leicester who had given seven advantages of using wardens rather than constables for the enforcement of parking regulations:

1 There is no mistaking the purpose for which a traffic warden patrols the streets. The deterrent effect of the distinctive uniform is considerable.
2 Traffic wardens are not subject to criticism by motorists of police officers enforcing traffic laws, namely that they ought to be catching criminals; that they are doing harm to the relationship between police and public, and so on.
3 Traffic wardens are always available for duty in connection with traffic. Their numbers are not reduced by varied shifts, assignment to specialist

[1] This is the system operating in the Hamburg Transport Community which encompasses municipal subways, trams, buses and ferries, a private bus company, taxis and German Federal Railway services. See Dr Ing F Pampel (1969), Paper to Thirty-eighth UITP Congress in London and V R Vuchic (1964), 'The Role of Public Transport in Hamburg,' *Traffic Quarterly*, xviii, 1, pp118–24.
[2] M Austin (1966), *Accident Black Spot*, p228.

tasks, training, and so on. Their days off can be taken on Sundays, public holidays and quiet days to the mutual benefit of the wardens and the service.

4 Their training lasts for only three weeks—two in the classroom and one on patrol.
5 Their pay is appreciably less than a constable.
6 Their pension is much less than a constable.
7 A five-day week and the limitation of duties to daytime hours attracts a high standard of woman candidate well fitted for this particular work.

The only disadvantages listed arose from limitations on the traffic wardens' powers of enforcement and for controlling moving traffic. Since 1966, of course, the powers of traffic wardens in London have been considerably broadened, and the police have pressed for further extensions.[1]

Nevertheless motoring offences have become a very large and onerous part of police work. Jackson, who distinguishes between 'real crime' (serious offences against people and property) and 'regulatory offences' (amongst which he rates the great bulk of motoring offences), gives the following striking statistics:

	1938	1968
Real crime	112 254	302 487
Regulatory offences	582 869	1122 753
of which: motor vehicles	380 697	998 015
bicycles	85 507	6 340

In magistrates courts in 1968, 64% of all those found guilty were involved in motoring offences.[2] Pointing out that the existence of regulatory offences presupposes a complete edifice of law making and administrative machinery to devise and implement the regulations, he was of the opinion that: 'There is no good reason why police officers should spend so much time on motoring offences; they do so because the division of work in the public service is that the police deal with everything criminal unless some other service is responsible for enforcement. The law might have developed in the way it did for Factory Acts, Public Health, Weights and Measures and many other topics where inspection and prosecution are carried out by officers of a central government department or local authorities.'[3]

It is suggested that as a logical and desirable institutional change, the

[1] For example, to be able to enforce bus lanes. See *Hansard HC Papers 107 (xviii)*, 1971–72, p421, Q1942.

[2] R M Jackson (1972), *Enforcing the Law* (Penguin edn), esp pp19–21, 352. His 'real crimes' are murder and manslaughter, wounding, assault, rape and indecent assaults, burglary and homebreaking, robbery, larceny and embezzlement, receiving and other frauds, and arson and malicious damage. Regulatory offences included drunkenness, vagrancy, offences against public health, education, labour, social security, weights and measures regulations or local by-laws.

[3] Jackson (1972), p373.

traffic functions of the Metropolitan and City of London Police forces in Greater London[1] should be transferred to a new civil 'traffic corps' under the control of the GLC and largely separate from the police. This move would set a precedent in the United Kingdom which might be followed by other forces in the provinces, although the benefits would probably be less outside the conurbations.

Much of the enforcement task, as with traffic management and highway maintenance and the proposed off-street parking licensing, could be managed by the boroughs on an agency basis for the GLC. Finance could still be provided 50% by precept and 50% from central government but the boroughs would more easily be able to pay for extra control measures, for example, to overcome local environmental problems.

The creation of this separate traffic corps under GLC control would bring substantial benefits to the effectiveness of traffic policies, to the public and in certain important ways to the police. First, the public image of the police would almost certainly be improved. As Peter Evans has said, 'good policing depends on contact with the public,'[2] but the contact must, of course, be of the right kind.

> Fifty years ago the policeman, except as a familiar figure in the streets, had little to do with the ordinary citizen. Most of us regarded him as a stolid bulwark between us and burglars or rowdy drunks. It was the coming of the motor-car more than anything else which makes it impossible nowadays for any of us to say that we shall never find ourselves up against the police.[3]

It is unlikely that brushes with the police over minor traffic offences do anything to improve public relations. On the contrary, they are likely to arouse criticism about the employment of fully trained constables on what are considered by most people to be matters of secondary importance to crime.

Second, the creation of a separate traffic force would enable the police to concentrate a greater proportion of their resources to the prevention and detection of crime and thus ease the growing problems experienced by the Metropolitan Police in recruiting and retaining sufficient manpower. It has sometimes been argued that police involvement in traffic control contributes to the effort against crime, but there seems little more point to this than in having trained police officers as publicans, garage mechanics or in any other occupation which would bring them into contact with the public.

Third, the traditional function of the police in advising local authorities on traffic matters has to a large extent become superfluous. This is par-

[1] The Metropolitan Police District extends well beyond Greater London where traffic functions could remain as at present, or the functions could be transferred to the county councils.

[2] *The Times*, 17 May 1972.

[3] C Pulling (ed) (1964), *Mr Punch and the Police*, pp22–3.

ticularly true in the case of the GLC which is the largest and most powerful local traffic authority in the country. It has been noted in earlier chapters that rather than pulling out of their advisory role, the Metropolitan Police have sought instead to acquire new technical expertise in the traffic field. This is illustrated in the following quotation from a senior police administrator:[1]

> At the end of the war, traffic management hadn't become as technical as it has now, and we could say to a local authority, 'the Commissioner cannot agree to the siting of a pedestrian-crossing at so-and-so street,' and that was that. Nowadays they would laugh at us, and start talking traffic flows. So we have had to learn the same language as County Hall and the Ministry. . . .

There is little value, however, in building up police knowledge simply to counter arguments put forward by local authorities. Indeed, traffic management became a technical matter because it cannot be carried out satisfactorily on the basis of subjective judgement alone. It is not envisaged, therefore, that the new traffic corps should concern itself with advising the GLC (or the boroughs) on any more than enforcement and related matters.

Fourth, there are distinct advantages to be gained from those responsible for traffic law making (i.e. the GLC) being given direct control over and responsibility for traffic law enforcement. It has become clear that the scale and impact of traffic and parking policies will grow in future years throughout London and that enforcement problems have already become a major hindrance to their success so far. It is therefore of the utmost importance that the GLC is fully aware—at both political and official levels—of the implications and feasibility of future policies and programmes in terms of enforcement. Direct control over the enforcement agency would provide the opportunity and the incentive for the GLC to plan the manpower and cost requirements for traffic supervision in relation to its policy programme. Also the present unsatisfactory situation where the police decide on priorities for enforcement (e.g. between traffic flow, pedestrians, bus priority schemes, environmental schemes) would be superseded by priorities drawn up by the GLC as part of its overall traffic and transport strategy.

Fifth, public service vehicle licensing (at present carried out by the police) would be with the same body as private vehicle licensing and the GLC could regulate taxis through a new executive body as recommended by the Maxwell Stamp Committee.[2]

A further benefit would be easier recruitment of manpower for traffic supervision and enforcement. A separate traffic corps would, like the

[1] Quoted in P Laurie (1970), *Scotland Yard: A Study of the Metropolitan Police*, p137.

[2] *Report of Departmental Committee on London Taxicabs Trade* (1970), Cmnd 4483. The Committee recommended a statutory controlling board appointed by the GLC (see paragraphs 6.24, 8.5, and p124).

present warden service, be able to draw upon a wider pool of labour than is possible for police constables for whom there are stricter entrance requirements of education, physical stature and age.

All these improvements will be of growing value as the pressure on road and parking space increases due to rising car ownership and other claims for better bus services and improved environmental conditions. There would, of course, be some problems in creating a separate body mostly arising from the need to define the respective responsibilities of the police and the traffic corps, and the links that should be established (if any) between them.

Some valuable continuity of methods and experience gained by the police over the years could be gained by selecting senior police officers for the top management positions of the new traffic corps, though policy matters would be the ultimate responsibility of the GLC, and by phased replacement of police officers. Continuous contact with the police could be maintained by equipping certain traffic personnel (e.g. the mobile traffic sections) with direct radio links. This would provide a useful source of immediate information for the police on, for example, reckless drivers likely to be connected with some criminal offence, people stealing vehicles or their contents, etc. It is not envisaged, however, that the creation of a separate traffic corps should mean less policemen on the streets; to the contrary, it should enable the total number of people engaged in supervision and enforcement of all kinds to be increased.

As far as the division of responsibilities is concerned, this could follow the present division between the Metropolitan Police Traffic ('B') Department and the rest of the force. As Laurie said in 1970:

> . . . the Traffic Department, with 1300 men, is almost a force of its own. It has its own garages, its own radio, organisation and boundaries. Its job is quite distinct from that of *A* and there is, in general terms, little organic contact between the two departments.[1]

The precise division of responsibility would probably need to be thoroughly reviewed before the traffic department was formally split from the rest of the force, but the difficulties are unlikely to outweigh the benefits to be gained. A senior police officer was quoted by Laurie as saying of the Traffic Department: 'With the stroke of a pen, it could be a separate force.'[2]

5 ORGANISATIONAL DEVELOPMENT FOR TRANSPORT PLANNING IN LONDON

In the introductory paragraphs to this chapter, stress was laid on the need to develop a comprehensive approach to planning and in particular to achieve the integration of all aspects of transport with land-use planning.

[1] Laurie (1970), p23. [2] Laurie (1970), p127.

The changes outlined in sections 1–4 are seen as important ways of facilitating and encouraging this at metropolitan and national levels. Further measures, however, are needed to foster not only the strategic transport planning role of the GLC but also the complementary role of the London boroughs.

In the following paragraphs organisational changes are suggested to improve the planning and management of LT services within the context of other transport facilities, to bring the land use and transport planning process into much closer harness, and to restructure certain government departments (central and local) as a way of removing or at least reducing the continuing adherence to limited, compartmentalised transport planning, and in particular to place road planning in balanced perspective with other aspects of urban planning.

The suggestions made are based on three principles. The first is that the planning structure should be capable of formulating sets of truly alternative strategies, and not simply, as in the past, variations on a common set of assumptions. The formulation, analysis and evaluation of these strategies is a task for an inter-professional staff; the choice between alternatives is a political one and should not be predetermined or prejudiced by any particular methods or professional bias employed in the preparation of the alternatives themselves. The second principle is that those who draw up and evaluate alternative plans should have a sufficient knowledge of or involvement in the different aspects of transport and land-use planning to appreciate and take account of their relationships. For example, the GLC since 1970 has acquired not only a responsibility for, but also a new understanding of, LT's problems and their implications; the suggested transfer of responsibility for the BR London rail services would enable and encourage the GLC to widen their approach still further. The third principle, which would contribute to the achievement of the first two, is that those professionally engaged in policy planning should not themselves undertake the detailed design, feasibility studies or execution of projects to the extent that they develop extensive specialist expertise in, and hence deep personal commitment to, particular projects or policies. There would, of course, be a need to ensure that the benefits of specialist research and experience are incorporated into the planning process. This, however, presents fewer difficulties than the present situation where the heavy commitment of officers to particular transport policies distorts not only the information fed to politicians, but also the interpretation of political decisions.

In short, the suggestions below seek to establish and maintain clear distinctions both between policy planning and policy implementation and between these professional activities as a whole and the political judgements and decisions based upon them.

(a) *The metropolitan level*

The proposed new transport grant structure for London would, if implemented, mean much greater responsibility for the GLC in deciding overall priorities for investment. It has also been argued that the GLC should become directly responsible for the planning of Trunk roads and BR's rail services in London. For the same reasons, and to be consistent with the proposed changes, the GLC should take a much closer involvement in and more direct responsibility for the planning of investment, fares, and levels of service for the LT undertaking. It was said in Chapter 6 that the GLC had begun to make progress in the interpretation of its duties towards LT, moving from a preoccupation with the financial aspects arising from the 1969 Act, to a concern with the levels of service to be operated and, in the very broadest terms, with the technical and financial methods of achieving them. It is suggested that the GLC's role should continue to develop in this direction, and in particular should include the monitoring of changes in passenger demand and the effects of particular policies, the specifications of levels of service in some considerable detail, and (to a much greater degree than hitherto) the generation and evaluation of alternative policies and long-term plans. This would leave LT to fulfil its role as a technical and operating agency (analogous to the PTA–PTE division of responsibilities under the 1968 Act). At the same time it would improve the certainty of the position of GLC officers and members, giving them more confidence to attack policy matters, and bringing the GLC's great resources to bear on a wider range of questions.

Monitoring the services operated by the LT Executive should be, of course, an essential part of the process of deciding upon levels of service. The GLC should therefore keep an up-to-date picture not only of overall statistics such as passenger and bus mileage p.a. but also of passenger waiting times, the reliability and frequency of services, the incidence of overcrowding, and the effects of traffic management, highway and other schemes on passenger usage and convenience. Where LT are unable to operate the desired or planned level of service, or wish to alter services, it should be the Executive's duty to inform the GLC of the reasons. The GLC would then be in a position to direct the Executive as to the levels of service they required and the degree of co-ordination necessary with BR and other services. This might be highly specific in the case of Underground services but could be rather more flexible for bus services in which the planning considerations of the boroughs could play a larger part (see part (b) of this section).

The planning of LT expenditure, both capital and revenue, should be based not only on the information and research on levels of service and changes in potential and expressed passenger demand, but should also form part of the GLC's transport strategy and expenditure programme. This would give the GLC both the capacity and the responsibility not merely to meet demand but also to influence it. The Council would thus become more closely involved with the initiation and evaluation of alternative LT projects as part of the planning process. They should not, however, be involved in the detailed design or execution of projects, which would fall to the transport operator, the local planning authority and (perhaps) private sector developers.

The GLC's involvement in road and traffic planning should be on a similar plane to that proposed for public transport. Effective strategic transport planning must include the formulation and evaluation not just of alternative road patterns but of alternative approaches to the whole transport problem which present social choices in terms of personal mobility, land-use patterns and densities, priorities between transport and other expenditure and so on. It has been argued that a major hindrance to the development of such an approach (not just by the GLC but throughout government) has been the long-standing acceptance of road building as an executive function of government rather than as one element of transport policy. The existence of large numbers of people trained and employed in local (and central) government to plan and design roads has put tremendous force behind the pursuance of this particular option (even if administrative, social and political problems have meant that implementation has not kept pace with the road planners' desires) and at the same time has prejudiced the objective consideration of other options. The evolution of satisfactory transport planning requires that those responsible for it disentangle themselves from deep professional or personal commitment to particular aspects of transport—whether it be the design or construction of roads, bridges, tunnels, railways or buses—while being aware of the operations and problems of the executive agencies who undertake such work.

It is therefore suggested that the planning and transportation department of the GLC should divest itself of detailed involvement in the design, development and execution of all substantial road projects. Road planning as a separate activity (whatever the links with other separate activities) should be discontinued and should instead become an integral part of the strategic planning process in which road schemes are initiated and evaluated through the officer and committee structure together with other transport policy options. Moreover the roads programme[1] should be discontinued and replaced by a transport programme which details the allocation of the new block grant between different elements of transport expenditure.[2] Land use, social and economic considerations should play a more important part in transport planning and a priority for research should be the development of methods for evaluating alternative schemes and policies.

With the reduced executive role of the GLC in road planning, private or independent consultants with specialist knowledge and experience would be appointed to deal with a much higher proportion of technical design

[1] Drawn up in accordance with the DOE's procedures for grant purposes—see Chapter 3, page 84.

[2] This suggestion has been made by the House of Commons Expenditure Committee: 'The urban roads programme should be abolished and replaced by an urban transport programme linked to the comprehensive plans required in the context of the new grant proposals.' *Hansard HC Papers 57-1*, 1972–73, pxv, Recommendation 34.

work and feasibility investigations. Consultants have for many years, of course, played an important part in the operation of local government by providing manpower on a fixed contract basis when there are fluctuations in workload. They have also been employed on highly specialised work beyond the resources of local authorities, for example to examine the cost and feasibility of tunnel motorways in London.

Turning now to the question of manpower, a major hindrance to development of the GLC's transport planning role has been the scarcity of relevant expertise. Transport planning is a growing field in which many ideas, concepts and methods are still emerging, and there is already a great need for more people to train in and develop this work. This need will grow immensely along with the development of a corporate approach to planning, but it is considered most important that the institutional changes should not await the appearance of 'new' professional and technical manpower and techniques. Indeed, the necessary developments in this direction are likely to come about more quickly as a result of organisational changes. It is, however, largely for the Government in conjunction with academic institutions to stimulate education in transport planning. In view of the very small number of people with skill and experience in transport beyond that required in particular fields such as highway engineering and public transport operation, a good case can be made for establishing, at least in the early years, a close degree of co-operation and exchange between government and academic bodies. This could be particularly valuable in providing the necessary introduction of more people with a background in sociology and other social sciences into the transport planning field.

The established professional institutes will need to re-examine their roles (indeed, some of them have already begun to do so) and to consider whether, in the light of the new skills which will be required in the future, it is appropriate to maintain the divisions between their respective disciplines. Suggestions[1] that 'environmental sciences' should share a basic course, followed by courses in their respective specialist disciplines, would be in line with this approach. But regardless of broader educational and professional changes, the GLC and other authorities (such as the new metropolitan counties and the DOE) can act as pioneers and provide valuable training and testing grounds. Significant efforts have already been made in bringing together 'planners' and 'engineers' at County Hall, Whitehall, and elsewhere; given time and also a remit to take a comprehensive approach to the problems at hand, the individualistic and piecemeal approach of traditional departments of government, which has been at best inefficient and at worst counterproductive, will hopefully disappear.

(b) *Local level*

What has been said so far in this chapter has related mainly to transport

[1] For example, by Professor Donnison, Centre for Environmental Studies.

planning and management at the national and metropolitan levels and this section now turns to measures at the local, or borough, level which it is believed would greatly improve the functioning of the system as a whole. Two measures are put forward here: one is to create within the organisation of London borough councils the kind of transport planning structure suggested for the GLC; the other is to establish formal co-ordination machinery between the boroughs and the public transport operators. Other suggested changes concerning the role of the boroughs are dealt with separately in sections 6 and 7 below.

The London boroughs have played a major role in land use and highway and traffic planning at the local level, and the intention has been for them to perform this role within the context of the strategic structure plan for Greater London prepared by the GLC and approved by the Government. The suggestion in the first part of this section that the GLC should be organised so as to be able to take a comprehensive and balanced approach needs to be matched by similar changes at the borough level. In practice the boroughs have been the initiators of local highway schemes, and this should continue to be the case once the GLC's strategic framework has been established. But in transport the interests of the boroughs, like those of the GLC, have been strongly directed towards highways and traffic. The traditional role and influence of the engineering departments has contributed significantly to this approach, although the almost complete absence of powers and responsibilities for public transport and the limitation of co-ordination typically to *ad hoc* unilateral meetings of BR, LT and borough officers have also been important.

The aim should be to move towards a broad but integrated planning approach within each of the boroughs so that all aspects of transport can be considered together with other aspects of planning and, equally important, so that the boroughs can readily interpret and contribute to the development of the strategic framework prepared by the GLC.

As a major step in this direction it is suggested that the forward planning and maintenance or 'executive' functions of the borough engineering departments should be divided. Forward highway and traffic planning should be carried out by a department with responsibility for all aspects of local transport and land-use planning, and for the development of transport and other programmes of expenditure. Thus, as already suggested for the DOE and the GLC, sections dealing with road and traffic planning as separate units would cease to exist. The borough engineering departments would be responsible for giving technical advice and carrying out schemes within the established policy framework and programme of schemes. They would report directly to a 'works' committee on maintenance and other engineering functions of a continuing or routine character,[1] and would

[1] As suggested for the GLC, the use of consultants for specialist engineering and feasibility studies should continue and be extended both to overcome fluctuations in workload and to keep the establishment of highly specialised engineering staff to that required to carry out executive work.

largely be autonomous from the policy planning department for this purpose.

At the same time the committee structure of the London boroughs should be aligned to accommodate the distinction between policy planning and executive functions. The system of joint reporting by departments, for example, which has become common amongst the boroughs as a means of co-ordinating the highway, engineering and planning functions at chief officer level, tends to conceal basic choices which should be made by the elected members. The combination of planning functions within a single department, as suggested, should allow conflicting aims and policies to be transmitted to member level for resolution rather than (as so often at present) to become the source of inter-departmental rivalry.

Such changes have already been taking place in a few of the London boroughs, for example in Camden and Islington, although a full definition and realisation of the respective 'planning' and 'executive' roles has been slow to emerge. Attempts have also been made to improve local planning through joint working of engineering, planning and other departments, examples being the town centre redevelopment schemes for Wood Green, Hammersmith, Lewisham and Peckham. There seems no reason why the pooling of expertise and effort should not become the rule rather than the exception in the local planning process.

The second proposal for transport planning at the local level is that standing liaison panels between the boroughs and the public transport operators should be created. In the planning of new or redevelopment schemes, and in the preparation of local plans LT and BR have only been consulted, if at all, at a late stage in the process and the matters dealt with have all too often been confined to matters of detailed design or operation. Little attention has been paid to the implications for transport policy (indirect influences on the demand for services, for example) and the operators themselves have only recently begun to take an interest in such matters. It is clear, however, that as this particular aspect of co-ordination gains ground, as it has already done at the metropolitan level, better machinery will be required to cope with local aspects.[1]

A system of small liaison committees or panels consisting of BR, LT and borough officers appointed by the respective bodies, is proposed. There would be thirty-three in all, one for each of the boroughs and one for the City of London, although BR and LT representatives could serve on several panels, perhaps serving the same areas as the teams of the GLC's Planning and Transportation Department. Both operators would not usually be involved in individual schemes. (In north London, for example, where BR services are relatively few, the panels would often include only LT and borough officers.) The panels would discuss problems and oppor-

[1] The need for this has been partly recognised, for example, by the establishment of the Transport Facilities' Conference described in the case study on the 'Shoppers' Bus Experiment (Case Study *N*), although this is a quite different body from those envisaged here.

tunities at the earliest possible stages of the preparation and design of plans and schemes, irrespective of whether they were initiated by the boroughs, the operators or any other body. They would not be statutory bodies but, like the GLTG, they would deal with co-ordinating and consultation required by statute which could mean new legislation. It would be the function of the officers involved, moreover, to bring to the attention of their Board, Executive or Council any matter which required formal resolution; this would usually only occur after full discussion of the issues involved. The GLC would become involved at the formal stage wherever major alterations to the prescribed levels of public transport service would be likely to result, or where the issues themselves would have an influence on services. Where the GLC is responsible for the design and preparation of 'action area' plans or schemes (such as Thamesmead and Covent Garden) similar panels may need to be established on an *ad hoc* basis.

6 A NEW VOICE FOR THE INTERESTS OF PEDESTRIANS, CYCLISTS AND THE ENVIRONMENT

The adverse effects of motor traffic threaten alike pedestrians, cyclists and the quality of the environment in which people live. Despite their vulnerability, the expression of these three interests within the institutional system has been weak, and barely heard amongst the claims for new road and management schemes to ease the flow of motor traffic or even those for improved public transport. It is therefore suggested that they are given a new and stronger voice both within the GLC and each of the London boroughs through the appointment of officers with specific responsibilities for pedestrians and cyclists. The officers would also be concerned with environmental improvements which involve transport and particularly road traffic.

There is ample evidence to support the claim that the GLC has failed to meet its statutory obligations as traffic authority to provide for the convenience as well as the safety of pedestrians, while even the safety of cyclists has received little if any consideration in highway and traffic schemes. Environmental interests have received rather more attention, particularly by the London boroughs, although it appears that they have been defended and promoted most strongly in areas where environmental quality was already above average and especially areas with special architectural or historic merit. It is in such areas that local voluntary groups have been formed to press the local authorities for improvements or to protest about schemes which threaten local amenities. Representation of environmental interests should not, however, be confined to certain privileged areas and should certainly not be dependent upon the existence of local voluntary organisations to badger or shame the local authorities into action.

The protection and improvement of the environment should be regarded as a major responsibility of local authorities whose organisation should reflect both the character and the scale of the problems to be tackled. In most cases organisational and legislative changes would help to bring about this situation. In addition to new responsibilities for officers, new statutory obligations for local authorities to secure environmental improvements in their areas would provide extra stimulus; few exist at present.

A specific problem has been that 'environmental area' and pedestrianisation schemes have conflicted with the traffic interests represented by the GLC. This is dealt with further in the next section, but it is considered that the conflict could be reduced by the changes in the officer structure suggested here.

The evidence has shown that the poor representation of pedestrian, cycling, and environmental interests has been due largely to the attitudes of officers and elected members. They have been unwilling, or at least slow, to alter established methods and priorities to meet changing public opinion about the adverse effects of increasing motor traffic. The suggestions already put forward for the removal of inappropriate professional and departmental boundaries should remove some of the present obstacles to achieving a balanced approach to motor traffic and the other aspects of urban life with which it inevitably conflicts.

Nevertheless, progress in this direction may still be inadequate. In order to establish a more balanced set of priorities, some short-term restructuring of powers and responsibilities may well be justified. One approach would be for the GLC and the London borough councils to provide a new brief for their officers and departments calling for action on hitherto neglected aspects of urban transport policy. A bolder and probably more effective step would be to appoint new senior officers with special responsibilities: these officers would offer critical appraisals of traffic and highway schemes from their particular standpoint, but more importantly they would initiate and develop schemes specifically designed to improve conditions for pedestrians and cyclists and the quality of the environment. In many if not most situations, such schemes would present a direct challenge to the comparatively well represented interests of motor traffic and consequently the appointments must be of a sufficiently high status to make them effective.

Before discussing, in the next section, ways in which competing traffic and environmental interests might be better resolved at the political level it should be emphasised that the suggested appointment of officers with new powers and responsibilities are recognised to be inconsistent in some respects with the broader transport and land-use planning structure proposed in the earlier sections of this chapter. In their approach to transport problems the GLC and the London boroughs should not unduly favour pedestrians and cyclists any more than they should give overriding priority to other means of travel. Similarly, the environmental effects of transport should not influence decisions to the exclusion of other considerations such as road safety and social equitability. The proposal is therefore to be seen as an expedient designed to redress a serious imbalance which currently exists in the weight given to these different considerations.

7 TRAFFIC AND THE ENVIRONMENT: THE ROLES OF THE GLC AND THE LONDON BOROUGHS

This section is concerned with what has been identified as one of the most striking problems of the two-tier system of local government in London, namely the difficulty of reconciling conflicting local and metropolitan interests.[1] It deals with the problems of resolving conflicts at the political level (though not necessarily on party political lines) that arise in traffic management matters between, for example, the needs of local and through traffic, parked and moving vehicles, vehicular traffic and the maintenance of a pleasant environment. The previous two sections proposed measures to improve the representation of these various interests at officer level, but these will be more effective if the political machinery is developed to reconcile wide differences of view between the GLC and the London boroughs. The problem arises less frequently with major highway schemes because it is usually the Secretary of State for the Environment who takes the final decision; there is no such machinery for the majority of traffic management schemes—indeed it was the intention of the 1967 and 1969 Acts that the Minister should no longer have to deal with such matters.

Before considering possible improvements to the present system it may be helpful to recall the context within which the machinery for dealing with traffic management in London was set up. The Herbert Commission drew the general conclusion that the new London boroughs:

> should perform all local authority functions except those which can only be effectively performed over the wider area of Greater London or which could be better performed over that wider area.[2]

Traffic management was clearly identified as one such wider function:

> We have no doubt that all these [traffic management] matters should be the responsibility of the Council for Greater London, and that these powers should apply to all streets and roads whether main roads or otherwise, the Council being free to use the boroughs as its agents for the execution of works of this nature.[3]

At the time the Herbert Commission reported, however, the concept of 'traffic management' was relatively new and its purpose was narrowly defined: 'The main object of traffic management is to keep the traffic moving.'[4]

[1] Other studies have drawn attention to this problem in the fields of housing and land-use planning: see A A Nevitt and G Rhodes (ch7) and P Self (ch8) in G Rhodes (ed) (1972), *The New Government of London: The First Five Years.*

[2] Cmnd 1162 (1960), p192. [3] Cmnd 1162 (1960), p203. [4] Cmnd 1162 (1960), p108.

To the Commission the problems of providing traffic management measures in London were due almost entirely to the multiplicity of authorities that were involved, and the lack of a single body with overall responsibility for traffic. The MOT had held the same view, and it was to overcome these problems that the London Traffic Management Unit (LTMU) was formed, and became the precursor of the Traffic Branch of the Highways and Transportation department of the GLC, as traffic authority for London.

Since that time, the objectives of traffic management and the range of available techniques have widened considerably and may now embrace such matters as local environmental improvements, better facilities for pedestrians, priority for buses, better parking and loading facilities, and so on. All of these may directly conflict with the objective which Herbert identified for traffic management of maintaining the free movement of vehicles. Thus if traffic management is to assume this wider role and if, as at present, the sole powers and responsibilities are to lie with the GLC, then the metropolitan authority must be concerned with local problems and interests to an extent not foreseen and certainly not envisaged by the Herbert Commission or anybody else.

The chief conclusion to be drawn from the research in this book on traffic management is that the GLC has adhered too rigidly to the narrow traffic management role played by the LTMU. In practice the GLC has promoted traffic management schemes in the interests of traffic flow and has rarely approved schemes for other purposes which seemed to them likely to increase traffic delays.

The policy of designating environmental areas provides a clear example of the resulting difficulties (see Case Study *G*). In this case the GLC, while subscribing to the policy as part of the GLDP strategy, decided that the planning of environmental management schemes should be the responsibility of the boroughs.[1] Thus, since these schemes required the approval of the GLC, the situation obtained where the boroughs had the responsibility but no powers while the GLC had the powers but abrogated the responsibility. The result of this, which was described by several members and officers from the London boroughs during interviews, has been an almost complete absence of any traffic management schemes in London designed to improve local environmental conditions.

Whether or not the present distribution of powers and responsibilities, and the GLC's interpretation of them, is seen as satisfactory must, of course, ultimately depend upon a considered view of which of the conflicting interests as represented by the boroughs and the GLC (or indeed their different departments) should take priority; such a view should properly be established at the political level. There is a grave danger in the present arrangements, however, that undue weight will be given to the interests of traffic flow not because of any deliberate disregard of other interests, nor because of any particular urgency in solving individual traffic problems, but because of the relative powers, responsibilities and strengths of the

[1] GLC (1969), *GLDP Written Statement*, para5.11; 1972, Revised Statement, para5.6.31.

GLC and the London boroughs. The GLC, being larger and having greater resources, have tended to dominate the boroughs in the traffic management field and, being a metropolitan authority, are not well placed to understand or adequately represent local interests. Moreover, each and every scheme (including even minor modifications) requires their approval and the traffic order-making procedures are both time-consuming and inflexible.

The proposal put forward in the following paragraphs is designed to introduce a counter-balance in the present arrangements, so that what may be generally described as 'local interests' can be more effectively represented where political decisions on traffic schemes are being made. It is recognised, however, that the efficacy of any major change would be dubious if on the one hand the GLC were to adopt an entirely different approach to its traffic responsibilities or if, on the other hand, the weight of opinion returned to the view of the early 1960s that 'the main objective of traffic management is to keep the traffic moving.' Neither prospect seems likely: it would be difficult for the GLC to become more deeply involved in local problems and needs without encroaching upon the (rightful) role of the boroughs or massively increasing its manpower; and, while the concept of traffic management as an instrument of broad planning (not just traffic) policy has established a firm foothold at all levels of government, opinion has also been moving strongly towards the defence and promotion of local interests. The following quotation from the newsletter of a local amenity society in London provides an illustration of this latter point, and a small but probably typical example of the consequent disparity between local and GLC priorities:

> The Putney Society has . . . told the GLC that the High Street Traffic Management scheme has had the undesirable effect of turning some residential streets into through traffic routes. . . .
>
> . . . the Society is adding its voice to those calling for better pedestrian facilities in the High Street. We are asking for longer pedestrian phases at the traffic light-controlled crossings, and an all-red phase and a pedestrian crossing indicator at the junction of the High Street and Upper Richmond Road. . . .
>
> We realise that most of our proposals will have the effect of slowing somewhat the flow of traffic through Putney. But we make no apology for this. The [GLC] Scheme was undoubtedly devised to accommodate the Surrey commuter and we think the people of Putney also deserve some consideration. After all they're just passing through . . . we live here.[1]

The proposal, then, is for a new political forum to be established in London to decide upon traffic management schemes, whether initiated by a London borough or the GLC, which become contentious to the point of

[1] The Putney Society *Bulletin*, vol1, No.4, November 1971.

formal objections or open disagreement between the two levels of government. A statutory committee would be formed of elected representatives of the London borough councils and the GLC with the responsibility and power to take final decisions on such traffic matters. This 'Arbitration Committee' might also deal with minor highway schemes not subject to arbitration by the Secretary of State[1] but it would not deal with experimental traffic schemes,[2] and would have no power to consider schemes on which the GLC and a borough agreed. When considering individual cases, the particular borough or boroughs within which the scheme fell might be excluded. Decisions by the Committee would be made in the light of evidence submitted by the GLC,[3] the borough concerned and representations from interested voluntary or other bodies. If necessary a public inquiry could be held, but the Committee, and not the GLC (as is the case under the 1972 regulations) would take the final decision.

This Committee, it is believed, would enable London borough councillors (through their membership of it) to become more closely aware than at present of metropolitan issues and of the 'strategic' policies of the GLC and their local interpretation. Since these policies will have been approved (at any one time) by the Secretary of State for the Environment, and the Committee would have a major role in their interpretation and implementation, it is suggested that the Arbitration Committee should report annually on the decisions taken and their contribution to strategic and local policy. This in itself would help to meet the need for better monitoring of GLC plans and policies. The Secretary of State could have default powers over the Committee, but should exercise them to no greater extent than over any other locally elected body.

It is not expected that a Committee of the kind described would be a panacea for what must be recognised as one of the most difficult problems of a two-tier local government system. But there appear to be few alternative approaches that would offer a prospect of improving upon present arrangements. A division or sharing of responsibility between the two tiers, for example, whether on a geographical or a functional basis, could provide scapegoats for indecision over the very matters where a firm and speedy decision is most important; the appointment of either an independent body or group of officers would remove these highly political matters from the political arena; transferring traffic powers to the boroughs or the Secretary of State would simply mean a reversion to the pre-1965 situation where metropolitan interests were inadequately represented. If the boroughs and the GLC in every case were of the same view as to the correct balance between metropolitan and local interests there would, of course, be no reason to suggest changes to the GLC's traffic responsibilities, but such

[1] Under Highways Act 1959. Only schemes on Principal roads would be affected, i.e. those for which the GLC was the highway authority.

[2] That is, under section 9 of the *Road Traffic Regulation Act 1967*, ch76.

[3] Including representations on enforcement, public transport, and strategic land-use matters.

agreement would be difficult to maintain on a permanent basis. This is not altogether an adverse comment on the two-tier system because the explication of conflicting interests is essential to healthy local government; what is lacking is the political means whereby these conflicts can be effectively resolved. The suggested Arbitration Committee would be specifically constituted to meet this need: its London-wide representation should provide it with a metropolitan viewpoint while the experience of many of its members in borough affairs would give it an understanding of local aspects of a decision without being partial to the particular borough concerned. Nevertheless, the frequency with which matters were referred to the Committee would be gradually reduced if in time the process promoted an improved understanding between the GLC and the boroughs.

8 PUBLIC INVOLVEMENT IN TRANSPORT PLANNING AND MANAGEMENT

The question of public participation in transport planning and decision-making processes is a difficult one and deserves greater consideration than has so far been given either in this book or elsewhere. Difficulties arise, for example, in deciding which issues to throw open, what degree of public debate and involvement to invite and, most important of all, who 'the public' are as far as any particular issue is concerned. Those case studies in which people outside the statutory institutional system played a significant part show that participation has tended to be confined to areas containing an articulate and sometimes wealthy population. There is, therefore, a vast area where the interest and influence of groups and individuals could be extended and this should be deliberately encouraged.

The demand for participation, however, has grown because the public have come to feel that the decisions of transport planners do not reflect their best interests. The institutional changes already suggested would, it is believed, considerably increase the formal opportunities for the discussion and negotiation of transport, planning and environmental issues which have particularly aroused public dissatisfaction and concern. But, as Skeffington[1] suggested, plans which truly reflect public needs and preferences can best be drawn up with public collaboration. An open approach should be adopted where the public are consulted and problems set out for debate before plans reach any stage of commitment. The public should be kept fully informed of relevant issues at various stages in the planning process. Moreover, part of the task of the planner, whatever the field, is actively to promote public interest, and in areas where formal participation procedures have failed to produce a public response new methods should be sought.

The extent to which most of the authorities examined in this study kept the public informed of their intentions, their methods and their decisions

[1] MOHLG (1969), *People and Planning: Report of the Committee on Public Participation in Planning*, HMSO.

was far from satisfactory, and there should be more stringent legal requirements on public information and involvement. It is also important for authorities to solicit public opinion and reactions to policies. It might be valuable to employ research staff for this work. These efforts should be made not only by central and local government but also by others involved in transport decisions such as BR, the British Airports Authority and the Port of London Authority.

Public information is vital, but it is also important for channels to be kept open for public objections, complaints and suggestions. Under present legislation there are many transport matters which do not fall within the scope of the public objection and inquiry procedures. It is suggested that the Arbitration Committee already described would provide a useful means whereby public objections to traffic management and highway schemes[1] could be the subject of independent scrutiny, without involving central government.

As far as public transport is concerned, the opportunities for public objection and comment on rail closures and service alterations should be greatly improved. The TUCC, for example, can under present legislation only hear evidence relating to hardship that would arise from a proposed rail closure, and the possible ways of alleviating hardship should the railway be closed. There is no reason, however, why the public should not be able to object to the grounds for closure put up by the transport operators, as well as to the closure proposal itself. The public should therefore be given access to relevant information concerning operating costs, capital costs, alternative services, operating economies and so on, which at present remain confidential to the operator and the DOE, and the terms of reference of the TUCC should be broadened accordingly.

If, as suggested earlier, responsibility for BR services in London was transferred to the GLC, the function of the TUCC for London could at the same time be transferred to the LTPC, thus placing all public transport matters in London in the hands of one consumer body. Whether or not this is done, greater opportunities should be provided in future for public representations about proposed bus service alterations, and especially bus service withdrawals. Machinery should be established (e.g. under the LTPC) to hear representations and objections about a proposed change in service and to report on all matters raised to the GLC[2] before a final decision is taken.

Finally, provision for public involvement in transport planning and management should be regarded as an integral part of the process. Quite apart from the moral questions involved, any consequent delays in reach-

[1] That is, those that would at present fall outside the scope of inquiries held by the Secretary of State for the Environment.

[2] This is consistent with the earlier suggestion (page 633) that the GLC becomes more closely responsible for the actual services provided. It would apply equally if LT remained responsible for individual service changes but in this case the GLC should become arbiter in any dispute between LT and other bodies over service alterations.

ing a decision can be and often are justified by a better (or at least more confident) decision and by the avoidance of difficulties that arise in the longer term as people become dissatisfied with the decisions that are being taken on their behalf.

9 CO-ORDINATION MACHINERY

The extent and role of co-ordinating machinery may be regarded as one measure of the suitability and performance of the basic institutional structure. The suggested redistribution of powers and responsibilities would require the establishment of some new co-ordinating bodies and

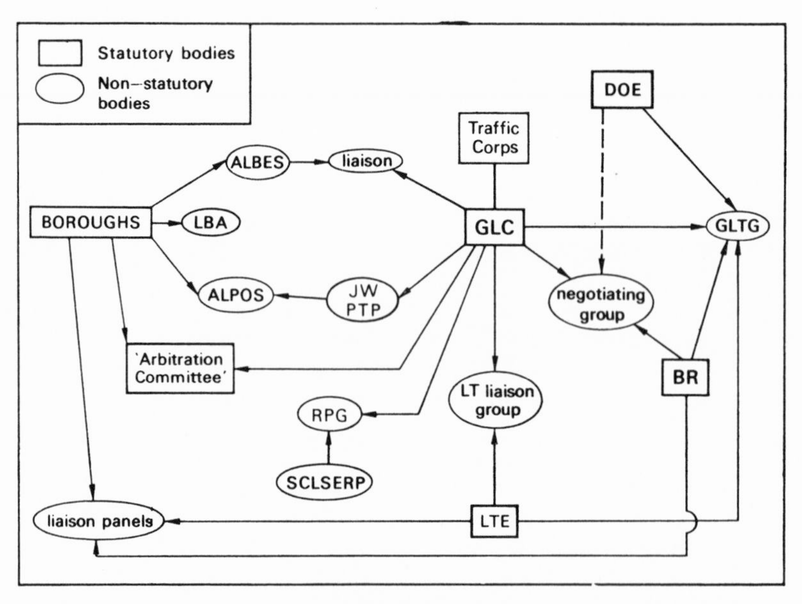

Figure 24 SUGGESTED CO-ORDINATING BODIES FOR TRANSPORT IN LONDON

would permit the abandonment of some existing ones, but there would overall be a simplification in that in most cases the 'bridging' function would be narrower and more specific than at present. Under the suggested arrangements, fewer statutory bodies would shoulder the load of integrated transport planning and management and so the need for major co-ordinating agencies would be reduced.

The resulting structure might resemble that in Figure 24 although, as already emphasised, it is not intended to be a blueprint for institutional change in London: each of the suggested changes could be implemented individually and would bring important benefits in their own right.[1] But in this final section the implications for co-ordinating machinery are summarised assuming that all the suggested measures are brought into effect.

Of major importance would be a greatly reduced role and work load for the Greater London Transport Group whose membership could remain the same (compare Figure 24 with Figure 5) in order to provide a top-level forum for discussions on responsibilities, strategy and major policy matters such as the future of London's dockland and the third London airport. The GLTG would not be required, as at present, to play a key role in transport planning and co-ordination. Much would depend on the interpretation by the various bodies, particularly the GLC and DOE, of their new responsibilities.

The transfer of traffic supervision and enforcement from the police to a new traffic corps under the direct control of the GLC would eliminate the need for the Joint Traffic Executive and its associated liaison groups (with the Association of London Borough Engineers and the Citrac group) (see Figure 5). There would, of course, need to be arrangements within the GLC whereby policy control of the traffic corps could be integrated with transport policy and traffic planning at both officer and member level.

Two further groups would disappear: the Highways Development Review Group whose separate existence to co-ordinate DOE and GLC road plans within Greater London would cease to be relevant not only as a result of the transfer of Trunk roads to the GLC, but also because there would be no place for road planning as a separate activity from transport planning; and the Public Transport Planning Group of BR and LT officers. Again, transport planning as a whole would be the responsibility of the GLC and separate co-ordination between BR and LT would be inappropriate. There might, however, continue to be meetings of LT and BR officers to consider common technical and operational problems.

Finally, some new co-ordinating machinery would be required. The Arbitration Committee on traffic management and highway schemes would in a sense be a co-ordinating body, although its powers and responsibilities, and constitution would be established by statute.

The transfer of responsibility for BR's London services to the GLC would require the establishment of a group of senior officers responsible to the senior management committee of the GLC to handle the complex and technical negotiations over the financing of services required by the GLC. This negotiating group might require a chairman independent of BR or the GLC perhaps from or appointed by the DOE. The DOE could also be represented, at least initially, to make use of experience and expertise already gained in the determination of grants for unremunerative rail services and through the operation of the Passenger Transport Authorities and Executives.

[1] The exception to this would be the suggested transport grant structure (section 1) which, to be fully effective, would require the transfer of responsibility for Trunk roads and BR services in London to the GLC.

Finally, the suggested local transport and land-use planning liaison panels would be numerous (i.e. one for each London borough and one for the City of London) although representatives from the transport operators would probably be able to cover several panels. Their work would be strictly local in character and concerned with the relationships between public transport and particular development proposals or local problems; their importance and influence would grow as the different authorities came to appreciate one another's problems and needs and as experience was gained in understanding the detailed relationship between urban form and transport facilities.

All the research material contained in this book, the conclusions from it and the suggestions for improvements to the institutional system put forward in this last chapter will, it is hoped, provide a useful contribution to the continuing but often elusive debate about the organisation of transport in large cities. Major reorganisation of government in London has, it is believed, created opportunities for tackling the city's transport problems in a way which respects and draws inspiration from the city's physical and social character. Further organisational developments in line with the principles of government which have already been established should enable London's transport difficulties to be alleviated more effectively than in the past. It is believed that the suggested changes will contribute to the evolution of more satisfactory arrangements for tackling the city's immense problems. If so, they will provide a valuable example to other major cities in Britain and to many cities in the rest of the world facing similar technical and social transport problems, particularly those that have or are considering two-tier systems of local government.

INDEX